Decision Theory Models for Applications in Artificial Intelligence:

Concepts and Solutions

L. Enrique Sucar
National Institute for Astrophysics, Optics and Electronics, Mexico

Eduardo F. Morales
National Institute for Astrophysics, Optics and Electronics, Mexico

Jesse Hoey
University of Waterloo, Canada

Information Science
REFERENCE

Managing Director:	Lindsay Johnston
Senior Editorial Director:	Heather Probst
Book Production Manager:	Sean Woznicki
Development Manager:	Joel Gamon
Development Editor:	Joel Gamon
Acquisitions Editor:	Erika Gallagher
Typesetters:	Mackenzie Snader
Print Coordinator:	Jamie Snavely
Cover Design:	Nick Newcomer, Greg Snader

Published in the United States of America by
Information Science Reference (an imprint of IGI Global)
701 E. Chocolate Avenue
Hershey PA 17033
Tel: 717-533-8845
Fax: 717-533-8661
E-mail: cust@igi-global.com
Web site: http://www.igi-global.com

Library of Congress Cataloging-in-Publication Data

Decision theory models for applications in artificial intelligence: concepts
and solutions / L. Enrique Sucar, Eduardo F. Morales and Jesse Hoey, editors.
    p. cm.
  Summary: "This book provides an introduction to different types of decision theory techniques, including MDPs, POM-DPs, Influence Diagrams, and Reinforcement Learning, and illustrates their application in artificial intelligence"-- Provided by publisher.
  Includes bibliographical references and index.
  ISBN 978-1-60960-165-2 (hardcover) -- ISBN 978-1-60960-167-6 (ebook) 1. Artificial intelligence--Statistical methods. 2. Bayesian statistical decision theory. I. Sucar, L. Enrique, 1957- II. Morales, Eduardo F. III. Hoey, Jesse.
  Q335.D43 2011
  006.3--dc22
                    2010054421

British Cataloguing in Publication Data
A Cataloguing in Publication record for this book is available from the British Library.

All work contributed to this book is new, previously-unpublished material. The views expressed in this book are those of the authors, but not necessarily of the publisher.

List of Reviewers

Concha Bielza, *Universidad Politécnica de Madrid, Spain*
Fabio Cozman, *University of Sao Paulo, Brazil*
Boris Defourny, *University of Liege, Belgium*
Javier Díez, *Universidad Nacional de Educación a Distancia, Spain*
Pantelis Elinas, *Australian Centre for Field Robotics, Australia*
Nando de Freitas, *University of British Columbia, Canada*
Marcel van Gerven, *Radboud University Nijmegen, Netherlands*
Phan H. Giang, *George Mason University, USA*
Robby Goetschalckx, *University of Waterloo, Canada*
Kevin Grant, *University of Lethbridge, Canada*
Jesse Hoey, *University of Waterloo, Canada*
Finn V. Jensen, *Aalborg University, Denmark*
Omar Zia Khan, *University of Waterloo, Canada*
Eduardo F. Morales, *INAOE, Mexico*
Rubén Morales-Menendez, *Tecnológico de Monterrey - Campus Monterrey, Mexico*
Abdel-Illah Mouaddib, *University of Caen, France*
Kasia Muldner, *University of British Columbia, Canada*
Julieta Noguez, *Tecnológico de Monterrey - Campus Ciudad de México, Mexico*
Alberto Reyes, *Instituto de Investigaciones Eléctricas, Mexico*
Claude Sammut, *University of New South Wales, Australia*
Eugene Santos, *Dartmouth College, USA*
Matthijs Spaan, *Delft University of Technology, Netherlands*
L. Enrique Sucar, *INAOE, Mexico*
Jason Williams, *AT&T Research, USA*

Table of Contents

Section 1
Fundamentals

L. Enrique Sucar, National Institute for Astrophysics, Optics and Electronics, Mexico
Eduardo Morales, National Institute for Astrophysics, Optics and Electronics, Mexico
Jesse Hoey, University of Waterloo, Canada

Luis Enrique Sucar, National Institute for Astrophysics, Optics and Electronics, Mexico

Pascal Poupart, University of Waterloo, Canada

Eduardo F. Morales, National Institute for Astrophysics, Optics and Electronics, México
Julio H. Zaragoza, National Institute for Astrophysics, Optics and Electronics, México

Section 2
Concepts

Matthew Hoffman, University of British Columbia, Canada
Nando de Freitas, University of British Columbia, Canada

Detailed Table of Contents

Section 1
Fundamentals

Chapter 1

L. Enrique Sucar, National Institute for Astrophysics, Optics and Electronics, Mexico
Eduardo Morales, National Institute for Astrophysics, Optics and Electronics, Mexico
Jesse Hoey, University of Waterloo, Canada

This chapter gives a general introduction to decision-theoretic models in artificial intelligence and an overview of the book.

Chapter 2

Luis Enrique Sucar, National Institute for Astrophysics, Optics and Electronics, Mexico

This chapter covers the fundamentals of probabilistic graphical models, in particular: (i) Bayesian networks, (ii) Dynamic Bayesian networks and (iii) Influence diagrams. For each it describes the representation and main inference techniques. For Bayesian networks and dynamic Bayesian networks it includes an overview of structure and parameter learning.

Chapter 3

Pascal Poupart, University of Waterloo, Canada

This chapter provides a gentle introduction to Markov decision processes as a framework for sequential decision making under uncertainty. It reviews fully and partially observable Markov decision processes, describes basic algorithms to find good policies and discusses modeling and computational issues that arise in practice.

Chapter 4

Eduardo F. Morales, National Institute for Astrophysics, Optics and Electronics, México
Julio H. Zaragoza, National Institute for Astrophysics, Optics and Electronics, México

This chapter provides a concise and updated introduction to Reinforcement Learning from a machine learning prespective. It gives the require background to undersand the chapters related to reinforcement learning in this book, and includes an overview of some of the latest trends in the area.

Section 2
Concepts

Chapter 5

Matthew Hoffman, University of British Columbia, Canada
Nando de Freitas, University of British Columbia, Canada

Semi-Markov decision processes are used to formulate many control problems and play a key role in hierarchical reinforcement learning. This chapter shows how to translate the decision making problem into a form that can instead be solved by inference and learning techniques. It establishes a formal connection between planning in semi-MDPs and inference in probabilistic graphical models.

Chapter 6

Boris Defourny, University of Liège, Belgium
Damien Ernst, University of Liège, Belgium
Louis Wehenkel, University of Liège, Belgium

This chapter presents the multistage stochastic programming framework for sequential decision making under uncertainty. It describes the standard technique for solving approximately multistage stochastic problems, which is based on a discretization of the disturbance space called scenario tree. It also shows how supervised learning techniques can be used to evaluate reliably the quality of an approximation.

Chapter 7

Omar Zia Khan, University of Waterloo, Canada
Pascal Poupart, University of Waterloo, Canada
James P. Black, University of Waterloo, Canada

It presents a technique to explain policies for factored MDPs by populating a set of domain-independent templates, and a mechanism to determine a minimal set of templates that, viewed together, completely justify the policy. The technique is demonstrated using the problems of advising undergraduate students in their course selection and assisting people with dementia in completing the task of handwashing.

Dynamic limited-memory influence diagrams (DLIMIDs) are a new type of decision-support model. Its main difference with other models is the restriction of limited memory, which means that the decision maker must make a choice based only on recent observations. This chapter presents several algorithms for evaluating DLIMIDs, shows a real-world model for a medical problem, and compares DLIMIDs with related formalisms.

This chapter introduces an approach for reinforcement learning based on a relational representation. The underlying idea is to represent states as set of first order relations, actions in terms of these relations, and policies over those generalized representations. The effectiveness of the approach is tested on a flight simulator and on a mobile robot.

Section 3
Solutions

A decision-theoretic tutor that helps students learn from Analogical Problem Solving is described. The tutor incorporates an innovative example-selection mechanism that tailors the choice of example to a given student. An empirical evaluation shows that this selection mechanism is more effective than standard selection approaches for fostering learning.

Chapter 11

This chapter describes how an intelligent tutor based on Dynamic Decision Networks is applied in an undergraduate Physics scenario, where the aim is to adapt the learning experience to suit the learners' needs. It employs Probabilistic Relational Models to facilitate the construction of the model. With this representation, the tutor can be easily adapted to different experiments, domains, and student levels.

This chapter presents AsistO, a simulation-based intelligent assistant for power plant operators that provides on-line guidance in the form of ordered recommendations. These recommendations are generated using Markov decision processes over an approximated factored representation of the plant. It also describes an explanation mechanism over these recommendations.

This chapter presents a general decision theoretic model of interactions between users and cognitive assistive technologies for various tasks of importance to the elderly populaton. The model is a POMDP whose goal is to work in conjuction with a user towards the completion of a given task. The model is used in 4 tasks: assisted handwashing, stroke rehabilitation, health monitoring, and wheelchair mobility.

Spoken dialog systems present a classic example of planning under uncertainty. Decision theory, and in particular partially-observable Markov decision processes, present an attractive approach to building spoken dialog systems. This chapter traces the history of POMDP-based spoken dialog systems, and sketches avenues for future work.

This chapter describes a novel framework based on functional decomposition that divides a complex problem into several sub-problems. Each sub-problem is defined as an MDP and solved independently, and their individual policies are combined to obtain a global policy. Resource and behavior conflicts between the individual policies are detected and solved. The framework is applied to task coordination in service robots, in particular for messenger robots.

Chapter 16

Aurélie Beynier, University Pierre and Marie Curie, France
Abdel-Illah Mouaddib, University of Caen, France

This chapter introduces problematics related to the decentralized control of multi-robot systems. It presents Decentralized Markov Decision Processes and discusses their applicability to real-world multi-robot applications. Then, it introduces OC-DEC-MDPs and 2V-DEC-MDPs which have been developed to increase the applicability of DEC-MDPs.

Foreword

Graphical models for handling uncertainty have been around for more than two decades. Most notably *Bayesian networks* have been widely known and applied. The extensive development of the theory of Bayesian networks has created new ways of specifying models for rational decision making, and over the past two decades we have also witnessed a rapid development of the theory of graphical models for sequential decision making.

Several excellent textbooks cover Bayesian networks. Focus in these books is belief updating in Bayesian networks and learning of models. However, I have for many years been missing a graduate textbook, which systematically introduces the concepts and techniques of graphical models for sequential decision making.

This book serves this purpose. Not only does it introduce the basic theory and concepts, but it also contains sections indicating new research directions as well as examples of real world decision models.

The two main obstacles for successful application of graphical decision models are complexity and insufficient insight in the domain for establishing a model. The book presents several approaches to overcoming these obstacles.

For the domain expert wanting to exploit graphical decision models for constructing a specific decision support system, this book is a useful hand book of the theory as well as of ideas, which may help establishing appropriate models.

To the young researcher: this book will give you a firm ground for working with graphical decision models. Read the book, and you will realize that the story is not over. There are lots of challenges waiting for you, and the book provides you an excellent starting point for en exiting journey into the science of graphical decision models.

Finn V. Jensen
Aalborg University, Denmark

Finn Verner Jensen *is Professor, PhD and Dr. Techn, and Knight of Dannebrog at the Department of Computer Science, Aalborg University in Denmark. Originally from Tnder, Denmark, he has cultivated his scientific interests since 1988, including probabilistic graphical models (PGMs) for decision making and diagnosis and data mining. He has 64 scientific publications (with academic referee) over the last ten years and three monographs on Bayesian networks and decision graphs (Springer-Verlag, New York). He was the co-designer of HUGIN, the first shell for Bayesian Networks and has achieved an H-index (Googlescholar) of 32. His industrial accomplishments include contributing to four patents which form the commercial basis for Dezide A/S, as well the before mentioned HUGIN. He is currently leader of three major research programs at Aalborg University, including the Machine Intelligence group at Aalborg University. His academic distinctions include being the Chair of the Board of Directors for The Association for Uncertainty in Artificial Intelligence (2005-2008), the Area editor for The International Journal of Approximate Reasoning and General Chair and co-chair of seven international conferences.*

Preface

Under the rational agent approach, the goal of artificial intelligence is to design rational agents that must take the best actions given the information available, their prior knowledge, and their goals. In many cases, the information and knowledge is incomplete or unreliable, and the results of their decisions are not certain, that is, they have to make decisions under uncertainty. An intelligent agent should try to make the *best* decisions based on limited information and limited resources. *Decision Theory* provides a normative framework for decision making under uncertainty. It is based on the concept of *rationality*, that is that an agent should try to maximize its utility or minimize its costs. Decision theory was initially developed in economics and operations research, but in recent years has attracted the attention of artificial intelligence researchers interested in understanding and building intelligent agents.

Decision Theory Models for Applications in Artificial Intelligence: Concepts and Solutions provides an introduction to different types of decision theory techniques, and illustrates their application in artificial intelligence. This book provides insights into the advantages and challenges of using decision theory models for developing intelligent systems. It includes a general and comprehensive overview of decision theoretic models in artificial intelligence, with a review of the basic solution techniques, a sample of more advanced approaches, and examples of some recent real world applications.

The book is divided into three parts: *Fundamentals, Concepts,* and *Solutions.* Section 1 provides a general introduction to the main decision-theoretic techniques used in artificial intelligence: Influence Diagrams, Markov Decision Processes and Reinforcement Learning. It also reviews the bases of probability and decision theory, and provides a general overview of probabilistic graphical models. Section 2 presents recent theoretical developments that extend some of the techniques in Section 1 to deal with computational and representational issues that arise in artificial intelligence. Section 3 describes a wide sample of applications of decision-theoretic models in different areas of artificial intelligence, including: intelligent tutors and intelligent assistants, power plant control, medical assistive technologies, spoken dialog systems, service robots, and multi-robot systems.

This book is intended for students, researchers and practitioners of artificial intelligence that are interested in decision-theoretic approaches for building intelligent systems. Besides providing a comprehensive introduction to the theoretical bases and computational techniques, it includes recent developments in representation, inference and learning. It is also useful for engineers and other professionals in different fields interested in understanding and applying decision-theoretic techniques to solve practical problems in education, health, robotics, industry and communications, among other application areas. The book includes a wide sample of applications that illustrate the advantages as well as the challenges involved in applying these techniques in different domains.

Acknowledgment

We will like to acknowledge the support of Project FONCICYT 95185, "Dynamic Probabilistic Graphical Models and Applications", sponsored by CONACYT, Mexico, and the European Union. Several chapters in this volume are related to this project, which concluded in June 2011.

We also acknowledge the professional work of all the reviewers, and the assistance of the publishers in the preparation of this volume.

Finally, we appreciate the support of our institutions during the edition of this book.

L. Enrique Sucar
National Institute for Astrophysics, Optics and Electronics, Mexico

Eduardo F. Morales
National Institute for Astrophysics, Optics and Electronics, Mexico

Jesse Hoey
University of Waterloo, Canada

Section 1
Fundamentals

Chapter 1
Introduction

L. Enrique Sucar
National Institute for Astrophysics, Optics and Electronics, Mexico

Eduardo Morales
National Institute for Astrophysics, Optics and Electronics, Mexico

Jesse Hoey
University of Waterloo, Canada

ABSTRACT

This chapter gives a general introduction to decision-theoretic models in artificial intelligence and an overview of the rest of the book. It starts by motivating the use of decision-theoretic models in artificial intelligence and discussing the challenges that arise as these techniques are applied to develop intelligent systems for complex domains. Then it introduces decision theory, including its axiomatic bases and the principle of maximum expected utility; a brief introduction to decision trees is also presented. Finally, an overview of the three main parts of the book –fundamentals, concepts and solutions– is presented.

ARTIFICIAL INTELLIGENCE AND DECISION THEORY

For achieving their goals, intelligent agents, natural or artificial, have to select a course of actions among many possibilities. That is, they have to take decisions based on the information they can obtain from their environment, their previous knowledge and their objectives. In many cases, the information and knowledge is incomplete or unreliable, and the results of their decisions are not certain, that is they have to take decisions under uncertainty. For instance: a medical doctor in an emergency, must act promptly even if she has limited information on the patient's state; an autonomous vehicle that detects what might be an obstacle in its way, must decide if it should turn or stop without being certain about the obstacle's distance, size and velocity; or a financial agent needs to select the best investment according to its vague predictions on expected return of the different alternatives and its clients' requirements. In all these cases, the agent should try to make the *best* decision based on limited information and resources (time, computational power, etc.). How can we determine which is the best decision?

Decision Theory provides a normative framework for decision making under uncertainty. It is

DOI: 10.4018/978-1-60960-165-2.ch001

based on the concept of *rationality*, that is that an agent should try to maximize its utility or minimize its costs. This assumes that there is some way to assign utilities (usually a number, that can correspond to monetary value or any other scale) to the result of each alternative action, such that the best decision is the one that has the highest utility. For example, if we wanted to select in which stock to invest $1000 for a year, and we knew which will be the price of each stock after a year, then we should invest in the stock that will provide the highest return. Of course we cannot predict with precision the price of stocks a year in advance, and in general we are not sure of the results of each of the possible decisions, so we need to take this into account when we calculate the value of each alternative. So in decision theory we consider the *expected utility*, which makes an average of all the possible results of a decision, weighted by their probability. Thus, in a nutshell, a rational agent must select the decision that maximizes its expected utility.

Decision theory was initially developed in economics and operations research (Neumann & Morgenstern, 1944), but in recent years has attracted the attention of artificial intelligent (AI) researchers interested in understanding and building intelligent agents. These intelligent agents, such as robots, financial advisers, intelligent tutors, etc., must deal with similar problems as those encountered in economics and operations research, but with two main differences.

One difference has to do with the size of the problems, which in artificial intelligence tend to be much larger, in general, than in traditional applications in economics; with many more possible *states* of the environment and in some cases also a larger number of actions or decisions for the agent. For example, consider a mobile robot that is moving in a large building and wants to decide the best set of movements that will take it from one place in the building to another. In this case

the world state could be represented as the position of the robot in the building, and the agent's actions are the set of possible motions (direction and velocity) of the robot. So the problem can be formulated as the selection of the best motion for each position in the building to reach the goal position (minimizing distance or time, for instance). In this case the number of states and actions are in principle infinite, or very large if we discretize them. The size of the problems in terms of states and actions imply a problem of computational complexity, in terms of space and time, so AI has to deal with these issues in order to apply decision theory to complex scenarios.

The other main difference has to do with knowledge about the problem domain, that is having a *model* of the problem according to what is required to apply decision theory techniques to solve it. This means, in general, knowledge of all the possible domain states and possible actions, and the probability of each outcome of a decision and its corresponding utility[1]. In many AI applications a model is not known in advance, and could be difficult to obtain. Returning to the robot navigation example, the robot might not have a precise model of the environment and might also lack a detailed model of its dynamics to exactly predict which will be its position after each movement. So AI researchers have to deal also with the problem of knowledge acquisition or learning.

The research on decision-theoretic models in artificial intelligence has focused on these two main issues: computational complexity and model acquisition; as well as in incorporating these theoretical advances in different applications of intelligent agents. In the rest of the book we will explore the theoretical and practical developments of this interaction between artificial intelligence and decision theory; but first we will review the basis of decision theory.

DECISION THEORY: FUNDAMENTALS

The principles of decision theory were initially developed in the classic text by Von Neuman and Morgensten, *Theory of Games and Economic Behavior* (Neumann & Morgenstern, 1944). They established a set of intuitive constraints that should guide the preferences of a rational agent, which are known as the axioms of utility theory. Before we list these axioms, we need to establish some notation.

In a decision scenario there are four elements:

- **Alternatives:** are the choices that the agent has and are under his control. Each decision has at least two alternatives (e.g. to do or not do some action).
- **Events:** these are produced by the environment or by other agents; are outside of the agent's control. Each random event has at least two possible results, and although we do not know in advance which result will occur, we can assign a probability to each one.
- **Outcomes:** are the results of the combination of the agents decisions and the random events. Each possible outcome has a different preference (utility) for the agent.
- **Preferences:** these are established according to the agent's goals and objectives and are assigned by the agent to each possible outcome. They establish a value for the agent for each possible result of its decisions.

As an example consider a virtual robot that navigates in a grid environment, see Figure 1. The virtual robot is in certain cell, and it can move to each 4 of the adjacent cells –up, down, left, right; its objective is to arrive to the goal cell. In this case the alternatives are the four possible actions that the robot can take in each cell. The events could be a failure in the robot or another agent

Figure 1. An example of a decision problem: a robot in a grid environment. The robot can move to the neighboring cells (as indicated by the arrows) an must select the best moves to avoid the obstacles (in gray) and reach the GOAL

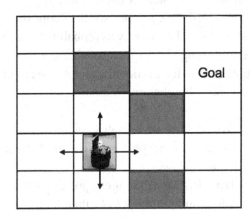

that gets in its way; both can prevent the robot from reaching the desired location. According to how likely these events are, there will be a certain probability that the robot reaches the desired cell or another cell. The outcomes are the result of the combination of the robot actions and the events. For example, if the robot moves to the cell to its right, the possible outcomes could be the that it arrives to the right cell, it stays in the same cell or it arrives to another adjacent cell. The preferences will be established according to the robot objectives. In this case, the robot will prefer the goal cell over all the other empty cells in the environment, and these over the cells that have obstacles.

In utility theory, these type of scenarios are called *lotteries*. In a lottery each possible outcome or *state*, A, has certain probability p and an associated preference to the agent which is quantified by a real number, U. For instance, a lottery L with two possible outcomes, A with probability p and B with probability $1 - p$, will be denoted as:

$$L = [p, A; 1 - p, B]$$

If an agent prefers A than B it is written as $A \succ B$, and if it is indifferent between both outcomes is denoted as $A \sim B$. In general a lottery can have any number of outcomes; an outcome can be an atomic state or another lottery.

Based on these concepts, we can define utility theory in an analogous way as probability theory, by establishing a set of reasonable constraints on preferences for a rational agent, these are the axioms of utility theory:

- **Order:** Given two states, an agent prefers one or the other or it is indifferent between them.
- **Transitivity:** If an agent prefers outcome A to B and prefers B to C, then it must prefer A to C.
- **Continuity:** If $A \succ B \succ C$, then there is some probability p such that the agent is indifferent between getting B with probability one, or the lottery $L = [p, A; 1 - p, C]$.
- **Substitutability:** If an agent is indifferent between two lotteries A and B, then the agent is indifferent between two more complex lotteries that are the same except that B is substituted for A in one of them.
- **Monotonicity:** There are two lotteries that have the same outcomes, A and B. If the agent prefers A, then it must prefer the lottery in which A has higher probability.
- **Decomposability:** Compound lotteries can be decomposed into simple ones using the rules of probability.

Then, the definition of a utility function follows from the axioms of utility.

- **Utility Principle**: If an agent's preferences follow the axioms of utility, then there is a real-valued utility function U such that:
  1. $U(A) \succ U(B)$ if an only if the agent prefers A over B,

  2. $U(A) = U(B)$ if an only if the agent is indifferent between A and B.
- **Maximum Expected Utility Principle**: The utility of a lottery is the sum of the utilities of each outcome times its probability:

$$U[p_1, S_1; p_2, S_2; P_3, S_3; .] = \sum_j p_j U_j$$

Based on this concept of a utility function, we can now define the expected utility (EU) of certain decision D taken by an agent, considering that there are N possible results of this decision, each with probability P:

$$EU(D) = \sum_{j=1}^{N} P(result_j(D)) U(result_j(D))$$

The principle of Maximum Expected Utility states that a rational agent should choose an action that maximizes its expected utility.

Although it seems straight-forward to apply this principle to determine the best decision, as the decision problems become more complex, involving several decisions, events and possible outcomes, it is not as easy as it seems; and a systematic approach is required to model and solve complex decision problems. One of the earliest modeling tools developed for solving decision problems are decision trees (Cole & Rowley, 1995).

Decision Trees

A decision tree is a graphical representation of a decision problem, which has three types of elements or nodes that represent the three basic components of a decision problem: decisions, uncertain events and results.

A *decision node* is depicted as a rectangle which has several *branches*, each branch represents each of the possible alternatives present in this decision point. At the end of each branch there could be another decision point, an event or a result.

An *event node* is depicted as a circle, and has also several branches, each branch represents one of the possible outcomes of this uncertain event. These outcomes correspond to all the possible results of this event, that is they should be mutually exclusive and exhaustive. A probability value is assigned to each branch, such that the sum of the probabilities for all the branches is equal to one. At the extreme of each branch there could another event node, a decision node or a result.

The *results* are annotated with the utility they express for the agent, and are usually at the end of each branch of the tree (the leaves).

Decision trees are usually drawn from left to right, with the root of the tree (a decision node) at the extreme left, and the leaves of the tree to the right. An example of a hypothetical decision problem (based on an example in (Borrás, 2001)) is shown in figure 2. It represents an investment decision with 3 alternatives: (i) Stocks, (ii) Gold, and (iii) No invest. Assuming that the investment is for one year, if we invest in stock, depending on how the stock market behaves (uncertain event), we could gain \$1000 or lose \$300, both with equal probability. If we invest in Gold, we have another decision, to have insurance or not. If we get insurance, then we are sure to gain \$200; otherwise we win or lose depending if the price of the gold is up, stable or down; this is represented as another event. Each possible outcome has a certain value and probability assigned, as shown in figure 2. What should the investor decide?

To determine the best decision for each decision point, according to the maximum expected utility principle, we need to *evaluate* the decision tree. The evaluation of a decision tree consists of determining the values of both types of nodes, decision and event nodes. It is done from right to left, starting from any node that has only results for all its branches:

Figure 2. An example of a decision tree (see text for details)

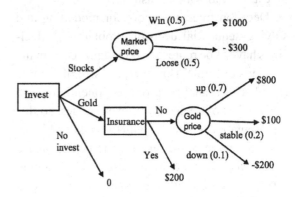

- The value of a decision node D is the maximum value of all the branches that emanate from it: $V(D) = \max_j U(result_j(D))$.

- The value of an event node E is the expected value of all the branches that emanate from it, obtained as the weighted sum of the result values multiplied by their probabilities:

$$V(E) = \sum_j P(result_j(E))U(result_j(E))$$

Following this procedure we can evaluate the decision tree of figure 2:

- **Event 1 - Market Price:**

$$V(E_1) = 1000 \times 0.5 - 300 \times 0.5 = 150$$

- **Event 2 - Gold Price:**

$$V(E_2) = 800 \times 0.7 + 100 \times 0.2 - 200 \times 0.1 = 560$$

- **Decision 2 - Insurance:**

$$V(D_2) = \max(200, 560) = 560$$

- **Decision 1 - Investment:**

$$V(D_1) = max(150, 560, 0) = 560$$

Thus, in this case the best decisions are to invest in Gold without insurance.

Decision trees are a tool for modelling and solving sequential decision problems, as decisions have to be represented in sequence as in the previous example. However, the size of the tree (number of branches) grows exponentially with the number of decision and event nodes, so this representation is practical only for *small* problems. An alternative modelling tool is the *Influence Diagram* (Howard & Matheson, 1984, Shachter, 1986), which provide a compact representation of a decision problem. Influence diagrams are introduced in Chapter 2.

Decision trees and influence diagrams are techniques for solving *simple* decision problems, where a few decisions are involved (usually less than 10). For more complex problems, in particular dynamic decision problems that involve a series of decisions in time (as the robot navigation example), there are other techniques, such as *Markov Decision Processes* (MDPs) and *Partially Observable Markov Decision Processes* (POMDPs). These are reviewed in Chapter 3.

In many domains the transition model is not known in advance and an agent must learn a policy from experience. For this case, several approaches have been proposed by the reinforcement learning community. These are reviewed in Chapter 4.

OVERVIEW

The book is organized in three sections: fundamentals, concepts, and solutions.

Fundamentals

The first section, fundamentals, provides a general introduction to the main decision-theoretic techniques used in artificial intelligence.

Probabilistic graphical models provide a framework for a compact representation of a joint probability distribution, and are incorporated in several advanced decision models, such as influence diagrams and factored Markov decision processes. Chapter 2 gives an overview of probabilistic graphical models and introduces influence diagrams. First, a brief review of probability theory is included. A general introduction to graphical models is given, and a more detailed description of certain types of graphical models is presented, in particular Bayesian networks and dynamic Bayesian networks. Then influence diagrams are introduced, including some of the more common solution techniques. Finally, a brief introduction to dynamic decision networks is presented, and their relation with Markov decision processes.

Chapter 3 provides an introduction to fully and partially observable Markov decision processes as a framework for sequential decision making under uncertainty. It reviews Markov decision processes (MDPs) and partially observable Markov decision processes (POMDPs), describes the basic algorithms to find good policies and discusses modeling and computational issues that arise in practice.

In many applications a decision model, such as an influence diagram or MDP, is not available, so an alternative is to learn directly a decision *policy* from experience using *Reinforcement Learning*. Chapter 4 provides a concise and updated introduction to reinforcement learning from a machine learning perspective. It gives the required background to understand the chapters related to reinforcement learning in the book, and includes an overview of some of the latest trends in the area.

Concepts

Section 2 presents recent theoretical developments that extend some of the techniques in Section 1, such as influence diagrams, Markov decision processes and reinforcement learning, to deal with computational and representational issues that arise in artificial intelligence. In some applications of artificial intelligence, it is not only important to make good decisions, but also to explain how the system arrived at these decisions; a novel method for automatically generating explanations for MDPs is also described.

Semi-Markov Decision Processes (SMDPs) are an extension of MDPs that generalize the notion of time by allowing the time intervals between states to vary stochastically. SMDPs are used to formulate many control problems and play a key role in hierarchical reinforcement learning. Chapter 5 shows how to translate a decision making problem into a form that can instead be solved by inference and learning techniques. It establishes a formal connection between planning in semi-MDPs and inference in probabilistic graphical models.

Multi-stage Stochastic Programming relies on mathematical programming and probability theory to solve complex decision problems. Chapter 6 presents the multi-stage stochastic programming framework for sequential decision making under uncertainty. It describes the standard techniques for solving approximately stochastic dynamic problems, which are based on a discretization of the disturbance space called a *scenario tree*. It also shows how supervised learning techniques can be used to evaluate the quality of an approximation.

Chapter 7 describes a technique to explain policies for factored Markov decision processes by populating a set of domain-independent templates, and a mechanism to determine a minimal set of templates that, viewed together, completely justified the policy. This technique is illustrated in two domains: advising students in their course selection and assisting people with dementia in completing the task of hand washing.

Dynamic limited-memory influence diagrams (DLIMIDs) are novel type of decision support models whose main difference with other models is the restriction of limited memory, which means that the decisions are based only on recent observations. Chapter 8 introduces DLIMIDs and presents several algorithms for evaluating them. The application of DLIMIDs is illustrated in a real-world medical problem, including a comparison with other formalisms.

Chapter 9 introduces an approach for reinforcement learning based on a relational representation. The basic idea is to represent states in the domain as sets of first order relations; actions and policies are also represented over those generalized representations. The approach is demonstrated in two applications: a flight simulator and a mobile robot.

Solutions

Section 3 describes a wide sample of applications of decision-theoretic models in different areas of artificial intelligence, including: intelligent tutors and intelligent assistants, power plant control, medical assistive technologies, spoken dialog systems, service robots, and multi-robot systems. As well as illustrating the practical aspects of using decision theory in AI, it also presents several developments that extend the techniques described in Section 1 and Section 2. These include: extending the expressive power of the models based on relational representations; making the solution techniques more efficient using abstraction and decomposition; and developing decentralized models for distributed applications, among others.

Chapter 10 describes a decision-theoretic tutor that helps students learn from analogical problem solving. The tutor incorporates a novel example–selection mechanism that tailors the choice of examples for a given student based on dynamic Bayesian networks. An empirical evaluation shows that this selection mechanism is more effective that standard approaches for fostering learning.

Chapter 11 presents an intelligent tutor based on dynamic decision networks applied to an undergraduate Physics scenario, where the aim is to adapt the learning experience to suit the learner's needs. It employs *Probabilistic Relational Models* to facilitate the construction of the models, such that the tutor can be easily adapted to different experiments, domains and student levels.

An intelligent assistant for power plant operators is introduced in Chapter 12. *AsistO* provides off-line training and on-line guidance to power plant operators in the form of ordered recommendations. These recommendations are generated using Markov decision processes over an approximate factored model of the power plant. It also describes an automatic explanation mechanism that explains the recommendations to the user.

Chapter 13 presents a general decision–theoretic model of interactions between users and cognitive assistive technologies for various tasks of importance to the elderly population. The model is a POMDP whose goal is to work in conjunction with the user towards the completion of a given task. It is applied to four tasks: assisted hand washing, stroke rehabilitation, health monitoring, and wheelchair mobility.

Spoken dialog systems present a classic example of planning under uncertainty. Thus, decision theory, and in particular partially–observable Markov decision processes, are an attractive approach to building spoken dialog systems. Chapter 14 traces the history of POMDP–based spoken dialog systems, and sketches avenues for future work.

Chapter 15 describes a novel framework based on functional decomposition of MDPs, and its application to task coordination in service robots. In this framework, a complex task is divided into several subtasks, each one defined as an MDP and solved independently; their policies are combined to obtain a global policy. Conflicts may arise as the individual policies are combined, so a technique for detecting and solving different types of conflicts is presented.

Chapter 16 introduces problems related to the decentralized control of multi–robot systems. It presents *Decentralized Markov Decision Processes* (DEC-MDPs) and discusses their applicability to real-world multi-robot applications. Then, it introduces OC-DEC-MDPs and 2V-DEC-MDPs which have been developed to increase the applicability of DEC-MDPs.

FINAL REMARKS

Sequential decision making is at the core of the development of many intelligent systems but it has been only recently that a large number of developments have been proposed and real world applications have been tackled. This book provides a general and comprehensive overview of decision theoretic models in artificial intelligence, with an overview of the basic solution techniques, a sample of more advanced approaches, and examples of some recent real world applications.

REFERENCES

Borrás, R. (2001). *Análisis de incertidumbre y riesgo para la toma de decisiones*. Orizaba, Mexico: Comunidad Morelos.

Cole, S., & Rowley, J. (1995). Revisiting decision trees. *Management Decision, 33*(8), 46–50.

Howard, R., & Matheson, J. (1984). Influence diagrams . In Howard, R., & Matheson, J. (Eds.), *Readings on the principles and applications of decision analysis*. Menlo Park, California: Strategic Decisions Group.

Neumann, J. V., & Morgenstern, O. (1944). *Theory of games and economic behavior*. Princeton University Press.

Shachter, R. D. (1986). Evaluating influence diagrams. *Operations Research, 34*(6), 871–882.

ENDNOTE

[1] What is a model according to different techniques will be defined more precisely in the next section and in the rest of the book

Chapter 2
Introduction to Bayesian Networks and Influence Diagrams

Luis Enrique Sucar
National Institute for Astrophysics, Optics and Electronics, Mexico

ABSTRACT

In this chapter we will cover the fundamentals of probabilistic graphical models, in particular Bayesian networks and influence diagrams, which are the basis for some of the techniques and applications that are described in the rest of the book. First we will give a general introduction to probabilistic graphical models, including the motivation for using these models, and a brief history and general description of the main types of models. We will also include a brief review of the basis of probability theory. The core of the chapter will be the next three sections devoted to: (i) Bayesian networks, (ii) Dynamic Bayesian networks and (iii) Influence diagrams. For each we will introduce the models, their properties and give some examples. We will briefly describe the main inference techniques for the three types of models. For Bayesian and dynamic Bayesian nets we will talk about learning, including structure and parameter learning, describing the main types of approaches. At the end of the section on influence diagrams we will briefly introduce sequential decision problems as a link to the chapter on MDPs and POMDPs. We conclude the chapter with a summary and pointers for further reading for each topic.

INTRODUCTION

We start by motivating the use of probabilistic graphical models and explaining their relevance to artificial intelligence. After a brief review of the basis of probability theory, we introduce the different types of models that will be covered in this book, which will be described in more detail later.

Motivation

Several important problems in Artificial Intelligence (AI), such as diagnosis, recognition, planning, among others, have to deal with *uncertainty*.

DOI: 10.4018/978-1-60960-165-2.ch002

Copyright © 2012, IGI Global. Copying or distributing in print or electronic forms without written permission of IGI Global is prohibited.

Exhibit 1.

$$P(D_i \mid S_1, S_2, \ldots, S_{20}) = P(D_i)P(S_1, S_2, \ldots, S_{20} \mid D_i) \, / \, P(S_1, S_2, \ldots, S_{20}) \tag{1}$$

Exhibit 2.

$$P(D_i \mid S_1, S_2, \ldots, S_{20}) = \frac{P(D_i)P(S_1 \mid D_i)P(S_2 \mid D_i)\ldots P(S_{20} \mid D_i)}{P(S_1, S_2, \ldots, S_{20})} \tag{2}$$

Probability theory provides a well established foundation for managing uncertainty, so it is natural to use it for reasoning under uncertainty in AI. However, if we apply probability in a naive way to the complex problems that are frequent in AI, we are soon deterred by computational complexity. For instance, assume that we want to build a probabilistic system for medical diagnosis, and we consider 10 possible diseases and 20 different symptoms; for simplicity assume that each symptom is represented as a binary variable (present or absent). One way to estimate the probability of certain disease, D_i, given a set of symptoms $S_1, S_2, \ldots, S_{20}$, is to use Bayes' rule (see section on Probability Theory) (see Exhibit 1).

The second term in the right hand of this equation will require storing a table of 10×2^{20} or approx. 10 million probabilities, which besides the memory problems, are very difficult to obtain either from an expert or from data. A way to simplify this problem is the common assumption that all the symptoms are independent given the disease, so we can apply instead what is called the *Naive Bayes Classifier* (see Exhibit 2).

In this case the number of required probabilities reduces drastically for the same term, as we require $20 \times (10 \times 2)$ entries, or 400 probability values (200 independent values, as some values can be deduced from others given the axioms of probability theory). However, the independence assumptions may not be valid, so the results could be not as good, and in some cases very bad!

Probabilistic Graphical Models (PGMs) provide a middle ground between these two extremes. The basic idea is to consider only those independence relations that are valid for certain problem, and include these in the probabilistic model to reduce complexity in terms of memory requirements and also computational time. A natural way to represent the dependence and independence relations between a set of variables is using graphs, such that variables that are *directly* dependent are connected; and the independence relations are implicit in this *dependency graph*. Before we go into a more formal definition of PGMs and discuss the different types of models, we will review some basic concepts in probability theory.

Probability Theory

Probability theory originated in the games of chance and has a long and interesting history. Several definitions or interpretations of probability have been proposed, starting from the *classical* one of Laplace, and including the *limiting frequency*, the *subjective*, the *logical* and the *propensity* interpretations (Gillies, 2000). We will consider the logical or normative approach and define probabilities in terms of the degree of plausibility of certain proposition given the available evidence (Jaynes, 2003). Based on Cox's work, Jaynes established some basic desiderata that these degrees of plausibility must follow (Jaynes, 2003):

Exhibit 3.

$$P(A_1 + A_2 + \cdots A_N \mid C) = P(A_1 \mid C) + P(A_2 \mid C) + \cdots + P(A_N \mid C) \tag{3}$$

Exhibit 4.

$$P(A_1, A_2, \ldots, A_N \mid B) = P(A_1 \mid B)P(A_2 \mid B) \cdots P(A_N \mid B) \tag{6}$$

1. Representation by real numbers.
2. Qualitative correspondence with common sense.
3. Consistency.

Based on this intuitive principles, we can derive the basic rules of probability:

- $P(A)$ is a continuous monotonic function in $[0,1]$.
- $P(A, B \mid C) = P(A \mid C) P(B \mid A, C)$ (product rule).
- $P(A \mid B) + P(\neg A \mid B) = 1$ (sum rule).

Where A, B, C are propositions (binary variables) and $P(A)$ is the probability of A given that C is known, which is called *conditional probability*. $P(A, B \mid C)$ is the probability of A AND B given C (logical conjunction) and $P(\neg A \mid C)$ is the probability of NOT A given C (logical negation). These rules are equivalent to the most commonly used Kolmogorov axioms (see (Jaynes, 2003)). From these basic rules or axioms, all conventional probability theory can be derived, so lets see some other important rules or theorems of probability.

The probability of the disjunction (logical sum) of two propositions is given by the *sum rule*[1]: $P(A + B \mid C) = P(A \mid C) + P(B \mid C) - P(A, B \mid C)$; if the propositions A and B are mutually exclusive given C, we can simplify it to: $P(A + B \mid C) = P(A \mid C) + P(B \mid C)$. This can be generalized for N mutually exclusive propositions to (see Exhibit 3).

In the case that there are N mutually exclusive and exhaustive hypothesis, $H_1, H_2, \ldots, H_N$, and if the evidence B does not favor any of them, then according to the principle of indifference: $P(H_i|B) = 1/N$.

According to the logical interpretation there are no *absolute* probabilities, all are conditional on some background information, B. $P(H|B)$ conditioned only on the background B is called a *prior* probability[2]; once we incorporate some additional information D we call it *posterior* probability, $P(H|D,B)$. From the product rule we obtain:

$$P(D, H \mid B) = P(D \mid H, B) P(H \mid B) = P(H \mid D, B) P(D \mid B) \tag{4}$$

From where we obtain:

$$P(H \mid D, B) = \frac{P(H \mid B)P(D \mid H, B)}{P(H \mid B)} \tag{5}$$

This last equation is known as *Bayes' rule* and the term $P(D|H,B)$ as the *likelihood*, $L(H)$.

In some cases the probability of H is not influenced by the knowledge of D, so it is said that H and D are *independent* given some background B, so then $P(H,D|B) = P(H|B)$. So in case A and B are independent the product rule can be simplified to: $P(A,B|C) = P(A|C)P(B|C)$, and this can be generalized to N mutually independent propositions (see Exhibit 4).

This is the condition assumed in the Naive Bayes classifier that we mentioned before. If two propositions are independent given just the back-

Exhibit 5.

$$P(A_1, A_2, \ldots, A_N \mid B) = P(A_1 \mid A_2, A_3, \ldots, A_N, B)P(A_2 \mid A_3, A_4, \ldots, A_N, B) \cdots P(A_N \mid B) \qquad (7)$$

ground information they are *marginally* independent; however if they are independent given some additional evidence, E, then they are *conditionally* independent: $P(H,D|B,E)=P(H|B,E)$. Probabilistic graphical models are based on these conditions of marginal and conditional independence as we will see in the next section.

The probability of a conjunction of N propositions, that is $P(A_1, A_2, \ldots, A_N|B)$, is usually called the *joint* probability. If we generalize the product rule to N propositions we obtain what is know as the *chain* rule (see Exhibit 5).

So the joint probability of N propositions can be obtained by this rule. Conditional independence relations between the propositions can be used to simplify this product; that is, for instance if A_1 and A_2 are independent given $A_3, \ldots, A_N, B$, then the first term in the right side of equation 7 can be simplified to $P(A_1|A_3, \ldots, A_N, B)$.

Random Variables. If we consider a finite set of exhaustive and mutually exclusive propositions[3], then a discrete variable X can represent this set of propositions, such that each value x_i of X corresponds to one proposition. If we assign a numerical value to each proposition x_i, then X is a *discrete random variable*. For example, the outcome of the toss of a die is a discrete random variable with 6 possible values 1,2,...,6. The probabilities for all possible values of X, $P(X)$, constitute the probability distribution of X. Considering the dice example, for a fair dice the probability distribution will be:

x	1	2	3	4	5	6
$P(x)$	1/6	1/6	1/6	1/6	1/6	1/6

This is an example of a *uniform* probability distribution. There are several probability distribu-

tions which have been defined, another common one is the *binomial* distribution. Assume we have an urn with N colored balls, red and black, of which M are red, so the fraction of red balls is $\pi = M/N$. We draw a ball at random, record its color, and return it to the urn, mixing the balls again (so that, in principle, each draw is independent of the previous one). The probability of getting r red balls in n draws is:

$$P(r \mid n, \pi) = \binom{n}{r}\pi^r(1-\pi)^{n-r}, \qquad (8)$$

where $\binom{n}{r} = \dfrac{n!}{r!(n-r)!}$. This is an example of a binomial distribution which applies when there are n independent trails, each with two possible outcomes (success or failure), and the probability of success is constant over all trials. There are many other distributions, we refer the interested reader to the additional reading section at the end of the chapter.

There are two important quantities that in general help to characterize a probability distribution. The expected value or *expectation* of a discrete random variable is the weighted average of the possible values, weighted according to their probabilities:

$$E(X \mid B) = \sum_{i=1}^{N} P(x_i \mid B)x_i \qquad (9)$$

The *variance* is defined as the expected value of the square of the variable minus its expectation:

$$Var(X \mid B) = \sum_{i=1}^{N} P(x_i \mid B)(x_i - E(X))^2 \qquad (10)$$

Intuitively, the variance gives a measure of how *wide* or *narrow* the probabilities are distributed for certain random variable.

So far we have considered discrete variables, however the rules of probability can be extended to continuous variables. If we have a continuous variable X, we can divide it into a set of mutually exclusive and exhaustive intervals, such that $P = (a < X \le b)$ is a proposition, so the rules derived so far apply to it. A *continuous random variable* can be defined in terms of a *probability density function*, $f(X|B)$, such that:

$$P(a < X \le b \mid B) = \int_a^b f(X \mid B)dx \qquad (11)$$

The probability density function must satisfy $\int_{-\infty}^{\infty} f(X \mid B)dx = 1$.

An example of a continuous probability distribution is the *Normal* or Gaussian distribution. This distribution plays an important role in many applications of probability and statistics, as many phenomena in nature have an approximately Normal distribution; and it is also prevalent in probabilistic graphical models due to its mathematical properties.

A Normal distribution is denoted as $N(\mu, \sigma^2)$, where μ is the *mean* (center) and σ is the *standard deviation* (spread); and is defined as:

$$f(X \mid B) = \frac{1}{2\sqrt{2\pi}} exp\{-\frac{1}{2\sigma^2}(x-\mu)^2\} \qquad (12)$$

After this brief review of probability theory, we are ready to define probabilistic graphical models.

Probabilistic Graphical Models

Given a set of (discrete) random variables, $X = X_1, X_2, ..., X_N$, the joint probability distribution, $P(X_1, X_2, ..., X_N)$ specifies the probability for each combination of values (the joint space). From it, we can obtain the probability of a variable(s) (marginal), and of a variable(s) given the other variables (conditional).

A *Probabilistic Graphical Model* is a compact representation of a joint probability distribution, from which we can obtain marginal and conditional probabilities. It has several advantages over a *flat*[4] representation:

- It is generally much more compact (space).
- It is generally much more efficient (time).
- It is easier to understand and communicate.
- It is easier to build (from experts) or learn (from data).

A graphical model is specified by two aspects: (i) a graph, $G(V,E)$, that defines the structure of the model; and a set of local functions, $f(Y_i)$, that defines the parameters, where Y_i is a subset of X. The joint probability is defined by the product of the local functions:

$$P(X_1, X_2, ..., X_N) = \prod_{i=1}^{M} f(Y_i) \qquad (13)$$

This representation in terms of a graph and a set of local functions (called *potentials*) is the basis for inference and learning in PGMs:

- **Inference:** obtain the marginal or conditional probabilities of any subset of variables Z given any other subset Y.
- **Learning:** given a set of data values for X (that can be incomplete) estimate the structure (graph) and parameters (local function) of the model.

There are different type of PGMs that are introduced below.

Table 1. Main types of PGMs

Type	Directed/Undirected	Static/Dynamic	Prob./Decisional
Bayesian Classifiers	D/U	S	P
Markov Chains	D	D	P
Hidden Markov Models	D	D	P
Markov Random Fields	U	S	P
Bayesian Networks	D	S	P
Dynamic Bayesian Networks	D	D	P
Kalman Filters	D	D	P
Influence Diagrams	D	S	D
MDPs	D	D	D
POMDPs	D	D	D

TYPES OF MODELS

We can classify probabilistic graphical models according to three dimensions:

1. Directed or Undirected
2. Static or Dynamic
3. Probabilistic or Decisional

The first dimension has to do with the type of graph used to represent the dependence relations. Undirected graphs represent symmetric relations, while directed graphs represent relations in which the direction is important. Given a set of random variables with the corresponding conditional independence relations, in general it is not possible to represent all the relations with one type of graph (Pearl, 1988), so both types of models are useful.

The second dimension defines if the model represents a set of variables at certain point in time (static) or across different times (dynamic).

Probabilistic models only include random variables, while decisional models also include decision and utility variables.

The most common classes of PGMs and their type according to the previous dimensions are summarized in Table 1.

In this chapter we will focus on Bayesian Networks, Dynamic Bayesian Networks, and

Figure 1. An example of a Bayesian network

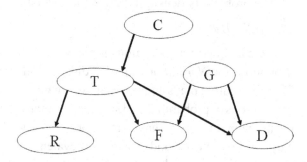

Influence Diagrams; which are the basis for several techniques and applications that are covered later. The next chapter introduces Markov decision processes (MDPs) and partially observable MDPs (POMDPs).

BAYESIAN NETWORKS

Representation

A Bayesian network (BN) (Pearl, 1988) represents the joint distribution of a set of n (discrete) variables, $X_1, X_2, \ldots, X_n$, as a directed acyclic graph (DAG) and a set of conditional probability tables (CPTs). Each node, that corresponds to a variable, has an associated CPT that specifies the probability of each state of the variable given its parents in the graph. The structure of the network implies a set of conditional independence assertions. Based on these conditional independence relations, BNs provide a powerful modeling technique for representing complex problems.

Figure 1 depicts an example of a simple BN. The structure of the graph implies a set of conditional independence assertions for this set of variables. For example, R is conditionally independent of C,G,F,D given T, that is:

$$P(R|C,T,G,F,D)=P(R|T) \qquad (14)$$

The conditional independence assertions implied by the structure of a BN should correspond to the conditional independence relations of the joint probability distribution, and vice versa. These are usually represented using the following notation. X is conditionally independent of Z given Y:

- In the probability distribution: $P(X|Y,Z)=P(X|Y)$.
- In the graph: $I<X|Y|Z>$.

In general it is not alway possible to have a *perfect mapping* of the independence relations between the graph (G) and the distribution (P), so we settle for what is called a *Minimal I–Map*: all the conditional independence relations implied by G are true in P, and if any arc is deleted in G this condition is lost (Pearl, 1988).

Conditional independence assertions can be verified directly from the structure of a BN using a criteria called *D–separation*. Before we define it, we consider the three basic BN structures for three variables and two arcs:

- Sequential: $X \to Y \to Z$.
- Divergent: $X \leftarrow Y \to Z$.
- Convergent: $X \to Y \leftarrow Z$.

In the first two cases, X and Z are conditionally independent given Y, however in the third case

this is not true. This last case, called *explaining away*, corresponds intuitively to having two *causes* with a common *effect*; knowing the effect and one of the causes, alters our belief in the other cause. These cases can be associated to the separating node in the graph, Y, so depending on the case, Y is sequential, divergent or convergent.

D-Separation

Given a graph G, the set of variables A is conditionally independent of the set B given the set C, if there is no trajectory in G between A and B such that:

1. All the convergent nodes are or have descendants in C.
2. All the other nodes are outside C.

For instance, for the BN in Figure 1, R is independent of C given T, but T and G are not independent given F.

According to the previous definition of D-separation, any node X is conditionally independent of all nodes in G that are not descendants of X given its parents in the graph, $Pa(X)$. The structure of a BN can be specified by the parents of each variable. For the example in Figure 1, its structure can be specified as:

1. $Pa(C) = \emptyset$
2. $Pa(T) = C$
3. $Pa(G) = \emptyset$
4. $Pa(R) = T$
5. $Pa(F) = T,G$
6. $Pa(D) = T,G$

Given this condition and using the chain rule, we can specify the joint probability distribution of the set of variables in a BN as the product of the conditional probability of each variable given its parents:

Figure 2. Parameters for the BN in Figure 1. It shows the CPTs for some of the variables in the example:
$P(C)$; $P(T|C)$; *and* $P(F|T,G)$. *We assume in this case that all variables are binary.*

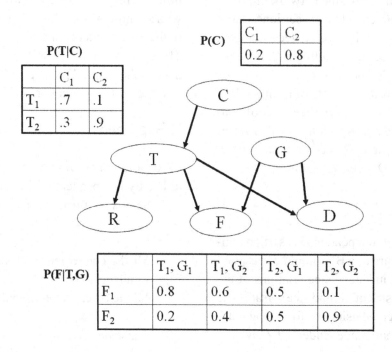

$$P(X_1, X_2, ., X_n) = \prod_{i=1}^{n} P(X_i \mid Pa(X_i)) \qquad (15)$$

For the example in Figure 1:

$P(C,T,G,R,F,D)=P(C)P(G)P(T|C)P(R|T)$
$P(F|T,G)P(D|T,G)$

The *Markov Blanket* of a node X, $MB(X)$, is the set of nodes that make it independent of all the other nodes in G, that is $P(X|G-X)=P(X|MB(X))$. For a BN, the Markov blanket of X can be:

- the parents of X,
- the children of X,
- and other parents of the children of X.

To complete the specification of a BN, we need to define its parameters. In the case of a BN, these parameters are the conditional probabilities of each node given its parents in the graph. If we consider discrete variables:

- Root nodes: vector of marginal probabilities.
- Other nodes: conditional probability table (CPT) of the variable given its parents in the graph.

Figure 2 shows some of the CPTs of the BN in Figure 1. In case of continuous variables we need to specify a function that relates the density function of each variable to the density of its parents (for example, Kalman filters consider Gaussian distributed variables and linear functions).

Inference Techniques: Singly and Multi-Connected Networks

Probabilistic inference consists of *propagating* the effects of certain evidence in a Bayesian network to estimate its effect in the unknown variables. That is, knowing the values for some subset E of variables in the model, the posterior probabilities of the other variables, H, are obtained. The subset

Figure 3. In a tree–structured BN, every node (B) divides the network into two conditionally independent subtrees, E+ and E−

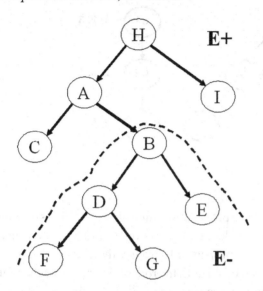

E could be empty, in this case we obtain the prior probabilities of all the variables.

If we compute these probabilities in a direct way (i.e., from the joint distribution), the computational complexity increases exponentially with respect to the number of variables, and the problem becomes intractable even with few variables. Many algorithms have been developed for making this process more efficient, which can be roughly divided into the following classes:

1. Probability propagation (Pearl's algorithm (Pearl, 1988)).
2. Variable elimination.
3. Conditioning.
4. Junction tree.
5. Stochastic simulation.

The probability propagation algorithm only applies to singly connected graphs (trees and polytrees[5]), although there is an extension for general networks called *loopy propagation* which does not guarantee convergence. The other four classes of algorithms work for any network structure, the

last one being an approximate technique while the other three are exact.

Next we briefly describe the probability propagation and the junction tree algorithms. For more information on the other methods we refer the interested reader to the further reading section at the end of this chapter.

Probability Propagation in Trees

We now describe the tree propagation algorithm proposed by Pearl, which provides the basis for several of the more advanced and general techniques.

Given certain evidence, E (subset of variables instantiated), the posterior probability for value i of any variable B, can be obtained by applying Bayes rule:

$$P(B_i \mid E) = P(B_i)P(E \mid B_i) / P(E) \qquad (16)$$

Given that the BN has a tree structure, any node divides the network into two independent subtrees, so we can separate the evidence into (see Figure 3):

E−: Evidence in the tree rooted at B.
E+: All the other evidence.

Then:

$$P(B_i \mid E) = P(B_i)P(E-, E+ \mid B_i) / P(E) \quad (17)$$

And given that $E+$ and $E-$ are independent given B_i, and applying Bayes' rule again, we obtain:

$$P(B_i \mid E) = \alpha P(B_i \mid E+)P(E- \mid B_i) \qquad (18)$$

Where α is a normalization constant. If we define the following terms:

$$\lambda(B_i) = P(E- \mid B_i) \qquad (19)$$

Figure 4. Transformation of a BN to a junction tree: (a) original net, (b) triangulated graph, (c) junction tree

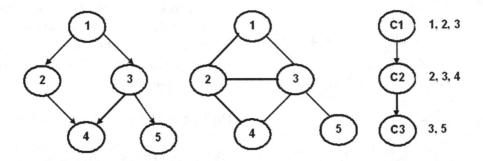

$$\pi(B_i) = P(B_i \mid E+) \tag{20}$$

Then eq. 18 can be written as:

$$P(B_i \mid E) = \alpha \pi(B_i)\lambda(B_i) \tag{21}$$

Equation 21 is the basis for a distributed propagation algorithm to obtain the posterior probability of all non-instantiated nodes. The computation of the posterior probability of any node B is decomposed in two parts: (i) the evidence coming from the children of B in the tree (λ), and the evidence coming from the parent of B (π). We can think of each node B in the tree as a simple processor that stores its vectors $\pi(B)$ and $\lambda(B)$, and its conditional probability table, $P(B|A)$. The evidence is propagated via a message passing mechanism, in which each node sends the corresponding messages to its parent and children in the tree. Message sent from node B to its parent A:

$$\lambda_B(Ai) = \sum_j P(B_j \mid A_i)\lambda(B_j) \tag{22}$$

Message sent from node B to its son S_k:

$$\pi_k(Bi) = \alpha \pi(B_j)\prod_{l \neq k} \lambda_l(B_j) \tag{23}$$

The propagation algorithm starts by assigning the evidence to the known variables, and then this is propagated through the message passing mechanism until the root of the tree is reached for the λ messages, and the leafs for the π messages. At the end of the propagation, each node has its updated λ and π vectors. The posterior probability of any variable B is obtained by combining these vectors using Eq. 21 and normalizing.

Probability propagation is a very efficient algorithm for tree structured BNs, the time complexity to obtain the posterior probability of all the variables in the tree is proportional to the *diameter* of the network (the number of arcs in the trajectory from the root to the more distant leaf). However, it only applies to singly connected networks. Next we will present a general algorithm that applies for any structure.

Junction Tree Algorithm

The junction tree method is based on a transformation of the a BN to a junction tree, where each node in this tree is a group or cluster of variables in the original network. Probabilistic inference is performed over this new representation. Following we give a brief overview of the basic algorithm, for more details see the additional readings section.

The transformation proceeds as follows:

1. Eliminate the directionality of the arcs.
2. Order the nodes in the graph.
3. Moralize the graph (add an arc between pairs of nodes with common children).
4. If necessary add additional arcs to make the graph *triangulated*.
5. Obtain the *cliques* of this graph (subsets of nodes that are fully connected and are not subsets of other fully connected sets).
6. Build a junction tree in which each node is a clique and its parent is any node that contains all common previous variables according to the ordering.

This transformation process is illustrated for a simple example in Figure 4.

Once the junction tree is built, inference is based on probability propagation over the junction tree, in an analogous way as for tree–structured BNs. Initially the joint probability (potential) of each macro node is obtained, and given some evidence, this is propagated to obtain the posterior probability of each junction. The individual probability of each variable is obtained from the joint probability of the appropriate junction via marginalization.

In the worst case probabilistic inference is NP-Hard (Cooper, 1990), and the complexity is proportional to the largest clique in the graph. However, in practice the graphs of BNs for real world problems are usually sparse graphs, and in this case the junction tree method and other techniques are very efficient even for models with hundreds of variables.

Learning

Learning a BN includes two aspects: learning the structure and learning the parameters. When the structure is known, parameter learning consists of estimating the CPTs from data. For structure learning there are two main types of methods: (i) global methods based on search and score, and (ii) local methods that use conditional independence

tests. Next we briefly describe both aspects, starting with parameter learning.

Parameter Learning

If we have *sufficient* and complete data for all the variables, and we assume the topology of the BN is known, parameter learning is straight forward. The CPT for each variable can be estimated from data based on the frequency of each value (or combination of values) obtaining a *maximum likelihood* (ML) estimator of the parameters. For example, to estimate the CPT of B given it has two parents, A,C:

$$P(B_i \mid A_j, C_k) \sim NB_i, A_j, C_k \, / \, NA_j, C_k \qquad (24)$$

where NB_i, A_j, C_k is the number of cases in the database[6] in which $B = B_i$, $A = A_j$ and $C = C_k$, and $NA_j C_k$ is the total number of cases in which $A = A_j$ and $C = C_k$.

If there is not sufficient data, a situation common in practice, we have uncertainty in the parameters. This uncertainty can be modeled using a second order probability distribution, and could be propagated in the inference process so we have an estimate of the uncertainty in the resulting probabilities. A second order probability distribution is a distribution of the uncertainty on the probability values or parameters. For binary variables, the uncertainty on the parameters can be modeled using a Beta distribution, and for multivalued variables by an extension of the Beta distribution known as the Dirichlet distribution.

Another common situation is to have incomplete data. There are two basic cases:

- **Missing Values:** In some registers there are missing values for one or more variables.
- **Hidden Nodes:** A variable or variables in the model for which there is no data at all.

In the case of missing values, there are several alternatives:

1. Eliminate the registers with missing values.
2. Consider an special "unknown" value.
3. Substitute the missing value by the most common value (mode) of the variable.
4. Estimate the missing value based on the values of the other variables in the corresponding register.

The first alternative is acceptable if there is sufficient data, otherwise we run the risk of discarding useful information. The second alternative can be applied if the "unknown" value has some meaning. The third alternative does not consider the other variables, so it could bias the model. In general, the best alternative is the fourth one. In this case we first learn the parameters of the BN based on the complete registers, and then complete the data and re-estimate the parameters, applying the following process. For each register with missing values:

1. Instantiate all the known variables in the register.
2. Through probabilistic inference obtain the posterior probabilities of the missing variables.
3. Assign to each variable the value with highest posterior probability.
4. Add this completed register to the database and re-estimate the parameters.

An alternative to the previous process is that instead of assigning the value with highest probability, we assign a *partial* case for each value of the variable proportional to the posterior probability.

For hidden nodes, an alternative to estimate their parameters is based on the *Expectation–Maximization* (EM) technique. Given a database with one or more hidden nodes, $H_1, H_2, \ldots, H_k$, the basic EM algorithm to estimate their CPTs is the following:

1. Obtain the CPTs for all the *complete* variables (the values of the variable and all its parents are in the database) based on a ML estimator.
2. Initialize the unknown parameters with random values.
3. Considering the actual parameters, estimate the values of the hidden nodes based on the known variables via probabilistic inference.
4. Use the estimated values for the hidden nodes to complete/update the database.
5. Re-estimate the parameters for the hidden nodes with the updated data.
6. Repeat 3–5 until converge (no significant changes in the parameters).

The EM algorithm optimizes the unknown parameters and gives a *local maximum* (the final estimates depend on the initialization).

Structure Learning

Structure learning consists on obtaining the topology of the BN from data. This is a complex problem because: (i) the number of possible structures is *huge* even with a few variables (it is super-exponential on the number of variables), and (ii) a very large database is required to obtain good estimates of the statistical measures on which all methods depend.

For the particular case of a tree structure, there is a method that guarantees the *best* tree. For the general case several methods have been proposed, which can be divided into two main classes:

1. Global methods: they perform a heuristic search over the space of network structures, starting from some initial structure, and generating variation of the structure at each step. The *best* structure is selected based on a score that measures how well the model represents the data, common scores are BIC (Cooper & Herskovitz, 1992) and MDL (Lam & Bacchus, 1994).

Table 2. Mutual information in descending order for the golf example

No.	Var 1	Var 2	Mutual Info.
1	temp.	outlook	.2856
2	play	outlook	.0743
3	play	humidity	.0456
4	play	wind	.0074
5	humidity	outlook	.0060
6	wind	temp.	.0052
7	wind	outlook	.0017
8	play	temp.	.0003
9	humidity	temp.	0
10	wind	humidity	0

2. Local methods: these are based on evaluating the (in)dependence relations between subsets of variables given the data, to sequentially obtain the structure of the network. The most well known variant of this approach is the PC algorithm (Spirtes, Glymour, & Scheines, 1993).

Both classes of methods obtain similar results with *enough* data. Local methods tend to be more sensitive when there is few data, and global methods tend to be more complex computationally.

Next we review two methods: the tree learning algorithm develop by Chow and Liu (Chow & Liu, 1968), and the PC algorithm (Spirtes et al., 1993). For more information on alternative techniques, see the additional readings section.

Tree Learning

Chow and Liu (Chow & Liu, 1968) developed a method for approximating any multi-variable probability distribution as a product of second order distributions, which is the basis for learning tree-structured BNs. The joint probability of *n* random variables can be approximated as:

$$P(X_1, X_2, .., X_n) = \prod_{i=1}^{n} P(X_i \mid X_{j(i)}) \qquad (25)$$

where $X_{j(i)}$ is the parent of X_i in the tree.

The problem is to obtain the *best* tree, that is the tree structure that better approximates the real distribution. A measure of how close is the approximation is based on the information difference between the real distribution (P) and the tree approximation (P^*):

$$DI(P, P^*) = \sum_X P(X) log(P(X) / P^*(X)) \qquad (26)$$

where $X = \{X_1, X_2, .., X_n\}$. So now the problem is to find the tree that minimizes DI.

The mutual information between any pair of variables is defined as:

$$I(X_i, X_j) = \sum_{X_i, X_j} P(X_i, X_j) log(P(X_i, X_j) / P(X_i)P(X_j)) \qquad (27)$$

Given a tree-structured BN with variables $X_1, X_2, .., X_n$, we define its *weight*, W, as the sum of the mutual information of the arcs (pairs of variable) that constitute the tree:

$$W(X_1, X_2, .., X_n) = \sum_{i=1}^{n} I(X_i, X_j) \qquad (28)$$

where X_j is the parent of X_i in the tree.

It can be shown (Chow & Liu, 1968) that minimizing DI is equivalent to maximizing W. Then, obtaining the optimal tree is equivalent to finding the *maximum weight spanning tree*, using the following algorithm:

1. Obtain the mutual information (I) between all pairs of variables (for *n* variables, there are $n(n-1)/2$ pairs).
2. Order the mutual informations in descending order.

3.   Select the pair with maximum *I* and connect the two variables with an arc, this constitutes the initial tree

4.   Add the pair with the next highest *I* to the tree, while they do not make a cycle; otherwise skip it and continue with the following pair.

5.   Repeat 4 until all the variables are in the tree (*n*−1 arcs).

This algorithm obtains the *skeleton* of the tree; that is, it does not provide the direction of the arcs in the BN. The directions of the links have to be obtained using external semantics or using higher order dependency tests (see below).

To illustrate the tree learning method consider the classic *golf* example with 5 variables: *play, outlook, humidity, temperature, wind*. Given some data, we obtain the mutual information shown in Table 2.

In this case we select the first 4 pairs (arcs) and obtain the tree in Figure 5, where the directions were assigned arbitrarily.

Rebane and Pearl (Rebane & Pearl, 1987) developed a method that can be used to direct the arcs in the skeleton, and in general learn a *polytree* BN. The algorithm is based on independence tests for variable triplets, and in this way it can distinguish *convergent* substructures; once one or more substructures of this type are detected in the skeleton, it can direct additional arcs applying the independence tests to neighboring nodes. However, there is not guarantee of obtaining the direction for all the arcs in the tree.

This same idea is used in the PC algorithm for learning general structures that we describe next.

The PC Algorithm

The PC algorithm (Spirtes et al., 1993) first recovers the skeleton (underlying undirected graph) of the BN, and then it determines the orientation of the edges.

To determine the skeleton, it starts from a fully connected undirected graph, and determines the

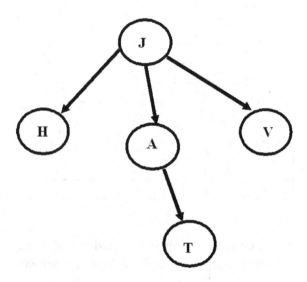

Figure 5. Tree structure obtained for the golf example (J is play, A is outlook, H is humidity, T is temperature, and V is wind)

conditional independence of each pair of variables given some subset of the other variables. For this it assumes that there is a procedure that can determine if two variables, *X,Y*, are independent given a subset of variables, **S**, that is, $I(X,Y|\mathbf{S})$. An alternative for this procedure is the conditional cross entropy measure. If this measure is below a threshold value set according to certain confidence level, the edge between the pair of variables is eliminated. These tests are iterated for all pairs of variables in the graph.

In the second phase the direction of the edges are set based on conditional independence tests between variable triplets. It proceeds by looking for substructures in the graph of the form *X−Z−Y* such that there is no edge *X−Y*. If *X,Y* are not independent given *Z*, it orients the edges creating a V-structure $X \rightarrow Z \leftarrow Y$. Once all the V-structures are found, it tries to orient the other edges based on independence tests and avoiding cycles. Algorithm 1 summarizes the basic procedure[7].

If the set of independences are faithful to a graph[8] and the independence tests are perfect, the

Algorithm 1. The PC algorithm

```
Require: Set of variables X, Independence test I
Return: Directed Acyclic Graph G
 1:  Initialize a complete undirected graph G'
 2:  i=0
 3:  repeat
 4:    for X ∈ X do
 5:      for Y ∈   ADJ(X) do
 6:        for S ⊆ ADJ(X) − {Y},| S |= i do
 7:          if I(X, Y | S) then
 8:            Remove the edge X-Y from G'
 9:          end if
 5:        for Y ∈   ADJ(X) do
10:          end for
11:        end for
12:      end for
13:      i=i+1
14:  until | ADJ(X) |≤ i, ∀X
15:  Orient edges in G'
16:  Return G
```

algorithm produces a graph equivalent to the original one (Spirtes et al., 1993).

DYNAMIC BAYESIAN NETWORKS

Representation

Bayesian networks usually represent the *state* of certain phenomena at an instant in time. However, in many applications, we want to represent the temporal evolution of certain process, that is, how the different variables evolve in time, known also as time series. An extension of BNs to model dynamic processes are called *dynamic Bayesian networks* (DBNs). A DBN consists of a *time slice* that represents the state of all the variables at certain time, t; a kind of snapshot of the evolving temporal process. For each temporal slice a dependency structure between the variables at that time is defined, called the *base network*. It

is usually assumed that this structure is duplicated for all the temporal slices (except the first slice, which can be different). Additionally, there are edges between variables from different slices, with their directions following the direction of time, defining the *transition network*. Usually DBNs are restricted to have directed links between consecutive temporal slices, known as a first order Markov model; although this is not necessary in general. An example of a DBN with 3 variables and 4 time slices is depicted in Figure 6.

Most of the DBNs consider in practice satisfy the following conditions:

- First order Markov model. The state variables at time t depend only on the state variables at time $t-1$.
- Stationary process. The structure and parameters of the model do no change over time.

Figure 6. An example of a DBN with 3 variables and 4 time slices. In this case the base structure is $X \rightarrow S \rightarrow E$ which is repeated across the 4 time slices.

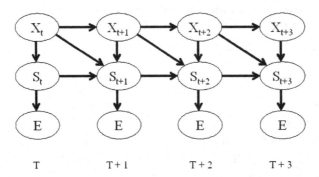

DBNs can be seen as a generalization of Markov chains and hidden Markov models (HMMs). A Markov chain is the simplest DBN, in which there is only one variable, X_t, per time slice, directly influenced only by the variable in the previous time. In this case the joint distribution can be written as:

$$P(X_1, X_2, ., X_T) = P(X_1)P(X_2 \mid X_1) \cdots P(X_T \mid X_{T-1})$$
(29)

A hidden Markov model has two variables per time stage, one that is known as the *state variable*, S; and the other as the *observation variable*, Y. It is usually assumed that S_t depends only on S_{t-1} and Y_t depends only on S_t. Thus, the joint probability can be factored as follows:

$$P(\{S_t, Y_t\}) = P(S_1)P(Y_1 \mid S_1)\prod_{t=2}^{T} P(S_t \mid S_{t-1})P(Y_t \mid S_t)$$
(30)

So Markov chains and HMMS are particular cases of DBNs, which in general can have N variables per time step, with any base and transition structures. Another particular variant of DBNs are Kalman Filters, which have also one state and one observation variable, but both variables are continuous. The basic Kalman filter assumes Gaussian distributions and linear functions for the transition and observation models.

Inference

There are several classes of inferences that can be performed with DBNs. Following we briefly mention the main types of inference, where **X** are the unobserved (hidden) variables, and **Y** are the observed variables:

- **Filtering:** Predict the next state based on past observations: $P(X_{t+1} \mid Y_{1:t})$.
- **Prediction:** Predict future states based on past observations: $P(X_{t+n} \mid Y_{1:t})$.
- **Smoothing:** Estimate the current state based on past and future observations (useful for learning): $P(X_t \mid Y_{1:T})$.
- **Decoding:** Find the most likely sequence of hidden variables given the observations:

$argmax(X_{1:T}) \, \mathrm{P}(X_{1:T} \mid \mathbf{Y}_{1:T})$.

Efficient inference methods have been developed for particular types of models, such as HMMs (Rabiner & Juang, 1993). However, for more complex models, inference becomes computationally intractable. In these cases we can apply approximate methods based on sampling, such as Markov chain Monte Carlo (Ghahramani,

Table 3. Learning dynamic Bayesian networks: 4 basic cases

Structure	Observability	Method
Known	Full	Maximum likelihood estimation
Known	Partial	Expectation–maximization (EM)
Unknown	Full	Search (global) or tests (local)
Unknown	Partial	EM and global or local

1998). A popular approximate method are *particle filters*, which approximate the state probability distribution (belief state) with a set of weighted *particles* or samples (Murphy, 2002).

Learning

As for BNs, learning dynamic Bayesian networks involves two aspects: (i) learning the structure or graph topology, and (ii) learning the parameters or CPTs for each variable. Additionally, we can consider two cases in terms of the observability of the variables: (a) full observability, when there is data for all the variables, and (b) partial observability, when some variables are unobserved or hidden, or we have missing data. So there are 4 basic cases for learning DBNs, see table 3.

For all the cases we can basically apply extensions of the methods for parameter and structure learning for Bayesian networks that we revised in the Section on Learning BNs. We describe one of these extensions below, for the case of unknown structure and full observability.

Structure Learning

Assuming that we have a time invariant DBN, we can consider that the model is defined by two structures: (i) the base structure, and (ii) the transition structure. Thus, we can divide the learning of a DBN in two parts, first learn the base structure, and then, given the base structure, learn the transition structure, see Figure 7.

For learning the base structure we can use all the available data for each variable, ignoring the

Figure 7. Learning a DBN: first we obtain the base structure (left), and then that transition structure (right)

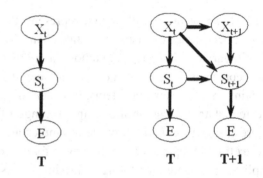

temporal information. This is equivalent to learning a BN, so we can apply any of the methods used for learning BNs.

For learning the transition network we consider the temporal information, in particular the data for all variables in two consecutive time slices, X_t and X_{t+1}. Considering the base structure, we can then learn the dependencies between the variables at time t and $t+1$ (assuming a first–order Markov model), and restricting the direction of the edges from the past to the future.

Here we have described in a simple, general way the two phases for learning a DBN, however there are several variants of this idea that have been developed, see the additional readings section.

There are some alternative BNs representations for describing temporal processes that have been developed, different from DBNs. An example of a different class of temporal Bayesian networks are *event networks* (Arroyo-Figueroa & Sucar, 1999, Galán, Arroyo-Figueroa, Díez, & Sucar,

Figure 8. Example of a simple ID with one decision node, D, one utility node, U, and 4 random nodes, A,B,C,D

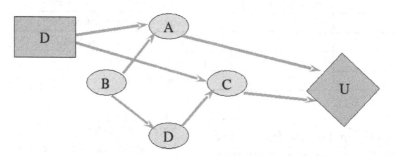

2007). In an event network, a node represents the *time* of occurrence of an event or state change of certain variable, in contrast to a node in a DBN that represents the state value of a variable at a certain time. For some problems, in which there are few state changes in the temporal range of interest, event networks provide a simpler and more efficient representation; however, for other applications such as monitoring or filtering, DBNs are more appropriate.

INFLUENCE DIAGRAMS

Introduction

Influence Diagrams (IDs) are a tool for solving decision problems that were introduce by Howard and Matheson (Howard & Matheson, 1984) as an alternative to decision trees to simplify modeling and analysis. From another perspective, we can view IDs as an extension of Bayesian networks that incorporates decision and utility nodes. In the following sections we present a brief introduction to IDs, including its representation and basic inference techniques, concluding with their extension to dynamic decision networks.

Representation

An influence diagram is a directed acyclic graph, *I*, that contains nodes that represent random, *X*, decision, *D*, and utility, *U*, variables:

- **Random nodes:** represent random variables as in BNs, with an associated CPT. These are represented as ovals.
- **Decision nodes:** represent decisions to be made. The arcs pointing towards a decision node are *informational*; that is, it means that the random or decision node at the origin of the arc must be known before the decision is made. Decision nodes are represented as rectangles.
- **Utility nodes:** represent the costs or utilities associated to the model. Associated to each utility node there is a function that maps each permutation of its parents to a utility value. Utility nodes are represented as diamonds. Utility nodes can be divided into *ordinary* utility nodes, whose parents are random and/or decision nodes; and *super-value* utility nodes, whose parents are ordinary utility nodes. Usually the super-value utility node is the (weighted) sum of the ordinary utility nodes.

An example of a simple ID with one decision and utility node is shown in figure 8.

There are three types of arcs in an ID:

Figure 9. A simplified model of the airport location problem represented as a simple ID. The decision node represents the different options for the location of a new airport, and the utility node represents the utility (or cost) which depends on several factors, which in turn depend on other random variables.

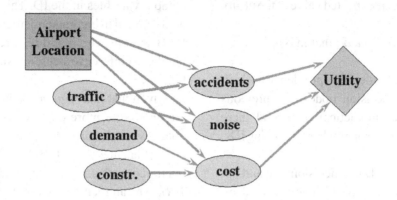

- **Probabilistic:** they indicate probabilistic dependencies, pointing towards random nodes.
- **Informational:** they indicate information availability, pointing towards decision nodes. That is, $X \rightarrow D$ indicates that value of X is known before the decision D is taken.
- **Functional:** they indicate functional dependency, pointing towards utility nodes.

In an ID there must be a directed path in the underlying directed graph that includes all the decision nodes, indicating the order in which the decisions are made. This order induces a partition on the random variables in the ID, such that if there are n decision variables, the random variables are partitioned into $n+1$ subsets. Each subset, R_i, contains all the random variables that are known before decision D_i and not known for previous decisions. Some of the algorithms for evaluating influence diagrams take advantage of these properties to make the evaluation more efficient.

IDs are used to aid a decision maker in finding the decisions that maximize its expected utility. That is, the goal in decision analysis is to find an *optimal policy*, $\pi = \{d_1, d_2, .., d_n\}$, which selects the best decisions for each decision node to maximize

the expected utility, $E_\pi(U)$. If there are several utility nodes, in general we consider that we have additive utility, so we will maximize the sum of these individual utilities:

$$E_\pi(U) = \sum_{u_i \in U} E_\pi(u_i) \qquad (31)$$

A more realistic example of an ID is depicted in Figure 9, which gives a simplified model of the problem of determining the location of a new airport, considering that the probability of accidents, the noise level and the estimated construction cost are the factors that directly affect the *utility*.

Evaluating an influence diagram is finding this sequence of best decisions or optimal policy.

Evaluation

We define a *simple* influence diagram as one that has a single decision node and a single utility node. In that case we can simple apply BN inference techniques to obtain the optimal policy following this algorithm:

1. For all $d_i \in D$:
   a. Set $D = d_i$.

    b.   Instantiate all the known random variables.

    c.   Propagate the probabilities as in a BN.

    d.   Obtain the expected value of the utility node, *U*.

2.   Select the decision, d_k, that maximizes *U*.

For more complex decision problems in which there are several decision nodes, the previous algorithm becomes impractical. In general, there are three main types of approaches for solving IDs:

- Transform the ID to a decision tree and apply standard solution techniques for decision trees.
- Solve directly the ID by variable elimination, applying a series of transformations to the graph.
- Transform the ID to a Bayesian network and use BN inference techniques.

Next we describe the last approach.

The idea to reduce an ID to a BN was originally proposed by Cooper (Cooper, 1988). The basic idea is to transform decision and utility nodes to random nodes, with an associated probability distribution. A decision node is converted to a discrete random variable by considering each decision, d_i, as a value for this variable; with a uniform distribution as CPT (a decision node has no parents as all incoming arcs are informational). A utility node is transformed to a binary random variable by *normalizing* the utility function so it is in the range from 0 to 1, that is:

$$P(u_i = 1 \mid Pa(u_i)) = val(Pa(u_i)) / maximum(val(Pa(u_i)))$$
(32)

where $Pa(u_i)$ are the parents of the utility node in the ID, and *val* is the value assigned to each combination of values of the parent nodes.

After the previous transformation, and considering a single utility node, the problem of finding the optimal policy reduces to finding the values of the decision nodes that maximize the probability of the utility node: $P(u=1|D,R)$, where *D* is the set of decision nodes, and *R* is the set of other random variables in the ID. This probability can be computed using standard inference techniques for BNs; however, it will require an exponential number of inference steps, one for each permutation of *D*.

Given that in a *regular* ID the decision nodes are ordered, a more efficient evaluation can be done by evaluating the decisions in (inverse) order (Shachter & Peot, 1992). That is, instead of maximizing $P(u=1|D,R)$, we maximize $P(D_j|u = 1,R)$. We can recursively optimize each decision node, D_j, starting from the last decision, continue with the previous decision, and so on, until we reach the first decision. This gives a much more efficient evaluation procedure. Additional improvements have been proposed to the previous algorithms based on *decomposable* IDs, see the additional readings section.

Traditional techniques for solving IDs make two important assumptions:

- **Total ordering:** all the decisions follow a total ordering according to a directed path in the graph.
- **Non forgetting:** all previous observations are remembered for future decisions.

These assumptions limit the applicability of IDs to some domains, in particular temporal problems that involve several decisions at different times. In some domains, such as in medical decision making, a total ordering of decisions is an unrealistic assumption in situations in which the decision maker does not know in advance what decision should be made first to maximize the expected utility. For a system that evolves over a large period of time, the number of observations grows linearly with the passing of time, so the non-forgetting requirement implies that the size of policies grows exponentially.

Figure 10. An example of a dynamic decision network with 4 decision epochs

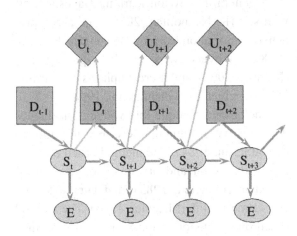

In order to avoid these limitations, Lauritzen and Nilsson (Lauritzen & Nilsson, 2001) proposed limited-memory influence diagrams (LIMIDs) as an extension of influence diagrams. The term limited-memory reflects the property that a variable known when making a decision is not necessarily remembered when making a posterior decision. Eliminating some variables reduces the complexity of the model so it solvable with a computer, although at the price of obtaining a sub-optimal policy. Chapter 8 presents an extension of LIMIDs to model dynamic domains with a periodic structure, named *Dynamic LIMIDs*.

Sequential Decision Problems

As for BNs, we can consider decision problems in which a series of decisions have to be taken at different time intervals, known as a *sequential decision problem*. A sequential decision problem can be modeled as *dynamic decision network* (DDN) –also known as *dynamic influence diagram*; which can be seen as an extension of a DBN, with additional decision and utility nodes for each time step, see Figure 10.

In principle, we can evaluate a DDN in the same way as an ID, considering that the decisions

have to be ordered in time. That is, each decision node D_t has incoming informational arcs from all previous decision nodes, D_{t-1}, D_{t-2}, etc. However, as the number of time epochs increases, the complexity increases and can become computationally intractable. Additionally, in some applications we do not know in advance the number of decision epochs, so in principle there might be an *infinite* number of decisions.

DDNs are closely related to *Markov decision processes* (MDPs). An MDP is a dynamic decision network which has a single random variable (*state*), decision node (*action*), and utility node (*reward*) per time epoch. In an MDP the state is observable, and the overall utility is a weighted sum of the rewards. There might be an infinite number of decision epochs, that is, an *infinite horizon*. Partially observable Markov decision processes extend MDPs by considering that the state is not directly observable, introducing an additional random variable per epoch (*observation*) such that the observation depends probabilistically on the state.

When there are a *large* number of states in an MDP (or states and observations in a POMDP), the model becomes too complex in terms of the number of parameters required to represent the transition (and observation) probability distribution. An alternative is to decompose the state into a number of variables (as in a Bayesian network), and represent the transition function as a two–stage dynamic Bayesian network. This type of models are known as *factored* MDPs (*factored* POMDPs).

MDPs and POMDPs are the topic of the next chapter.

SUMMARY

Probabilistic graphical models provide a compact representation of a joint probability distribution, from which we can obtain marginal and conditional probabilities. PGMs are represented in terms of a graph and a set of local functions. Their power derives from an explicit representation of conditional independence relations, which makes these models more expressive, and is the basis for efficient inference techniques. There are several types of PGMs, in this chapter we have reviewed three of them: Bayesian networks, dynamic Bayesian networks and influence diagrams.

Bayesian networks are DAGs that model a set of random variables, parameterized by a set of conditional probability tables. These models are commonly used to predict or estimate certain variables given some evidence. There are several methods for probabilistic inference in BNs, as well as for learning the structure and parameters from data. Dynamic Bayesian networks extend BNs to model temporal data. DBNs are used to represent compactly the transition function in *factored* Markov decision processes.

Influence diagrams incorporate, besides random variables, decisions and utilities; and are used to aid a decision maker in determining the decisions that maximize its expected utility. There alternative algorithms to evaluate an ID, that is finding the optimal sequence of decisions or optimal policy. Dynamic decision networks extend IDs by considering a sequence of decisions in time.

These models are incorporated in several of the more complex representations and applications that will be covered in the rest of the book.

FURTHER READING

A wide and unconventional introduction to probability theory from a logical perspective is presented in (Jaynes, 2003).

The classical book on Bayesian networks is (Pearl, 1988), which is still a very good introduction to the field. Other general books on Bayesian networks are (R. E. Neapolitan, 1990, Jensen, 2001). The book by Jensen (Jensen, 2001) also includes influence diagrams. A more recent account with emphasis on inference techniques is given in (Darwiche, 2009). Koller and Friedman

(Koller & Friedman, 2009) give a wider introduction to probabilistic graphical models.

A general review on learning Bayesian networks is (R. Neapolitan, 2004); and a comprehensive tutorial on learning BNs is (Heckerman, 2008). An overview of DBNs is presented in (Murphy, 2002), and more emphasis on learning DBNs is given by (Ghahramani, 1998).

The basic technique for evaluating influence diagrams were originally described in (Howard & Matheson, 1984). The method based on variable elimination and arc inversion was introduced in (Olmsted, 1983), and later extended and formalised in (Shachter, 1986). The method based on a transformation to a BN is described in (Cooper, 1988). A survey on the evaluation of influence diagrams is presented in (Crowley, 2004). A general reference on decision analysis is (Clemen & Reilly, 2001).

ACKNOWLEDGMENT

I appreciate the comments and suggestions of Javier Díez, Jesse Hoey and Eduardo Morales on earlier drafts of this chapter. This work was supported in part by FONCICYT Project 95185 and INAOE.

REFERENCES

Arroyo-Figueroa, G., & Sucar, L. (1999, July). A temporal Bayesian network for diagnosis and prediction. In K. Laskey & H. Prade (Eds.), *Proc. of the Fifteenth Conference on Uncertainty in Artificial Intelligence* (pp. 13–20). Stockholm, Sweden: Morgan Kaufmann Publishers, San Francisco, CA.

Chow, C., & Liu, C. (1968). Approximating discrete probability distributions with dependence trees. *IEEE Transactions on Information Theory*, *14*, 462–467. doi:10.1109/TIT.1968.1054142

Clemen, R., & Reilly, T. (2001). *Making hard decisions*. Pacific Grove, CA: Duxbury.

Cooper, G. (1988). A method for using belief networks as influence diagrams. In *Proceedings of the Twelfth Conference on Uncertainty in Artificial Intelligence*, (pp. 55–63).

Cooper, G. (1990). The computational complexity of probabilistic inference using Bayesian networks. *Artificial Intelligence, 42*, 393–405. doi:10.1016/0004-3702(90)90060-D

Cooper, G., & Herskovitz, E. (1992). A Bayesian method for the induction of probabilistic networks from data. *Machine Learning, 9*(4), 309–348. doi:10.1007/BF00994110

Crowley, M. (2004). *Evaluating influence diagrams*. Retrieved from http://www.cs.ubc.ca/~crowley/papers/aiproj.pdf

Darwiche, A. (2009). *Modeling and reasoning with Bayesian networks*. Cambridge University Press. doi:10.1017/CBO9780511811357

Galán, S. F., Arroyo-Figueroa, G., Díez, F. J., & Sucar, L. E. (2007). Comparison of two types of event Bayesian networks: A case study. *Applied Artificial Intelligence, 21*(3), 185–209. doi:10.1080/08839510601170754

Ghahramani, Z. (1998). Learning dynamic Bayesian networks. *Lecture Notes in Computer Science, 1387*, 168–197. doi:10.1007/BFb0053999

Gillies, D. (2000). *Philosophical theories of probability*. London, UK: Routledge.

Heckerman, D. (2008). A tutorial on learning with Bayesian networks. *Innovations in Bayesian Networks*, 33–82.

Howard, R., & Matheson, J. (1984). Influence diagrams. In Howard, R., & Matheson, J. (Eds.), *Readings on the principles and applications of decision analysis*. Menlo Park, CA: Strategic Decisions Group.

Jaynes, E. T. (2003). *Probability theory: The logic of science*. Cambridge, UK: Cambridge U Press. doi:10.1017/CBO9780511790423

Jensen, F. (2001). *Bayesian networks and decision graphs*. New York, NY: Springer-Verlag.

Koller, D., & Friedman, N. (2009). *Probabilistic graphical models: Principles and techniques*. MIT Press.

Lam, W., & Bacchus, F. (1994). Learning Bayesian belief netwoks: An aproach based on the MDL principle. *Computational Intelligence, 10*, 269–293. doi:10.1111/j.1467-8640.1994.tb00166.x

Lauritzen, S., & Nilsson, D. (2001). Representing and solving decision problems with limited information. *Management Science, 47*, 1235–1251. doi:10.1287/mnsc.47.9.1235.9779

Murphy, K. (2002). *Dynamic Bayesian networks: Representation, inference and learning*. PhD dissertation, University of California, Berkeley, Berkeley, CA.

Neapolitan, R. (2004). *Learning Bayesian networks*. New Jersey: Prentice Hall.

Neapolitan, R. E. (1990). *Probabilistic reasoning in expert systems*. New York, NY: John Wiley & Sons.

Olmsted, S. M. (1983). *On representing and solving decision problems*. Unpublished doctoral dissertation, Engineering-Economic Systems Dept., Stanford University, CA, U.S.A.

Pearl, J. (1988). *Probabilistic reasoning in intelligent systems: networks of plausible inference*. San Francisco, CA: Morgan Kaufmann.

Rabiner, L., & Juang, B. (1993). *Fundamentals of speech recognition. Signal Processing Series*. New Jersey, USA: Prentice Hall.

Rebane, G., & Pearl, J. (1987). The recovery of causal poly-trees from statistical data. In L. N. Kanal, T. S. Levitt, & J. F. Lemmer (Eds.), *Uncertainty in artificial intelligence* (pp. 175–182). Elsevier. Retrieved from http://www2.sis.pitt.edu/~dsl/UAI/UAI87/Rebane.UAI87.html

Shachter, R. D. (1986). Evaluating influence diagrams. *Operations Research, 34*(6), 871–882. doi:10.1287/opre.34.6.871

Shachter, R. D., & Peot, M. (1992). Decision making using probabilistic inference methods. In *Proc. of the Eight Conference on Uncertainty Artificial Intelligence* (pp. 276–283).

Spirtes, P., Glymour, C., & Scheines, R. (1993). *Causation, prediction, and search*. Berlin, Germany: Springer-Verlag.

ENDNOTES

[1] $A+B$ denotes logical sum or disjunction.

[2]   It is common to write $P(H)$ without explicit mention of the conditioning information, in this case we assume that there is still some context under which probabilities are considered even if it is not written explicitly.

[3]   This means that one and only one of the propositions has a value TRUE.

[4]   A flat representation of a joint probability distribution with N random variables consists of an N–dimensional table in which the probabilities of the conjunction of all variables for each value of these variables are specified.

[5]   A polytree is a singly connected DAG in which some nodes have more than one parent; in a directed tree, each node has at most one parent.

[6]   The database is a table that contains data of the variables in the BN, usually with N rows and M columns, where N is the number of instances or registers, and M is the number of variables.

[7]   Where $ADJ(X)$ is the set of nodes adjacent to X in the graph, and $I(X,Y|S)$ is a *True* if X and Y are independent given S according to some statistical test.

[8]   That is, that the independence relations can be represented as a DAG.

Chapter 3
An Introduction to Fully and Partially Observable Markov Decision Processes

Pascal Poupart
University of Waterloo, Canada

ABSTRACT

The goal of this chapter is to provide an introduction to Markov decision processes as a framework for sequential decision making under uncertainty. The aim of this introduction is to provide practitioners with a basic understanding of the common modeling and solution techniques. Hence, we will not delve into the details of the most recent algorithms, but rather focus on the main concepts and the issues that impact deployment in practice. More precisely, we will review fully and partially observable Markov decision processes, describe basic algorithms to find good policies and discuss modeling/computational issues that arise in practice.

INTRODUCTION

A central goal of artificial intelligence is the design of automated systems that can robustly accomplish a task despite uncertainty. Such systems can be viewed abstractly as taking inputs from the environment and producing outputs toward the realization of some goals. An important problem is the design of good control policies that produce suitable outputs based on the inputs received. For instance, a thermostat is an automated system that regulates the temperature of a room by controlling a heating device based on information provided by heat sensors. For such a simple system, a reactive control policy can maintain the temperature more or less constant by turning on and off the

DOI: 10.4018/978-1-60960-165-2.ch003

heating device when the temperature is below or above some target. For more complicated systems, effective control policies are often much harder to design. Consider a system designed to assist elderly persons suffering from memory deficiencies. Memory loss can severely hamper the ability of a person to accomplish simple activities of daily living such as dressing, toileting, eating, taking medication, etc. An automated system could help a person regain some autonomy by guiding a person with some audio prompts that remind the person of the next steps in the course of an activity. Suppose the system is equipped with sensors (e.g., video-cameras and microphones) to monitor the user, and actuators (e.g., speakers) to communicate with the user. The design of a suitable prompting strategy is far from obvious. In particular, the information provided by the sensors tends to be inaccurate due to the noisy nature of image and sound processing. Furthermore, that information may be incomplete due to the limited scope of the sensors. For example, although cameras and microphones allow the system to observe movements and utterances made by a user, they do not reveal the intentions nor the state of mind of people. Ideally, if the system could read minds, the design of effective prompting strategies could be eased significantly. Instead, the system must infer the state of the user based on the limited and noisy information provided by sensors. The effects of actuators may also be quite uncertain. For example, users may not always follow the prompts depending on their mood, their physical or mental weariness, etc. The system should then have the ability to take into account this uncertainty in its strategy.

In summary, the design of an effective prompting strategy is complicated by uncertainty in the action effects and the sensor measurements, as well as the interdependencies induced by the sequential nature of the task. Many other tasks such as mobile robot navigation, spoken dialog management, resource allocation, maintenance

scheduling, planning and design of experiments also include sequential decision making problems under uncertainty. Hence, the goal of this chapter is to introduce Markov decision processes as a principled and flexible framework to tackle sequential decision making problems under uncertainty.

Markov decision processes (MDPs) were initially formalized in Operations Research (Bellman, 1957) to optimize various tasks with a sequential nature and some uncertainty. The idea is to specify a task formally by modeling explicitly each component including the uncertainty. Once a model of the task is specified, a computer optimizes a policy to perform the task. In general, it is often easier to specify a model and let a computer optimize a policy instead of trying to manually specify a policy. Hence this chapter describes the components of an MDP and some algorithms that can be used to optimize a policy.

MDPs can be divided in two groups: fully observable MDPs (when there is uncertainty about the action effects only) and partially observable MDPs (when there is uncertainty about the action effects and sensor measurements). Following common practice in the literature, we will use the MDP acronym to refer to fully observable problems and POMDP (partially observable Markov decision process) to refer to partially observable problems. Naturally, POMDPs are more expressive since uncertainty in the sensor measurements allow us to model problems where the underlying state cannot be fully recognized, but as a result the algorithms to optimize the policy are more complicated.

This chapter is organized as follows. In Section 2, we describe the components of an MDP and the three main classes of algorithms that can be used to optimize a policy. Section 3 considers the more general POMDPs and describes the model components as well as the solution algorithms. Section 4 gives an overview of some of the issues to deploy MDP applications in practice. Finally we conclude in Section 5.

MARKOV DECISION PROCESSES

In this section, we introduce Markov decision processes (MDPs) as a framework to model and solve planning problems with uncertainty. We first describe the MDP model and then review the three main classes of algorithms to optimize a policy. We also explain how factored representations can be used to model large problems in a modular way.

Model

MDPs provide a rich framework to model uncertainty in a planning problem. They allow action effects to be modeled probabilistically and state preferences to be quantified. In this section, we provide a formal description of Markov decision processes, their limitations and Bellman's equation, which characterizes optimal solutions.

Components

Formally, an MDP is specified by a tuple $<S,A,T,R,h,\gamma>$. We now describe each one of those 6 components. In practice, each component is specified by a domain expert or learned from data.

State Space S

The world is modeled by a set S of distinct states s. The number of states may be finite, countably infinite or uncountably infinite. Unless otherwise stated, we will focus on discrete models with a finite number of states. In this section, we also assume that states are fully observable. This assumption will be relaxed in the next section when we consider partially observable Markov decision processes (POMDPs).

Action Space A

An agent seeks to influence the future states by executing actions a from the set A. Again, A can be finite, countably infinite or uncountably infinite, but we will assume that it is finite unless otherwise stated. Roughly speaking, the agent's goal is to choose actions that will influence the world in such a way that desirable states are visited more frequently.

Transition Function T

MDPs allow action effects with uncertainty to be modeled. From the agent's point of view, this means that the world has a certain probability of making a transition to any state in S as a result of an action execution. The stochastic nature of action effects is captured by the transition function T. Let

$$T(s',a,s) = \Pr(s' \mid s,a)$$

denote the probability that the world makes a transition to state s' when action a is executed in state s.

Reward Function R

The preferences of the agent are encoded in the reward function R. This function indicates how much utility $R(s,a)$ is earned by an agent when the world is in state s and action a is executed. The reward function is a powerful tool that quantifies the agent's preference for each state-action pair.

Horizon h and Discount Factor γ

In decision theory, the goal of an agent is to maximize the expected utility earned over some time frame. The horizon h defines this time frame by specifying the number of time-steps the agent must plan for. The horizon can be finite or infinite. A discount factor γ is also used to indicate how rewards earned at different time-steps should be weighted. In general, the more delayed a reward is, the smaller will be its weight. Therefore, γ is a constant in $[0,1]$ indicating by how much a reward should be scaled down for every time-step delay.

Figure 1. Graphical model representation of an MDP

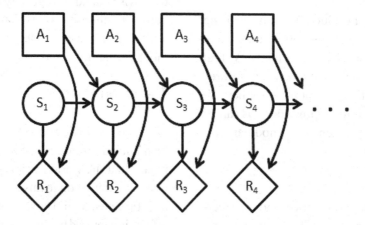

A reward earned k steps in the future is scaled down by γ^k as if there was some inflation at each step. We can also interpret $1-\gamma$ as a probability that the process may terminate early. This is useful in situations where external factors may cause the process to terminate at each step with some small probability before reaching the horizon h. Unless otherwise indicated, we assume infinite horizon MDPs with a discount factor strictly less than 1.

Graphical Model

We can represent an MDP with the probabilistic graphical model shown in Figure 1. Following the convention of influence diagrams, circles indicate random variables, squares indicate decision variables and diamonds indicate utility variables. Each slice corresponds to a different time step. The arcs indicate direct influences between the variables. For instance, S_t depends on S_{t-1} and A_{t-1} and the dependencies are quantified by the transition function $\Pr(S_t|S_{t-1},A_{t-1})$. Similarly, R_t depends on S_t and A_t which indicates that $R_t(S_t,A_t)$ is a utility function that takes S_t and A_t as arguments.

Markovian and Stationary Assumptions

It is interesting to note that by definition MDPs assume two important properties: *Markovian* and *stationary* dynamics. A process is Markovian when the variables at a given time-step depend only on variables at the current and previous time-step, but not other time-steps in the past. The fact that S_t depends only on A_{t-1} and S_{t-1}, implies that previous states and actions do not influence S_t (i.e., $\Pr(S_t|S_{t-1},A_{t-1},S_{t-2},A_{t-2}\ldots) = \Pr(S_t \mid S_{t-1},A_{t-1})$ $\forall S_{t-2},A_{t-2}\ldots$). Similarly, the rewards are Markovian since each reward depends only on the current state and action (i.e., $R_t(S_t,A_t)$).

A process is stationary when the dependencies are the same at every time step (i.e., time independent). Since the transition and reward functions are assumed to be the same at each step (i.e., $\Pr\left(S_t|S_{t-1},A_{t-1}\right) = \Pr\left(S_{t+k}|S_{t-1+k},A_{t-1+k}\right)$ and $R\left(S_t,A_t\right) = R\left(S_{t+k},A_{t+k}\right)\forall t,k$), the MDP is a stationary process.

The Markovian and stationary assumptions are very useful in practice to represent the process compactly and to optimize policies efficiently. The Markovian property ensures that the transition and reward functions have bounded dependencies since each variable can only depend on the other variables in the same or immediately preceding time step. As a result, the transition and reward functions require only $O(|S|^2|A|)$ and $O(|S||A|)$ parameters respectively. The stationary property ensures that a single transition function and a single reward function are sufficient to encode the dynamics for all time steps.

While the Markovian and stationary assumptions seem restrictive, it is always possible to satisfy them by defining states that capture enough information. For the Markovian property, we can always extend the state definition to include past states and actions until all relevant information to predict the next state and determine the current reward is included. Similarly, a non-stationary process can always be converted into a stationary process by including the external factors that influence the process into the state definition. Naturally, the expansion of the state definition until the process becomes Markovian and stationary may lead to an explosion of states. Hence, there is a tradeoff. Chapter 5 also discusses semi-Markov decision processes for continuous time decision problems.

Policies

Given an MDP specified by the tuple $<S,A,T,R,h,\gamma>$, the goal is to find a policy π that maximizes the expected sum of discounted rewards. In its most general form, a policy can be any mapping from histories of past states and actions to the next action. However, because the process is Markovian, it is sufficient to condition the choice of action on the last state only. Since the last state is sufficient to predict future states and rewards, then it is also sufficient to choose the next action. Hence, we consider the space of policies $\pi : S \rightarrow A$ that are mappings from states to actions. Furthermore, when a mapping is optimal for a time step then it is also optimal for all time-steps since the process is stationary and infinite. Intuitively, if choosing action a in state s at time-step t is optimal, then a is also optimal at all other time-steps where s is the state since the agent

will face the same process for an infinite number of steps.

Bellman's Equation

The value of a policy is given by the expected sum of discounted rewards earned while executing the policy. Since the value may change depending on the starting state, we can define the value function $V^\pi(s)$ as follows:

$$V^\pi (s) = \sum_{t=0}^{\infty} \gamma^t E_\pi [R(s_t, \pi (s_t))] \quad \forall s$$

The value function can also be written recursively as the sum of the current reward with the expected discounted future rewards given again by the value function.

$$V^\pi (s) = R\left(s, \pi (s)\right)$$
$$+\gamma \sum_{s'} \Pr\left(s'|s, \pi (s)\right) V^\pi \left(s'\right) \forall s$$

Hence the value function can be computed by solving a system of $|S|$ linear equations (as above) with $|S|$ unknowns corresponding to $V^\pi(s)$ for each s. A policy π^* is optimal when $V^{\pi^*} (s) \geq V^\pi (s) \forall s, \pi$. Such a policy maximizes the expected sum of discounted rewards and its value function satisfies Bellman's equation:

$$V^{\pi^*} (s) = \max_a R\left(s, a\right)$$
$$+\gamma \sum_{s'} \Pr\left(s'|s, a\right) V^{\pi^*} \left(s'\right) \forall s$$

Solution Algorithms

We now present four classic algorithms to optimize policies: value iteration, policy iteration, linear

Table 1. Value iteration

Inputs: MDP, $\in$

Output: π

$n \leftarrow 0$

$V^0\left(s\right) \leftarrow 0 \quad \forall s$

Repeat

$n \leftarrow n+1$

$V^n\left(s\right) \leftarrow \max_a R\left(s,a\right) + \gamma \sum_{s'} \Pr\left(s'|s,a\right) V^{n-1}\left(s'\right) \quad \forall s$

Until $\max_s |\, V^n(s) - V^{n-1}(s) \leq \varepsilon$

Extract policy: $\pi\left(s\right) \leftarrow argmax_a R\left(s,a\right) + \gamma \sum_{s'} \Pr\left(s'|s,a\right) V\left(s'\right) \quad \forall s$

---

programming and forward search. Most modern algorithms are variants of these basic algorithms.

Value Iteration

A simple way of finding the optimal value function is by dynamic programming. More precisely, decisions are optimized in reverse order by starting at the horizon and going backwards. Intuitively, it is easy to optimize a decision when there is no other decision that follows. Once the last decision is optimized, it is also easy to optimize the preceding decision given an optimal policy for the last decision. More generally, it is easy to optimize a decision once all subsequent decisions have already been optimized and are assumed fixed.

Table 1 describes value iteration, which iteratively computes the optimal value function $V^n(s)$ for n stages to go. The algorithm starts with $V^0(s)$ set to 0. Then, for an increasing number of stages to go $V^n(s)$ is obtained by applying the right hand side of Bellman's equation to $V^{n-1}(s)$. As $n \rightarrow \infty$, V^n converges to V^*. Since it is not

feasible to perform an infinite number of iterations, the algorithm terminates when the largest difference between V^n and V^{n-1} at all states is smaller than some threshold $\in$. This guarantees that $\left\|V^n - V^*\right\|_\infty \leq 2\varepsilon / (1-\gamma)$. Finally, a policy is obtained from V^n by performing a one-step lookahead corresponding to Bellman's equation.

Policy Iteration

Instead of iteratively computing the value function and then extracting a policy, we can directly optimize a policy by policy iteration (Table 2). The algorithm alternates between two steps: policy evaluation and policy improvement. The evaluation step finds the value function of the current policy by solving a system of linear equations. The improvement step is guaranteed to find a better policy if one exists. The algorithm terminates when two consecutive policies are identical, indicating that no improvement is possible and therefore that the policy must be optimal.

Table 2. Policy iteration

Inputs: MDP

Output: π^n

Initialize π^0 randomly

$n \leftarrow 0$

Repeat

Policy evaluation: $V(s) = R(s, \pi^n(s)) + \gamma \sum_{s'} \Pr(s'|s, \pi^n(s)) V(s') \quad \forall s$

Policy improvement: $\pi^{n+1}(s) \leftarrow argmax_a R(s, a) + \gamma \sum_{s'} \Pr(s'|s, a) V(s') \quad \forall s$

$n \leftarrow n + 1$

Until $\pi^n = \pi^{n+1}$

Table 3. Linear programming

Inputs: MDP

Output: π

Solve LP: $\min_{\bar{V}} \sum_{s} \bar{V}(s) \, s.t. \quad \bar{V}(s) \geq R(s, a) + \gamma \sum_{s'} \Pr(s'|s, a) \bar{V}(s') \forall s, a$

Extract policy: $\pi(s) \leftarrow argmax_a R(s, a) + \gamma \sum_{s'} \Pr(s'|s, a) \bar{V}(s') \quad \forall s$

Linear Programming

A third approach consists of linear programming (Table 3). The idea is to search for the smallest upper bound $\bar{V}$, on V^*. This explains why the objective minimizes $\bar{V}$. A sufficient condition to ensure that a value function V is an upper bound consists of verifying that a step of value iteration applied to V produces a lower value function. This explains why the constraint verifies that $\bar{V}$ is greater than equal to one step of value iteration applied to $\bar{V}$.

It is interesting to note that since an optimal policy can be obtained by linear programming, then policy optimization for fully observable MDPs can always be done in polynomial time with respect to the number states and actions.

Forward Search

The three preceding algorithms pre-compute a policy. In other words, an entire policy is computed offline before its execution begins. However, when there is very little time between the formulation of the MDP and the execution of the

Figure 2. Expectimax search tree

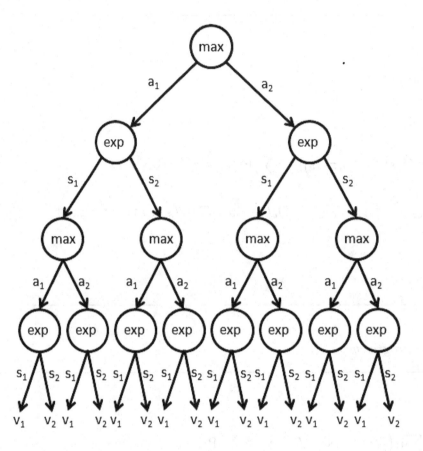

first action, it may be necessary to optimize the policy while executing it. A simple approach consists of optimizing the choice of the next action between each time step by doing a forward search. The idea is to simulate all possible courses of actions up to a certain number of steps in the future and to execute the initial action that leads to the best expected discounted total reward. Figure 2 describes a search tree where the edges are labeled with actions and states in alternation. The edges at the root correspond to the actions that can be taken initially. The second level of edges corresponds to the states that can be reached by each action. The following levels of edges alternate between actions and states in the same way that an agent would alternate between executing an action and reaching a state. The optimal

initial action for a planning horizon of half the depth of the tree can be computed in a bottom up fashion. At each leaf, we store the reward for the last state and action of the path that reaches that leaf. Interior nodes with outgoing action edges are labeled by "max" to indicate that the maximum of the children is computed. The interior nodes with outgoing state edges are labeled by "exp" to indicate that an expectation of the children is computed. More precisely, we compute the sum of the current reward with the discounted expected value of the children's value: $R(s,a) + \gamma \sum_{s} \Pr(s'|s,a) V^{child}(s')$. The action that maximizes the value at the root is the best action to execute next. Table 4 describes a depth first search algorithm that performs this computation for a horizon of h steps.

Table 4. Forward search

Inputs: MDP, s, h

Outputs: $< a^*, V^* >$

If $h = 0$ then
return $V^* = 0$
Else

$$Q(s,a) = R(s,a) + \gamma \sum_{s'} \Pr(s'|s,a) \, forwardSearch(MDP, s', h-1) \, \forall s, a \text{ Return}$$

$a^* = \arg \max_a Q(s,a)$ and $V^* = \max_a Q(s,a)$

End

The computational complexity of forward search is $O\left((|A||S|)^h\right)$ since the branching factor is $|S||A|$ at each time step. While the algorithm scales exponentially in the planning horizon, it is simple and works well in domains where a small number of look ahead steps is sufficient to choose good actions. The running time can be speeded up by memorizing the states already visited and reducing the number of branches by sparse sampling (for the expectation nodes) (Kearns, Mansour et al., 1999) or branch and bound (for the max nodes).

In practice, it is generally best to combine forward search with an offline algorithm. For instance, value iteration can be used to pre-compute an approximate value function before the execution of the first action. This value function can be used to approximate the values of the leaves of the search tree. As a result, a shallower search may be sufficient to select a good action at each step.

Factored Representation

In many application domains, the state space and action space may be very large. This usually arises due to one of two common reasons: discretization of continuous variables into many values or states/actions defined by the joint assignment of several variables. In this section, we focus on the latter case.

Consider a robotic domain where the states correspond to possible poses of the robot and the actions to different controls. A pose may be specified by the spatial coordinates and orientation of each part of the robot. In general, there is one state variable for each degree of freedom of the robot and a state corresponds to a joint assignment of values for those variables. Similarly, a control may be specified by the forces and moments applied to each part of the robot. Hence, there is one action variable for each type of force and an action corresponds to a joint assignment of forces to the variables. MDPs with states and actions defined by several variables are often referred to as factored MDPs because the transition function typically factors into a product of conditional probability distributions. We now explain how factored MDPs are formally specified and how a factored representation impacts solution algorithms such as value iteration. Chapters 7 and 12 present application domains that feature factored MDPs, and Chapters 13 and 14 include applications of factored POMDPs.

Factored Components

Factored MDPs are specified by a tuple $<S,A,T,R,h,\gamma>$ that is very similar to the tuple for flat MDPs. From now on we will use bold letters to denote sets. For instance, $S = \{S_1, S_2, \ldots, S_N\}$ is the set of state variables (instead of the state space). The state space is the cross product of the domains of the state variables (i.e., $\times_{n=1}^{N} dom(S_n)$). Similarly, $A = \{A_1, A_2, \ldots, A_M\}$ is the set of action variables and the action space is given by the cross product of the domains of the action variables (i.e., $\times_{m=1}^{M} dom(A_m)$). The transition function is compactly represented by a product of the conditional probability distributions for each state variable given its parents. In other words,

$$T = \{\Pr(S'_1 | pa(S'_1)), \Pr(S'_2 | pa(S'_2)), \ldots, \Pr(S'_N | pa(S'_N))\}$$

where $pa(S'_i)$ is the set of variables that are parents of S'_i and

$$\Pr(s'|s,a) = \prod_n \Pr(s'_n \mid s_{\downarrow pa(S'_n)}, a_{\downarrow pa(S'_n)}).$$

Here, bold lower case letters denote a joint assignment of values for a set of variables. For instance $s = <s_1, s_2, \ldots, s_N>$ and $a = <a_1, a_2, \ldots, a_M>$ are joint assignments of values corresponding to a state and an action. Furthermore, $s_{\downarrow pa(S_n)}$ and $a_{\downarrow pa(S_n)}$ indicate partial joint assignments that are restricted to the set of variables consisting of the parents of S_n. Similarly, the reward function is compactly represented by a sum of local utility functions that each depend on a subset of the state and action variables. In other words $R = \{R_1, R_2, \ldots, R_K\}$ is a set of reward variables and the reward function is $R(S, A) = \sum_k U_k(pa(R_k))$. Here, for each reward variable R_k, we define a local utility function $U(pa(R_k))$ that maps each joint assignment of the parents of R_k to some utility value for R_k. The horizon h and the discount γ are the same as for flat MDPs. The probabilistic graphical model of factored MDPs (Figure 3) differs from flat MDPs only in the fact that several variables are used for the states, actions and rewards. The edges are problem dependent.

Factored Value Iteration

Factored MDPs permit a compact representation of large MDPs when states or actions are naturally defined by joint assignments to a set of variables. While the size of the conditional probability distributions and the local utility functions grows exponentially with the number of parents for each variable, graphical models are typically sparse and the number of parents is often small and bounded. As a result, the factored representation is often exponentially smaller than the original flat representation. This is particularly useful for large MDPs, but we also need efficient algorithms that can exploit the factored representations. Unfortunately, finding the optimal policy of a factored MDP is EXP-hard (Lusena, Goldsmith et al., 2001). This holds for exact and approximate algorithms in the sense that finding a near optimal policy with an arbitrarily small additive bound on the loss in value is EXP-hard (Lusena, Goldsmith et al., 2001).

That being said, it is still desirable to devise algorithms that can exploit the factored representation to obtain good policies as efficiently as possible even though (near) optimality cannot be guaranteed in polynomial time. We now describe how to adapt value iteration to factored MDPs. Recall that the main operation performed in value iteration is a Bellman backup to compute the optimal value function V^n from V^{n-1}:

$$V^n(s) \leftarrow \max_a R(s,a)$$
$$+\gamma \sum_{s'} \Pr(s'|s,a) V^{n-1}(s')$$

The complexity of the above equation is linear in the number of actions and quadratic in the number of states. However, since the number of states and actions is exponential in the number

Figure 3. Graphical model of a factored MDP

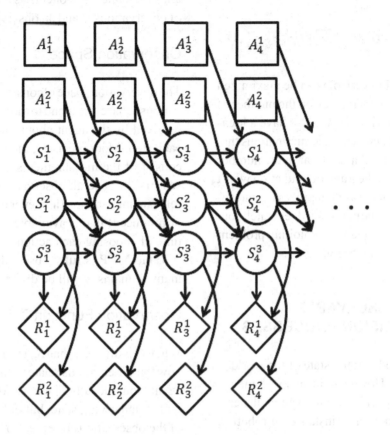

of variables, it is desirable to exploit the factored representation. Substituting the reward function by the sum of local utility functions and the transition function by the product of conditional probability distributions yields

$$V^n(\boldsymbol{s}) \leftarrow \max_{a_1, a_2, \ldots, a_M} \sum_{k=1}^{K} U\big(\boldsymbol{s}_{\downarrow pa(R_k)}, \boldsymbol{a}_{\downarrow pa(R_k)}\big)$$

$$+ \gamma \sum_{s_1', s_2', \ldots, s_N'} \prod_{n=1}^{N} \Pr\left(s_n' \mid \boldsymbol{s}_{\downarrow pa\left(S_n'\right)}, \boldsymbol{a}_{\downarrow pa\left(S_n'\right)}\right) V^{n-1}(\boldsymbol{s}')$$

If we distribute the maximization of action variables over the sum of utility terms and distribute the summation of state variables over the product of conditional distributions, we may be able to save on computation. Such a distribution is essentially the same as the distribution per-formed in variable elimination for inference queries in Bayesian networks. In the best case scenario, it is possible to reduce the complexity of a Bellman backup to $O(|S|log|\underline{S}|log|A|)$ instead of $O(|S|^2|A|)$. Consider the case where each state and action variable is binary. Let the transition function be composed of a set of independent processes that do not depend on any action (i.e.,

$$\Pr\big(\boldsymbol{s}'|\boldsymbol{s}, \boldsymbol{a}\big) = \prod_{n=1}^{N} \Pr(s_n' \mid s_n)$$ and let each utility function depend on a separate state and action variable (i.e., $R(\boldsymbol{s}, \boldsymbol{a}) = \sum_{n=1}^{N} U(s_n, a_n)$). In that case, the maximization of action variables and the summation of state variables can be distributed as follows:

$$V^n(s) \leftarrow \sum_{k=1}^{K} \max_{a_k} U(s_k, a_k)$$

$$+\gamma \sum_{s_1} \Pr\left(s_1' | s_1\right) \sum_{s_2} \Pr\left(s_2' | s_2\right) \ldots \sum_{s_N} \Pr\left(s_N' | s_N\right) V^{n-1}(s')$$

Since each action variable can be maximized independently, the dependency on the number of actions is only logarithmic. We also have a logarithmic number of state variable summations that each involve a factor that is linear in the number of states. In general, the transition function won't factor into a set of independent processes and action variables cannot be maximized separately, but savings can still be reaped by exploiting problem specific conditional independencies.

PARTIALLY OBSERVABLE MARKOV DECISION PROCESSES

So far, we assumed that the state of the world is fully observable. However, in many domains, only noisy and partial information about the current state is available. For instance, in robotics, noisy range sensors, cameras and microphones provide measurements that are not exact and do not reveal the entire state. Partially observable Markov decision processes (POMDPs) provide a natural framework to model such problems.

POMDP Model

In this section, we describe how to extend fully observable MDPs into partially observable MDPs.

POMDP Components

A partially observable Markov decision process (POMDP) is essentially a fully observable MDP with observations that are correlated with the underlying state. Since the underlying state is not directly observable, actions must be chosen based on the observations. Formally, a POMDP is defined by a tuple $<S, A, O, T, Z, R, h, \gamma>$ that con-

tains the same components as an MDP with a set of observations O and an observation function Z.

Observation Space O

The observation space O consists of a set of observations o that correspond to the bits of information received by the agent about the environment at each step. More precisely, the observations may consist of the measurements provided by some sensors. In general, observations consist of any relevant information (however it may be obtained or produced) that is available to the agent at the time of choosing each action. Note that when $O = S$, the MDP is fully observable. However, in many domains O will be different than S.

Observation Function Z

When O is different than S, it is important to know how the observations relate to the states since the agent would ideally like to choose actions based on the underlying state, but only has knowledge of the observations received so far. The observation function describes the correlation between observations, states and actions by a conditional distribution over observations o' given the last state s' and action a (i.e., $Z(o',a,s') = Pr(o'|a,s')$). Similar to the transition function and the reward function, the observation function is also assumed to be Markovian (i.e.,

$$\Pr\left(O_{t+1} | S_{t+1}, A_t, S_t, A_{t-1}, \ldots\right) = \Pr\left(O_{t+1} | S_{t+1}, A_t\right) \forall S_t, A_{t-1}$$

and stationary (i.e.

$$\Pr\left(O_{t+1} | S_{t+1}, A_t\right) = \Pr\left(O_{t+1+k} | S_{t+1+k}, A_{t+k}\right) \forall k).$$

Graphical Model

Figure 4 illustrates the graphical model for POMDPs, which is the same as for MDPs with an additional set of random variables for the

Figure 4. Graphical model representation of a POMDP

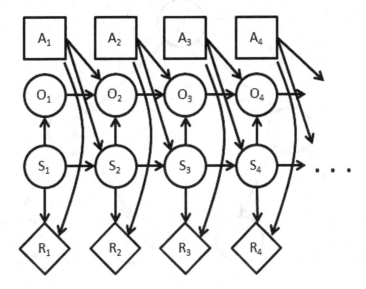

observations. The arcs from states and actions to observations indicate the probabilistic dependency of observations on states and actions.

Policies

Since the underlying state is not observable in POMDPs, we cannot specify policies as a mapping from states to actions. Instead, actions must be chosen based on the history of past observations and actions (i.e.,

$$\pi : A_0, O_1, A_1, O_2, \ldots, A_{t-1}, O_t \to A_t).$$

Such a mapping can be represented by a tree where each path corresponds to a history and the actions are stored in the nodes. Figure 5 shows a 3-step policy such that the root indicates the initial action, the children indicate the actions that should be executed for each observation and the leaves indicate the actions that should be executed for each history of two observations and actions. Since the process is Markovian (i.e., transition, reward and observation functions depend only on the state

and action of the current and immediately preceding time step), an interesting question is whether it is sufficient to choose actions based only on the last observation and action. It turns out that this is not the case. An optimal policy may need to take into account observations and actions that are arbitrarily far in the past. This is problematic since the history of past observations and actions cannot be bounded and the size of policy trees grows exponentially with the length of histories.

One solution to this problem is to consider finite state controllers. A controller consists of a graph where the nodes are labeled with actions and edges are labeled with observations (see Figure 6 for an example). A controller can be viewed as a cyclic policy tree where branches are allowed to merge. Similar to a policy tree, a controller encodes a policy by storing actions in each node and treating the paths that arrive to a node as the histories that map to the action stored in that node. It is interesting to note that even when a controller has a finite number of nodes, it is possible to encode a policy with unbounded histories since cyclic paths lead to potentially infinite

Figure 5. Three-step policy tree for a POMDP of two actions and two observations

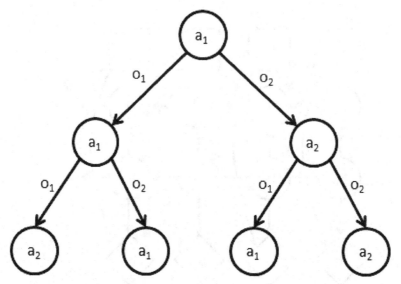

histories. That being said, not all policies can be represented by a controller of a fixed size. Nevertheless, fixed size controllers are quite attractive in practice because the amount of memory required is bounded and for many problems a small amount of memory is sufficient to obtain very good policies.

Alternatively, one can also consider policies that are mappings from distributions over states (also known as beliefs) to actions (i.e., $\pi : B \rightarrow A$ where B is the belief space). Although the underlying state cannot be observed, we can infer a distribution over states based on the history of past observations and actions. Suppose that at time step 0, the agent has an initial belief b_0. After executing a_0 and observing o_1 the agent can use the transition and observation functions to revise its belief according to Bayes' theorem as follows:

$$b_1\left(s'\right) = \sum_s b_0\left(s\right) \Pr\left(s'|s, a_0\right) \Pr(o_1 \mid a_0, s')$$

Similarly, at every time step t the agent can update its belief b_t based on the previous belief b_{t-1}, the last action a_{t-1} and the last observation o_t. It can be shown that the belief b_t is a sufficient statistic of the history of past actions and observations up to time t. The equivalence between histories and beliefs is quite interesting because beliefs have a fixed length while the length of histories grows with the planning horizon. This is possible because beliefs live in a continuous space (i.e., simplex of distributions over states) and therefore an unbounded number of histories can be embedded into the continuous belief space.

We can also think of the beliefs as information states. Since the states are not observable in POMDPs, we are free to define the states in any way we want as long as we can define Markovian and stationary transition and reward functions. Beliefs can indeed be considered as states and doing this gives rise to a belief state MDP that is equivalent to the original POMDP. For any POMDP $<S, A, O, T, Z, R, \gamma, h>$, there is an equivalent belief state MDP $< \hat{S}, \hat{A}, \hat{T}, \hat{R}, \gamma, h >$ where

Figure 6. Finite state controller for a POMDP of two actions and two observations

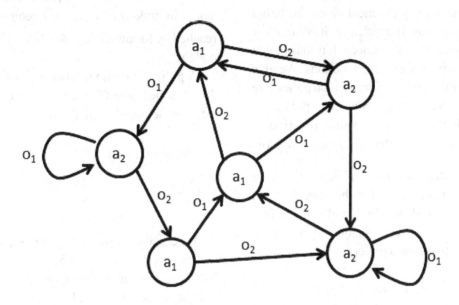

$\hat{S} = B = \Delta S$ (ΔS indicates the simplex of probability distributions over S),

$\hat{A} = A$,

$\hat{T}(b', b, a) = \Pr(o' \mid b, a)$

when $b' = <b, a, o'>$ and 0 otherwise,

$\hat{R}(b, a) = \sum_s b(s) R(s, a).$

This belief MDP is equivalent to the original POMDP in the sense that replacing the beliefs by their corresponding history in the optimal policies of the belief MDP leads to optimal policies for the POMDP. Since the belief MDP is a fully observable MDP and therefore it has an optimal policy that is Markovian and stationary, it will often be easier to work with the belief MDP instead of the POMDP. As we will see shortly, several POMDP algorithms are actually defined with respect to the equivalent belief MDP.

Value Function

POMDP value functions can be expressed in a similar way as MDP value functions when working with belief MDPs. Recall that the value V^π of a policy π is given by the expected sum of discounted rewards earned while executing the policy. In the case of belief MDPs, the value function and the rewards are defined with respect to beliefs:

$$V^\pi(b_0) = \sum_{t=0}^{\infty} \gamma^t E_\pi[R(b_t, \pi(b_t))] \ \forall b_0$$

The value function can be written recursively as the sum of the current reward with the expected discounted future rewards given again by the value function.

$$V^\pi(b) = R(b, \pi(b))$$
$$+ \gamma \sum_{o'} \Pr(o' \mid b, \pi(b)) V^\pi(b_o^a) \forall b$$

Here b_o^a is the updated belief according to Bayes theorem after executing a and observing *o'*. While the above equation is fine theoretically, it is not immediately practical since the belief space is continuous. In particular, it is not clear how to represent value functions. It turns out that policy trees have linear value functions. We give a proof by induction. Consider a trivial policy tree of just one node labeled *a*. Since this policy executes a single action, its value function is $V(b) = \sum_s b(s)R(s,a)$, which is linear in *b*. Now assume that all policy trees of depth *d* have a linear value function in *b*. Then the value function of a policy tree of depth *d* + 1 is also linear in *b* since it is the linear combination of the value functions of its subtrees of depth *d*:

$$V^{tree}(b) = \sum_s b(s)[R(s,a(root))$$
$$+\gamma \sum_{o'} \Pr(o'|s,a(root)) V^{subtree(o')}(b_{o'}^{a(root)})]$$

In the above equation, *a(root)* is the action stored at the root of the tree and *subtree(o')* is the subtree reached by following the edge labeled by *o'*. Similarly, the value function of a controller can be represented by a set Γ of linear functions (also known as α-functions). There is one linear function $\alpha_n(b)$ per node *n* in the controller since we can think of each node as the root of a cyclic policy tree. Since these functions are linear, they are typically represented by a vector $\alpha_n(s)$ of the same name (i.e., $\alpha_n(b) = \sum_s b(s)\alpha_n(s)$). Hence, depending on whether we are referring to the function or its vector representation, we will use the expression α-function or α-vector. Due to the cyclic nature of controllers, α-vectors can be defined recursively, yielding the following set of linear equations:

$$\alpha_n(s) = R(s,\beta(n))$$
$$+\gamma \sum_{s',o'} \Pr(s'|s,\beta(n)) \Pr(o'|s',\beta(n)) \alpha_{\phi(n,o')}(s') \forall n,s$$

In the above equation $\beta(n)$ returns the action stored in node *n* and $\phi(n,o')$ returns the node reached by following the edge labeled by *o'* from node *n*.

A policy is optimal when its value function $V^*(b)$ is the highest for all beliefs *b* and therefore satisfies Bellman's equation:

$$V^{\pi^*}(b) = \max_a R(b,a)$$
$$+\gamma \sum_{o'} \Pr(o'|b,a) V^{\pi^*}(b_{o'}^a) \forall b$$

We can also show that V^* is piece-wise linear and convex (Smallwood & Sondik, 1973). Figure 7 shows an example of an optimal value function. It is piece-wise linear and convex because it corresponds to the upper surface of a set of linear functions. Intuitively, there is one linear function per policy tree. Since different policy trees are better for different starting beliefs, we simply take the highest function at each belief, which corresponds to the upper surface. We will explain in the next section how to compute the linear pieces that compose the optimal value function by value iteration.

Solution Algorithms

The optimization of a POMDP policy is a notoriously hard problem. In general, finding the optimal policy for finite horizon problems is PSPACE-Complete (Papadimitriou & Tsitsiklis, 1987). As a result, most approaches focus on approximations and try to exploit problem specific structure. There are three broad classes of algorithms to optimize the policy of a POMDP: forward search, value iteration and policy search. Forward search techniques are online in the sense that they optimize the policy as it is executed, while value iteration and policy search techniques pre-compute a policy offline.

Figure 7. Optimal value function V^* for a one-dimensional belief space

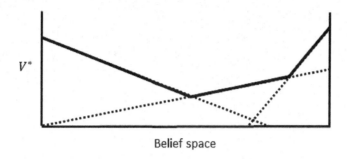

Belief space

Value Iteration

It is possible to define a value iteration algorithm (Table 5) that computes the optimal value function for an increasing horizon. The algorithm builds the linear pieces of the optimal value function by considering all possible policy trees. Initially, for zero steps to go, the set Γ^0 of linear functions that defines the value function contains only a constant zero function. At n steps to go, the set Γ^n is formed by computing the linear functions associated with all n step policy trees. This is done recursively by augmenting the n-1 step policy trees. A new root is created and an existing n-1 step policy tree is selected as the subtree for each observation. The algorithm doesn't explicitly build policy trees, but the α-vectors associated with the trees are computed directly in a similar fashion. In the inner-most loop of value iteration in Table 5, α-vectors are constructed by adding the reward vector associated with the action at the root and the α-vectors associated with the n-1 step policy trees for each observation. In the algorithm, the operator $\oplus$ is used to indicate the cross sums of different sets of vectors (i.e.,

$$S_1 \oplus S_2 = \{v_1 + v_2 \mid v_1 \in S_1, v_2 \in S_2\})$$. The algorithm returns a set Γ of α-vectors whose upper surface represents the value function $V(b) = \max_{\alpha \in \Gamma} \alpha(b)$. Although the α-vectors correspond to the value of some policy trees, these policy trees are rarely constructed explicitly. Instead, a mapping π from beliefs to actions is inferred. More precisely, actions are selected greedily for each belief by computing a one-step look ahead according to Bellman's equation:

$$\pi(b) = \arg\max_a R(b,a) + \gamma \sum_o \Pr(o' \mid b,a) \max_{\alpha \in \Gamma} \alpha(b_o^a)$$

Hence, the execution of the policy induced by Γ is performed by alternating between updating the belief according to Bayes' theorem and selecting the best action according to Bellman's equation.

Let's analyze the complexity of value iteration. Since there are $|A|$ possible reward vectors (one for each action) and $|\Gamma^{n-1}|$ possible α-vectors for each observation, the number of n-step α-vectors is $|\Gamma^n| = |A||O|^{|\Gamma^{n-1}|}$. The overall computational complexity of value iteration is $O(|S|^2|A|^{|O|^h})$ since there are $|A|^{|O|^h}$ policy trees for a planning horizon of h steps and the matrix operations involved are quadratic in $|S|$. This is clearly intractable since the complexity is exponential in $|O|$ and doubly exponential in h. However, recall that for any belief b, the optimal value is given by the policy tree that has the highest value (i.e., $V^*(b) = \max_{\alpha \in \Gamma^h} \sum_s b(s)\alpha(s)$). Hence, we only need

Table 5. Value iteration

Inputs: POMDP, $\in$

Output: Γ^n

$n \leftarrow 0$

$\Gamma^0 \leftarrow \{0\}$

Repeat

$n \leftarrow n + 1$

$\Gamma^n \leftarrow \{\}$ For each $a \in A$ do

$\Gamma^n \leftarrow \Gamma^n \bigcup \oplus_{o'} \{\frac{R(s,a)}{|O|} + \gamma \sum_s \Pr\left(o' \mid s', a\right) \Pr\left(s' \mid s, a\right) \alpha\left(s'\right) \mid \alpha \in \Gamma^{n-1}\}$ End for

Until $\max_b \mid \max_{\alpha \in \Gamma^n} \alpha\left(b\right) - \max_{\alpha' \in \Gamma^{n-1}} \alpha'\left(b\right) \mid \leq \varepsilon$

the α-vectors that are optimal for some belief and therefore are part of the upper surface. Several variants of value iteration have been proposed that prune Γ^n at each step to retain only the vectors that form the upper surface (Zhang & Liu, 1996; Kaelbling, Littman et al., 1998). While these variants scale better, for most problems the number of α-vectors still tends to grow exponentially with the planning horizon.

For many problems, since there is only one initial belief b_0 for which we need a policy, we can restrict our attention to the belief points that are reachable from b_0. This has led to several variants of value iteration that are known as *point-based value iteration* algorithms (Pineau, Gordon et al., 2006). More precisely, these algorithms compute a set Γ of α-vectors that are optimal for a set B of belief points. Since we only need one optimal α-vector per belief, the size of Γ can be bounded by the size of B. Unless B includes all reachable belief points, Γ may not contain all α-vectors necessary to represent the optimal value function, but in practice, a reasonable num-

ber of α-vectors is often sufficient to obtain a very good policy. Table 6 describes a prototypical point-based value iteration algorithm. For each belief b from a set B, a Bellman backup is computed to obtain an optimal α-vector at b. Point-based value iteration algorithms differ mostly in how the set of beliefs is selected, but in general they all try to select beliefs that are reachable from b_0 (Spaan & Vlassis, 2005; Smith & Simmons, 2005; Pineau, Gordon et al., 2006; Shani, Brafman et al., 2007; Kurniawati, Hsu et al., 2008; Poupart, Kim et al., 2011).

Policy Search

Instead of calculating a value function from which a policy π is inferred, we can directly optimize a policy. Several policy search techniques consider the space of controllers to perform their search. Consider the following parameterization for a controller. Let $\beta : N \rightarrow A$ be a mapping that indicates which action shall be executed in each node. Also, let $\phi : N \times O \rightarrow N$ be a mapping

Table 6. Point-based value iteration

Inputs: POMDP, $\in$

Output: Γ^n

Select a set B of beliefs b

$n \leftarrow 0$
$\Gamma^0 \leftarrow \{0\}$

Repeat

$n \leftarrow n + 1$

$\Gamma^n \leftarrow \{\}$ For each $b \in B$ do $\alpha_{ao'} \leftarrow \underset{\alpha \in \Gamma^{n-1}}{\mathrm{argmax}}\, \alpha(b)\, \forall a, o'$

$a^* \leftarrow \underset{a}{\max}\, R(b, a) + \gamma \sum_{o'} \Pr\left(o'|b, a\right) \alpha_{ao'}(b_o^a)$

$\alpha(b) \leftarrow R(b, a^*) + \gamma \sum_{o'} \Pr\left(o'|b, a^*\right) \alpha_{a^*o'}(b_o^{a^*})$

$\Gamma^n \leftarrow \Gamma^n \bigcup \{\alpha\}$ End for

Until $\underset{b \in B}{\max} \,|\, \underset{\alpha \in \Gamma^n}{\max}\, \alpha(b) - \underset{\alpha' \in \Gamma^{n-1}}{\max}\, \alpha'(b)\,| \leq \varepsilon$

---

that indicates which node should be reached from each node after receiving an observation. Table 7 describes policy iteration, which is a basic policy search technique that alternates between policy evaluation and policy improvement (Hansen, 1997; Hansen, 1998). Given a controller encoded by an action mapping β and a successor node mapping ϕ, the value function of this controller is computed by solving a linear system of equations that yields an α-vector for each node n. The policy improvement step augments the controller with some new nodes corresponding to all the root nodes that could be created to form new policy trees that use the existing policy trees as children. Since there are $|A|$ possible actions and $|\Gamma|$ possible subtrees for each observation,

$|A||\Gamma|^{|O|}$ new nodes are created. The policy improvement step is similar to a step of value iteration, however policy trees are constructed explicitly. The complexity of policy iteration is the same as value iteration (i.e., $O(|S|^2 |A|^{|O|^h})$) since the number of nodes created at each iteration is identical to the number of α-vectors computed in value iteration. Policy iteration typically needs fewer iterations than value iteration to converge because policies are evaluated immediately at each iteration, but value iteration takes less time per iteration because policies are not evaluated in a separate step. Nevertheless, these differences do not change the fact that both algorithms are equally intractable.

Table 7. Policy iteration

Inputs: POMDP, ε

Output: controller $< \beta, \phi >$

Initialize controller $< \beta, \phi >$ arbitrarily

Repeat

Policy evaluation:

$$\alpha_n(s) = R(s, \beta(n)) + \gamma \sum_{s',o'} \Pr(s'|s, \beta(n)) \Pr(o'|s', \beta(n)) \alpha_{\phi(n,o')}(s') \forall n \in N, s \in S \text{ Policy improvement:}$$

Create a set N_{new} of $|A||\Gamma|^{|O|}$ new nodes corresponding to all possible mappings $\beta : N_{new} \rightarrow A$ and $\phi : N_{new} \times O \rightarrow N$ $N \leftarrow N \bigcup N_{new}$

Until value function improvement $\leq \varepsilon$

Similar to value iteration, it is possible to improve the running time of policy iteration by pruning the nodes that are not optimal for any belief, however the complexity typically remains exponential. We can also exploit the fact that in many problems we only care about finding a good policy for a specific initial belief b_0. However, instead of focusing the search on a set of reachable beliefs which would implicitly bound the number of nodes and α-vectors, we can directly bound the size of the controller. To that effect, we can formulate an optimization problem that finds the best action mapping β and the best successor node mapping ϕ for a fixed number of nodes. When the number of nodes is bounded, the best controller may be stochastic. Intuitively, if the number of nodes is insufficient, it may be the case that the same node needs to be used in different beliefs where different actions would be preferable. In situations like that, randomizing the choice of action is often better than deterministically choosing only one action. Hence, we consider stochastic controllers parameterized by an action distribution $\Pr(a|n)$ and a successor node distribution $\Pr(n'|n,o')$. Table 8 describes a non-convex optimization problem to find the best action and

successor node distributions for a fixed number of nodes. Several algorithms including gradient descent (Meuleau, Kim et al., 1999), bounded policy iteration (Poupart & Boutilier, 2003), stochastic local search (Braziunas & Boutilier, 2004), expectation maximization (Toussaint, Harmeling et al., 2006) and sequential quadratic programming (Amato, Bernstein et al., 2007) have been proposed, however, due to the non-convex nature of the problem, none of the algorithms can reliably find the global optimum. Several techniques have been proposed to escape local optima by adding new nodes to the controller (Poupart & Boutilier, 2003; Poupart, Lang et al., 2011).

Forward Search

Similar to fully observable MDPs, we can define online forward search techniques for POMDPs viewed as belief MDPs. The idea is to build an "expectimax" search tree where the edges are labeled by actions and observations in alternation and the nodes are labeled by maximization and expectation in alternation. Each node is also associated with the belief obtained by following the sequence of past actions and observations on the

Table 8. Bounded controller optimization

Inputs: POMDP, ε

Output: stochastic controller $< \Pr(a \mid n), \Pr(n' \mid n, o') >$

Solve non-convex optimization problem

$$\max_{\{\Pr(a|n), \Pr(n'|n,o'), \alpha_n(s)\}} \sum_s b_0(s)\alpha_1(s)$$

s.t. $\alpha_n(s) = \sum_a \Pr(a|n)[R(s,a) + \gamma \sum_{s',o',n'} \Pr(s'|s,a)\Pr(o'|s',a)\Pr(n'\mid n,o')\alpha_{n'}(s')] \forall n, s$

$\sum_a \Pr(a|n) = 1 \forall n$ and $\sum_{n'} \Pr(n'|n,o') = 1 \forall n, o'$

Table 9. POMDP Forward Search

Inputs: POMDP, b, d

Output: a^*, v^*

If $d = 0$ then $a^* \leftarrow \underset{a}{\operatorname{argmax}} R(b,a)$

$v^* \leftarrow \underset{a}{\max} R(b,a)$ Else $v_{a,o'} \leftarrow forwardSearch\left(POMDP, b_o^a, d-1\right) \ \forall a, o'$

$a^* \leftarrow \underset{a}{\operatorname{argmax}} R(b,a) + \gamma \sum_{o'} \Pr(o' \mid b,a)v_{a,o'}$

$v^* \leftarrow \underset{a}{\max} R(b,a) + \gamma \sum_{o'} \Pr(o'|b,a)v_{ao'}$

End

path to the node. Table 9 describes how to compute the expected values at each node in a bottom up fashion. The action that yields the highest value at the root will be the next action executed. For a search depth d, the computational complexity is $O(|S|^2(|A||O|)^d)$. However, significant portions of the tree may be pruned by sampling observations instead of enumerating all observations and ignoring actions that are provably suboptimal (Kearns, Mansour et al., 1999; Ross, Pineau et al., 2008, Silver & Veness, 2010).

CHALLENGES FOR DEPLOYMENT IN APPLICATIONS

In this section, we discuss various challenges for the deployment of MDP and POMDP algorithms in applications. Since MDPs and POMDPs assume that a model is given (i.e., transition, observation and reward functions), then the first question that needs to be answered in an application is: where does the model come from? We discuss several lines of work that address this question in Section

4.1. Once a model is obtained, then the algorithms described in this chapter can be applied to optimize a policy. However, as we discussed, scalability is an issue, especially for POMDPs. Hence, Section 4.2 provides an overview of some of the efforts to tackle ever larger problems. Once a policy is computed, the next challenge that is often faced by practitioners is the acceptance of the policy. Since the model used to compute a policy may not be accurate, the solution algorithm may be approximate and users are often reluctant to follow advice from a computer, how can we convince users to trust the resulting policy? Section 4.3 discusses some work to devise "robust" policies and to explain action choices to users.

Where does the Model come from?

The transition, observation and reward functions can either be obtained before the policy is optimized or while optimizing and executing the policy. The former is the traditional approach used in Operations Research, while the latter is the subject of Reinforcement Learning, which is discussed in Chapter 4.

Let's consider the construction of a model before policy optimization. In general, models can be estimated from data, specified by hand or both. When data is available, the transition and observation functions can be estimated with learning techniques for Dynamic Bayesian Networks (DBNs) discussed in the previous chapter. Recall that the transition model of a flat MDP is a Markov process, which corresponds to a DBN with a single chain of variables (i.e., the state variables). When the states are fully observable, then the transition distribution can be estimated very easily by the relative frequencies

$$\Pr(s'|s,a) = \frac{\#(s',s,a)}{\#(s,a)},$$ which corresponds to

maximizing the likelihood of the data. Similarly, for factored MDPs, the transition model is a multivariate DBN (i.e., multiple state variables)

and the conditional probabilities of each variable can be estimated by the relative frequencies (i.e.,

$$\Pr(X|pa(X)) = \frac{\#(X,pa(X))}{\#(pa(X))}).$$ For POMDPs,

model estimation is more complicated since the states are hidden. Nevertheless, the transition and observation models correspond together to an input output hidden Markov model (IOHMM) (Bengio & Frasconi, 1996), which is a special type of DBN. The parameters can also be estimated by maximum likelihood, but using techniques for incomplete data or semi-supervised learning such as expectation maximization (Dempster, Laird et al., 1977).

In factored problems, the structure of the DBN that encodes the transition and observation models can be learned from data by various structure learning techniques. In the case of partially observable models, the number of hidden states may not be known since the states are never observed. Hence they can also be learned from data with model selection techniques. That being said, in many situations, it is best to use a hybrid approach where part of the model is manually specified by a human expert while the rest is learned from data. In general, humans can easily specify the qualitative aspects of the model (e.g., the graphical structure of the DBN and the number of hidden states), but have a harder time with the quantitative parts (e.g., the conditional probabilities). In contrast, learning algorithms for the parameters are well established and scale well, while structure learning is much more complex both computationally and statistically. Hence, it is common practice to ask a domain expert to specify the structure of the model and in some cases, some bounds on the parameters, but to let learning algorithms estimate the precise values of the conditional probabilities.

Similarly, the reward function can be estimated from data or specified manually. For estimation from data, there are two important lines of work: preference elicitation and inverse reinforcement learning. In preference elicitation, the reward function is estimated based on some queries about the preferences of the user for some outcomes (Regan & Boutilier., 2011a). Common queries include comparative queries and standard gamble queries where a user is asked to compare the value of an outcome to another outcome or a gamble with respect to several outcomes. The answers to those queries are the data from which the reward function can be estimated. More precisely, the answers provide bounds on the numerical values of the rewards. Given a space of admissible reward functions, it is possible to optimize an MDP to maximize a lower bound on the optimal value function or to minimize the worst-case regret (Regan & Boutilier., 2010; Oh & Kim, 2011; Regan & Boutilier., 2011b).

Instead of directly querying a domain expert, inverse reinforcement learning estimates the reward function by observing the expert (Ng & Russell, 2000; Abbeel & Ng, 2004; Neu & Szepesvari, 2007; Choi & Kim, 2011). More precisely, we observe an expert execute a policy that is assumed to be optimal (or near optimal) and the problem is to infer what reward function the expert is implicitly maximizing. Most of the time, the problem is ill defined since a policy can usually be explained by more than one reward function. Hence, it is often necessary to use additional prior knowledge to express a bias that will break ties.

In summary, the transition and observation models can be obtained from data by maximizing likelihood, specified by hand or both. The reward function can be estimated by preference elicitation, inverse reinforcement learning or manually. More generally, reinforcement learning can be used to optimize a policy directly with or without estimating a model.

Can we Tackle ever Larger Domains?

Many application domains are quite complex and therefore lead to large MDPs and POMDPS. Hence it becomes important to use an algorithm that scales well. For instance, the state, action and observation spaces may be very large when they are continuous or defined by the cross product of several variables. In the latter case, such models are typically referred to as factored MDPs and POMDPs since the transition and observation distributions are factored into a product of conditional distributions. Similarly, the reward function could be decomposed into a sum of local utility functions. The number of states, actions and observations grows exponentially with the number of variables since states, actions and observations correspond to all possible joint assignments of the variables.

The key to scalability is to exploit structure. Practical problems are not random and therefore typically exhibit some kind of structure. For instance, factored models often exhibit a fair amount of conditional independence and context specific independence. Hence, an approach to exploit this structure consists of using algebraic decision diagrams (ADDs) as the underlying data structure for all computation instead of vectors and matrices (Hoey, St-Aubin et al., 1999; Shani, Poupart et al., 2008; Sim, Kim et al., 2008). An ADD consists of a tree where the branches are allowed to merge. Similar to a vector that stores a mapping from indices to values, an ADD stores a mapping from variable assignments to values. Figure 8 gives an example of a vector and an ADD that encode the same function. For the ADD, the values are stored in the leaves and each path corresponds to a joint assignment of the variables. When a vector contains identical values, a more compact ADD can often be used to represent the same function by merging branches that lead to the same leaf. Several value iteration algorithms that use ADDs as the underlying structure have been devised for factored MDPs and POMDPs. In general, their scalability depends on the amount of conditional and context-specific independence present in the problem. In particular, the size of the ADD representation of the value functions and α-vectors will depend on the number of repeated values. Extensions to exploit affine transformations (e.g., AADDs (Sanner & McAllester, 2005)) and represent continuous functions (i.e., XADD (Sanner, Delgado et al., 2011)) have also been developed.

An alternative representation to compactly represent value functions consists of linear combinations of basis functions (Schuurmans & Patrascu, 2001; Guestrin, Koller et al., 2003; Kveton, Hauskrecht et al., 2006). Since the value function is the sum of rewards over the planning horizon, perhaps we can approximate it by a weighted sum of small functions often referred to as basis functions. This approach has the advantage that vectors that do not feature repeated values may still be represented compactly. Furthermore, linear combinations of basis functions can be used in value iteration, policy iteration and linear programming, as well as discrete and continuous domains. Scalability depends on the number of basis functions necessary to achieve a good fit.

Another line of work considers hierarchical models to decompose a complex planning problem into several smaller problems (Parr & Russell, 1997; Dietterich, 1998; Sutton, Precup et al., 1999; Pineau, Gordon et al., 2003, Hansen & Zhou, 2003). Each small problem can be solved in isolation using any algorithm and the resulting policies are then treated as extended actions into higher level planning problems. Hierarchical decompositions typically lead to temporal and spatial abstractions. In the low level problems, it may be possible to ignore some state variables, effectively reducing the size of the state space. In the higher level problems, it may be possible to reduce the planning horizon since the actions are lower level policies that extend over several time steps that are now combined into one higher level time step.

There is no perfect algorithm that scales for all problems. However with enough domain knowledge, it is often possible to choose a suitable algorithm that exploits the right structure to find a good policy in the desired amount of time.

Can we Trust the Resulting Policy?

Once a policy is obtained, users and decision makers may question its correctness. In some application domains, actions are executed by users. For instance, in recommender systems, decision support tools and assistive technologies, the role of the policy is to recommend a course of action, however users often like to make the final decision and sometimes question the recommendation. In other application domains such as robotics, spoken dialog management and autonomic computing, the policy is executed by the computer and there is no human in the loop. Nevertheless, stake holders may question how good the policy is before deploying it. In fact, since the model is never perfect and solution algorithms are rarely exact, there is a need for explicit guarantees about the quality of the policy.

As discussed in Section 4.1, the model may be obtained from data and/or prior knowledge. As a result, it is at best an approximation of the true model. If the values of the parameters come with bounds, it is possible to optimize the policy with respect to all models that satisfy the bounds. More precisely, we can search for the policy that has the highest lower bound. Optimization techniques have been developed to that effect for MDPs with bounded transition functions (Satia, Lave Jr., 1970; White III & El-Deib, 1994; Delgado, Sanner et al., 2011). We can also search for the policy that minimizes the worst regret given a space of bounded reward functions (Regan & Boutilier., 2010; Oh & Kim, 2011; Regan & Boutilier., 2011b).

To help with scalability, approximate algorithms are often used, especially for POMDPs. While the resulting policies are generally good, it is often important to bound the errors due to the approximation. To that effect, several algorithms provide lower and upper bounds on the value of the function returned (Smith & Simmons, 2005; Kurniawati, Hsu et al., 2008; Sim, Kim et al., 2008; Poupart, Kim et al., 2011). For instance,

Figure 8. Vector and algebraic decision diagram (ADD) representation of the same function

S_1	S_2	S_3	V
t	t	t	1
t	t	f	2
t	f	t	3
t	f	f	4
f	t	t	3
f	t	f	4
f	f	t	5
f	f	f	5

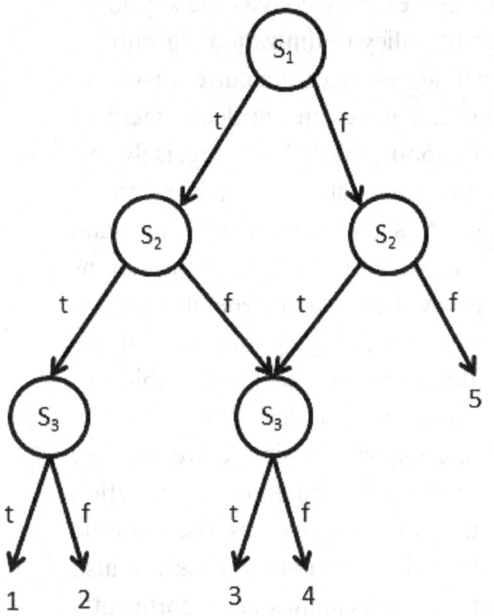

most algorithms that approximate POMDP value functions with a parsimonious set of value functions actually produce a lower bound. Although upper bounds are not as critical as lower bounds, they indicate the degree of sub-optimality of a policy. A few algorithms give lower and upper bounds on the optimal value function (Smith & Simmons, 2005; Kurniawati, Hsu et al., 2008; Sim, Kim et al., 2008; Poupart, Kim et al., 2011).

In some situations, the lower and upper bounds are difficult to appreciate for the end user since these bounds are based on a reward function that does not have an obvious scale except for the engineer who designed it or elicited it. Furthermore, decision makers often prefer to make the final decision and therefore will have a tendency to question the actions recommended even in the presence of bounds. One strategy consists of returning a set of actions (instead of a single action) to the decision maker, who can then make the final decision about the action that will be executed. This set of actions can be obtained by finding the set of policies that are ε-optimal for a given ε (Fard & Pineau, 2011). Another strat-

egy consists of providing an explanation about the action recommended. While the best kind of explanation is problem dependent, some approaches can automatically generate explanations for any MDP by reporting the most relevant state variable (Elizalde, Sucar et al., 2008) or the expected frequency with which some key states (or groups of states) can be reached (Khan, Poupart et al., 2009). Chapters 7 and 12 give more details on policy explanation techniques.

CONCLUSION

In this chapter, we introduced fully and partially observable Markov decision processes as a principled and flexible framework for sequential decision making under uncertainty. This framework can be seen as the combination of dynamic Bayesian networks (for sequential reasoning) and influence diagrams (for decision making) that were described in the previous chapter. We described the main classes of solution algorithms and gave an example of a prototypical algorithm in each class. While these basic algorithms are not the most advanced ones, they convey the key ideas in the design of policy optimization algorithms. We also discussed some of the current work to address important issues in the deployment of (PO)MDPs in applications. More precisely, we discussed some approaches to obtain a model, some strategies to scale solution algorithms and some techniques to help users accept the actions recommended by a computer generated policy. The question of optimizing a policy without any model or while learning a model is the subject of Chapter 4 on reinforcement learning.

To keep the exposition simple we focused on planning problems with finite state, action and observation spaces as well as discrete time steps. Infinite and continuous models are also possible, but the mathematics are significantly more complex. Nevertheless, some work has explored MDPs with continuous states and actions (Feng, Dearden et al., 2003; Kveton, Hauskrecht et al., 2006; Meuleau, Benazera et al., 2009), POMDPs with continuous states, actions and observations (Thrun, 1999; Hoey & Poupart, 2005; Porta, Vlassis et al., 2006) as well as continuous time planning problems (Howard, 1971; Guo & Hernandez-Lerma, 2009). Chapter 5 also presents some solution techniques for continuous time semi-Markov decision processes. We also assumed that the objective is to maximize the discounted sum of rewards, but maximizing the average rewards is also common (Puterman, 2005). In some application domains, it is also natural to consider multiple objectives where the goal is to maximize one of the objectives, while imposing some bounds on the other objectives (Altman, 1999; Piunovskiy & Mao, 2000; Kim, Lee et al., 2011).

Finally, we assumed the presence of a single decision maker. However, with the increasing popularity of distributed systems, there may be several decision makers with different objectives and different sources of information. When the decision makers are cooperative and share a common objective, but cannot communicate to exchange sensory information as they execute a policy, decentralized (PO)MDPs (DEC-MDPs and DEC-POMDPs) provide a suitable framework to optimize a policy that will be executed in a decentralized way (Bernstein, Amato et al., 2009; Amato, Berstein et al., 2010). Chapter 16 also describes some work based on DEC-MDPs. When the decision makers are competitive in the sense that they do not share the same objective, then interactive POMDPs (I-POMDPs) provide a flexible framework (Gmytrasiewicz & Doshi, 2005).

REFERENCES

Abbeel, P., & Ng, A. (2004). Apprenticeship learning via inverse reinforcement learning, *International Conference on Machine Learning (ICML)*, Banff, Alberta, (pp. 1-8).

Altman, E. (1999). *Constrained Markov Decision Processes*. Boca Raton, FL: Chapman & Hall/CRC.

Amato, C., Bernstein, D. S., & Zilberstein, S. (2007). *Solving POMDPs using quadratically constrained linear programs. International Joint Conferences on Artificial Intelligence* (pp. 2418–2424). IJCAI.

Amato, C., Bernstein, D. S., & Zilberstein, S. (2010). Optimizing fixed-size stochastic controllers for POMDPs and decentralized POMDPs. *Autonomous Agents and Multi-Agent Systems, 21*(3), 293–320. doi:10.1007/s10458-009-9103-z

Bellman, R. (1957). A Markov decision process. *Indiana University Mathematics Journal, 6*(4), 679–684. doi:10.1512/iumj.1957.6.06038

Bengio, Y., & Frasconi, P. (1996). Input/output HMMs for sequence processing. *IEEE Transactions on Neural Networks, 7*(5), 1231–1249. doi:10.1109/72.536317

Bernstein, D. S., Amato, C., Hanse, E. A., & Zilberstein, S. (2009). Policy iteration for decentralized control of Markov decision processes. [JAIR]. *Journal of Artificial Intelligence Research, 34,* 89–132.

Braziunas, D., & Boutilier, C. (2004). Stochastic local search for POMDP controllers. *National Conference on Artificial Intelligence (AAAI)*, San Jose, California, (pp. 690-696).

Choi, J., & Kim, K.-E. (2011). Inverse reinforcement learning in partially observable domains. [JMLR]. *Journal of Machine Learning Research, 12,* 691–730.

Delgado, K. V., Sanner, S., & Nunes de Barros, L. (2011). Efficient solutions to factored MDPs with imprecise transition probabilities. [AIJ]. *Artificial Intelligence, 175*(9-10), 1498–1527. doi:10.1016/j.artint.2011.01.001

Dempster, A., Laird, L., & Rubin, D. (1977). Maximum likelihood from incomplete data via the EM algorithm. *Journal of the Royal Statistical Society. Series B. Methodological, 39*(1), 1–38.

Dietterich, T. (1998). The MAXQ method for hierarchical reinforcement learning. *International Conference on Machine Learning*, (pp. 118-126).

Elizalde, F., Sucar, L. E., Luque, M., Diez, F. J., & Reyes, A. (2008). Policy explanation in factored Markov decision processes. *European Workshop on Probabilistic Graphical Models*, (pp. 97-104).

Fard, M. M., & Pineau, J. (2011). Non-deterministic policies in Markovian decision processes. [JAIR]. *Journal of Artificial Intelligence Research, 40,* 1–24.

Feng, Z., Dearden, R., Meuleau, N., & Washington, R. (2004). Dynamic programming for structured continuous Markov decision problems. *International Conference on Uncertainty in Artificial Intelligence (UAI)*, (pp. 154-161).

Gmytrasiewicz, P., & Doshi, P. (2005). A framework for sequential planning in multiagent settings [JAIR]. *Journal of Artificial Intelligence Research, 24,* 49–79.

Guestrin, C., Koller, D., Parr, R., & Venkataraman, S. (2003). Efficient solution algorithms for factored MDPs. [JAIR]. *Journal of Artificial Intelligence Research, 19,* 399–468.

Guo, X., & Hernandez-Lerma, O. (2009). Continuous time Markov decision processes. *Applications of Mathematics, 62,* 9–18.

Hansen, E. A. (1997). *An improved policy iteration algorithm for partially observable MDPs. Advances in Neural Information Processing systems* (pp. 1015–1021). Denver, Colorado: NIPS.

Hansen, E. A. (1998). Solving POMDPs by searching in the policy space. *International Conference on Uncertainty in Artificial Intelligence (UAI)*, Madison, Wisconsin, (pp. 211-219).

Hansen, E. A., & Zhou, R. (2003). Synthesis of hierarchical finite-state controllers for POMDPs. *International Conference on Automated Planning and Scheduling (ICAPS)*, (pp. 113-122).

Hoey, J., & Poupart, P. (2005). *Solving POMDPs with continuous or large discrete observation spaces. International Joint Conferences on Artificial Intelligence* (pp. 1332–1338). IJCAI.

Hoey, J., St-Aubin, R., Hu, J. A., & Boutilier, C. (1999). SPUDD: stochastic planning using decision diagrams. *International Conference on Uncertainty in Artificial Intelligence (UAI)*, (pp. 279-288).

Howard, R. A. (1971). *Dynamic Probabilistic Systems (Vol. II)*. New York, NY: John Wiley & Sons.

Kaelbling, L. P., Littman, M., & Cassandra, A. R. (1998). Planning and acting in partially observable stochastic domains. *Artificial Intelligence, 101,* 99–134. doi:10.1016/S0004-3702(98)00023-X

Kearns, M., Mansour, Y., & Ng, A. Y. (1999). *A sparse sampling algorithm for near-optimal planning in large Markov decision processes. International Joint Conferences on Artificial Intelligence* (pp. 1324–1331). Stockholm, Sweden: IJCAI.

Khan, O. Z., Poupart, P., & Black, J. P. (2009). Minimal sufficient explanations for factored Markov decision processes. *International Conference on Automated Plannning and Scheduling (ICAPS)*.

Kim, D., Lee, J., Kim, K.-E., & Poupart, P. (2011). *Point-Based Value Iteration for Constrained POMDPs. International Joint conferences on Artificial Intelligence* (pp. 1968–1974). IJCAI.

Kurniawati, H., Hsu, D., & Lee, W. (2008). SARSOP: Efficient point-based POMDP planning by approximating optimally reachable belief spaces. *International Conference on Robotics: Science and Systems (RSS)*.

Kveton, B., Hauskrecht, M., & Guestrin, C. (2006). Solving factored MDPs with hybrid state and action variables. [JAIR]. *Journal of Artificial Intelligence Research, 27*, 153–201.

Lusena, C., Goldsmith, J., & Mundhenk, M. (2001). Nonapproximability results for partially observable Markov decision processes. [JAIR]. *Journal of Artificial Intelligence Research, 14*, 83–103.

Meuleau, N., Benazera, E., Brafman, R.I., & Hansen, E.A. & Mausam. (2009). A Heuristic Search Approach to Planning with Continuous Resources in Stochastic Domains. [JAIR]. *Journal of Artificial Intelligence Research, 34*, 27–59.

Meuleau, N., Kim, K.-E., Kaelbling, L. P., & Cassandra, A. R. (1999), Solving POMDPS by searching the space of finite policies, *International Conference on Uncertainty in Artificial Intelligence (UAI)*, Stockholm, Sweden, (pp. 417-426).

Neu, G., & Szepesvari, C. (2007) Apprenticeship learning using inverse reinforcement learning and gradient methods. *International Conference on Uncertainty in Artificial Intelligence (UAI)*, Vancouver, Canada, (pp. 295-302).

Ng, A., & Russell, S. (2000). Algorithms for inverse reinforcement learning. *International Conference on Machine Learning (ICML)*, Stanford, California, (pp. 663-670).

Oh, E., & Kim, K.-E. (2011). A geometric traversal algorithm for reward-uncertain MDPs. *International Conference on Uncertainty in Artificial Intelligence (UAI)*, Barcelona, Spain.

Papadimitriou, C. H., & Tsitsilis, J. N. (1987). The complexity of Markov decision processes. *Mathematics of Operations Research, 12*(3), 441–450. doi:10.1287/moor.12.3.441

Parr, R., & Russell, S. J. (1997). *Reinforcement learning with hierarchies of machines. Advances in Neural Information Processing Systems*. NIPS.

Pineau, J., Gordon, G., & Thrun, S. (2006). Anytime point-based approximations for large POMDPs. [JAIR]. *Journal of Artificial Intelligence Research, 27*, 335–380.

Pineau, J., Gordon, G. J., & Thrun, S. (2003) Policy-contingent abstraction for robust robot control. *International Conference on Uncertainty in Artificial Intelligence (UAI)*, (pp. 477-484).

Piunovskiy, A. B., & Mao, X. (2000). Constrained Markovian decision processes: the dynamic programming approach. *Operations Research Letters, 27*(3), 119–126. doi:10.1016/S0167-6377(00)00039-0

Porta, J. M., Vlassis, N. A., Spaan, M. T. J., & Poupart, P. (2006). Point-Based Value Iteration for Continuous POMDPs. [JMLR]. *Journal of Machine Learning Research, 7*, 2329–2367.

Poupart, P., & Boutilier, C. (2003). *Bounded finite state controllers, Advances in Neural Information Processing Systems*. Vancouver, Canada: NIPS.

Poupart, P., Kim, K. E., & Kim, D. (2011). Closing the Gap: Improved Bounds on Optimal POMDP Solutions, *International Conference on Automated Planning and Scheduling (ICAPS)*, Freiburg, Germany.

Poupart, P., Lang, T., & Toussaint, M. (2011). Analyzing and Escaping Local Optima in Planning as Inference for Partially Observable Domains. *European Conference on Machine Learning (ECML)*, Athens, Greece.

Puterman, M. (2005). *Markov Decision Processes: Discrete Stochastic Dynamic Programming* (2nd ed.). New York, NY: John Wiley & Sons.

Regan, K., & Boutilier, C. (2010). Robust policy computation in reward-uncertain MDPs using nondominated policies. *National Conference on Artificial Intelligence (AAAI)*.

Regan, K., & Boutilier, C. (2011a). *Eliciting additive reward functions for Markov decision processes. International Joint Conferences on Artificial Intelligence* (pp. 2159–2164). Barcelona, Spain: IJCAI.

Regan, K., & Boutilier, C. (2011b). *Robust Online Optimization of Reward-Uncertain MDPs. International Joint Conferences on Artificial Intelligence* (pp. 2165–2171). Barcelona, Spain: IJCAI.

Ross, S., Pineau, J., Paquet, S., & Chaib-Draa, B. (2008). Online planning algorithms for POMDPs. [JAIR]. *Journal of Artificial Intelligence Research, 32*, 663–704.

Sanner, S., Delgado, K. V., & de Barros, L. N. (2011). Symbolic dynamic programming for discrete and continuous state MDPs. *International Conference on Uncertainty in Artificial Intelligence (UAI)*, Barcelona, Spain.

Sanner, S., & McAllester, D. (2005). Affine algebraic decision diagrams (AADDs) and their application to structured probabilistic inference. *International Joint Conference on Artificial Intelligence (IJCAI)*.

Satia, J. K., & Lave, R. E. Jr. (1970). Markovian decision processes with uncertain transition probabilities. *Operations Research, 21*, 728–740. doi:10.1287/opre.21.3.728

Schuurmans, D., & Patrascu, R. (2001). *Direct value-approximation for factored MDPs. Advances in Neural Information Processing Systems* (pp. 1579–1586). Vancouver, BC: NIPS.

Shani, G., Brafman, R. I., & Shimony, S. E. (2007). *Forward search value iteration for POMDPs. International Joint Conferences on Artificial Intelligence* (pp. 2619–2624). IJCAI.

Shani, G., Poupart, P., Brafman, R. I., & Shimony, S. E. (2008). Efficient ADD Operations for Point-Based Algorithms. *International Conference on Automated Planning and Scheduling (ICAPS)*, pp. 330-337.

Silver, D., & Veness, J. (2010). *Monte Carlo planning in large POMDPs, Advances in Neural Information Processing Systems*. Vancouver, BC: NIPS.

Sim, H. S., Kim, K.-E., Kim, J. H., Chang, D.-S., & Koo, M.-Y. (2008). Symbolic heuristic search value iteration for factored POMDPs. *National Conference on Artificial Intelligence (AAAI)*, pp. 1088-1093.

Smallwood, R. D., & Sondik, E. J. (1973). The optimal control of partially observable Markov processes over a finite horizon. *Operations Research, 21*, 1071–1088. doi:10.1287/opre.21.5.1071

Smith, T., & Simmons, R. G. (2005). Point-based POMDP algorithms: improved analysis and implementation, *International Conference on Uncertainty in Artificial Intelligence (UAI)*, pp. 542-547.

Spaan, M. T. J., & Vlassis, N. A. (2005). Perseus: randomized point-based value iteration for POMDPs. [JAIR]. *Journal of Artificial Intelligence Research, 24*, 195–220.

Sutton, R., Precup, D., & Singh, S. P. (1999). Between MDPs and semi-MDPs: a framework for temporal abstraction in reinforcement learning. [AIJ]. *Artificial Intelligence, 112*(1-2), 181–211. doi:10.1016/S0004-3702(99)00052-1

Thrun, S. (1999). Monte Carlo POMDPs. [NIPS]. *Advances in Neural Information Processing Systems*, 1064–1070.

Toussaint, M., Harmeling, S., & Storkey, A. (2006). Probabilistic inference for solving (PO) MDPs, *Technical Report EDI-INF-RR-0934*, School of Informatics, University of Edinburgh.

White, C. C. III, & El-Deib, H. K. (1994). Markov decision processes with imprecise transition probabilities. *Operations Research, 42*(4), 739–749. doi:10.1287/opre.42.4.739

Zhang, N. L., & Liu, W. (1996). Planning in stochastic domains: problem characteristics and approximation. *Technical Report HKUST-CS96-31*, Hong Kong University of Science and Technology.

Chapter 4
An Introduction to Reinforcement Learning

Eduardo F. Morales
National Institute for Astrophysics, Optics and Electronics, México

Julio H. Zaragoza
National Institute for Astrophysics, Optics and Electronics, México

ABSTRACT

This chapter provides a concise introduction to Reinforcement Learning (RL) from a machine learning perspective. It provides the required background to understand the chapters related to RL in this book. It makes no assumption on previous knowledge in this research area and includes short descriptions of some of the latest trends, which are normally excluded from other introductions or overviews on RL. The chapter provides more emphasis on the general conceptual framework and ideas of RL rather than on presenting a rigorous mathematical discussion that may require a great deal of effort by the reader. The first section provides a general introduction to the area. The following section describes the most common solution techniques. In the third section, some of the most recent techniques proposed to deal with large search spaces are described. Finally, the last section provides some final remarks and current research challenges in RL.

INTRODUCTION

Reinforcement Learning (RL) has become one of the most active research areas in Machine Learning[1]. In general terms, its main objective is to learn how to map states to actions while maximizing a reward signal. In reinforcement learning an au-tonomous agent follows a trial-and-error process to learn the optimal action to perform in each state in order to reach its goals. The agent chooses an action in each state, which may take the agent to a new state, and receives a reward. By repeating this process, the agent eventually learns which is the best action to perform to obtain the maximum expected accumulated reward. In general, in each iteration (see Figure 1), the agent perceives its cur-

DOI: 10.4018/978-1-60960-165-2.ch004

Figure 1. Reinforcement learning process

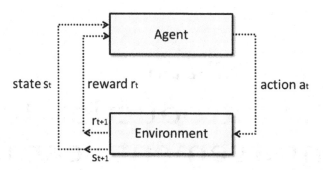

rent state ($s \in S$), selects an action ($a \in A$), possibly changing its state, and receives a reward signal ($r \in R$). In this process, the agent needs to obtain useful experiences regarding states, actions, state transitions and rewards to act optimally and the evaluation of the system occurs concurrently with the learning process.

This approach appeals to many researchers because if they want to teach an agent how to perform a task, instead of programming it, which may be a difficult and time-consuming process, they only need, in principle, to let the agent learn how to do it by interacting with the environment.

To illustrate this learning process, suppose that we want a mobile robot to learn how to reach a particular destination in an indoor environment. We can characterize this navigation problem as a RL problem. The states can be defined in terms of the information provided by the sensors of the robot, for instance, if there is an obstacle in front of the robot or not. We can have a finite set of actions per state, such as *go-forward, go-backward, go-left* and *go-right*, and the goal may be to go to a particular place (see Figure 2). Each time the robot executes an action there is some uncertainty on the actual next state as the wheels of the robot often slip on the ground or one wheel may turn faster than another, leaving the robot in a possibly different expected state. Upon reaching a goal state, the robot receives a positive reward and similarly receives negative regards in undesirable

states. The robot must choose its actions in order to increase in the long turn the total accumulated rewards. By following a trial and error process the robot learns after several trials which is the best action to perform on each state to reach the destination point and obtain the maximum expected accumulated reward.

Deciding which action to take in each state is a sequential decision process. In general, we have a non-deterministic environment (the same action in the same state can produce different results). However, it is assumed to be stationary (i.e., the transition probabilities do not change over time). This sequential decision process can be characterized by a Markov Decision Process or MDP. As described in Chapter 3, an MDP, $M = <S,A,P,R>$, can be described as follows:

- A finite set of states (S)
- A finite set of actions (A_s) per state (s)
- A reward function $R : S \times A \rightarrow R$
- A transition function P that represent the probability of reaching state $s' \in S$ given an action $a \in A$ taken at state $s \in S : P(s'|s,a)$.

In many settings, the agent receives a constant reward until reaching a terminal state. For instance, the robot moves through the environment and it is until it crashes or reaches a goal state that it receives a distinctive reward. This introduces the credit-assignment problem, i.e., if the robot

Figure 2. Reinforcement Learning process with a mobile robot where the robot may have different possible actions per state and the goal is to learn how to go to a particular destination while receiving the maximum total expected reward

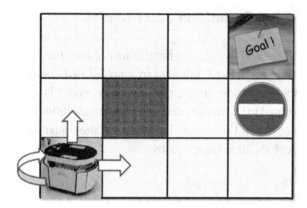

eventually reaches a good (bad) state, we would like to know which actions are responsible for that. Two distinctive features of RL are that: it follows a trial and error process, which means that it should follow an exploration strategy, and that there is a delayed reward, which introduces this credit-assignment problem. We will first introduce different reward models, then talk about exploration-exploitation strategies and then describe the concepts of value functions and policies that are needed to understand how the RL algorithms work.

Reward Models

Given a state $s_t \in S$ at some time t and an action $a_t \in A_{s_t}$, the agent receives a reward r_{t+1} and moves to the next state s_{t+1}. The idea in RL is not to maximize the immediate rewards but the long term accumulated reward. We can denote the total received rewards after certain time i as:

$$R_t = r_{t+1} + r_{t+2} + r_{t+3} + \ldots + r_{t+i}$$

If there is a terminal state, it is said that we have *episodic* tasks, otherwise these tasks are considered *continuous*. In this last case, we cannot impose an upper limit in the accumulated rewards, so an alternative way is to geometrically reduce the contributions of the rewards as they become more distant: <<:

$$R_t = r_{t+1} + \gamma r_{t+2} + \gamma^2 r_{t+3} + \ldots = \sum_{k=0}^{\infty} \gamma^k r_{t+k+1}$$

where γ is known as the *discount rate* and it is between: $0 \leq \gamma < 1$.

Since we have a probabilistic transition function, what we want is to maximize the expected accumulated reward, and in general, we can have the following models:

Finite Horizon: the agent tries to optimize the expected accumulated reward on the next h steps, without considering what happens afterward:

$$E(\sum_{t=0}^{h} r_t)$$

where r_t refers to the reward received after t steps in the future.

This model can be used in two forms: (i) *stationary policy*: where in the first state it takes h next steps, in the next, it takes $h-1$ steps, etc., until the end. The main problem is that it is not always possible to know how many steps to take. (ii) *Receding-horizon control*: it always takes the next h steps.

Infinite Horizon: the rewards received by the agent are geometrically reduced according to a discount factor γ ($0 \leq \gamma < 1$):

$$E(\sum_{t=0}^{\infty} \gamma^t r_t)$$

Average Reward: the idea is to optimize in the long run the average reward:

$$lim_{h\to\infty}E(\frac{1}{h}\sum_{t=0}^{h}r_t)$$

One problem with this optimization criterion is that it cannot distinguish between policies that receive a big reward at the beginning or at the end of the episode.

The most widely used model is *infinite horizon* and it is the one we will assume from now on.

Exploration and Exploitation

One important aspect in RL is that it must explore the environment to gather information in order to build a policy. We do not want to leave unexplored areas but we also want to use the accumulated knowledge to make better decisions. In this sense, there is a balance between exploration and exploitation. To gain more rewards an agent can follow certain actions that are known to produce high immediate rewards, however, in order to know which is the best action it has to explore the environment. In many cases the exploration strategy depends on the time that the agent has interacted with the environment.

Some common strategies to select actions and explore the environment are:

- $\varepsilon-greedy$: where most of the time the selected action is the one with the largest estimated accumulated reward but with probability ε an action is randomly selected.
- *Softmax*: where the probability of selecting an action depends on its estimated accumulated reward. The most common being the Boltzmann or Gibbs distribution, which selects an action on state s with probability:

$$\frac{e^{Q_t(s,a)/\tau}}{\sum_{b=1}^{n}e^{Q_t(s,b)/\tau}}$$

where τ is a positive parameter (temperature), n is the number of possible actions at state s, and Q is a value function that represents the estimated accumulated rewards and which is described in the following section.

Value Functions and Policies

In general the actions determine not only the immediate reward, but also in a probabilistic way, the next state. In RL the transition model is assumed to be Markovian, so the state transitions do not depend on previous states, and the transition probabilities are given by:

$$P(s' \mid s,a) = P(s_{t+1} = s' \mid s_t = s, a_t = a)$$

The expected reward value is:

$$R(s' \mid s,a) = E\{r_{t+1} \mid s_t = s, a_t = a, s_{t+1} = s'\}$$

The total expected reward depends on the current state and on the selection of actions in future states. The selection of actions per state is given by a *policy*. More formally, a policy π is a mapping of each state $s \in S$ and action $a \in A(s)$ to the probability $\pi(s,a)$ of taking the action a in state s.

One of the goals in RL is to estimate how good it is to be in a state (or being in a state and perform an action). The notion of "goodness" is defined in terms of future rewards or expected accumulated rewards which are represented as *value functions*. The value function of a state s, denoted by $V^\pi(s)$, represents the total expected accumulated reward that the agent can receive starting at state s and following policy π. Similarly, the value function of a state s taking action a, is denoted as $Q^\pi(s,a)$ and represents the total expected accumulated reward that the agent can receive starting at state s, taking action a and following a policy π. The idea is to find the policy that produces the maximum value functions rather than the maximum immediate rewards. The rewards are given by the environment, but the value functions need to be estimated (learned) with experience. *Reinforcement learning learns value functions while interacting with the environment.*

The value function for a state s using an infinite discounted reward model can be expressed as:

$$V^{\pi}(s) = E_{\pi}\{R_t \mid s_t = s\} = E_{\pi}\left\{\sum_{k=o}^{\infty} \gamma^k r_{t+k+1} \mid s_t = s\right\}$$

Likewise, the value function of a state s with action a and policy π ($Q^{\pi}(s,a)$) can be expressed as:

$$Q^{\pi}(s,a) = E_{\pi}\{R_t \mid s_t = s, a_t = a\}$$
$$= E_{\pi}\left\{\sum_{k=o}^{\infty} \gamma^k r_{t+k+1} \mid s_t = s, a_t = a\right\}$$

If we expand the expression for $V^{\pi}(s)$:

$$V^{\pi}(s) = E_{\pi}(R_t \mid s_t = s)$$
$$= E_{\pi}(\sum_{k=o}^{\infty} \gamma^k r_{t+k+1} \mid s_t = s)$$
$$= E_{\pi}(r_{t+1} + \gamma \sum_{k=o}^{\infty} \gamma^k r_{t+k+2} \mid s_t = s)$$
$$= \sum_a \pi(s,a) \sum_{s'} P(s' \mid s,a)\left[R(s' \mid s,a) + \gamma E_{\pi}(\sum_{k=o}^{\infty} \gamma^k r_{t+k+2} \mid s_t = s)\right]$$
$$= \sum_a \pi(s,a) \sum_{s'} P(s' \mid s,a)\left[R(s' \mid s,a) + \gamma V^{\pi}(s')\right]$$

$$(1)$$

where $\pi(s,a)$ is the probability of taking action s in state s under policy π.

We can similarly derive an equivalent expression for $Q^{\pi}(s,a)$:

$$Q^{\pi}(s,a) = \sum_{s'} P(s' \mid s,a)\left[R(s' \mid s,a) + \gamma V^{\pi}(s')\right]$$

$$(2)$$

The last two equations form the basis of the RL algorithms as value functions are normally updated in terms of the immediate rewards and value functions of the following state.

If we choose different policies we obtain different value functions. For instance, a mobile robot may choose a right-hand wall-following policy from which particular value functions are obtained for particular mazes. A left-hand wall-following policy produces different value functions. In general, given a particular policy we can evaluate the associated value functions for each state or state-action pair.

In practice, we want to produce the best policies, i.e., those that produce the largest expected accumulated rewards. A policy π is defined to be better than or equal to a policy π' if its expected return is greater or equal to that of π' for all states.

$$\pi \geq \pi' \text{ if } V^{\pi}(s) \geq V^{\pi'}(s) \text{ for all } s \in S$$

There is always at least one policy that is better than or equal to all other policies, i.e., an *optimal policy*, π^*. The optimal policy shares the optimal state value function V^* and the optimal state-action value function Q^* and can be expressed as:

$$V^*(s) = max_{\pi} V^{\pi}(s) \text{ and } Q^*(s,a) = max_{\pi} Q^{\pi}(s,a)$$

Considering Eqs. 1 and 2, the optimal value functions can be expressed recursively with the Bellman optimality equations as:

$$V^*(s) = max_a \sum_{s'} P(s' \mid s,a)[R(s' \mid s,a) + \gamma V^*(s')]$$

Similarly, for Q values:

$$Q^*(s,a) = \sum_{s'} P(s' \mid s,a)[R(s' \mid s,a) + \gamma V^*(s')]$$

or

Algorithm 1. TD(0) algorithm

```
Initialize V(s) arbitrarily and π to the policy to evaluate
for each episode do
    Initialize s
   repeat
     for each step in the episode do
        a ← action given by π for s
        Perform action a; observe the reward r and the next state s'
```
$$V(s) \leftarrow V(s) + \alpha[r + \gamma V(s') - V(s)]$$
$$s \leftarrow s'$$
```
     end for
    untils is a terminal state
 end for
```

$$Q^*(s,a) = \sum_{s'} P(s' \mid s,a)[R(s' \mid s,a) + \gamma \max_{a'} Q^*(s',a')]$$

$$V(s_t) \leftarrow V(s_t) + \alpha\left[r_{t+1} + \gamma V(s_{t+1}) - V(s_t)\right]$$

So the obvious question now is: how can we learn such policies? In the next section we review some common techniques.

SOLUTION TECHNIQUES

There are tree principal ways of solving MDPs: (i) Dynamic Programming, (ii) Monte Carlo, and (iii) Temporal Differences or Reinforcement Learning. Dynamic Programming methods, based on policy and value iteration are clearly described in Chapter 3. The main idea behind Monte Carlo methods is to simulate experiences, collect statistics and return the averages of the accumulated rewards obtained from the simulated experiences for each state or state-action pair. In this chapter we will concentrate only on RL algorithms.

The idea of the RL techniques is to update the value functions with the next step using the error or difference between successive predictions. Their main advantage is that they represent incremental algorithms that are easy to compute.

The simplest method TD(0) updates $V(s_t)$ as follows:

The TD(0) algorithm is described in Algorithm 1. In general, TD methods update the existing value function using the immediate reward and the estimated value function of the next state. In this case the target is based on the immediate next step information ($r + \gamma V(s')$) which is compared with the actual estimate ($V(s)$), producing a *TD error* which is used to update the current value function. Updating based on existing estimates is also known as *bootstrapping*.

RL can be used for control problems, where we want to learn a value function based on state-action pairs. As previously mentioned, there is a trade-off between exploration and exploitation and the approaches fall into two categories: *on-policy* and *off-policy* strategies. An on-policy approach learns the value of the policy that is used to make the decisions and update value functions based strictly on experience. An off-policy approach learns the value of a policy other that the one used to make the decisions, it can update the estimated value functions using hypothetical actions, which may not have actually been tried. We will first review an on-policy strategy (SARSA) and then an off-policy strategy (Q-learning).

Algorithm 2. SARSA algorithm

```
Initialize Q (s, a) arbitrarily
for each episode do
      Initialize s
      Select an a from s using the policy given by Q (e.g., ε-greedy)
      repeat
            for each step in episode do
                  Perform action a, observe r, s'
                  Choose a' and s' using the policy derived from Q
```
$$Q(s,a) \leftarrow Q(s,a) + \alpha[r + \gamma Q(s',a') - Q(s,a)]$$
$$s \leftarrow s'; a \leftarrow a'$$
```
            end for
      until s is a terminal state
end for
```

In SARSA, we update value functions considering an action as follows:

$$Q(s_t, a_t) \leftarrow Q(s_t, a_t)$$
$$+\alpha[r_{t+1} + \gamma Q(s_{t+1}, a_{t+1}) - Q(s_t, a_t)]$$

The algorithm is almost the same as TD(0) and is described in Algorithm 2, however, in this case we are continuously estimating the Q values for a particular policy π, but at the same time we are changing the policy π in a greedy approach considering the Q values. It can be proved that this strategy converges to the optimal policy and action-value function as long as we visit all the state-action pairs an infinite number of times.

One of the most important developments in Reinforcement Learning was an *off-policy* algorithm known as Q-learning. The main idea is to update the value functions as follows (Watkins, 1989):

$$Q(s_t, a_t) \leftarrow Q(s_t, a_t)$$
$$+\alpha[r_{t+1} + \gamma max_{a_{t+1}} Q(s_{t+1}, a_{t+1}) - Q(s_t, a_t)]$$

The algorithm is described in Algorithm 3 and it follows an off-policy strategy which means that this algorithm approximates the optimal action-value function independently of the policy being followed.

Another different RL approaches are the Actor-Critic methods. In essence, these are TD methods that have two separate memory structures, one of them is used to represent the policy an the other one is used to represent the value function. In this kind of methods the policy structure is known as the actor, because its goal is to select actions, and the estimated value function is known as the critic; the critic qualifies the actions made by the actor. In Actor-Critic methods learning is always on-policy since the critic must learn about and qualify the policy currently followed by the actor. The evaluation or critique takes the form of a TD error. This (usually scalar) signal is the only output of the critic and its work is to model the learning in both the actor and the critic. The main idea in Actor-Critic methods is to use the TD error $(r+V(s')-V(s))$ to change the policy which is responsible for choosing the actions. If the TD error is positive then the tendency to select the correct action is increased, otherwise it is decreased, this tendency is normally changed by increasing (or decreasing) its probability of being selected.

Algorithm 3. Q-learning algorithm

```
Initialize Q (s, a) arbitrarily
for each episode do
        Initialize sRepeatfor each step in episode do
            Select an a from s using the policy given by Q (e.g., ε-greedy)
                Perform action a, observe r, s'
```
$$Q(s,a) \leftarrow Q(s,a) + \alpha[r + \gamma max_{a'} Q(s',a') - Q(s,a)]$$

$$s \leftarrow s';$$

```
            end for
        until s is a terminal state.
end for
```

SOME RECENT DEVELOPMENTS

In order to obtain an adequate policy, traditional RL techniques need to visit all the states (or state-action pairs) several times. This, however, is only possible in very restricted domains. With large state and action spaces traditional RL techniques require large computational resources and long convergence times.

Since the number of possible states grows exponentially in the number of features (*curse of dimensionality* (Bellman, 1957)), researchers have proposed different approaches to tackle this problem. Some of the most common approaches are: (i) update several value functions at the same time, (ii) approximate value functions with continuous functions, (iii) learn and use a model to generate new experiences, (iv) employ abstractions and/or hierarchies, and (v) provide additional guidance to the agent. We review these approaches in the following sections.

Update Several Value Functions

In traditional RL each step updates a single value function using the immediate reward. This means that if the agent is two steps away from a state with a very high reward it has to wait until the immediate state is updated to obtain information about such desirable state. One idea is to propagate information among the visited states in what is called *eligibility traces*.

The idea of eligibility traces is to consider the *n* next states (or change the *n* previous states) and update several value functions.

As stated previously:

$$R_t = r_{t+1} + \gamma r_{t+2} + \gamma^2 r_{t+3} + ... + \gamma^{T-t-1} r_T$$

What temporal difference methods do is to use the estimated accumulated reward expressed as the value function:

$$R_t = r_{t+1} + \gamma V_t(s_{t+1})$$

which makes sense since $V_t(s_{t+1})$ replace the next terms ($\gamma r_{t+2} + \gamma^2 r_{t+3} ...$).

However, it also makes sense to use the value function after two known rewards:

$$R_t = r_{t+1} + \gamma r_{t+2} + \gamma^2 V_t(s_{t+2})$$

and in general for *n* future steps.

In practice, rather than waiting *n* steps to update (*forward view*), you can update backwards on the visited states (*backward view*). It can be proved

Algorithm 4. SARSA (λ) with eligibility traces

```
Initialize Q (s, a) arbitrarily y e(s, a) - 0∀s,a for each episode do
    Initialize s, a
        repeat
            for each step in episode do
                Take action a and observe r, s'
                    Select an a from s using the policy derived from Q (e.g.,
                    ε -greedy)
```
$$\delta \leftarrow r + \gamma Q(s',a') - Q(s,a)$$
$$e(s,a) \leftarrow e(s,a) + 1$$
```
            for all s, a do
```
$$Q(s,a) \leftarrow Q(s,a) + \alpha\delta e(s,a)$$
$$e(s,a) \leftarrow \gamma\lambda e(s,a)$$
```
            end for
```
$$s \leftarrow s';a \leftarrow a'$$
```
            end for
        until s is a terminal state.
end for
```

that both approaches are equivalent. In the backward view, you store information over the visited states (the eligibility trace) and use the TD error to update the visited value functions associated with the visited states backwards (discounted by distance).

To implement this idea, each state or state-action pair is associated with an extra variable, representing the *eligibility trace* denoted by $e_t(s)$ or $e_t(s,a)$. This value is decremented with the length of the trace created on each episode.

Initially all the $e_t(s) = 0$. For *TD*(λ) we mark only the visited states:

$$e_t(s) = \begin{cases} \gamma\lambda e_{t-1}(s) & \text{if } s \neq s_t \\ \gamma\lambda e_{t-1}(s) + 1 & \text{if } s = s_t \end{cases}$$

and we update the value functions over the visited states using information from the TD errors.

For SARSA we mark the visited state-action pairs as following:

$$e_t(s,a) = \begin{cases} \gamma\lambda e_{t-1}(s,a) & \text{if } s \neq s_t \\ \gamma\lambda e_{t-1}(s,a) + 1 & \text{if } s = s_t \end{cases}$$

and update as described before. *SARSA*(λ) is described in Algorithm 4. In this case the reinforcements are accumulated each time the state-action pair is visited and decay gradually when the state-action pair is not visited. At each step in an episode the TD error is propagated backwards to each previously visited state-action pair according to their current eligibility trace value.

For Q-learning, however, we need to be careful since some movements are exploratory movements. The problem is that the agent can reach undesirable states through exploratory actions that can propagate negative rewards along good paths. Some options are to maintain the trace until the first exploratory action is taken, ignoring exploratory actions, or using a more complicated scheme that considers all the possible actions per state.

Approximate Value Functions

So far we have assumed that the value functions are stored in tabular forms. This works fine for small domains, but it is impractical for domains with a large number of states like chess (10^{120}) or backgammon (10^{50}) or for continuous spaces.

One option is to use an implicit representation; a function. For instance, in games a function is used to estimate the utility of a state with a weighted linear function over a set of attributes (f_i's):

$$V(i) = w_1 f_1(i) + w_2 f_2(i) + \ldots + w_n f_n(i)$$

In chess there are approximately 10 weights, so there is a significant compression. This representation also allows to generalize over non visited states.

There are many possible options to represent functions and in general there is a trade off between expressibility and tractability since models represented in more expressive languages are more difficult to learn.

There are several examples of different choices for expressing value functions, such as neural networks (Bertsekas & Tsitsiklis, 1996), decision trees (Chapman & Kaelbling, 1991), SVMs (Dietterich & Wang, 2002), different Kernels (Ormoneit & Sen, 2002) and Gaussian processes (Peters, Vijayakumar, & Schaal, 2003b).

In this chapter, we will only illustrate the approach with a linear combination of basis functions $\phi_1, \phi_2, \ldots, \phi_n$ of the form $\sum_{i=1}^{n} w_i \phi_i$ where the weights ($w_i \in \vec{\Theta}$) need to be learned.

Many supervised learning systems try to minimize the mean squared error (MSE) under certain input distribution. If $\vec{\Theta}_t$ denotes the parameters' vector of the function we want to learn, gradient descent techniques adjust the values of such parameters in the direction that produces the maximum reduction in the error.

$$
\begin{aligned}
\vec{\Theta}_{t+1} &= \vec{\Theta}_t - \frac{1}{2}\alpha \nabla_{\overline{\Theta}_t}[V^\pi(s_t) - V_t(s_t)]^2 \\
&= \vec{\Theta}_t + \alpha[V^\pi(s_t) - V_t(s_t)]\nabla_{\overline{\Theta}_t} V_t(s_t)
\end{aligned}
$$

where α is a positive parameter $0 \le \alpha \le 1$ and $\nabla_{\overline{\Theta}} f(\Theta_t)$ denotes a vector of partial derivatives.

Since we do not know $V^\pi(s_t)$ we have to approximate it. We can do it with eligibility traces and update the function $\Theta\tau$ as follows:

$$\vec{\Theta}_{t+1} = \vec{\Theta}_t + \alpha \delta_t \vec{e}_t$$

where δ_t is the TD error:

$$\delta_t = r_{t+1} + \gamma V_t(s_{t+1}) - V_t(s_t)$$

and $\vec{e}_t$ is a vector of eligibility traces, one for each component $\vec{\Theta}_t$, that is updated as:

$$\vec{e}_t = \gamma\lambda\vec{e}_{t-1} + \nabla_{\overline{\Theta}_t} V_t(s_t)$$

with $\vec{e}_0 = 0$. It has been shown that in many cases trying to find an approximate value function can diverge (Baird, 1995)

Other approaches have been used to relate or represent interactions among features in different ways. They include coarse coding (Hinton, 1984), tile coding (Lim & Kim, 1991), radial basis functions (Poggio & Girosi, 1989) and Kanerva coding (Kanerva, 1993).

Learn and Use a Transition Model

With eligibility traces we propagate the TD error through visited states. If we could have a transition function, then we could propagate among all states, which is what value iteration and policy iteration do.

RL visits many state-action pairs while learning to approximate value functions, however the information about these state transitions is lost.

Algorithm 5. Dyna-Q algorithm

```
Initialize Q (s, a) and Model(s,a)∀s ⊂ S,a ∈ A
loop
     s ← actual state
     a ← ε − greedy(s,a)
     Take action a observe s' and r
     Q(s,a) ← Q(s,a) + α[r + γmaxₐ'Q(s',a') − Q(s,a)]
     Model(s,a) ← s'r
     for N times do
          s ← previous state randomly selected
          a ← random action taken in s
          s'r ← Model(s,a)
          Q(s,a) ← Q(s,a) + α[r + γmaxₐ'Q(s',a') − Q(s,a)]
     end for
end loop
```

One idea is use this information to construct a transition model while learning. This is appealing for several reasons: (i) we can converge much faster to an optimal policy with a transition model, (ii) we do not need in general a very precise transition model and we can refine it as we learn, and (iii) the transition model can guide the exploration strategy towards states with poor transition models.

With a transition model, we can predict the next state and plan. What is interesting is that we can use planning also for learning. For a learning system, it does not matter if the state-action pairs and rewards are from real or simulated experiences.

Given a model of the environment, we can randomly select a state-action pair, use the model to select the next state, obtain a reward and update a Q value as if it was part of an episode. This can be repeated until convergence to Q^*.

Dyna-Q combines experience with planning to learn faster a policy. The idea is not only to learn from experience, but also to learn and use a model while learning to simulate experience (see Algorithm 5).

Dyna-Q randomly selects previously visited state-action pairs. However, better planning can be performed if it is focused on particular state-action pairs. For instance, starting in the goal states and going backwards or in any state with a large change on its value function. The idea behind *prioritized sweeping* is to focus the simulation on states that significantly changed their value function (see Algorithm 6). The aim is to simulate new experience only on state-action pairs whose Q values change above a certain pre-defined threshold value.

More recently, some related approaches have been suggested, such as E^3 (Kearns, 1998) and R-MAX (Brafman & Tennenholtz, 2002), where again the idea is to learn while updating a model of its environment by gathering statistics. In E^3 an internal mechanism is used to decide whether to explore or exploit while R-MAX backs up optimistic rewards through the value function so that the learned policy effectively plans to visit insufficiently explored states.

Algorithm 6. Prioritized sweeping

```
Initialize Q (s, a) and  Model(s,a)∀s ∈ S,a ∈ A  and QueueP = Ø
loop
        s ← actual state
        a ← ε − greedy(s,a)
        take action a and observe s' and r
         Model(s,a) ← s'r
        p ←| r + γ max_a' Q(s',a') − Q(s,a) |
        if  p > θ then
                then insert s, a in QueueP with priority p
        end if
        while QueueP≠Ø do
                for N times do
                        s,a ← first(QueueP)
                        s',r ← Model(s,a)
                        Q(s,a) ← Q(s,a) + α[r + γ max_a Q(s',a') − Q(s,a)]
                        for all s̄,ā which predicts to reach s do
                                r̄ ← predicted reward
                                p ← r̄ + γ max_a Q(s,a) − Q(s̄,ā) |
                                        if  p > θ, then add s̄,ā to Queue with priority p
                        end for
                end for
        end while
end loop
```

ABSTRACTIONS AND HIERARCHIES

A common approach in Artificial Intelligence to tackle complex problems is to use abstractions (Dzeroski, Raedt, & Driessens, 2001, Chapman & Kaelbling, 1991, Cocora, Kersting, Plagemanny, Burgardy, & Raedt, 2006, Morales, 2003) and/or to divide the problem in sub-problems (Ormoneit & Sen, 2002, Ryan, 1998, Torrey, Shavlik, Walker, & Maclin, 2008, Dietterich, 2000), perhaps using a hierarchy (Govea & Morales, 2006, Cuaya & Muñoz-Meléndez, 2007). RL has not been an exception and several approaches have been suggested along these lines.

One common approach is state aggregation (Singh, Jaakkola, & Jordan, 1996, Otterlo, 2003), in which several "similar" states are joined and

they all receive the same value, thereby reducing the state space.

Another possibility is to divide the problem in sub-problems (Dietterich, 2000), learn a policy for each sub-problem and then join these policies to solve the original problem. There has been several approaches around this idea. One of them learns sequences of primitive actions (policies) and treat them as an abstracted action (e.g., Macros or Options (Sutton & Barto, 1989)). Another possibility is to learn sub-policies at a low level within a hierarchy and use them to learn policies at a higher level in the hierarchy (e.g., MAXQ (Dietterich, 2000), HEXQ (Hengst, 2002)).

Actions can also have variable duration, so it is possible to have abstractions over the action sequences, in what is called semi-Markov decision processes of SMDPs (Sutton, Precup, & Singh, 1999).

An alternative approach is based on the definition of finite state machines, in which the RL task is to decide which machine to use in a hierarchical abstract machine or HAM (Parr & Russell, 1998).

More recently, authors have used first-order representations for RL, which can have more abstract states and produce transferable policies. The idea is to use first-order representations to reason about objects and relations between objects (see (Otterlo, 2009)).

In general some abstractions can introduce partial observability and at an abstract level the problem may not longer be Markovian. Even with convergence at the abstract level does not mean convergence to an optimal solution at a primitive level.

ADDITIONAL GUIDANCE

Besides dividing or abstracting the RL problem, some approaches have focused on speeding up the learning process in order to develop control policies in reasonable times for very complex domains by including additional guidance or feedback from the user.

One commonly used approach is to "observe" a person (expert) perform a task (rather than asking him/her how to do it) and save logs with information of the performed actions and then use this information to guide the RL policy search process. The same idea has been developed under different flavors known as Behavioural Cloning (BC) (Bratko, Urbančič, & Sammut, 1998), Apprenticeship Learning (Abbeel & Ng, 2004) and Programming by Demonstration (Billard, Calinon, Dillmann, & Schaal, 2008).

The simplest approach is to use the information from the trace-logs to update the value functions and then follow the RL process with the initial value functions already updated with information of the traces (Singh, Sutton, & Kaelbling, 1996).

Other approaches use the traces to try to derive a reward function in what is known as *inverse Reinforcement Learning* (Ng & Russell, 2000). In this case, rather than trying to derive a direct mapping from states to the actions of the expert, they derive a reward function that penalizes deviations from the desired trajectories, trying to recover the expert's true and unknown reward function (see also (Schaal, 1997, Abbeel & Ng, 2004)).

An alternative approach is to use the given traces to learn a set of possible actions to perform on each state and then use RL to decide which is the best action among such reduced subset of actions ((Morales & Sammut, 2004, J. Zaragoza, 2010), see also Chapter 9).

Another approach to provide additional guidance is through the reward function. Reward shaping attempts to mold the conduct of the agent by adding additional rewards that encourage a behavior consistent with some prior knowledge (Ng, Harada, & Russell, 1999, Marthi, 2007, Grzes & Kudenko, 2009). As the shaping rewards offer localized advice, the time to exhibit the intended behavior can be greatly reduced. Since given an adequate reward shaping function may not be easy for some domains, feedback from the user can be used to provide such guidance. The user may critique sub-sequences of given traces (e.g., (Judah, Roy, Fern, & Dietterich, 2010, Argall, Browing, & Veloso, 2007)) or the system may try to learn a model from the user's feedback (e.g, (Knox & Stone, 2010)) and use that information to adjust the current policy. An alternative approach, called dynamic reward shaping, is to provide on-line feedback from the user to change the reward function during the learning process (Tenorio-Gonzalez, Morales, & Pineda, 2010).

Other Approaches

Reinforcement Learning research has grown in multiple areas. In particular there is substantial research in multi-agent systems, where the idea is to develop a control policy for a group of agents that combine their efforts to perform a common task. Here an agent has to take into account the consequences of the actions of the other agents while trying to find out its right sequence of actions that, eventually, will lead the group to the goal. Similarly, RL has been used in adversarial games or competitive MDPs where there is a sequential decision problem with several decision makers. In this setting the transition probabilities depend on the current state and the actions chosen by all the agents, however, the immediate reward can be a different function for each player. Here the policy of each player is referred to as a strategy and the overall performance metric depends on the strategies selected by all the players. When all the players want to optimize their own objective normally the solutions of the algorithms arrive to the Nash equilibrium (see for example (Littman, 1994) for zero-sum games).

As described in Chapter 3, there has been an increasing interest in developing algorithms for partially observable states in MDPs in what are called POMDPs. This has also been the case for RL and it is known as Partially Observable Reinforcement Learning (PORL) in which the agent has to deal with the uncertainty on its current state while learning a policy (lbling, Littman, & Cassandra, 1998). This setting is common in mobile robots where the sensors are normally noisy and the robot may have some uncertainty of its current state.

Another productive line of research has been the incorporating of a Bayesian framework into RL (Strens, 2000, Dearden, Friedman, & Russell, 1998). This has also been extended into multiple tasks in a hierarchical approach (Wilson, Fern, Ray, & Tadepalli, 2007) and has been incorporated also into inverse RL (Ramachandran, 2007). Very recently there have been interest in combining RL with optimal control and dynamic programming techniques for inverse RL (Theodorou, Buchli, & Schaal, 2010).

Finally, there has been some interesting work on how to transfer policies to similar domains to avoid learning from scratch (Fernandez & Veloso, 2006, Sunmola & Laboratory, 2006, Ferguson & Mahadevan, 2006).

FINAL REMARKS

Reinforcement learning is a very active research area that has been used in several areas of artificial intelligence and that has produced some very interesting results in real–world applications. These range from elevator scheduling (Crites & Barto, 1995), job-shop scheduling (Zhang & Dietterich, 1995), the AGV routing problem (Tadepalli & Ok, 1998), to areas such as Backgammon (Tesauro, 1992), humanoid control (Peters, Vijayakumar, & Schaal, 2003a), and control of helicopters (Tang, Singh, Goehausen, & Abbeel, 2010, Abbeel, Coates, & Ng, 2010).

A general introductory reference is the excellent book by Sutton and Barto (Sutton & Barto, 1989). An on-line version of the book can be found on Sutton's webpage. An earlier comprehensive survey up to 1966 is (Kaelbling, Littman, & Moore, 1996) which is also available from Kaelbling's webpage. There are other more recent surveys, such as (Gosavi, 2008).

There is a large body of literature on specific topics such as transfer learning in RL (Taylor & Stone, 2009) or relational reinforcement learning (Otterlo, 2009), and a continuous flow of current research papers on mayor machine learning forums.

ACKNOWLEDGMENT

The authors would like to thank Enrique Muñoz de Cote, Enrique Sucar and Jesse Hoey for their useful comments on an earlier version of this chapter.

REFERENCES

Abbeel, P., Coates, A., & Ng, A. Y. (2010). Autonomous helicopter aerobatics through apprenticeship learning. *The International Journal of Robotics Research, 29*(13), 1608–1639. doi:10.1177/0278364910371999

Abbeel, P., & Ng, A. Y. (2004). Apprenticeship learning via inverse reinforcement learning. In *Proceedings of the twenty-first international conference on machine learning.* ACM Press.

Argall, B., Browing, B., & Veloso, M. (2007). Learning by demonstration with critique from a human teacher. In *2nd Conf. on Human-Robot Interaction* (pp. 57–64).

Baird, L. (1995). Residual algorithms: Reinforcement learning with function approximation. In *Proceedings of the Twelfth International Conference on Machine Learning* (pp. 30–37). Morgan Kaufmann.

Bellman, R. (1957). *Dynamic programming.* Princeton, NJ: Princeton University Press.

Bertsekas, D. P., & Tsitsiklis, J. (1996). *Neurodynamic programming.* Belmont, MA: Athena Scientific.

Billard, A., Calinon, S., Dillmann, R., & Schaal, S. (2008). *Robot programming program by demonstration.* MIT Press.

Brafman, R. I., & Tennenholtz, M. (2002). R-max - A general polynomial time algorithm for near-optimal reinforcement learning. *Journal of Machine Learning Research, 3*, 213–231.

Bratko, I., Urbančič, T., & Sammut, C. (1998). Behavioural cloning: phenomena, results and problems. Automated systems based on human skill. In *Proc. of the International Federation of Automatic Control Symposium.* Berlin.

Chapman, D., & Kaelbling, L. (1991). Input generalization in delayed reinforcement learning: An algorithm and performance comparison. In *Proc. of the International Joint Conference on Artificial Intelligence* (p. 726-731). San Francisco, CA: Morgan Kaufmann.

Cocora, A., Kersting, K., Plagemanny, C., Burgardy, W., & Raedt, L. D. (2006). Octuber). Learning relational navigation policies. *Journal of Intelligent & Robotic Systems*, 2792–2797.

Crites, R. H., & Barto, A. G. (1995). *Improving elevator performance using reinforcement learning* (pp. 1017–1023). Proc. of the Neural Information Processing Systems.

Cuaya, G., & Muñoz-Meléndez, A. (2007, September). *Control de un robot hexapodo basado en procesos de decision de markov.* Primer Encuentro de Estudiantes en Ciencias de la Computación (CIC-IPN).

Dearden, R., Friedman, N., & Russell, S. (1998). Bayesian q-learning. In *Proc. of the AAAI Conference on Artificial Intelligence* (pp. 761–768). AAAI Press.

Dietterich, T. G. (2000). Hierarchical reinforcement learning with the maxq value function decomposition. *Journal of Artificial Intelligence Research, 13*, 227–303.

Dietterich, T. G., & Wang, X. (2002). Batch value function approximation via support vectors. In *Advances in Neural Information Processing Systems* (pp. 1491–1498). Cambridge, MA: MIT Press.

Dzeroski, S., Raedt, L. D., & Driessens, K. (2001). Relational reinforcement learning. *Machine Learning, 43*(2), 5-52.

Ferguson, K., & Mahadevan, S. (2006). Proto-transfer learning in markov decision processes using spectral methods. In *Proc. of the ICML Workshop on Transfer Learning.*

Fernandez, F., & Veloso, M. (2006). Probabilistic policy reuse in a reinforcement learning agent. In *Proceedings of the Fifth International Joint Conference on Autonomous Agents and Multiagent Systems* (pp. 720–727). ACM Press.

Gosavi, A. (2008). Reinforcement learning: A tutorial survey and recent advances. *INFORMS Journal on Computing*, 1–45.

Govea, B. V., & Morales, E. (2006). *Learning navigation teleo-operators with behavioural cloning.*

Grzes, M., & Kudenko, D. (2009). Theoretical and empirical analysis of reward shaping in reinforcement learning. In *Proc. of the International Conference on Machine Learning and Applications* (p. 337-344).

Hengst, B. (2002). Discovering hierarchy in reinforcement learning with hexq. In *Proceedings of the Nineteenth International Conference on Machine Learning* (pp. 243–250). Morgan Kaufmann.

Hinton, G. (1984). *Distributed representations* (Tech. Rep. No. CMU-CS-84-157). Pittsburgh, PA: Carnegie-Mellon University, Department of Computer Science.

Judah, K., Roy, S., Fern, A., & Dietterich, T. G. (2010). Reinforcement learning via practice and critique advice. In *Proceedings of the Twenty-Fourth AAAI Conference on Artificial Intelligence* (pp. 481–486). AAAI Press.

Kaelbling, L. P., Littman, M. L., & Moore, A. W. (1996). Reinforcement learning: A survey. *Journal of Artificial Intelligence Research, 4*, 237–285.

Kanerva, P. (1993). Sparse distributed memory and related models. In Hassoun, M. (Ed.), *Associate neural memories: Theory and implementation* (pp. 50–76). New York, NY: Oxford University Press.

Kearns, M. (1998). Near-optimal reinforcement learning in polynomial time. In *Machine learning* (pp. 260–268). Morgan Kaufmann.

Knox, W. B., & Stone, P. (2010). Combining manual feedback with subsequent MDP reward signals for reinforcement learning. In *Proc. of 9th int. Conf. on Autonomous Agents and Multiagent Systems* (pp. 5–12).

lbling, L. P. K., Littman, M. L., & Cassandra, A. R. (1998). Planning and acting in partially observable stochastic domains. *Artificial Intelligence, 101*, 99–134.

Lim, C., & Kim, H. (1991). Cmac-based adaptive critic self-lerning control. *IEEE Transactions on Neural Networks, 2*, 530–533. doi:10.1109/72.134290

Littman, M. L. (1994). Markov games as a framework for multi-agent reinforcement learning. In *Proceedings of the Eleventh International Conference on Machine Learning* (pp. 157–163). Morgan Kaufmann.

Marthi, B. (2007). Automatic shaping and decomposition of reward functions. In *Proceedings of the International Conference on Machine Learning*. ICML.

Morales, E. (2003). Scaling up reinforcement learning with a relational representation. In *Proc. of the Workshop on Adaptability in Multi-Agent Systems* (p. 15-26).

Morales, E., & Sammut, C. (2004). Learning to fly by combining reinforcement learning with behavioural cloning. In *Proc. of the Twenty-First International Conference on Machine Learning* (p. 598-605).

Ng, A. Y., Harada, D., & Russell, S. (1999). Policy invariance under reward transformations: Theory and application to reward shaping. In *Proceedings of the Sixteenth International Conference on Machine Learning* (pp. 278–287). Morgan Kaufmann.

Ng, A. Y., & Russell, S. (2000). Algorithms for inverse reinforcement learning. In *Proc. 17th International Conf. on Machine Learning* (pp. 663–670). Morgan Kaufmann.

Ormoneit, D., & Sen, S. (2002, November-December). Kernel-based reinforcement learning. *Machine Learning, 49*(2-3), 161–178. doi:10.1023/A:1017928328829

Parr, R., & Russell, S. (1998). Reinforcement learning with hierarchies of machines. [MIT Press.]. *Advances in Neural Information Processing Systems, 10*, 1043–1049.

Peters, J., Vijayakumar, S., & Schaal, S. (2003a). Reinforcement learning for humanoid robotics. In *Proceedings of the Third IEEE-RAS International Conference on Humanoid Robots* (pp. 1–20).

Peters, J., Vijayakumar, S., & Schaal, S. (2003b, September). Reinforcement learning for humanoid robotics. *Proc. of the Third IEEE-RAS International Conference on Humanoid Robots, Karlsruhe, Germany*, (pp. 29-30).

Poggio, T., & Girosi, F. (1989). A theory of networks for approximation and learning. Laboratory, Massachusetts Institute of Technology, 1140.

Ramachandran, D. (2007). Bayesian inverse reinforcement learning. In *Proceedings of the 20th International Joint Conference on Artificial Intelligence* (pp. 2586–2591).

Ryan, M. (1998). Rl-tops: An architecture for modularity and re-use in reinforcement learning. In *Proc. of the Fifteenth International Conference on Machine Learning* (p. 481-487). San Francisco, CA: Morgan Kaufmann.

Schaal, S. (1997). Learning from demonstration. In *Advances in Neural Information Processing Systems, 9*. MIT Press.

Singh, S., Jaakkola, T., & Jordan, M. (1996). Reinforcement learning with soft state aggregation. In *Neural Information Processing Systems 7*. Cambridge, MA: MIT Press.

Singh, S., Sutton, R. S., & Kaelbling, P. (1996). Reinforcement learning with replacing eligibility traces. In *Machine learning* (pp. 123–158).

Strens, M. (2000). A Bayesian framework for reinforcement learning. In *Proceedings of the Seventeenth International Conference on Machine Learning* (pp. 943–950). ICML.

Sunmola, F. T., & Laboratory, W. C. (2006). Model transfer for Markov decision tasks via parameter matching. In *Workshop of the UK Planning and Scheduling Special Interest Group.*

Sutton, R., & Barto, A. (1989). *Reinforcement learning an introduction.* Cambridge, MA: MIT Press.

Sutton, R., Precup, D., & Singh, S. (1999). Between mdps and semi-mdps: A framework for temporal abstraction in reinforcement learning. *Artificial Intelligence, 112*, 181–211. doi:10.1016/S0004-3702(99)00052-1

Tadepalli, P., & Ok, D. (1998). Model-based average reward reinforcement learning. In *Artificial intelligence* (pp. 881–887). AAAI Press/MIT Press.

Tang, J., Singh, A., Goehausen, N., & Abbeel, P. (2010). Parameterized maneuver learning for autonomous helicopter flight. In *Proc. of the International Conference on Robotics and Automation* (pp. 1142–1148).

Taylor, M. E., & Stone, P. (2009). Transfer learning for reinforcement learning domains: A survey. *Journal of Machine Learning Research, 10*(1), 1633–1685.

Tenorio-Gonzalez, A. C., Morales, E. F., & Pineda, L. V. (2010). Dynamic reward shaping: Training a robot by voice. In *Proc. of the Ibero-American Conference on Artificial Intelligence* (pp. 483-492).

Tesauro, G. (1992, May). Practical issues in temporal difference learning. *Machine Learning, 8,* 257–277. doi:10.1007/BF00992697

Theodorou, E., Buchli, J., & Schaal, S. (2010). A generalized path integral control approach to reinforcement learning. *Journal of Machine Learning Research, 11,* 3137–3181.

Torrey, L., Shavlik, J., Walker, T., & Maclin, R. (2008). Relational macros for transfer in reinforcement learning. *ILP,* 254-268.

van Otterlo, M. (2003). Efficient reinforcement learning using relational aggregation. In *Proc. of the Sixth European Workshop on Reinfocement Learning.* Nancy, France.

van Otterlo, M. (2009). *The logic of adaptive behavior: Knowledge representation and algorithms for adaptive sequential decision making under uncertainty in first-order and relational domains.* The Netherlands: IOS Press.

Watkins, C. (1989). *Learning from delayed rewards.* Unpublished doctoral dissertation. Cambridge, MA: Cambridge University.

Wilson, A., Fern, A., Ray, S., & Tadepalli, P. (2007). Multi-task reinforcement learning: A hierarchical bayesian approach. In *Proceedings of the 24th International Conference on Machine Learning* (p. 1015). ACM Press.

Zaragoza, J. H. (2010). Relational reinforcement learning with continuous actions by combining behavioral cloning and locally weighted regression. *Journal of Intelligent Learning Systems and Applications, 2,* 69–79. doi:10.4236/jilsa.2010.22010

Zhang, W., & Dietterich, T. G. (1995). Value function approximations and job-shop scheduling. In *Proceedings of the Workshop on Value Function Approximation,* Carnegie-Mellon University, School of Computer Science (pp. 95–206).

ENDNOTE

[1] This can be clearly appreciated by considering the percentage of articles and special workshops in this area in some of the main Machine Learning conferences e.g., *International Conference on Machine Learning (*www.icml2010.org*), Neural Information Processing Systems (*nips.cc*), European Conference on Machine Learning and Principles and Practice of Knowledge Discovery in Databases (*www.ecmlpkdd2010. org*)* and special issues in some well-known journals e.g., *Machine Learning Journal (*www.springer.com/computer/ai/journal/10994*), Journal of Machine Learning Research (*jmlr.csail.mit.edu*), Computational Intelligence (*www.wiley.com/bw/journal.asp?ref=0824-7935*)*.

Section 2
Concepts

Chapter 5
Inference Strategies for Solving Semi-Markov Decision Processes

Matthew Hoffman
University of British Columbia, Canada

Nando de Freitas
University of British Columbia, Canada

ABSTRACT

Semi-Markov decision processes are used to formulate many control problems and also play a key role in hierarchical reinforcement learning. In this chapter we show how to translate the decision making problem into a form that can instead be solved by inference and learning techniques. In particular, we will establish a formal connection between planning in semi-Markov decision processes and inference in probabilistic graphical models, then build on this connection to develop an expectation maximization (EM) algorithm for policy optimization in these models.

INTRODUCTION

Researchers in machine learning have long attempted to join the fields of inference and learning with that of decision making. Influence diagrams, for example, explicitly cast the decision making process as inference in a graphical model Cooper (1988); Shachter (1988). However, while these methods are a straight-forward application of infer-ence techniques they only apply to finite-horizon problems and only learn non-stationary policies.

For goal-directed decision problems, more general techniques such as that of Attias (2003) exist for finding the *maximum a posteriori* action sequence. (This technique was later extended by Verma & Rao (2006) to compute the *maximal probable explanation*.) It is crucial to note, however, that these approaches are not optimal in an expected reward sense. Instead, they can

DOI: 10.4018/978-1-60960-165-2.ch005

be interpreted as maximizing the probability of reaching the goal.

While it is well known in the optimal control literature that there exists a fundamental duality between inference and control for the special case of linear-quadratic Gaussian models (Kalman, 1960), this result does not hold in general. Extending these ideas to more general models has been attempted by locally approximating the optimal solution Toussaint (2009); Todorov & Li (2005).

A key step in realizing general inference-based approaches while still maintaining optimality with respect to expected rewards was originally addressed by Dayan & Hinton (1997) for immediate reward decision problems. In particular this work proposes an expectation maximization (EM) approach to the problem which works by optimizing a lower bound on the expected rewards. This technique was then greatly formalized by Toussaint & Storkey (2006) who extend it to the infinite-horizon case (see also Toussaint et al., 2006). This line of research has since enjoyed substantial success in the field of robotics (Peters & Schaal, 2007; Kober & Peters, 2008; Vijayakumar et al., 2009), where empirical evidence has indicated that these methods can often outperform traditional stochastic planning and control methods as well as more recent policy gradient schemes.

The focus of this chapter is two-fold: to act as an introduction to the "planning as inference" methodology and to show how to extend these techniques to semi-Markov Decision Processes (SMDPs). SMDPs are an extension of the MDP formalism that generalize the notion of time—in particular, by allowing the time-intervals between state transitions to vary stochastically. This allows us to handle tradeoffs not only between actions based on their expected rewards, but also based on the amount of time that each action takes to perform.

SMDPs are interesting problems in their own right, with applications to call admission control and queueing systems (see e.g. Singh et al., 2007; Das et al., 1999). This formalism also serves as a natural platform in robotics for building complex motions from sequences of smaller motion "templates" as evidenced by Neumann et al. (2009). Finally, SMDPs are a crucial building block for hierarchical reinforcement learning methods Ghavamzadeh & Mahadevan (2007); Sutton et al. (1998); Dietterich (2000). While this chapter serves as an introductory text to the paradigm of inference and learning, and its application to SMDPs, we hope that future work in this area will leverage advances in structured inference techniques for hierarchical tasks of this nature.

The first section of this work will describe the basic mixture of MDPs model that we build on while the second section will show how to extend this to the SMDP formalism. We then describe an EM algorithm for solving these problems. Finally, in the last section we apply this approach to a small SMDP example.

A Mixture of Finite-Time MDPs

Following the notation of Hoffman, de Freitas, et al. (2009) an MDP can be succinctly described via the following components:

- an initial state model $p(x_0)$,
- a state transition model $p(x_{n+1}|x_n, u_n)$,
- an immediate reward model $r(x_n, u_n)$,
- and finally a stochastic policy $\pi_\theta(u_n \mid x_n)$.

In this model, $n = 1, 2, \ldots$ is a discrete-time index, $\{x_n\}$ is the state process, and $\{u_n\}$ is the action process. The model further assumes a randomized policy, but one can also easily adopt a deterministic policy $\pi_\theta(u \mid x) = \delta_{\phi_\theta(x)}(u)$, where δ denotes the Dirac function and ϕ is a deterministic mapping from states to actions. (By this same reasoning we can also encode knowledge of the initial state using a Dirac mass.) We will assume that the policy-parameters are real-valued, i.e. $\theta \in \mathbb{R}^d$.

Having defined the model, our objective is to maximize the expected future reward with respect to the parameters of the policy θ :

$$J(\theta) = \mathbb{E}\Big[\sum_{n=0}^{\infty} \gamma^n \, r(x_n, u_n) \,\Big|\, \theta\Big], \qquad (1)$$

where $0 < \gamma < 1$ is a discount factor. In order to ease notation later we will also note that for a given θ this model induces a Markov chain over state/action pairs $z_n = (x_n, u_n)$. The transition probabilities for this "extended state space" can then be written as

$$p_\theta(z_0) \& = p(x_0)\,\pi_\theta(u_0 \mid x_0) \qquad \text{and}$$

$$p_\theta(z_{n+1} \mid z_n) = p(x_{n+1} \mid x_n, u_n)\,\pi_\theta(u_{n+1} \mid x_{n+1}),$$

where the joint distribution over any finite k-length sequence of state/action pairs is defined as

$$p_\theta(z_{0:k} \mid k) = p_\theta(z_0)\prod_{n=1}^{k} p_\theta(z_n \mid z_{n-1}) \qquad (2)$$

Finally, we will also write the rewards as $r(z) = r(x,u)$.

In order to transform the problem into one that is more amenable to inference methods we will first note that any maximum of $(1 - \gamma)J(\theta)$ is also a maximum of $J(\theta)$, as this extra multiplicative term just rescales the expected reward. Now, by expanding (1) we can write the (rescaled) expected reward as

$$(1-\gamma)J(\theta)$$
$$= (1-\gamma)\int \Big[p_\theta(z_0)\prod_{n=1}^{\infty} p_\theta(z_n \mid z_{n-1})\Big]\Big[\sum_{k=0}^{\infty} \gamma^k \, r(z_k)\Big] dz_{0:\infty}$$

and by exchanging the order of integration and summation we arrive at:

$$= \int (1-\gamma)\gamma^0 p_\theta(z_0 \mid k = 0)\, r(z_0)\, dz_0$$
$$+ \int (1-\gamma)\gamma^1 p_\theta(z_{0:1} \mid k = 1)\, r(z_1)\, dz_{0:1} + \dots$$
$$= \sum_{k=0}^{\infty} \int \underbrace{(1-\gamma)\gamma^k}_{time\ prior} \, \underbrace{p_\theta(z_{0:k} \mid k)}_{state/action\ prior} \, r(z_k)\, dz_{0:k}$$

It is for this reason that the additional factor of $(1-\gamma)$ was introduced. Under this formulation the discounting terms can be seen as a geometric distribution $p(k) = (1-\gamma)\gamma^k$ and the expected reward under this random time-horizon can be written as

$$(1-\gamma)J(\theta) = \mathbb{E}_{k,z_{0:k}}\Big[r(z_k) \mid \theta\Big],$$
$$p(k, z_{0:k}) = p(k)\, p(z_{0:k} \mid k). \qquad (3)$$

As originally noted by Toussaint & Storkey (2006), we can now view this problem as an infinite mixture of finite horizon MDPs where rewards only occur at the end of a chain whose length is given by the random variable k. A diagram of this interpretation is shown in Figure 1. We must emphasize, however, that we have not changed the model nor the form of the expected rewards, but are instead departing from the standard *interpretation* of these types of decision problems. The classical approach to these problems is to take the expectation of an infinite-length trajectory and sum over increasingly discounted rewards (i.e. the rewards are worth less as time passes due to the discount factor). Instead we are taking the expectation with respect to a *finite-length* trajectory whose length is stochastic with probability equal to the discounting associated with this length. We then evaluate the expected reward only at the end of this chain, but by taking the expectation with respect to k we are essentially summing over the rewards at all such trajectory lengths. Note in particular that this is still an infinite-horizon problem!

This formulation is the basis for many inference and learning approaches to solving MDPs. In the next sections we will show how to extend this formulation in the context of SMDPs and will

Figure 1. Illustration of the mixture of finite horizon MDPs. Expected rewards are computed by mixing over individual MDPs with probability p(k) and taking reward $r_k = r(x_k; u_k)$.

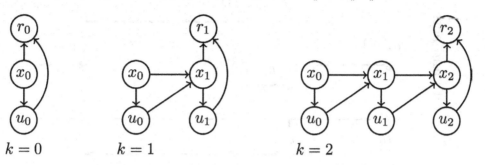

then describe an Expectation-Maximization (EM) algorithm for optimizing the parameters θ. We will first note, however, that these techniques are quite general and can be applied in both discrete[1] and continuous state-spaces (Toussaint & Storkey, 2006; Hoffman, de Freitas, et al., 2009). As we will briefly see later these methods can also be applied to situations where the models themselves are unknown and can only be sampled from (Kober & Peters, 2008; Vlassis & Toussaint, 2009). Finally, it is also possible to derive Markov chain Monte Carlo (MCMC) methods to optimize via sampling in parameter space. While we will omit discussion of these methods entirely we can point the interested reader towards (Hoffman et al., 2007; Hoffman, Kück, et al., 2009) for an introduction. This further enables the solution of planning problems using generic inference algorithms Goodman et al. (2008).

An Extension to Semi-MDPs

Formally we can define an SMDP as a continuous-time controlled stochastic process $z(t) = (x(t),u(t))$ consisting, respectively, of states and actions at every point in time t. In particular we will assume that the system transitions at random *arrival times* t_n and that the process is stationary in between jumps, i.e. $x(t) = x_n$ and $u(t) = u_n$ for all $t \in [t_n, t_{n+1})$. Here each of the state/action pairs evolves according to models defined in Section for MDPs. What makes this model a *semi*-MDP

is the use of random transition times. In order to handle this generalization we will introduce random *sojourn times* $s_n > 0$ which represent the amount of time spent in the nth state. We will then assume the following distribution:

- a time model $p(s_n | x_n, u_n)$,
- where $t_n = t_{n-1} + s_n$ and $t_0 = 0$.

Importantly, the conditional probability for sojourn times does not include the duration of the previous interval. See Figure 2 for an illustration of this process. More generally, we could also allow the sojourn times s_n to depend on the next state x_{n+1}. While the methods we will describe are fully capable of handling this situation, we will ignore this dependency for notational simplicity. Finally, we can write the joint probability over sequences of states/action pairs and sojourn times as

$$p_\theta(z_{0:k}, s_{0:k}) = p_\theta(z_0)\, p(s_0 \mid z_0)\prod_{n=1}^{k} p(s_n \mid z_n)\, p_\theta(z_n \mid z_{n-1})$$

$$(4)$$

for any choice of horizon k.

Just as in the standard MDP formulation we must also specify a reward function $r(z) = r(x,u)$ over states and actions. However, unlike in an MDP our discounting behaves differently in order to take into account the variable time in each state. In particular, we will discount the reward continuously over our entire trajectory, which

Figure 2. Relationship between arrival times t_n, sojourn times s_n and the system state $(x_n; u_n)$

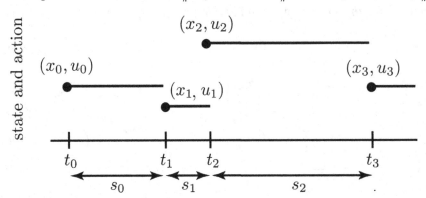

because of the jump-Markov nature of our transitions will simplify to

$$
\begin{aligned}
J(\theta) &= \mathbb{E}\left[\int_0^\infty \beta e^{-\beta t}\, r(z(t))\, dt \,\Big|\, \theta\right] \\
&= \mathbb{E}\left[\sum_{n=0}^\infty e^{-\beta t_n}\left(1 - e^{-\beta s_n}\right) r(z_n) \,\Big|\, \theta\right]
\end{aligned}
\tag{5}
$$

Here $\beta > 0$ is a discount rate which is analogous to the discount factor in an MDP. In fact, when the sojourn times are deterministically given by $s_n = 1$ we recover a standard infinite-horizon, discounted MDP with a discount factor of $\gamma = e^{-\beta}$. Those readers more familiar with continuous-time control problems may note that in the first line of the expected reward definition we have introduced an additional multiplicative term of β. We do this so that later we can give the discount factors a more intuitive interpretation as a probability distribution, and we point out that since this is a multiplicative constant it will not change the optimal policy parameters of the system.

Based on the intuition developed earlier for MDPs we can interpret the discount terms in (5) as a distribution over random time horizons k and write the following joint distribution over paths and path lengths:

$$
p_\theta(k, z_{0:k}, s_{0:k}) = e^{-\beta(s_0 + \ldots + s_{k-1})}\left(1 - e^{-\beta s_k}\right) p_\theta(z_{0:k}, s_{0:k})
\tag{6}
$$

This distribution is not, however, nearly as straightforward as that in the MDP case. Nor is there the simple division between path-lengths and paths.

Proposition 1. *The joint distribution introduced in (6) is properly defined and normalized, i.e. it integrates to 1.*

In theory we can integrate out each of the infinitely many trajectory and time variables to see that for any k the marginal over path lengths is given by

$$
p_\theta(k) = \mathbb{E}[e^{-\beta s_0}]\cdots\mathbb{E}[e^{-\beta s_{k-1}}](1 - \mathbb{E}[e^{-\beta s_k}])
$$

Given this marginal we can consider an infinite sequence of non-identical Bernoulli trials, where $p_n = \mathbb{E}[e^{-\beta s_n}]$ is the probability that the nth trial fails. Note, we need not compute this quantity in practice.

Due to the restriction that sojourn times are greater than zero we know that each such quantity lies in the range $0 < p_n \leq 1$. With this in mind, we can then see that $p_\theta(k)$ is the probability that this sequence of trials has its first success after k-1 failures. As a result the marginal distribution over K can be properly defined as a conjunction of Bernoulli random variables and thus the full joint (i.e.\ not integrating over the trajectory and time variables) must be similarly well defined and integrate to 1.

Finally, given the joint distribution $p_\theta(k, z_{0:k}, s_{0:k})$ we can rewrite our objective from (5) as the *expected final reward* under this distribution, i.e.

$$
\begin{aligned}
J(\theta) &= \int p_\theta(z_{0:\infty}, s_{0:\infty}) \Big[\sum_{k=0}^\infty e^{-\beta t_k}(1 - e^{-\beta s_k}) r(z_k) \Big] ds_{0:\infty} \, dz_{0:\infty} \\
&= \sum_{k=0}^\infty \int p_\theta(z_{0:k}, s_{0:k}) e^{-\beta t_k}(1 - e^{-\beta s_k}) r(z_k) \, ds_{0:k} \, dz_{0:k} \\
&= \sum_{k=0}^\infty \int p_\theta(k, z_{0:k}, s_{0:k}) r(z_k) \, ds_{0:k} \, dz_{0:k} \\
&= \mathbb{E}_{k, z_{0:k}}\big[r(z_k) \,|\, \theta \big].
\end{aligned}
\tag{7}
$$

Similar to the MDP case we have obtained this result by exchanging the order of integration and summation and pulling the discount factor into the previously introduced distribution from (6). In the next section we will take this one step further and treat the reward terms $r(z_k)$ as the likelihood of some "imaginary event". We can then use this to develop an EM algorithm for finding the most likely policy parameters under this "data".

Finally, as an aside, we should note how the formulations of this section simplify in the MDP case, and more importantly why these simplifications do not hold for SMDPs. In particular, for an MDP it is not necessary to reason about times s_n (since these are deterministically set to 1) and the joint distribution (6) can be factorized as

$$
p_\theta(k, z_{0:k}) = p(k)\, p_\theta(z_{0:k} \,|\, k).
$$

Here the conditional distribution is given by (4) and the "time prior" $p(k)$ is given by a geometric distribution with success probability $\gamma = e^{-\beta}$, i.e. the constant discount factor. This factorization is what allowed Toussaint & Storkey (2006) to reformulate the infinite-horizon MDP problem as a mixture of finite-time MDPs, where the random variable k acts as an indicator variable. Unfortunately this interpretation does not hold in the case of more general SMDPs. By looking at the discount factors in (6) we can see that the

probability of a specific trajectory length k is a function of all sojourn times $s_{0:k}$, and as a result the distribution over the random variable k depends on an infinite number of sojourn times. However, while the SMDP formalism does not have as clean of a probabilistic interpretation as MDPs, we can still apply this model by working directly with the joint distribution.

AN EM ALGORITHM FOR SMDPs

Expectation-Maximization (EM) is an algorithm formulation that is used to compute maximum likelihood estimates in the presence of unobserved or hidden variables. In our case, the unobserved variables consist of the trajectory length k along with the state/action pairs and their corresponding sojourn times, $z_{0:k}$ and $s_{0:k}$ respectively. The observed variables for this model are then implicitly given by the reward function—i.e. we are assuming some *imaginary* random variable was observed where the likelihood of this observation conditioned on our hidden variables is given by $r(z_k)$. Note, treating the rewards as likelihoods does place some restrictions on their allowable forms. While they need not sum to 1, they must be positive. However, for finite models or models which are bounded below this is easily obtainable by adding some constant term.

Given this interpretation we can introduce the following quantities which are necessary for deriving the EM algorithm:

- The *complete data likelihood* is the likelihood of both our observed and unobserved data; here given by $r(z_k)\, p_\theta(k, z_{0:k}, s_{0:k})$.
- The *incomplete data likelihood* is the integral of the complete data likelihood with respect to the hidden variables; here given by $\mathbb{E}[r(z_k)\,|\,\theta]$.
- Finally, the *predictive distribution* over the hidden variables is given by the "posterior"

that takes into account both the prior and likelihood, and is thus the ratio of complete and incomplete likelihoods.

In particular, we will write the predictive distribution using the following notation:

$$\tilde{p}_\theta(k, z_{0:k}, s_{0:k}) = \frac{r(z_k)\, p_\theta(k, z_{0:k}, s_{0:k})}{\mathbb{E}[r(z_k)\mid\theta]} \qquad (8)$$

Given these quantities the EM algorithm is an iterative procedure which at iteration i computes the *expected* complete data log-likelihood, parameterized by θ, under the previous iteration's policy parameters $\theta^{(i-1)}$. This quantity, which we will denote with $Q(\theta, \theta^{(i-1)})$, is then optimized with respect to the policy parameters in order to obtain $\theta^{(i)}$. We can summarize this procedure as:

$$Q(\theta, \theta^{(i-1)}) = \mathbb{E}\Big[\log\{p_\theta(k, z_{0:k}, s_{0:k})\, r(z_k)\}\,\Big|\,\theta^{(i-1)}\Big],$$
$$\text{(E-step)}$$

$$\theta^{(i)} = \arg\max_\theta Q(\theta, \theta^{(i-1)}), \qquad \text{(M-step)}$$

This EM procedure is known to locally maximize the incomplete data likelihood (see Dempster et al., 1977; McLachlan & Krishnan, 1997) and hence will maximize our original objective $J(\theta)$.

Before deriving the E-step in more detail we will first take a brief look at the quantities that are actually needed in order to perform the maximization in the M-step. We can first let θ' denote the previous iteration's parameter estimate and rewrite the Q-function as

$$Q(\theta, \theta') = \mathbb{E}\Big[\log\Big\{\textstyle\prod_{n=0}^{k}\pi_\theta(z_n)\Big\}\,\Big|\,\theta'\Big] +$$
$$\mathbb{E}\Big[\log\Big\{r(z_k)\,p(x_0)\textstyle\prod_{n=1}^{k}p(x_n\mid z_{n-1})\Big\}\,\Big|\,\theta'\Big] +$$
$$\mathbb{E}\Big[\log\Big\{\textstyle\prod_{n=0}^{k}p(s_n\mid z_n)\Big\}\,\Big|\,\theta'\Big]$$

where we have expanded the complete data likelihood and separated those terms which do and do not depend on θ. Since only the first of these three quantities depends on θ we can drop the others and expand this expectation:

$$= \sum_{k=0}^{\infty}\int\Big[\sum_{n=0}^{k}\log\pi_\theta(z_n)\Big]\tilde{p}_{\theta'}(k, z_{0:k})\, dz_{0:k} + \text{const.}$$
$$= \sum_{k=0}^{\infty}\sum_{n=0}^{k}\int\log\pi_\theta(z_n)\,\tilde{p}_{\theta'}(k, z_n)\, dz_n + \text{const.}$$
$$(9)$$

Finally, in order to optimize the Q-function with respect to the policy parameters θ we will also need to evaluate the gradient

$$\nabla_\theta Q(\theta, \theta') = \sum_{k=0}^{\infty}\sum_{n=0}^{k}\int \tilde{p}_{\theta'}(k, z_n)\nabla_\theta \log \pi_\theta(z_n)\, dz_n.$$
$$(10)$$

Ultimately, this expansion informs how we will derive the steps required for the EM algorithm. In the E-step we need to construct the distribution $\tilde{p}_{\theta'}(k, z_n)$ and in the M-step we will compute the expectation of the gradient $\nabla \log \pi_\theta(z_n)$ under this distribution. We should note that this is the same form of the marginal distribution that would be computed in the E-step for a standard MDP. We will see shortly, however, that the computations necessary to compute this distribution are different due the integration over sojourn-times. In the next two subsections we will discuss these steps in more detail.

The E-Step

As noted in the previous section, we need to construct the marginals $\tilde{p}_\theta(k, z_n)$ in order to compute the gradient of the expected complete log-likelihood. In this section, we will derive an efficient method for recursively constructing this distribution. We start by writing the marginal distribution as the integral of the predictive distribution with respect to all those terms other than k and z_n,

$$\tilde{p}_\theta(k, z_n) = \int \tilde{p}_\theta(k, z_{0:k}, s_{0:k})\, dz_{0:n-1}\, dz_{n+1:k}\, ds_{0:k}.$$

This integral can then be broken into those components that come before and after n respectively, and we can then see that the marginal distribution is proportional to

$$\tilde{p}_\theta(k, z_n) \propto \int e^{-\beta(s_0 + \dots + s_{n-1})}\, p_\theta(z_{0:n}, s_{0:n-1})\, dz_{0:n-1}\, ds_{0:n-1} \times$$
$$\propto \int e^{-\beta(s_n + \dots + s_{k-1})}(1 - e^{-\beta s_k})\, r(z_k)\, p_\theta(z_{n+1:k}, s_{n:k} \mid z_n)\, dz_{n+1:k}\, ds_{n:k}.$$
$$(11)$$

We should emphasize the fact that we are *not* integrating over z_n, which enables us to break the original integral into two independent integrals. Here we have also omitted the constant of proportionality, given by the expected reward $\mathbb{E}[r(z_k)]$.

In an analogy to the forward-backward algorithm for hidden Markov models we will call the two sets of integrals from (11) "forward" and "backward" messages, denoting them as $\alpha_\theta(z_n)$ and $\beta_\theta(z_n \mid \tau = k - n)$ respectively[2]. Using these messages we can then write the marginal distribution as

$$\tilde{p}_\theta(k, z_n) = \frac{1}{\mathbb{E}[r(z_k)]} \alpha_\theta(z_n)\, \beta_\theta(z_n \mid k - n)$$
$$(12)$$

Intuitively the forward messages are integrating information forward in time from the initial-state distribution where the nth such message is the state/action distribution at step n weighted by the expected discounting up to step n-1. Meanwhile, the backward messages are integrating information backward from the rewards and can be seen as the expected reward at step k given the state/action pair at step n (weighted by the expected discounting between n and k). It is crucial to note,

however, that these messages are not probability distributions due to the way the discount factors have been split between the forward and backward components, namely:

$$\underbrace{e^{-\beta(s_0 + \dots + s_{n-1})}}_{forward}\ \underbrace{e^{-\beta(s_n + \dots + s_{k-1})}(1 - e^{-\beta s_k})}_{backward}.$$

This causes no technical (or conceptual) difficulties, though, because when combined in (12) these messages form the desired probability distribution. This is similar in spirit to techniques used to maintain numerical stability when working with hidden Markov models (Bishop, 2006).

At this point, we can also more fully describe the use of the τ term in defining the backward messages. The reason behind this notation stems from the fact that naively computing these messages for each choice of k and n turns out to involve a great deal of redundant computation. Under the predictive distribution defined in (8) the reward factors only interact with the end of a finite-length trajectory. As a result the backward messages depend only on the difference $\tau = k$-n, i.e. how far in the future the rewards are obtained. Because of this, we can instead define the backward messages purely in terms of the "time-to-go". This notation was originally presented by Toussaint & Storkey (2006), but here the messages are generalized to account for the fact that in the semi-Markov setting the kth reward introduces a factor over the state and action z_n and duration s_n at every epoch n prior to k.

Finally, by integrating the components of the first integral in (11) successively we can recursively define the forward messages as

$$\alpha_\theta(z_0) = \mu(x_0)\, \pi_\theta(u_0 \mid x_0),$$
$$\alpha_\theta(z_n) = \int \alpha_\theta(z_{n-1})\, p_\theta(z_n \mid z_{n-1})\, dz_{n-1} \qquad (13)$$
$$\times \int e^{-\beta s_{n-1}}\, p_\theta(s_{n-1} \mid z_{n-1})\, ds_{n-1}.$$

Here we can see that we have the standard MDP forward message recursion multiplied by an additional integral due to the sojourn times. Similarly, we can recursively define the backwards messages as

$$\beta_\theta(z_n \mid 0) = r(z_n) \int (1 - e^{-\beta s_n}) p_\theta(s_n \mid z_n) ds_n,$$

$$\beta_\theta(z_n \mid \tau) = \int \beta_\theta(z_{n+1} \mid \tau - 1) p_\theta(z_{n+1} \mid z_n) dz_{n+1}$$

$$\times \int e^{-\beta s_n} p_\theta(s_n \mid z_n) ds_n. \tag{14}$$

Again we can see that these messages can be seen as two integrals, one corresponding to the standard MDP message and a sojourn time message. Given the format of these two messages we can further introduce what we call an "expected discount factor"

$$\gamma(z) = \int e^{-\beta s} T(s \mid z) ds \tag{15}$$

which corresponds to the integral over sojourn times noted above. We can consider this term as a generalization of the MDP formalism wherein discount factors are no longer constant and instead depend on the current state and the action taken from that state. Further, we can see that for any exponential-family distribution this integral will exist in closed form.

The M-Step

The M-step requires us to maximize the Q-function with respect to the policy parameters θ. If possible we can analytically maximize this function by solving for the fixed point of $\nabla_\theta Q(\theta, \theta') = 0$. If this is not possible we can still evaluate the gradient at the current set of policy parameters $\nabla_\theta Q(\theta', \theta')$ and follow the resulting ascent direction, resulting in a generalized EM algorithm (GEM). When this procedure is iterated, both of these methods are known to

locally maximize the incomplete data likelihood (again, for more details see McLachlan & Krishnan, 1997).

While EM methods are, in general, only able to guarantee local convergence it can be shown via its relation to policy iteration that these methods exhibit global convergence for discrete models when using exact/analytic inference (see Toussaint et al. (2006) for more details). In more general continuous settings no such guarantees can be made, however as noted by Hoffman, de Freitas, et al. (2009) a sufficiently exploratory initial policy does seem to have a tempering effect. This is especially true if the exact EM updates can be used, as additional exploratory noise does not cause the dramatic increase in variance associated with sample-based methods (such as policy gradients).

Monte Carlo EM

It is also possible to perform a Monte Carlo approximation during the E-step in order to optimize these problems when either the necessary distributions are unknown or the updates cannot be computed in closed form. As is derived for MDPs in (Kober & Peters, 2008; Vlassis & Toussaint, 2009), we can sample from the initial-state and transition distributions in order to approximate the Q-function. Given M trajectories $\{z_{0:k}^{(i)}, s_{0:k}^{(i)}\}_{i \leq M}$ sampled from $p_{\theta'}(z_{0:k}, s_{0:k})$ we can approximate the joint distribution for any $n < k$ with

$$\tilde{p}_{\theta'}(k, z_n) \approx \frac{1}{MA} \sum_{i=1}^M \left[e^{-\beta t_k^{(i)}} \left(1 - e^{-\beta s_k^{(i)}} \right) \right] r(z_k^{(i)}) \delta_{z_n^{(i)}}(z_n),$$

where A is a proportionality constant, given by $E[r(z_k)]$ as noted earlier. If we assume some maximum time-horizon K_{max} we can approximate the Q-function as

$$Q(\theta, \theta') \approx \sum_{i=1}^{M} \sum_{k=0}^{K_{\max}} \sum_{n=0}^{k} \left[e^{-\beta t_k^{(i)}} \left(1 - e^{-\beta s_k^{(i)}} \right) \right] r(z_k^{(i)}) \log \pi_\theta(z_n^{(i)})$$

$$- \sum_{i=1}^{M} \sum_{n=0}^{K_{\max}} \log \pi_\theta(z_n^{(i)}) \sum_{k=n}^{K_{\max}} \left[e^{-\beta t_k^{(i)}} \left(1 - e^{-\beta s_k^{(i)}} \right) \right] r(z_k^{(i)}).$$

This function can then be optimized using the same techniques as in the standard M-step.

DISCRETE MODELS WITH GAMMA-DISTRIBUTED TIME

The methods presented in previous sections, as with all EM-based procedures, provide a "meta-algorithm" which depends upon the exact models in use. In this section we present a simple model for the purposes of illustrating the procedure. Again, for a more advanced treatment of these methods in the context of MDPs we refer the reader to (Hoffman, de Freitas, et al., 2009; Toussaint et al., 2006; Toussaint, 2009; Kober & Peters, 2008).

We will now consider a model where the states and actions are discrete and sojourn times are given by a Gamma distribution. While simple, this model nonetheless presents an interesting scenario for planning and control domains because it can naturally be extended to cases when we want to reason about more complex distributions over the time to complete an action. In our experiments, we define the discrete transition, initial-state, and reward models according to

$$\mu_x = p(x_0 = x),$$
$$P_{xux'} = p(x_{n+1} = x' \mid x_n = x, u_n = u), \text{ and}$$
$$R_{xu} r = (x, u)$$

where the sojourn times are Gamma-distributed according to

$$p(s_n \mid x_n = x, u_n = u) = \Gamma(s_n; k_{xu}, \sigma_{xu})$$

Finally, we will assume a discrete policy where $\theta_{xu} = \pi_\theta(u \mid x)$.

Under this formulation the forward and backward messages will be representable as matrices, and by dropping the θ index we will let α_{xu}^n and β_{xu}^τ denote the n-step forward message and τ-step backward messages respectively. By plugging initial state, transition, and reward matrices into (13) and (14) we can explicitly write these messages as:

$$\alpha_{xu}^n = \theta_{xu} \sum_{x',u'} \alpha_{x'u'}^{n-1} P_{x'u'x} \gamma_{x'u'}, \qquad \alpha_{xu}^0 = \theta_{xu} \mu_x; \tag{16}$$

$$\beta_{xu}^\tau = \gamma_{xu} \sum_{x',u'} \beta_{x'u'}^{\tau-1} P_{xux'} \theta_{x'u'}, \qquad \beta_{xu}^0 = R_{xu}(1 - \gamma_{xu}) \tag{17}$$

To make notation easier we will also introduce a forward message defined only over states, $\bar{\alpha}_x = \sum_u \alpha_{xu}$. In this setting the expected discount factor noted earlier can be written as the matrix

$$\gamma_{xu} = \int \Gamma(s; k_{xu}, \sigma_{xu}) e^{-\beta s} \, ds$$
$$= \int s^{k_{xu}-1} \frac{\exp\left(-(\beta + \sigma_{xu}^{-1})s\right)}{\Gamma(k_{xu}) \sigma_{xu}^{k_{xu}}} \, ds = (1 + \beta \sigma_{xu})^{-k_{xu}}.$$

This particular form arises purely from the use of Gamma-distributed sojourn times, and in fact we can imagine extending this to continuous spaces using functions $k(x,u)$ and $\sigma(x,u)$.

At every iteration, for a given set of parameters θ', the E-step consists of calculating the forward and backward messages given by Equations (16,17. By plugging these terms into the Q-function defined in (9) we can write

$$Q(\theta, \theta') = \frac{1}{\mathbb{E}[r(z_k)]} \sum_{k=0}^{\infty} \sum_{n=0}^{k} \sum_{u,x} (\log \theta_{xu}) \theta'_{xu} \, \bar{\alpha}_x^n \, \beta_{xu}^{k-n}$$

$$= \frac{1}{\mathbb{E}[r(z_k)]} \sum_{u,x} (\log \theta_{xu}) \theta'_{xu} \Big[\sum_{n=0}^{\infty} \bar{\alpha}_x^n \Big] \Big[\sum_{\tau=0}^{\infty} \beta_{xu}^{\tau} \Big],$$

where the second equality can be obtained by rearranging the sums over k and n. This alternate formulation is particularly useful in discrete models where the sum over forward and backward messages can expressed as finite quantities, i.e. a vector and a matrix respectively. Further, given this formulation we can optimize the Q-function for each state x individually, which is possible because in discrete domains we can find the optimal action to take for each state regardless of the probability of visiting that state. By taking the gradient of the log-policy $\nabla \log \pi_{\theta}(u \mid x) = \theta_{xu}^{-1}$ and solving $\nabla Q(\theta, \theta') = 0$ for θ, subject to the constraint that $\sum_{u} \theta_{xu} = 1$ for each x, we arrive at the following solution methods:

$$\theta_{xu} \propto \theta'_{xu} \sum_{\tau=0}^{\infty} \beta_{xu}^{\tau}, \tag{EM}$$

$$\theta_{xu} = \delta_{m(x)}(u) \text{ where } m(x) = \arg \max_{u'} \sum_{\tau=0}^{\infty} \beta_{xu'}^{\tau}.$$
$$\text{(greedy-EM)}$$

Here the EM solution is performing exactly the optimization described above, while the greedy-EM solution, however, myopically chooses for each state x the one action u that maximizes the total future rewards when taken from that state. In particular, the greedy solution can be seen as iterations which correspond to repeated M-steps which skip intermediate E-steps as is shown by Toussaint et al. (2006), and in this sense this method is equivalent (again only for discrete models) to policy iteration. In larger discrete models, however, the EM approach has the advantage over policy iteration in that it is possible to prune computation (by using the forward messages α) in

a principled manner; see Toussaint et al. (2006) for more details.

Results on various discrete models. The top-left plot shows convergence of the described algorithms on a randomly generated, dense model; the top-right plot shows performance on a model of the same size but with grid-like transitions and more structured transition times. The bottom-left plot shows performance on a larger grid domain. The bottom-right shows the learned policy in the larger domain. For both grid domains there is a single large reward (denoted with a dot) and transitions taken outside of the edge states (denoted with grey) have a larger expected sojourn time.

We first test these algorithms on a small, 16-state, 5-action domain with randomly generated transition and sojourn parameters, as well as a randomly generated reward model. The principal challenge of this domain, over other discrete domains, is to take advantage of the structure in the sojourn time distribution. The top-left plot of Figure 3 displays convergence properties of the described algorithms as well as a comparison to a standard policy-gradient method (see e.g. Baxter & Bartlett, 2001). In particular we should note that the resulting model was densely connected which allows for quick travel across the space, and explains the very good performance of the stochastic policy gradient algorithm. Also shown for policy gradients are error-bars corresponding to one standard deviation. The other methods don't need error bars because they are deterministic.

Building upon these results, the top-right plot shows the algorithms learning in a more structured environment. In particular the model used has grid-structured transitions on a small 4-by-4 grid. This model is especially interesting because we specify different Gamma-distributions for the inner nodes than the outer nodes such that the inner nodes move much more slowly. Also, we use a sparse reward model where most states have negligible reward and one state has high reward. The most important thing to note from this subfigure is that the policy gradient method starts to

Figure 3. Results on various discrete models. The top-left plot shows convergence of the described algorithms on a randomly generated, dense model; the top-right plot shows performance on a model of the same size but with grid-like transitions and more structured transition times. The bottom left plot shows performance on a larger grid domain. The bottom-right shows the learned policy in the larger domain. For both grid domains there is a single large reward (denoted with a dot) and transitions taken outside of the edge states (denoted with grey) have a larger expected sojourn time.

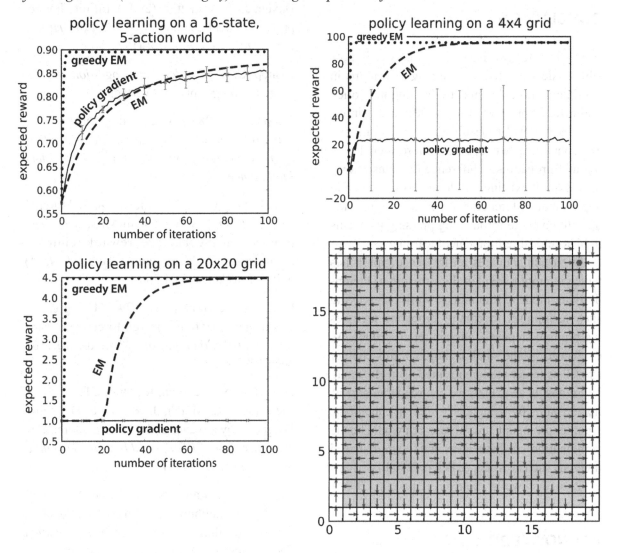

break down under this sparse transition and reward model, even though the size of the state and action spaces are the same as in the previous example.

Lastly the bottom-left plot of this figure displays the progress of these algorithms on a much larger 20-by-20 grid, i.e. one in which there are 2000 state/action pairs. Similar to the previous

example there is a single (relatively) large reward in the upper right corner of the grid and inner nodes with much slower sojourn times. Here we see that the EM algorithms vastly out-perform the policy gradient method and the learned policy successfully skirts the outside edge of the state-space in order to most quickly get to the high reward.

Here the policy gradient method has relatively low-variance because it is not able to make any progress (i.e. it is stuck exploring a plateau with very little gradient information).

CONCLUSION

In this chapter, we have shown how it is possible to design effective planning algorithms in continuous-time domains by framing the policy optimization problem in an SMDP as one of inference in a related probabilistic graphical model. The connection between the reinforcement learning and probabilistic inference domains allows us to exploit existing developments in exact and approximate inference, and will perhaps provide us with leverage for tackling pressing problems in hierarchical reinforcement learning.

Of particular interest are inference approaches which attempt to exploit the structure of the underlying models. Preliminary work on applying such techniques to control problems includes the pruning steps of Toussaint et al. (2006). As evidenced by the small example in this chapter as well as larger continuous models in Hoffman, de Freitas, et al. (2009) we can see large performance gains by using exact inference methods. Another promising area of research would be the combination of these ideas with sample-based methods such as Kober & Peters (2008), perhaps via Rao-Blackwellization (de Freitas et al., 2004).

ACKNOWLEDGMENT

We would like to thank Peter Carbonetto and Arnaud Doucet for helpful contributions to an earlier version of this report. We would also like to thank Peter for his help in generating Figure 2. Finally, we would like to thank the editors and reviewers of this chapter for their helpful comments.

REFERENCES

Attias, H. (2003). Planning by probabilistic inference. In *Proceedings of the International Conference on Artificial Intelligence and Statistics.*

Baxter, J., & Bartlett, P. (2001). Infinite-horizon policy-gradient estimation. *Journal of Artificial Intelligence Research, 15*(4).

Bishop, C. (2006). *Pattern recognition and machine learning.* Springer-Verlag.

Cooper, G. (1988). A method for using belief networks as influence diagrams. In *Proceedings of the Conference on Uncertainty in Artificial Intelligence.*

Das, T., Gosavi, A., Mahadevan, S., & Marchalleck, N. (1999). Solving semi-Markov decision problems using average reward reinforcement learning. *Management Science, 45*(4). doi:10.1287/mnsc.45.4.560

Dayan, P., & Hinton, G. (1997). Using expectation-maximization for reinforcement learning. *Neural Computation, 9*(2). doi:10.1162/neco.1997.9.2.271

de Freitas, N., Dearden, R., Hutter, F., Morales-Menendez, R., Mutch, J., & Poole, D. (2004). Diagnosis by a waiter and a Mars explorer. *Proceedings of the IEEE, Special Issue on Sequential State Estimation, 92*(3).

Dempster, A., Laird, N., & Rubin, D. (1977). Maximum likelihood from incomplete data via the em algorithm. *Journal of the Royal Statistical Society. Series B, Statistical Methodology, 39*(1).

Dietterich, T. (2000). Hierarchical reinforcement learning with the MAXQ value function decomposition. *Journal of Artificial Intelligence Research, 13*(1).

Ghavamzadeh, M., & Mahadevan, S. (2007). Hierarchical average reward reinforcement learning. *Journal of Machine Learning Research, 8.*

Goodman, N., Mansinghka, V., Roy, D., Bonawitz, K., & Tenenbaum, J. (2008). Church: A language for generative models. In *Proceedings of the Conference on Uncertainty in Artificial Intelligence.*

Hoffman, M., de Freitas, N., Doucet, A., & Peters, J. (2009). An expectation maximization algorithm for continuous Markov decision processes with arbitrary reward. In *Proceedings of the International Conference on Artificial Intelligence and Statistics.*

Hoffman, M., Doucet, A., de Freitas, N., & Jasra, A. (2007). Bayesian policy learning with trans-dimensional MCMC. In *Advances in Neural Information Processing Systems.*

Hoffman, M., Kück, H., de Freitas, N., & Doucet, A. (2009). New inference strategies for solving Markov decision processes using reversible jump MCMC. In *Proceedings of the Conference on Uncertainty in Artificial Intelligence.*

Kalman, R. (1960). A new approach to linear filtering and prediction problems. *Journal of Basic Engineering, 82*(1).

Kober, J., & Peters, J. (2008). Policy search for motor primitives in robotics. In *Advances in Neural Information Processing Systems.*

McLachlan, G., & Krishnan, T. (1997). *The EM algorithm and extensions.* New York, NY: Wiley.

Neumann, G., Maass, W., & Peters, J. (2009). Learning complex motions by sequencing simpler motion templates. In *Proceedings of the International Conference on Machine Learning.*

Peters, J., & Schaal, S. (2007). Reinforcement learning for operational space control. In *Proceedings of the IEEE International Conference on Robotics and Automation.*

Shachter, R. (1988). Probabilistic inference and influence diagrams. *Operations Research, 36*(4). doi:10.1287/opre.36.4.589

Singh, S., Tadic, V., & Doucet, A. (2007). A policy gradient method for semi-Markov decision processes with application to call admission control. *European Journal of Operational Research, 178*(3), 808–818. doi:10.1016/j.ejor.2006.02.023

Sutton, R., Precup, D., & Singh, S. (1998). Between MDPs and semi-MDPs: A framework for temporal abstraction in reinforcement learning. *Artificial Intelligence, 112*(1).

Todorov, E., & Li, W. (2005). A generalized iterative LQG method for locally-optimal feedback control of constrained nonlinear stochastic systems. In *Proceedings of the 2005 American Control Conference.*

Toussaint, M. (2009). Robot trajectory optimization using approximate inference. In *Proceedings of the International Conference on Machine Learning.*

Toussaint, M., Harmeling, S., & Storkey, A. (2006). *Probabilistic inference for solving (PO) MDPs.* (Tech. Rep. No. EDI-INF-RR-0934). University of Edinburgh, School of Informatics Research.

Toussaint, M., & Storkey, A. (2006). Probabilistic inference for solving discrete and continuous state Markov decision processes. In *Proceedings of the International Conference on Machine Learning.*

Verma, D., & Rao, R. (2006). Planning and acting in uncertain environments using probabilistic inference. In *Intelligent robots and systems.*

Vijayakumar, S., Toussaint, M., Petkos, G., & Howard, M. (2009). Planning and moving in dynamic environments: A statistical machine learning approach. In *Creating brain like intelligence: From principles to complex intelligent systems.* Springer-Verlag.

Vlassis, N., & Toussaint, M. (2009). Model-free reinforcement learning as mixture learning. In *Proceedings of the 26th International Conference on Machine Learning*.

ADDITIONAL READING

For further discussion on the connection between planning and inference problems we direct the reader towards the tutorial of Toussaint et al. (2006). In (Hoffman et al., 2009a) this approach is also applied to a continuous state/action domain. An application of these approaches to the model-free case is given in the works of (Vlassis and Toussaint, 2009) as well as (Kober and Peters, 2008). Finally, a related approach is applied in (Hoffman et al., 2009b) in order to obtain a fully-Bayesian solution to the problem. Additional details on the use of SMPDs are given by (Singh et al., 2007) and (Ghavamzadeh and Mahadevan, 2007) for the case of queueing systems. Finally, the works of (Sutton et al., 1998) and (Dieterich, 2000) give additional details on the applications of SMDPs to hierarchical planning.

KEY TERMS AND DEFINITIONS

Complete Data: In the context of the Expectation-Maximization algorithm, this refers to the combination of hidden and observed data.

Expectation Maximization: An algorithm for performing maximum-likelihood parameter learning in models with hidden data.

Incomplete Data: In the context of the EM algorithm, this refers to the data that has been observed. The likelihood of this data is thus given by the integral of the complete data likelihood taken with respect to the hidden data.

Semi-Markov Decision Problem: An MDP extension in which the time of each action is variable, and specified by a stochastic model.

ENDNOTES

[1] For discrete models the integrals become sums (i.e. integration with respect to the counting measure).

[2] The notation here is slightly confusing in that we have a term β denoting the continuous discount factor and $\beta_\theta(\cdot \mid \tau)$ denoting the backward messages. This confusion, however, seems unavoidable as both of these terms are unanimously used in their respective literatures. To somewhat alleviate this confusion we note that the backward messages are *always* subscripted.

Chapter 6
Multistage Stochastic Programming:
A Scenario Tree Based Approach to Planning under Uncertainty

Boris Defourny
University of Liège, Belgium

Damien Ernst
University of Liège, Belgium

Louis Wehenkel
University of Liège, Belgium

ABSTRACT

In this chapter, we present the multistage stochastic programming framework for sequential decision making under uncertainty. We discuss its differences with Markov Decision Processes, from the point of view of decision models and solution algorithms. We describe the standard technique for solving approximately multistage stochastic problems, based on a discretization of the disturbance space called scenario tree. We insist on a critical issue of the approach; the decisions can be very sensitive to the parameters of the scenario tree, whereas no efficient tool for checking the quality of approximate solutions exists. In this chapter, we show how supervised learning techniques can be used to evaluate reliably the quality of an approximation, and thus facilitate the selection of a good scenario tree. The framework and solution techniques presented in the chapter are explained and detailed on several examples. Along the way, we define notions from decision theory that can be used to quantify, for a particular problem, the advantage of switching to a more sophisticated decision model.

DOI: 10.4018/978-1-60960-165-2.ch006

INTRODUCTION

This chapter addresses decision problems under uncertainty for which complex decisions can be taken in several successive stages. By complex decisions, it is meant that the decisions are structured by numerous constraints or lie in high-dimensional spaces. Problems where this situation arises include capacity planning, production planning, transportation and logistics, financial management, and others (Wallace & Ziemba, 2005). While those applications are not currently mainstream domains of research in artificial intelligence, where many achievements have already been obtained for control problems with a finite number of actions and for problems where the uncertainty is reduced to some independent noise perturbing the dynamics of the controlled system, the interest for applications closer to operations research — where single instantaneous decisions may already be hard to find and where uncertainties from the environment may be delicate to model — and for applications closer to those addressed in decision theory — where complex objectives and potentially conflicting requirements have to be taken into account — seems to be growing in the machine learning community, as indicated by a series of advances in approximate dynamic programming motivated by such applications (Powell, 2007; Csáji & Monostori, 2008).

Computing strategies involving complex decisions calls for optimization techniques that can go beyond the simple enumeration and evaluation of the possible actions of an agent. Multistage stochastic programming, the approach presented in this chapter, relies on mathematical programming and probability theory. It has been recognized by several industries — mainly in energy (Kallrath, Pardalos, Rebennack, & Scheidt, 2009) and finance (Dempster, Pflug, & Mitra, 2008) — as a promising framework to formulate complex problems under uncertainty, exploit domain knowledge, use risk-averse objectives, incorpo-

rate probabilistic and dynamical aspects, while preserving structures compatible with large-scale optimization techniques.

Even for readers primarily concerned by robotics, the development of these techniques for sequential decision making under uncertainty is interesting to follow. Puterman (1994), the early roots of sequential decision processes, recalls the role of the multi-period inventory models from the industry in the development of the theory of Markov Decision Processes (Chapter 3 of this book). We could also mention the role of applications in finance as a motivation for the early theory of multi-armed bandits and for the theory of sequential prediction, now an important field of research in machine learning.

The objective of the chapter is to provide a functional view of the concepts and methods proper to multistage stochastic programming.

To communicate the spirit of the approach, we use examples that are short in their description. We use the freely available optimization software Cvx (Grant & Boyd, 2008, 2009), which has the merit of enabling occasional users of optimization techniques to conduct their own numerical experiments in MATLAB (The MathWorks, Inc., 2004).

We cover our recent contributions on scenario tree selection and out-of-sample validation of optimized models (Defourny, Ernst, & Wehenkel, 2009), which suggest partial answers to issues concerning the selection of approximations/discretization of multistage stochastic programs, and to issues concerning the efficient comparison among those approximations.

Many details relative to optimization algorithms and specific problem classes have been left aside in our presentation. A more extensive coverage of these aspects can be found in Birge and Louveaux (1997); Shapiro, Dentcheva, and Ruszczyński (2009). These excellent sources also present many examples of formulations of stochastic programming models. Note, however, that there is no such thing as a general theory on multistage stochastic programming that would allow the many approximation/discretization schemes proposed in the technical literature (referenced later in the chapter) to be sorted out.

BACKGROUND

Now, even if we insist on concepts, our presentation cannot totally escape from the fact that multistage stochastic programming uses optimization techniques from mathematical programming, and can harness advances in the field of optimization.

To describe what a mathematical program is, simply say that there is a function F, called the objective function, that assigns to $x \in X$ a real-valued cost $F(x)$, that there exists a subset C of X, called the feasibility set, describing admissible points x (by functional relations, not by enumeration), and that the program formulates our goal of computing the minimal value of F on C, written $\min_C F$, and a solution $x^* \in C$ attaining that optimal value, that is, $F(x^*) = \min_C F$. Note that the set of points $x \in C$ such that $F(x) = \min_C F$, called the optimal solution set and written $\operatorname{argmin}_C F$, need not be a singleton. Obviously, many problems can be formulated in that way, and what makes the interest of optimization theory is the clarification of the conditions on F and C that make a minimization problem well-posed ($\min_C F$ finite and attained) and efficiently solvable. For instance, in the chapter, we speak of convex optimization problems. To describe this class, imagine a point $\bar{x} \in C$, and assume that for each $x \in C$ in a neighborhood of $\bar{x}$, we have $F(x) \geq F(\bar{x})$. The class of convex problems is a class for which any such $\bar{x}$ belongs to the optimal solution set $\operatorname{argmin}_C F$. In particular, the minimization of F over C with F an affine function of $x \in \mathbb{R}^n$ (meaning that F has values $F(x) = \sum_{i=1}^{n} a_i x_i + a_0$) and $C = \{x : g_i(x) \leq 0, h_j(x) = 0 \text{ for } i \in I, j \in J\}$ for some index sets I, J and affine functions g_i, h_j, turns out to be a convex problem (linear

programming) for which huge instances — in terms of the dimension of x and the cardinality of I, J — can be solved. Typically, formulation tricks are used to compensate the structural limitations on F, C by an augmentation of the dimension of x and the introduction of new constraints $g_i(x) \leq 0$, $h_j(x) = 0$. For example, minimizing the piecewise linear function $f(x) = \max\{a_i x + b_i : i \in I\}$ defined on $x \in \mathbb{R}$, with $I = \{1, \ldots, m\}$ and $a_i, b_i \in \mathbb{R}$, is the same as minimizing the linear function $F(x, t) = t$ over the set $C = \{(x, t) \in \mathbb{R} \times \mathbb{R} : a_i x + b_i - t \leq 0, i \in I\}$. The trick can be particularized to $f(x) = |x| = \max\{x, -x\}$.

For more on applied convex optimization, we refer to Boyd and Vandenberghe (2004). But if the reader is ready to accept that conditions on F and C form well-characterized classes of problems, and that through some modeling effort one is often able to formulate interesting problems as an instance of one of those classes, then it is possible to elude a full description of those conditions.

Stochastic programming (Dantzig, 1955) is particular from the point of view of approximation and numerical optimization in that it involves a representation of the objective F by an integral (as soon as F stands for an expected cost under a continuous probability distribution), a large, possibly infinite number of dimensions for x, and a large, possibly infinite number of constraints for defining the feasibility set C. In practice, one has to work with approximations F', C', and be content with an approximate solution $x' \in \operatorname{argmin}_{C'} F'$. Multistage stochastic programming (the extension of stochastic programming to sequential decision making) is challenging in that small imbalances in the approximation can be amplified from stage to stage, and that x' may be lying in a space of dimension considerably smaller than the initial space for x. Special conditions might be required for ensuring the compatibility of an approximate solution x' with the initial requirement $x \in C$.

One of the main messages of the chapter is that it is actually possible to make use of supervised learning techniques (Hastie, Tibshirani, &

Friedman, 2009) to lift x' to a full-dimensional approximate solution $\tilde{x} \in C$, and then use an estimate of the value $F(\tilde{x})$ as a feedback signal on the quality of the approximation of F, C by F', C'.

The computational efficiency of this lifting procedure based on supervised learning allows us to compare reliably many approximations of F and C, and therefore to sort out empirically, for a given problem or class of problems at hand, the candidate rules that are actually relevant for building better approximations. This new methodology for guiding the development of discretization procedures for multistage stochastic programming is exposed in the present chapter.

We recall that supervised learning aims at generalizing a finite set of examples of input-output pairs, sampled from an unknown but fixed distribution, to a mapping that predicts the output corresponding to a new input. This can be viewed as the problem of finding parameters maximizing the likelihood of the observed pairs (if the mapping has a parametric form); alternatively this can be viewed as the problem of selecting, from a hypothesis space of controlled complexity, the hypothesis that minimizes the expectation of the discrepancy between true outputs and predictions, measured by a certain loss function. The complexity of the hypothesis space is determined by comparing the performance of learned predictors on unseen input samples. Common methods for tackling the supervised learning problem include: neural networks (Hinton, Osindero, & Teh, 2006), support vector machines (Steinwart & Christman, 2008), Gaussian processes (Rasmussen & Williams, 2006), and decision trees (Breiman, Friedman, Stone, & Olshen, 1984; Geurts, Ernst, & Wehenkel, 2006). A method may be preferable to another depending on how easily one can incorporate prior knowledge in the learning algorithm, as this can make the difference between rich or poor generalization abilities.

Note that supervised learning is integrated to many approaches for tackling the reinforcement learning problem (Chapter 4 of this book). The literature on this aspect is large: see, for instance, Lagoudakis and Parr (2003); Bagnell, Kakade, Ng, and Schneider (2004); Ernst, Geurts, and Wehenkel (2005); Langford and Zadrozny (2005); Munos and Szepesvári (2008).

Organization of the Chapter

The chapter is organized as follows. We begin by presenting the multistage stochastic programming framework, the discretization techniques, and the considerations on numerical optimization methods that have an influence on the way problems are modeled. Then, we compare the approach to Markov Decision Processes, discuss the curse of dimensionality, and put in perspective simpler decision making models based on numerical optimization, such as two-stage stochastic programming with recourse or Model Predictive Control. Next, we explain the issues posed by the dominant approximation/discretization approach for solving multistage programs (which is suitable for handling both discrete and continuous random variables). A section is dedicated to the proposed extension of the multistage stochastic programming framework by techniques from machine learning. The proposal is followed by an extensive case study, showing how the proposed approach can be implemented in practice, and in particular how it allows to infer guidelines for building better approximations of a particular problem at hand. The chapter is complemented by a discussion of issues arising from the choice of certain objective functions that can lead to inconsistent sequences of decisions, in a sense that we will make precise. The conclusion indicates some avenues for future research.

THE DECISION MODEL

This section describes the multistage stochastic programming approach to sequential decision making under uncertainty, starting from elementary considerations. The reader may also want to take a look at the example at the end of this section (and to the few lines of MATLAB code that implement it).

From Nominal Plans to Decision Processes

In their first attempt towards planning under uncertainty, decision makers often set up a course of actions, or *nominal plan* (reference plan), deemed to be robust to uncertainties in some sense, or to be a wise bet on future events. Then, they apply the decisions, often deviating from the nominal plan to better take account of actual events. To further improve the plan, decision makers are then led to consider (i) in which parts of the plan flexibility in the decisions may help to better fulfill the objectives, and (ii) whether the process by which they make themselves (or the system) "ready to react" impacts the initial decisions of the plan and the overall objectives. If the answer to (ii) is positive, then it becomes valuable to cast the decision problem as a sequential decision making problem, even if the net added value of doing so (benefits minus increased complexity) is unknown at this stage. During the planning process, the adaptations (or *recourse decisions*) that may be needed are clarified, their influence on prior decisions is quantified. The notion of nominal plan is replaced by the notion of *decision process*, defined as a course of actions driven by observable events. As distinct outcomes have usually antagonist effects on ideal prior decisions, it becomes crucial to determine which outcomes should be considered, and what importance weights should be put on these outcomes, in the perspective of selecting decisions under uncertainty that are not regretted too much after the dissipation of the uncertainty by the course of real-life events.

Incorporating Probabilistic Reasoning

In the *robust optimization* approach to decision making under uncertainty, decision makers are concerned by worst-case outcomes. Describing the uncertainty is then essentially reduced to drawing the frontier between events that should be considered and events that should be excluded from consideration. In that context, outcomes under consideration form the *uncertainty set*, and decision making becomes a game against some hostile opponent that selects the worst outcome from the uncertainty set. The reader will find in Ben-Tal, El Ghaoui, and Nemirovski (2009) arguments in favor of robust approaches.

In a *stochastic programming* approach, decision makers use a softer frontier between possible outcomes, by assigning weights to outcomes and optimizing some aggregated measure of performance that takes into account all these possible outcomes. In that context, the weights are often interpreted as a probability measure over the events, and a typical way of aggregating the events is to consider the expected performance under that probability measure.

Furthermore, interpreting weights as probabilities allows *reasoning under uncertainty*. Essentially, probability distributions are conditioned on observations, and Bayes' rule from probability theory (Chapter 2 of this book) quantifies how decision makers' initial beliefs about the likelihood of future events — be it from historical data or from bets — should be updated on the basis of new observations.

Technically, it turns out that the optimization of a decision process contingent to future events is more tractable (read: suitable to large-scale operations) when the "reasoning under uncertainty" part can be decoupled from the optimization process itself. Such a decoupling occurs in particular when the probability distributions describing future events are not influenced in any way by the decisions selected by the agent, that is, when the uncertainty is exogenous to the decision process. Examples of applications where the uncertainty can be treated as an exogenous process include capacity planning (especially in the gas and electricity industries), and asset and liability management. In both case, historical data allows to calibrate a model for the exogenous process.

The Elements of the General Decision Model

We are now in a position to describe the general decision model used throughout the chapter, and introduce some notations. The model is made of the following elements.

1. A sequence of random variables $\xi_1, \xi_2, \ldots,$ ξ_T defined on a probability space (Ω, B, P). For a rigorous definition of the probability space, see e.g. Billingsley (1995). We simply recall that for a real-valued random variable ξ_t, interpreted, in the context of the rigorous definition of the probability space, as a B-measurable mapping from Ω to R with values $\xi_t(\omega)$, the probability that $\xi_t \leq v$, written $P\{\xi_t \leq v\}$, is the measure under P of the set $\{\omega \in \Omega: \xi_t(\omega) \leq v\} \in B$. One can write $P(\xi_t \leq v)$ for $P\{\xi_t \leq v\}$ when the measure P is clear from the context. If $\xi_1, \ldots, \xi_T$ are real-valued random variables, the function of $(v_1, \ldots, v_T)$ with values $P\{\xi_1 \leq v_1, \ldots, \xi_T \leq v_T\}$ is the joint distribution function of $\xi_1, \ldots, \xi_T$. The smallest closed set Ξ in R^T such that $P\{(\xi_1, \ldots, \xi_T) \in \Xi\} = 1$ is the support of measure P of $(\xi_1, \ldots, \xi_T)$, also called the support of the joint distribution. If the random variables are vector-valued, the joint distribution function can be defined by breaking the random variables into their scalar components. For simplicity, we may assume that the random variables have a joint density (with respect the Lebesgue measure for continuous random variables, or with respect to the counting measure for discrete random variables), written $P(\xi_1, \ldots, \xi_T)$ by a slight abuse of notation, or $p(\xi_1, \ldots, \xi_T)$ if the measure P can be understood from the context. As several approximations to P are introduced in the sequel and compared to the

exact measure P, we always stress the appropriate probability measure in the notation.

The random variables represent the uncertainty in the decision problem, and their possible realizations (represented by the support of measure P) are the possible observations to which the decision maker will react. The probability measure P serves to quantify the prior beliefs about the uncertainty. There is no restriction on the structure of the random variables; in particular, the random variables may be dependent. When the realization of $\xi_1,$ $\ldots, \xi_{t-1}$ is known, there is a residual uncertainty represented by the random variables $\xi_t, \ldots, \xi_T$, the distribution of which in now conditioned on the realization of $\xi_1, \ldots, \xi_{t-1}$.

For example, the evolution of the price of resources over a finite time horizon T can be represented, in a discrete-time model, by a random process $\xi_1, \ldots, \xi_T$, with the dynamics of the process inferred from historical data.

2. A sequence of decisions $u_1, u_2, \ldots, u_T$ defining the decision process for the problem. Some models also use a decision u_{T+1}. We will assume that u_2 is valued in a Euclidian space R^m (the space dimension m, corresponding to a number of scalar decisions, could vary with the index t, but we will not stress that in the notation).

For example, a decision u_t could represent quantities of resources bought at time t.

3. A convention specifying when decisions should actually be taken and when the realizations of the random variables are actually revealed. This means that if ξ_{t-1} is observed before taking a decision u_t, we can actually adapt u_t to the realization of ξ_{t-1}. To this end, we identify *decision stages*: see Table 1. A row of the table is read as follows: at decision stage $t > 1$, the decisions $u_1, \ldots, u_{t-1}$ are already implemented (no modification is possible), the realization of the random variables $\xi_1, \ldots, \xi_{t-1}$ is known, the realization of the random variables $\xi_t, \ldots, \xi_T$ is still unknown but a density $P(\xi_t, \ldots, \xi_T \mid \xi_1, \ldots, \xi_{t-1})$ conditioned on the realized value of $\xi_1, \ldots, \xi_{t-1}$ is available, and the current decision to take concerns the value of u_t. Once such a con-

Table 1. Decision stages, setting the order of observations and decisions

Stage	Available information for taking decisions			Decision
	Prior decisions	Observed outcomes	Residual uncertainty	
1	none	none	$P(\xi_1,...,\xi_T)$	u_1
2	u_1	ξ_1	$P(\xi_2,...,\xi_T|\xi_1)$	u_2
3	u_1, u_2	ξ_1, ξ_2	$P(\xi_3,...,\xi_T|\xi_1,\xi_2)$	u_3
...				...
T	$u_1,...,u_{T-1}$	$\xi_1,...,\xi_{T-1}$	$P(\xi_T|\xi_1,...,\xi_{T-1})$	u_T
optional:				
$T+1$	$u_1,...,u_T$	$\xi_1,...,\xi_T$	none	(u_{T+1})

vention holds, we need not stress in the notation the difference between random variables ξ_t and their realized value, or decisions as functions of uncertain events and the actual value for these decisions: the correct interpretation is clear from the context of the current decision stage.

The adaptation of a decision u_t to prior observations $\xi_1, ..., \xi_{t-1}$ will always be made in a deterministic fashion, in the sense that u_t is uniquely determined by the value of $(\xi_1, ..., \xi_{t-1})$.

A sequential decision making problem has more than two decision stages inasmuch as the realizations of the random variables are not revealed simultaneously: the choice of the decisions taken between successive observations has to take into account some residual uncertainty on future observations. If the realization of several random variables is revealed before actually taking a decision, then the corresponding random variables should be merged into a single random vector; if several decisions are taken without intermediary observations, then the corresponding decisions should be merged into a single decision vector. This is how a problem concerning several time periods could actually be a two-stage stochastic program, involving two large decision vectors u_1 (first-stage decision, constant), u_2 (recourse decision, adapted to the observation of ξ_1). What is called a *decision* in a stochastic programming model may thus actually correspond to several

actions implemented over a certain number of discrete time periods.

4. A sequence of feasibility sets $U_1, ..., U_T$ describing which decisions $u_1, ..., u_T$ are admissible. When $u_t \in U_t$, one says that u_t is feasible. The feasibility sets $U_2, ..., U_T$ may depend, in a deterministic fashion, on available observations and prior decisions. Thus, following Table 1, U_t may depend on $\xi_1, u_1, \xi_2, u_2, ..., \xi_{t-1}$ in a deterministic fashion. Note that prior decisions are uniquely determined by prior observations, but for convenience we keep track of prior decisions to parameterize the feasibility sets.

An important role of the feasibility sets is to model how decisions are affected by prior decisions and prior events. In particular, a situation with no possible recourse decision (U_t empty at stage t, meaning that no feasible decision $u_t \in U_t$ exists) is interpreted as a catastrophic situation to be avoided at any cost.

We will always assume that the planning agent knows the set-valued mapping from the random variables $\xi_1, ..., \xi_{t-1}$ and the decisions $u_1, ..., u_{t-1}$ to the set U_t of feasible decisions u_t.

We will also assume that the feasibility sets are such that a feasible sequence of decisions $u_1 \in U_1$, ..., $u_T \in U_T$ exists for all possible joint realizations of $\xi_1, ..., \xi_T$. In particular, the fixed set U_1 must be nonempty. A feasibility set U_t parameterized only by variables in a subset of $\{\xi_1, ..., \xi_{t-1}\}$ must be nonempty for any possible joint realization of those variables. A feasibility set U_t also parameterized by variables in a subset of $\{u_1, ..., u_{t-1}\}$ must be implicitly taken into account in the definition of the prior feasibility sets, so as to prevent immediately a decision maker from taking a decision at some earlier stage that could lead to a situation at stage t with no possible recourse decision (U_t empty), be it for all possible joint realizations of the subset of $\{\xi_1, ..., \xi_{t-1}\}$ on which U_t depends, or for some possible joint realization only. These implicit requirements will affect in particular the definition of U_1.

For a technical example, interpret $a \pm b$ for any vectors $a, b \in \mathbb{R}^q$ as a shorthand for the componentwise inequalities $a_i \geq b_i, i = 1, ..., q$, assume that $u_{t-1}, u_t \in \mathbb{R}^m$, and take $U_t = \{u_t \in \mathbb{R}^m: u_t \pm 0, A_{t-1}u_{t-1} + B_t u_t = h_t(\xi_{t-1})\}$ with $A_{t-1}, B_t \in \mathbb{R}^{q \times m}$ fixed matrices, and h_t an affine function of ξ_{t-1} with values in $\mathbb{R}^q$. If B_t is such that $\{B_t u_t : u_t \pm 0\} = \mathbb{R}^q$, meaning that for any $v \in \mathbb{R}^q$, there exists some $u_t \pm 0$ with $B_t u_t = v$, then this is true in particular for $v = h_t(\xi_{t-1}) - A_{t-1}u_{t-1}$, so that U_t is never empty. More details on this kind of sufficient conditions in the stochastic programming literature can be found in Wets (1974).

One can use feasibility sets to represent, for instance, the dynamics of resource inflows and outflows, assumed to be known by the planning agent.

5. A performance measure, summarizing the overall objectives of the decision maker, that should be optimized. It is assumed that the decision maker knows the performance measure. In this chapter, we write the performance measure as the expectation of a function f that assigns some scalar value to each realization of $\xi_1, ..., \xi_T$ and $u_1, ..., u_T$, and assume that the expectation is well-defined.

For example, one could take for f a sum of scalar products $\sum_{t=1}^{T} c_t \cdot u_t$, where c_1 is fixed and where c_t depends affinely on $\xi_1, ..., \xi_{t-1}$. The function f would represent a sum of instantaneous costs over the planning horizon. The decision maker would be assumed to know the vector-valued mapping from the random variables $\xi_1, ..., \xi_{t-1}$ to the vector c_t, for each t.

Besides the expectation, more sophisticated ways to aggregate the distribution of f into a single measure of performance have been investigated (Pflug & Römisch, 2007). An important element considered in the choice of the performance measure is the tractability of the resulting optimization problem.

The planning problem is then formalized as a mathematical programming problem. The formulation relies on a particular representation of the random process $\xi_1, ..., \xi_T$ in connection with the decision stages, commonly referred to as the *scenario tree*.

The Notion of Scenario Tree

Let us call *scenario* an outcome of the random process $\xi_1, ..., \xi_T$. A *scenario tree* is an explicit representation of the branching process induced by the gradual observation of $\xi_1, ..., \xi_T$, under the assumption that the random variables have a finite discrete support. It is built as follows. A *root node* is associated to the first decision stage and to the initial absence of observations. To the root node are connected children nodes associated to stage 2, one child node for each possible outcome of the random variable ξ_1. Then, to each node of stage 2 are connected children nodes associated to stage 3, one for each outcome of ξ_2 given the observation of ξ_1 relative to the parent node. The branching process construction goes on until the last stage is reached; at this point, the outcomes associated to the nodes on the unique path from the root to a leaf define together a particular scenario, that can be associated to the leaf.

The probability distribution of the random variables is also taken into account. Probability masses are associated to the nodes of the scenario tree. The root node has probability 1, whereas children nodes are weighted by probabilities that represent the probability of the value to which

Figure 1. (From left to right) Nested partitioning of the event space Ω, starting from a trivial partition representing the absence of observations. (Rightmost) Scenario tree corresponding to the partitioning process.

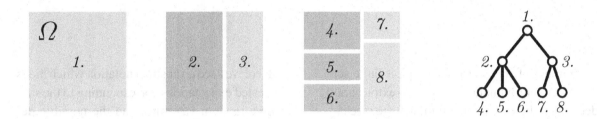

they are associated, conditioned on the value associated to their ancestor node. Multiplying the probabilities of the nodes of the path from the root to a leaf gives the probability of a scenario.

Clearly, an exact construction of the scenario tree would require an infinite number of nodes if the support of $(\xi_1, ..., \xi_T)$ is discrete but not finite. A random process involving continuous random variables cannot be represented as a scenario tree; nevertheless, the scenario tree construction turns out to be instrumental in the construction of approximations to nested continuous conditional distributions.

Branchings are essential to represent residual uncertainty beyond the first decision stage. At the planning time, the decision makers may contemplate as many hypothetical scenarios as desired, but when decisions are actually implemented, the decisions cannot depend on observations that are not yet available. We have seen that the decision model specifies, with decision stages, how the scenario actually realized will be gradually revealed. No branchings in the representation of the outcomes of the random process would mean that after conditioning on the observation of ξ_1, the outcome of $\xi_2, ..., \xi_T$ could be predicted (anticipated) exactly. Under such a representation, decisions spanning stages 2 to T would be optimized on the anticipated outcome. This would be equivalent to optimizing a nominal plan for u_2,

..., u_T that fully bets on some scenario anticipated at stage 2.

To visualize how information on the realization of the random variables becomes gradually available, it is convenient to imagine nested partitions of the event space (Figure 1): refinements of the partitions appear gradually at each decision stage in correspondence with the possible realizations of the new observations. To each subregion induced by the partitioning of the event space can be associated a constant recourse decision, as if decisions were chosen according to a piecewise constant decision policy. On Figure 1, the surface of each subregion could also represent probabilities (then by convention the initial square has a unit surface and the thin space between subregions is for visual separation only). The dynamical evolution of the partitioning can be represented by a scenario tree: the nodes of the tree corresponds to the subregions of the event space, and the edges between subregions connect a parent subregion to its refined subregions obtained by one step of the recursive partitioning process.

Ideally, a scenario tree should cover the totality of possible outcomes of a random process. But unless the support of the distribution of the random variables is finite, no scenario tree with a finite number of nodes can represent exactly the random process and the probability measure, as we already mentioned, while even if the support is finite, the number of scenarios grows exponentially with

Exhibit 1.

```
S:    minimize      E{ f (ξ, π(ξ)) }
      subject to        πₜ (ξ) ∈ Uₜ (ξ)           ∀ t,
                        π(ξ)    non-anticipative.
```

the number of stages. How to exploit finite scenario tree approximations in order to extract good decision policies for general multistage stochastic programming problems involving continuous distributions will be extensively addressed in this chapter.

The Finite Scenario-Tree Based Approximation

In the general decision model, the agent is assumed to have access to the joint probability distributions, and is able to derive from it the conditional distributions listed in Table 1. In practice, computational limitations will restrict the quality of the representation of P. Let us however reason at first at an abstract and ideal level to establish the program that an agent would solve for planning under uncertainty.

For brevity, let ξ denote $(\xi_1, ..., \xi_T)$, and let $\pi(\xi)$ denote a *decision policy* mapping realizations of ξ to realizations of the decision process $u_1, ..., u_T$. Let $\pi_t(\xi)$ denote u_t viewed as a function of ξ. To be consistent with the decision stages, the policy must be a *non-anticipative policy*, in the sense that u_t cannot depend on observations relative to subsequent stages. Equivalently one can say that π_1 must be a constant-valued function, π_2 a function of ξ_1, and in general π_t a function of ξ_1, ..., ξ_{t-1} for $t = 2,...,T$.

The planning problem can then be stated as the search for a non-anticipative policy π, restricted by the feasibility sets U_t, that minimizes an expected total cost f spanning the decision stages and determined by the scenario ξ and the decisions $\pi(\xi)$ (Exhibit 1).

Here we used an abstract notation which hides the nested expectations corresponding to the successive random variables, and the possible decomposition of the function f among the different decision stages indexed by t. It is possible to be even more general by replacing the expectation operator by a functional Φ assigning single numbers in $R \cup \{\pm\infty\}$ to distributions. We also stressed the possible dependence of U_t on $\xi_1, u_1, \xi_2, u_2, ...,$ ξ_{t-1} by writing $U_t(\xi)$.

A program more amenable to numerical optimization is obtained by representing $\pi(\cdot)$ by a set of optimization variables for each possible argument of the function. That is, for each possible outcome $\xi^k = (\xi_1^k,..., \xi_T^k)$ of ξ, one associates the optimization variables $(u_1^k,..., u_T^k)$, written u^k for brevity. The non-anticipativity of the policy can be expressed by a set of equality constraints: for the first decision stage we require $u_1^k = u_1^j$ for all k, j, and for subsequent stages $(t>1)$ we require $u_t^k = u_t^j$ for each (k,j) such that $(\xi_1^k,..., \xi_{t-1}^k) \equiv (\xi_1^j,..., \xi_{t-1}^j)$.

A finite-dimensional approximation to the program S is obtained by considering a finite number n of outcomes, and assigning to each outcome a discrete probability p^k. This yields a formulation on a scenario tree covering the scenarios ξ^k (Exhibit 2).

Once again we used a simple notation ξ^k for designating outcomes of the process ξ, which hides the fact that outcomes can share some elements according to the branching structure of the scenario tree.

Non-anticipativity constraints can also be accounted for implicitly. A partial path from the root (depth 0) to some node of depth t of the scenario tree identifies some outcome $(\xi_1^k,..., \xi_t^k)$ of $(\xi_1,$

Exhibit 2.

```
S':    minimize        ∑ᵀₖ₌₁ pᵏf (ξ ᵏ, uᵏ)
       subject to      uₜᵏ ∈ Uₜ (ξ ᵏ)        ∀ k, ∀ t,
                       u₁ᵏ = u₁ʲ             ∀ k, j ,
                       uₜᵏ = uₜʲ whenever    (ξ₁ᵏ, …,  ξₜ₋₁ᵏ) ≡ (ξ₁ʲ, …,  ξₜ₋₁ʲ) .
```

..., ξ_t). To the node can be associated the decision u_{t+1}^k, but also all decisions u_{t+1}^j such that $(\xi_1^k, \dots, \xi_t^k) \equiv (\xi_1^j, \dots, \xi_t^j)$. Those decisions are redundant and can be merged into a single decision on the tree, associated to the considered node of depth t (the reader may refer to the scenario tree of Figure 1).

The finite scenario tree approximation is needed because numerical optimization methods cannot handle directly problems like S, which cannot be specified with a finite number of optimization variables and constraints. The approximation may serve to provide an estimate of the optimal value of the original program; it may also serve to obtain an approximate first-stage decision u_1. Several aspects regarding the exploitation of scenario-tree approximations and the derivation of decisions for the subsequent stages will be further discussed in the chapter.

Finally, we point out that there are alternative numerical methods for solving stochastic programs (usually two-stage programs), based on the incorporation of the discretization procedure into the optimization algorithm itself, for instance by updating the discretization or carrying out importance sampling within the iterations of a given optimization algorithm (Norkin, Ermoliev, & Ruszczyński, 1998), or by using stochastic subgradient methods (Nemirovski, Juditsky, Lan, & Shapiro, 2009). Also, heuristics for finding policies directly have been suggested: a possible idea (akin to direct policy search procedures in Markov Decision Processes) is to optimize a combination of feasible non-anticipative basis policies $\pi^j(\xi)$ specified beforehand (Koivu & Pennanen, 2010).

Numerical Optimization of Stochastic Programs

The program formulated on the scenario tree is solved using numerical optimization techniques. In principle, it is the size, the class and the structure of the program that determine which optimization algorithm is suitable. The size depends on the number of optimization variables and the number of constraints of the program. It is therefore influenced by the number of scenarios, the planning horizon, and the dimension of the decision vectors. The class of the program depends on the range of the optimization variables (set of permitted values), the nature of the objective function, and the nature of the equality and inequality constraints that define the feasibility sets. The structure depends on the number of stages, the nature of the coupling of decisions between stages, the way random variables intervene in the objective and the constraints, and on the joint distribution of the random variables (independence assumptions or finite support assumptions can sometimes be exploited). The structure determines whether the program can be decomposed in smaller parts, and where applicable, to which extent sparsity and factorization techniques from linear algebra can alleviate the complexity of matrix operations.

Note that the history of mathematical programming has shown a large gap between the complexity theory concerning some optimization algorithms, and the performance of these algorithms on problems with real-world data. A notable example (not directly related to stochastic programming, but striking enough to be mentioned here) is the traveling salesman problem (TSP).

The TSP consists in finding a circuit of minimal cost for visiting n cities connected by roads (say that costs are proportional to road lengths). The dynamic programming approach, based on a recursive formulation of the problem, has the best known complexity bound: it is possible to find an optimal solution in time proportional to $n^2 2^n$. But in practice only small instances ($n \approx 20$) can be solved with the algorithm developed by Bellman (1962), due to the exponential growth of a list of optimal subpaths to consider. Linear programming approaches based on the simplex algorithm have an unattractive worst-case complexity, and yet such approaches have allowed to solve large instances of the problem — $n = 85900$ for the record on pla85900 obtained in 2006 — as explained in Applegate, Bixby, Chvátal, and Cook (2007).

In today's state of computer architectures and optimization technologies, multistage stochastic programs are considered numerically tractable, in the sense that numerical solutions of acceptable accuracy can be computed in acceptable time, when the formulation is convex. The covered class includes linear programs (LP) and convex quadratic programs (QP), which are similar to linear programs but have a quadratic component in their objective. A problem can be recognized to be convex if it can be written as a convex program; a program $\min_C F$ is convex if (i) the feasibility set C is convex, that is, $(1-\lambda) x + \lambda y \in C$ whenever $x, y \in C$ and $0 < \lambda < 1$ (Rockafellar, 1970, page 10); (ii) the objective function F is convex on C, that is, $F((1-\tau) x + \tau y) \leq (1-\tau) F(x) + \tau F(y)$, $0 < \tau < 1$, for every $x, y \in C$ (Rockafellar, 1970, Theorem 4.1). We refer to Nesterov (2003) for an introduction to complexity theory for convex optimization and to interior-point methods.

Integer programs (IP) and mixed-integer programs (MIP) are similar to linear programs but have integrality requirements on all (IP) or some (MIP) of their optimization variables. The research in stochastic programming for these classes is mainly focused on two-stage models: computationally-intensive methods for preprocessing pro-

grams so as to accelerate the repeated evaluation of integer recourse decisions (Schultz, Stougie, & Van der Vlerk, 1998); convex relaxations (Van der Vlerk, 2010); branch-and-cut strategies (Sen & Sherali, 2006). In large-scale applications, the modeling and numerical optimization aspects are closely integrated: see, for instance, the numerical study of Verweij et al. (2003). Solving multistage stochastic mixed-integer models is extremely challenging, but significant progress has been made recently (Escudero, 2009).

In our presentation, we focus on convex problems, and use MATLAB for generating the data structure and values of the scenario trees, and CVX for formulating and solving the resulting programs — CVX is a modeling tool: it uses a language close to the mathematical formulation of the models, leading to codes that are slower to execute but less prone to errors.

Example

To fix ideas, we illustrate the scenario tree technique on a trajectory tracking problem under uncertainty with control penalization. In the proposed example, the uncertainty is such that the exact problem can be posed on a small finite scenario tree.

Say that a random process $\xi = (\xi_1, \xi_2, \xi_3)$, representing perturbations at time $t = 1,2,3$, has 7 possible realisations (scenarios), denoted by ξ^k, $1 \leq k \leq 7$, with known probabilities p^k (Table 2).

The random process is fully represented by the scenario tree of Figure 2 (Left) — the first possible outcome is $\xi^1 = (-4, -3, 0)$ and has probability $p^1 = 0.1$. Note that the random variables ξ_1, ξ_2, ξ_3 are not mutually independent.

Assume that an agent can choose actions $v_t \in R$ at $t = 1, 2, 3$ (the notation v_t instead of u_t is justified in the sequel). The goal of the agent is the minimization of an expected sum of costs $E\{ \sum_{t=1}^{3} c_t (v_t, x_{t+1}) \mid x_1 = 0 \}$. Here $x_t \in R$ is the state of a continuous-state, discrete-time dy-

Table 2.

k	1	2	3	4	5	6	7
ξ_1^k	-4	-4	-4	3	3	3	3
ξ_2^k	-3	2	2	-3	0	0	2
ξ_3^k	0	-2	1	0	-1	2	1
p^k	0.1	0.2	0.1	0.2	0.1	0.1	0.2

Figure 2. (Left) Scenario tree representing the 7 possible scenarios for a random process $\xi = (\xi_1, \xi_2, \xi_3)$. The outcomes ξ_t^k are written in bold, and the scenario probabilities p^k are reported at the leaf nodes. (Middle) Optimal actions v_t for the agent, displayed scenario per scenario, with frames around scenarios passing by a same tree node. (Right) Visited states x_t under the optimal actions, treated as artificial decisions (see text).

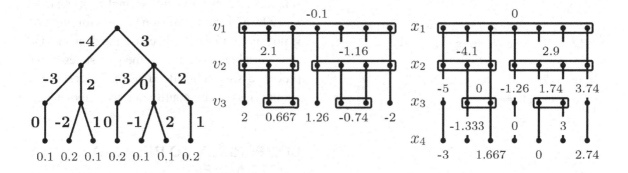

Exhibit 3.

```
Minimize       ∑_{k=1}^7 p^k [ ∑_{t=1}^3  (d_{t+1}^k + (v_t^k)²/4) ]
subject to      - d_{t+1}^k ≤ x_{t+1}^k - α_{t+1}^k ≤ d_{t+1}^k        ∀ k, t ,
                 x_1^k = 0,   x_{t+1}^k = x_t^k + v_t^k + ξ_t^k         ∀ k, t ,
                 v_1^1 = v_1^2 = v_1^3 = v_1^4 = v_1^5 = v_1^6 = v_1^7, v_2^1 = v_2^2 = v_2^3 ,    v_2^4 = v_2^5
= v_2^6 = v_2^7, v_3^2 = v_3^3 ,    v_3^5 = v_3^6 .
```

namical system, that starts from the initial state $x_1 = 0$ and follows the state transition equation $x_{t+1} = x_t + v_t + \xi_t$. Costs $c_t(v_t, x_{t+1})$, associated to the decision v_t and the transition to the state x_{t+1}, are defined by $c_t = (d_{t+1} + v_t^2/4)$ with $d_{t+1} = |x_{t+1} - \alpha_{t+1}|$ and $\alpha_2 = 2.9, \alpha_3 = 0, \alpha_4 = 0$ ($\alpha_{t=1}$: nominal trajectory, chosen arbitrarily; d_{t+1}: tracking error; $v_t^2/4$: penalization of control effort).

An optimal policy mapping observations ξ_1, ..., ξ_{t-1} to decisions v_t can be obtained by solving

the following convex quadratic program over variables $v_t^k, x_{t+1}^k, d_{t+1}^k$, where k runs from 1 to 7 and t from 1 to 3, and over x_1^k trivially set to 0 (Exhibit 3).

Here, the vector of optimization variables (v_1^k, x_1^k) plays the role of u_1^k, the vector (v_t^k, x_t^k, d_t^k) plays the role of u_t^k for $t = 2, 3$, and the vector (x_4^k, d_4^k) plays the role of u_4^k, showing that the decision process $u_1, ..., u_{T+1}$ of the general multistage stochastic programming model can in fact

Exhibit 4.

```
% problem data
xi    = [-4 -4 -4  3  3  3  3;...
         -3  2  2 -3  0  0  2;...
          0 -2  1  0 -1  2  1];
p     = [.1.2.1.2.1.1.2];
a     = [2.9 0 0]';
x1    = 0;  n  =  7;   T  =  3;
% call cvx toolbox
cvx_begin
 variables x(T+1,n) d(T,n) v(T,n)
 minimize(sum(sum(d*diag(p)))...
    + sum(sum((v.^2)*diag(p)))/4);
 subject to
  -d <= x(2:T+1,:)-a(:,ones(1,n));
  x(2:T+1,:)-a(:,ones(1,n)) <=  d;
  x(1,:)       == x1;
  for t=1:T
    x(t+1,:) ==...
       x(t,:)+v(t,:)+xi(t,:);
  end
  v(1,2:n)   ==   v(1,1);
  v(1,2:n)   ==   v(1,1);
  v(2,2:3)   ==   v(2,1);
  v(2,5:n)   ==   v(2,4);
  v(3,3)     ==   v(3,2);
  v(3,6)     ==   v(3,5);
cvx_end
% display solution
cvx_optval, v, x
```

include state variables and more generally any element that serves to evaluate costs conveniently.

The following code allows to formulate and solve the program using MATLAB and CVX. It is almost a direct transcription of the program formulation, with variables and constraints defined in matrix form (column indices are relative to scenarios). Note that CVX replicates scalars if needed in componentwise constraints (Exhibit 4).

The code should return the optimal objective value +7.3148. The corresponding optimal solution is depicted on Figure 2. In the next section, we will discuss the differences between stochastic programming approaches and Markov Decision Processes. In this example, observe that the final solution can be recast as mappings $\tilde{\pi}_t$ from x_t to v_t, namely, $\tilde{\pi}_1 (0) = -0.1$, $\tilde{\pi}_2 (-4.1) = 2.1$, $\tilde{\pi}_2 (2.9) = -1.16$, $\tilde{\pi}_3 (-5) = 2$, $\tilde{\pi}_3 (-1.26) = 1.26$, $\tilde{\pi}_3 (0) = 0.667$, $\tilde{\pi}_3 (1.74) = -0.74$, $\tilde{\pi}_3 (3.74) = -2$. Hence in this case, the convenient assumption of an agent able to observe ξ_t instead of the system state x_t is not a fundamental restriction. Observe also that finding in this example the optimal mapping from x_t to v_t by a Markov Decision Process formulation is not straightforward, because the decision and state variables — to which the past states of the process ξ_t should be added, as the process is not memoryless — are continuous and unbounded.

COMPARISON TO RELATED APPROACHES

This section discusses several modeling and algorithmic complexity issues raised by the multistage stochastic programming framework and scenario-tree based decision making.

The Exogenous Nature of the Random Process

A frequent assumption made in the stochastic programming framework is that decision makers do not influence by their decisions the realization of the random process representing the uncertainty. The random process is said to be an *exogenous process*. This allows to simulate, select and organize in advance possible realizations of the exogenous process, before any observation is actually made, and then optimize jointly (by opposition to individually for each scenario) the decisions contingent to the possible realizations.

The need to decouple the description of uncertainties and the optimization of decisions might appear at first as a strong limitation on the situations that can be modeled and treated by stochastic programming techniques. This impression is in part justified for a large family of problems of control theory in which the uncertainty is identified to some zero-mean noise perturbing the observations or the dynamics of the system, or when the uncertainty is understood as the uncertainty on the value of system parameter. However, in another large family of sequential decision making problems under uncertainty, major sources of uncertainty are precisely the ones that are the less influenced by the behavior of the decision makers (weather, interest rates evolution, accidental pollution, new regulations, for example). We also note that random processes strongly influenced by the behavior of the decision makers can sometimes be handled by incorporating them to the initial decision process and treating them as a virtual decision process.

A probabilistic reasoning based on a subset of possible scenarios could easily be tricked by an adversarial random process that would exploit one of the scenarios discarded during the planning process. In many practical problems however, the environment is not totally adversarial. In situations where the environment is mildly adversarial, it is often possible to choose measures of performances that are more robust to bad outcomes, and that can still be optimized in a tractable way. We will come back to issues posed by risk-sensitive models for sequential decision making at the end of the chapter.

Finally, it is easier in terms of sample complexity to learn a model (find model parameters from finite data sets) for an exogenous process than for an endogenous process. Learning a model for an exogenous process is possible from observations of the process, such as time series, whereas learning a model for an endogenous process forces us to be able to simulate possible state transitions for every possible action, or at least to have at one's disposal a fairly exhaustive data set relating actions to state transitions.

The scheduling of electric power units (Carpentier, Cohen, & Culioli, 1996; Sen, Yu, & Genc, 2006) and the management of cash flows, assets and liabilities (Dempster et al., 2008) are example of sequential decision making problems with exogenous processes following sophisticated models.

Comparison to Markov Decision Processes

In Markov Decision Processes (MDP), the decision maker seeks to optimize a performance criterion decomposed into a sum of instantaneous rewards. The information state of the decision maker at time t coincides with the state x_t of a dynamical system For simplicity, we do not consider in this discussion partial observability (POMDP) or risk-sensitivity, for which the system state need not be the information state of the agent. Optimal decision policies are often found by a reasoning based on the dynamic programming principle, to which is essential the notion of state as a sufficient statistic for representing the complete history of the system's evolution and agent's beliefs.

Multistage stochastic programming problems could be viewed as a subclass of finite-horizon Markov Decision Processes, by identifying the growing history of observations $\xi_1, ..., \xi_{t-1}$ to the agent's state. However, the mathematical assumptions under the MDP and the stochastic programming formulations are in fact quite different. Complexity results suggest that the algorithmic resolution of MDPs is efficient when the decision space is finite and small (Littman, Dean, & Kaelbling, 1995; Kearns, Mansour, & Ng, 2002), while for the scenario-tree based stochastic programming framework, the resolution is efficient when the optimization problem is convex — in particular the decision space is continuous — and the number of decision stages is small (Shapiro, 2006).

One of the main appeals of stochastic programming techniques is their ability to deal efficiently with high-dimensional continuous decision spaces structured by numerous constraints, and with sophisticated, non-memoryless random processes. At the same time, if stochastic programming models have traditionally been used for optimizing long-term decisions that are implemented once and have lasting consequences, for example in network capacity planning \shortcite{sen94}, they are now increasingly used in the context of near-optimal control strategies that Bertsekas (2005) calls *limited-lookahead* strategies. In this usage, at each decision stage an updated model over the remaining planning horizon is rebuilt and optimized on the fly, from which only the first-stage decisions are actually implemented. Indeed, when a stochastic program is solved on a scenario tree, the initial search for a decision policy degenerates into the search for sequences of decisions relative to the scenarios covered by the tree. The first-stage decision does not depend on observations and can thus always be implemented on any new scenario, whereas the recourse decisions relative to any particular scenario in the tree could be infeasible on a new scenario, especially if the feasibility sets depend on the random process.

The Curse of Dimensionality

The *curse of dimensionality* is an algorithmic-complexity phenomenon by which computing optimal policies on higher dimensional input spaces requires an exponential growth of computational resources, leading to intractable problem formulations. In dynamic programming, the input space is the state space or a reduced parametrization of it. In practice the curse of dimensionality limits attempts to cover inputs to spaces embedded in R^d with d at most equal to 5~10.

Approximate Dynamic Programming methods (ADP) (Bertsekas, 2005) and Reinforcement Learning approaches (RL) (Sutton & Barto, 1998)

help to mitigate the curse of dimensionality, for instance by attempting to cover only the regions of the input space that are actually reached under an optimal policy. An exploratory component may be added to the original dynamic programming solution strategy so as to discover the interesting regions of the input space by testing decisions. Those approaches work well in several cases:

- The structure of a near-optimal policy is known a priori. For example, policy search methods work well when a near-optimal policy can be described by a small number of parameters. Value-function based methods work well when there is a finite and rather small set of actions, known a priori, that are the elementary building blocks of a near-optimal policy, and are used to drive the exploratory phase. Such situations are often exploited in robotics. For instance, the fundamental building blocks of near-optimal policies can be reduced to a limited number of motor primitives optimized separately.

- The structure of the optimization problem is such that the promising decisions and input space regions identifiable early in the exploratory phase correspond to those that are actually relevant for a near-optimal policy. This ensures the practical success of optimistic exploratory strategies, that refine decisions within regions identified as promising. This situation typically arises in problems where the stochastic part comes from a noise process that slightly disturbs the dynamics of the system.

Stochastic programming algorithms do not rely on the covering of the state space of dynamic programming. Instead, they rely on the covering of the random exogenous process, which needs not correspond to the complete state space (see how the auxiliary state x_t is treated in the example of the previous section). The complement of the state space and the decision space are "explored" during the optimization procedure itself. The success of the approach will thus depend on the tractability of the joint optimization in those spaces, and not on insights on the structure of near-optimal policies.

In multistage stochastic programming approaches, the curse of dimensionality is present when the number of decision stages increases, and in face of high-dimensional exogenous processes. Therefore, methods that one could call, by analogy to ADP, *approximate stochastic programming methods*, will attempt to cover only the realizations of the exogenous random process that are truly needed to obtain near-optimal decisions. These methods work with a number of scenarios that does not grow exponentially with the dimension of the exogenous process and the number of stages.

The Value of Multistage Stochastic Programming

Due to the curse of dimensionality, multistage stochastic programming is in competition with more tractable decision models. At the same time it provides a unifying framework between several simplified decision making paradigms, that we now describe.

Reduction to Model Predictive Control

A radical simplification consists in discarding the detailed probabilistic information on the uncertainty, taking a nominal scenario, and optimizing decisions on the nominal scenario. As the common practice for defining a nominal scenario is to replace random variables by their expectation, the resulting problem on the nominal scenario is called the *expected value problem*, the solution of which constitutes a nominal plan. Even if the nominal plan could be used as an {\em open-loop decision policy}, that is, implemented over the complete planning horizon, decision makers will usually want to recompute the plan at the next

decision stage by solving an updated expected value problem on a new nominal scenario that incorporates the observations. In the control community, the approach is known as Model Predictive Control (MPC). We refer the reader with a background in reinforcement learning to Ernst, Glavic, Capitanescu, and Wehenkel (2009) for discussions on this area of research.

An indicator of the value of multistage programming decisions over model predictive control decisions is given by the *value of the stochastic solution* (VSS). To make the notion precise, let us define successively:

- V^*, the optimal value of the multistage stochastic program $\min_\pi E\{ f(\xi, \pi(\xi)) \}$. For notational simplicity, we adopt the convention that $f(\xi, \pi(\xi)) = \infty$ if the policy π is anticipative or yields infeasible decisions.

- $\zeta = (\zeta_1, \ldots, \zeta_T)$, the nominal scenario.

- u^ζ, the optimal solution to the expected value problem $\min_u f(\zeta, u)$. Note that the optimization is over a single fixed sequence of feasible decisions; the problem data is determined by ζ.

- u_1^ζ, the first-stage decision of u^ζ.

- V^ζ, the optimal value of the multistage stochastic program $\min_\pi E\{ f(\xi, \pi(\xi)) \}$ subject to the additional constraint $\pi_1(\xi) = u_1^\zeta$ for all ξ. If by a slight abuse of notation, we write π_1, viewed as an optimization variable, for the value of the constant-valued function π_1, then the additional constraint is simply $\pi_1 = u_1^\zeta$. By definition, V^ζ is the value of a policy implementing the first decision from the expected value problem, and then selecting optimal recourse decisions for the subsequent decision stages. The recourse decisions differ in general from those that would be selected by a policy optimal for the original multistage program.

The VSS is then defined as the difference $V^\xi - V^* \geq 0$. For maximization problems, it would be defined by $V^* - V^\xi \geq 0$. Birge and Louveaux (1997) describe special cases (with two decision stages, and restrictions on the way randomness affects problem data) for which it is possible to compute bounds on the VSS. They also come to the conclusion, from their survey of works studying the VSS, that there is no rule that can predict a priori whether the VSS is low or high for a given problem instance — for example increasing the variance of random variables may increase or decrease the VSS.

Reduction to Two-Stage Stochastic Programming

A less radical simplification consists in discarding the distinction between recourse stages, keeping in the model a first stage (associated to full uncertainty) and a second stage (associated to the full knowledge of the realized scenario). A multistage model degenerates into a two-stage model when the scenario tree has branchings only at one stage (we have already described how random variables and decisions should be merged if observations and decisions are not intertwined). The situation arises for instance when scenarios are sampled over the full horizon independently: the tree has then branchings only at the root. Huang and Ahmed (2009) define the *value of multistage programming* (VMS) as the difference of the optimal values of the multistage model versus the two-stage model. The authors establish bounds on the VMS and describe an application (in the semiconductor industry) where the VMS is high. Note however that a generalization of the notion of VSS would rather quantify how multistage decisions outperform two-stage decisions when those two-stage decisions are implemented with model rebuilding at each stage, in the manner of the Model Predictive Control scheme.

Reduction to Heuristics based on Parametric Optimization

As an intermediate simplification between the expected value problem and the reduction to a two-stage model, it is possible to optimize sequences of decisions separately on each scenario. The decision maker can then use some averaging, consensus or selection strategy to implement a first-stage decision inferred from the so-obtained ensemble of first-stage decisions. Here again, the model should be rebuilt with updated scenarios at each decision stage.

The problem of computing optimal decisions separately for each scenario is known as the *distribution problem*. The problem appears in the definition of the *expected value of perfect information* (EVPI), which quantifies the additional value that a decision maker could reach in expectation if he or she were able to predict the future. To make the notion precise, let V^* denote as before the optimal value of the multistage stochastic program $\min_\pi \mathrm{E}\{ f(\xi, \pi(\xi)) \}$ over non-anticipative policies π; let $V(\xi)$ denote the optimal value of the deterministic program $\min_u f(\xi, u)$; and let V^A be the expected value of $V(\xi)$, according to the distribution of ξ. Observe that V^A is also the optimal value of the program $\min \pi^A \mathrm{E}\{ f(\xi, \pi^A(\xi)) \}$ over anticipative policies π^A, the optimization of which is now decomposable among scenario subproblems. The EVPI is then defined as the difference $V^* - V^A \geq 0$. For maximization problems, it is defined by $V^A - V^* \geq 0$. Intuitively, the EVPI is high when having to delay adaptations to final outcomes due to a lack of information results in high costs.

The EVPI is usually interpreted as the price a decision maker would be ready to pay to know the future (Raiffa & Schlaifer, 1961; Birge, 1992). The EVPI also indicates how valuable the dependence of decision sequences is on the particular scenario they are optimized over. Mercier and Van Hentenryck (2007) show on an example with low EVPI how a strategy based on a particular aggregation of decisions optimized separately on deterministic scenarios can be arbitrarily bad. Thus even if the EVPI is low, heuristics based on the decisions of anticipative policies can perform poorly.

This does not mean that the approach cannot perform well in practice. Van Hentenryck and Bent (2006) have studied and refined various aggregation and regret-minimization strategies on a series of stochastic combinatorial problems already hard to solve on a single scenario, as well as schemes that build a bank of pre-computed reference solutions and then adapt them online to accelerate the optimization on new scenarios. They show that their strategies perform well on vehicle routing applications.

Remark on the Progressive Hedging Algorithm

The progressive hedging algorithm (PHA) of Rockafellar and Wets (1991) is a decomposition method that computes the solution to a multistage stochastic program on a scenario tree by solving repeatedly separate subproblems on the scenarios covered by the tree. First-stage decisions and other decisions coupled by non-anticipativity constraints are obtained by aggregating the decisions of the concerned scenarios, in the spirit of the heuristics based on the distribution problem presented above. The algorithm modifies the scenario subproblems at each iteration to make the decisions coupled by non-anticipativity constraints converge towards a common and optimal decision.

As the iterations are carried out, first-stage decisions evolve from decisions hedged by the aggregation strategy to decisions hedged by the multiple recourse decisions computed on the scenario tree. Therefore, the progressive hedging algorithm shows that there can be a smooth conceptual transition between the decision model based on the distribution problem and the decision model based on the multistage stochastic programming problem.

Example

We illustrate the computation of the VSS and the EVPI on an artificial multistage problem, with numerical parameters chosen in such a way that the full multistage model is valuable. By valuable we mean that the presented simplified decision-making schemes will output first-stage decisions that are suboptimal. If those decisions were implemented, and subsequently the best possible recourse decisions were applied, the value of the objective over the full horizon would be significantly suboptimal.

Let w_1, w_2, w_3 be mutually independent random variables uniformly distributed on $\{+1, -1\}$. Let $\xi = (\xi_1, \xi_2, \xi_3)$ be a random walk such that $\xi_1 = w_1$, $\xi_2 = w_1 + w_2$, $\xi_3 = w_1 + w_2 + w_3$. Let the 8 equiprobable outcomes of ξ form a scenario tree and induce non-anticipativity constraints (the tree is a binary tree of depth 3). Consider the decision process $u = (u_1, u_2, u_3)$ with $u_2 \in R$ and $u_t = (u_{t1}, u_{t2}) \in R^2$ for $t = 1, 3$. Then consider the multistage stochastic program (Exhibit 5).

The non-anticipativity constraints C1, C2, C3, which are convenient to state the problem, indicate in practice the redundant optimization variables that can be eliminated.

- The optimal value of the multistage stochastic program is $V^* = 0.35$ with optimal first-stage decision $u_1^* = (1, 0)$.

- The *expected value problem* for the mean scenario $\zeta = (0,0,0)$ is obtained by setting momentarily $\xi^k = \zeta$ for all k and adding the constraints C2': $u_2^k = u_2^1$ for all k and C2': $u_3^k = u_3^1$ for all k. Its optimal value is 1 with first-stage decision $u_1^\zeta = (0,0)$. When equality constraints are made implicit the problem can be formulated using 5 scalar optimization variables only.

- The *two-stage relaxation* is obtained by relaxing the constraints C2, C3. Its optimal value is 0.6361 with $u_1^k @ u_1^{II} = (0.6111, 0.3889)$.

Exhibit 5.

$$\text{Maximize} \quad (1/8) \sum_{k=1}^{8} \{[0.8 \ u_{11}{}^k - 0.4(u_2{}^k/2$$
$$+ \ u_{31}{}^k - \xi_3{}^k)^2] + u_{32}{}^k \xi_3{}^k + [1 - u_{11}{}^k - u_{12}{}^k]\}$$

subject to

$$u_{11}{}^k + u_{12}{}^k \leq 1 \qquad \forall \ k$$
$$- u_{11}{}^k \leq u_2{}^k \leq u_{11}{}^k \qquad \forall \ k$$
$$- u_{1j}{}^k \leq u_{3j}{}^k \leq u_{1j}{}^k \qquad \forall \ k \text{ and } j = 1, 2$$

C1: $\quad u_1{}^k = u_1{}^1 \qquad\qquad\qquad\qquad \forall \ k$

C2: $\quad u_2{}^k = u_2{}^{k+1} = u_2{}^{k+2} = u_2{}^{k+3} \qquad \text{for } k = 1, 5$

C3: $\quad u_3{}^k = u_3{}^{k+1} \qquad\qquad\qquad\qquad \text{for } k = 1, 3, 5, 7.$

- The *distribution problem* is obtained by relaxing the constraints C1, C2, C3. Its optimal value is $V^A = 0.6444$. The two extreme scenarios $\xi^1 = (1, 2, 3)$ and $\xi^8 = (-1, -2, -3)$ have first-stage decisions $u_1{}^1 = u_1{}^8 = (0.7778, 0.2222)$ and value -0.0556. The 6 other scenarios have $u_1{}^k = (0.5556, 0.3578)$ and value 0.8778, $k = 2,...,7$. Note that in general, (i) scenarios with the same optimal first-stage decision and values may still have different recourse decisions, and (ii) the first-stage decisions can be distinct for all scenarios.

- The EVPI is equal to $V^A - V^* = 0.2944$.

- Solving the multistage stochastic program with the additional constraint C1$^\zeta$: $u_1{}^k = u_1{}^\zeta$ for all k yields an upper bound on the optimal value of any scheme using the first-stage decision of the expected value problem. This value is $V^\zeta = -0.2$.

- The VSS is equal to $V^* - V^\zeta = 0.55$.

- Solving the multistage stochastic program with the additional constraint C1^{II}: $u_1{}^k = u_1{}^{II}$ for all k yields an upper bound on the optimal value of any scheme using the first-stage decision of the two-stage relaxation model. This value is $V^{II} = 0.2431$. Thus, the value of the multistage model over a two-stage model, in our sense (distinct from the VMS of Huang and Ahmed (2009)), is at least $V^* - V^{II} = 0.1069$.

To summarize, observe the collapse of the optimal value from $V^* = 0.35$ to $V^{II} = 0.2431$ (with the first-stage decision of the two-stage model) and then to $V^\zeta = -0.2$ (with the first-stage decision of the expected value model).

We can also consider the anticipative decision sequences of the distribution problem, and check if there exists plausible strategies that could exploit the set of first-stage decisions to output a good first-stage decision (with respect to any decision-making scheme for the subsequent stages).

- Selection strategy: Solving the multistage stochastic program with a constraint that enforces one of the first-stage decisions extracted from the distribution problem yields the following results: optimal value 0.3056 if $u_1{}^k = (0.7778, 0.2222)$, optimal value 0.2167 if $u_1{}^k = (0.5556, 0.3578)$. But one has to concede that in contrast to other simplified models, for which we solve multistage programs only to measure the quality of a suboptimal first-stage decision, the selection strategy needs good estimates of the different optimal values to actually output the best decision.

- Consensus strategy: The outcome of a majority vote out of the set of the 8 first-stage decisions would be the decision $(0.5556, 0.3578)$ associated to the scenarios 2 to 7. With value 0.2167, this turns out to be the worst decision between (0.7778,0.2222) and (0.5556,0.3578).

- Averaging strategy: The mean first-stage decision of the set of 8 first-stage decisions is $\bar{u}_1 = (0.6111,0.3239)$. Solving the multistage program with $u_1^k = \bar{u}_1$ for all k yields the optimal value 0.2431.

The best result is the value 0.3056 obtained by the selection strategy. Note that we are here in a situation where the multistage program and its variants could be solved exactly, that is, with a scenario tree representing the possible outcomes of the random process exactly.

PRACTICAL SCENARIO-TREE APPROACHES

We now focus on a practical question essential to the deployment of a multistage stochastic programming model: if a problem has to be approximately represented by a scenario tree in order to compute a decision strategy, how should a tractable and at the same time representative scenario-tree approximation be selected for a given problem?

After some background on discretization methods for two-stage stochastic programming, we pose the scenario tree building problem in an abstract way and then discuss the antagonist requirements that make its solution very challenging. Then we review the main families of methods proposed in the literature to build tractable scenario-tree approximations for a given problem, and highlight their main properties from a theoretical point of view.

Given the difficulty of determining a priori good scenario-tree approximations for many problems of practical interest (a difficulty which is to some extent surprising, given the practical success of related approximation methods for two-stage stochastic programming), there is a growing consensus on the necessity of being able to test a posteriori the quality of scenario-tree based approximations on a large independent sample of new scenarios. We present in this light a standard strategy based on the so-called shrinking-horizon approach — the term is used, for instance, in Balasubramanian and Grossmann (2003).

Approximation Methods in Two-Stage Stochastic Programming

Let S denote a two-stage stochastic program, where the uncertainty is modeled by a random vector ξ, possibly of high-dimension, following a certain distribution with either a discrete support of large cardinality, or a continuous support. Let S' be an approximation to S, where ξ is approximated by a random vector ξ' that follows a distribution with a finite discrete support, the cardinality of the support being limited by the fact that to each possible realization of ξ' is associated optimization variables for representing the corresponding recourse decisions. To obtain a good approximation, one would ideally target the problem of finding a finite discrete distribution for ξ' (values for the support and associated probability masses) such that any first-stage decision u_1' optimal for S' yields on S a minimal regret, in the sense that with optimal recourse decisions, the value on S of the solution made of u_1' and of optimal recourse decisions is close to the exact optimal value of S. By analogy to the VSS, we could also say that the distribution for ξ' should minimize the value of the exact program S with respect to the approximate program S'.

Many authors have found it more convenient to restrict the attention on the problem of finding a finite discrete distribution for ξ' such that the optimal value of S' is close to the optimal value of S, and the solutions u_1' optimal for S' are close to solutions optimal for S. For this approach to work, one might want to impose some weak form of continuity of the objective of S with respect to solutions. One may also want to ensure that small perturbations of the probability measure for ξ have a bounded effect on the perturbation of optimal solutions u_1.

An interesting deterministic approach (Rachev & Römisch, 2002) known as the *method of probability metrics* consists in analyzing the structure of optimal policies for a given problem class, the structure of the objective when the optimal policy is implicitly taken into account, and inferring from it a relevant measure of distance between two distributions, based on worst-case differences among objectives in a class of functions having the identified structure (or in a larger class if this is technically convenient for the computation of the distance measure). Finding a good approximation to a two-stage stochastic program is then reformulated as the problem of finding a discrete distribution minimizing the relevant probability distance to the original distribution. Note that probability distance minimization problems can be difficult to solve, especially on high-dimensional distributions. Thus, the approach, which reformulates the approximation problem as the optimal quantization of the initial probability distribution, can have essentially two sources of suboptimality with respect to the ideal approximation problem: (i) the class of functions over which worst-case distances are evaluated are as large as needed for the tractable computation of the distance; (ii) the minimal distance between probability measures is not necessarily attained in practice. Despite these limitations, the approach has been shown to work well. Moreover, the reduction of the initial approximation problem to an optimal quantization problem indicates the relevance of existing work on vector quantization and probability density estimation (MacKay, 2003, Chapter 20), and on discretization methods explored in approximate dynamic programming.

Randomized approaches are based on Monte Carlo sampling and its many extensions, including variance reduction techniques, and quasi Monte Carlo techniques. All these techniques have more or less been tried for solving two-stage stochastic programs: Infanger (1992), for instance, investigates importance sampling. They have been shown to work well in practice. Random approximations based on Monte Carlo have been shown to be consistent, in the sense that with an infinite number of samples, optimal solutions to discretized programs can converge to solutions optimal for S. More detailed results can be found in Shapiro (2003b).

Challenges in the Generation of Scenario Trees

In two-stage stochastic programming, the large or infinite set of recourse decisions of the original program is reduced to a finite set of recourse decisions for the approximation. Hence the exact and approximate solutions lie in different spaces and cannot be compared directly. Still, recourse decisions can be treated implicitly, as if they were already incorporated to the objective function, and as if the only remaining element to optimize were the first-stage decision.

In multistage stochastic programming, we face the same issue: we cannot compare solutions directly. But now, treating all recourse decisions implicitly leads to a dilution of exploitable structural properties of the objective. The classes of functions respecting those weak properties are larger. Worst-case distances between functions in such classes may cease to guide satisfactorily a discretization procedure. In addition, discretization problems are posed over larger spaces, making them more difficult to solve, even approximately.

For these reasons, rather than presenting the generation of scenario trees as a natural extension of discretization methods for two-stage stochastic programming, with the incorporation of branchings for representing the nested conditional probability densities, we state the problem in a more open way, which also highlights complexity aspects:

Construct a tractable algorithm A that:

- given a multistage stochastic program S: $\min_\pi \mathrm{E}\{ f(\xi, \pi(\xi)) \}$ defined over a probability space (Ω, B, P) with objective f (including by convention the constraints) and non-anticipative policies $\pi(\xi)$,
- will produce an approximate finite-dimensional surrogate program of the form S' : $\min_u \sum_{k=1}^n p^k g(\xi^k, u^k)$, defined over some reduced space (Ω', B', P') and objective g, and from which a surrogate policy $\hat\pi(\xi)$ subject to non-anticipativity constraints may be computed in a tractable way,
- with the goal of making the regret R @ $\mathrm{E}\{ f(\xi, \hat\pi(\xi)) \}$ - $\min_\pi \mathrm{E}\{ f(\xi, \pi(\xi)) \} \geq 0$ as small as possible.

Notice that we allow, for the sake of generality, that the surrogate program may refer to a function g different from the original objective f, and that we impose that the algorithm A, the solving strategy associated to the problem S', as well as the evaluation of the induced policy $\hat\pi$ on any new scenario, are all tractable. At this stage, we do not specify how $\hat\pi$ is inferred or understood; $\hat\pi$ needs to be introduced here only to be able to write a valid expression for the regret on the original multistage program.

Depending on situations, the problem S (random process model and function f) can be described analytically, or be only accessible through sampling and/or simulation. The problem S' will be described by a scenario tree and the choice of the function g, under limitations intrinsically due to the tractability of the optimization of the approximate program.

As we have seen, there are many derived decision-making schemes and usages of the multistage stochastic programming framework. Also, various classes of optimization programs can be distinguished — with the main distinctions being

between two-stage and multistage settings, and among linear, convex, and integer/mixed-integer formulations — and thus several possible families of functions over which one might attempt to minimize a worst-case regret.

In the stochastic programming literature, several scenario tree generation strategies have been studied. The scenario tree generation problem is there often viewed in one or another of two reduced ways with respect to the above definition, namely

1. as the problem of finding a scenario tree with an associated optimal value $\min_u \sum_{k=1}^n p^k f(\xi^k, u^k)$ close to the exact optimal value $\min_\pi \mathrm{E}\{ f(\xi, \pi(\xi)) \}$, or

2. as the problem of finding a scenario tree with its associated optimal first-stage decision $\hat u_1$ close to a first-stage decision π_1 optimal for the exact program.

Indeed, version (i) is useful when the goal is merely to estimate the optimal value of the original program S, while version (ii) is useful when the goal is to extract only the first stage decision, assuming that later on, recourse decisions are recomputed using a similar algorithm, given the new observations.

The generic approximation problem that we have described is more general, since it covers also the case where the scenario tree approach may be exploited offline to extract a complete policy $\hat\pi(\xi)$ that may then be used later on, in a stand-alone fashion for decision making over arbitrary scenarios and decision steps, be it in the real world or in the context of Monte Carlo simulations.

To give an idea of theoretical results established in the scenario tree generation literature, we now briefly discuss two representative trends of research: work that study Monte Carlo methods for building the tree, and work that seek to minimize in a deterministic fashion a certain measure of discrepancy between the original process and the approximate process represented by the scenario tree.

Monte Carlo Scenario Tree Sampling Methods

Monte Carlo methods have several advantages: they are easy to implement and they scale well with the dimension, in the sense that with enough samples, one can get close to the statistical properties of high-dimensional target distributions with high probability. The major drawback of (pure) Monte Carlo methods is the variance of the results (optimal value and solutions of the approximate programs) in small-sample conditions.

Let us describe the Sample Average Approximation method (SAA) (Shapiro, 2003b), which uses Monte Carlo for generating the scenario tree. One starts by building the branching structure of the tree. Note that the method does not specify how to carry out that step. Practitioners often use the same branching factor for each node relative to a given decision stage. They also often concentrate the branchings at early stages: the branching factor is high at the root node and then decreases with the index of the decision stage. The next step of the method consists in sampling the node values according to the distributions conditioned on the values of the ancestor nodes. The procedure, referred to as *conditional sampling*, is implemented by sampling the realizations of random variables at stage t before sampling those of stage $t+1$. Distinct realizations are assigned to distinct nodes, which are given a conditional probability equal to the inverse of the branching factor. The last step consists in solving the program on the so-obtained scenario tree and thus, although part of the description of the SAA method, does not concern the generation of the tree itself.

Consider scenario trees obtained by conditional sampling. For simplicity assume a uniform branching factor n_t at each stage t, so that the number of scenarios is $n = \prod_{t=1}^{T} n_t$. Shapiro (2006)

shows under some technical assumptions that if we want to guarantee, with a probability at least $1-\alpha$, that implementing the first-stage decision $\hat{u}_1$ optimized on a scenario tree of size n while implementing subsequently optimal recourse decisions conditionally to the first-stage decision will yield an objective value ε-close to the exact optimal value, then the size n of the tree we use for that purpose has to grow exponentially with the number of stages. The result goes against the intuition that by asking for ε-optimality with probability $1-\alpha$ only, one could get moderate sample complexity requirements. Now, as the exponential growth of the number of scenarios is not sustainable, one can only hope solving multistage models in small-sample conditions, and obtain solutions that at least with the SAA method may vary from tree to tree and be of uncertain value for the real problem. Perhaps surprisingly, it is not possible to obtain valid statistical bounds for that uncertain value by imposing as first-stage decision the tested first-stage decision and reoptimizing recourse decisions on several new random trees (Shapiro, 2003a).

Deterministic Scenario Tree Optimization Methods

There exists various deterministic techniques for selecting jointly the scenarios of the tree. Note that there is a part of numerical experimentation in the development of scenario tree methods, and a risk of overestimating the domain of validity of the proposed methods, since research efforts are oriented by experiments on particular problems.

Moment-matching methods (Høyland, Kaut, & Wallace, 2003) attempt to produce discrete distributions with some statistical moments matching those of a target distribution. Moment matching may be done at the expense of other statistics, such as the number and the location of the modes, that might also be important. Hochreiter and Pflug (2007) gives an example illustrating that risk.

The theoretical analysis underlying probability metrics methods, that we have described in the context of two-stage stochastic programming, was initially believed to be easily extended to the multistage case (Heitsch & Römisch, 2003); but then it turned out that more elaborated measures of probability distances, integrating the intertemporal aspect of observations, were needed (Heitsch & Römisch, 2009). These elaborated metrics are more difficult to compute and to minimize, so that well-justified discretizations of multistage programs are more difficult to obtain.

We can also mention methods that come with approximation guarantees, such as bounds on the suboptimality of the approximation (Kuhn, 2005). However, they are applicable under very specific assumptions concerning the problem class and the type of randomness. Quasi Monte Carlo techniques are perhaps among the more generally applicable methods (Pennanen, 2009).

Most deterministic methods end up with the formulation of difficult optimization problems, such as nonconvex or NP-hard problems (Høyland et al., 2003; Hochreiter & Pflug, 2007), with computationally demanding tasks (such as multidimensional integrations), especially for high-dimensional random processes.

The field is still in a state where the scope of existing methods is not well defined, and where the algorithmic description of the methods is incomplete, especially concerning the branching structure of the trees. That the domains of applicability are not known or overestimated makes it delicate to select a sophisticated deterministic technique for building a scenario tree on a new problem.

The Need for Testing Scenario-Tree Approximations

Theoretical analyses of scenario tree generation algorithms, often based on worst-case reasonings or large deviation theory, provide guarantees on the quality of approximate solutions that are usu-

ally too loose in practice or equivalently call for intractable scenario tree sizes. Hence they do not really solve the basic question of how to build a priori small scenario trees in a generic, scalable, and computationally efficient way, potentially jeopardizing the practical relevance of the multistage extension of stochastic programming for sequential decision making under uncertainty. Now if we are ready to renounce to worst-case guarantees embedded in the scenario tree generation method, new tools are needed for computing, a posteriori, guarantees on the value of a given numerical approximation scheme.

If we want to assess on an independent test set of scenarios the performance of decisions optimized on a scenario tree, a difficulty arises: first-stage decisions can be tested but subsequent recourse decisions are only defined for the scenarios covered by the scenario tree. Therefore, it is necessary to extend the approach so as to allow one to test solutions on new scenarios, at a computational cost low enough to allow the validation on large numbers of test scenarios.

We have to stress that this extension is not really necessary for two-stage stochastic programming. First, approximations of two-stage models yield constant first-stage decisions, that are implementable on any scenario, while recourse decisions on new scenarios can then often be found analytically, or by running a myopic one-stage optimization procedure for each new scenario, or by implementing a known recourse procedure that the initial two-stage model was only approximating for optimizing the first-stage decisions — a strategy found efficient in capacity planning (Sen, Doverspike, & Cosares, 1994). Thus, testing is generally straightforward for two-stage models. Second, finite-dimensional approximations of two-stage stochastic programming models do not use scenario trees. They only use a finite set of outcomes. Theoretical results show that in the two-stage situation, statistical confidence bounds on the quality of an approximate solution can be computed (Mak, Morton, & Wood, 1999). These results break down in the multistage case, giving its true interest to guarantees based on testing (Shapiro, 2003a).

The Inference of Shrinking-Horizon Decision Policies

Several authors have proposed to use a generic scheme similar to Model Predictive Control to assess the performances associated to a particular algorithm A for building the scenario tree (Kouwenberg, 2001; Chiralaksanakul, 2003). The scheme can be sketched as follows.

1. Generate a scenario tree using algorithm A, solve the resulting program, extract from its solution the first-stage decision u_1 ;
2. Generate a test sample of m mutually independent scenarios by sampling realizations of the random process.
3. For each scenario of the test sample, obtain sequentially the recourse decisions $u_2, ..., u_T$, where each decision u_t is treated as a first-stage decision computed by taking as an initial condition the past decisions $u_1, ..., u_{t-1}$ and the history $\xi_1, ..., \xi_{t-1}$ of the test scenario, by conditioning the joint distribution of $\xi_t, ..., \xi_T$ on the history, by using the algorithm A to build a new scenario tree that approximates the random process $\xi_t, ..., \xi_T$, by solving the program formulated on this tree over the optimization variables relative to the decisions $u_t, ..., u_T$, and by discarding all but the decision $u_t = \pi_t(\xi_1, ..., \xi_{t-1})$.
4. Estimate the overall performance of the scheme on the test sample by forming the empirical average $V_{TS}(A) = m^{-1} \sum_{j=1}^{m} f(\xi^j, u^j)$, where the sum runs over the indices relative to the scenarios in the test sample TS and their associated decision sequences $u^j = (u_1^j, ..., u_T^j)$.

The statistical estimator $V_{TS}(A)$ provides an unbiased estimation of the value of the scenario tree building algorithm A in the context of the other approximations involved in the numerical computations of the sequences of decisions, such as simplifications of the objective function or early stopping at low-accuracy solutions.

The estimator may have a high variance, but we can expect a high positive correlation between estimators $V_{TS}(A)$, $V_{TS}(A')$ relative to distinct algorithm variants A, A' on the same test sample TS, allowing a reliable comparison of the relative performance of the two variants on the problem instance at hand.

The validation is generic in the sense that it can be applied to any algorithm A, but also in the sense that it addresses the general scenario tree building problem in the larger context of the decision making scheme actually implemented in practice.

Synthesis

In the preceding subsections we have formulated and analyzed the problem of inferring a good scenario tree approximation for a given multistage stochastic programming problem. We have seen that the state of the art does not currently provide strong enough methods with broad enough practical coverage and good enough theoretical guarantees in terms of the quality of the approximate solutions derived in this way.

Researchers in the field were thus led to suggest the use of the shrinking-horizon recursive procedure for exploiting the scenario-tree based approach in practice. However, evaluating the resulting performance estimator on an independent sample of scenarios is extremely demanding, as it requires, for each test scenario and at each stage of recourse decisions, the automatic construction of a new scenario tree and the optimization of the resulting program on the tree. Doing this is still beyond the possibility of available computational approaches when considering the solution of large-scale problems.

For these reasons, there is currently no scalable off-the-shelf method for generating and testing scenario-tree based approximations of multistage stochastic programs, and the framework of stochastic programming based on scenarios trees has in this way, in spite of its theoretical appeal, lost its practical attractiveness during the last years in many environments dealing with large-scale systems (Powell & Topaloglu, 2003; Van Hentenryck & Bent, 2006).

MACHINE LEARNING BASED APPROACH

In this section we propose an approach for solving stochastic programming problems based on the idea of generating in a lazy fashion a large number of random tractable scenario-tree based approximations. The approach is lazy in the sense that instead of recommending a careful analysis of the structure of the problem at hand, and instead of devoting all computational resources to the construction of a single scenario tree, we recommend a multiplication of solution attempts through the generation of several approximations. The method works by extracting, from the solutions of these approximations, datasets that combine realizations of the random process and decision sequences, and by processing these datasets by a supervised learning method, so as to infer policies that can be later on tested efficiently on a large sample of new independent scenarios. These policies can be jointly exploited to infer multistage decision strategies that achieve good performances in a very generic way.

In this section, we describe our solution approach in general. Practical implementation details are easier to discuss on a concrete problem; this will be done in the next section.

Motivation

Our approach is motivated by two complementary and intimately related considerations induced by our analysis of the state of the art in approximation methods for stochastic programming, and their confrontation to the problems addressed in the field of machine learning in the last years.

The first motivation is derived from the need for intensive testing of decision-making policies for multistage programs. This need is primarily a consequence of the lack of tight theoretical results that would provide broadly usable, a priori guarantees on scenario-tree based methods. A posteriori testing of decisions by the shrinking-horizon approach is not a viable option, given its internal use of additional scenario trees, and its overall computational complexity. With respect to this motivation, machine learning offers a multitude of ways of extracting policies that are easy to test in an automatic way on a large number of independent samples. Keeping the sample set large is an unavoidable requirement for the statistical significance of performance estimators evaluated on high-dimensional random vectors and/or long scenarios, and thus ultimately for the practical use of the framework.

The second motivation has to do with the intrinsic nature of the finite scenario-tree approximation for multistage stochastic programming. The variance in the quality of the optimal decisions that may be inferred from finite approximations suggests that such problems are essentially *ill-posed* in the same sense as inverse problems addressed in machine learning are also ill-posed: small perturbations in the values of a finite data set used for the empirical estimation of an expectation leads to large variations (instability) of the predictor optimal with respect to the empirical expectation. Therefore, regularization techniques and principles from statistical learning theory (Vapnik, 1998), such as the structural risk minimization principle, may help to extract solutions from small scenario-tree approximations in a sound way from the theoretical point of view, and in an efficient way from the practical point of view.

To summarize the main ideas of the following subsections, we propose an approach that (i) allows to test small scenario trees quickly and reliably, (ii) is likely to offer better ways of exploiting individual scenario-tree approximations, and (iii) in the end allows to revisit the initial question of generating, solving, ranking and exploiting tractable scenario trees for solving complex multistage decision-making problems.

Inference and Evaluation of a Policy from a Scenario Tree

Cheap estimators of the quality of a scenario tree can be constructed by resorting to supervised learning techniques (Defourny et al., 2009). The basic principle consists in inferring a suboptimal policy by first learning a sequence of decision predictors $(\hat{\pi}_1, \ldots, \hat{\pi}_T)$ from a data set of examples of information state/decision pairs. The information states are extracted from the nodes of the scenario tree; they correspond to the partial scenario histories in the tree, but they could also be represented differently, for instance by features, or by a state in the sense of dynamic programming. The decisions are also extracted from the nodes of the tree; they are the optimal decisions computed on the tree. The predictions are then corrected in an ad-hoc fashion using a cheap repair procedure, denoted for simplicity by M_t, so as to obtain feasible decisions $u_t = M_t(\hat{\pi}_t(\xi_1, \ldots, \xi_{t-1})) \in U_t$ evaluated and implemented online on new scenarios. Repair procedures are also suggested in Küchler and Vigerske (2010) as a means of restoring the feasibility of decisions extracted from a tree and directly applied on test scenarios.

Formally, the decision predictor $\hat{\pi}_t$ is defined as a map from inputs $X_t = (\xi_1, \ldots, \xi_{t-1})$ to outputs $Y_t = u_t$ learned from a dataset $D_t = \{(X_t^k, Y_t^k)\}_{k=1,\ldots,n}$ of input-output pairs extracted from the scenario tree and its associated optimized decisions. The

nature of the repair procedure varies with the feasibility constraints that should be enforced. It is necessary when standard supervised learning algorithms are unable to meet the constraints exactly. The decisions and observations on which U_t depend are passed in arguments of the repair procedure. An example of repair procedure is the projection of a predicted decision on the corresponding feasibility set. It is also possible to resort to simple problem-dependent heuristics for restoring feasibility.

This leads to the following inference and validation scheme:

1. Generate a scenario tree using an algorithm A, solve the resulting program, extract from its solution the first-stage decision u_1, and the datasets D_t of partial-scenario/stage-t-decision pairs.

2. Learn the decision predictors $\hat{\pi}_t$ from the dataset D_t, for $t = 2, \ldots, T$.

3. Generate a test sample of m mutually independent scenarios by sampling realizations ξ^j of the random process ξ.

4. For each scenario ξ^j of the test sample, set $u_1^j = u_1$ and obtain sequentially the recourse decisions $u_2^j, \ldots, u_T^j$, where each decision u_t^j is obtained by first evaluating $\hat{\pi}_t(\xi_1^j, \ldots, \xi_{t-1}^j)$ and then restoring feasibility by the repair procedure M_t.

5. Estimate the overall performance of the scheme on the test sample by forming the empirical average $V_{TS}(A) = m^{-1} \sum_{j=1}^{m} f(\xi^j, u^j)$, where the sum runs over the indices relative to the scenarios in the test sample and their associated decision sequences $u^j = (u_1^j, \ldots, u_T^j)$.

The estimator $V_{TS}(A)$ computed in this way reflects the quality of the scenario tree, the learned policy and the repair procedure. We expect however that scenario tree variants can be ranked reliably, despite the variance of the estimator due to the choice of the test sample, and despite a new source of bias due to the simplified representation of the decision policy by the supervised learning strategy. The value $V_{TS}(A)$ is obtained by simulating an explicit policy that generates feasible decisions, and thus always provides a pessimistic bound (upper bound for minimization, lower bound for maximization) on the performance of the best policy that could be inferred from the current scenario tree. Hence a reliable bound on the achievable performance for the sequential decision making strategy is provided, up to the standard error of the test-sample estimator. (The standard error can be reduced by increasing m, under the assumption that the initial problem has a finite optimal value.) The pessimistic bound can be made tighter by testing various policies obtained from the same scenario tree but with different learning algorithms and/or repair procedures. The best combination of algorithms and learning parameters is then retained. In principle, the value of the best policy should be evaluated again on a new independent test sample.

Note that a learned policy is not necessarily always worse than a shrinking-horizon policy using the same first-stage decision u_1, as the regularization that occurs during the supervised learning step could actually improve the quality of the recourse decisions $u_2, ..., u_T$.

Note also that the input space of the learned policy is a simple matter of convenience. As long as the policy remains non-anticipative, the input space can be reparameterized, typically by letting appear explicitly past decisions, state variables, and additional features derived from the information state and that might facilitate the generalization of the decisions in the data sets, or later, the online evaluation of the learned predictors.

Simple Monte Carlo Based Search of Scenario Trees

We are now ready to sketch a workable and generic scheme for obtaining approximate solutions to multistage stochastic programs with performance guarantees. The scheme builds on the procedure of the previous section, which allows to extract a policy from any scenario tree and from optimal solutions for the approximate program associated with the tree, and allows to estimate the value of the policy by Monte Carlo simulation with a sufficient accuracy. In its most elementary version, the scheme consists in generating a possibly large set of randomized scenario-tree approximations for a given problem S, ranking them according to the estimated value of their corresponding policy, and identifying in this way automatically the best scenario tree among the considered sample of trees.

More specifically, we propose the following algorithm.

1. Generate a large test sample TS of mutually independent scenarios for the problem under consideration.
2. Generate the branching structure for a scenario tree randomly. The procedure may use any valuable insight on good branching structures (in general or specific to the problem).
3. Use an existing scenario tree generation method to instantiate the values and probabilities of the nodes of the tree, for example, the Monte Carlo based method SAA already described. That the generation of the values defining the scenarios could be integrated to the construction of the branching structure is not really relevant: the two phases are separated here to stress that they are carried out independently. The construction of the tree is independent of the test sample TS.
4. Solve the approximate program derived from the so-obtained scenario tree.
5. Extract from the solution the datasets of information state/decision pairs that are necessary to learn a suboptimal policy for the recourse decisions, and then associate to the scenario tree the score V_{TS} corresponding

to the average performance of that policy on the test sample.

6.   Return to step 2 until a stopping criterion is met. Output the first-stage decision u_1 from the scenario tree with the best score, and the guarantee that u_1 yields at least $V^*_{TS'}$ up to some standard error, with the corresponding learned policy as a certificate. Here $V^*_{TS'}$ is ideally the estimation of the value of the best policy on a new, very large test sample TS' of mutually independent scenarios.

As this procedure performs a kind of model selection on the basis of scores measured on the test sample TS, an unbiased estimation of the performance of the selected first-stage decision u_1 and associated recourse policy calls for a new independent test sample TS'. The initial test sample TS should then be called a *validation sample*, according to the standard machine learning terminology. In our numerical experiments, we merely used a very large validation sample TS in order to evaluate various policies and estimate their respective performances in a reliable way.

In applications where the only information about the random process is a finite set of realizations, the method could be extended as follows: one would split the set of realizations into a test set serving as the test sample TS, and a learning set LS from which a generative model G_{LS} for the random process would be inferred, that is, a best possible estimate for P. The scenario trees would then be built by querying new samples from the generative model.

Discussion

The generic procedure presented in this section is based on various open ingredients that may be largely exploited for the design of a wide class of algorithms in a very flexible way. Namely, the "meta-parameters" are (i) the scenario tree sampling scheme, (ii) the (possibly regularized)

optimization technique used to extract from a scenario tree a dataset, (iii) the precise supervised learning algorithm used to obtain the decision strategies from the datasets, (iv) the repair procedure used to restore the feasibility of the decisions on new scenarios.

The main ideas of the proposed scheme are evaluated in the case study section on a family of problems proposed by other authors. We illustrate how one may adjust the scenario tree generation algorithm and the policy learning algorithm to one's needs, and by doing so we also illustrate the flexibility of the proposed approach and the potential of the combination of scenario-tree based decision making with supervised learning. In particular, the efficiency of supervised learning strategies makes it possible to rank large numbers of policies inferred from large numbers of randomly generated scenario trees.

Although we do not illustrate this in the present work, we would like also to stress that the scenario tree sampling scheme may be coupled in various other ways with the inference of policies by machine learning. For example, one could seek to use sequential Monte Carlo techniques inspired from the importance sampling literature, in order to progressively guide the scenario tree sampling and machine learning methods towards regions of high interest, given the quality of the policies inferred from scenarios trees at previous iterations. Also, instead of using each dataset obtained from each scenario tree to extract a single policy, one could extract multiple policies from a single dataset, or use several datasets and learning algorithms to extract a single policy, in the spirit of the wide range of model combination and perturbation schemes from the machine learning literature (Dietterich, 2000).

Exhibit 6.

```
Minimize      ρ⁻¹ log E { exp{-ρ ∑ᵀₜ₌₁ ξₜ₋₁ ·πₜ (ξ)} }
subject to    0 ≤ πₜ (ξ) ≤ 1   and  ∑ᵀₜ₌₁ πₜ (ξ) ≤ Q,
                 π   non-anticipative.
```

CASE STUDY

We will show the interest of the approximate solution techniques presented in the chapter by applying them to a family of multistage stochastic programs. Implementation choices difficult to discuss in general terms, such as choices concerning the supervised learning of a policy for the recourse decisions, and the choices for the random generation of the trees, will be illustrated on a concrete case.

The section starts by the formulation of a multistage stochastic program that various researchers have presented as difficult for scenario tree methods (Hilli & Pennanen, 2008; Koivu & Pennanen, 2010; Küchler & Vigerske, 2010). Several instances of the problem will be addressed, including instances on horizons considered as almost unmanageable by scenario tree methods.

Problem Description

We consider a multistage problem adapted from Hilli and Pennanen (2008), interpreted in that paper as the valuation of an electricity swing option. In this chapter, we interpret the problem rather as the search for risk-aware strategies for distributing the sales of a commodity over T stages in a flexible way adapted to market prices. A risk-aware objective is very interesting for our purposes, but it is difficult to justify it in a context of option valuation. The formulation of the problem is as follows (Exhibit 6).

The objective uses the exponential utility function, with risk aversion coefficient ρ. Such objectives are discussed at the end of the chapter.

In our formulation of the problem, there is no constant first-stage decision to optimize. We begin directly by the observation of ξ_0, followed by a recourse decision $u_1 = \pi_1 (\xi_0)$. Observations and decisions are intertwined so that in general $u_t = \pi_t (\xi_0, ..., \xi_{t-1})$. The random variable ξ_{t-1} is the unitary profit ($\xi_{t-1} > 0$) or loss ($\xi_{t-1} < 0$) that can result from the sale of the commodity at time t. Potential profits and losses fluctuate in time, depending on market conditions (we later select a random process model for market prices to complete the problem specification). The commodity is sold in quantity $u_t = \pi_t (\xi_0, ..., \xi_{t-1})$ at time t, meaning that the quantity u_t can depend on past and current prices. The decision is made under the knowledge of the potential profit or loss at time t, given by $\xi_{t-1} \cdot u_t$, but under uncertainty of future prices. This is by the way why scenario tree techniques must be used with great care on this problem when the planning horizon is long: as soon as the scenarios cease to have branchings, there is no more residual uncertainty on future prices, and the optimization process wrongly identifies opportunities anticipatively. Those spurious future opportunities may significantly degrade the quality of previous decisions.

We seek strategies where the sales per stage are bounded (constraint $0 \leq \pi_t (\xi) \leq 1$). The constraint can model a bottleneck in the production process. Notice also that bounded sales are consistent with the model assumption of an exogenous random process: very large sales are more likely to influence the market prices on long planning horizons. The scalar Q bounds the total sales (we assume $Q \geq 1$). It represents the initial stock of commodity,

Exhibit 7.

```
Minimize        - E {  ∑(t=1..T) ξ_{t-1} · π_t (ξ) }
subject to      0 ≤ π_t (ξ) ≤ 1   and   ∑(t=1..T) π_t (ξ) ≤ Q,
                π   non-anticipative,
```

the sale of which must be distributed optimally over the horizon T.

When the risk aversion coefficient ρ tends to 0, the problem reduces to the search of a risk-neutral strategy. This case has been studied by Küchler and Vigerske (2010). It admits a linear programming formulation (Exhibit 7): and an exact analytical solution (which thus serves as a reference):

$$\pi_t^{ref}(\xi) = \begin{cases} 0 & if \ t \leq T - Q \ or \ \xi_{t-1} \leq 0, \\ 1 & if \ t > T - Q \ and \ \xi_{t-1} > 0. \end{cases}$$

In a first experiment, we will take the numerical parameters and the process ξ selected in Hilli and Pennanen (2008) (to ease the comparisons): $\rho = 1$, $T = 4$, $Q = 2$, $\xi_t = (\exp\{b_t\} - K)$ where $K = 1$ is the fixed cost (or the strike price, when the problem is interpreted as the valuation of an option) and b_t is a random walk: $b_0 = \sigma \cdot \varepsilon_0$, $b_t = b_{t-1} + \sigma \cdot \varepsilon_t$, with $\sigma = 0.2^{-1/2}$ and ε_t following a standard normal distribution N (0, 1).

In a second experiment over various values of the parameters (ρ, Q, T) with T up to 52, we will take for ξ the process selected in Küchler and Vigerske (2010) (because otherwise on long horizons the price levels of the first process blow out in an unrealistic way, making the problem rather trivial): $\xi_t = (\xi_t' - K)$ with $\xi_t' = \xi_{t-1}' \exp\{\sigma \cdot \varepsilon_t - \sigma^2/2\}$ where $\sigma = 0.07$, $K = 1$, and ε_t following a standard normal distribution. Equivalently $\xi_t = (\exp\{b_t - (t + 1) \sigma^2/2\} - K)$ with b_t a random walk such that $b_0 = \sigma \cdot \varepsilon_0$ and $b_t = b_{t-1} + \sigma \cdot \varepsilon_t$.

Algorithm for Generating Small Scenario Trees

At the heart of tree selection procedure relies our ability to generate scenario trees reduced to a very small number of scenarios, with interesting branching structures. As the trees are small, they can be solved quickly and then scored using the supervised learning policy inference procedure. Fast testing procedures make it possible to rank large numbers of random trees.

The generation of random branching structures has not been explored in the classical stochastic programming literature; we thus have to propose a first algorithm in this section. The algorithm is developed with our needs in view, with the feedback provided by the final numerical results of the tests, until results on the whole set of considered numerical instances suggest that the algorithm suffices for the application at hand. We believe that the main ideas behind this algorithm will be reused in subsequent work for addressing the representation of stochastic processes of higher dimensions. Therefore, in the following explanations we put more emphasis on the methodology we followed than on the final resulting algorithm.

Method of Investigation

The branching structure is generated by simulating the evolution of a branching process. We will soon describe the branching process that we have used, but observe first that the probability space behind the random generation of the tree structure is not at all related to the probability space of the random process that the tree approximates. It is the values and probabilities of the nodes that are later chosen in accordance to the target probability distribution, either deterministically or randomly, using any new or existing method.

For selecting the node values, we have tested different deterministic quantizations of the one-dimensional continuous distributions of random variables ξ_t, and alternatively different quantizations of the gaussian innovations ε_t that serve to define $\xi_t = \xi_t(\varepsilon_t)$, as described by the relations given in the previous section. Namely, we have tested the minimization of the quadratic distortion (Pages & Printems, 2003) and the minimization of the Wasserstein distance (Hochreiter & Pflug, 2007). On the considered problems we did not notice significant differences in performance attributable to a particular deterministic variant.

What happened was that with deterministic methods, performances began to degrade as the planning horizon was increased, perhaps because trying to preserve statistical properties of the marginal distributions ξ_t distorts other statistics of the joint distribution of $(\xi_0, ..., \xi_{T-1})$, especially in higher dimensions. Therefore, for treating instances on longer planning horizons, we switched to a crude Monte Carlo sampling for generating node values.

By examining trees with the best scores in the context of the present family of problems, we observed that several statistics of the random process represented by those trees could be very far from their theoretical values, including first moments. This might suggest that it is very difficult to predict without any information on the optimal solutions which properties should be preserved in small scenario trees, and thus which objective should be optimized when attempting to build a small scenario tree. If we had discovered a correlation between some features of the trees and the scores, we could have filtered out bad trees without actually solving the programs associated to these trees, simply by computing the identified features.

Description of the Branching Processes

We now describe the branching process used in the experiments made with deterministic node values. Let $r \in [0,1]$ denote a fixed probability of creating a branching. We start by creating the root node of the tree (depth 0), to which we assign the conditional probability 1. With probability r we create 2 successor nodes to which we assign the values ± 0.6745 and the conditional probabilities 0.5 (the values given here minimize the Wasserstein distance between a two mass point distribution and the standard normal distribution for ε_t). With probability $(1-r)$ we create instead a single successor node to which we assign the value 0 and the conditional probability 1; this node is a degenerate approximation of the distribution of ε_t. Then we take each node of depth 1 as a new root and repeat the process of creating 1 or 2 successor nodes to these new roots randomly. The process is further repeated on the nodes of depth 2,..., T-1, yielding a tree of depth T for representing the original process $\varepsilon_0, ..., \varepsilon_{T-1}$. The scenario tree for ξ is derived from the scenario tree for ε.

For problems on larger horizons, it is difficult to keep the size of the tree under control with a single fixed branching parameter r — the number of scenarios would have a large variance. Therefore, we used a slightly more complicated branching process, by letting the branching probability r depend on the number of scenarios currently developed. Specifically, let N be a target number of scenarios and T a target depth for the scenario tree with the realizations of ξ_t relative to depth $t+1$. Let n_t be the number of parent nodes at depth t; this is a random variable except at the root for which $n_0 = 1$. During the construction of the tree, parent nodes at depth $t<T$ are developed and split in $v=2$ children nodes with a probability $r_t = n_t^{-1}(v-1)^{-1}(N-1)/T$. Parent nodes have a single child node with a probability $1-r_t$. If $r_t > 1$, we set $r_t = 1$ and all nodes are split in $v=2$ children nodes. Thus in general $r_t = \min\{1, n_t^{-1}(v-1)^{-1}(N-1)/T\}$.

Exhibit 8.

$$\mathrm{E}\ \{\ \exp\{-\sum\nolimits_{t'=1}^{T} \xi_{t'-1} \cdot u_{t'}\ \}\ |\ \xi_0,\ \dots,\ \xi_{t-1}\ \}$$

$$=\exp\{-\sum\nolimits_{t'=1}^{t-1} \xi_{t'-1} \cdot u_{t'}\ \}\ \cdot$$

$$\mathrm{E}\ \{\ \exp\{-\sum\nolimits_{t'=t}^{T} \xi_{t'-1} \cdot u_{t'}\ \}\ |\ \xi_0,\ \dots,\ \xi_{t-1}\ \},$$

Algorithm for Learning Policies

Solving a program on a scenario tree yields a dataset of scenario/decision sequence pairs(ξ, u). To infer a decision policy that generalizes the decisions of the tree to test scenarios, we have to learn mappings from $(\xi_0, \dots, \xi_{t-1})$ to u_t and ensure the compliance of the decisions with the constraints. To some extent the procedure is thus problem-specific. Here again we insist on the methodology.

Dimensionality Reduction

We try to reduce the number of features of the input space. In particular, we can try to get back to a state-action space representation of the policy (and postprocess datasets accordingly to recover the states). Note that in general needed states are those that would be used by an hypothetical reformulation of the optimization problem using dynamic programming. Here the objective is based on the exponential utility function. By the property that (Exhibit 8) we can see that decisions at $t' = 1, \dots, t$-1 scale by a same factor the contribution to the return brought by the decisions at $t' = t, \dots, T$. Therefore, if the feasibility set at time t can be expressed from state variables, the decisions at $t' = t, \dots, T$ can be optimized independently of the decisions at $t' = 1, \dots, t$-1. This suggests to express u_t as a function of the state ξ_{t-1} of the process ξ, and of an additional state variable ζ_t defined by $\zeta_0 @ Q, \zeta_t @ Q - \sum_{t'=1}^{t-1} u_{t'}$,

that allows to reformulate the constraint $\sum_{t'=1}^{T} u_{t'} \le Q$ as $\sum_{t'=t}^{T} u_{t'} \le \zeta_t$.

Feasibility Guarantees Sought Before Repair Procedures

We try to map the output space in such a way that the predictions learned under the new geometry and then transformed back using the inverse mapping comply with the feasibility constraints. Here, we scale the output u_t so as to have to learn the fraction $y_t = y_t (\xi_{t-1}, \zeta_t)$ of the maximal allowed output $\min(1, \zeta_t)$, which summarizes the two constraints of the problem. Since $\zeta_0 = Q$, we distinguish the cases $u_1 = y_1 (\xi_0) \cdot 1$ and $u_t = y_t (\xi_{t-1}, \zeta_t) \cdot \min(1, \zeta_t)$. It will be easy to ensure that fractions y_t are valued in $[0,1]$ (thus we do not need to define an a posteriori repair procedure).

Input Normalization

It is convenient for the sequel to normalize the inputs. From the definition of ξ_{t-1} we can recover the state of the random walk b_{t-1}, and use as first input $x_{t1} @ (\sigma^2 t)^{-1/2} b_{t-1}$, which follows a standard normal distribution. Thus for the first version of the process ξ, instead of ξ_{t-1} we use $x_{t1} = \sigma^{-1} t^{1/2} \log(\xi_{t-1} + K)$, and for the second version of the process ξ, instead of ξ_{t-1} we use $x_{t1} = \sigma^{-1} t^{1/2} \log(\xi_{t-1} + K) + \sigma t^{1/2}/2$. Instead of the second input ζ_t (for $t > 1$) we use $x_{t2} @ \zeta_t / Q$, which is valued in $[0,1]$. Therefore, we rewrite the fraction $y_t (\xi_{t-1}, \zeta_t)$ as $g_t (x_{t1}, x_{t2})$.

Exhibit 9.

$$g_t(x_{t\,1}, x_{t\,2}) = \text{logsig}\{\ \gamma_t\ +\ \sum_{j=1}^{L} w_{t\,j}$$
$$\cdot\ [$$
$$\text{tansig}(\beta_{t\,j}\ +\ \sum_{k=1}^{2} v_{t\,j\,k} x_{t\,k})\ ]\ \},$$

Hypothesis Space

We have to choose the hypothesis space for the learned fractions g_t defined previously. Here we find it convenient to choose the class of feed-forward neural networks with one hidden layer of L neurons (Exhibit 9): sqqwith weights v_{tjk} and $w_{t\,j}$, biases $\beta_{t\,j}$ and γ_t, and activation functions $\text{tansig}(x)=(2(1+e^{-2x})^{-1}-1)\in[-1,+1]$ and $\text{logsig}(x) = (1+e^{-x})^{-1} \in [0, 1]$, a usual choice for imposing the output ranges $[-1, +1]$ and $[0, 1]$ respectively.

Since the training sets are extremely small, we take $L = 2$ for g_1 (which has only one input $x_{1\,1}$) and $L = 3$ for g_t ($t >1$).

We recall that artificial neural networks have been found to be well-adapted to nonlinear regression. Standard implementations of neural networks (construction and learning algorithms) are widely available, with a full documentation from theory to interactive demonstrations (Demuth & Beale, 1993). We report here the parameters chosen in our experiments for the sake of completeness; the method is largely off-the-shelf.

Details on the Implementation

The weights and biases are determined by training the neural networks. We used the Neural Network toolbox of MATLAB with the default methods for training the networks by backpropagation — the Nguyen-Widrow method for initializing the weights and biases of the networks randomly, the mean square error loss function, and the Levenberg-Marquardt optimization algorithm. We used $[-3, 3]$ for the estimated range of $x_{t\,1}$,

corresponding to 3 standard deviations, and $[0, 1]$ for the estimated range of $x_{t\,2}$.

Trained neural networks are dependent on the initial weights and biases before training, because the loss minimization problem is nonconvex. Therefore, we repeat the training 5 times from different random initializations. We obtain several candidate policies (to be ranked on the test sample). In our experiments on the problem with $T=4$, we randomize the initial weights and biases of each network independently. In our experiments on problems with $T>4$, we randomize the initial weights and biases of $g_1(x_{1\,1})$ and $g_2(x_{2\,1}, x_{2\,2})$, but then we use the optimized weights and biases of g_{t-1} as the initial weights and bias for the training of g_t. Such a warm-start strategy accelerates the learning tasks. Our intuition was that for optimal control problems, the decision rules π_t would change rather slowly with t, at least for stages far from the terminal horizon.

We do not claim that using neural networks is the only or the best way of building models g_t that generalize well and are fast in exploitation mode. The choice of the MATLAB implementation for the neural networks could also be criticized. It just turns out that these choices are satisfactory in terms of implementation efforts, reliability of the codes, solution quality, and overall running time.

Remark on Approximate Solutions

An option of the proposed testing framework that we have not discussed, as it is linked to technical aspects of numerical optimization, is that we can form the datasets of scenario/decisions pairs using inexact solutions to the optimization programs as-

Figure 3. First experiment: scores on the test sample associated to the random scenario trees (lower is better). The linear segments join the best scores of policies inferred from trees of equivalent complexity.

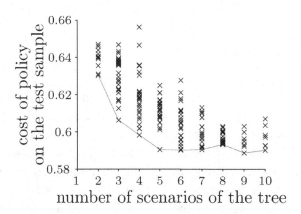

sociated to the trees. Indeed, simulating a policy based on any dataset will still give a pessimistic bound on the optimal solution of the targeted problem. The tree selection procedure will implicitly take this new source of approximation into account. In fact, every approximation one can think of for solving the programs could be tested on the problem at hand and thus ultimately accepted or rejected, on the basis of the performance of the policy on the test sample, and the time taken by the solver to generate the decisions of the dataset.

Numerical Results

We now describe the numerical experiments we have carried out and comment on the results.

Experiment on the Small-Horizon Problem Instance

First, we consider the process ξ and parameters (ρ, Q, T) taken from Hilli and Pennanen (2008). We generate a sample of $m=10^4$ scenarios drawn independently, on which each learned policy will be tested. We generate 200 random tree structures as described previously (using $r=0.5$ and rejecting structures with less than 2 or more than 10 scenarios). Node values are set by the deterministic

method, thus the variance in performance that we will observe among trees of similar complexity will come mainly from the branching structure. We form and solve the programs on the trees using Cvx, and extract the datasets. We generate 5 policies per tree, by repeatedly training the neural networks from random initial weights and biases. Each policy is simulated on the test sample and the best of the 5 policies is retained for each tree.

The scenarios $\xi^k=(\xi_0^k, \xi_1^k, \xi_2^k)$ are shifted vertically to distinguish them when they pass through common values, written on the left. Scenario probabilities p^k are indicated on the right.

The result of the experiment is shown on Figure 3. Each point is relative to a particular scenario tree. Points from left to right are relative to trees of increasing size. We report the value of $m^{-1}\sum_{j=1}^{m} \exp\{-\sum_{t=1}^{T} \xi_{t-1}^j \cdot \hat{\pi}_t(\xi^j)\}$ for each learned policy $\hat{\pi}$, in accordance with the objective minimized in Hilli and Pennanen (2008). Lower is better. Notice the large variance of the test sample scores among trees with the same number of scenarios but different branching structures.

The tree selection method requires a single lucky outlier to output a good valid upper bound on the targeted objective — quite an advantage with respect to approaches based on worst-case

Figure 4. Small trees (5,6,7,9 scenarios) from which good datasets could be obtained

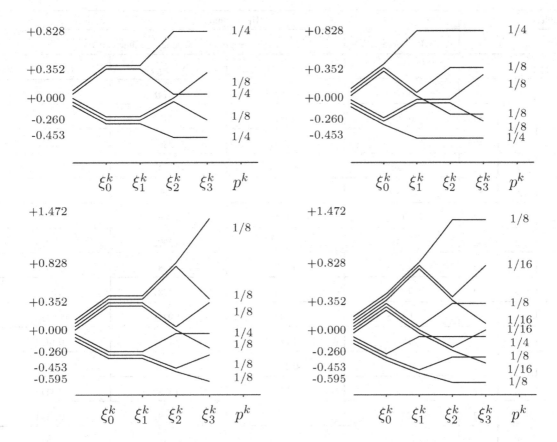

reasonings for building a single scenario tree. With a particular tree of 6 scenarios (best result: 0.59) we already reach the guarantee that the optimal value of our targeted problem is less or equal to $\log(0.59) \approx -0.5276$. On Figure 4, we have represented graphically some of the lucky small scenario trees associated to the best performances. Of course, tree structures that perform well here may not be optimal for other problem instances.

The full experiment takes 10 minutes to run on a pc with a single 1.55 GHz processor and 512 Mb RAM. By comparing our bounds to those reported in Hilli and Pennanen (2008) — where validation experiments taking up to 30 hours with a single 3.8Ghz processor, 8Gb RAM have been carried out — we deduce that we reached essentially the quality of the optimal solution.

Experiment on Large-Horizon Problem Instances

Second, we consider the process ξ taken from Küchler and Vigerske (2010) and a series of 15 sets of parameters for (ρ, Q, T). We repeat the following experiment on each (ρ, Q, T) with 3 different parameter values for controlling the size of the random trees: generate 25 random trees (we recall that this time the node values are also randomized), solve the resulting 25 programs, learn 5 policies per tree (depending on the random initialization of the neural networks), and report as the best score the lowest of the resulting 125 values computed on the test sample.

Table 3 reports values corresponding to the average performance $\rho^{-1} \log \{m^{-1} \sum_{j=1}^{m} \exp\{-\rho$

Table 3. Second experiment: Best upper bounds for a family of problem instances

Problem			Upper bounds[1]			
ρ	Q	T	Reference[2]	Value of the best policy[3], in function of N		
				$N = 1 \cdot T$	$N = 5 \cdot T$	$N = 25 \cdot T$
0	2	12	-0.1869	-0.1837	-0.1748	-0.1797
	2	52	-0.4047	-0.3418	-0.3176	-0.3938
	6	12	-0.5062	-0.5041	-0.4889	-0.4930
	6	52	-1.1890	-1.0747	-1.0332	-1.1764
	20	52	-3.6380	-3.5867	-3.5000	-3.4980
0.25	2	12	-0.1750	-0.1716	-0.1661	-0.1700
	2	52	-0.3351	-0.3210	-0.3092	-0.3288
	6	12	-0.4363	-0.4371	-0.4381	-0.4365
	6	52	-0.7521	-0.7797	-0.7787	-0.8030
	20	52	-1.4625	-1.8923	-1.9278	-1.9128
1	2	12	-0.1466	-0.1488	-0.1473	-0.1458
	2	52	-0.2233	-0.2469	-0.2222	-0.2403
	6	12	-0.3078	-0.3351	-0.3385	-0.3443
	6	52	-.03676	-0.5338	-0.5291	-0.5354
	20	52	-0.5665	-0.9625	-0.9757	-0.9624

[1]Estimated on a test sample of $m = 10000$ scenarios. On a same row, lower is better.

[2]Defined by $\pi_t^{ref}(\xi)$ and optional for the risk-neutral case $\rho = 0$.

[3]On random trees of approximately N scenarios.

$\sum_{t=1}^{T} \xi_{t-1}^{j} \cdot \hat{\pi}_t(\xi^j)\} \}$ obtained for a series of problem instances, the numerical parameters of which are given in the first column of the table, for different policies selected among random trees of 3 different nominal sizes, so as to investigate the effect of the size of the tree on the performance of the learned policies. One column is dedicated to the performance of the analytical reference policy π^{ref} on the test sample.

In the case $\rho = 0$, the reference value provided by the analytical optimal policy suggests that the best policies are close to optimality. In the case $\rho = 0.25$, the reference policy is now suboptimal.

It still slightly dominates the learned policies when $Q = 2$, but not anymore when $Q = 6$ or $Q = 20$. In the case $\rho = 1$, the reference policy is dominated by the learned policies, except perhaps when $Q = 2$ and the trees are large. That smaller trees are sometimes better than large trees may be explained by the observation that multiplying the number of scenarios by 25, as done in our experiments, does not fundamentally change the order of magnitude of size of the tree, given the required exponential growth of the number of scenarios with the number of stages.

This experiment shows that even if the scenario tree selection method requires generating and solving several trees, rather than one single tree, it can work very well. In fact, with a random tree generation process that can generate a medium size set of very small trees, there is a good likelihood in the problem that at least one of those trees will lead to excellent performances. Large sets of scenario trees could easily be processed simply by parallelizing the tree selection procedure. Overall, the approach seems promising in terms of the usage of computational resources.

TIME INCONSISTENCY AND BOUNDED RATIONALITY LIMITATIONS

This section discusses the notion of dynamically consistent decision process (time-consistency), which is relevant to sequential decision making with risk-sensitivity — by opposition to the optimization of the expectation of a total return over the planning horizon, which can be described as risk-indifferent, or risk-neutral.

Time-Consistent Decision Processes

We will say that an objective induces a dynamically consistent policy, or time-consistent policy, if the decisions selected by a policy optimal for that objective coincide with the decisions selected by a policy recomputed at any subsequent time step t and optimal for the same objective with decisions and observations prior to t set to their realized value (and decisions prior to t chosen according to the initial optimal policy).

Time-consistent policies are not necessarily time-invariant: we simply require that the optimal mappings π_t from information states i_t to decisions u_t at time t, evaluated from some initial information state at $t=0$, do not change if we take some decisions following these mappings, and then decide to compute them again from the current

information state. We recall that in the Markov Decision Process framework, the information state i_t is the current state x_t, and in the multistage stochastic programming framework, i_t is the current history $\xi_1, ..., \xi_{t-1}$ of the random process, with t indexing decision stages. We say that a decision process is time-consistent if it is generated by a time-consistent policy.

A close notion of time-consistency can also be defined by saying that the preferences of the decision maker among possible distributions for the total return over the planning horizon can never be affected by future information states that the agent recognizes, at some point in the decision process, as impossible to reach (Shapiro, 2009; Defourny, Ernst, & Wehenkel, 2008).

In the absence of time-consistency, the following situation may arise (the discussion is made in the multistage stochastic programming framework). At time $t=1$, an agent determines that for each possible outcome of a random variable ξ_2 at time $t=2$, the decision $u_2 = a$ at time $t=2$ is optimal (with respect to the stated objective and constraints of the problem, given the distribution of ξ_2, ξ_3, ..., and taking account of optimized recourse decisions u_3, u_4, ... over the planning horizon). Then at time $t=2$, having observed the outcome of the random variable ξ_1 and conditioned the probability distributions of ξ_2, ξ_3, ... over this observation, and in particular, having ruled out all scenarios where ξ_1 differs from the observed outcome, the agent finds that for some possible realizations of ξ_2, $u_2 = a$ is not optimal.

The notion of time-consistency already appears in Samuelson (1937), who states: "as the individual moves along in time there is a sort of perspective phenomenon in that his view of the future in relation to his instantaneous time position remains invariant, rather than his evaluation of any particular year" (page 160). Several economists have rediscovered and refined the notion (Strotz, 1955; Kydland & Prescott, 1977), especially when trying to apply expected utility theory, valid for comparisons of return distributions viewed from a single initial information state, to sequential decision making settings, where the information state evolves.

In fact, if an objective function subject to constraints can be optimized by dynamic programming, in the sense that a recursive formulation of the optimization is possible using value functions (on an augmented state space if necessary, and irrespectively of complexity issues), then an optimal policy will satisfy the time-consistency property. This connection between Bellman's principle (1957) and time-consistency is well-established (Epstein & Schneider, 2003; Artzner, Delbaen, Eber, Heath, & Ku, 2007). By definition and by recursion, a value function is not affected by states that have a zero probability to be reached in the future; when the value function is exploited, a decision u_t depends only on the current information state i_t. Objectives that can be optimized recursively include the expected sum of rewards, and the expected exponential utility of a sum of rewards (Howard & Matheson, 1972), with discount permitted, although the recursion gets more involved (Chung & Sobel, 1987). A typical example of objective that cannot be rewritten recursively in general is the variance of the total return over several decision steps. This holds true even if the state fully describes the distribution of total returns conditionally to the current state. Note, however, that a nice way of handling a mean-variance objective on the total return is to relate it to the expected exponential utility: if R denotes a random total return, $\Phi_\rho\{R\}$ $= E\{R\} - (\rho/2) \operatorname{var}\{R\} \approx -\rho^{-1} \log E\{\exp(-\rho R)\}$. The approximation holds for small $\rho>0$. It is exact for all $\rho>0$ if R follows a Gaussian distribution.

Limitations of Validations Based on Learned Policies

In our presentation of multistage stochastic programming, we did not discuss several extensions that can be used to incorporate risk awareness in the decision making process. In particular, a whole branch of stochastic programming is concerned with the incorporation of *chance constraints* in models (Prékopa 1995), that is, constraints to be satisfied with a probability less than 1. Another line of research involves the incorporation of modern risk measures such as the *conditional value-at-risk* at level α (expectation of the returns relative to the worst α-quantile of the distribution of returns) (Rockafellar & Uryasev, 2000). An issue raised by many of these extensions, when applied to sequential decision making, is that they may induce time-inconsistent decision making processes (Boda & Filar, 2006).

The validation techniques based on supervised learning that we have proposed are not adapted to time-inconsistent processes. Indeed, these techniques rely on the assumption that the optimal solution of a multistage stochastic program is a sequence of optimal mappings π_t from reachable information states $(\xi_1, ..., \xi_{t-1})$ to feasible decisions u_t, uniquely determined by some initial information state at which the optimization of the mappings takes place. We believe, however, that the inability to address the full range of possible multistage programming models should have minor practical consequences. On the one hand, we hardly see the point of formulating a sophisticated multistage model with optimal recourse decisions unrelated to those that would be implemented if the corresponding information states are actually reached. On the other hand, it is always possible to simulate any learned policy, whatever the multistage model generating the learning data might be, and score an empirical return distribution obtained with the simulated policy according to any risk measure important for the application. Computing a policy and sticking to it, even if preferences are changing over time, is a form of precommitment (Hammond, 1976).

Finally, let us observe that a shrinking-horizon policy can be time-inconsistent for two reasons: (i) the policy is based on an objective that cannot induce a time-consistent decision process; (ii) the policy is based on an objective that could be reformulated using value functions, but anyway the implicit evaluation of these value functions changes over time, due to numerical approximations local to the current information state. Similarly, if an agent uses a supervised-learning based policy to take decisions at some stage and is then allowed to reemploy the learning procedure at later stages, the overall decision sequence may appear as dynamically inconsistent. The source (ii) of inconsistency appears rather unavoidable in a context of bounded computational resources; more generally, it seems that bounded rationality (Simon, 1956) would necessarily entail dynamical inconsistency.

CONCLUSION

In this chapter, we have presented the principles of the multistage stochastic programming approach to sequential decision making under uncertainty, and discussed the inference and exploitation of decision policies for comparing various approximations of a multistage program in the absence of tight theoretical guarantees.

Sequential decision making problems under uncertainty form a rich class of optimization problems with many challenging aspects. Markov Decision Processes and multistage stochastic programming are two frameworks for addressing such problems. They have been originally studied by different communities, leading to a separate development of new approximation and solution techniques. In both fields, research is done so as to extend the scope of the framework to new problem classes: in stochastic programming, there is research on robust approaches (Dupacova, 1987; Delage & Ye, 2010), decision-dependent random processes (Goel & Grossmann, 2006), nonconvex problems (Dentcheva & Römisch, 2004); in Markov Decision Processes, many efforts are directed at scaling dynamic programming (or policy search) to problems with high-dimensional continuous state spaces and/or decision spaces (Ng

& Jordan, 1999; Ghavamzadeh & Engel, 2007; Antos, Munos, & Szepesvári, 2008).

It is likely that a better integration of the ideas developed in the two fields will ultimately yield better solving strategies for large-scale problems having both continuous and discrete aspects. Both fields have foundations in empirical process theory, and can benefit from advances in Monte Carlo methods, especially in variance reduction techniques (Singh et al., 2007; Coquelin, Deguest, & Munos, 2009; Hoffman, Kueck, Doucet, & de Freitas, 2009).

ACKNOWLEDGMENT

This paper presents research results of the Belgian Network DYSCO (Dynamical Systems, Control, and Optimization), funded by the Interuniversity Attraction Poles Programme, initiated by the Belgian State, Science Policy Office. The scientific responsibility rests with its authors. Damien Ernst is a Research Associate of the Belgian FRS-FNRS of which he acknowledges the financial support. This work was supported in part by the IST Programme on the European Community, under the PASCAL2 Network of Excellence, IST-2007-216886. This publication only reflects the authors' views.

REFERENCES

Antos, A., Munos, R., & Szepesvári, C. (2008). Fitted Q-iteration in continuous action-space MDPs. In *Advances in Neural Information Processing Systems 20 (NIPS-2007)* (pp. 9–16). Cambridge, MA: MIT Press.

Applegate, D. L., Bixby, R. E., Chvátal, V., & Cook, W. J. (2007). *The traveling salesman problem: A computational study*. Princeton, NJ: Princeton University Press.

Artzner, P., Delbaen, F., Eber, J.-M., Heath, D., & Ku, H. (2007). Coherent multiperiod risk adjusted values and Bellman's principle. *Annals of Operations Research, 152*(1), 5–22. doi:10.1007/s10479-006-0132-6

Bagnell, D., Kakade, S., Ng, A. Y., & Schneider, J. (2004). Policy search by dynamic programming. In *Advances in Neural Information Processing Systems 16 (NIPS-2003)* (pp. 831–838). Cambridge, MA: MIT Press.

Balasubramanian, J., & Grossmann, I. E. (2003). Approximation to multistage stochastic optimization in multiperiod batch plant scheduling under demand uncertainty. *Industrial & Engineering Chemistry Research, 43,* 3695–3713. doi:10.1021/ie030308+

Bellman, R. (1962). Dynamic programming treatment of the travelling salesman problem. *Journal of the ACM, 9,* 61–63. doi:10.1145/321105.321111

Ben-Tal, A., El Ghaoui, L., & Nemirovski, A. (2009). *Robust optimization*. Princeton, NJ: Princeton University Press.

Bertsekas, D. P. (2005). *Dynamic programming and optimal control* (3rd ed.). Belmont, MA: Athena Scientific.

Billingsley, P. (1995). *Probability and measure* (3rd ed.). New York, NY: Wiley-Interscience.

Birge, J. R. (1992). The value of the stochastic solution in stochastic linear programs with fixed recourse. *Mathematical Programming, 24,* 314–325. doi:10.1007/BF01585113

Birge, J. R., & Louveaux, F. (1997). *Introduction to stochastic programming*. New York, NY: Springer.

Boda, K., & Filar, J. A. (2006). Time consistent dynamic risk measures. *Mathematical Methods of Operations Research, 63,* 169–186. doi:10.1007/s00186-005-0045-1

Boyd, S., & Vandenberghe, L. (2004). *Convex optimization*. Cambridge, UK: Cambridge University Press.

Breiman, L., Friedman, J., Stone, C. J., & Olshen, R. A. (1984). *Classification and regression trees.* Boca Raton, FL: Chapman and Hall/CRC.

Carpentier, P., Cohen, G., & Culioli, J. C. (1996). Stochastic optimization of unit commitment: A new decomposition framework. *IEEE Transactions on Power Systems, 11,* 1067–1073. doi:10.1109/59.496196

Chiralaksanakul, A. (2003). *Monte Carlo methods for multi-stage stochastic programs*. Unpublished doctoral dissertation, University of Texas at Austin, Austin, TX.

Chung, K.-J., & Sobel, M. (1987). Discounted MDP's: Distribution functions and exponential utility maximization. *SIAM Journal on Control and Optimization, 25*(1), 49–62. doi:10.1137/0325004

Coquelin, P.-A., Deguest, R., & Munos, R. (2009). Particle filter-based policy gradient in POMDPs. In *Advances in Neural Information Processing Systems 21 (NIPS-2008)* (pp. 337–344). Cambridge, MA: MIT Press.

Csáji, B., & Monostori, L. (2008). Value function based reinforcement learning in changing Markovian environments. *Journal of Machine Learning Research, 9,* 1679–1709.

Dantzig, G. B. (1955). Linear programming under uncertainty. *Management Science, 1,* 197–206. doi:10.1287/mnsc.1.3-4.197

Defourny, B., Ernst, D., & Wehenkel, L. (2008, December). *Risk-aware decision making and dynamic programming.* Paper presented at the NIPS-08 Workshop on Model Uncertainty and Risk in Reinforcement Learning, Whistler, BC.

Defourny, B., Ernst, D., & Wehenkel, L. (2009). Bounds for multistage stochastic programs using supervised learning strategies. In *Stochastic Algorithms: Foundations and Applications. Fifth International Symposium, SAGA 2009* (pp. 61-73). Berlin, Germany: Springer-Verlag.

Delage, E., & Ye, Y. (2010). Distributionally robust optimization under moment uncertainty with application to data-driven problems. *Operations Research, 58*(3), 596–612. doi:10.1287/opre.1090.0741

Dempster, M. A. H., Pflug, G., & Mitra, G. (Eds.). (2008). *Quantitative fund management*. Boca Raton, FL: Chapman & Hall/CRC.

Demuth, H., & Beale, M. (1993). *Neural network toolbox for use with Matlab.*

Dentcheva, D., & Römisch, W. (2004). Duality gaps in nonconvex stochastic optimization. *Mathematical Programming, 101*(3), 515–535. doi:10.1007/s10107-003-0496-1

Dietterich, T. G. (2000). Ensemble methods in machine learning. In *Proceedings of the First International Workshop on Multiple Classifier Systems* (pp. 1-15). Berlin, Germany: Springer-Verlag.

Dupacova, J. (1987). The minimax approach to stochastic programming and an illustrative application. *Stochastics, 20,* 73–88. doi:10.1080/17442508708833436

Epstein, L., & Schneider, M. (2003). Recursive multiple-priors. *Journal of Economic Theory, 113,* 1–13. doi:10.1016/S0022-0531(03)00097-8

Ernst, D., Geurts, P., & Wehenkel, L. (2005). Tree-based batch mode reinforcement learning. *Journal of Machine Learning Research, 6,* 503–556.

Ernst, D., Glavic, M., Capitanescu, F., & Wehenkel, L. (2009). Reinforcement learning versus model predictive control: A comparison on a power system problem. *IEEE Transactions on Systems, Man, and Cybernetics. Part B, Cybernetics, 39*(2), 517–529. doi:10.1109/TSMCB.2008.2007630

Escudero, L. F. (2009). On a mixture of the fix-and-relax coordination and Lagrangian substitution schemes for multistage stochastic mixed integer programming. *Top (Madrid), 17,* 5–29. doi:10.1007/s11750-009-0090-7

Geurts, P., Ernst, D., & Wehenkel, L. (2006). Extremely randomized trees. *Machine Learning, 63,* 3–42. doi:10.1007/s10994-006-6226-1

Ghavamzadeh, M., & Engel, Y. (2007). Bayesian policy gradient algorithms. In *Advances in Neural Information Processing Systems 19 (NIPS-2006)* (pp. 457–464). Cambridge, MA: MIT Press.

Goel, V., & Grossmann, I. E. (2006). A class of stochastic programs with decision dependent uncertainty. *Mathematical Programming, 108,* 355–394. doi:10.1007/s10107-006-0715-7

Grant, M., & Boyd, S. (2008). Graph implementations for nonsmooth convex programs. In Blondel, V., Boyd, S., & Kimura, H. (Eds.), *Recent advances in learning and control. Lecture Notes in Control and Information Sciences* (*Vol. 371*, pp. 95–110). London, UK: Springer-Verlag.

Grant, M., & Boyd, S. (2009, February). *CVX: Matlab software for disciplined convex programming (web page and software).* Retrieved from http://stanford.edu/~boyd/cvx

Hammond, P. J. (1976). Changing tastes and coherent dynamic choice. *The Review of Economic Studies, 43,* 159–173. doi:10.2307/2296609

Hastie, T., Tibshirani, R., & Friedman, J. (2009). *The elements of statistical learning: Data mining, inference, and prediction* (2nd ed.). New York, NY: Springer.

Heitsch, H., & Römisch, W. (2003). Scenario reduction algorithms in stochastic programming. *Computational Optimization and Applications, 24,* 187–206. doi:10.1023/A:1021805924152

Heitsch, H., & Römisch, W. (2009). Scenario tree modeling for multistage stochastic programs. *Mathematical Programming, 118*(2), 371–406. doi:10.1007/s10107-007-0197-2

Hilli, P., & Pennanen, T. (2008). Numerical study of discretizations of multistage stochastic programs. *Kybernetika, 44,* 185–204.

Hinton, G. E., Osindero, S., & Teh, Y.-W. (2006). A fast learning algorithm for deep belief nets. *Neural Computation, 18,* 1527–1554. doi:10.1162/neco.2006.18.7.1527

Hochreiter, R., & Pflug, G. C. (2007). Financial scenario generation for stochastic multi-stage decision processes as facility location problems. *Annals of Operations Research, 152,* 257–272. doi:10.1007/s10479-006-0140-6

Hoffman, M., Kueck, H., Doucet, A., & de Freitas, N. (2009). New inference strategies for solving Markov decision processes using reversible jump MCMC. In *Proceedings of the Twenty-Fifth Conference on Uncertainty in Artificial Intelligence (UAI-2009)* (pp. 223-231). AUAI Press.

Howard, R. A., & Matheson, J. (1972). Risk-sensitive Markov decision processes. *Management Science, 18*(7), 356–369. doi:10.1287/mnsc.18.7.356

Høyland, K., Kaut, M., & Wallace, S. W. (2003). A heuristic for moment matching scenario generation. *Computational Optimization and Applications, 24,* 169–185. doi:10.1023/A:1021853807313

Huang, K., & Ahmed, S. (2009). The value of multistage stochastic programming in capacity planning under uncertainty. *Operations Research, 57,* 893–904. doi:10.1287/opre.1080.0623

Infanger, G. (1992). Monte Carlo (importance) sampling within a Benders decomposition algorithm for stochastic linear programs. *Annals of Operations Research, 39,* 69–95. doi:10.1007/BF02060936

Kallrath, J., Pardalos, P. M., Rebennack, S., & Scheidt, M. (Eds.). (2009). *Optimization in the energy industry.* Berlin, Germany: Springer-Verlag. doi:10.1007/978-3-540-88965-6

Kearns, M. J., Mansour, Y., & Ng, A. Y. (2002). A sparse sampling algorithm for near-optimal planning in large Markov Decision Processes. *Machine Learning, 49*(2-3), 193–208. doi:10.1023/A:1017932429737

Koivu, M., & Pennanen, T. (2010). Galerkin methods in dynamic stochastic programming. *Optimization, 59,* 339–354. doi:10.1080/02331931003696368

Kouwenberg, R. (2001). Scenario generation and stochastic programming models for asset liability management. *European Journal of Operational Research, 134,* 279–292. doi:10.1016/S0377-2217(00)00261-7

Küchler, C., & Vigerske, S. (2010). Numerical evaluation of approximation methods in stochastic programming. *Optimization, 59,* 401–415. doi:10.1080/02331931003700756

Kuhn, D. (2005). *Generalized bounds for convex multistage stochastic programs. Lecture Notes in Economics and Mathematical Systems (Vol. 548).* Berlin, Germany: Springer-Verlag.

Kydland, F. E., & Prescott, E. C. (1977). Rules rather than discretion: The inconsistency of optimal plans. *The Journal of Political Economy, 85,* 473–492. doi:10.1086/260580

Lagoudakis, M. G., & Parr, R. (2003). Reinforcement learning as classification: Leveraging modern classifiers. In *Proceedings of the Twentieth International Conference on Machine Learning (ICML-2003)* (pp. 424-431). Menlo Park, CA: AAAI Press.

Langford, J., & Zadrozny, B. (2005). Relating reinforcement learning performance to classification performance. In *Proceedings of the Twenty-Second International Conference on Machine Learning (ICML-2005)* (pp. 473-480). New York, NY: ACM.

Littman, M. L., Dean, T. L., & Kaelbling, L. P. (1995). On the complexity of solving Markov decision problems. In *Proceedings of the Eleventh Conference on Uncertainty in Artificial Intelligence (UAI-1995)* (pp. 394-402). San Francisco, CA: Morgan Kaufmann.

MacKay, D. J. C. (2003). *Information theory, inference and learning algorithms*. Cambridge, UK: Cambridge University Press.

Mak, W.-K., Morton, D. P., & Wood, R. K. (1999). Monte Carlo bounding techniques for determining solution quality in stochastic programs. *Operations Research Letters*, *24*(1-2), 47–56. doi:10.1016/S0167-6377(98)00054-6

Mercier, L., & Van Hentenryck, P. (2007). Performance analysis of online anticipatory algorithms for large multistage stochastic integer programs. In *Proceedings of the Twentieth International Joint Conference on Artificial Intelligence (IJCAI-07)* (pp. 1979-1984). San Francisco, CA: Morgan Kaufmann.

Munos, R., & Szepesvári, C. (2008). Finite-time bound for fitted value iteration. *Journal of Machine Learning Research*, *9*, 815–857.

Nemirovski, A., Juditsky, A., Lan, G., & Shapiro, A. (2009). Stochastic approximation approach to stochastic programming. *SIAM Journal on Optimization*, *19*, 1574–1609. doi:10.1137/070704277

Nesterov, Y. (2003). *Introductory lectures on convex optimization*. Dordrecht, The Netherlands: Kluwer Academic Publishers.

Ng, A. Y., & Jordan, M. (1999). PEGASUS: A policy search method for large MDPs and POMDPs. In *Proceedings of the Sixteenth Conference on Uncertainty in Artificial Intelligence (UAI-2000)* (pp. 406-415). San Francisco, CA: Morgan Kaufmann.

Norkin, V. I., Ermoliev, Y. M., & Ruszczyński, A. (1998). On optimal allocation of indivisibles under uncertainty. *Operations Research*, *46*, 381–395. doi:10.1287/opre.46.3.381

Pages, G., & Printems, J. (2003). Optimal quadratic quantization for numerics: The Gaussian case. *Monte Carlo Methods and Applications*, *9*, 135–166. doi:10.1515/156939603322663321

Pennanen, T. (2009). Epi-convergent discretizations of multistage stochastic programs via integration quadratures. *Mathematical Programming*, *116*, 461–479. doi:10.1007/s10107-007-0113-9

Pflug, G. C., & Römisch, W. (2007). *Modeling, measuring and managing risk*. Hackensack, NJ: World Scientific Publishing Company. doi:10.1142/9789812708724

Powell, W. B. (2007). *Approximate dynamic programming: Solving the curses of dimensionality*. Hoboken, NJ: Wiley-Interscience. doi:10.1002/9780470182963

Powell, W. B., & Topaloglu, H. (2003). Stochastic programming in transportation and logistics. In Ruszczyński, A., & Shapiro, A. (Eds.), *Stochastic programming. Handbooks in operations research and management science* (*Vol. 10*, pp. 555–635). Amsterdam, The Netherlands: Elsevier.

Prékopa, A. (1995). *Stochastic programming*. Dordrecht, The Netherlands: Kluwer Academic Publishers.

Puterman, M. L. (1994). *Markov decision processes: Discrete stochastic dynamic programming*. Hoboken, NJ: Wiley.

Rachev, S. T., & Römisch, W. (2002). Quantitative stability in stochastic programming: The method of probability metrics. *Mathematical Programming, 27*(4), 792–818.

Raiffa, H., & Schlaifer, R. (1961). *Applied statistical decision theory*. Cambridge, MA: Harvard University Press.

Rasmussen, C. E., & Williams, C. K. I. (2006). *Gaussian processes for machine learning*. Cambridge, MA: MIT Press.

Rockafellar, R. T. (1970). *Convex analysis*. Princeton, NJ: Princeton University Press.

Rockafellar, R. T., & Uryasev, S. (2000). Optimization of conditional value-at-risk. *Journal of Risk, 2*(3), 21–41.

Rockafellar, R. T., & Wets, R. J.-B. (1991). Scenarios and policy aggregation in optimization under uncertainty. *Mathematics of Operations Research, 16*, 119–147. doi:10.1287/moor.16.1.119

Samuelson, P. A. (1937). A note on measurement of utility. *The Review of Economic Studies, 4*(2), 155–161. doi:10.2307/2967612

Schultz, R., Stougie, L., & Van der Vlerk, M. H. (1998). Solving stochastic programs with integer recourse by enumeration: A framework using Gröbner basis reduction. *Mathematical Programming, 83*, 229–252. doi:10.1007/BF02680560

Sen, S., Doverspike, R. D., & Cosares, S. (1994). Network planning with random demand. *Telecommunication Systems, 3*, 11–30. doi:10.1007/BF02110042

Sen, S., & Sherali, H. (2006). Decomposition with branch-and-cut approaches for two-stage stochastic mixed-integer programming. *Mathematical Programming, 106*, 203–223. doi:10.1007/s10107-005-0592-5

Sen, S., Yu, L., & Genc, T. (2006). A stochastic programming approach to power portfolio optimization. *Operations Research, 54*, 55–72. doi:10.1287/opre.1050.0264

Shapiro, A. (2003a). Inference of statistical bounds for multistage stochastic programming problems. *Mathematical Methods of Operations Research, 58*(1), 57–68. doi:10.1007/s001860300280

Shapiro, A. (2003b). Monte Carlo sampling methods. In Ruszczyński, A., & Shapiro, A. (Eds.), *Stochastic programming. Handbooks in operations research and management science* (*Vol. 10*, pp. 353–425). Amsterdam, The Netherlands: Elsevier.

Shapiro, A. (2006). On complexity of multistage stochastic programs. *Operations Research Letters, 34*(1), 1–8. doi:10.1016/j.orl.2005.02.003

Shapiro, A. (2009). On a time-consistency concept in risk averse multistage stochastic programming. *Operations Research Letters, 37*, 143–147. doi:10.1016/j.orl.2009.02.005

Shapiro, A., Dentcheva, D., & Ruszczyński, A. (2009). *Lectures on stochastic programming: Modeling and theory*. Philadelphia, PA: SIAM. doi:10.1137/1.9780898718751

Simon, H. A. (1956). Rational choice and the structure of the environment. *Psychological Review, 63*, 129–138. doi:10.1037/h0042769

Singh, S. S., Kantas, N., Vo, B.-N., Doucet, A., & Evans, R. J. (2007). Simulation-based optimal sensor scheduling with application to observer trajectory planning. *Automatica, 43*, 817–830. doi:10.1016/j.automatica.2006.11.019

Steinwart, I., & Christman, A. (2008). *Support vector machines*. New York, NY: Springer.

Strotz, R. H. (1955). Myopia and inconsistency in dynamic utility maximization. *The Review of Economic Studies, 23*, 165–180. doi:10.2307/2295722

Sutton, R. S., & Barto, A. G. (1998). *Reinforcement learning, an introduction.* Cambridge, MA: MIT Press.

The MathWorks, Inc. (2004). *Matlab.* Retrieved from http://www.mathworks.com

Van der Vlerk, M. H. (2010). Convex approximations for a class of mixed-integer recourse models. *Annals of Operations Research, 177,* 139–151. doi:10.1007/s10479-009-0591-7

Van Hentenryck, P., & Bent, R. (2006). *Online stochastic combinatorial optimization.* Cambridge, MA: MIT Press.

Vapnik, V. N. (1998). *Statistical learning theory.* New York, NY: John Wiley & Sons.

Verweij, B., Ahmed, S., Kleywegt, A., Nemhauser, G., & Shapiro, A. (2003). The sample average approximation method applied to stochastic routing problems: A computational study. *Computational Optimization and Applications, 24*(2-3), 289–333. doi:10.1023/A:1021814225969

Wallace, S. W., & Ziemba, W. T. (Eds.). (2005). *Applications of stochastic programming.* Philadelphia, PA: SIAM. doi:10.1137/1.9780898718799

Wets, R. J.-B. (1974). Stochastic programs with fixed recourse: The equivalent deterministic program. *SIAM Review, 16,* 309–339. doi:10.1137/1016053

ADDITIONAL READING

For an introduction to convex optimization, we suggest Boyd and Vandenberghe (2004). A large collection of results in convex optimization can be found in Rockafellar (1970). For an introduction to statistical learning, we suggest Hastie, Tibshirani, and Friedman (2009). For a general view of results in stochastic programming and multistage stochastic programming, we suggest Shapiro, Dentcheva, and Ruszczyński (2009). For a general view of risk-averse decision making criteria we suggest Pflug and Römisch (2007).

KEY TERMS AND DEFINITIONS

Model Selection: Identification of a best learned policy by comparing the empirical mean performance of learned policies on a test sample of independent scenarios.

Non-Anticipative Policy: Mapping from scenarios to sequences of decisions, defined for all possible scenarios, such that the rule for determining a decision at time t takes as input only quantities that can be observed at time t, namely the part of the scenario observed up to time t (or an equivalent representation thereof).

Policy Learning: Estimation of a non-anticipative policy from examples of scenarios paired to sequences of decisions, where the examples are obtained jointly by solving a large optimization program parameterized by the scenarios.

Scenario: A joint realization of an ordered collection of random variables having a fixed joint probability distribution and assumed to be gradually observed by a decision maker.

Scenario Tree: A finite collection of probability-weighted scenarios, that begin to differ at various stages so as to represent approximately, for planning purpose, the possible conditional distributions given past observations that the decision maker could face.

Chapter 7
Automatically Generated Explanations for Markov Decision Processes

Omar Zia Khan
University of Waterloo, Canada

Pascal Poupart
University of Waterloo, Canada

James P. Black
University of Waterloo, Canada

ABSTRACT

Explaining policies of Markov Decision Processes (MDPs) is complicated due to their probabilistic and sequential nature. We present a technique to explain policies for factored MDPs by populating a set of domain-independent templates. We also present a mechanism to determine a minimal set of templates that, viewed together, completely justify the policy. These explanations can be generated automatically at run-time with no additional effort required from the MDP designer. We demonstrate this technique using the problems of advising undergraduate students in their course selection and assisting people with dementia in completing the task of handwashing. We also evaluate these automatically generated explanations for course-advising through a user study involving students.

INTRODUCTION

In many situations, a sequence of decisions must be taken by an individual or system (e.g., course selection by students, inventory management by a store, etc.). However, deciding on a course of action is notoriously difficult when there is

DOI: 10.4018/978-1-60960-165-2.ch007

uncertainty in the effects of the actions and the objectives are complex. As described earlier, Markov decision processes (MDPs) provide a principled approach for automated planning under uncertainty. While the beauty of an automated approach is that the computational power of machines can be harnessed to optimize difficult sequential decision-making tasks, there are two drawbacks with this approach. First, experts find it difficult to create accurate models or debug inaccurate models. Second, users find it difficult to understand the reasoning behind an automated recommendation. Both of these issues are key bottlenecks to the widespread use of MDPs. Thus, there is a need for explanations that enhance the expert's understanding and user's trust of these recommendations.

It is difficult to design MDPs because real-world MDPs often have hundreds of thousands, if not millions of states. There are no existing tools for experts to examine and/or debug their models. The current design process involves successive iterations of tweaking various parameters to achieve a desirable output. At the end, the experts still cannot verify if the policy is indeed reflecting their requirements accurately. Users also have to trust the policy by treating it as a black box, with no explanations whatsoever regarding the process of computing the recommendation or the confidence of the system in this recommendation. They cannot observe which factors have been considered by the system while making the recommendation. The system also cannot accept suggestions from the user to modify the policy and update the model to reflect this preference. Our approach on providing a minimal set of explanations will help in alleviating some of these problems. But first, we briefly describe the process of designing transition and reward functions that will help us better appreciate the complexity of creating MDPs and hence motivate the need for explanations.

Challenges in Designing Transition Functions

It is not trivial to encode transition functions for a real-world problem, even using a factored transition model. Experts can attempt to handcraft a transition function, but this is likely to be a tedious process. Further, it is even more likely that their encoding will be erroneous, and they will have to undergo a laborious process of finding and

rectifying these errors. It is possible to resort to historical data to learn transitions regarding the model. Transition functions can be learnt from data by frequency counting. Frequency counting for learning transitions is equivalent to parameter learning through maximum likelihood. Different issues exist with such an approach. First, the distribution learnt from the historical data may not be similar to the distribution being encountered by the MDP. Second, there may not be enough data to learn distributions. The lack of sufficient data can also result in missing rare events in the learned model. Another approach to learning transition functions is based on Bayesian reinforcement learning. A distribution over all possible transition models is maintained, and the distribution is updated as more evidence is accumulated.

Challenges in Designing Reward Functions

Reward functions can also be hand-crafted by experts, but this is also a tedious process that is prone to mistakes. Experts may easily identify different attributes that contribute towards the utility. Specifying numerical values for the utilities of these attributes is more complicated. Unlike transition probabilities, utilities may not be expressed explicitly, unless utility is a tangible concept such as time or money. For such cases, it is not possible to learn the reward function from historical data since utilities act as hidden variables.

Inverse reinforcement learning (Russell, 1998) deals with the problem of observing the behaviour of an expert to determine the reward function that is being maximized by the expert. This problem has been studied to infer a decision maker's utility function by treating the previous decisions (or actions) as constraints on the possible utility function (Chajewska, Koller, & Ormoneit, 2001) and representing these constraints using an influence diagram (Nielsen & Jensen, 2004). More specifically, this problem has also been studied in the context of MDPs, but the key issue is that it is not always possible to recover a unique reward function. For a given set of observed behaviours, many possible reward functions can lead to an optimal policy, most notable among them being a function that assigns zero or any other constant reward to every state (Ng & Russell, 2000). Preference elicitation techniques have also been considered to derive numerical values of utility (Boutilier, 2003). Boutilier, Poupart & Schuurmans (2006) present an approach based on minimax regret to elicit utilities. Regret can be considered the opportunity loss or difference between the current outcome and the possible outcome of another approach. This approach minimizes maximum regret over all possible utility functions to reduce the effect in worst-case scenarios. The objective of this work is not to elicit the complete utility function, but to retrieve enough information so that in the worst case, the loss due to uncertainty about the utility function is below a certain level.

The above discussion regarding the design of transition and reward functions demonstrates the complexity involved in developing an MDP model. Explanations for experts in this environment can help them verify their models and act as tools to isolate problems or correct the model to reflect their desired outcome. This would speed up the process of creating accurate MDP models. Explanations for users would allow them to understand the reasoning behind the recommendation and increase their trust in the model. The users can even learn about the inadequacy of the MDP if the explanation lacks additional information the users may wish to consider while making the decision, and thus inform them of when to not trust the recommendations.

In this chapter, we describe a technique to explain MDP policies. The key objective is to automatically create generic explanations that are domain-independent and can be used in different applications. Just like MDPs can be solved using domain-independent techniques (like value iteration), this technique can be used to explain MDP policies in different domains without any

domain-specific changes, using an approach that treats explanation as a dialogue. For experts, this would imitate the interaction between an architect and a builder to ensure that the end result is according to the specification of the architect. For users, it would imitate the process of consultation with an expert in which the user can ask follow-up questions to clarify any confusion.

BACKGROUND

Merriam-Webster defines explanation as the process of explaining[1]. Explain is defined as to make known, or to make plain or understandable, or to give reason for or cause of, or to show the logical development or relationships[2]. In terms of intelligent systems, explanation may be considered to be giving the reason or cause of the choice made by the system to make it understandable to the user. This definition of explanation focuses on identifying the cause for arriving at a particular decision, though in philosophy explanations may also be functional (describing a function) or intentional (describing the intention) (Sormo, Cassens, & Aamodt, 2005).

Explanandum and *explanans* are terms used to refer to different parts of an explanation (Hempel & Oppenheim, 1948). *Explanandum* refers to the concept that needs to be explained, and *explanans* refers to the concepts that provide the explanation. The different types of *explanandum* for intelligent decision-making systems can include the data being used to make the decision, the reasoning that led to the current decision, and the decision chosen as a result of the reasoning process. The explanation of data would require elaborating why the world is as it is. In terms of MDPs, this would mean explaining why the transition or reward functions are as they are specified. The explanation of the reasoning of the decision would require elaborating how the decision was actually chosen. In terms of MDPs, this would mean demonstrating the process of computing the optimal policy for the

MDP. The explanation of decision would require elaborating why a certain decision was chosen. In terms of MDPs, this would mean explaining why the optimal policy for the MDP provides the best possible sequence of actions for the user.

It has been shown that explanations are needed either when the system performs an action that is not in accordance with the user's mental image (Gregor & Benbasat, 1999), or when the cost of failure is high (Sormo, Cassens, & Aamodt, 2005). In this chapter, both of these goals, understanding and verifying the model, serve as motivations for explanations in MDPs. While explanations can also be provided by the system on its own, the focus in this document is on the case where an explanation is triggered by a request from the user.

Characteristics and Types of Explanations

Wick and Thompson (1992) have identified different characteristics for explanations in expert systems, namely audience, goals, and focus. These characteristics are also relevant to explanations for decision-theoretic techniques such as MDPs.

The audience of the explanations can be experts, knowledge engineers or end-users. Experts understand the domain completely and are interested in explanations that describe the knowledge available to the system. The knowledge engineers or designers are concerned primarily with the correct operation of the system and require explanations that make the operation of the system transparent. End-users are more concerned with understanding the recommendation made by the system. While this separation can be useful, in most cases the knowledge engineers for the MDPs will also need to be experts and vice versa. In the rest of the document, experts and designers will be used interchangeably to refer to a single entity that performs both roles. The actual term used, along with the context, will indicate the more dominant role.

The goals for explanations are verification, duplication and ratification. Verification can be performed by examining an explanation that presents the system's knowledge in an accurate manner. Experts will be more concerned about verification of the system through the explanations. For MDPs, this will mean verifying that the specified model results in the correct policy. Duplication requires transfer of knowledge to the user, such that the user can arrive at the same conclusion using this information. It is of more concern to experts trying to understand the model to ensure they have the correct information. This goal may not be relevant for explanations in MDPs because it is not generally possible to perform the calculations involved in computing the policy manually. Ratification refers to enhancing the credibility of the system in the eyes of the users by providing appropriate explanations.

The focus of explanations determines the content of the explanation. The focus can either be the process or the solution. If the focus is the process then details of how the system arrived at a certain conclusion need to be presented in the explanation. If the focus is the solution, then it is more relevant to justify the conclusion by providing arguments in its favour.

The characteristics of explanations provide insights into the types of explanations that are more useful for different types of audience. Experts would be more interested in verifying the model by focusing on the process, whereas the users would be more interested in ratification through focus on the solution.

Chandrasekaran, Tanner, and Josephson (1989) have identified three different types of explanations. Type 1 explanations provide information about why certain decisions were or were not made. Type 2 explanations justify the system's knowledge base through some domain principles. Type 3 explanations highlight the control behaviour and problem-solving strategy. For MDPs, Type 1 would explain the policy, and Type 2 would explain the transition and reward functions and the discount factor, whereas Type 3 would be similar to Type 1 since the only control strategy for MDPs is to maximize expected utility.

Previous Research on Explanations

Explanations for intelligent systems have been considered an essential component of intelligent systems from their very outset. The primary focus of previous work on explanations has been to enhance user confidence regarding the recommendations made by the system. We now list various strategies to develop explanations for intelligent systems and examine their utility for MDPs.

Canned Explanations

Error messages can be considered the most primitive form of explanations. These are displayed by the system when a certain event occurs. Their only purpose is to notify the user regarding detection of that event. The biggest issue with such an approach is that the designer needs to anticipate all possible questions and then explicitly provide answers to every such question. With changes in model, the explanations (error messages) also need to be changed manually.

Execution Traces

The first approaches to explanations in expert systems were based on presenting the execution traces to the users. This technique was used by the MYCIN expert system (Clancey, 1983) for medical diagnosis. It provided users with answers to certain type of "Why" questions. They were answered by listing the rule that required certain information being asked from the user as well as by providing a trace of the execution of that rule indicating the conclusion that rule could lead to. There are also other proposals to examine the code being run, and describe it in English as an execution trace (Swartout, 1977). Such systems answer explanations of Type 1.

The issue with providing an execution trace is that it can yield too much information, not necessarily all of which is relevant to understanding the final decision. Also it is not necessary that the structure of the expert system lends itself to user comprehension. Hence, while such techniques may be useful in debugging the system, they cannot always be used in explanations to users.

Justification and Strategic Explanations

Another criticism of explanation systems based on execution traces has been that they do not provide justifications in their explanations. At best, they can only explain the reasoning through which the system arrived at a conclusion, but they cannot be used to convey the rationale behind that reasoning. To understand that reason, the system needs to know the rationale the designer had in mind that led to the creation of those rules. While the expert system can function and arrive at the correct conclusions by just knowing the rules, it is not possible to justify these conclusions without external domain knowledge.

These kinds of explanations were needed especially for intelligent tutoring systems, in which the goal is to transfer knowledge to the user. Xplain (Swartout, 1983) was one of the first systems to provide justifications of its decisions to users. To provide justifications, it maintained a knowledge base in addition to the rules used by the expert system. The knowledge base provided domain-specific information, called deep-knowledge by its designers, used for creating justifications. Such systems answer explanations of Type 2. It may be noted that an extra step is required to create the knowledge base for generating justifications.

The execution traces coupled with a knowledge base for domain-specific information may not be sufficient to explain the working of an expert system to the user. Users will understand the different rules that were executed, and why those rules were consistent with the domain principles, but they may lack strategic information such as the ordering of those rules. NEOMYCIN (Clancey, 1983), an extension to MYCIN, addressed this problem by retaining strategic information of this nature, as well as requiring the designer to label different phases of the reasoning process explicitly. Examples of such phases could include establishing a hypothesis space, or exploring and refining that hypothesis space. Thus, the user was then given an explanation that included information about the high-level goals or sub-goals of the system relevant to the rule under consideration. Such systems answer explanations of Type 3. Again, there is an additional burden on the designer of the system to record such information along with the rules or to explicitly divide the expert system's execution into such stages.

Similarity Based Measures

Of late, different systems have started providing explanations based on similarity with other situations or cases known to the user. Quite a few recommender systems are based on collaborative filtering techniques in which users are grouped in different clusters based on their similarity on certain aspects. The system assumes that similar users have similar preferences. Thus, a user is recommended items (e.g., movies, books or songs) based on whether other users similar to her liked those items. Explanations for such recommendations (Herlocker, 2000; Tintarev & Masthoff, 2007) convey how many users liked this item, or the attributes on which other users, who liked this item, were similar to the current user.

Case-based reasoning systems function on the principle of identifying other situations or events, called cases, that are most similar to the current case and then identifying the decisions taken in those cases. The users are then presented those cases as explanation for the chosen decision. Various similarity measures can be defined with the simplest being that the nearest neighbor is chosen as an explanation (Aamodt & Plaza, 1994). Another example of similarity can be the nearest

neighbor that lies between the current instance and the nearest unlike case, which in some cases can serve as a better explanation (Doyle, Cunningham, Bridge & Rahman, 2004).

Similar cases have also been used as explanations for systems that use a complex mathematical technique, such as neural networks or regression (Nugent & Cunningham, 2005). In this case, the training data of the system is searched for a similar case with a similar result that can be presented to the user. Such explanations can be considered a form of reconstructive explanation, since the actual reason behind the choice is the mathematical technique rather than the similarity to the case in the training data. Explanations based on similarity measures cannot be used for MDPs since there is not always training data available for MDPs.

Explanations for Probabilistic Systems

The explanations of the previous section provide a good starting point for explaining MDPs, but do not serve the purpose completely. None of the systems discussed are stochastic, like MDPs. In most cases, the policy is already known to the designer, unlike MDPs in which the policy is computed. Also, none of them need to focus on a sequence of inter-related decisions, which is more complicated than explaining a single isolated decision. The complex numerical computations involved in finding optimal policies also make it difficult for users to gain an insight into the decision-making process.

While there has been a lot of work on explanations for intelligent systems, such as expert and rule-based systems, there has not been much work for probabilistic and decision-theoretic systems. The main reason behind this discrepancy is the difference in processes through which they arrive at their conclusions. For probabilistic and decision-theoretic systems, there are well-known axioms of probability and theorems from utility theory that are applied to perform inference or to compute a policy. Since these systems are based on a principled approach, experts do not need to examine the reasoning trace to determine if the inference or policy computation process is correct. The trace would essentially refer to concepts such as Bayes' theorem, or the principle of maximum expected utility, or other axioms of probability and utility theory. These techniques are well-known, and if it is assumed that they have been coded correctly, then there is no doubt that they will yield the correct result. This is in clear contrast with expert and rule-based systems in which no similar principled approach is being followed. The experts need to examine what rules have been triggered as a result of the current state, and whether their sequence of instantiation and then execution is correct. This explains the large number of projects to generate explanations for expert and rule-based systems. On the other hand, for probabilistic and decision-theoretic systems, the requirement is to highlight portions of the input that lead to a particular result rather than to explain the principles behind these techniques. In the past, decision-theoretic approaches have not been scalable for real-world problems which explains the lack of literature on explanations for MDPs and POMDPs. Recently, decision-theoretic systems have been used for some real-world problems (Boger et al., 2006; Montemerlo, Pineau, Roy, Thrun, & Verma, 2002; Pedersen, Bualat, Lees, Smith, & Washington, 2003), which now motivates the need for explanations in them.

Explanations for Bayesian Networks

Lacave & Díez (2002) provide a survey of different techniques in this area, and define three different types of explanations that are generated for Bayesian networks. The first type is related to explanation of evidence, in which the system explains what values of observed variables led to a certain conclusion. This technique is known as abduction. The second type is related to the explanation of the model in which the static knowledge, encoded in the Bayesian network, is presented or displayed to the user. The third technique refers to the explanation of reasoning in which the user is told how the inference process unfolds. This can be done by showing the reasoning process that led to certain results (possibly including intermediate results), or by showing the reasoning process that led to rejection of a hypothesis (possibly including intermediate results), or by providing knowledge to the user about hypothetical situations in which the result would have changed, if certain variables in the current state were different.

A similar categorization can be used for explanation in MDPs. The explanation of evidence can refer to explaining the current state, and even the observation function in the case of POMDPs. The explanation of the model can refer to explaining the transition and reward functions. Finally, the explanation of reasoning can refer to explaining the process through which the optimal policy is computed.

Explanations for Influence Diagrams

Lacave, Luque, and Díez (2007) present different approaches to explain graphical models, including Bayesian networks and influence diagrams. Their explanations are geared to users with a background in decision analysis, and they present utilities of different actions graphically and numerically. This assumes that the audience is familiar with the concept of utility. This work cannot be used for users who are not likely to have knowledge of the underlying model or utilities. This work can be used to assist experts, and the authors mention that they have used it to construct and debug models to help medical doctors in diagnosis and decision-making. Similar techniques may be used to debug and validate the transition function, however, there is still a need to explain the policy and to support modifying the original transition if the policy is incorrect.

Explanations for MDPs

There has been very little work on explanation of policies generated using MDPs. The only other work we are aware on explanation of MDPs is by Elizalde et al. (2007; 2008a; 2008b). In their work, an explanation comprises three components: an optimal action, a relevant variable, and explaining why the optimal action is the best in terms of the relevant variable. They identify the relevant variable by determining which variable affects the utility function the most. Two heuristics are provided to determine a relevant variable. In the first method, they keep the rest of the state fixed and only change the values of one variable under consideration. By doing this, they measure the difference in the maximum and minimum values of the utilities of the states which are similar for all other variables except for the variable being considered. This process is repeated for all variables, and the variable with the largest difference between the maximum and minimum value is then considered relevant. In the second heuristic, they examine the optimal action for different states, such that only the value of the variable under consideration is changed and other values are kept fixed. They consider a variable more relevant if the optimal policy changes more frequently by changing the value of that variable, while keeping the values of other variables fixed.

Such explanations belong to the category of reconstructive explanations of Type 1, since they do not mirror the reasoning process. They provide intuition regarding the optimal action by discussing the relevant variable and its possible impact. This technique provides a first step towards explanations for MDPs by exploring whether users can always be satisfied by only showing a single relevant variable. It is conceivable that multiple relevant variables may need to be combined to construct a more meaningful and intuitive explanation. It will also be interesting to explore the long-term effects of the optimal action, rather than only focusing on the change of utility while identifying a relevant variable. We present our work on generating explanations for MDPs next.

AUTOMATIC EXPLANATIONS FOR MARKOV DECISION PROCESSES

We want to present an explanation that answers the question, "Why has this recommendation been made?" We populate generic templates with domain-specific information from the MDP. The templates are populated at run-time, with a subset of these included in the explanation.

Various methods for computing a policy for an MDP have been discussed in a previous chapter on Markov Decision Processes. An alternate method to evaluate a policy involves occupancy frequencies (Poupart, 2005). The discounted occupancy frequency (hereafter referred as simply occupancy frequency) $\lambda_{s_0}^\pi(s')$ is the expected number of times we reach state s' from starting state s_0 by executing policy π. Occupancy frequencies can be computed by solving Eq. 1.

$$\lambda_{s_0}^\pi = \delta(s', s_0) + \gamma \sum_{s \in S} \Pr(s' \mid s, \pi(s)) \pi_s^\pi(s') \quad (1)$$

where $\delta(s', s_0)$ is a Kroenecker delta which assigns 1 when $s' = s$ and 0 otherwise. In certain domains, it will be impossible to revisit a state so the occupancy frequency will lie in $[0, 1]$. But the frequency is not a probability so it can lie in $[0, h]$, where h is the horizon.

In factored MDPs, a set of state variables define the state space, with the state of the MDP determined by the values of all state variables. We define the set of states obtained by assigning values to a subset of state variables as a scenario. We can define occupancy frequencies for scenarios $\lambda_{s_0}^\pi(sc)$, as the expected number of times we reach a scenario sc, from starting state s_0, by executing policy π *i.e.*, $\lambda_{s_0}^\pi(sc) = \sum_{s \in sc} \lambda_{s_0}^\pi(s)$. The dot product of occupancy frequencies and rewards gives the value of a policy, as shown in Eq. 2.

$$V^\pi(s_0) = \sum_{s \in S} \lambda^\pi_{s_0}(s) R(s, \pi(s)) \qquad (2)$$

We use this formulation of the value function while generating our explanations.

Explanation Templates

The reward function reflects the preference amongst different states or scenarios. Rewards are generally assigned to states or scenarios that have certain semantic value associated with them. The policy for an MDP is computed by maximizing the sum of expected discounted rewards. Our explanations indicate how this expectation is being maximized by executing the optimal action. Our approach anticipates the effects of an action and shows the contributions of those effects to the sum of expected rewards. The expected reward is the sum of products of the occupancy frequency of each state/scenario with its reward. A sample explanation for choosing an action could be that the frequency of reaching a scenario is highest (or lowest). This is especially useful when this scenario also has a relatively high (or low) reward. Below we describe templates in which the italicized phrases (scenarios and their probabilities) are populated at run-time.

- **Template 1:** *"ActionName is the only action that is likely to take you to $Var_1 = Var_1, Var_2 = Var_2, Var_3 = Var_3$ about λ times, which is higher (or lower) than any other action"*
- **Template 2:** *"ActionName is likely to take you to $Var_1 = Var_1, Var_2 = Var_2, Var_3 = Var_3$ about λ times, which is as high (or low) as any other action"*
- **Template 3:** *"ActionName is likely to take you to $Var_1 = Var_1, Var_2 = Var_2, Var_3 = Var_3$ about λ times"*

The frequency λ can be higher than 1 if a state can be revisited. While the frequencies are discounted they still represent an expectation of the number of times a state will be visited. To understand this, consider an alternate yet equivalent representation of the discount factor in which $1-\gamma$ is the termination probability, i.e., the probability of the MDP terminating at each step.

While these templates provide a method to present explanations, multiple templates can be populated even for non-optimal actions; a non-optimal action may have the highest frequency of reaching a scenario with a high reward, but it still may not have the maximum expected utility. Thus, we need to identify a set of templates to include in the explanation to justify the optimal action. This is our main contribution in this work.

Minimum Sufficient Explanations (MSE)

We define an explanation as sufficient if it can prove that the recommendation is optimal, i.e., the selected templates show the action is optimal without needing additional templates. A sufficient explanation cannot be generated for a non-optimal action since an explanation for another action (i.e., optimal action) will have a higher utility. A sufficient explanation is also minimal if it includes the minimum number of templates needed to ensure it is sufficient. The sufficiency constraint is useful for designers of MDPs trying to debug their model. The minimality constraint is useful for users trying to understand the policy with as little information as is necessary. If needed, we can relax the minimality or sufficiency constraints and provide more or less templates depending upon the audience.

Let s_0 be the state where we need to explain why $\pi^*(s_0)$ is an optimal action. Let $\pi^{s_0,a}$ be defined as $\pi^{s_0,a} = \begin{cases} a & \text{if } s = s_0 \\ \pi^*(s) & \text{Otherwise} \end{cases}$ where a is a sub-optimal action. Note that $\pi^{s_0,a}$ and π^* are equivalent if $a = \pi^*(s_0)$. We can express the expected utility of executing this policy, as $V^{\pi^{s_0,a}}$. This is equivalent to the action-value function (Sutton, 1998), also known as the Q-function, $Q^\pi(s_0, a)$. Since a template is populated by a frequency and a state/scenario, let us define a term t which encapsulates this information as $t(s, \pi^*, s_0) = \lambda^{\pi^*}_{s_0}(s)R(s, \pi^*(s))$. Now V^π can be computed as Eq. 3, by rewriting Eq. 2.

$$V^{\pi^*} = \sum_{s \in S} t(s, \pi^*, s_0) \tag{3}$$

The MSE comprises a subset of the terms in Eq. 3. For this reason, the expected utility of the terms included in the MSE, V^{MSE}, cannot exceed that of the optimal action, V^{π^*}, but must be higher than that of any other action, i.e., $V^{\pi^*} \geq V^{\text{MSE}} \geq Q^{\pi^*}(s_0, a) \quad \forall a \neq \pi^*(s_0)$. In the worst case, all terms will have to be included in the explanation. To compute the MSE, we arrange all terms in Eq. 3 in descending order, and then select the first k terms of this sequence, necessary to ensure that $V^{\text{MSE}} \geq Q^{\pi^*}(s_0, a)$. We can compute V^{MSE} using Eq. 4.

$$V^{\text{MSE}} = \sum_{i \leq k} t_i + \sum_{i > k} \bar{r}\lambda^{\pi^*}_{s_0}(s_i) \tag{4}$$

V^{MSE} comprises two components. First, we include the expected utility from all the terms in the MSE, i.e., $\sum_{i \leq k} t_i$. Second, for every term not included in the MSE, we need to consider its worst case by adding utility computed by using the minimum possible reward, $\bar{r}$, to the MSE. The second component is needed to ensure sufficiency if rewards are negative, and minimality otherwise.

In Eq. 4, the total number of terms will equal the size of the state space. This can be computationally prohibitive for large state spaces. Typi-

cally, factored MDPs are used in such cases. Also, the reward function can be decomposed and defined by a set R of reward variables $\Re$ such that the sum of their values r is the reward at any given state. Let $sc_{R=r}$ define the scenario for which reward variable R has value r, and $V^{\pi^*}_f$ represent the utility of executing π^* for a factored MDP. Using these definitions, we can now compute the value of a policy using a term involving scenarios, instead of states. In Eq. 4, $\bar{r}$ represents the minimum value for the reward function. With multiple reward variables, every variable may have its own minimum value which can be used instead. Let $\bar{r}_i$ define the minimum value for the reward variable used in term i in the sorted sequence. Now, we can rewrite Eq. 3 and 4 as Eq. 5 and 6 respectively.

$$V^{\pi^*}_f = \sum_{R \in \Re} \sum_{r \in \text{dom}(R)} r\lambda^{\pi^*}_{s_0}(sc_{R=r}) \tag{5}$$

$$V^{\text{MSE}}_f = \sum_{i \leq k} t_i + \sum_{i > k} \bar{r}_i\lambda^{\pi^*}_{s_0}(sc_i) \tag{6}$$

The number of terms is now significantly lower since we only need a single term per value of each reward variable. This allows us to compute an MSE even for domains with large state spaces.

We know that the optimal policy is invariant to positive linear transformations on the reward function. We also want this property in the MSE to ensure that the MSE only changes if the model has changed. This will assist designers in debugging the model efficiently.

Proposition: MSE remains invariant under affine transformations of the reward function.

Proof: Let $\hat{V}^\pi_f$ denote the expected utility for any policy π when rewards have been scaled by adding any constant c. If we substitute r by $r+c$ in Eq. 5, we get $\hat{V}^\pi_f = V^\pi_f + c \sum_{R \in \Re} \sum_{r \in \text{dom}} (R)\lambda^{\pi^*}_{s_0}(sc_{R=r})$. Since occupancy frequencies computed for an MDP must add up to the horizon ($\sum_{r\in\text{dom}} (R)\lambda^\pi(sc_{R=r}) = h$), so $\hat{V}_f^\pi = V_f^\pi + ch \mid R \mid$, where $\mid R \mid$ is the total number of reward variables. Similarly, $\hat{V}_f^{\text{MSE}} = V_f^{\text{MSE}} + ch \mid R \mid$. Since $V_f^{\text{MSE}} \geq V_f^\pi$, thus $\hat{V}_f^{\text{MSE}} \geq \hat{V}_f^\pi$ for any constant c. Also $\hat{V}_f^{\text{MSE}}$ will comprise the same scaled reward values and frequencies as those in V_f^{MSE} otherwise the explanation would not remain either sufficient or minimal. For discounted domains, the frequencies will add up to the expected discounted horizon instead of h. A similar proof can also be presented for the case where rewards are multiplied by a positive constant.

Workflow and Algorithm for Explanations

The basic workflow for our explanation process is as follows. The designer identifies the states and actions, and specifies the transition and reward functions of an MDP. The optimal policy is computed by using a technique such as value iteration. Now the designer/user can consult an optimal policy to determine an optimal action and request an explanation. Our system will compute an MSE using the algorithm given below.

1. Compute $sc_{R=r}$, the scenario which comprises the set of all states that lead to each value r of each reward variable R. This information is directly available from the dependencies encoded in the reward function. For each assignment of value r to variable R, note the set of states that receive reward r to compute the scenario.

2. For every scenario $sc_{R=r}$, compute the occupancy frequency $\lambda_{s_0}^{\pi^*}(sc_{R=r})$ for every action. The occupancy frequency for a scenario is computed efficiently by summing the occupancy frequencies of each state in it using variable elimination. The recurrence is terminated after a number of steps equal

to the horizon of the MDP or when convergence is achieved (due to the discount factor) for infinite horizon problems.

3. Compute the term $t(s,\pi^*,s_0)$ and $\bar{r}_i\lambda_{s_0}^{\pi^*}(sc_i)$ for every scenario $sc_{R=r}$. They respectively represent the advantage and disadvantage of including and excluding a term from the MSE.

4. Sort $t_i - \bar{r}_i\lambda_{s_0}^{\pi^*}(sc_i)$ in descending order and select the first k terms from this sequence to include in the MSE for which $V^{\text{MSE}} \geq Q^{\pi^*}(s_0,a) \quad \forall a \neq \pi^*(s_0)$. Note that t_i and $\bar{r}_i\lambda_{s_0}^{\pi^*}(sc_i)$ respectively represent the advantage and disadvantage associated with including and excluding a term from the MSE, so their difference indicates the benefit of this term in the explanation versus excluding it.

5. Present each term in then explanation to user in one of the defined templates. Choose templates using the following criteria.
   a. Use template 1 if the optimal action has the highest (or lowest) expected frequency to reach that scenario by a significant margin.
   b. Use template 2 if the optimal action has the highest (or lowest) expected frequency, but not by a significant margin.
   c. Use template 3 if neither of the previous templates can be used.

The pseudo code for above algorithm is shown in Figure 1. The expensive step in the algorithm is Step 2 that involves computing the occupancy frequencies. The rest are basic arithmetic operations and logical comparisons except sorting the sequence of terms in Step 4. Computing occupancy frequencies is similar to policy evaluation whose complexity is that of solving a linear system of equations, which is cubic in the state space. To speed up computation, we compute occupancy

Figure 1. Pseudo code to compute minimal sufficient explanations

```
//Inputs:  Starting State: s₀, Optimal Policy: π*
//Outputs: Minimal Sufficient Explanation, MSE
ComputeMSE(s₀,π*)
   for R in R
   |  for r in R
   |  |  sc[r,R] = ComputeScenarios(r,R)
   |  |  λ[r,R] = ComputeOccupancyFrequency(sc[r,R])
   |  |  term[sc, π*,s₀]= λ[r,R]*r
   |  |  loss[sc, πᵃ,s₀]= λ[r,R]*rₘᵢₙ
   |  |  net[sc,r,R] = term[sc, π*,s₀] - loss[sc, πᵃ,s₀]
   |  end
   end
   sortedNet = sortDescending(net)
   V_MSE = 0; V_templates = 0; V_notemplates = sum(loss); k=1; MSE, Terms={}
   do
       |     add sc[r,R], λ[r,R] for sortedNet[k] in Terms
       |     V_templates   += sortedNet[k]
       |     V_notemplates -= sortedNet[k]
       |     V_MSE = V_templates + V_notemplates
       |     k++
   while (V_MSE < V_rest)
   MSE = generateTemplates(Terms)
   return MSE
//end computeMSE
```

frequencies by performing variable elimination using algebraic decision diagrams (ADD). ADDs provide a compact representation that automatically aggregates states with identical values/frequencies, needed for scenarios, thereby significantly reducing the running time. More details on the use of ADDs in MDPs can be found in (Hoey, St-aubin, Hu, & Boutilier, 1999).

Discussion

For any given state, an MSE is guaranteed to exist; in the worst case it will need to include all the terms in the MSE from Eq. 4 or Eq. 6. Thus, the upper bound on the number of templates displayed to the user is constrained by the number of terms t_i, which will depend on the structure of the

MDP being explained. A relatively large number of terms in the MSE will indicate that the effect of the optimal action is not substantially different from that of at least one other action. We can also argue that for every term there is at least one template that can be used to present the information to the user since Template 3 can always be used. While template 3 may not seem to provide much information in itself, it does indicate that there are better or worse actions available if the scenario being depicted is of particular interest to the user or designer.

Our technique can be used in finite and discounted infinite horizon problems. For discounted MDPs, the frequencies are discounted so if their value appears non-intuitive, the user may have to be explained that a discount factor is being used.

If an infinite horizon MDP is only discounted for computational convenience, the explanation may again appear non-intuitive. As explained, we also cater to the case where multiple goals are expressed through different reward variables.

In model checking, safety and liveness properties are used to debug or validate models. While our approach does not explicitly indicate whether an action is chosen because it leads to a dead-end or is optimal because it is the only action that avoids a dead-end, this information is implicit in the MSE since a dead-end would be a scenario with low reward, and the optimal action would have a low frequency of reaching it.

EXPERIMENTS

We ran experiments on two different domains. The first domain is related to course advising and the MDP provides advice to students about the choice of elective courses. The second domain is focused on assisting people with dementia in the task of handwashing. We briefly discuss these domains below.

Course Advising Domain

Our course-advising MDP has 4 core courses and 7 elective courses (from which the student has to choose), with each course having 4 possible letter grades and belonging to a certain area. It has 21 possible actions, with each action representing a pair of elective courses. The objective is to pass 6 elective courses in 3 terms by taking at least one course in 3 different areas. The transition model was obtained by using historical data collected over several years (for 14,000 undergraduate students) at our university. The reward function provides rewards for completing different degree requirements with the reward function decomposed in two different variables, one for each degree requirement, with 2 values per variable. The horizon of this problem is 3 steps, each step

representing one term and it is undiscounted. Explanations for this domain are intended for students wishing to determine which courses to register in the next term.

Handwashing Domain

We also ran our experiments on the handwashing POMDP developed by Hoey et al. (Hoey, Bertoldi, Poupart, & Mihailidis, 2007) available online[3], to assist people with dementia in handwashing. We converted their POMDP into an MDP, assuming all states are observable and changing variable names and values to make them more user-friendly. The horizon for this domain is 100 steps and discount factor is 0.95. There are three different reward variables in the reward function with 19 distinct values for rewards. Explanations for this domain are intended for a caregiver/nurse to evaluate the validity of the prompt, and not for the person washing hands.

Experimental Results

We computed MSEs for different starting states in the course advising and handwashing MDPs. The results are shown in Table 1 and Table 2 that display the mean and standard deviations. We can see that the MSE generally contains very few terms for both domains, more evident in the handwashing domain in which there was a total of 19 terms, and only 6 were needed for any given optimal action in 382 different starting states generated randomly. It is natural to expect an explanation to be more complicated if two policies have similar effects. We estimate the complexity of an explanation by the number of terms included in it. Also we define two policies to have similar effects if the ratio of their normalized expected utilities is close to 1. We can see from both tables that if the ratio between the expected utility of the second best policy, $Q^{\pi^*}(s_0, a')$, and optimal pol policies, V^{π^*}, is high then the expla-

Table 1. Explanations for course advising domain (reward variables=2, values per variable=2+2, max. terms=4)

Terms in MSE	1	2	3-4
Frequency	134	48	0
Mean $\pm$ STD of $Q^{\pi^*}(s_0, a') / V^{\pi^*}$	0.46 $\pm$ 0.41	0.81 $\pm$ 0.24	-

Table 2. Explanations for course advising domain (reward variables=3, values per variable=2+2+15, max. terms=19)

Terms in MSE	1	2	3	4	5	6	7-19
Frequency	0	142	94	119	2	25	0
Mean $\pm$ STD of $Q^{\pi^*}(s_0, a') / V^{\pi^*}$	-	0.51 $\pm$ 0.22	0.62 $\pm$ 0.10	0.68 $\pm$ 0.94	0.61 $\pm$ 0.15	0.69 $\pm$ 0.05	-

nation includes more terms. On the other hand, if the ratio is low it means that the optimal action is much superior and we can see that fewer terms are needed in the MSE. This result is in line with our intuition.

Two sample explanations, one from each domain, are shown below.

- Action *TakeCS343&CS448* is the best action because:-
  - It is likely to take you to *CoursesCompleted=6, TermNumber=Final* about *0.86* times, which is as high as any other action
- Action *DoNothingNow* is the best because:-
  - It is likely to take you to *handswashed=YES, planstep=Clean&Dry* about *0.71* times, which is the higher than any other action
  - It is likely to take you to *prompt=NoPrompt* about *12.71* times, which is as high as any other action

The occupancy frequency in the last template is higher than 1 because it is possible to visit a state multiple times with a reward for not issuing a prompt every time.

We precomputed the optimal policy for both domains since they do not need to be recomputed for every explanation. We were able to compute explanations for the course advising and handwashing problems in approximately 1 and 4 seconds respectively on a Pentium IV 1.66 GHz laptop with 1GB RAM using Java on Windows XP with the optimal policy and second best action precomputed. Note that the course advising problem has 117.4 million states and the handwashing problem has 207,360 states. The simpler reward function (two reward variables with two values each) in the course advising domain resulted in faster execution despite a larger number of states.

EVALUATION THROUGH USER STUDY

Evaluating explanations is a non-trivial task. The evaluation would clearly depend on the objective of the explanation. We have mentioned that the primary objective of the explanation is to answer the question about why a certain action is optimal for a given situation. However, secondary objectives such as enhancing user trust, educating users about the rationale behind the choice, and indicating the absence of any obvious errors, also influence how an explanation is evaluated. Even if the objective is clearly stated, the success of explanations cannot be directly observed. To demonstrate the usability of our explanations, we conducted a user study to evaluate explanations for course advising with advisors and students. The objective of this user study was to understand whether the students found automatically generated explanations beneficial and receive their feedback for improvement.

Interview with Student Advisors

We presented our explanations for several states to undergraduate advisors and sought their feedback. The advisors noted that students not performing well would benefit from our explanations as they would help them focus on requirements they are likely to not fulfill. They also mentioned that grade-conscious students would also appreciate our explanations. The advisors considered the model used by the MDP, i.e., the transition probabilities, as a useful tool to validate or correct their perception about various courses being easy or hard. They were apprehensive that it would be difficult for an online system to replace them as they consider more factors than completing degree requirements, which include preferences such as student's interests, career path, difficulty level of the course, stereo-types about areas, courses or professors. There has been some research on preference elicitation to model student preferences for course advising in MDPs (Royalty, Holland, Dekhtyar, & Goldsmith, 2002), so we explained that it is possible to extend our model to include such factors, but it is outside the scope of our work on explaining MDPs. The explanations resembled the sample explanations presented earlier in the chapter. For the purpose of our user study, students were asked to assume that they had certain preferences. This allowed us to conduct the user study without conducting preference elicitation.

User Study with Students

We recruited 37 students from our university's Computer Science department and showed 5 recommendations with explanations for different states. For each explanation, they were asked to rate the explanations on various factors such as comprehension, trust-worthiness and usefulness. They responded by filling out questionnaires detailing their ratings. For 3 states, the explanation was computed by our technique and for the other 2, the explanations were provided by advisors.

The results regarding the user's perceptions of our explanations are shown in Figure 2. 59% (65/111) of the respondents indicated that they were able to understand our explanation without any other information. Most of the students who wanted more information either wanted to know the occupancy frequencies for some other actions to get a comparison, or knowledge about the technique used to compute the transition probabilities. For the first concern, we can provide this information as it is already computed in Step 2 of algorithm for the MSE. For the second concern, we attribute this curiosity to our audience, mostly students in CS interested in understanding the system. In 76% (84/111) of the cases, it was believed that the explanation provided by our system was accurate. A few students wanted to know our sample size to judge the accuracy. Quite a few respondents, 69% (77/111), indicated that they would require extra information beyond that presented in the explanation. When asked what other type of information they may be interested in, we discovered that they considered the model inadequate and wanted a richer model that was able to cater to preferences such as student's interest, future career plans, and level of difficulty rather than the explanation being inadequate for

Figure 2. User perception of MDP-based explanations

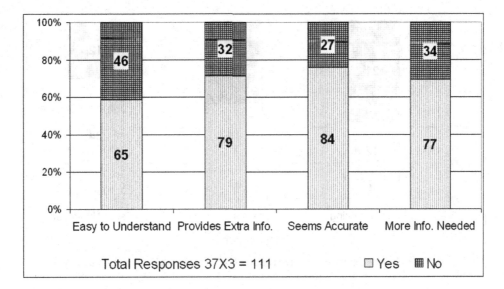

the existing model. An important indicator of the usefulness of these explanations is that 71% (79/111) of the students mentioned that the explanation provided them with extra information that helped in making a decision. Another indicator of their influence is that while students initially disagreed 23% (26/111) of the times with the recommendation, in 35% (9/26) of these cases our explanation convinced them to change their mind and agree with the recommendation. In most of the other cases, again the students disagreed because their final decision depended upon some factor, not modeled by our system, so their opinion could not have been changed by any explanation.

To compare our explanations with advisor explanations, we asked students whether they preferred our explanation, the advisor explanation, or having access to both of them simultaneously. These results are shown in Figure 3. 57% (21/37) students found that the most convincing option was to access both explanations, as opposed to 32% in favor of only advisor explanations and 11% in favor of only our explanations. Similarly, 46% (17/37) students considered both explanations viewed together as more trust-worthy as opposed to having only advisor explanations

(38%) or only our explanations (16%). As expected, most of the students (65% or 24/37) found it easier to understand advisor explanations as they were more personal and human-oriented. This is understandable since the advisors employ domain-specific constructs in their explanations while our explanations are totally generic. However, a few students (32%) also indicated that having a combination of the two would be easier to understand. Finally, we also asked students if they were provided access to our system over the Internet, in addition to the option of discussing their choices with an undergraduate advisor, would they use our system. 86% of them mentioned they would use it from home while trying to determine their choice of courses, 89% mentioned they would use it before meeting with an advisor to examine different options for themselves, and 70% mentioned they would use it after meeting with advisors to arrive at a final decision. Among the 30%, who indicated they would not use it after meeting advisors, many expected the advisors to incorporate the information from our explanations in their advice and thus considered it redundant to check it themselves. In any case, these numbers are very

Figure 3. Comparison of MDP-based and advisor explanations

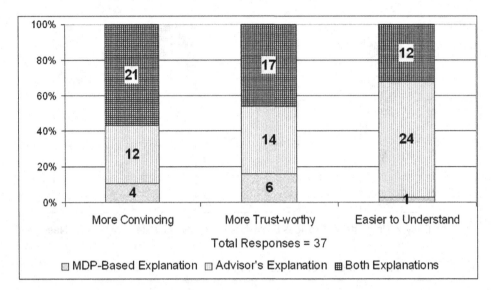

encouraging as they show substantial interest in our explanations.

The explanations generated by our system are generic, while those provided by the advisors are domain-specific. Our results show that these two types of explanations are complementary and students would like to access our explanations in addition to consulting advisors. A recurring theme during the user study was students inquiring about a facility to compare different choices, i.e., asking the question "Why is action *a* better than action *b*?", especially if their preferred action was different from the recommended action. We have extended our system to answer such questions by presenting the MSE for the recommended action *a* using the policy π and then populating the templates for the same terms for their preferred action *b*. The comparison demonstrates how *a* is better than *b* as $V^{\mathrm{MSE}} \geq Q^{\pi^*}(s_0, b)$.

FUTURE RESEARCH DIRECTIONS

We have described a mechanism to generate explanations for factored MDPs in any domain without requiring any additional effort from the MDP designer. We introduced the concept of a minimal sufficient explanation through which an action can be explained using the fewest possible terms. We showed that our explanations can be generated in near-real time for different domains. We also conducted a user study to evaluate the effectiveness of our explanations for course advising. The users appreciated the extra information provided by our generic explanation but also required some domain-specific information. Most of the students considered the combination of our explanation with the advisor explanation more effective than either one alone.

Injecting domain-specific information in explanations increases user-acceptance, though requires additional effort from the designers. As future work, a generic mechanism to represent domain-specific information can be developed. Another extension of this work can be related to partially observable MDPs. The complication in such explanations is to cater for the observation function rather than having a single known current state for which the optimal policy has been computed and is being executed.

REFERENCES

Aamodt, A., & Plaza, E. (1994). Case-based reasoning: Foundational issues, methodological variations, and system approaches. *AI Communications*, 7(1), 39–59.

Boger, J., Hoey, J., Poupart, P., Boutilier, C., Fernie, G., & Mihailidis, A. (2006, April). A planning system based on Markov decision processes to guide people with dementia through activities of daily living. *IEEE Transactions on Information Technology in Biomedicine*, 10(2), 323–333. doi:10.1109/TITB.2006.864480

Boutilier, C. (2003, August 9—15). On the foundations of expected expected utility. *Eighteenth International Joint Conference on Artificial Intelligence* (pp. 285-290). Acapulco, Mexico.

Boutilier, C., Patrascu, R., Poupart, P., & Schuurmans, D. (2006). Constraint-based optimization and utility elicitation using the minimax decision criterion. *Artificial Intelligence*, *170*(8), 686–713. doi:10.1016/j.artint.2006.02.003

Chajewska, U., Koller, D., & Ormoneit, D. (2001, June 28-July 1). Learning an agent's utility function by observing behavior. *Eighteenth International Conference on Machine Learning* (pp. 35–42). Williamstown, MA: Morgan Kaufmann.

Chandrasekaran, B., Tanner, M. C., & Josephson, J. R. (1989). Explaining control strategies in problem solving. *IEEE Expert: Intelligent Systems and Their Applications*, 4(1), 9–15, 19-24.

Clancey, W. J. (1983). The epistemology of a rule-based expert system – A framework for explanation. *Artificial Intelligence*, *20*, 215–251. doi:10.1016/0004-3702(83)90008-5

Doyle, D., Cunningham, P., Bridge, D., & Rahman, Y. (2004). *Advances in case-based reasoning* (pp. 157–168). Berlin, Germany: Springer. doi:10.1007/978-3-540-28631-8_13

Elizalde, F., Sucar, E., Luque, M., Díez, J., & Reyes, A. (2008a). *Policy explanation in factored Markov decision processes*. Fourth European Workshop on Probabilistic and Graphical Models.

Elizalde, F., Sucar, E., Reyes, A., & deBuen, P. (2007). *An MDP approach for explanation generation*. Workshop on Explanation-Aware Computing with American Association of Artificial Intelligence.

Elizalde, F., Sucar, L. E., Noguez, J., & Reyes, A. (2008b). *Integrating probabilistic and knowledge-based systems for explanation generation*. European Conference on Artificial Intelligence 2008 Workshop on Explanation Aware Computing.

Gregor, S., & Benbasat, I. (1999). Explanations from intelligent systems: Theoretical foundations and implications for practice. *Management Information Systems Quarterly*, 23(4), 497–530. doi:10.2307/249487

Hempel, C. G., & Oppenheim, P. (1948). Studies in the logic of explanation. *Philosophy of Science*, *15*, 135–175. doi:10.1086/286983

Herlocker, J. (1999). *Explanations in recommender systems*. Computer Human Interaction 1999 Workshop on Interacting with Recommender Systems.

Hoey, J., St-Aubin, R., Hu, A., & Boutilier, C. (1999, July 30 to August 1). SPUDD: Stochastic planning using decision diagrams. *Uncertainty in Artificial Intelligence* (pp. 279–288). Stockholm, Sweden.

Hoey, J., von Bertoldi, A., Poupart, P., & Mihailidis, A. (2007). *Assisting persons with dementia during handwashing using a partially observable Markov decision process*. International Conference on Computer Vision Systems.

Lacave, C., & Díez, F. J. (2002). A review of explanation methods for Bayesian networks. *The Knowledge Engineering Review*, *17*, 107–127. doi:10.1017/S026988890200019X

Lacave, C., Luque, M., & Díez, F. (2007). Explanation of Bayesian networks and influence diagrams in Elvira. *IEEE Transactions on Systems, Man, and Cybernetics*, *37*(4), 952–965. doi:10.1109/TSMCB.2007.896018

McGuinness, D., Glass, A., Wolverton, M., & da Silva, P. (2007). *Explaining task processing in cognitive assistants that learn*. National Conference on Artificial Intelligence Spring Symposium on Interaction Challenges for Intelligent Assistants.

Montemerlo, M., Pineau, J., Roy, N., Thrun, S., & Verma, V. (2002, July 28-August 1). Experiences with a mobile robotic guide for the elderly. *Eighteenth National Conference on Artificial Intelligence* (pp. 587–592). Edmonton, AB, Canada.

Ng, A. Y., & Russell, S. J. (2000, June 29 to July 2). Algorithms for inverse reinforcement learning. *Seventeenth International Conference on Machine Learning* (pp. 663–670). Stanford, CA: Morgan Kaufmann Publishers Inc.

Nielsen, T. D., & Jensen, F. V. (2004). Learning a decision maker's utility function from (possibly) inconsistent behavior. *Artificial Intelligence*, *160*(1), 53–78. doi:10.1016/j.artint.2004.08.003

Nugent, C., & Cunningham, P. (2005). A case-based explanation system for black-box systems. *Artificial Intelligence Review*, *24*(2), 163–178. doi:10.1007/s10462-005-4609-5

Pedersen, L., Bualat, M. G., Lees, D., Smith, D. E., & Washington, R. (2003, May). *Integrated demonstration of instrument placement, robust execution and contingent planning*. International Symposium on Artificial Intelligence, Robotics and Automation for Space. Tokyo, Japan.

Poupart, P. (2005). *Exploiting structure to efficiently solve large scale partially observable markov decision processes*. Unpublished doctoral dissertation, University of Toronto.

Royalty, J., Holland, R., Dekhtyar, A., & Goldsmith, J. (2002). *POET, the online preference elicitation tool*. In National Conference on Artificial Intelligence Workshop on Preferences in Artificial Intelligence and Constraint Programming: Symbolic Approaches.

Sørmo, F., Cassens, J., & Aamodt, A. (2005). Explanation in case-based reasoning—Perspectives and goals. *Artificial Intelligence Review*, *24*(2), 109–143. doi:10.1007/s10462-005-4607-7

Sutton, R. S., & Barto, A. G. (1998). *Reinforcement learning: An introduction*. Cambridge, MA: MIT Press.

Swartout, W. R. (1977, August). A digitalis therapy advisor with explanations. Fifth International Joint Conference on Artificial Intelligence. Cambridge, MA, USA.

Swartout, W. R. (1983). Xplain: A system for creating and explaining expert consulting programs. *Artificial Intelligence*, *21*, 285–325. doi:10.1016/S0004-3702(83)80014-9

Tintarev, N., & Masthoff, J. (2007). A survey of explanations in recommender systems. *International Conference on Data Engineering Workshop on Recommender Systems & Intelligent User Interfaces*.

Wick, M. R., & Thompson, W. B. (1992). Reconstructive expert system explanation. *Artificial Intelligence*, *54*(1-2), 33–70. doi:10.1016/0004-3702(92)90087-E

ADDITIONAL READING

Gregor, S., & Benbasat, I. (1999). Explanations from intelligent systems: Theoretical foundations and implications for practice. *Management Information Systems Quarterly, 23*(4), 497–530. doi:10.2307/249487

Herlocker, J. (1999). Explanations in recommender systems. *Computer Human Interaction 1999 Workshop on Interacting with Recommender Systems*

Lacave, C., & Díez, F. J. (2002). A review of explanation methods for Bayesian networks. *The Knowledge Engineering Review, 17*, 107–127. doi:10.1017/S026988890200019X

Sørmo, F., Cassens, J., & Aamodt, A. (2005). Explanation in case-based reasoning—perspectives and goals. *Artificial Intelligence Review, 24*(2), 109–143. doi:10.1007/s10462-005-4607-7

KEY TERMS AND DEFINITIONS

Explanation: An explanation is a combination of templates, with each template indicating the effect of explained action w.r.t. various states or scenarios.

Minimum Sufficient Explanation: An MSE is an explanation that has the minimum number of templates needed to ensure the value of the explanation is greater than the value of any other action.

Occupancy Frequency: $(\lambda_{s_0}^{\pi}(s'))$, the expected number of times we reach state (s') from starting state (s_0) by executing a particular policy (π).

Scenario: a collection of states obtained by not assigning values to a subset of state variables in a factored MDP.

Template: A template reports the occupancy frequency of a state or scenario and compares this frequency to other alternate actions.

Term: $(t(s, \pi^*, s_0))$ the product of the reward $(R(s, \pi^*(s)))$ and occupancy frequency $(\lambda_{s_0}^{\pi^*}(s))$ for a particular state or scenario (s or sc).

ENDNOTES

[1]   http://www.merriam-webster.com/dictionary/explanation
[2]   http://www.merriam-webster.com/dictionary/explain
[3]   http://www.cs.uwaterloo.ca/~ppoupart/software/symbolicPerseus/problems/handwashing/

Chapter 8
Dynamic LIMIDS

Francisco J. Díez
UNED, Spain

Marcel A. J. van Gerven
Radboud University Nijmegen, The Netherlands

ABSTRACT

One of the objectives of artificial intelligence is to build decision-support models for systems that evolve over time and include several types of uncertainty. Dynamic limited-memory influence diagrams (DLIMIDs) are a new type of model proposed recently for this kind of problems. DLIMIDs are similar to other models in assuming a multi-stage process that satisfies the Markov property, i.e., that the future is independent of the past given the current state. The main difference with those models is the restriction of limited memory, which means that the decision maker must make a choice based only on recent observations, but this limitation can be circumvented by the use of memory variables. We present several algorithms for evaluating DLIMIDs, show a real-world model for a medical problem, and compare DLIMIDs with related formalisms, such as LIMIDs, dynamic influence diagrams, and POMDPs.

INTRODUCTION

One of the main goals of artificial intelligence is to create computer programs that make optimal decisions in situations characterized by uncertainty. A particular family of problems of this type is to make decisions about a system that evolves over time. For instance, a patient suffering from a chronic disease goes to the doctor several times a year, and in each visit the doctor observes some

symptoms and signs, orders some tests, and selects a treatment for the patient. In the same way, a robot must decide which action to perform at each moment, which may include analyzing an image, moving to a destination, picking up an object, recharging its batteries, or any combination of them. A similar problem would be the control of an industrial plant, in which the decisions might be to perform a test, to open or close a valve, to replace a component, etc.

One of the first modeling tools for decision analysis and decision support were probabilistic

DOI: 10.4018/978-1-60960-165-2.ch008

decision trees (Raiffa, 1968). Even though they are still the standard method in some fields, such as medicine and economy, they are very difficult to build, even for medium-size problems. For this reason, they are not considered as a suitable tool for artificial intelligence. Influence diagrams, initially proposed in the field of economy (Howard & Matheson, 1984), are much more powerful as a modeling tool, and for this reason they have become very popular in artificial intelligence. However, they are not suitable for solving temporal problems, such as the three examples presented above. One of the reasons is that influence diagrams require a total ordering of decisions, which is an unrealistic assumption in many situations in which the decision maker does not know in advance what decision should be made first to maximize the expected utility. A second drawback, especially important in the case of temporal reasoning, is that in an influence diagram each policy depends—at least in principle—on all the past observations. For a system that evolves over a large period of time, the number of observations usually grows linearly with the passing of time, which implies that the size of policies grows superexponentially.

In order to avoid these two limitations, Lauritzen and Nilsson (2001) presented limited-memory influence diagrams (LIMIDs) as an extension of influence diagrams. The term *limited-memory* name reflects the property that a finding known when making a decision is not necessarily "remembered" when making a posterior decision. Eliminating some variables from the domain of some policies may reduce the complexity of the model to the point of making it solvable with a computer, albeit at the price of reducing the quality of the policies.

In their original formulation, LIMIDs did not have an explicit representation of time, nor the possibility of indicating that the structure of the model repeats itself periodically. As a consequence, the size of a LIMID aimed at modeling a system that evolves over a long period of time

would grow linearly with the duration of the process. In order to overcome this limitation, we developed DLIMIDs (dynamic LIMIDs) as a type of temporal model for decision analysis and decision support in problems with uncertainty and a periodic structure (van Gerven & Díez, 2006, van Gerven, Díez, Taal, & Lucas, 2007).

Independently, Markov decision processes (MDPs) were developed around the mid-20th century as a model for finding the optimal policy in situations where outcomes are partly random and partly under the control of a decision maker (Bellman, 1957). The main limitation of this model was the assumption that the state of the system is always known with certainty, which is unrealistic in most cases. The relaxation of this assumption led to the emergence of partially observable Markov decision processes (POMDPs) (Åström, 1965), in which the state of the system is not directly observable, but there is a variable that correlates probabilistically with it. The main problem of MDPs and POMDPs is that the variable that represents the state of the system may take a huge number of values, which complicates significantly the evaluation of the models. A partial remedy to this problem was to use several variables to represent the state of the system, rather than only one; this led to factored MDPs (Boutilier, Dearden, & Goldszmidt, 1995, 2000) and factored POMDPs (Boutilier & Poole, 1996).

DLIMIDs can be seen as a generalization of factored POMDPs, as they allow to have several decisions per time slice, which may be useful for many real-world problems. For example, the DLIMID in Figure 1 represents the follow-up of a chronic patient, such that in each consultation the doctor decides whether to perform a test *and*, depending on its result, whether to apply a therapy, while a POMDP would assume that the doctor can either do the test *or* apply the therapy, but not both, which would introduce a severe mismatch between the reality and the model.[1] The downside of this increase in representational power is that some of the algorithms developed in the last years, which

Figure 1. A DLIMID for the treatment of patients that may or may not have a disease D. The disease can be identified by a finding F, which is the result of a laboratory test L, having an associated cost, that is captured by the utility function U. Based on the finding, we decide whether or not to perform treatment T. If the patient does not have the disease then this has an associated utility U'.

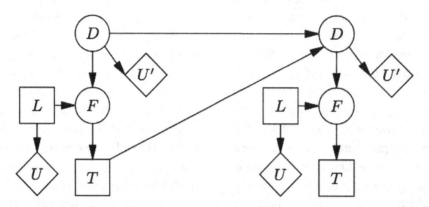

allow to solve very large POMDPs (see (Poupart, 2005) and references therein), can not be applied to DLIMIDs, at least at the moment.

The rest of this chapter is structured as follows. First, we present the basic properties of DLIMIDs. Then, we describe several algorithms for evaluating DLIMIDs, either with finite or infinite horizon. The next section shows a DLIMID for a real-world problem: the follow-up of patients with carcinoid tumors. Then, we analyze the similarities and differences between DLIMIDs and other models, such us LIMIDs, dynamic influence diagrams, and factored POMDPs. Finally, we summarize the conclusions and discuss several lines for future research.

DYNAMIC LIMITED-MEMORY INFLUENCE DIAGRAMS (DLIMIDS)

Definition of DLIMID

A *dynamic limited memory influence diagram* (DLIMID) is a tuple $L=(h,\mathbf{C},\mathbf{D},\mathbf{U},G,P,U,\gamma)$. In this tuple, $h \in \mathbb{N}^+ \cup \{+\infty\}$, is the *horizon*. $\mathbf{C}$ is a set of chance variables. $\mathbf{D}$ is a set of decision variables (actions). We assume in this chapter that

all the variables in $\mathbf{C}$ and $\mathbf{D}$ are discrete. $\mathbf{U}$ is the set of utility variables (rewards). Variables are indexed by time: $t \in \{1,\dots,h\}$.

G is an acyclic directed graph containing a node for each variable X^t; for this reason we will use the terms variable and node interchangeably. The parents of a variable X^t in the graph are denoted by $Pa(X^t)$. Two additional restrictions of the graph are that utility nodes cannot have children and that links to the past, i.e., of the form $X^t \rightarrow Y^{t'}$ with $t' > t$, are not allowed.[2]

P is a set of conditional probability distributions such that for each chance variable X^t and each configuration of its parents, $pa(X^t)$, there is a conditional probability distribution of the form $P(x^t|pa(X^t))$. The set P induces a joint probability distribution for the variables in $\mathbf{C}$, conditioned on the decisions, as follows:

$$P(\mathbf{c} \mid \mathbf{d}) = \prod_{C \in \mathbf{C}} P(c \mid pa(C)) \qquad (1)$$

In this equation, c is the result of projecting configuration $(\mathbf{c},\mathbf{d})$ onto C and $pa(C)$ is the result of projecting $(\mathbf{c},\mathbf{d})$ onto $Pa(C)$. The next equations in this chapter must be understood in the same way.

Similarly, the set *U* contains, for each node U^t, a function $u(pa(U^t))$ that maps each configuration of the parents of U^t in the graph onto a real number. These utilities are sometimes called *rewards*.

Therefore, the meaning of an arc $X \to Y$ in *G* is determined by the type of *Y*. If *Y* is a chance variable, then the conditional probability distribution associated with *Y* is conditioned on *X*, as in Equation 1. If *Y* is a utility node, it means that the utility function associated with node *Y* depends on variable *X*. If *Y* is a decision, then *X* represents information that is present to the decision maker prior to deciding upon *Y*, which in turn implies that *X* is observable.[3]

Finally, $\gamma \in (0,1]$ is the *discount factor*. Usually $\gamma < 1$, which implies that delayed rewards are less valuable to the decision maker.

The subgraph that contains all the nodes X^t having the same temporal index *t* and the links between them is known as the *t*-th *slice*. We use C^t, D^t, and U^t to denote the chance, decision, and utility nodes at the *t*-th slice, respectively.

If there is a $k \in \mathbb{N}^+$ such that every link $X^t \to Y^{t'}$ satisfies that $t' - t \leq k$, which means that all the parents of a node Y^t are in the *t'*-th slice or in the previous *k* slices, we say that the DLIMID is *of k-th order*. In practice, it is usual to work with first-order DLIMIDs (*k*=1).

Stationary DLIMIDs

A DLIMID of order *k* is *stationary* if the (*k*+1)-th slice and the next slices have the same structure and the same parameters. Put formally, for each $t > k+1$,

- there is a link $X^t \to Y^t$ if and only if there is a link $X^{k+1} \to Y^{k+1}$,
- $P(x^t \mid pa(X^t)) = P(x^{k+1} \mid pa(X^{k+1}))$, and
- $U^t(pa(U^t)) = U^{k+1}(pa(U^{k+1}))$.

Given that the slices repeat themselves after the *k*-th, we can have a compact representation in which we only represent the first *k*+1 slices. If the horizon *h* of the DLIMID is finite, we can unroll it completely by cloning the last slice $h - (k+1)$ times.

In the case of a first-order DLIMID, which is the most common case, stationarity means that only the first slice differs from the others and, hence, we can represent the DLIMID by only the first two time slices; this compact form of DLIMIDs is very similar to the standard representation of (factored) MDPs and POMDPs.

Alternatively, a DLIMID can be represented by a *temporal LIMID* (TLIMID), which consists of a prior model $\mathcal{L}_0$, representing the initial state of the system, and a transition model $\mathcal{L}_t$, representing the evolution over time; this representation is very similar to the representation of dynamic Bayesian networks using 2TBNs (Murphy, 2002, Sec. 2.2).[4]

Policies and Strategies

A link $X \to D$, where *X* is a chance variable or a decision and *D* is a decision, means that the value of *X* is known when making decision *D*. For this reason, the parents of *D* are also called *informational predecessors*.[5] A *stochastic policy* for a decision $D \in \mathbf{D}$ is defined as a distribution $P_D(d|pa(D))$ that maps each configurations of $Pa(D)$ to a distribution over alternatives (i.e., actions) for *D*; thus, $P_D(d|pa(D))$ is the probability of choosing option (action) *d* when the information available is $pa(D)$. If P_D is degenerate (consisting of ones and zeros only) then we say that the policy is *deterministic*.

A *strategy* is a set of policies $\Delta = \{P_D : D \in \mathbf{D}\}$, which induces the following joint distribution over the variables in $\mathbf{C} \cup \mathbf{D}$:

$$P_\Delta(\mathbf{c}, \mathbf{d}) = P(\mathbf{c} \mid \mathbf{d}) \prod_{D \in \mathbf{D}} P_D(d \mid pa(D)) \qquad (2)$$

$$= \prod_{C \in \mathbf{C}} P(c \mid pa(C)) \prod_{D \in \mathbf{D}} P_D(d \mid pa(D)). \qquad (3)$$

If we group the variables that belong to the same time slice, this equation can be rewritten as

$$P_\Delta(\mathbf{c}, \mathbf{d}) = \prod_{t=0}^{h} \prod_{X \in \mathbf{X}^t} P_\Delta(x \mid pa(X)) \qquad (4)$$

$$= \prod_{t=0}^{h} P_\Delta(\mathbf{x}^t \mid pa(\mathbf{X}^t)) \qquad (5)$$

where $P_\Delta(c|pa(C)) = P(c|pa(C))$ for each chance variable, $P_\Delta(d|pa(D)) = P_D(d|pa(D))$ for each decision, X^t is the set of chance and decision nodes in the t-th slice ($(\mathbf{X}^t = \mathbf{C}^t \cup \mathbf{D}^t)$, and $Pa(X^t)$ is the set of nodes that have a child in the t-th slice but do not belong to that slice.

We define

$$\mathcal{U}_t(\mathbf{c}^t, \mathbf{d}^t) = \sum_{U^t \in \mathbf{U}^t} u(pa(U^t)), \qquad (6)$$

which means that the utility for the t-th time slice for a configuration (c^t, d^t) of $\mathbf{C}^t \cup \mathbf{D}^t$ is the sum of the utility functions of the utility nodes at that slice. The *utility* of a configuration $(\mathbf{c}, \mathbf{d})$ of $\mathbf{C} \cup \mathbf{D}$ is defined as

$$\mathcal{U}(\mathbf{c}, \mathbf{d}) = \sum_{t=0}^{h} \gamma^t \, \mathcal{U}_t(\mathbf{c}^t, \mathbf{d}^t)$$

and the *expected utility* of a strategy Δ as

$$\mathrm{EU}(\Delta) = \sum_{\mathbf{c}} \sum_{\mathbf{d}} P_\Delta(\mathbf{c}, \mathbf{d}) \cdot \mathcal{U}(\mathbf{c}, \mathbf{d}) \qquad (7)$$

$$= \sum_{\mathbf{x}^0} \cdots \sum_{\mathbf{x}^h} \prod_{t=0}^{h} P_\Delta(\mathbf{x}^t \mid pa(\mathbf{X}^t)) \sum_{t'=0}^{h} \gamma^{t'} \, \mathcal{U}_{t'}(pa(\mathbf{U}^{t'}))$$
$$(8)$$

The *optimal strategy* is the one that maximizes the expected utility:

$$\Delta^* = \arg\max_\Delta \mathrm{EU}(\Delta). \qquad (9)$$

A strategy is said to be *stationary* if it repeats itself after a certain time. The optimal strategy for an infinite-horizon first-order stationary DLIMID is stationary, because the optimal policy for a decision only depends on the current state of the system and on the expected rewards, which are stationary.

Memory Variables

An important shortcoming of the limited-memory assumption is that it may lead to neglecting important findings obtained in the past. For instance, let us consider the case of a patient who showed an allergic reaction to a drug in the past. If we forget this fact and administer the same drug again, we may cause more harm than benefit. Apparently, a situation like this cannot be addressed with stationary DLIMIDs, because a stationary DLIMID is, by definition, of k-th order, and therefore it cannot have an informational link $F^t \to D^{t'}$ with $t' - t > k$; i.e., when making decision D at time t' we cannot take into account the value of a finding F^t in a distant past. In particular, in a first-order DLIMID, the informational predecessors of a decision variable D^t can only occur in time-slices t or $t-1$. Thus, the limited-memory assumption implies that observations made earlier in time will not be taken into account and, as a result, states that are qualitatively different can appear the same to the decision maker, which leads to suboptimal decisions. This phenomenon is sometimes refered to as perceptual aliasing (Whitehead & Ballard, 1991).

However, there is a way of circumventing this problem: to introduce in the DLIMID *memory variables* that represent a summary of the observed history. In the above example we may have a binary variable M indicating whether this patient has ever had an allergic reaction to that drug or not. This way, in a k-th order stationary LIMID, we can add a memory variable M, of type chance ($M \in \mathbf{C}$), whose parents are in the previous k slices. The domain of M and the conditional probability tables for each M^t will depend on the meaning that the knowledge engineer assigns to this variable. If F is Boolean and the purpose of M were to "remember" whether F has ever taken a positive value, the parents of M^t would be M^{t-1} and F^t, and the conditional probability table for M^t would be,

$$P(+m^t \mid m^{t-1}, f^t) = \begin{cases} 1 & \text{if } (m^{t-1} = +m^{t-1}) \vee (f^t = +f^t) \\ 0 & \text{otherwise}. \end{cases}$$

Alternatively, if M is intended to "remember" the last k' values of finding F, with $k' \leq k$, the parents of M^t will be $\{F^{t-k'-1}, \ldots, F^t\}$. For example, if variable F represents the result of a dichotomous test, it may take on three values, $\{u, n, p\}$, where u stands for *unobserved* (test not performed), n for *negative*, and p for *positive*, and we wish to remember the last three values of F ($k = 3$) then the domain of M will be $\Omega_M = \{u, n, p\} \times \{u, n, p\} \times \{u, n, p\}$, i.e., M will have 27 possible values. The value of M^t represented by upn means that the test was not performed at time $t-2$, gave a positive result at $t-1$, and a negative result at t.

Memory variables are not necessarily associated to chance variables: we can also "remember" whether we have made a decision (chosen a particular option) at any moment in the past. However, the parents of a memory variable M must be observable variables and, optionally, other memory variables: if one of the parents of M were unobservable, the value of M would be unknown and it could not be an informational predecessor for any decision; if the parents of M

were only other memory variables, the value of M could not be updated with new information.

The advantage of memory variables is that they allow us to keep information from the distant past and, at the same time, to fulfill *the Markov condition*, which states that the future is independent of the past given the present, i.e., the current state of the system. This is just the function of memory variables, to augment the state of the system by including information from the past.

It is not always easy to decide the number of memory variables that should be introduced in a DLIMID and the meaning of each one. We cannot think of any algorithmic procedure to make this decision. It is the knowledge engineers who, using the available domain knowledge, their common sense, and their experience, should make the best modeling decisions. We will later explain how we have built the memory variables for a real-world medical problem.

Evaluation of DLIMIDs

The evaluation of a decision model consists of finding the optimal strategy (or, at least, a near-optimal strategy) and its expected utility. We analyze two cases: finite-horizon DLIMIDs and stationary DLIMIDs, which include as a particular case infinite-horizon DLIMIDs. Most of the algorithms are based on an exploration of the space of strategies, for which they need to compute the expected utility of some of them. For this reason, we discuss in the first place how to perform this computation.

Evaluation of Finite-Horizon DLIMIDs

Computing the Expected Utility of a Strategy

In this section we explain two methods for computing the expected utility of a strategy in the case of a first-order finite-horizon DLIMID. These methods can be extended to higher order DLIMIDs, but the mathematics become more complicated.

Backward Evaluation

A DLIMID can be evaluated backwards by applying the following theorem. The proof can be found in the appendix.

Theorem 1. *The expected utility of a finite-horizon first-order DLIMID is*

$$\text{EU} = \sum_{\mathbf{x}^0} P_\Delta(\mathbf{x}^0)\left[\mathcal{U}_0(\mathbf{x}^0) + V_\Delta^0(\mathbf{x}^0)\right], \quad (10)$$

where $V_\Delta^0(\mathbf{x}^0)$ is given by the following definition:

$$V_\Delta^i(\mathbf{x}^i) = \begin{cases} \gamma \sum_{\mathbf{x}^{i+1}}\begin{bmatrix} P_\Delta(\mathbf{x}^{i+1}\mid\mathbf{x}^i)\,\mathcal{U}_{i+1}(\mathbf{x}^i,\mathbf{x}^{i+1}) \\ +V_\Delta^{i+1}(\mathbf{x}^{i+1}) \end{bmatrix} & \text{if } 0 \le i < h-1 \\ \gamma \sum_{\mathbf{x}^h} P_\Delta(\mathbf{x}^h\mid\mathbf{x}^{h-1})\,\mathcal{U}_h(\mathbf{x}^{h-1},\mathbf{x}^h) & \text{if } i = h-1. \end{cases}$$
$$(11)$$

In this theorem, $\mathcal{U}_0(\mathbf{x}^0)$ represents the immediate reward obtained from configuration $\mathbf{x}^0$ at $t=0$, while $V_\Delta^i(\mathbf{x}^i)$ is the accumulated value of future rewards for the state $\mathbf{x}^i$ at the i-th time slice. Equation 11 amounts to computing the expected value by eliminating the time-slices backwards, from the horizon ($t = h$) to the present ($t = 0$). In fact, it is essentially the same value-iteration procedure used to evaluate a strategy in MDPs and POMDPs.

Please note that, according to the proof of this theorem, V_Δ^i does not need to be defined on X^i, the whole set of chance and decision variables in the i-th slice, but on the subset of those variables that have children in the next time slice.

Forward Evaluation

Alternatively, the following theorem allows us to evaluate a DLIMID forwards.

Theorem 2. *The expected utility of a finite-horizon first-order DLIMID is*

$$\text{EU}(\Delta) = \sum_{t=0}^{h} \gamma^t\, R_t, \quad (12)$$

where

$$R_t = \begin{cases} \sum_{\mathbf{x}^0} P(\mathbf{x}^0)\,\mathcal{U}_0(\mathbf{x}^0) & \text{if } t = 0 \\ \sum_{\mathbf{x}^t}\sum_{\mathbf{x}^{t-1}} P_\Delta(\mathbf{x}^{t-1})\,P_\Delta(\mathbf{x}^t\mid\mathbf{x}^{t-1})\,\mathcal{U}_t(\mathbf{x}^{t-1},\mathbf{x}^t) & \text{if } t > 0. \end{cases}$$
$$(13)$$

In this latter equation, $P(\mathbf{x}^0)$, $\mathrm{U}_0(\mathbf{x}^0)$, and $U_t(\mathbf{x}^{t-1},\mathbf{x}^t)$ are parameters of the model, $P_\Delta(\mathbf{x}^t\mid\mathbf{x}^{t-1})$ can be obtained immediately for each strategy Δ, and $P_\Delta(\mathbf{x}^{t-1})$ can be computed recursively as follows:

$$P_\Delta(\mathbf{x}^t) = \begin{cases} \sum_{\mathbf{x}^1} P_\Delta(\mathbf{x}^1\mid\mathbf{x}^0)\,P(\mathbf{x}^0) & \text{if } t = 1 \\ \sum_{\mathbf{x}^{t-1}} P_\Delta(\mathbf{x}^t\mid\mathbf{x}^{t-1})\,P_\Delta(\mathbf{x}^{t-1}) & \text{if } t > 1. \end{cases}$$
$$(14)$$

This theorem can be easily turned into an algorithm that evaluates the DLIMID from the present ($t = 0$) to the future: for each slice, it computes R_t which is accumulated as indicated by Equation 12, and $P_\Delta(\mathbf{x}^t)$ which will be used in the evaluation of the next slice.

In fact, we do not need the joint probability of all the chance and decision variables in the t-th slice, but just the marginal probability of the subset of those variables having children in the next one. This is equivalent to using the interface algorithm proposed by Kevin Murphy (2002) for dynamic Bayesian networks.

Finding the Optimal Strategy

Having two methods for computing the expected utility of each strategy, we can apply Equation 9 to determine the optimal strategy, but as the space of strategies grows superexponentially with the size of the problem, we should use some heuristic to guide the search. Given that finite-horizon

DLIMIDs are a particular case of LIMIDs[6], one possibility is to apply the Single Policy Updating (SPU) method proposed by Lauritzen and Nilsson (2001) for LIMIDs, which proceeds iteratively by updating the policy of one decision each time, until it reaches a maximum.

A policy in a LIMID is said to be *locally optimal* if the strategy it makes part of can not be optimized by replacing it with a different policy for the same decision—see (Lauritzen & Nilsson, 2001). A policy p_j for decision D can be seen as a set of rules, such that each rule selects an option (an action) for a configuration of the informational predecessors of D, which are its parents, $Pa(D)$. Given a strategy Δ that contains p_j as a policy, we define $p_j' * \Delta$ as the strategy obtained by replacing p_j with p_j' In the case of LIMIDs, it is possible to find a locally optimal policy by finding the optimal rule for each configuration, independently of the others, because the rules in the same policy do not interact. Therefore, we "only" need to evaluate cm^r different policies at each decision variable D, where c denotes the cardinality of Ω_D, and r is the number of informational predecessors of D, assuming that the cardinality of $\Omega_{D'}$ equals m for all $D' \in Pa(D)$.

The problem of SPU and other heuristic-search methods is the risk of getting trapped in local maxima. However, there are some LIMIDs, called "soluble LIMIDs" in (Lauritzen & Nilsson, 2001, Sec. 4), for which it is possible to find a complete ordering of the decisions such that SPU is guaranteed to find an optimal strategy, without falling in local maxima. A question open for future research is to find the conditions under which a finite-horizon DLIMID with several decisions per time slice is "soluble".

If the DLIMID is first-order, stationary, and has a large horizon, it can be evaluated approximately by assuming that the policy is stationary, as if the horizon were infinite. In the next section we describe three algorithms for stationary first-order DLIMIDs.

Evaluation of Stationary DLIMIDs

In this section we describe three algorithms that find stationary strategies for DLIMIDs. They apply to infinite-horizon first-order DLIMIDs, whose optimal strategies are stationary, for the reasons discussed above. These algorithms also serve to find near-optimal strategies for stationary first-order DLIMIDs having a large horizon, because in this case the policy is stationary if we are far enough from the horizon.

Each algorithm is based on a different way of exploring the space of strategies, trying to maximize the expected utility. For this reason, we discuss first how to compute the expected utility of a given strategy.

Computing the Expected Utility of a Strategy

One possibility to compute the expected utility of a strategy for an infinite-horizon DLIMID is to apply Cooper's (1988) transformation to convert the pair {DLIMID, strategy} into a dynamic Bayesian network (Dean & Kanazawa, 1989, Boutilier et al., 1996), which can then be evaluated with the methods proposed in (Murphy, 2002). In particular, a first-order DLIMID expressed in the form of a TLIMID can be converted into a two time-slice Bayesian network (2TBN), as depicted in Figure 2. This is the approach that we used in (van Gerven et al., 2007), because we were using the BNT software (Murphy, 2001).

A more efficient approach would be to evaluate the DLIMID and the strategy directly with one of the above proposed methods for finite-horizon DLIMIDs. Those methods also apply to infinite-horizon DLIMIDs having a true discount, i.e., $\gamma < 1$, because in this case the contribution of each slice to the expected utility decreases exponentially with time. In fact, for a given t, the total contribution of the slices such that $t' > t$ is at most $u_{max} \, \gamma^{t+1} / (\gamma - 1)$, where u_{max} is the

Figure 2. Converting between different representations

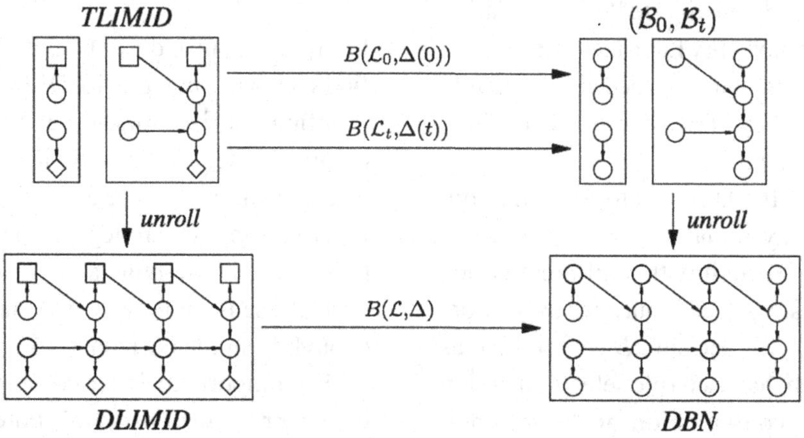

maximum utility obtainable from one slice. Therefore, given an infinite-horizon DLIMID, if we wish to compute the expected utility of a strategy with a maximum error ε, it suffices to unroll a DLIMID with horizon h, where,

$$h = \log_\gamma \frac{\epsilon(1-\gamma)}{u_{\max}}. \qquad (15)$$

Another possibility is to select the horizon by using domain knowledge, as we did when evaluating the DLIMID for carcinoid tumors.

Single Policy Updating

As we said, the SPU method proposed by Lauritzen and Nilsson (2001) for LIMIDs can be applied directly to finite-horizon DLIMIDs because the latter are a particular case of the former. Given that the number of policies in a stationary strategy is also finite, we can use the same optimization scheme for this problem, i.e., we can iterate over the set of policies updating them one by one in an attempt to approach the optimal strategy. If the DLIMID is expressed in the form of a TLIMID, SPU can proceed as indicated by Algorithm 1.

Nevertheless, there is an important difference with the previous case. In a LIMID, a locally optimal policy can be found by updating each rule independently of the others, because the rules inside the same policy do not interact. But in the case of a stationary policy for a DLIMID, the optimal rule for decision D^t (for a configuration of its parents) depends on the rules applied in future decisions. As a consequence, it is not possible to find an optimal policy for D^t by optimizing each of its rules independently of the others. This implies that instead of evaluating cm^r different policies at each decision variable D, as in the case of LIMIDs, now we need to evaluate $c^{(m^r)}$, which makes SPU unfeasible even for many small problems.

Single Rule Updating

Given the impossibility of iterating over the set of all policies for each decision in a DLIMID, we proposed a hill-climbing method, called *single rule updating* (SRU). A deterministic policy can be viewed as a mapping $p_j : \Omega_{\pi(D_j)} \rightarrow \Omega_{D_j}$, describing, for each configuration of the informational predecessors of a decision variable D_j, an action $a \in \Omega_{D_j}$. Each pair $(\mathbf{x}, a) \in p_j$ is called a *decision rule*. Instead of exhaustively searching over all possible policies for each decision variable, we try to increase the expected utility by

Algorithm 1. Single policy updating for TLIMIDs

```
input: TLIMID T, initial random strategy Δ⁰, stopping criterion K
Δ = Δ⁰, euMax = EUᴷ (Δ⁰).
repeat
        euMaxOld = euMaxforj = 1 to ndofor all policies pⱼ' for Δ at Dⱼdo
                Δ = pⱼ' * Δ
                if EUᴷ(Δ') > euMaxthen
                        Δ = Δ'andeuMax = EUᴷ(Δ')
                end ifend for
        end for
untileuMax = euMaxOld
return Δ
```

local changes to the decision rules within the policy; i.e., at each step we change one decision-rule within the policy, and accept the change when the expected utility increases. We use $(\mathbf{x}, a') * p_j$ to denote the replacement of $(\mathbf{x},a)$ by $(\mathbf{x}, a')$ in p_j Similarly to SPU, we keep iterating until there is no further increase in the expected utility. Using SRU, we decrease the number of policies that need to be evaluated in each *local* cycle for a decision node to only cm^r where notation is as before, albeit at the expense of replacing the exhaustive search by a hill-climbing strategy, which increases the risk of ending up in a local maximum, and having to run local cycles until convergence. SRU based on a TLIMID T with initial strategy Δ^0 is then defined by Algorithm 2.

As explained in the previous section, in the case of LIMIDs—and finite-horizon DLIMIDs, in particular—there is no difference between SPU and SRU, because the way of finding a locally maximum policy is to optimize each single rule in that policy. But in the case of a stationary policy—for example, in the case of an infinite-horizon DLIMID—SRU does not even guarantee that the strategy obtained is locally maximal.

Simulated Annealing

In order to improve upon the strategies found by SRU, we resort to *simulated annealing* (SA) (Kirkpatrick, Gelatt Jr, & Vecchi, 1983), which is a heuristic search method that tries to avoid getting trapped into local maximum solutions found by hill-climbing techniques. SA chooses candidate solutions by looking at neighbors of the current solution as defined by a *neighborhood function*. Local maxima are avoided by sometimes accepting worse solutions according to an *acceptance function*. We propose to use the following acceptance function,

$$P(a(\Delta') = \text{yes} \mid eu, eu', t) = \begin{cases} 1 & \text{if } eu' > eu \\ e^{\frac{eu'-eu}{T(t)}} & \text{otherwise}, \end{cases}$$
(16)

where $a(\Delta')$ stands for the acceptance of the proposed strategy Δ', $eu' = \text{EU}^\kappa(\Delta')$, $eu = \text{EU}^\kappa(\Delta)$ for the current strategy Δ, and T represents the temperature in an *annealing schedule* defined as[7]

$$T(t+1)=\alpha \cdot T(t),$$
(17)

Algorithm 2. Single rule updating for TLIMIDs

```
input: TLIMID T, initial random strategy Δ⁰, stopping criterion K
Δ = Δ⁰; euMax = EUᴷ(Δ⁰)
repeat
 euMaxOld = euMax
 forj = 1 to ndo
        repeat
          euMaxLocal = euMax
          for all configurations x of π (Dⱼ) do
             for all actions a' ∈ Ω_Dⱼ do
                  pⱼ' = (x, a') * pⱼ
                  Δ' = pⱼ' * Δ
                  if EUᴷ(Δ') > euMaxthen
                      Δ = Δ' and euMax = EUᴷ(Δ')
                  end if
               end for
             end for
          untileuMax = euMaxLocal
     end for
untileuMax = euMaxOld
return Δ
```

where $T(0)=\beta$ with $\alpha<1$ and $\beta>0$. The annealing schedule ensures that initially a random search through the space of strategies is performed, which gradually changes into a hill-climbing search. We refer to (Eglese, 1990) for a discussion about choices that can be made for SA parameters α and β. With respect to strategy finding in dynamic LIMIDs, we propose an initial simulated annealing scheme and a subsequent application of SRU in order to greedily find a local maximum solution (van Gerven & Díez, 2006, van Gerven et al., 2007). Let θ denote a random variable that is repeatedly chosen uniformly at random between 0 and 1, and let T_{min} stand for the minimum temperature for which we perform the annealing. SA based on a TLIMID T with initial strategy Δ^0 is then defined by Algorithm 3.

An experiment with a small LIMID for a hypothetical problem, using 20 different initial strategies Δ^0, showed that in most of the cases

SA yields better strategies than SRU. It also showed that in general it is possible to reach an additional increase in the expected utility by applying SRU after SA. Further experiments, based on a real-world medical example, are described below.

REAL-WORLD EXAMPLE: TREATMENT OF CARCINOID TUMORS

Construction of the Model

We have applied DLIMIDs to the problem of treatment selection for high-grade carcinoid tumor patients. Our aim is to validate if the treatment strategy that is used in practice will also be found by a decision-theoretic model, thereby confirming the quality of the employed strategy.

Algorithm 3. Simulated annealing for TLIMIDs

```
input: TLIMID T, initial random strategy Δ₀, stopping criterion K,
            annealing schedule T, minimum temperature T_min
Δ = Δ⁰; t = 0, eu = EUᴷ(Δ)
repeat
    select a random decision variable D_j
     select a random decision rule (x, a) ∈ p_j
     select a random action a' ∈ Ω_{D_j}, a' ≠ ap'_j = (x, a') * p_j
    Δ' = p'_j * Δ
    eu' = EUᴷ(Δ')
    ifθ ≤ P (a(Δ') = yes | eu, eu', t) then
            Δ = Δ'
            eu = eu'
    end if
    t = t + 1
untilT(t) < Tm_{in}
return SRU(T, Δ, K)
```

A carcinoid tumor is a type of neuroendocrine tumor that is predominantly found in the midgut and is normally characterized by the production of excessive amounts of biochemically active substances, such as serotonin (Modlin, Kidd, Latich, Zikusoka, & Shapiro, 2005). These neuroendocrine tumors are often differentiated according to the histological findings (Capella, Heitz, Hofler, Solcia, & Kloppel, 1995) and in a small minority of cases tumors are of high-grade histology, which, although biochemically much less active than low-grade carcinoids, show much more rapid tumor progression. Therefore, carcinoid treatment that concentrates on reducing biochemical activity is not considered applicable, and more aggressive chemotherapy in the form of an etoposide and cisplatin-containing scheme is the only remaining treatment option (Moertel, Kvols, O'Connell, & Rubin, 1991). The dynamic decision problem then becomes whether or not to administer chemotherapy at each decision moment.

Since patients return to the clinic for follow-up every three months, we assume that each time slice represents patient status at three-month intervals, at which time treatment can be adjusted. As some patients can live up to almost ten years, we would need a dynamic (i.e., periodic) model containing at least 40 stages. As we discuss below, a dynamic influence diagram for this problem would be unfeasible, because the last decisions should consider a large amount of findings, which would lead to intractable domain sizes. Building an ordinary LIMID would also be cumbersome, even if it had stationary parameters, because we would need to explicitly represent the 40 time slices. Additionally, the SPU algorithm for LIMIDs would need to iterate over the 40 decisions, which may lead to a very slow convergence. We will come back to this point later.

For these reasons, we decided to model the evolution of high-grade carcinoid tumor by means of a DLIMID. According to an expert physician who contributed the domain knowledge, the pathophysiology of the disease is such that the current state of the patient depends mainly on the evolution of the disease in the last few months. Therefore, we decided to build a first-order model, enhanced with some memory variables if

Figure 3. A TLIMID for high-grade carcinoid tumor pathophysiology. Chemotherapy has not yet been given at the initial time, which renders the tumor response to chemotherapy (RESP) independent of all other variables at $\mathcal{L}_0$.

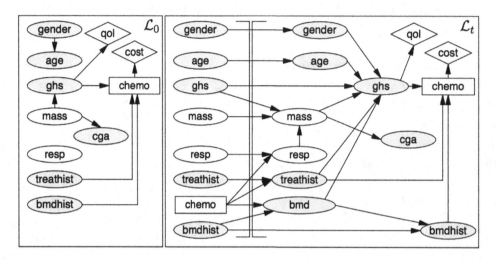

Figure 4. Tumor mass

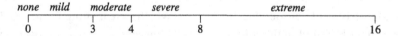

necessary. As the horizon chosen for this problem was only ten years, it seemed unnecessary to take into account the direct effect of age on the parameters of the model,[8] and consequently it would make sense that the model be stationary. All this implies that the DLIMID might be represented by a TLIMID. The structure of the resulting model is shown in Figure 3, where shaded nodes indicate observable variables.[9]

In this model, the patient's *general health status* (ghs) is of central importance. In oncology, one way to estimate the general health status is by means of the *performance status* (Oken et al., 1982), which is distinguished into *normal* (0), *mild complaints* (1), *ambulatory* (2), *nursing care* (3), *intensive care* (4), and *death* (5). Modeling the evolution of ghs is a non-trivial task; it depends on the current general health status, and on patient properties such as age, and gender, since these

are risk factors that may lead to patient death due to causes other than the disease. Furthermore, ghs is influenced by the tumor mass (mass) and the treatment strategy. Tumor mass has a negative influence on the general health status and is the first cause of death for patients with high-grade carcinoid tumors. Hepatic metastases normally account for the majority of the tumor mass and the primary tumor does not normally contribute significantly to the tumor mass. Tumor mass is expressed in terms of standard units, ranging from a patient with just a primary localization (mass = 0) to a patient that shows the maximal amount of metastases (mass = 16), as depicted in Figure 4.

Most patients with high-grade tumors have extensive metastatic disease when admitted to the hospital. If there is no tumor response due to treatment then the physician estimates an exponential growth in tumor mass: $x(t) = x_0 \cdot e^{1.41t}$. If

Table 1. The WHO criteria for tumor response

Tumor Response	Criteria
Complete remission (*cr*)	Disappearance of all lesions.
Partial remission (*pr*)	More than 50% decrease in tumor mass.
Progressive disease (*pd*)	More than 25% increase in lesions, or a new lesion.
Stable disease (>*sd*)	Neither *pr* nor *pd*.

there is a tumor response due to treatment then we will see a reduction in tumor mass according to Table 1. If no chemotherapy is given, then we use *nt* (no treatment) to denote the absence of tumor response. Finally, if ghs = *dead* then there is no change in tumor mass.

Chemotherapy (CHEMO) with states {*none, reduced, standard*} is the only available treatment to reduce tumor growth, where a reduced dose is at 75% of the standard dose. We use TREATHIST with states {0, 1, 2, 3} as a memory variable to represent the patient's relevant treatment history, such that TREATHIST = *i* represents continued chemotherapy over the past *i* trimesters. Reductions in tumor mass due to chemotherapy are often described by means of the WHO criteria for tumor response (RESP), as defined in Table 1. In (Moertel et al., 1991), 17% of patients that received chemotherapy showed complete regression, 50% showed partial regression and the remaining 33% of patients showed stable disease. Hence, none of the patients who received chemotherapy for the first time showed progressive disease. For reduced chemotherapy, we estimated that 5% of patients show complete regression, 45% show partial regression and the remaining 50% of patients show stable disease. If a patient has been treated previously, then the effectiveness of treatment changes. In case RESP($t-1$) is either *pr* or *cr*, then it is assumed that continued chemotherapy will lead to stable disease (*sd*). If, on the other hand, RESP($t-1$)=*sd* then continued chemotherapy will become less effective. Even when chemotherapy is discontinued, we expect some residual effect of chemotherapy due to the knock-out effect

on tumor-cells. It is estimated that after three months, the effect of chemotherapy is at 70% of its normal effectiveness.

Note that chemotherapy may have both positive and negative effects on general health status. Positive due to reductions in tumor mass, and negative due to severe bone-marrow depression (bmd) and damage associated with prolonged chemotherapy. Severe bone-marrow depression may cause patient death due to associated neutropenic sepsis and/or internal bleeding, and it has been reported that 5 out of 45 patients experienced grade 4 leucopenia due to chemotherapy (Moertel et al., 1991). We therefore estimate that 11% of patients will experience life-threatening forms of bone-marrow depression when given standard chemotherapy. When reduced dose chemotherapy is administered, we estimate that in the order of 3% of patients will be affected. We use bmdhist, with states *no-bmd* and *bmd*, as a memory variable to represent whether or not the patient has experienced bmd in the past. No decision variable has been defined that determines whether or not to assess bmd status, since this status is assumed to be given by routine laboratory tests.

The global utility is defined as a discounted additive combination of the *quality of life* (qol) and the cost of chemotherapy (cost):

$$\mathcal{U} = \sum_{t=0}^{n} \gamma^t (\text{qol}^t(\text{ghs}^t) - \text{cost}^t(\text{chemo}^t)).$$

Our measure of quality of life is based on *quality-adjusted life-years*, or QALYs (Weinstein

Table 2. Quality-adjustment weights for ghs

ghs	0	1	2	3	4	5
weight	0.214	0.184	0.168	0.121	0.109	0.000

& Stason, 1977), which simultaneously captures gains in quantity and quality of life (Drummond, Sculpher, Torrance, O'Brien, & Stoddart, 2005). QALYs are computed by multiplying a *quality-adjustment weight* for each health state by the discounted time spent in this state. We associate quality-adjustment weights with the states of ghs based on the *quality of well-being* scale (Kaplan & Anderson, 1988), taking into account that each time slice stands for a three-month period (Table 2). We have associated a small economical cost with chemotherapy, that is regarded insignificant compared with the benefit gained in terms of quality of life.

In our model, we used a discounting factor of 0.95 as suggested in (Haddix, Teutsch, Schaffer, y Dunet, 1996), such that the three-month discount factor is $\gamma \approx 0.987$. The expected utility then becomes:

$$EU(\Delta) = E_\Delta \left(\sum_{t=0}^{n} \gamma^t \mathrm{qol}(\mathrm{ghs}^t) \right)$$

$$- E_\Delta \left(\sum_{t=0}^{n} \gamma^t \mathrm{cost}^t(\mathrm{chemo}^t) \right) \qquad (18)$$

The first term in Equation 18 is the discounted quality-adjusted life expectancy (QALE) and the second term is the discounted expected cost of treatment. The goal of our model then is to find a policy for chemotherapy that maximizes this expression.

The physician has indicated that the informational predecessors of chemo are given by ghs, treathist and bmdhist, where both treathist and

bmdhist are used as memory variables within the model. Changes in treatment history are specified as follows. Given that chemo equals *standard* or *reduced*, treathist increases from x to $x + 1$ until the maximum of 3 is reached, and given that chemo=*none*, treathist decreases from x to $x - 1$ until the minimum of 0 is reached. In order to represent whether or not a patient has ever experienced bone-marrow depression, we assume that bmdhist = *no-bmd* if bmd = *no* and bmdhist = *no-bmd*. Otherwise, it is assumed that bmdhist=*bmd*. Note that in this case, memory variables can "remember" findings from an arbitrarily distant past, by restricting ourselves to consider only whether severe bone-marrow depression has ever occurred, regardless of the moment at which it occurred. Contrary to what may be expected, the chromogranin A test (cga), a correlate of tumor mass, is not regarded to be an informational predecessor by the physician, since a patient who is known to have a high-grade carcinoid tumor is treated as often as possible, irrespective of the current state of the tumor.

Experimental Results

Our aim is to find a treatment strategy for high-grade carcinoid tumors using the developed model and the described algorithms. We have applied the simulated annealing scheme, followed by SRU, as suggested above.[10] Since the informational predecessors are equal for chemo in $\mathcal{L}_0$ and $\mathcal{L}_t$, we assume that $\Delta_0 = \Delta_t$. We use Δ to denote this strategy, containing a stationary policy for chemo. The number of possible policies for chemo is then given by:

$$\Omega_{\mathrm{CHEMO}}^{\Omega_{\mathrm{ghs}} \cdot \Omega_{\mathrm{treathist}} \cdot \Omega_{\mathrm{bmdhist}}} = 3^{5 \cdot 4 \cdot 2} \approx 1.22 \cdot 10^{19}.$$

Note that single policy updating would require an exhaustive search through this space of possible policies, which is clearly computationally intractable. For our model, we have used a horizon

$h = 40$, based on the observation that ten-year survival is rarely attained for this aggressive form of cancer—please remind that the cycle length in our model is 3 months.

After some initial experiments, we chose $\alpha = 0.995$, $\beta = 0.5$ and $T_{min} = 1.225 \cdot 10^{-3}$ for the simulated annealing parameters.

The SA algorithm was repeated twenty times, starting from random initial strategies. It consistently found the same treatment strategy Δ, with an expected utility of 1.795. Figure 5 shows the subsequent values of EU*(Δ) of the strategies found during one of these experiments. The figure depicts how the initial explorative behavior of the simulated annealing scheme gradually changes into a hill-climbing strategy. The application of single rule updating after the simulated annealing phase caused a small increase in expected utility from 1.795 to 1.798. For this particular example, the solution found by simulated annealing (followed by SRU) was the same as the solution found by SRU alone, although this does not hold in general.

A strategy for a DLIMID can be represented by a *policy graph* (Meuleau, Kim, Kaelbling, & Cassandra, 1999); a finite state controller that depicts state transitions, where states represent actions and transitions are induced by observa-tions. The policy graph for this medical problem is shown in Figure 6.

DISCUSSION: RELATED MODELS

DLIMIDs vs. LIMIDs

As stated above, finite-horizon DLIMIDs are a particular case of the LIMIDs proposed by Lauritzen and Nilsson (2001), the main difference being that in DLIMIDs variables have a temporal interpretation, such that each X representing a real-world property, a decision, or a utility, leads to a set of variables $\{X^1, \ldots, X^h\}$. Stationary DLIMIDs have the advantage that they can be represented compactly, especially when the order, k, is small. In practice, it is usual to use first-order DLIMIDs ($k = 1$), which means that all the time slices are the same after the second one. This way, DLIMIDs can model dynamic systems that evolve over long periods of time, including the possibility of having infinite horizons,[11] which makes DLIMIDs very similar to POMDPs in their expressive power.

In contrast, LIMIDs are not appropriate for that kind of problems. Certainly, the idea of using LIMIDs to represent a problem that repeats itself periodically was implicit in the work by Lauritzen and Nilsson (2001)—see especially the "pigs ex-

Figure 5. Change in EU(Δ) *for the treatment strategies, selected during simulated annealing, followed by single rule updating at the end*

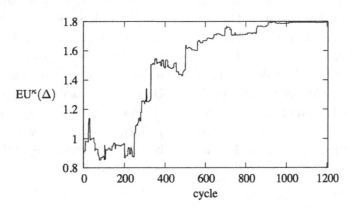

Figure 6. Policy graph for the best strategy that was found by simulated annealing, where o_1 = ghs>3, o_2 = ghs≤3 ∧ bmdhist=no−bmd and o_3 = ghs≤3 ∧ bmdhist=bmd.

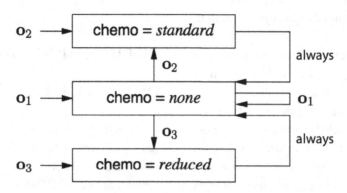

ample" in their paper—, but they did not address that issue. For a problem such as the evolution of carcinoid tumors, that required around 40 time slices, building a non-stationary LIMID would be a daunting task, and building a stationary LIMID would be tedious, because of the need to represent explicitly all the slices; when evaluating such a model, the SPU algorithm would not scale-up properly, and even if our computer were able to evaluate it, non-stationary policies would be difficult to communicate to human users.

On the contrary, it was relatively easy to build the DLIMID for carcinoid tumors (see again the TLIMID in Figure 3), and the stationary policy, shown in Figure 6, is very easy to understand.

With respect to the quality of the returned policies, DLIMIDs must use SRU or simulated annealing, which have a higher risk of getting trapped in local maxima than the SPU method used for LIMIDs. However, a LIMID for a system that evolves over a large period of time would have a huge number of decisions, which in turn increases the risk of local maxima. An issue for future research would be to study which model, LIMIDs or DLIMIDs, would reach higher expected utilities in this type of problems. Nevertheless, we do not think that any knowledge engineer would be willing to build a LIMID for such a problem, as a DLIMID would be much easier to build.

DLIMIDs vs. DIDs

Both IDs and finite-horizon DLIMIDs are particular cases of LIMIDs, and dynamic influence diagrams (DIDs) are the intersection of IDs and finite-horizon DLIMIDs. Therefore we can make the trivial assertion that all the problems that can be solved with DIDs can also be solved with DLIMIDs. However, there are some DLIMIDs that are not DIDs, either because there is not a complete ordering of the decisions in each time slice, or because the information available when making a decision cannot be older than a certain time lapse (i.e., memory is limited), or both. In particular, we have already seen in that in a DLIMID of k-th order the information available when making decision D^t contains, at most, the observations made between moments $t − k$ and t (both inclusive).

The no-forgetting assumption, which DIDs include by definition, is the main shortcoming of this kind of models, because it makes the computational complexity grow superexponentially with the horizon of the problem, h. As a consequence, DIDs can only solve problems with very limited horizons. On the contrary, DLIMIDs can handle problems of very large horizons, even infinite, because the complexity of the policies they consider is bounded.

DLIMIDs vs. POMDPs

DLIMIDs and factored POMDPs are very similar in their structure: both contain chance variables (some of which are observable and some are not), decisions, and utility nodes. An advantage of DLIMIDs is that they may include several decisions per time slice, as shown in Figure 1. Modeling this problem with a POMDPs would amount to assuming that the doctor can either order a test or apply a therapy in each visit, but not both, which would make the model differ significantly from the real problem, thus invalidating its conclusions. In many domains, it may be an important reason for building a DLIMID instead of a POMDP.

Given that the DLIMID for carcinoid tumors presented above only contains one decision per time slice, it can be viewed and evaluated as a POMDP, which has two unobservable variables (the mass of the tumor, mass, and the response to the treatment, resp), seven observable variables (the seven shaded ovals on the right part of Figure 3), one decision (chemo), and two rewards (quality of life, qol, and the cost of the chemotherapy).

The main difference would be in the returned policies. In a DLIMID, the policy for a decision D depends on its informational predecessors, $Pa(D)$, which are a subset of the observable variables.[12] Therefore, if all the informational predecessors are discrete, then the domain of the policy is discrete, as in the case of fully observable MDPs.[13] In our medical model, the informational predecessor for the only decision, chemo, are the global health state (ghs) and two memory variables, bmdhist and treathist, that represent the antecedents of severe bone-marrow depression and the previous treatments; however, after the evaluation it turned out that the policy does not depend on treathist. Reciprocally, we might have included more variables in the domain of the policy, as we discuss below.

On the contrary, in the most usual way of solving POMDPs, the policy depends on the belief states of the unobservable variable and the solution

is expressed as a partition of the belief space. In a factored POMDP, the policy may depend on both the belief state of unobservable variables and on the configuration of observable variables, which makes the solution much more difficult to communicate. This is an advantage of evaluating this model as a DLIMID, because the policy shown in Figure 6 is very clear and intuitive.

However, an alternative way to solve a POMDP is to build a finite-state controller (Hansen, 1998, Meuleau et al., 1999). The solution returned by these kinds of algorithms is, to a certain extent, similar to that returned by our algorithms for DLIMIDs. However, there are still significant differences. The main one is that in the case of POMDPs the structure of the strategy (the finite-state controller) is not imposed by the knowledge engineer; it is the algorithm that finds it by performing a search over a space of finite-state controllers. On the contrary, in the case of DLIMIDs it is the knowledge engineer who decides which of the observable variables—maybe remembered by means of memory variables—will be taken into account when making a decision. This restriction may reduce the quality of the policies returned by the algorithms that evaluate a DLIMID, but, on the other hand, may have the advantage of leading to more intuitive policies. For instance, the fact that a patient experienced an allergic reaction in the past may be sufficient to decide not to administer the same drug again, and this can be evident when analyzing the resulting policy. In contrast, in a finite-state controller for the same problem the antecedent of allergic reaction may be represented by several controller states, which may be much more difficult to detect when trying to explain the policy to a human user.

Put another way, when building a DLIMID we have to decide which variables are allowed to make part of the domain of each decision, i.e., to be "observed"—or, better, "remembered"—by the decision maker at each moment. In our DLIMID the decision about chemotherapy was based on three observations: ghs, bmdhist, and treathist.

We can see in Figure 3 that there is an information link from each of them to the decision node therapy. We did not draw links from age or gender to therapy because we assumed, using domain knowledge, that the treatment policy does not depend directly on the patient's gender and age. But perhaps it was a wrong assumption. This difficulty of selecting the informational predecessors of each decision in a DLIMID is avoided when building a POMDP, but, on the other hand, DLI-MIDs give us more flexibility, because the fewer variables we include for each decision, the faster the algorithms will be and the easier the policies will be to understand for human users. This way, we can reach a trade-off between computational complexity, intuitiveness of the solutions, and higher expected utilities, while in POMDPs we do not have this kind of freedom.

We would like to conclude this section with a remark about memory variables. We said at the beginning of the paper that POMDPs do not need memory variables, because they store the history of observations implicitly in the belief state of non-observable variables. Then, one might think that when evaluating the model for carcinoid tumors as a POMDP we can get rid of the two memory variables bmdhist and treathist without affecting the performance of the model. However, this is not true, because in this case the model would not take into account the influence of chemotherapy into the global health state, which is mediated by variables bmd and treathist—see Figure 3. If we removed bmdhist and treathist from the POMDP, we would need to add unobservable variables to represent two features specific of each patient: the response to chemotherapy and the probability of suffering from severe bone-marrow depression. Therefore, building POMDPs avoids the difficulty to make modeling decisions about memory variables, but may require to include additional unobservable variables in the model; choosing the domain and obtaining the conditional probabilities for such variables may be as difficult as introducing memory variables.

CONCLUSION AND FUTURE WORK

Both POMDPs and DLIMIDs are designed for Markovian infinite-horizon problems in which only some of the variables can be observed. DLI-MIDs can be seen as a generalization of factored POMPDs, as they allow to have several decisions per time slice. In fact, a DLIMID having only one decision per time slice, such as the carcinoid model presented in this paper, can be interpreted and solved as a POMDP, and vice versa. Therefore, we can say that they are not two different types of models, but two ways of evaluating a model.

There are, however, subtle differences from the point of view of knowledge engineering. DLIMIDs in general need memory variables to summarize past observations, while POMDPs summarize the whole observed history implicitly in the belief state the unobservable variables. However, it does not imply that when interpreting and evaluating a DLIMID as a POMDP we can always remove the memory variables; it may be necessary to replace them with hidden variables.

If a POMDP is evaluated as a DLIMID without introducing memory variables, in general we will obtain a much lower expected utility. But if is an open issue to determine if a model including memory variables gives higher expected utilities when evaluated as a DLIMID than when evaluated as a POMDP, or vice versa. It would also be interesting to study which policies are easier to understand by human users.

Another line for future research is the development of new algorithms for DLIMIDs that avoid as much as possible getting trapped in local maxima without incurring excessive computational costs. A possibility would be the application of well-known optimization methods such as genetic algorithms or tabu search.

In turn, memory variables are the subject of several open research topics. As mentioned above, the evaluation of the DLIMID for carcinoid tumors showed that the policy does not depend on treathist, but perhaps if we had modeled this variable such that it summarized previous treatments in a different way, it would be relevant for the policy and might have led to a higher expected utility. In same way, the inclusion of more variables in the policy for decision chemo, such as age and gender, might also increase the expected utility. It is a possibility that should be tested empirically. Another open line is the comparison of memory variables with the states of finite-state controllers built by some POMDP algorithms.

We might also compare the expected utility obtained when evaluating the carcinoid model as a DLIMID with that obtained when evaluating it as a POMDP. There are several algorithms for DLIMIDs and many for POMDPs, based on different approximations and heuristic techniques. Thus, we have a chance to trade-off reduction in expected utility in order to save time and space.

It would also be interesting to analyze how intuitive the policies returned by each model are for human users. For our carcinoid model, the policy obtained when evaluating it as a DLIMID (see Figure 6) is very easy to understand, but other policies containing more variables in their domains might attain higher expected utilities, as mentioned above; this is another possible trade-off: intuitiveness vs. quality of the policy. On the other hand, we believe that these DLIMID policies, having discrete domains, would be much more intuitive for human users than the POMDP policies based on partitions of the belief state, but it is something that we should prove empirically. We should also compare our algorithms with those proposed for building finite-state controllers that represent near-optimal policies for POMDPs.

There is, finally, another research line also related with recent methods that are able to solve very large POMDPs, much larger than the DLIMIDs that can be solved with the algorithms presented in this paper. It would be very interesting and useful to adapt them to DLIMIDs that contain several decisions per time slice, which can be considered as an extension of factored POMDPs.

ACKNOWLEDGMENT

The first author was supported by grants TIN2006-11152 and TIN2009-09158, of the Spanish Ministry of Science and Technology, and by FONCICYT grant 85195.

The second author was supported by the Dutch Institute Madrid, by the Protocure II project under grant number IST-FP6-508794, and by The Netherlands Organization for Scientific Research (NWO) under grant number 612.066.201.

A significant part of this chapter was published previously at the journal of Artificial Intelligence in Medicine (van Gerven et al., 2007).

REFERENCES

Åström, K. J. (1965). Optimal control of Markov decision processes with incomplete state estimation. *Journal of Mathematical Analysis and Applications*, *10*, 174–205. doi:10.1016/0022-247X(65)90154-X

Bellman, R. E. (1957). *Dynamic programming*. Princeton, NJ: Princeton University Press.

Boutilier, C., Dean, T., & Hanks, S. (1996). Planning under uncertainty: Structural assumptions and computational leverage. In Ghallab, M., & Milani, A. (Eds.), *New directions in AI planning* (pp. 157–171). Amsterdam, The Netherlands: IOS Press.

Boutilier, C., Dearden, R., & Goldszmidt, M. (1995). Exploiting structure in policy construction. In *Proceedings of the 14th International Joint Conference on Artificial Intelligence (IJCAI–95)* (p. 1104-1111). Montreal, Canada.

Boutilier, C., Dearden, R., & Goldszmidt, M. (2000). Stochastic dynamic programming with factored representations. *Artificial Intelligence*, *121*(1-2), 49–107. doi:10.1016/S0004-3702(00)00033-3

Boutilier, C., & Poole, D. (1996). Computing optimal policies for partially observable decision processes using compact representations. In W. J. Clancey & D. Weld (Eds.), *Proceedings of the Thirteenth National Conference on Artificial Intelligence (AAAI-96)* (pp. 1168–1175). Portland, OR: AAAI Press.

Capella, C., Heitz, P. U., Hofler, H., Solcia, E., & Kloppel, G. (1995). Revised classification of neuroendocrine tumours of the lung, pancreas and gut. *Virchows Archiv, 425*(6), 547–560. doi:10.1007/BF00199342

Cooper, G. F. (1988). A method for using belief networks as influence diagrams. In R. Shachter, T. Levitt, L. N. Kanal, & J. F. Lemmer (Eds.), *Proceedings of the Fourth Workshop on Uncertainty in Artificial Intelligence* (pp. 55–63). New York, NY: Elsevier Science.

Dean, T., & Kanazawa, K. (1989). A model for reasoning about persistence and causation. *Computational Intelligence, 5*(3), 142–150. doi:10.1111/j.1467-8640.1989.tb00324.x

Drummond, M. F., Sculpher, M. J., Torrance, G. W., O'Brien, B. J., & Stoddart, G. L. (2005). *Methods for the economic evaluation of health care programmes* (3rd ed.). Oxford, UK: Oxford University Press.

Eglese, R. W. (1990). Simulated annealing: A tool for operational research. *European Journal of Operational Research, 46,* 271–281. doi:10.1016/0377-2217(90)90001-R

Haddix, A., Teutsch, S., Shaffer, P., & Dunet, D. (1996). *Prevention effectiveness: A guide to decision analysis and economic evaluation.* Oxford, UK: Oxford University Press.

Hansen, E. A. (1998). Solving POMDPs by searching in policy space. In *Proceedings of the 14th Conference on Uncertainty in Artificial Intelligence (UAI'98)* (pp. 211–219). Madison, WI: Morgan Kaufmann, San Francisco, CA.

Howard, R. A., & Matheson, J. E. (1984). Influence diagrams. In Howard, R. A., & Matheson, J. E. (Eds.), *Readings on the principles and applications of decision analysis* (pp. 719–762). Menlo Park, CA: Strategic Decisions Group.

Kaplan, R. M., & Anderson, J. P. (1988). A general health policy model: Update and applications. *Health Services Management Research, 23*(2), 203–235.

Kirkpatrick, S., Gelatt, C. D. Jr, & Vecchi, M. P. (1983). Optimization by simulated annealing. *Science, 220,* 671–680. doi:10.1126/science.220.4598.671

Lauritzen, S. L., & Nilsson, D. (2001). Representing and solving decision problems with limited information. *Management Science, 47,* 1235–1251. doi:10.1287/mnsc.47.9.1235.9779

Meuleau, N., Kim, K. E., Kaelbling, L. P., & Cassandra, A. R. (1999). Solving POMDPs by searching the space of finite policies. In *Proceedings of the 15th Conference on Uncertainty in Artificial Intelligence (UAI'99)* (pp. 417–426). Stockholm, Sweden: Morgan Kaufmann, San Francisco, CA.

Modlin, I. M., Kidd, M., Latich, I., Zikusoka, M. N., & Shapiro, M. D. (2005). Current status of gastrointestinal carcinoids. *Gastroenterology, 128,* 1717–1751. doi:10.1053/j.gastro.2005.03.038

Moertel, C. G., Kvols, L. K., O'Connell, M. J., & Rubin, J. (1991). Treatment of neuroendocrine carcinomas with combined etoposide and cisplatin. Evidence of major therapeutic activity in the anaplastic variants of these neoplasms. *Cancer, 68*(2), 227–232. doi:10.1002/1097-0142(19910715)68:2<227::AID-CNCR2820680202>3.0.CO;2-I

Murphy, K. (2001). The Bayes Net Toolbox for Matlab. *Computing Science and Statistics, 33,* 1–20.

Murphy, K. (2002). *Dynamic Bayesian networks: Representation, inference and learning.* Unpublished doctoral dissertation, Computer Science Division, University of California, Berkeley.

Oken, M. M., Creech, R. H., Tormey, D. C., Horton, J., Davis, T. E., & McFadden, E. T. (1982). Toxicity and response criteria of the eastern cooperative oncology group. *American Journal of Clinical Oncology, 5*, 649–655. doi:10.1097/00000421-198212000-00014

Poupart, P. (2005). *Exploiting structure to efficiently solve large scale partially observable Markov decision processes.* Unpublished doctoral dissertation, Dept. of Computer Science, University of Toronto, Canada.

Raiffa, H. (1968). *Decision analysis. Introductory lectures on choices under uncertainty.* Reading, MA: Addison-Wesley.

van Gerven, M. A. J., & Díez, F. J. (2006). Selecting strategies for infinite-horizon dynamic LIMIDs. In M. Studený & J. Vomlel (Eds.), *Proceedings of the Third European Workshop on Probabilistic Graphical Models (PGM'06)* (pp. 131-138). Prague, Czech Republic.

van Gerven, M. A. J., Díez, F. J., Taal, B. G., & Lucas, P. J. F. (2007). Selecting treatment strategies with dynamic limited-memory influence diagrams. *Artificial Intelligence in Medicine, 40*, 171–186. doi:10.1016/j.artmed.2007.04.004

Weinstein, M., & Stason, W. (1977). Foundations of cost-effectiveness analysis for health and medical practices. *The New England Journal of Medicine, 296*(13), 716–721. doi:10.1056/NEJM197703312961304

Whitehead, S. D., & Ballard, D. H. (1991). Learning to perceive and act by trial and error. *Machine Learning, 7*, 45–83. doi:10.1007/BF00058926

KEY TERMS AND DEFINITIONS

DLIMID (Dynamic LIMID): A LIMID having a periodic structure.

ID (Influence Diagram): A decision model containing three types of nodes—chance, decision, and utility. It assumes that the information available when making a decision is available ("remembered") for subsequent decisions.

LIMIDs (Limited Memory Influence Diagram): A decision model similar to an ID; however, some of the information available when making a decision may be "forgotten" when making subsequent decisions.

MDP (Markov Decision Process): A periodic model in which the state of the systems at each time point is represented by a variable; the reward obtained at each time point depends on the state of the system and on the option chosen by the decision maker. It is assumed that the decision maker knows with certainty the state of the system when making the decision.

POMDP (Partially Observable Markov Decision Process): It is similar to an MDP in that it contains a variable that represents the state of the systems at each time point, and a reward that depends on the state of the system and on the option chosen by the decision maker; the difference is that the state of the system is not known with certainty, but indirectly, by its relation with an observed variable. decision.

ENDNOTES

[1] One might try to avoid this limitation by assigning several time slices to each visit, but it would give rise to other problems, such as how to measure the quality-adjusted life time when the cycle length of the POMDP is not a constant.

[2] As well as in the case of LIMIDs, and unlike the case of influence diagrams, we do not require that there is directed path passing

by all the decision nodes. It implies that in LIMIDs and DLIMIDs there is not a total ordering of the decisions.

[3]   However, the reverse is not true: it is not necessary that an observable variable makes part of the informational predecessors of any decision. For instance, in Figure 3 the age and gender of the patient are observable, but they are not taken into account when making the decision about chemotherapy, because their impact is mediated by the variable ghs (global health state), which is also observable. In LIMIDs and LIMIDs, contrary to the case of influence diagrams and POMDPs, it is the knowledge engineer who decides which of the observable variables will be treated as such in the model.

[4]   2TBNs were introduced in (Boutilier, Dean, & Hanks, 1996). The reason for representing a DLIMID as a TLIMID is the possibility of converting it into a 2TBN, as explained below.

[5]   In a DLIMID, the informational predecessors or a decision are only its parents, as it is the case in LIMIDs, while in an influence diagram the informational predecessors of a decision are its parents and the parents of any decision made before D—see (Lauritzen & Nilsson, 2001, van Gerven et al., 2007).

[6]   The main difference between finite-horizon DLIMIDs and other LIMIDs is that the latter do not have necessarily a temporal indexing of variables nor a periodic graphical structure. The rest of the properties of DLIMIDs

stated above can be taken as the definition of LIMID—see (Lauritzen & Nilsson, 2001).

[7]   In this equation, the time t refers to diffent iterations of the annealing schedule. It has nothing to do with the time associated with each slice in the DLIMID.

[8]   Actually, age influences decisions indirectly due to its influence on general health status.

[9]   The model was built with Hugin Developer™: http://www.hugin.com.

[10]   The proposed algorithms were implemented using Intel's Probabilistic Networks Library (PNL): http://www.intel.com/technology/computing/pnl.

[11]   Certainly, in practice we never have an infinite horizon, but when the horizon is very large, the policy is stationary for decisions that are far enough from the horizon, which implies that in that case we can treat the problem as if the horizon were infinite, as we have discussed in previous sections.

[12]   Please note that the algorithms for the evaluation of DLIMIDs allow that the policies depend on unobservable variables. However, such policies would be useless, because it would impossible to make a decision based on information that is not available.

[13]   In this sense, DLIMIDs are similar to factored MDPs, but the latter assume that all the variables are observable and that policies depend on all the variables. Therefore, factored MDPs are inapropriate for many problems that can be modeled more accurately with POMDPs or DLIMIDs.

APPENDIX: PROOFS OF THE THEOREMS

In the case of a first-order DLIMID, the parents of the nodes in the t-th slice are either in the same slice or in the previous one. It implies that $P_\Delta(\mathbf{x}^t \mid pa(\mathbf{X}^t)) = P_\Delta(\mathbf{x}^t \mid \mathbf{x}^{t-1})$ and $\mathcal{U}_t(pa(\mathbf{U}^t)) = \mathcal{U}_t(\mathbf{x}^{t-1}, \mathbf{x}^t)$, and Equation 8 can be rewritten as:

$$\mathrm{EU}(\Delta) = \sum_{\mathbf{x}^0} \cdots \sum_{\mathbf{x}^h} P(\mathbf{x}^0) \prod_{t=1}^{h} P_\Delta(\mathbf{x}^t \mid \mathbf{x}^{t-1}) \left[\mathcal{U}_0(\mathbf{x}^0) + \sum_{t'=1}^{h} \gamma^{t'} \mathcal{U}_t(\mathbf{x}^{t'-1}, \mathbf{x}^{t'}) \right].$$

When $t > 0$, does not depend on xt. Therefore,

$$\sum_{\mathbf{x}^1} \cdots \sum_{\mathbf{x}^h} \prod_{t=1}^{h} P_\Delta(\mathbf{x}^t \mid \mathbf{x}^{t-1}) \cdot \mathcal{U}_0(\mathbf{x}^0) = \mathcal{U}_0(\mathbf{x}^0) \sum_{\mathbf{x}^1} \cdots \sum_{\mathbf{x}^h} \prod_{t=1}^{h} P_\Delta(\mathbf{x}^t \mid \mathbf{x}^{t-1}) = \mathcal{U}_0(\mathbf{x}^0),$$

$$\sum_{\mathbf{x}^i} P_\Delta(\mathbf{x}^i \mid \mathbf{x}^{i-1}) = 1.$$

because As a consequence,

$$\mathrm{EU}(\Delta) = \sum_{\mathbf{x}^0} P(\mathbf{x}^0) \left[\mathcal{U}_0(\mathbf{x}^0) + \sum_{\mathbf{x}^1} \cdots \sum_{\mathbf{x}^h} \prod_{t=1}^{h} P_\Delta(\mathbf{x}^t \mid \mathbf{x}^{t-1}) \sum_{t'=1}^{h} \gamma^{t'} \mathcal{U}_t(\mathbf{x}^{t'-1}, \mathbf{x}^{t'}) \right]. \quad (19)$$

We will use this equation to prove both theorems.

Proof of Theorem 1

First, we have that

$$\mathrm{EU}(\Delta) = \sum_{\mathbf{x}^0} P(\mathbf{x}^0)$$

$$\left[\mathcal{U}_0(\mathbf{x}^0) + \sum_{\mathbf{x}^1} \cdots \sum_{\mathbf{x}^{h-1}} \prod_{t=1}^{h-1} P_\Delta(\mathbf{x}^t \mid \mathbf{x}^{t-1}) \sum_{t'=1}^{h} \gamma^{t'} \sum_{\mathbf{x}^h} P_\Delta(\mathbf{x}^h \mid \mathbf{x}^{h-1}) \mathcal{U}_t(\mathbf{x}^{t'-1}, \mathbf{x}^{t'}) \right].$$

If $0 < t' \leq h - 1$., then $\mathcal{U}_t(\mathbf{x}^{t'-1}, \mathbf{x}^{t'})$ does not depend on $\mathbf{x}^h$. Therefore,

$$\sum_{t'=1}^{h-1} \gamma^{t'} \sum_{\mathbf{x}^h} P_\Delta(\mathbf{x}^h \mid \mathbf{x}^{h-1}) \cdot \mathcal{U}_t(\mathbf{x}^{t'-1}, \mathbf{x}^{t'})$$

$$= \gamma^{t'} \sum_{t'=1}^{h-1} \mathcal{U}_t(\mathbf{x}^{t'-1}, \mathbf{x}^{t'}) \sum_{\mathbf{x}^h} P_\Delta(\mathbf{x}^h \mid \mathbf{x}^{h-1})$$

$$= \gamma^{t'} \sum_{t'=1}^{h-1} \mathcal{U}_t(\mathbf{x}^{t'-1}, \mathbf{x}^{t'})$$

and

$$\mathrm{EU}(\Delta) = \sum_{\mathbf{x}^0} P(\mathbf{x}^0) \left[\mathcal{U}_0(\mathbf{x}^0) + \sum_{\mathbf{x}^1} \cdots \sum_{\mathbf{x}^{h-1}} \right.$$

$$\prod_{t=1}^{h-1} P_\Delta(\mathbf{x}^t \mid \mathbf{x}^{t-1}) \sum_{t'=1}^{h-1} \gamma^{t'} \mathcal{U}_{t'}(\mathbf{x}^{t'-1}, \mathbf{x}^{t'})$$

$$\left. + \gamma^h \sum_{\mathbf{x}^h} P_\Delta(\mathbf{x}^h \mid \mathbf{x}^{h-1}) \, \mathcal{U}_{t'}(\mathbf{x}^{h-1}, \mathbf{x}^h) \right].$$

Because of the definition of V_Δ^i (cf. Eq. 11), we have:

$$\mathrm{EU}(\Delta) = \sum_{\mathbf{x}^0} P(\mathbf{x}^0) \left[\mathcal{U}_0(\mathbf{x}^0) + \sum_{\mathbf{x}^1} \cdots \sum_{\mathbf{x}^{h-1}} \prod_{t=1}^{h-1} P_\Delta(\mathbf{x}^t \mid \mathbf{x}^{t-1}) \left[\sum_{t'=1}^{h-1} \gamma^{t'} \mathcal{U}_{t'}(\mathbf{x}^{t'-1}, \mathbf{x}^{t'}) \atop + \gamma^{h-1} V_\Delta^{h-1}(\mathbf{x}^{h-1}) \right] \right]$$

$$= \sum_{\mathbf{x}^0} P(x^0) \left[\mathcal{U}_0(\mathbf{x}^0) \sum_{\mathbf{x}^1} \cdots \sum_{\mathbf{x}^{h-2}} \prod_{t=1}^{h-2} P\Delta(\mathbf{x}^t \mid \mathbf{x}^{t-1}) \left[\sum_{t'=1}^{h-2} \gamma^{t'} \mathcal{U}_{t'}(\mathbf{x}^{t'-1}, \mathbf{x}^{t'}) \atop + \gamma^{h-1} \sum_{\mathbf{x}^{h-1}} P_\Delta(\mathbf{x}^t \mid \mathbf{x}^{t-1}) \left[\mathcal{U}_{h-1}(\mathbf{x}^{h-2}, \mathbf{x}^{h-1}) \atop + V_\Delta^{h-1}(\mathbf{x}^{h-1}) \right] \right] \right]$$

$$= \sum_{\mathbf{x}^0} P(x^0) \left[\mathcal{U}_0(\mathbf{x}^0) \sum_{\mathbf{x}^1} \cdots \sum_{\mathbf{x}^{h-2}} \prod_{t=1}^{h-2} P_\Delta(\mathbf{x}^t \mid \mathbf{x}^{t-1}) \left[\sum_{t'=1}^{h-2} \gamma^{t'} \mathcal{U}_{t'}(\mathbf{x}^{t'-1}, \mathbf{x}^{t'}) \atop + \gamma^{h-2} V_\Delta^{h-2}(\mathbf{x}^{h-2}) \right] \right]$$

and we apply the same procedure again and again, until we arrive at:

$$\mathrm{EU}(\Delta) = \sum_{\mathbf{x}^0} P_\Delta(\mathbf{x}^0) \left[\mathcal{U}_0(\mathbf{x}^0) \atop + \sum_{\mathbf{x}^1} P_\Delta(\mathbf{x}^1 \mid \mathbf{x}^0) \left[\gamma \mathcal{U}_1(\mathbf{x}^0, \mathbf{x}^1) + \gamma V_\Delta^1(\mathbf{x}^1) \right] \right]$$

$$= \sum_{\mathbf{x}^0} P_\Delta(\mathbf{x}^0) \left[\mathcal{U}_0(\mathbf{x}^0) + V_\Delta^0(\mathbf{x}^0) \right],$$

which proves the theorem.

Proof of Theorem 2

From Equation 19 we have:

$$\text{EU}(\Delta) = \sum_{\mathbf{x}^0} P(\mathbf{x}^0)\, \mathcal{U}_0(\mathbf{x}^0)$$

$$+ \left[\sum_{t=1}^{h} \gamma^t \sum_{\mathbf{x}^0} P(\mathbf{x}^0) \sum_{\mathbf{x}^1} \cdots \sum_{\mathbf{x}^h} \prod_{t'=1}^{h} P_\Delta(\mathbf{x}^{t'} \mid \mathbf{x}^{t'-1})\, \mathcal{U}_t(\mathbf{x}^{t-1}, \mathbf{x}^t) \right].$$

We define R_t', where $1 \le t \le h$, as follows:

$$R_t' = \sum_{\mathbf{x}^1} \cdots \sum_{\mathbf{x}^h} P(\mathbf{x}^0) \prod_{t'=1}^{h} P_\Delta(\mathbf{x}^{t'} \mid \mathbf{x}^{t'-1})\, \mathcal{U}_t(\mathbf{x}^{t-1}, \mathbf{x}^t).$$

Because of this definition and the definition of R_0 in Equation 13, we have that

$$\text{EU}(\Delta) = R_0 + \sum_{t=1}^{h} \gamma^t R_t'.$$

Therefore, to prove the theorem it suffices to show that $R_t' = R_t$ for $1 \le t \le h$.
If $t' > t$, then $\mathcal{U}_t(\mathbf{x}^{t-1}, \mathbf{x}^t)$ does not depend on $\mathbf{x}^{t'}$ and, consequently,

$$R_t' = \sum_{\mathbf{x}^0} P(\mathbf{x}^0) \sum_{\mathbf{x}^1} \cdots \sum_{\mathbf{x}^t} \prod_{t'=1}^{h} P_\Delta(\mathbf{x}^{t'} \mid \mathbf{x}^{t'-1})\, \mathcal{U}_t(\mathbf{x}^{t-1}, \mathbf{x}^t) \left[\sum_{\mathbf{x}^{t+1}} \cdots \sum_{\mathbf{x}^h} \prod_{t'=t+1}^{h} P_\Delta(\mathbf{x}^{t'} \mid \mathbf{x}^{t'-1}) \right]$$

$$\sum_{\mathbf{x}^0} P(\mathbf{x}^0) \sum_{\mathbf{x}^1} \cdots \sum_{\mathbf{x}^t} \prod_{t'=1}^{h} P_\Delta(\mathbf{x}^{t'} \mid \mathbf{x}^{t'-1})\, \mathcal{U}_t(\mathbf{x}^{t-1}, \mathbf{x}^t)$$

By reordering the sums, we have that

$$R'_t = \sum_{\mathbf{x}^t} \sum_{\mathbf{x}^{t-1}} P_\Delta(\mathbf{x}^t \mid \mathbf{x}^{t-1}) \mathcal{U}_t(\mathbf{x}^{t-1}, \mathbf{x}^t) \sum_{\mathbf{x}^{t-2}} P_\Delta(\mathbf{x}^{t-1} \mid \mathbf{x}^{t-2}) \cdots \sum_{\mathbf{x}^1} P(\mathbf{x}^2 \mid \mathbf{x}^1) \sum_{\mathbf{x}^0} P(\mathbf{x}^1 \mid \mathbf{x}^0) P(\mathbf{x}^0)$$

$$= \sum_{\mathbf{x}^t} \sum_{\mathbf{x}^{t-1}} P_\Delta(\mathbf{x}^t \mid \mathbf{x}^{t-1}) \mathcal{U}_t(\mathbf{x}^{t-1}, \mathbf{x}^t) \sum_{\mathbf{x}^{t-2}} P_\Delta(\mathbf{x}^{t-1} \mid \mathbf{x}^{t-2}) \cdots \sum_{\mathbf{x}^1} P(\mathbf{x}^2 \mid \mathbf{x}^1) P(\mathbf{x}^1)$$

$$= \sum_{\mathbf{x}^t} \sum_{\mathbf{x}^{t-1}} P_\Delta(\mathbf{x}^t \mid \mathbf{x}^{t-1}) \mathcal{U}_t(\mathbf{x}^{t-1}, \mathbf{x}^t) \sum_{\mathbf{x}^{t-2}} P_\Delta(\mathbf{x}^{t-1} \mid \mathbf{x}^{t-2}) \cdots P(\mathbf{x}^2)$$

and finally

$$R_{t'} = \sum_{\mathbf{x}^t} \sum_{\mathbf{x}^{t-1}} P_\Delta(\mathbf{x}^t \mid \mathbf{x}^{t-1})\, \mathcal{U}_t(\mathbf{x}^{t-1}, \mathbf{x}^t)\, P_\Delta(\mathbf{x}^{t-1}) = R_t,$$

which completes the proof.

Chapter 9
Relational Representations and Traces for Efficient Reinforcement Learning

Eduardo F. Morales
National Institute for Astrophysics, Optics and Electronics, México

Julio H. Zaragoza
National Institute for Astrophysics, Optics and Electronics, México

ABSTRACT

This chapter introduces an approach for reinforcement learning based on a relational representation that: (i) can be applied over large search spaces, (ii) can incorporate domain knowledge, and (iii) can use previously learned policies on different, but similar, problems. The underlying idea is to represent states as sets of first order relations, actions in terms of those relations, and to learn policies over such generalized representation. It is shown how this representation can produce powerful abstractions and that policies learned over this generalized representation can be directly applied, without any further learning, to other problems that can be characterized by the same set of relations. To accelerate the learning process, we present an extension where traces of the tasks to be learned are provided by the user. These traces are used to select only a small subset of possible actions increasing the convergence of the learning algorithms. The effectiveness of the approach is tested on a flight simulator and on a mobile robot.

INTRODUCTION

Sequential decision making under uncertainty has been studied in fields such as decision-theoretic planning (Puterman, 1994), reinforcement learning (Sutton & Barto, 1989) and economics. The idea is to decide on each state, which is the best action to perform, given uncertainty on the outcomes of the actions and trying to obtain the maximum benefit in the long run. Optimal sequence decision making can be formalized as a Markov decision process or MDP, where several dynamic programming techniques have been developed (Puterman, 1994). These techniques, obtain optimal policies, i.e., the best action to perform

DOI: 10.4018/978-1-60960-165-2.ch009

on each state, however, they require knowing a transition model. Reinforcement learning (RL), on the other hand, can learn optimal or near optimal policies while interacting with an external environment, without a transition model (Sutton & Barto, 1989). In either case, the representation used in traditional models for MDPs require all the possible states to be explicitly represented. This restricts its applicability to only very simple domains as the number of possible states grows exponentially with the number of relevant variables. In order to cope with this curse of dimensionality several approaches have been suggested in recent years. Some of these methods include, function approximation (e.g., (Chapman & Kaelbling, 1991)), hierarchical (e.g., (Dietterich, 2000)) and temporal abstraction (e.g., (Sutton, Precup, & Singh, 1999a)), and factored representations (e.g., (Kaelbling, Littman, & Cassandra, 1998)). Despite recent advances, there is still on-going research into trying to deal more effectively with large search spaces, to incorporate domain knowledge, and to transfer previously learned policies to other related problems. Most work, however, uses a propositional framework and still do not scale well as many domains are more clearly defined in terms of objects and relations.

Suppose we want to learn a policy to play a simple chess endgame from a particular side. Even for learning how to win in a simple and deterministic endgame like king-rook vs. king (KRK), there are more than 175,000 not-in-check legal positions. The number of possible actions for the king-rook side is in general 22 (8 for the king and 14 for the rook), which sum up to nearly 4 million possible state-action pairs. Even with modern computers, learning directly in this representation is just too slow. In this domain, however, there are many states that are essentially the same, in the sense that they all share the same set of relations. For a chess player, the exact location of each piece is not as important as the relations that hold between the pieces to decide which movement to perform (see also (Charness, 1977, Groot, 1965)). For

instance, in the KRK domain, whenever the two kings are *in_opposition* (in the same rank or file with one square in between), the rook is in the file/rank that divides both kings, and the rook is at least two squares apart from the opposite king (i.e., it is safe to check), a good move is to check the opposite king to force it to move towards a border (see Figure 1). This action is applicable to all the chess board positions where the previously mentioned relations hold between the pieces, and already captures more than 1,000 chess positions with a white rook. In fact, it is applicable to chess boards of different sizes.

In this chapter, a relational representation for reinforcement learning is used to represent a small set of abstract states with a set of properties (e.g., *in_opposition, rook_divides*, etc.), represent actions in terms of such properties (e.g., If *in_opposition* And *rook_divides* Then *check*) and learn which action to apply on each state.

There has been a growing interest in using first-order logic for modeling MDPs (e.g., (Driessens & Ramon, 2003, Dzeroski, Raedt, & Driessens, 2001, Fern, Yoon, & Givan, 2003, Morales, 2003, Otterlo, 2009)). The use of a relational representation has many advantages. In particular, logical expressions may contain variables and consequently make abstractions of many specific grounded states or transitions. This considerably reduces the number of states and actions and simplifies the learning process that can be carried out at the abstract level. Furthermore, it is possible to transfer policies to other instances and to other, although similar, domains.

Since the seminal work by Dzeroski et al. (Dzeroski et al., 2001, Driessens, Ramon, & Blockeel, 2001, Driessens & Dzeroski, 2002) an increasing number of systems have been proposed in the literature. In particular, at the same time and independently, three related approaches defined abstract states and actions in terms of relations (Kersting & Raedt, 2003, Morales, 2003, Otterlo, 2003). In this chapter, an extended and more formal description of the approach described in

Figure 1. Forcing the opponent king to move towards a border

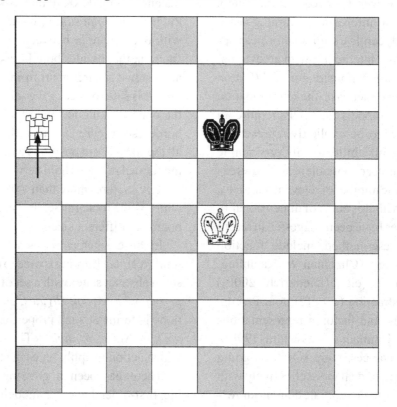

(Morales, 2003) is given including other tests and results. A more complete description of recent relational reinforcement learning algorithms is given in (Otterlo, 2009).

This chapter also shows that we can significantly reduce the convergence time of the learning process by using traces, provided by the user, of the task we want the agent to learn. Finally, it is shown how to transform a discrete actions policy into a continuous actions policy using Locally Weighted Regression.

The objectives of this chapter are to formalize the use of relational representations in reinforcement learning, show their benefits, describe an approach to produce faster convergence times and show the capabilities on two challenging domains; a flight simulator and a mobile robot.

This chapter is organized as follows. It first introduces the basic setting and standard notation. An overview of the most relevant related work is given next. It then describes in detail the proposed relational representation and how to apply a reinforcement learning algorithm over this representation. It then shows how to learn a subset of relational actions from traces provided by the user to speed-up the learning process. This chapter provides experimental evidence of the proposed approach in a flight simulator and a robotics domain. Conclusions and suggests future research directions are given at the end of the chapter.

Preliminaries

Logic

A first-order alphabet Σ is a set of predicate symbols p with arity $m \geq 0$ and a set of function symbols f with arity $n \geq 0$. If $m = 0$ then p is called a proposition and if $n = 0$, f is called a constant.

An atom $p(t_1,\ldots,t_m)$ is a predicate symbol p followed by a bracketed m-tuple of terms t_i. A term is a variable or a constant. A conjunction is a set of (possibly negated) atoms. A substitution τ is a set of assignments of terms t_i to variables V_i, $\Theta = \{V_1 / t_1, \ldots, V_l / t_l\}$. A term, atom or conjunction is called ground if it contains no variables. For more information, on Logic and Logic Programming see, for instance, (Lloyd, 1987).

Markov Decision Processes

A Markov Decision Process (MDP) is a tuple $M = <S,A,T,R>$, where S is a set of states, A is a set of actions, $A(s) \in A$ is a set of actions for each state $s \in S$, T is the transition function $T : S \times A \times S \rightarrow [0,1]$ and R is the reward function $R : S \times A \times S \rightarrow R$. A transition from state $s \in S$ to state $s' \in S$ caused by some action $a \in A(s)$ occurs with probability $P(s'|a,s)$ and receives a reward $R(s,a,s')$. A policy $\pi : S \rightarrow A$ for M specifies which action $a \in A(s)$ to execute when an agent is in some state $s \in S$, i.e., $\pi(s) = a$.

A solution for a given MDP $M = <S,A,T,R>$ consists of finding a policy that maximizes the long-time reward sequence. A deterministic policy $\pi : S \rightarrow A$ specifies which action $a \in A(s)$ to perform on each state $s \in S$. The policy is associated with a value function $V^\pi : S \rightarrow R$. For each state $s \in S$, $V^\pi(s)$ denotes the expected accumulated reward that will be obtained from state s and following the actions suggested by π. This can be expressed in a discounted infinite horizon by:

$$V^\pi(s) = E_\pi \left(\sum_{t=0}^{\infty} \gamma^t R(s_t) \mid s_t = s \right)$$

Similarly, the action-value function for policy π, denoted by $Q^\pi(a,s)$ is defined as:

$$Q^\pi(s,a) = E_\pi \left(\sum_{t=0}^{\infty} \gamma^t R(s_t) \mid s_t = s, a_t = a \right)$$

The expression for V can be recursively defined in terms of the Bellman Equation:

$$V^\pi(s) = \sum_{s' \in S} P(s \mid \pi(s), s') \left(R(s) + \gamma V^\pi(s') \right).$$

For more information on Markov Decision Process and Reinforcement Learning see (Puterman, 1994, Sutton & Barto, 1989).

Several approaches have been suggested in the literature to learn optimal policies and value functions in RL. In this chapter we used a modified Q-learning approach over an abstracted space based on a relational representation.

Related Work

Other researchers have also turned their attention towards abstracting the search space in different ways in order to tackle larger problems. State aggregation clusters "similar" states together and assigns them the same value, effectively reducing the state space. Work on tile-coding (e.g., (Lim & Kim, 1991)), coarse coding (e.g., (Hinton, 1984)), radial basis functions (e.g., (Poggio & Girosi, 1990)), Kanerva coding (e.g., (Kanerva, 1993)), and soft-state aggregation (e.g., (Singh, Jaakkola, & Jordan, 1996)) are some of the representatives of this approach. In this paper, we also do state aggregation, but we use a relational representation, grouping together states that share the same set of relations. This has several advantages over previous approaches: (i) it is easy to define useful and powerful abstractions, (ii) it is easy to incorporate domain knowledge, and (iii) the learned policies can be directly used to other similar domains without any further learning, which is not possible with previous approaches.

Relational Reinforcement Learning (RRL) (Dzeroski et al., 2001, Driessens et al., 2001, Driessens & Dzeroski, 2002) uses a relational representation for states and actions; however their main focus has been on approximating value functions with a relational representation. This extends previous work on incremental regression trees (e.g., (Chapman & Kaelbling, 1991)) to a relational representation. One disadvantage with an incremental tree approach is that once a split in the tree is decided it cannot be undone, which makes the approach highly dependent on the initial sequence of experiments. Recently, Croonenborghs *et al.* (Croonenborghs, Driessens, & Bruynooghe, 2007) extended this work and introduced a method to learn relational options for transfer learning in RL. They first learn a relational policy with the RRL approach presented in (Sutton, Precup, & Singh, 1999b) where the goal is to decompose and learn tasks as a set of options. An option can be viewed as a subroutine, consisting of an option policy that specifies which action to execute for a subset of the environment states. Besides learning these sets of options for the tasks they also generate examples or traces guided from the learned sets of options. They do this in order to provide some help or guidance to the person or method that generates the examples. These examples and the sets of options are given to *TILDE* (Blockeel & Raedt, 1998) to learn relational decision trees that allow the knowledge from the learned policies to be transferred between similar domains. Unfortunately the method was only applied to the blocks world and the actions from the sets of options are discrete.

The closest research work to the relational reinforcement learning approach described in this chapter, which is a clearer formalization of what was introduced in (Morales, 2003), was independently proposed by Kersting and De Raedt (Kersting & Raedt, 2003, 2004) and by van Otterlo (Otterlo, 2003, 2004). The three approaches introduced similar abstractions based on predicates. In fact, all three transform the

underlying relational MDP into a much smaller abstract MDP that is solved using modifications of traditional reinforcement learning algorithms.

Kersting and De Raedt (Kersting & Raedt, 2003, 2004) introduced a first-order probabilistic STRIPS-like language to specify an MDP on a relational domain. An abstract policy is an ordered set of rules that can be seen as an abstraction of a Q-value table. Van Otterlo (Otterlo, 2003, 2004) abstraction is also a conjunction of first-order literals (with negation). Our approach and van Otterlo's use a slightly more powerful state abstraction, than Kersting and De Raedt, as they can include negation and arbitrary state predicates.

Kersting and Driessens (Kersting & Driessens, 2008) proposed a method to learn Parametric Policy Gradients for learning tasks. This model-free policy gradient approach deals with relational and propositional domains. They represent policies as weighted sums of regression models grown in a stage-wise optimization. Each regression model can be viewed as defining several new feature combinations. The idea is to start with an initial policy for a given task. Then calculate the gradient (through Friedmanns gradient boosting (Friedman, 2001)) values of this policy and move or adapt the parameters of the initial policy into the direction of the gradient. This method is recursively applied until no improvement on the policy is achieved. The method can developed control policies with continuous actions and deals with continuous states. It was applied to the blocks world and for teaching a robot how to traverse through a one-dimensional corridor. However the method is complex as it needs to compute the gradient of initially as many regression models as possible feature combinations (which for real robots with several sensors each of them providing readings at very high sample rates might become infeasible) and the method can lead to local maxima.

In (Raedt, Kimmig, & Toivonen, 2007) the authors developed ProbLog which is a probabilistic extension of Prolog. All clauses (facts) are labeled with the probability that they are true and these probabilities are mutually independent. Once a clause is tested as true, its probability value is calculated (given its parents from the derivation tree or previous clause's probability values) and then propagated to the subsequent clauses. Besides allowing relational representations the method is useful when we need to know the probability of a given predicate (which can be an action or state predicate) in order to make choices when having incomplete or uncertain information, however, there is no straightforward way to make ProbLog learn tasks that require the execution of continuous actions.

Another approach for tasks planning using a relational representation is the Planning Domain Definition Language (PDDL) (McDermott, 1998) which is an attempt to standardize planning domain and problem description languages. It was first developed by Drew McDermott mainly to make the 1998/2000 International Planning Competitions possible[1]. The learning task is defined by objects, predicates, the initial state, the goal specification, and actions/operators to change the state of the world. The language also allows the use of temporal logic where predicates are evaluated until some condition is achieved. The inference mechanisms of PDDL allow users to generate the sets of actions that make the goal specifications true. These goal specifications are evaluated true when their previous predicates are also evaluated true. By using this relational domain (through first order predicate logic) the learned tasks can be transferred between similar domains. PDDL was recently extended to specify MDPs (Younes & Littman, 2004), however, the user is responsible for specifying the transition and reward functions, as well as the actions. In this chapter the transition and reward function are not given in advance and the agent is able to learn the action from human traces.

Other languages have been defined to combine probability with first-order logic, such as Markov Logic Networks (Richardson & Domingos, 2006), Probabilistic Relational Models (Getoor, Koller,

Taskar, & Friedman, 2000), FOCIL (Natarajan et al., 2005) and Bayesian Logic Programs (Kersting, Raedt, & Kramer, 2000) among others (see also (Getoor & Taskar, 2007)). This chapter provides an extended and more formal description of the approach given in (Morales, 2003), with other tests and results. A key issue in all these relational MDPs is the representation of states and actions which is normally provided by the user. A clear distinction of this chapter with previous approaches is the incorporation of Behavioral Cloning, to learn relational actions and produce faster convergence times. It also introduces two extensions, one is an exploration strategy to complete the information provided by human traces (illustrated with a flight simulator) and the other one is an on-line process to transform a discrete actions policy into a continuous actions policy (illustrated with a mobile robot).

Relational Representation for Reinforcement Learning

The key idea underlying relational reinforcement learning is to use relations instead of flat symbols. In this work, states are represented as sets of predicates that can be used to characterize a particular state and which may be common to other states. This representation allows us to:

- Create powerful abstractions, as states are characterized by a set of predicates. This makes it useful for large search spaces and applicable to relational domains.
- Learn policies which are, in general, independent of the exact position of the agent and the goal. This allows us to transfer policies to different problems where the same relations apply without any further learning, which is not possible with a propositional representation.

Exhibit 1.

```
r_action(2,S,rook,sq(D,E),sq(I,J),State1,State2):-
        rook_divs(S,king,sq(B,C),S,rook,sq(D,E),OS,king,sq(G,H),State1),
        opposition(S,king,sq(B,C),OS,king,sq(G,H),State1),
        make_move(S,rook,sq(D,E),sq(I,J),State1,State2),
        not threatkR(OS,king,sq(G,H),S,rook,sq(I,J),State2),
        l_patt(OS,king,sq(G,H),S,king,sq(B,C),S,rook,sq(I,J),State2).
```

Definition 1: *A relational state or r-state, s_R, is a conjunction of logical atoms.*

The extension of an *r-state* is the set of states that are covered by its description. That is, an *r-state* represents a set of states, where each state is represented by a conjunction of ground facts. More formally an *r-state*, s_R, represents all the states $s \in S$ for which there is a substitution Θ such that $s_R\Theta \subseteq s$. In our framework, each state $s \in S$ is an instance of one and only one *r-state*, which creates a partition over the state space S. In the chess domain, individual predicates could be *rook_threatened, kings_in_opposition, rook_divides_kings*, etc., which involve, in this case, the relative position of one, two or three pieces. A conjunction of these predicates represent an *r-state*, one of which could be *kings_in_opposition and rook_divides_kings*, that covers all the chess positions where these two relations hold (more than 3,000 positions). Once a set of relations has been defined, the search space in the relational space is completely defined.

The set of actions also use a first-order relational representation, similar to STRIPS operators or PDDL actions (McDermott, 1998).

Definition 2: *A relational action or r-action, $a_R(s_R)$, is a set of pre-conditions, a generalized action, and possibly a set of post-conditions. The pre-conditions are conjunctions of relations that need to hold for the r-action to be applicable, and the post-conditions are conjunctions of relations that need to hold after a particular primitive action is* performed. *The generalized action represents all the instantiations of primitive actions that satisfy the conditions.*

For example, the following *r-action* (Exhibit 1), using Prolog notation, with id number 2 (first argument), says to move the rook of side S, from square (D,E) to square (I,J) if the rook divides the two kings and both kings are in opposition (pre-conditions), provided the rook is not threatened after the move and the three pieces form an L-shaped pattern (post-conditions) (see Figure 1).

For an *r-action* to be properly defined, the following condition must be satisfied: *If an r-action is applicable to a particular instance of an r-state, then it should be applicable to all the instances of that r-state*. This is not a problem for *r-actions* without post-conditions, as the pre-conditions are subsets of relations used to represent *r-states*, and consequently applicable to all the instances. This assures that *r-actions* associated with a particular *r-state* are always applicable in that *r-state*.

Similarly to the representation of states, the actions can be provided by the user. In this chapter, however, it is shown that once a set of relations has been defined, it is possible to induce the *r-actions* using a Behavioral Cloning approach, as described below. Each *r-action* can have different instantiations, resulting in different instantiations of the resulting *r-state*. When several possible instantiations of actions are possible, one is chosen randomly (uniform distribution). As can be seen, even assuming a deterministic policy in a relational

Figure 2. A non deterministic r-action, where two possible actions are possible satisfying all the conditions of the r-action

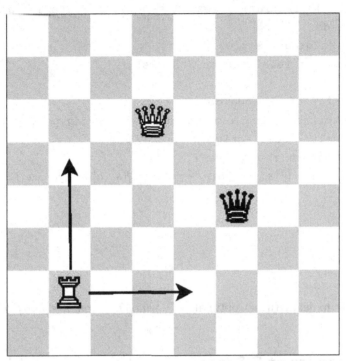

representation, the policy is still non deterministic at the ground level since different action instances can be selected. For example, an *r-action* could be to move the rook to divide both kings either horizontally or vertically. Figure 2 shows this case where there are two equally possible rook moves to divide both kings, both possible states are instances of the same *r-state*.

Once *r-state*s and *r-action*s are defined, a relational transition function can be defined giving the probability of being at state s_R, given that an action $a_R(s_R)$ is applied in *r-state* s_R.

Definition 3: *A relational transition or r-transition $P(s_R|a_R, s_R)$ is defined by an r-state, an r-action and the resulting r-state, where each resulting instance in s_R has a uniform probability of occurring.*

A reward function is defined as in traditional MDP, giving a real number for each state $R_R : S \rightarrow R$. The same reward is given to all the instances of an *r-state* s_R.

Definition 4: *A relational MDP, or r-MDP, is a tuple $M_R = <S_R, A_R, T_R, R_R>$ where S_R is a set of r-states, $A_R(S_R)$ is a set of r-actions (one per r-state), T_R is an r-transition and R_R is the reward function.*

To summarize, abstract states are created with a set of properties expressed in a relational representation and a set of actions, using such properties, are defined for each abstract state. Reinforcement learning is then used to decide which action to perform on each state. The main advantages of the approach are that it is relatively easy to express and incorporate background knowledge, powerful abstractions can be achieved, and it is possible to re-use a previously learned policy on other instances of the problem and even on similar, although different, problems. The following

Algorithm 1. The rQ-learning algorithm

```
Initialize Q(s_R, a_R) arbitrarily (where s_R is an r-state and a_R is an r-action)
for each episode do
    Initialize s {a ground state}
    s_R ← rel(s) {set of relations on state s}
    Repeat
        for each step of episode do
            Choose from using a persistently exciting policy (e.g., greedy)
            Randomly choose action a applicanle in
            Take action a, observe r, s'
```

$$Q\left(s_R, a_R\right) \leftarrow Q\left(s_R, a_R\right) + \alpha(r_R + \gamma max_{a_R'} Q(s_R', a_R') - Q(s_R, a_R))$$

$$s_R \leftarrow s_R'$$

```
        end for
    untils is terminal
end for
```

section describes how to learn (near) optimal policies for r-MDPs.

Reinforcement Learning on R-Space

For any Markov decision process, the objective is to find the optimal policy, i.e., one which achieves the highest cumulative reward among all policies. The main purpose to learn in an *r-space* is to reduce the size of the search space, and take all the advantages of a richer representation language. However, in the *r-space* there is no guarantee that the defined *r-actions* are adequate to find an optimal sequence of primitive actions and suboptimal policies can be produced. We can however, defined optimality in terms of an *r-space*.

A policy consistent with our representation, which we will refer to as an *r-space* policy (π_R), is a scheme for deciding which *r-action* to select when entering an *r-state*. An *r-space* optimal policy (π_R^*) is a policy that achieves the highest cumulative reward among all *r-space* policies.

Definition 5: *A deterministic policy for an r-MDP, called r-space policy,* $\pi_R : S_R \rightarrow A_R$ *specifies*

which *r-action*, $a_R(s_R)$, *to perform on each r-state*, s_R.

The expected reward, in this case, is the expected *average* reward over all the instances of the *r-state*. When several *r-actions* are applicable in a particular *r-state*, the best policy will prefer the *r-actions* which lead to an *r-state* with the best expected average reward.

The rQ-Learning Algorithm

This paper focuses on applying Q-learning (Watkins, 1989) in *r-space*, although a similar argument can be applied to other reinforcement learning algorithms, such as TD(λ) or SARSA (Sutton & Barto, 1989). Algorithm 1 gives the pseudo-code for the rQ-learning algorithm. This is very similar to the Q-learning algorithm, but the states and actions are characterized by relations. The algorithm still takes primitive actions (*a*'s) and moves over primitive states (*s*'s), but learns over *r-state-r-action* pairs.

It will be shown, empirically, that obtaining an *r-space* policy is good enough to solve complex problems and that in many cases, it also corresponds to the optimal policy at the ground level, although this depends on the description of the *r-space*. Also, since we are learning over generalized actions and states, the same policy is applicable to different instances of the problem and sometimes to other problems where the same set of relations hold. Even with an abstract representation, reinforcement learning can take a considerable time to converge to a suitable policy. In the following section, it is shown how to accelerate the learning process using traces provided by users.

Accelerating the Learning Process

So far, we have assumed that the r-actions are defined by the user. One way to learn *r-actions* is from log traces of humans, or other computer systems, solving a task. Behavioural Cloning (BC) induces control rules from traces of skilled operators, e.g., (Sammut, Hurst, Kedzier, & Michie, 1992, Michie, Bain, & Hayes-Michie, 1990, Bratko, Urbančič, & Sammut, 1998). The general idea is that if the human is capable of performing a task, rather than asking him/her to explain how it is performed, he/she is asked to perform it. Machine Learning is then used to produce a symbolic description of the skill.

In this chapter we use logs of human traces to learn and identify only a subset of potentially relevant actions and then use reinforcement learning over this abstracted and reduced search space to learn a policy. Our approach can use traces from several experts, which may choose different actions. The traces provided by the user(s) are transformed into a relational representation. From these relational traces a set of *r-actions* is learned for each *r-state*. The BC approach can learn good and bad *r-actions* but then relational reinforcement learning is used to decide which are the best *r-actions* to use on each *r-state*. In this sense, it is an incremental approach, as new traces can be given at any time.

Contrary to other related approaches, like Programming by Demonstration, we are not limited by the quality of the traces provided by the user, as we accept traces from several users and of different quality and our reinforcement learning algorithm finds which is the best action to perform on each state. Also we are focusing the search space to a limited number of actions which significantly reduces the convergence times of reinforcement learning.

In order to learn a new *r-action* each frame in the human trace is transformed, if necessary, to a set of predefined predicates, and the action performed by the user is observed. The action may also need to be transformed into a predicate. A new *r-action* is constructed with the conjunction of the above predicates, unless the control action is an instance of an already defined *r-action* (see also (Morales, 1997) for a similar approach used in chess end-games). The predicates that are true in the current frame are used as conditions that need to be satisfied in order to consider such action. In general, an *r-action* has the following format (Exhibit 2), where *predicate* $i,s1(Args_i, State1)$ is a predicate that needs to be true for the action to be executed (a precondition) and may have some particular arguments (*Args*) and *predicate_action*(*Action,State1*), is the predicate that performs the action. In some domains, like chess, it is possible to predict the next state after the action is executed and extract predicates that can then be used as post-conditions. In that case, an *r-action* has the following format (Exhibit 3), where *State2* contains information of the next state after the action has been executed and *predicate j,s2* is a post-condition.

In general, a trace will contain low level information of the domain. For example, a trace in chess will consist of board positions (e.g., white in rook in position g3, black king in b6, etc.) with plies (e.g., white rook moves from g3 to g6). A trace in robotics will consist of sensors' information (e.g., laser reading 1 is 0.32, laser reading 2 is 0.31,..., sonar1 reading is 2.78, sonar2 reading is 3.18,

Exhibit 2.

```
r_action(Action,State1):-
        predicate1,s1 (Args1,State1),
        predicate2,s1 (Args2,State1),
        ...
        predicate_action(Action,State1).
```

Exhibit 3.

```
r_action(Action,State1,State2):-
        predicate 1,s1 (Args1,State1),
        predicate 2,s1 (Args2,State1),
        ...
        predicate_action(Action,State1,State2),
        predicate 1,s2 (Args3,State2),
        predicate 2,s2 (Args4,State2),
        ...
```

etc.) and movement information (e.g., speed is 5.1 cm/sec). This information is transformed into predicates such as, *rook_threatened*, *in_opposition* and *make_move* for chess or *door_detected*, *obstacle_detected* and *go_forward* or *turn_right* for robotics, from which the *r-actions* are build.

The approach only learns the *r-actions* used in the traces. This substantially reduces the learning process, as only a subset of actions are considered per state, but can also generate sub-optimal policies as not all the applicable actions are considered per state. It is also possible that some *r-states* are never visited. These issues are later discussed in this chapter. Algorithm 2 summarizes the behavioral cloning approach used for reinforcement learning.

Experiments

We illustrate the approach in two challenging domains and illustrate two possible improvements to the proposed approach. The first domain is a flight simulator, where the goal is to learn how to fly an aircraft. In this experiment we illustrate how to incorporate an exploration strategy to produce more robust policies. The second domain is a mobile robot, where the goal is to learn navigation tasks. In this experiment we show how to transform a discrete action policy into a continuous action policy.

Learning to Fly

Trying to learn how to control an aircraft is a challenging task for reinforcement learning as it may typically involve 20 to 30 variables, most of them continuous, describing an aircraft moving in a potentially "infinite" three dimensional space.

A flight simulator based on a high fidelity model of a high performance aircraft (a Pilatus PC-9 acrobatic air plane) was used in our experiments.[2] The PC-9 is an extremely fast and maneuverable aircraft used for pilot training. The model, provided by the Australian Defense Science and Technology Organization (DSTO), is based on wind tunnel and in-flight performance data. Since the flight simulator is of an acrobatic aircraft, small changes in control can result in large deviations in the aircraft position and ori-

Algorithm 2. Behavioral cloning approach for reinforcement learning

```
Given a set a trace-logs (Each composed of a set of frames) of the task we
want to learn for each frame do
    Transform the information of the frame into a relational representation (r-
    state) using a pre-defined set of Predicates
    Transform the information from the action performed by the user into a re-
    lational representation (predicate-action)
    Construct, if new, an r-action with the conjunction of the r-state and the
    predicate-action
end for
```

entation. This chapter only deals with controlling the ailerons and elevators, which are the two most difficult tasks to learn. In all the experiments, it was assumed that the aircraft was already in the air with a constant throttle, flat flaps and retracted gear. Turbulence was added during the learning process (both behavioral cloning and reinforcement learning) as a random offset to the velocity components of the aircraft, with a maximum displacement of 10*ft/s* in the vertical direction and 5*ft/s* in the horizontal direction.[3]

The goal is to learn how to fly through a sequence of ways points, each way point with a tolerance of 100*ft* vertically and horizontally. Thus the aircraft must fly through a "window" centered at the way point.

We decided to divide the task into two independent reinforcement learning problems: (i) forward-backward movements to control the elevation of the aircraft and (ii) left-right movements to control the roll and heading of the aircraft. We assume that in normal flight, the aircraft is approximately level so that the elevators have their greatest effect on elevation and the ailerons on roll.

To characterize the states for elevation control the following predicates and discretized values were defined:

- *distance_goal*: relative distance between the plane and the current goal. Possible values: *close* (less than 100 ft), *near* (be-

tween 100 and 1,000 ft), and *far* (more than 1,000 ft).

- *elevation_goal*: difference between current elevation of the aircraft and the goal elevation, considering the plane's current inclination. Possible values: *far_up* (more than 30°), *up* (between 5° and 30°), *in_front* (between 5° and -5°), *down* (between -5° and -10°), and *far_down* (less than -30°).

For aileron control, in addition to *distance_goal*, the following predicates and discretized values were also defined:

- *orientation_goal*: relative difference between current yaw of the aircraft and goal yaw, considering the current orientation of the plane. Possible values: *far_left* (less than -30°), *left* (between -5° and -30°), *in_front* (between -5° and 5°), *right* (between 5° and 30°), and *far_right* (more than 30°).
- *plane_rol*: current inclination of the plane. Possible values: *far_left* (less than -30°), *left* (between -5° and -30°), *horizontal* (between -5° and 5°), *right* (between 5° and 30°), and *far_right* (more than 30°).
- *plane_rol_trend*: current trend in the inclination of the plane. Possible values: *inc* (more than +1), *std* (between +1 and −1), *dec* (less than −1).

Exhibit 4.

```
r_action(Num,el,State,move_stick(StickMove)) ←
        distance_goal(State,DistGoal) | ∧
        elevation_goal(State,ElevGoal) ∧
        move_stick(StickMove).
```

Exhibit 5.

```
r_action(Num,al,State,move_stick(StickMove)) ←
        distance_goal(State,DistGoal) ∧
        orientation_goal(State,Orient_Goal) ∧
        plane_rol(State,PlaneRol) ∧
        plane_rol_trend(State,RolTrend) ∧
        move_stick(StickMove).
```

The ranges of the discretized values were chosen arbitrarily at the beginning of the experiments and defined consistently across different variables with no further tuning. The exact values appear not to be too relevant, but further tests are needed.

The actions were discretized as follows. The X component of the stick can have the following values: *farleft* (if stick X component value is less than -0.1), *left* (if it is between -0.1 and -0.03), *nil* (between -0.03 and 0.03), *right* (between 0.03 and 0.1), and *farright* (greater than 0.1). For the Y component of the stick movements the following discretization was used: *fardown* (above 0.4), *down* (between 0.3 and 0.4), *nil* (between 0.2 and 0.3), *up* (between 0.1 and 0.2), and *farup* (below 0.1). These discretizations were based on the actions performed by human pilots. These predicates were used to construct, from human traces, a set of aileron and elevation *r-actions*. Elevation *r-actions* have the following format (Exhibit 4): where *Num* is an identification number, *StickMove* is one of the possible values for stick on the Y coordinate, *DistGoal* is one of the possible values for *distance_goal*, and *ElevGoal* is one of the possible values for *elevation_goal*. For elevation there can be 75 possible *r-actions* (3 possible values for *DistGoal*, 5 for *ElevGoal*, and 5 for *StickMovement*).

Similarly, the format for the aileron *r-actions* is as follows (Exhibit 5):where there can be 1,125 possible aileron *r-actions*.

A total of 222 *r-actions* (180 for aileron and 42 for elevation) were learned after 5 consecutive mission logs over the flight plan shown in Figure 3.

Exploration Mode

As we are learning only from seen cases, there may be some states descriptions not covered by the *r-actions* but which may occur in other flight maneuvers. To compensate for this, the learned *r-actions* were used to fly the aircraft to try to reach previously unseen situations. In cases where there were several applicable *r-actions*, one was chosen randomly. Whenever the aircraft reached a new state description (where there was no applicable *r-action*), the system prompted the user for a suitable action, from which a new *r-action* was induced. Also the user was able to perform a different action in any state if he/she wished, even if there were some applicable *r-actions*. Exploration mode continued until almost no new *r-actions* were learned, which was after 20 consecutive explor-

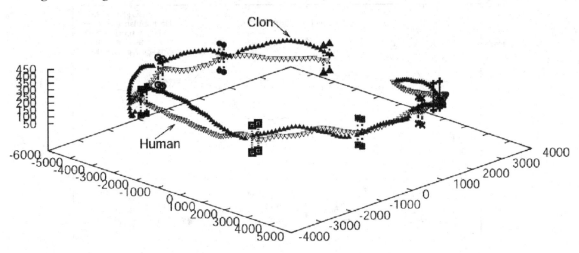

atory flights. In total, 407 *r-actions* were learned, 359 for aileron (out of 1,125 which is ≈32%) and 48 for elevation (out of 75, which is ≈64%). So although, we are still learning a substantial number of *r-actions* behavioral cloning helps us to learn only a subset of the possible *r-actions* (only one third) focusing the search space and simplifying the subsequent reinforcement learning task (an average of 1.6 *r-actions* per aileron state and 3.2 per elevation state).

When performing an *r-action*, the actual value of the stick position was assigned as the mid point of the intervals, except for the extreme ranges, as follows. For the X coordinate: *farleft* = −0.15, *left* = −0.05, *nil* = −0.01, *right* = 0.05, and *farright* = 0.15. For the Y coordinate: *fardown* = 0.45, *down* = 0.35, *nil* = 0.25, *up* = 0.15, and *farup* = 0.05. This discrete actions policy was adequate to learn a reasonable flying strategy as it will be shown in the experimental results. We will describe, in the robotics domain, how to transform this type of policies into policies with continuous actions.

Once the state has been abstracted and the *r-actions* induced, rQ-learning is used to learn a suitable policy to fly the aircraft.

Results

In all the experiments, the Q values were initialized to -1, $\epsilon = 0.1, \gamma = 0.9, \alpha = 0.1$, and $\lambda = 0.9$. The experiments were performed on the 8 goals mission shown in Figure 3. If the aircraft increases its distance to the current goal, after 20 time steps have elapsed from the previous goal, it is assumed that it has passed the goal and it changes to the next goal.

The following experiments were performed:

1. Positive reinforcement (+20) was given only when crossing a goal within 100 ft. with negative rewards otherwise (-1). In case the aircraft crashed or got into a state with no applicable *r-action*, a negative reward was given (-10). The experiments were performed with the maximum level of turbulence.

2. Same as (1) without turbulence.

3. Same as (1) but only with the *r-actions* learned from the original traces, i.e., without the exploration stage (222 *r-actions* in total).

4. Same as (1) but we automatically generate all the possible *r-actions* per state (5 with our

Figure 4. Learning curve for aileron for the different experimental set-ups while training

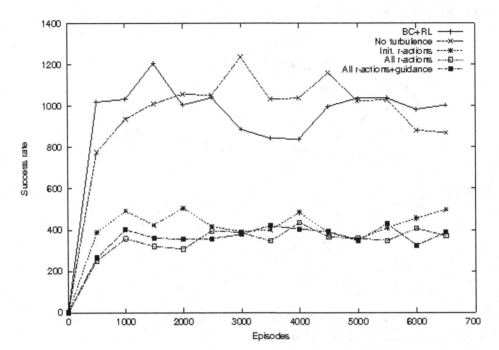

discretization scheme) with 1200 *r-actions* in total.

5. Same as (4) but we use the original traces to "seed" Q-values, providing initial guidance.

Figures 4 and 5 show the learning curves of the above experiments for aileron and elevation respectively. In particular, how many times the aircraft crosses successfully the eight goals with maximum turbulence (every 500 flights) for aileron and elevation control. We continued the experiments for 20,000 episodes without any clear improvements in any of the experiments after the first 3,000 episodes.

As can be seen from the figures, without focusing the search with behavioral cloning, reinforcement learning is unable to learn an adequate strategy in a reasonable time. In complex environments, spurious actions can very easily lead an agent to miss the goal. In this particular domain, going away from the current goal at some intermediate state can lead the agent into a situation where it is impossible to recover and reach the goal without first going away from the goal. The exploratory phase, where new *r-actions* were learned using random exploration, also proved to be useful as the initial traces substantially biased the learning process and limited its applicability.

The policy learned in experiment 1 after 1,500 flights was able to fly the whole mission successfully. Its robustness was tested under different turbulence conditions. Figure 3 shows a human trace of the mission and the trace followed by the learned policy. Table 1 shows the results, averaged over 100 trials, of flying the learned policy on the mission with different levels of turbulence. Two columns are shown per turbulence level, one with percentages passing the way point within 100 ft. (which was used in the reward scheme) and one with 200 ft. The important point to note is that the aircraft can recover even if it misses one or more goals, and although it occasionally misses some of the goals, it gets quite close to them, as can be seen from Figure 3.

Figure 5. Learning curve for elevation for the different experimental set-ups while training

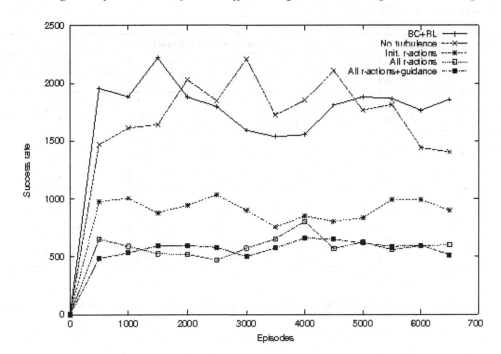

The learned policies were then tested on a completely different mission, consisting of four way points. The intention was to try maneuvers not previously seen before. The new mission included: a right turn[4], a sharper left climb turn of what it has previously seen before, another quick right turn, and a sharp descending right turn.

Figure 6 shows a human trace and the trace using the previously learned policy (experiment 1) on the new mission with the maximum level of turbulence. The learned policy of the previous mission is clearly able to fly the aircraft on a completely new mission. Table 2 shows the performance of the policy on this new mission with different turbulence levels averaged over 100 trials.

An Application in Mobile Robots

Our second experiment consists of teaching a mobile robot how to perform navigation tasks in office–like environments with continuous actions.

To define a representation in terms of common objects found in office-like environments, like rooms, corridors, walls, doors, and obstacles, we first transform the low-level information from sensors into high-level predicates representing such objects. This transformation process is based on the work developed in (Hernández & Morales, 2006), where they defined natural landmarks, such as: (1) discontinuities, defined as an abrupt variation in the measured distance of two consecutive laser readings, (2) corners, defined as the location where two walls intersect and form and angle, and (3) walls, identified from laser sensor readings using the Hough transform. We also add obstacles identified through sonars and defined as any detected object between certain range. We also used the work described in (Herrera-Vega, 2009) to identify the robot's current location such as room, corridor and/or intersection. These natural landmarks, along with the robot's actual location, are used to automatically characterize

Table 1. Performance of the learned policy of experiment 1 after 1,500 episodes with different levels of turbulence on the eight goals mission

Stage	Turbulence (m/s)/Tolerance					
	0/	0/	5/	5/	10/	10/
	100	200	100	200	100	200
Goal1	0	100	31	75	49	89
Goal2	100	100	16	41	26	46
Goal3	0	100	53	62	51	70
Goal4	0	0	23	35	27	46
Goal5	0	100	57	91	59	95
Goal6	0	0	16	33	24	47
Goal7	100	100	47	74	33	66
Goal8	0	100	35	58	45	61
Aver.	25	75.0	34.75	58.625	39.25	65.0

Figure 6. Flight path trace for a human and for the learned policy on a new mission with 4 goals

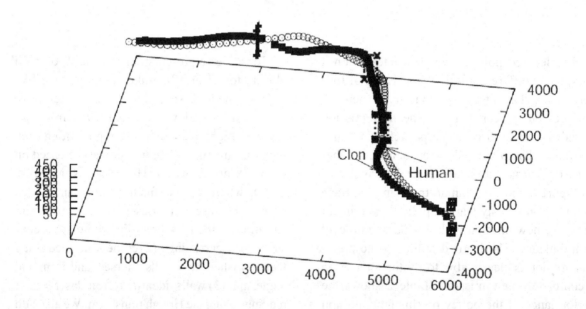

the relational states that describe the environment in real–time.

The predicates used for developing the robot's r-states are:

- *place*: This predicate returns the robot's location, which can be *in-room*, *in-door*, *in-corridor* and *in-intersection*.

- *doors_detected*: This predicate returns the orientation and distance to doors. A door is characterized by identifying a right dis-

Table 2. Performance of the learned policy on a different mission with different levels of turbulence

Stage	Turbulence (m/s)/Tolerance					
	0/	0/	5/	5/	10/	10/
	100	200	100	200	100	200
Goal1	0	100	66	99	74	100
Goal2	100	100	17	39	29	44
Goal3	100	100	38	70	46	70
Goal4	0	100	51	77	39	58
Aver.	50	100	43	71.25	47	68

continuity (*r*) followed by a left disconti-
nuity (*l*) from the natural landmarks. The
door's orientation angle and distance values are calculated by averaging the values
of the right and left discontinuities angles
and distances. The discretized values used
for door orientation are: *right* (door's angle between -67.5° and -112.5°), *left* (67.5
to 112.5°), *front* (22.5° to -22.5°), *back*
(157.5° to -157.5°), *right-back* (-112.5°
to -157.5°), *right-front* (-22.5° to -67.5°),
left-back (112.5° to 157.5°) and *left-front*
(22.5° to 67.5°). The discretized values
used fro distance are: *hit* (door's distance
between 0*m*. and 0.3*m*.), *close* (0.3*m*. to
1.5*m*.), *near* (1.5*m*. to 4.0*m*.) and *far* (>
4.0*m*). For example, if a right (number 1
in Figure 7) and left (number 3 in Figure
7) discontinuities are obtained from the
robot's sensors, then the following predicate is produced *doors_detected*([*front*,
close, -12.57, 1.27]), which corresponds
to the orientation (first and third argument
in symbolic and numeric representation)
and distance (second and fourth argument)
descriptions of a detected door (see Figure
7). For every pair of right and left discontinuities a list with these orientation and
distance descriptions is generated.

- *walls_detected*: This predicate returns the
length, orientation and distance to walls
(type *w* landmarks).[5]

The possible values for the wall's size are:
small (length between 0.15*m*. and 1.5*m*.), *medium*
(1.5*m*. to 4.0*m*.) and *large* (> 4.0*m*.).

- *corners detected*: This predicate returns the
orientation and distance to corners (type *c*
landmarks).[6]
- *obstacles_detected*: This predicate returns
the orientation and distance to obstacles
(type *o* landmarks).[7]
- *goal_position*: This predicate returns the
relative orientation and distance between
the robot and the current goal. It receives
the parameter the robot's current position
and the goal's current position, though as
a trigonometry process, the orientation and
distance values are calculated and then
discretized.[8]
- *goal_reached*: This predicate indicates if
the robot is in its goal position. Possible
values are *true* or *false*.

The previous predicates tell the robot if it is in
a room, a corridor or an intersection, detect walls,
corners, doors, obstacles and corridors and give a
rough estimate of the direction and distance to the
goal. The action predicates receive as parameters
the odometer's speed and angle readings, and are
defined as follows:

Figure 7. Robot sensing its environment through laser and sonar sensors and corresponding natural landmarks

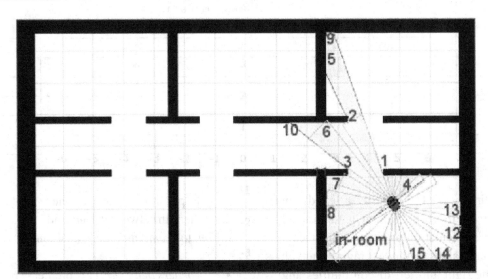

- *go*: This predicate returns the robot's actual moving action. Its possible values are *forward* and *back*.
- *turn*: This predicate returns the robot's actual turning action. Its possible values are *right* and *left*.

Similarly to the flight simulator domain, initial traces are given to the system which uses the previously defined predicates to induce a set of *r-actions* and used them to learn a discrete actions policy. In the following section we describe a real-time post-processing stage that can be applied to the previous approach to produce policies with continuous actions.

Relational Policies with Continuous Actions

This stage refines the coarse actions from the discrete actions policy previously generated. This is achieved using Locally Weighted Regression (LWR). The idea is to combine discrete actions' values give by that policy with the action's values previously observed in traces and stored in a database *DB*. This way the robot follows the policy learned with rQ-learning, but the actions are tuned through the *LWR* process.

What we do is to detect the robot's actual *r*-state. For this *r*-state the discrete actions policy determines the action to be executed (Figure 8(a)). Before performing the action, the robot searches in the *DB* for all the registers that share this same *r-state* description (Figure 8(b)). Once found, the robot gets all of the numeric orientation and distance values from these registers. These orientation and distance values are used to perform a triangulation process. This process allows us to estimate the relative position of the robot from previous traces with respect to the robot's actual position. Once this position has been estimated, a weight is assigned to the previous traces action's values. This weight depends on the distance of the robot from the traces with respect to the actual robot's position (Figure 8(c)). These weights are used to perform the *LWR* that produces continuous *r-actions* (Figure 8(d)).

Once all the distance values (d_i) are calculated for all the registers in the *DB* with the same *r-state*, we apply a Gaussian kernel $w_i(d_i) = exp(-d_i^2)$

Figure 8. Continuous actions developing process. (a) r-state and corresponding r-action. (b) A trace segment. (c) Distances and weights. (d) Resulting continuous action.

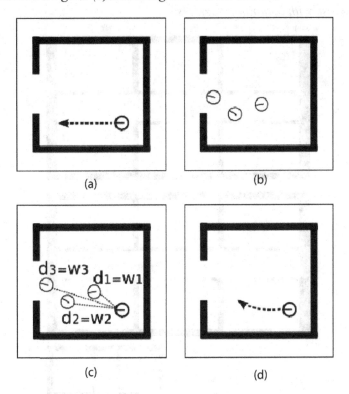

(a)

(b)

(c)

(d)

to obtain a new weight w_i for each relevant register.

Then, every weight w_i is multiplied by the corresponding speed and angle values ($w_i \times speed_{DBi}$ and $w_i \times angle_{DBi}$) of the *r-state-r-action* pairs retrieved from the *DB*. The resulting values are added to the *r-action* ($rA_t = \{disc\_speed, disc\_angle\}$) values of the policy obtained by rQ-learning in order to transform this discrete *r-action* into a continuous action that is executed by the robot. This process is applied to every register read from the *DB* with the same *r-state* description and is repeated every time the robot reaches a new *r-state*.

The main advantage of our approach is the simple and fast strategy to produce continuous actions policies that are able to produce smoother and shorter paths in different environments.

Results. Experiments were carried out in simulation (*Player/Stage* (Vaughan, Gerkey & Howard, 2003)) and with a real robot[9]. Both

robots (simulated and real) are equipped with a 180° front *SICK* laser sensor and an array of 4 back sonars at -170°, -150°, 150° and 170°. The laser range is 8.0*m* and the sonar range is 6.0*m*. The tasks to perform in these experiments were: (i) *navigating* through the environment and (ii) *following* a moving object.

The policy learning process was carried out in the Map 1 shown in Figure 9. For each of the two tasks a set of 15 traces was generated in this map. For the *navigation* tasks, the robot and the goal's global position (for the *goal_position* predicate) were calculated using the work developed in (Hernández & Morales, 2006). For the *following* tasks we used a second robot which orientation and angle was calculated through laser sensor.

We applied our Behavioral Cloning approach to all the traces, to define *r-states* and induce relevant *r-actions*. Then, *rQ-learning* was applied to learn the policies. For generating the policies,

Figure 9. Tasks examples from Maps 1 (size 15.0m. ×8.0m.) and 2 (size 20.0m. ×14.0m.). (a) Navigation task with discrete actions. (b) Navigation task with continuous actions. (c) Following task with discrete actions. (d) Following task with continuous actions.

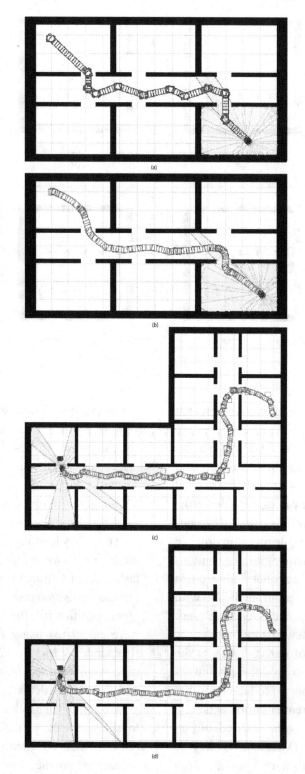

Q-values were initialized to -1, $\in$ = 0.1, γ =0.9 and α = 0.1. Positive reinforcement, *r*, (*+100*) was given when reaching a goal (within 0.5 m.), negative reinforcement (*-20*) was given when the robot hit an element and no reward value was given otherwise (*0*). To generate the continuous actions policy, Locally Weighted Regression was applied on-line using a Gaussian kernel. Once the policies were learned, experiments were executed in the training map with different goal positions and in two new and unknown environments for the robot (Map 2 shown in Figure 9(c) and Map 3 shown in Figure 10). A total of 120 experiments were performed: 10 different navigation and 10 following tasks in each map, executed first with the discrete actions policy from the first stage and then with the continuous actions policy from the second stage. Each experiment has a different distance to cover and requires the robot to traverse through different places. The minimum distance to cover was *2m.* (Manhattan distance), and it was gradually increased up to 18*m.*

Figure 9 shows a *navigation* (Map 1) and a *following* task (Map 2) performed with discrete (left figures) and continuous (right figures) actions, respectively.

Figure 10 shows a *navigation* and a *following* task performed with the real robot, with the discrete and with the continuous actions policy.

We cannot guarantee that the user visited all the possible *r-states*. If the robot reaches an unseen *r-state*, it asks for guidance to the user. Through a joystick, the user indicates the robot which action to execute and the robot stores this new *r-state-r-action* pair in *DB*. The number of unseen *r-states* decreases with the number of experiments.

We evaluated the performance of the discrete and continuous actions policies in three aspects:

1. How close the paths of the tasks are to the paths performed by a user
2. How close the paths o the tasks are from obstacles in the environment
3. What are the execution times of the policies

Figure 11(a)[10] shows results in terms of quality of the performed tasks with the real robot. This comparison is made against tasks performed by humans. All of the tasks performed in the experiments with the real robot, were also performed by a human using a joystick (Figures 10(c), 10(f)), and logs of the paths were saved. The graph shows the normalized squared error between these logs and the trajectories followed by the robot.

Figure 11(b) shows results in terms of how much the robot gets closer to obstacles. This comparison is made using the work developed in (Romero, Morales, & Sucar, 2001). In that work, values were given to the robot according to its proximity to objects or walls. The closer the robot is to an object or wall the higher the cost it is given. Values were given as follows: if the robot is very close to an object (0*m.* to 0.3*m*).a value of -100 was given, if the robot is close to an object (0.3*m.* to 1.0*m*) a value of -3 was given, if the robot is near an object (1.0*m.* to 2.0*m*) a value of -1, otherwise a value of 0 is given. As can be seen in the figure, quadratic error and penalty values for continuous actions policies are lower than those with discrete actions.

Execution times, shown in Figure 12, with the real robot were also registered. Continuous actions policies execute faster paths than the discrete actions policy despite our triangulation and Locally Weighted Regression processes.

In summary, the continuous actions policies are more similar to human traces, are smoother, safer and faster than the discrete actions policies.

CONCLUSION AND FUTURE WORK

This work introduces an abstraction based on a relational representation for reinforcement learning. The user defines a set of properties to characterize a domain and to abstract the state space. The idea is to capture some relevant properties of the domain that can be used in different instances of the domain and sometimes to solve different, although

Figure 10. Navigation and following tasks examples from Map 3 (size 8.0m. ×8.0m.). (a) Navigation task with discrete actions. (b) Navigation task with continuous actions. (c) Navigation task performed by user. (d) Following task with discrete actions. (e) Following task with continuous actions. (f) Following task performed by user.

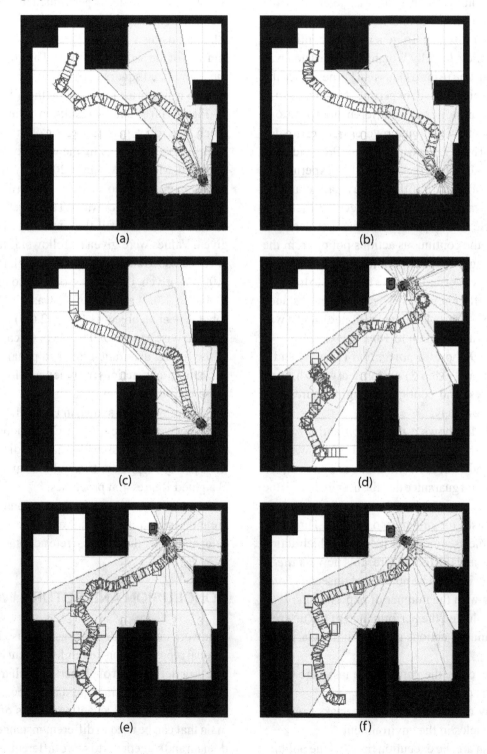

Figure 11. Navigation and following results of the tasks performed by the real robot. (a) Squared error value. (b) Penalty values

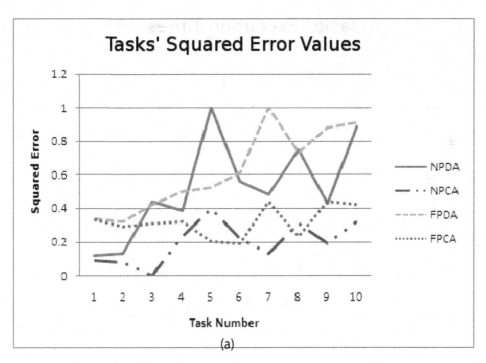

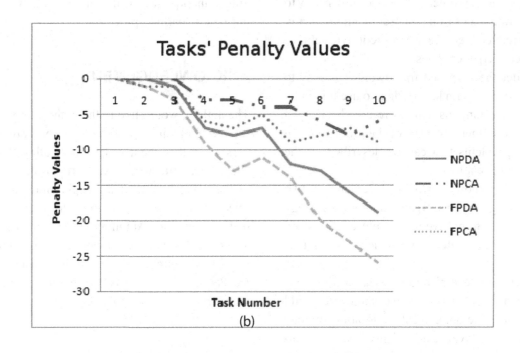

Figure 12. Execution times results

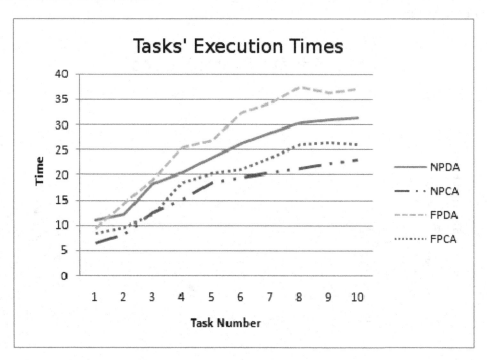

closely related, problems. It is also shown how to incorporate traces from the user to automatically learn a reduced set of relational actions to achieve faster convergence times.

Under the proposed framework it is easy to incorporate domain knowledge, to use it in large application domains, and to re-use the learned policies on other instances of the problem or on related problems that can be described by the same set of relations.

We also showed two improvements in two challenging domains: (i) an exploration strategy to learn how to behave in unexplored states and (ii) an on-line strategy to produce a continuous actions policy.

There are several future research directions that we are considering. In particular, we would like to improve our current exploration strategy to identify in advance non-visited states to complete the traces provided by the user. We are also considering how to include partial observability in our current framework. Finally, we are plan-

ning to incorporate the user in a more active way during the learning process.

ACKNOWLEDGEMENT

The authors would like to thank the anonymous referees for their helpful comments on a previous version of this chapter. The first author thanks Claude Sammut for his support and comments in the development of the flight simulator application and the support from the ARC Centre of Excellence for Autonomous Systems (CAS). The second author was supported by a grant from CONACyT number 212418 for his Master studies. Part of this work was also supported by grant number 84162 from CONACyT.

REFERENCES

Blockeel, H., & Raedt, L. D. (1998, June). Top-down induction of logical decision trees. *Artificial Intelligence, 101*, 285–297. doi:10.1016/S0004-3702(98)00034-4

Bratko, I., Urbančič, T., & Sammut, C. (1998). Behavioural cloning: Phenomena, results and problems. automated systems based on human skill. In *IFAC Symposium*. Berlin.

Chapman, D., & Kaelbling, L. (1991). Input generalization in delayed reinforcement learning: an algorithm and performance comparison. In *Proc. of the International Joint Conference on Artificial Intelligence* (pp. 726-731). San Francisco, CA: Morgan Kaufmann.

Charness, N. (1977). Human chess skill. In Frey, P. (Ed.), *Chess skill in man and machine* (pp. 35–53). Springer-Verlag.

Croonenborghs, T., Driessens, K., & Bruynooghe, M. (2007, June). Learning relational options for inductive transfer in relational reinforcement learning. In *Proceedings of the 17th Conference on Inductive Logic Programming* (pp. 88–97). Springer.

de Groot, A. (1965). *Thought and choice in chess*. The Hague, The Netherlands: Mouton.

Dietterich, T. (2000). Hierarchical reinforcement learning with the maxq value function decomposition. *Journal of Artificial Intelligence Research, 13*, 227–303.

Driessens, K., & Dzeroski, S. (2002). Integrating experimentation and guidance in relational reinforcement learning. In *Proc. of the Nineteenth International Conference on Machine Learning* (p. 115-122). Morgan Kaufmann.

Driessens, K., & Ramon, J. (2003). Relational instance based regression for relational reinforcement learning. In *Proc. of the International Conference on Machine Learning (icml'03)*.

Driessens, K., Ramon, J., & Blockeel, H. (2001). Speeding up relational reinforcement learning through the use of an incremental first order decision tree learner. In *Proc. of the 13th. European Conference on Machine Learning (ecml-01)* (p. 97-108). Springer.

Dzeroski, S., Raedt, L. D., & Driessens, K. (2001). Relational reinforcement learning. *Machine Learning, 43*(2), 5–52. doi:10.1023/A:1007694015589

Fern, A., Yoon, S., & Givan, R. (2003). Approximate policy iteration with a policy language bias. In *Proc. of the Neural and Information Processing Conference (NIPS'03)*.

Friedman, J. H. (2001). Greedy function approximation: A gradient boosting machine. *Annals of Statistics, 29*(5), 1189–1232. doi:10.1214/aos/1013203451

Getoor, L., Koller, D., Taskar, B., & Friedman, N. (2000). Learning probabilistic relational models with structural uncertainty. In *Proceedings of the ICML-2000 Workshop on Attribute-Value and Relational Learning: Crossing the Boundaries* (pp. 13–20).

Getoor, L., & Taskar, B. (2007). *Introduction to statistical relational learning: Adaptive computation and machine learning*. Boston, MA: MIT Press.

Hernández, S. F., & Morales, E. F. (2006, Setpember). Global localization of mobile robots for indoor environments using natural landmarks. *Proc. of the IEEE 2006 ICRAM*, (pp. 29-30).

Herrera-Vega, J. (2009). *Mobile robot localization in topological maps using visual information*. Master's thesis (to be published).

Hinton, G. (1984). *Distributed representations* (Tech. Rep. No. CMU-CS-84-157). Pittsburgh, PA: Carnegie-Mellon University, Department of Computer Science.

Kaelbling, L., Littman, M., & Cassandra, A. (1998). Planning and acting in partially observable stochastic domains. *Artificial Intelligence, 101*(1-2). doi:10.1016/S0004-3702(98)00023-X

Kanerva, P. (1993). Sparse distributed memory and related models. In Hassoun, M. (Ed.), *Associate neural memories: Theory and implementation* (pp. 50–76). New York, NY: Oxford University Press.

Kersting, K., & Driessens, K. (2008, July). Nonparametric policy gradients: A unified treatment of propositional and relational domains. In *Proceedings of the 25th International Conference on Machine Learning* (vol. 307, pp. 456–463). ACM.

Kersting, K., & Raedt, L. D. (2003). Logical Markov decision programs. In *Proc. of the IJCAI-03 Workshop on Learning Statistical Models of Relational Data.*

Kersting, K., & Raedt, L. D. (2004). Logical markov decision programs and the convergence of td(λ). In *Proc. of the Conference on Inductive Logic Programming.*

Kersting, K., Raedt, L. D., & Kramer, S. (2000). Interpreting Bayesian logic programs. In *Proceedings of the Work-In-Progress Track at the 10th International Conference on Inductive Logic Programming* (pp. 138–155).

Lim, C., & Kim, H. (1991). Cmac-based adaptive critic self-lerning control. *IEEE Transactions on Neural Networks, 2*, 530–533. doi:10.1109/72.134290

Lloyd, J. (1987). *Foundations of logic programming* (2nd ed.). Berlin, Germany: Springer-Verlag.

McDermott, D. V. (1998). *The planning domain definition language manual.* Technical Report 98-003, Department of Computer Science, Yale University.

Michie, D., Bain, M., & Hayes-Michie, J. (1990). Cognitive models from subcognitive skills. In Grimble, M., McGhee, J., & Mowforth, P. (Eds.), *Knowledge-based systems in industrial control* (pp. 71–90). Peter Peregrinus. doi:10.1049/PB-CE044E_ch5

Morales, E. (1997). On learning how to play. In van den Herik, H., & Uiterwijk, J. (Eds.), *Advances in computer chess 8* (pp. 235–250). The Netherlands: Universiteit Maastricht.

Morales, E. (2003). Scaling up reinforcement learning with a relational representation. In *Proc. of the Workshop on Adaptability in Multi-Agent Systems (aorc-20 03)* (p. 15-26).

Natarajan, S., Tadepalli, P., Altendorf, E., Dietterich, T. G., Fern, A., & Restificar, A. (2005). Learning first-order probabilistic models with combining rules. In *ICML '05: Proceedings of the 22nd International Conference on Machine Learning* (pp. 609–616). New York, NY: ACM.

Poggio, T., & Girosi, F. (1990). Regularizationn algorithms for learning that are equivalent to multilayer networks. *Science, 247*, 978–982. doi:10.1126/science.247.4945.978

Puterman, M. (1994). *Markov decision processes: Discrete stochastic dynamic programming.* New York, NY: Wiley.

Raedt, L. D., Kimmig, A., & Toivonen, H. (2007, January). Problog: A probabilistic prolog and its application in link discovery. In *Proceedings of 20th International Joint Conference on Artificial Intelligence* (pp. 2468–2473). AAAI Press.

Richardson, M., & Domingos, P. (2006). Markov logic networks. *Machine Learning, 62*(1-2), 107–136. doi:10.1007/s10994-006-5833-1

Romero, L., Morales, E., & Sucar, L. E. (2001). An exploration and navigation approach for indoor mobile robots considering sensor's perceptual limitations. *Proc. of the IEEE ICRA*, (pp. 3092-3097).

Sammut, C., Hurst, S., Kedzier, D., & Michie, D. (1992). Learning to fly. In *Proc. of the Ninth International Conference on Machine Learning* (p. 385-393). Morgan Kaufmann.

Singh, S., Jaakkola, T., & Jordan, M. (1996). Reinforcement learning with soft state aggregation. In *Neural information processing systems 7*. Cambridge, MA: MIT Press.

Sutton, R., & Barto, A. (1989). *Reinforcement learning: An introduction*. Cambridge, MA: MIT Press.

Sutton, R., Precup, D., & Singh, S. (1999a). Between MDPs and semi-MDPs: A framework for temporal abstraction in reinforcement learning. *Artificial Intelligence, 112*, 181–211. doi:10.1016/S0004-3702(99)00052-1

Sutton, R., Precup, D., & Singh, S. (1999b). Between MDPs and semi-MDPs: A framework for temporal abstraction in reinforcement learning. *Artificial Intelligence, 112*, 181–211. doi:10.1016/S0004-3702(99)00052-1

van Otterlo, M. (2003). Efficient reinforcement learning using relational aggregation. In *Proc of the Sixth European Workshop on Reinforcement Learning*. Nancy, France.

van Otterlo, M. (2004). Reinforcement learning for relational mdps. In A. Nowé, T. Lenaerts, & K. Steenhaut (Eds.), *Proc. of the Machine Learning Conference of Belgium and The Netherlands* (pp. 138-145).

van Otterlo, M. (2009). *The logic of adaptive behavior: Knowledge representation and algorithms for adaptive sequential decision making under uncertainty in first-order and relational domains*. The Netherlands: IOS Press.

Vaughan, R., Gerkey, B., & Howard, A. (2003). On device abstractions for portable, reusable robot code. *Proc. of the 2003 IEEE/RSJ IROS*, (pp. 11-15).

Watkins, C. (1989). *Learning from delayed rewards*. Unpublished doctoral dissertation, Cambridge University, Cambridge, MA.

Younes, H., & Littman, M. (2004). *Ppddl1.0: An extension to pddl for expressing planning domains with probabilistic effect*s. Technical Report CMU-CS-04-167, Department of Computer Science, Carnegie-Mellon University.

ENDNOTES

1   www.ida.liu.se/~TDDA13/labbar/planning/2003/writing.html

2   The flight simulator application was done while the first author was on sabbatical leave at the University of New South Wales, Australia.

3   Although this is not a strictly accurate model of turbulence, it is a reasonable approximation for these experiments.

4   The training mission involved only left turns.

5   The values used for orientation and distance are the same as with doors.

6   The values used for orientation and distance are the same as with doors.

7   The values used for orientation and distance are the same as with doors.

8   The values used for orientation and distance are the same as with doors.

9   An ActivMedia GuiaBot, www.activrobots.com

10   *NPDA*: Navigation Policy with Discrete Actions, *NPCA*: Navigation Policy with Continuous Actions, *FPDA*: Following Policy with Discrete Actions, *FPCA*: Following Policy with Continuous Actions.

Section 3
Solutions

Chapter 10
A Decision-Theoretic Tutor for Analogical Problem Solving

Kasia Muldner
Arizona State University, USA

Cristina Conati
University of British Columbia, Canada

ABSTRACT

We describe a decision-theoretic tutor that helps students learn from Analogical Problem Solving (APS), i.e., from problem-solving activities that involve worked-out examples. This tutor incorporates an innovative example-selection mechanism that tailors the choice of example to a given student so as to trigger studying behaviors that are known to foster learning. The mechanism relies on a two-phase decision-theoretic process, as follows. First, a probabilistic user model corresponding to a dynamic Bayesian network simulates how a given student will use an example to solve a problem and what she will learn from doing so. Second, this simulation is quantified via an expected utility calculation, enabling the tutor to select the example with the highest expected utility for maximizing learning and problem-solving outcomes. Once an example is presented to a student, the user model generates an assessment of the student's APS, enabling the selection mechanism to have up to date information on the student. Our empirical evaluation shows that this selection mechanism is more effective than standard selection approaches for fostering learning from APS. Here, we provide a comprehensive technical description of the example-selection mechanism, as well as an overview of its evaluation and a discussion of some of the challenges related to our decision-theoretic approach.

INTRODUCTION

Intelligent Tutoring Systems (ITSs) are computer applications that employ artificial intelligence techniques to instruct students in an "intelligent way" (VanLehn, 1988). Although there isn't an accepted definition of the term "intelligent", a characteristic shared by many ITSs is that they possess knowledge and reasoning capabilities to adapt instruction to the needs of each individual student. This functionality is motivated by research demonstrating that students learn more effectively from tailored, one-on-one instruction, as

DOI: 10.4018/978-1-60960-165-2.ch010

compared to standard classroom instruction (Bloom, 1984). Achieving the goal of computer-based individualized instruction, however, is extremely challenging. To tailor pedagogical interventions to students' needs, an ITS needs information on students' states of interest, such as the evolution of knowledge as a result of interaction with a tutor (to provide appropriate instructional scaffolding), affective states (to generate empathic tutorial responses), and general learning and reasoning skills, or *meta-cognitive skills* (to provide instruction that promotes general learning abilities in addition to domain-dependent expertise). Information on the relevant student states can be difficult to obtain unobtrusively, making student modeling a process permeated with uncertainty. Uncertainty also permeates the selection of appropriate tutorial actions, because even if the tutor were able to obtain perfect information on the current state of the student, the effects of each available tutorial action cannot be unequivocally predicted from its theoretical underpinnings.

It is quite common for ITSs to deal with the uncertainty in student modeling by relying on formal approaches for reasoning under uncertainty (for an overview, see (Woolf, 2008)). Less common is to explicitly take uncertainty into account during action selection: most ITSs perform action selection based on ad-hoc heuristics. For instance, a common approach for deciding the content of a hint is to (1) *a priori* associate hints with the domain principles needed to solve the problem, (2) at run-time identify the principle the student is likely to need help on and display the associated hint (e.g., (Conati et al., 2002). Such ad-hoc approaches can run the risk of sub-optimal pedagogical action selection, because they do not take into the account the fact that there is uncertainty about the effect of the available tutorial actions, and they do not explicitly represent how this uncertainty, together with the uncertainty on the student state, impact the decision-making process. An alternative for generating individual-

ized instruction is to rely on a decision-theoretic approach, where an ITS's decision with respect to tutorial action selection depends on both what it believes (represented using probability theory) and what it wants (represented using utility theory). The advantage of this approach is that the selected tutorial action is guaranteed to be optimal, given the available information about the student and the preferences for the tutor's behavior[1].

In this chapter, we describe a decision-theoretic ITS, namely the Example Analogy (EA)- Coach. The tutor targets meta-cognitive skills needed to learn from a specific type of instructional activity: solving problems in the presence of worked-out examples, also referred to as *Analogical Problem Solving* (APS). We chose this activity since examples play a key role in cognitive skill acquisition: students rely heavily on examples when learning a new skill (Pirolli and Anderson, 1985; Reed, Dempster et al., 1985; Novick, 1995; VanLehn, 1998) and examples are more effective aids to problem solving than general procedures alone (Reed and Bolstad, 1991) or hints on the instructional material (Ringenberg and VanLehn, 2006). However, many students do not use examples effectively during APS (Reed, Dempster et al., 1985; VanLehn, 1998) and so support is needed to maximize learning and problem solving for these students.

A key factor influencing APS outcomes is which example a student chooses to help solve the target problem. For instance, if the example is very different from the problem, then it will clearly not be useful because it cannot provide guidance on how to generate the problem solution (Novick, 1995). However, a very similar example can also be detrimental if a student uses it to simply copy the problem solution (VanLehn 1990). Because novices have difficulty selecting appropriate examples (Novick, 1988; Reed, Willis et al., 1994), the EA-Coach takes over the selection task. To choose the optimal example for a given student, one that fosters problem solving and learning by encouraging the meta-cognitive skills needed for APS, the system relies on a two-step decision-theoretic process that tailors the choice of example to a given student's needs, as follows. First, the EA-Coach student model generates a *simulation* of how a student will solve a problem in the presence of a candidate example and what she[2] will learn from doing so. Second, the system quantifies the model's prediction via a multi-attribute utility function. After repeating these two steps for all the available examples, this process allows the tutor to select the example with the highest expected utility (EU) for enabling successful learning and problem solving. Once the example is presented, the model generates an *assessment* of how the student's knowledge and meta-cognitive skills evolve as she uses the example, allowing the selection mechanism to have up to date information on the student when a new example needs to be presented.

While we have described aspects of the system's decision-theoretic process (Muldner and Conati, 2007b) and its evaluation (Muldner & Conati, to appear) elsewhere, this chapter provides a comprehensive technical overview of our approach, including unpublished details on the student model, an integrated description of the simulation and assessment processes, and novel discussion of some of the challenges related to our approach.

We will begin with an overview of the related work, followed by a description of the EA-Coach, including the target meta-cognitive skills and system architecture. Next, we will present the decision-theoretic example-selection mechanism, and then describe how the selected example is used by the student model to generate an assessment of a student's APS. After summarizing the findings from the evaluation of the EA-Coach, we will conclude a discussion of some of the challenges related to the design and evaluation of decision-theoretic systems.

RELATED WORK

While it is fairly common for various types of adaptive systems to utilize probabilistic approaches for user modeling (e.g., (Bunt et al., 2004; Arroyo et al., 2005)), it is more rare for these systems to rely on decision theory for action selection, although doing so is becoming more common (e.g., (Pack and Horvitz, 2000; Gajos et al. 2008)). Here, we focus on a sub-class of decision-theoretic adaptive systems, namely ITSs, since these are the topic of this chapter. Traditionally, ITSs have provided support for cognitive skills needed during problem solving (e.g., (Conati et al., 2002; Heffernan et al., 2009)). In the past decade or so, there has also been growing interest in supporting other aspects necessary for learning, such as affect (e.g., (Boyer et al., 2008; Conati and Maclaren, 2009; Robinson et al., 2009)) and meta-cognitive skills (e.g., (Conati and VanLehn 2000; Bunt et al., 2004; Merten and Conati, 2007; Chi and VanLehn, 2008; Roll et al., in press; Rau et al., 2009)). We now describe a representative sample of the latter class of systems, since they are most related to the EA-Coach.

The INQPRO (Ting, Zadeh et al., 2006) ITS helps students acquire meta-cognitive scientific inquiry skills by targeting hypothesis generation in the domain of introductory science. To support the inquiry process, INQPRO provides tailored meta-cognitive interventions that are intended to assist students in generating effective hypotheses. To decide which intervention to generate, INQPRO relies on a Bayesian network supplemented with utility and decision nodes, i.e., a decision network. Like INQPRO, some tutors take a decision-theoretic approach for action selection, but do not support meta-cognitive skills (Pek and Poh, 2000; Mayo and Mitrovic, 2001). All these tutors deliver their support during pure problem solving, without access to examples. For instance, the CAPIT (Mayo and Mitrovic, 2001) tutor helps students acquire punctuation skills via two forms of support: (1) selection of appropriate problems for students to work on and (2) provision of hints. CAPIT includes a student model corresponding to a dynamic Bayesian network, used to infer information about the student's knowledge. In order to decide which problem or hint to select, CAPIT first uses the Bayesian network to predict the impact of a candidate tutorial action (i.e., a problem or error message). The network's prediction is then quantified via a single-objective utility function, allowing CAPIT to select the tutorial action with the maximum expected utility. Another tutor that supports learning by selecting problems for students via a decision network is iTutor (Pek and Poh, 2000).

Instead of selecting problems for students, some tutors focus on tutorial action selection related to feedback provision. One such ITS is the Decision Theoretic (DT)-Tutor (Murray, Van-Lehn et al., 2004). As is the case for CAPIT and iTutor, DT-Tutor's student model corresponds to a dynamic Bayesian network. DT-Tutor uses the network's prediction as input to a linearly additive multi-attribute utility function to calculate a candidate tutorial action's expected utility in terms of its impact on a student's knowledge, problem-solving progress and affective state. Another ITS relying on multi-attribute decision theory (MAUT) is F-SMILE (Kabassi and Virvou, 2006), which provides instruction about the Windows operating system. In contrast to the ITSs described above, the F-SMILE weights for the MAUT calculation are derived from a user study. Specifically, 10 experts observed video recordings of novice users performing a set of standard file manipulation tasks. The experts were asked to state their preference for tutorial interventions in response to student actions, and this information was used to set the weights for the MAUT function. The overall pedagogical utility of F-SMILE has yet to be evaluated with actual users.

To date, existing tutors have not targeted meta-cognitive skills during APS, making the EA-Coach the only decision-theoretic tutor to provide support for a certain APS-specific skill (described below). On the other hand, the EA-Coach supports the meta-cognitive skill of self-explanation, i.e., the process of explaining instructional material to one self. This skill is supported by a variety of ITSs (e.g., (Conati and VanLehn, 2000; Bunt et al., 2004; Rau et al., 2009; Wylie et al., 2009)). In contrast to the EA-Coach, however, these other tutors do not rely on decision theory for action selection. Furthermore, instead of selecting examples, the standard approach for supporting self-explanation has been to provide students with tools that they can use to derive the explanations and/or provide prompts encouraging self-explanation.

THE EA-COACH: OVERVIEW

The EA-Coach provides adaptive support to encourage two meta-cognitive skills (also referred to as *tendencies* below) that cognitive science shows are needed to learn effectively from APS:

- *min-analogy*, e.g., solving the problem on one's own as much as possible instead of by copying from examples (VanLehn, 1998);
- *self-explanation*, the process of explaining instructional material to oneself. The EA-Coach targets a specific type of self-explanation, referred to as *Explanation-based learning of correctness* (EBLC) that can be used to learn new domain principles from partial domain knowledge and pre-existing common-sense knowledge (Chi and VanLehn 1991; VanLehn, 1999) - for an example of EBLC, please see (VanLehn, 1999). For simplicity, we refer to EBLC as *self explanation* from this point on.

Min-analogy and self-explanation are beneficial for learning because they allow students to discover their knowledge gaps during problem solving and fill them using examples. Unfortu-

Figure 1. EA-Coach architecture

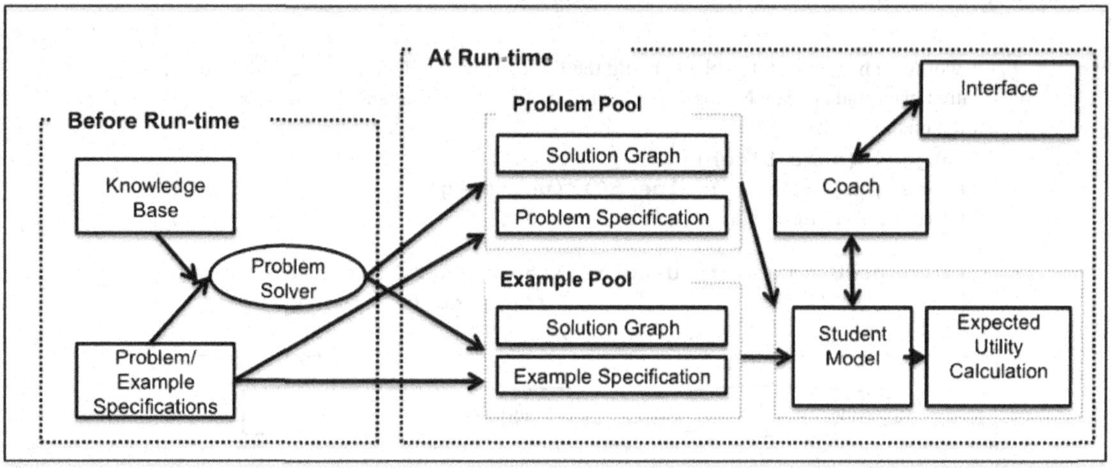

nately, some students often engage in shallower studying processes that hinder learning, such as copying as much as possible from examples without any proactive reasoning (e.g., (VanLehn, 1998)). The EA-Coach is designed to provide support for these students by supplying them with examples that discourage shallow studying while promoting min-analogy and self-explanation, as we describe in the following sections. While other meta-cognitive skills, such as effective help seeking (Roll et al., in press), may also be relevant to APS, for the time being we focus on min-analogy and self-explanation because they are the skills that have been extensively studied in Cognitive Science with relation to APS (e.g., (VanLehn, 1998; VanLehn 1999)).

The EA-Coach Architecture

To select examples tailored to each student's needs, the EA-Coach needs to assess the impact of a given example on that student's min-analogy and self-explanation behaviors. To do so, the system needs a formal representation of the problems and examples in the target domain. It also needs to encode a given student's domain knowledge and relevant meta-cognitive skills in a computational model that can be used to guide the tailoring of

instructional support. These requirements are implemented in the EA-Coach architecture, shown in Figure 1[3].

The knowledge base contains a rule-based representation of the system's target domain, introductory Newtonian physics. Before run time, the *problem solver*[4] uses the problem or example *specification* and the *knowledge base rules* to automatically generate the corresponding solution, stored in the problem/ example pools. The system encodes the solutions in a structure called the *solution graph*, a dependency network representing how each solution step derives from previous steps and rules in the knowledge base, based on (Conati et al., 2002)). Figure 2 shows how a portion of the problem in Figure 3a, which asks the student to find the normal force on a block being pushed by a worker, is derived. For instance, the rule node '*Rule: normal-force*' (encoding a normal force exists) and the step node '*Step: block-is-the-body*' (encoding that the body to apply Newton's Second Law is the *block*) derive the problem solution step '*Step:normal-exists*' (encoding that a normal force exists on the block). In addition to step and rule nodes, the solution graph also includes other auxiliary nodes used to, for instance, structure the solution process (these will not be discussed here - details may be found in (Muldner,

Figure 2. Simplified fragment of the formal specification (top) and simplified fragment of the corresponding solution graph (bottom) for the problem in Figure 3

A workman pushes a 50 kg. block along the floor inclined 0 degrees. He pushes it hard, with a magnitude of 120 N, applied at an angle of 25 degrees as shown. Find the normal force on the block.

```
(object (name block))
(mass (obj block) (value 50) (units kg))
(surface (name floor) (incline 0))
   ...
(goal-problem (is find-normal)(applied-to block)
                             (applied-by floor))
```

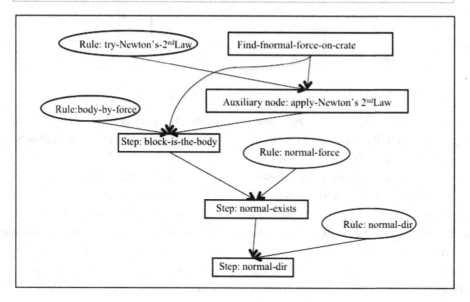

2007a)). The number of nodes encoded in the solution graphs varies according to the particular physics topic. For the problems/examples used in the EA-Coach evaluation described below, all problems related to Newton's Second Law; each problem/example solution graph corresponded to about 100 nodes.

At run time, students interact with the system via an *interface* that includes two windows (see Figure 3 (a) and (b)). In the *problem* window, students solve physics problems by typing equations and drawing free-body diagrams (Figure 3a). The *Coach* provides immediate feedback on a student's problem-solving entries by coloring them green (if correct) or red (if incorrect). As students work on a problem, they can use the '*Get*

Example' button to ask for an example. In response, the EA-Coach *example-selection mechanism* (Figure 1) chooses an example from its example pool and presents it in the *example window* (Figure 3b). The various elements of the example specification and solution in this window are presented via the so-called *masking interface* (see Figure 4), i.e. covered by boxes that disappear momentarily when moused over.

The selection mechanism aims to select an example that best meets the following two objectives: (1) *Learning objective:* the example triggers the student's learning of the target physics domain by encouraging min-analogy and self-explanation; (2) *Problem-solving success objective:* the example helps the student generate the target prob-

Figure 3. EA-Coach interface, (a) Problem window and (b) Example window

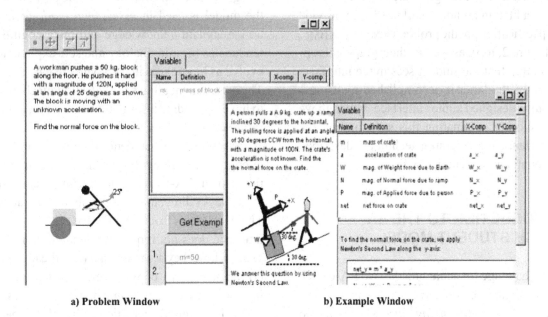

a) Problem Window　　　　　　　　　　b) Example Window

Figure 4. Masking interface over the example window shown in Figure 3b

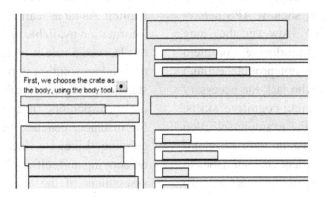

lem solution. To meet these two objectives, the mechanism relies on its two components, the *student model* and *EU (Expected Utility) calculation* (see Figure 1).

Before we describe the example-selection mechanism and its components, we should point out that the design and implementation of the EA-Coach was a labor-intensive endeavor. This is generally the case with any ITS: In addition to the coding effort required for implementing the system, including the design of pedagogical interventions, human experts are also needed for specifying the target domain knowledge. In our work, we relied on an established source, i.e., the Andes ITS knowledge base (Conati et al., 2002), which was designed over several months with a team of human physics expert tutors. With the EA-Coach, once the system was designed and implemented, further effort was needed to populate the problem and example pools. While some of this effort was alleviated by the fact that the system's internal representation, the solution graph, is automatically generated by the problem solver, a human author is still needed to provide the specifications of the problems/examples (e.g., see Figure 2, top), as well as their graphical representation that the student sees in the interface. Currently, the latter is accomplished by using a specially-designed author interface, although we are exploring automating this step through the natural language generation techniques described in (Conati and Carenini, 2001).

INTRODUCTION TO THE EA-COACH STUDENT MODEL

A key challenge for achieving the two EA-Coach example-selection objectives presented above (*learning, problem-solving success*) relates to achieving a balance between them for different learners. Examples that are not highly similar to the target problem may support the learning objective by discouraging shallow APS behaviors such as pure copying. However, they may also hinder students from producing a problem solution because they do not provide enough scaffolding for students who lack the necessary domain knowledge or meta-cognitive skills. Thus, it is essential that the example-selection mechanism take into account both problem/example similarity and student characteristics to chose an example tailored to a student's needs. To meet this requirement, the selection mechanism relies on the EA-Coach component responsible for representing and reasoning about the student, i.e., the student model.

During the example-selection process, the student model is used in *simulation mode* to predict how each example in the EA-Coach pool will influence a student's APS behaviors (min-analogy, self-explanation), as well as subsequent learning and problem-solving outcomes, given the student's existing knowledge and meta-cognitive skills. This simulation forms the basis of the system's ability to adapt the choice of example

to a given student. Once an example is presented, the model is used in *assessment mode* to infer how a student's knowledge and meta-cognitive tendencies for min-analogy and self-explanation evolve as he engages in APS with the EA-Coach. This assessment allows the selection mechanism to have up-to-date information on the student for future example selections.

Assessing how a student's knowledge and meta-cognitive skills evolve throughout her interaction with the EA-Coach is challenging because the model lacks direct information about the student. This lack stems from the fact that the EA-Coach interface does not require students to explicitly express how they are reasoning (i.e., the interface does not capture copying/self-explanation, for instance via specially designed tools). This design allows for a natural interaction with the EA-Coach, but it means that the information available to the model is much more ambiguous than if the system constrained students to make all their reasoning explicit. As far as learning is concerned, the only information available to the model that a student has learned a rule is when he generates the corresponding solution step. However, generating a step does not guarantee that a student has learned the corresponding rule, because a student could, for instance, generate the step by guessing or copying. Likewise, lack of direct information on copying and self-explanation complicates the assessment of the corresponding min-analogy and self-explanation tendencies, as does lack of understanding in the cognitive science community on how these tendencies evolve throughout APS. During simulation mode, the model has even less information than during assessment. That is, the model aims to infer how a student will solve the problem and learn from it solely based on information on problem/example similarity and the current assessment of the student's cognitive and meta-cognitive skills.

The fact that the model only has access to indirect information about the student introduces a good deal of uncertainty to the student-modeling process. Uncertainty also permeates the relationships between meta-cognitive behaviors and learning (e.g., self-explanation increases the likelihood of learning but does not guarantee it (Chi, 2000)). To handle this uncertainty, the EA-Coach relies on *dynamic Bayesian networks (DBN)* (Dean and Kanazawa, 1989), a formal framework for reasoning under uncertainty. This framework makes it possible to model the temporal evolution of probabilistic events – students' knowledge and meta-cognitive tendencies in the case of the EA-Coach.

Student Model Construction

A key challenge with using Bayesian networks for the modeling task corresponds to building the network, including specifying its structure and parameters. To address this challenge, the EA-Coach relies on the approach taken by Andes, an ITS for physics problem solving without access to examples (Conati, Gertner et al., 2002). Specifically, when a student opens a problem, the system automatically creates the student model Bayesian network, as follows. First, the EA-Coach obtains the network *structure* from the problem's solution graph. Recall that the solution graph encodes how each solution step is derived from previous steps and physics rules (see Figure 2). In the student model, this information is used to represent the likelihood that a student can generate the various steps in the problem solution given her current knowledge. Second, the network *parameters* are realized by supplementing the graph nodes with probability distributions over the nodes' values, as follows (all nodes have binary *True/False* values):

- Rule nodes represent the probability P that the student knows the rule.
- Step nodes represent the probability P the student can generate the solution step.

Priors over rule nodes are defined either using existing data on a student's physics knowledge,

population data or a uniform distribution when no data is available. The conditional probabilities for the step nodes are defined by relying on simple AND-type logic, following the approach in (Conati et al., 2002). Specifically, the probabilities between a step node and its parents rely on a *noise* and a *leak* parameter to encode the following assumptions:

- The 'noise' parameter α models that there is a non-zero probability a problem step is false even if all parents are true. This encodes the possibility that even if the student does have the necessary prerequisites to generate the step, she may not generate it.
- The 'leak' β parameter models that there is a non-zero probability a problem step is true even if some of its parents are false. This encodes the possibility that even if the student does not have the necessary prerequisites to generate the step, she may still generate the step by using alternate means, such as guessing or asking a friend.

As we noted above, Andes automatically creates the model when a student opens a problem. When the student is done problem solving and so closes the problem, Andes stores the model's assessment corresponding to the posterior probabilities of the rule nodes. This allows the student model to have up-to-date information on the student each time he opens a problem to work on: the posterior probabilities are used as the priors for the rules corresponding to the newly-opened problem. While the EA-Coach follows the Andes approach to construct and parameterize its initial student model, it differs in three key ways from the Andes model. First, the EA-Coach uses a dynamic Bayesian network instead of a static network like Andes does. Second, the EA-Coach model includes additional nodes to assess APS-specific behaviors, like copying and self explanation. Third, while both models generate an assessment of the student while she is solving a problem, only the EA-Coach model is used to generate a simulation of APS.

For the Bayesian network-related functionality, the EA-Coach makes use of the *Smile* (Structural Modeling, Inference and Learning Engine) library (Smile, 2010). Smile corresponds to a set of portable C++ classes implementing graphical decision-theoretic methods, provided by the Decision Systems Laboratory at the University of Pittsburg (this well-established toolkit has thousands of users worldwide, see http://genie.sis.pitt.edu/ for details). The specific inference algorithm the EA-Coach uses corresponds to Smile's cluster-update algorithm.

THE EA-COACH EXAMPLE-SELECTION MECHANISM

The EA-Coach student model plays a key role in the operation of the system by formally representing the uncertainty between student observable behaviors and their internal states. However, the fact that the model's information is permeated with uncertainty complicates the decision regarding which example to select, since it means that the tutor needs to consider not only which outcome is desirable but also how likely it is to happen (Clement, 1996). To handle the uncertainty in the decision-making process, the EA-Coach relies on a decision-theoretic process designed to select an example with the highest expected utility in terms of meeting the *learning* and *problem-solving success* selection objectives. This process consists of two phases, repeated for each candidate example:

(*Simulation Phase*) First, the EA-Coach uses its student model in simulation mode, i.e., to predict how a student will solve a given problem in the presence of the candidate example and what the student will learn from doing so. This entails obtaining the posterior probabilities of learning and problem solving outcomes given a particular example, as we shall see shortly.

(*Expected Utility Calculation Phase*) Given this prediction, the EA-Coach uses a utility function to quantify the candidate example's expected utility in terms of meeting the learning and problem-solving success objectives.

Once the simulation and utility calculation phases are repeated for each example in the system's example pool, the example with the highest expected utility for learning and problem-solving success is presented to the student.

Simulation Phase: Prediction of Student APS Behaviors

We will illustrate the simulation phase by relying on a specific scenario. Suppose a student opens the problem in Figure 3a and asks for an example. Opening the problem triggers the automatic construction of the EA-Coach dynamic Bayesian network (DBN) student model from the target problem's solution graph, as described in the previous section (a fragment of the network is shown in slice *t*, Figure 5, left). Initially, this network contains all of the solution graph rule and step nodes (*'Rule', 'Step'* nodes in slice *t*, Figure 5), as well as nodes to model a student's APS tendency for min-analogy and self-explanation (*MinAnalogyTend and SETend* in slice *t*, Figure 5). In this network, unless otherwise stated all nodes have Boolean values.

To predict the impact of the example on learning and problem solving, a special *'simulation'* slice is added to the network (Figure 5, slice *t +1*, *simulation slice,* assuming the candidate example is the one shown in Figure 3b). The simulation slice contains all the rule and step nodes of the initial slice (*pre-simulation* slice from now on)[5], as well as additional nodes included to model students' APS behaviors: *similarity, copy and self-explanation (SE)* nodes. We now describe these three types of nodes and how they are used to generate a prediction of learning and problem-solving success.

Figure 5. Simplified fragment of the EA-Coach student model

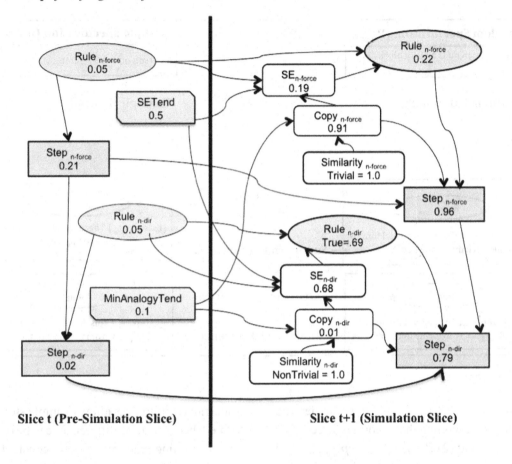

Slice t (Pre-Simulation Slice)   **Slice t+1 (Simulation Slice)**

Representing Problem/Example Similarity in the Student Model

Similarity nodes are added to the simulation slice to represent the similarity between the problem and candidate example. This similarity, in turn, is used to generate a prediction of copying and self-explanation behaviors, as well as subsequent learning and problem-solving outcomes. The model's design for generating this prediction is based on cognitive science research showing that (1) problem/example differences hinder learning and problem solving if students lack the skills to bridge them (Novick, 1995); (2) examples that are highly similar to the target problem support problem-solving success, but interfere with learning because they allow the solution to be generated by copying from the example (Reed, Dempster et al., 1985). What cognitive science research has yet to specify is whether certain examples can help students to *both* solve the target problem and learn from doing so, or how student characteristics interact with similarity to influence APS outcomes. To complete the design of the student model, it was therefore necessary to formulate our own hypotheses.

We begin with some terminology. It is common practice to define a pair of problem/example steps as *structurally identical* if they are generated by the same rule, and *structurally different* otherwise (Reed, Dempster et al., 1985; Novick, 1995). To make this concrete, Figure 6 shows solution fragments for the physics problem/example pair in Figure 3, which includes two structurally-identical

Figure 6. Problem/example relations for the problem/example pair in Figure 3

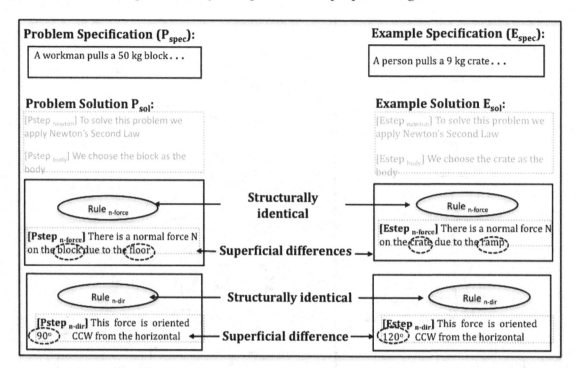

pairs of steps: (1) $Pstep_{n\text{-}force}$ / $Estep_{n\text{-}force}$ derived from the rule encoding that a normal force exists ($Rule_{n\text{-}force}$), and (2) $Pstep_{n\text{-}dir}$ / $Estep_{n\text{-}dir}$ derived from the rule encoding the normal force direction ($Rule_{n\text{-}dir}$).

Two structurally-identical steps may be *superficially* different. In cognitive science literature, superficial similarity is determined through the terms and/or constants making up the problem/ example specifications and solution steps (e.g., $Pstep_{n\text{-}force}$ / $Estep_{n\text{-}force}$ include two superficial differences, *block* vs. *crate* and *floor* vs. *ramp*, see Figure 6; $Pstep_{n\text{-}dir}$ / $Estep_{n\text{-}dir}$ include one superficial difference corresponding to the direction of the normal force, *90°* vs. *120°*). We have extended this definition by further classifying superficial differences as *trivial* or *non-trivial*, based on the type of transfer from example to problem that they allow. A formal definition may be found in (Conati, Muldner et al., 2006; Muldner, 2007a), here it suffices to say that trivial

superficial differences allow example steps to be copied, because these differences can be resolved by substituting example-specific constants with ones needed for the problem solution. The substitution is possible because the constants corresponding to the two respective differences (*block/ crate* and *floor/ramp*) appear in the example/ problem solutions and specifications, which provides a guide for their substitution (Anderson, 1993) (as is the case for $Pstep_{n\text{-}force}$ / $Estep_{n\text{-}force}$, Figure 6). In contrast, non-trivial differences require more in-depth reasoning such as self-explanation to be resolved. This is because the example constant corresponding to the difference is missing from the example specification, making it less obvious what it should be replaced with (as is the case for $Pstep_{n\text{-}dir}$ / $Estep_{n\text{-}dir}$, Figure 6, since the difference corresponding to the direction of the normal force, i.e., *90°* vs. *120°*, does not appear in the problem/example specification and thus needs to be reconciled by the student via self explanation).

Our classification of the various types of problem/example similarity forms the basis of several key hypotheses, as follows. If there is a structural difference between the problem and the example with respect to a given step, then the example cannot be used to generate the necessary step. In contrast, superficial differences between two structurally-identical problem/example steps do not block transfer of the example step. Since the two steps are generated by the same rule, the student can either learn the rule from the example and apply it to generate the problem step, or copy the example step without learning the rule. Because trivial differences are easily resolved, they encourage copying for students with poor domain knowledge and APS meta-cognitive skills. In contrast, non-trivial differences encourage min-analogy and self-explanation because they do not allow the problem solution to be generated by simple problem/example constant substitution. We evaluated these hypotheses in a series of pilot evaluations (Muldner & Conati, in press), which provided encouraging indications that our assumptions were appropriate.

To embed these hypotheses into the EA-Coach student model's operation, for each *step* node in the simulation slice, the system adds a corresponding similarity node and follows the definitions we presented above to set its value to either *None* (structural difference), *Trivial* or *NonTrivial*. Thus, as is illustrated in Figure 5, the value of the $Similarity_{n\text{-}force}$ node is *Trivial* because it relates to a problem step that is trivially different from the corresponding example solution step. The value of the $Similarity_{n\text{-}dir}$ node is *NonTrivial* because the problem step it is linked to includes a non-trivial difference with the corresponding example solution step.

To set the similarity node values, the system compares the problem/example solution graphs and specifications according to the algorithm in Figure 7. The most expensive step in this algorithm is Step 3, i.e., *locate corresponding rules in the example* (once these are located, the corresponding step(s) derived by a rule can be located in constant time). If a naïve data structure is used to store the rules, then Step 3 has a complexity of $O(N)$, although this reduces to $O(\log N)$ if a more sophisticated structure such as a sorted list is utilized. Thus, the overall complexity of setting the similarity varies between $O(N^2)$ and $O(N\log N)$, depending on the implementation.

Currently, the similarity nodes are placed in the same time slice as the copy and self-explanation nodes (i.e., slice t+1, *simulation slice*, see Figure 5). An alternative configuration could involve placing all the similarity nodes in the first time slice (i.e., slice t in Figure 5). We did not implement this for two reasons. First, during assessment mode, the current configuration affords the possibility that more than one example is used to aid solving a single target problem, something that is not supported by the configuration where all the similarity nodes are placed in the first time slice. Second, the similarity node placement represents a temporal relation between the similarity, copy and self explanation nodes, i.e., that problem/example similarity at time *t* impacts copying and self-explanation at time *t*. We feel that conceptually, this makes more sense than to place the node in a previous time slice as this would imply that problem/example similarity from the past influenced future copying /self explanation. Note that the second argument is at a conceptual level, since in practical terms, the inference outcome would be the same for either configuration given a fixed problem/example pair.

Prediction of Copying During APS

During the simulation phase, a *copy* node is added for each problem solution step in the simulation slice. Copy nodes allow the student model to predict whether the student will generate the corresponding problem solution step by copying from the example, according to our hypotheses

Figure 7. EA-Coach algorithm used to determine the value of the similarity nodes

[Step 1] locate the problem step node *sp* that the similarity node is linked to the problem's solution graph,

[Step 2] Identify the rule *R* that generated *sp*,

[Step 3] Check if rule *R* is in the example's solution graph:

[Case 3a: *Structurally different; Value = None*] If *R* is not in the example's solution graph, then a structural difference exists between the problem and example with respect to *sp*. Set the value of the similarity node to *None*.

[Case 3b: *Structurally identical; Value = Trivial or NonTrivial*] If *R* is in the example's solution graph, then the problem/example are structurally identical with respect to *sp*. Identify the type of superficial relation (trivial, non-trivial) between the problem and example with respect to *sp*:

[Step 4] Identify the set of nodes $S=\{se_1...se_n\}$ in the example's solution graph that were derived by *R*.

[Step 5] Identify which node *se* in *S* to compare with *sp*:

[Case 5a] If $|S|=1$, this is straightforward, i.e., $se = se_1$.

[Case 5b] If $|S|>1$, then use heuristics to identify *se* (see (Muldner, 2007a)).

[Step 6] Assess the superficial similarity between *sp* and *se* and set the similarity node value accordingly. This involves comparing *sp/se*'s formal representation of the problem/example solution terms stored in the solution graph nodes (see Blind for review, 2007a], and setting the similarity node according to our definitions. In particular, the value of the similarity node is set to *NonTrivial* if *sp* and *se* include at least one non-trivial difference and to *Trivial* otherwise. Given a superficial difference between *sp* and *se*, to determine if it is *trivial* or *non-trivial*, the system checks if (1) the example constant corresponding to the difference appears in the example specification, and (2) has a corresponding constant in the problem specification; if (1) and (2) are true, then the difference is assessed as *trivial*, and otherwise, as *non-trivial*.

regarding similarity's impact on copying. To generate this prediction, the model takes into account: (1) the similarity between the problem step the copy node is linked to and the corresponding step in the example solution, captured by the parent similarity node, and (2) the student's tendency for min-analogy, captured by the parent min-analogy tendency node.

Following our hypotheses regarding the impact of similarity presented above, the conditional probability table (CPT from now on) for a copy node encodes the assumption that if the value of the parent similarity node is *NonTrivial* or *None*, then the probability of the corresponding problem solution step being generated by copying is virtually zero, because the example does not afford students the opportunity to do so. If the value of the parent similarity node is *Trivial*, then the probability of copying depends upon

the student's tendency for min-analogy. If the tendency is low, then the probability of copying is high, and vice-versa.

The impact of these factors is shown in Figure 5. The probability the student will generate the problem step corresponding to node '$Step_{n\text{-}force}$' by copying is high (simulation slice, '$Copy_{n\text{-}force}$', *True*=.91). This is because the problem/example similarity allows for it (simulation slice, '$Similarity_{n\text{-}force}$'=*Trivial*,) and the student has a low tendency for min-analogy (pre-simulation slice, '*MinAnalogyTend*', *True*=.1). In contrast, the probability that the student will generate the problem step corresponding to node '$Step_{n\text{-}dir}$' by copying is very low (simulation slice, '$Copy_{n\text{-}dir}$', *True*=.01), despite the student's tendency to copy. This is because the non-trivial difference (simulation slice, '$Similarity_{n\text{-}dir}$'=*NonTrivial*) between the problem step and corresponding example step blocks copying.

The copy node DBN parameters, as well as the other node parameters described in subsequent sections, are based on relevant APS literature and represent our best first estimate of the impact of factors such as student characteristics/similarity on the variable under consideration. For instance, the copy node CPT parameters encode that even if the students' tendency for min-analogy is *true*, indicating that the student does not tend to copy, there is some probability that she will copy (currently 0.2 in the CPT). Likewise, a student who has a high tendency for copying will not copy is encoded with a probability of 0.05 in the copy CPT. These parameters encode the uncertainty inherent to modeling copying in an ITS that does not force students to use explicit tools for the copying process, which could determine exactly when copying did or did not occur. Note that there is currently less uncertainty in the model about a student who has a tendency to copy actually copying, as compared to a student who does not have a tendency to copy. This is based anecdotal evidence we obtained from our various pilot studies, where (1) some students, presumably with a very low min-analogy tendency, copied virtually everything and (2) even the "good" students, i.e., ones who likely had a high min-analogy tendency, copied sometimes. Future work will involve any necessary refinements, such as using machine learning, i.e., learning the conditional probability table parameters from data, for instance via the Expectation Maximization (EM) algorithm (Dempster, Laird et al., 1977). As with many learning algorithms, EM affords the possibility of learning individual model parameters for each student. Doing so, however, may not be practical in many situations, since it requires that substantial data is first collected for each student, and then the model is created from that data. Thus, researchers are investigating how to build generalizable models that transfer to new populations (e.g., (Cooper, Muldner et al., 2010)). Future refinements may also include

the structure of the network. For instance, the network does not currently include a link between copying and knowledge. Although it may be the case that knowledge somehow mediates student copying along with analogy tendency, this has yet to be investigated, and thus for the time being our network does not include that link.

Prediction of Self-Explanation During APS

In addition to similarity and copy nodes, a third type of node added to the simulation slice is the self-explanation (SE) node. One SE node is added for each rule node in the simulation slice that is used in the example solution (i.e., when there are *both* a problem and an example step that are derived by that rule). SE nodes allow the simulation to predict whether the student will learn the corresponding rule through self-explanation from the example, according to our hypotheses regarding the impact of similarity on self-explanation. To generate this prediction, the model takes into account: (1) the probability the student knows the rule, captured by corresponding rule node in the pre-simulation slice; (2) the probability the student will generate the problem solution step derived by this rule by copying, captured by the corresponding copy node; (3) the student's tendency for self-explanation, captured by the parent SE-tendency node.

The SE node CPT encodes the assumption that if the student already knows the rule, then self-explanation is not necessary and the probability of it occurring is thus low. If the student does not know the rule, then the probability that he will reason via self-explanation to derive it depends on two factors: his tendency for this type of reasoning, and the probability that he will generate the corresponding problem step by copying from the example. If the probability of generating the step by copying is low, it is more likely that the student will engage in self explanation, although this probability is mediated by the model's belief in the student's self-explanation tendency. In particular, if the student has a low tendency for self explanation then the probability that he will engage in it is low, even if he does not copy.

The impact of these factors is shown in Figure 5. The model predicts that the student is unlikely to learn via self-explanation the rule corresponding to the '$Rule_{n\text{-}force}$' node in the simulation slice (simulation slice, '$SE_{n\text{-}force}$', *True*=.19). This is because of the high probability that the student will copy the corresponding solution step (simulation slice, '$Copy_{n\text{-}force}$', *True*=.91), and the moderate probability of her having tendency for self-explanation (pre-simulation slice, '*SETend*', *True*=.5). In contrast, a low probability of copying (simulation slice, '$Copy_{n\text{-}dir}$', *True*=0.01) combined with a moderate tendency for self-explanation (pre-simulation slice, '*SETend*', *True*=.5) increases the probability for self-explanation (simulation slice, '$SE_{n\text{-}dir}$', *True*=.68).

Note that the network's structure with respect to self-explanation and copying means that the two are not mutually exclusive, i.e., one can reason via self-explanation and still copy. Although this seems unlikely, cognitive science research does not provide clear answers on how self-explanation and copying interact, and so we wanted to account for this possibility in our network.

Prediction of Learning and Problem-Solving Success During APS

The student model's prediction of copying and self-explanation in the presence of an example influences its prediction of learning and problem-solving outcomes. In particular, rule node probabilities in the simulation slice represent the model's prediction regarding whether the student will learn the corresponding rules in the presence of the candidate example. To generate this prediction, the model takes into account (1) whether the student already knows the rule (captured by the temporal link to the corresponding rule node in the pre-simulation slice); (2) will generate the step

by copying; (3) has the necessary prerequisites to generate the step on her own.

A rule node CPT encodes that learning of the rule is predicted to occur if the probability of the rule being known is low in the pre-simulation slice and the simulation predicts the student will reason via self-explanation to learn the rule (e.g., as is the case for rule '$Rule_{n\text{-}dir}$' in the simulation slice in Figure 5). Even in this case, however, learning is not guaranteed to occur, since cognitive science research shows that students may require several attempts before correct principles are inferred (Chi, 2000); this is modeled through the noise parameters described above.

The probabilities for the problem steps in the simulation slice represent the probability that the student will generate those steps in the problem-solving interface. To generate this prediction, the model takes into account: (1) the node's past value; (2) whether the student will generate the step by copying; (3) whether the student has the necessary prerequisites to generate the step on her own (i.e., knows the rule for deriving the step and can generate all prerequisite steps).

A step node CPT encodes that if a problem step is not already generated in the pre-simulation slice6, the student will generate it either if she copies from the example (as is the case for '$Step_{n\text{-}force}$' node in the simulation slice in Figure 5) or by the application of her own knowledge (as is the case for '$Step_{n\text{-}dir}$' node in the simulation slice in Figure 5).

Above, we described how evidence corresponding to problem/example similarity is used to obtain the posterior probabilities that represent a prediction of learning and problem solving success in the presence of that example. We now show how this prediction is used to choose an optimal example.

Expected Utility Calculation Phase

Once the simulation phase is completed for a candidate example, the EA-Coach selection mechanism

Figure 8. The EA-Coach utility model

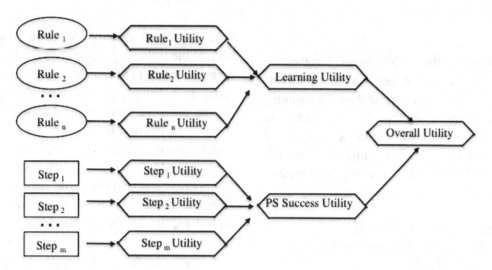

quantifies the student model's prediction in terms of the candidate example's expected utility. Since the EA-Coach has two objectives when choosing an example, i.e., learning and problem-solving success, the selection outcome is characterized by two attributes encoding how these objectives are achieved. For instance, an outcome could be that an example is likely to support problem-solving success, but not learning. When an outcome is characterized by more than one attribute, a factor that needs to be taken into account during the decision-making process is how the attributes compare in terms of importance. Such decision problems are handled by multi-attribute utility theory (MAUT) (Keeney and Raiffa, 1976; Clement, 1996). The EA-Coach relies on a particular kind of multi-attribute utility function, a linearly additive one, which has the following form:

$$U(x_1, x_2, \ldots, x_n) = \sum_{i=1}^{n} w_i U(x_i)$$

where (1) x_i are the attributes; (2) $U(x_1, x_2, \ldots, x_n)$ is the utility of the outcome described as a function of the attributes $x_1, x_2, \ldots, x_n$; (3) $U(x_i)$ is the utility of an attribute x_i; (4) w_i is the weight assigned to that attribute encoding its importance.

As is illustrated graphically in Figure 8, the EA-Coach obtains an overall expected utility for a candidate example by combining utilities for learning and problem-solving success. These are in turn obtained by combining utilities for the individual rules and problem steps.

The expected utility (*EU*) for learning each individual rule in the problem solution (captured by the nodes '*Rule₁ Utility*', ..., '*Ruleₙ Utility*' in Figure 8) is calculated as the sum of the probability *P* of each possible learning outcome for that rule (i.e., value of a rule node), multiplied by the utility *U* of that outcome:

$EU(Rule_i) = P(known(Rule_i)) \cdot U(known(Rule_i))$
$+P(\neg known(Rule_i)) \cdot U(\neg known(Rule_i))$

Since we define $U(known(Rule_i))=1$ and $U(\neg known(Rule_i))=0$, the expected utility of a rule corresponds to the probability that the rule is known. An example's overall expected utility for learning (captured by the node '*Learning Utility*' node in Figure 8) is calculated as the weighted sum of the expected utilities for learning the individual rules:

$$\sum_{i}^{n} EU(Rule_i) \cdot w_i$$

Currently all the weights *w* are assigned an equal value (i.e., 1/n, where *n* is the number of rules in the network), representing the assumption that all rules are equally important. The same approach is used to obtain the measure for the problem-solving success objective. First, the expected utility (*EU*) of each step being generated is calculated:

$EU(\text{Step}_i) = P(generated(\text{Step}_i)) \cdot U(generated(\text{Step}_i)) + P(\neg generated(\text{Step}_i)) \cdot U(\neg generated(\text{Step}_i))$

We define $U(generated(\text{Step}_i))=1$ and $U(\neg generated(\text{Step}_i))=0$, thus an example's overall expected utility for problem-solving success is the weighted sum of the expected utilities for the individual facts (captured by the node '*PS Success Utility*' node in Figure 8):

$$\sum_{i}^{m} EU(\text{Step}_i) \cdot w_i$$

Again, the weights are assigned an equal value (i.e., 1/m, where *m* is the number of steps in the network), representing the assumption that all the steps are equally important. To obtain an example's overall expected utility (captured by the node '*Overall Utility*' node in Figure 8), the EA-Coach combines the expected utilities for learning and problem-solving success in a weighted sum:

Overall EU(example) = EU(Learning) $\cdot w_1$ + *EU(PS Success)* $\cdot w_2$

The weights w_1 and w_2 are currently set to the same value (i.e., 1/2), making learning and problem-solving success equally important.

Summary

The EA-Coach example-selection process involves the following two phases for each candidate example: (1) *Simulation phase*: generating a prediction of how the student will solve a problem in the presence of the candidate example and what she will learn from it; (2) *Expected utility calculation phase*: quantifying this prediction via a linearly additive multi-attribute utility function to obtain the candidate example's expected utility. When a candidate example's expected utility is calculated, its simulation slice is discarded from the network. The simulation and utility calculation phases are repeated for each example in the framework's pool and the example with the highest expected utility is presented to the student. Currently, for the Newton's Second Law-type problems and examples (e.g., see Figure 3) stored in the EA-Coach knowledge base and used in the evaluation described shortly, obtaining a single example's expected utility requires approximately 0.07 seconds (when running non-optimized code on a Macbook Pro4 – there was little or no difference between various target problems and/or examples since as we mentioned all of them involved roughly same-size networks).

USING THE EA-COACH STUDENT MODEL IN ASSESSMENT MODE

During example selection, the DBN student model is used in *simulation mode* to predict the impact of a given example on APS. Once the example with the highest expected utility is selected, the student model is used in *assessment mode* to assess how the student actually uses the example to solve the target problem and how her knowledge and meta-cognitive tendencies evolve as a result. Doing so enables the selection mechanism to have up to date information on the student the next time she asks for an example. Although the same network and parameters are used in assessment mode as during simulation mode, there are two key differences between the modes.

(1) In contrast to simulation mode, in assessment mode the DBN student model generates its appraisal as a response to student actions. Specifically, a new slice is added to the network each time a student produces a correct problem-solving entry. While updating the network given an incorrect entry would allow the system to assess when students did not know a particular rule, doing so is problematic. This is because the EA-Coach does not constrain students' solution entries, making it possible for students to generate many different types of incorrect entries. The system currently does not have a model to capture how incorrect entries map to the correct rules in its knowledge base, which is needed to determine which step the student was trying to generate (and so which step node to clamp to *false* in the DBN). We are working on integrated a limited version of the mapping, implemented in Andes (Conati et al., 2002), into the EA-Coach. The issue of if and how to represent buggy knowledge is a long standing challenge in the ITS community; many tutors do not include such a representation and so face the same issue with respect to incorrect entries as the EA-Coach (for further discussion of this issue see (Heffernan et al., 2008)).

(2) In contrast to simulation mode, in assessment mode the DBN student model has evidence on student actions, including problem-solving entries and example-viewing actions, captured by the masking interface.

We will illustrate the network operation in assessment mode with the following scenario. Suppose a student opens the problem in Figure 3a, which results in the construction of a dynamic Bayesian network based on that problem's solution graph (see slice t in Figure 9). Next, the student asks for an example and the EA-Coach presents her with the one shown in Figure 3b. The student then generates a correct problem-solving entry corresponding to specifying the normal force. In response, the system adds a new slice to the dynamic Bayesian network (see slice $t+1$, Figure 9). This slice initially contains the same solution graph and APS tendencies nodes as the slice before it. In the newly added slice (see slice $t+1$, Figure 9), the EA-Coach:

- adds a similarity, a copy and an SE node, and links them to the step and rule nodes corresponding to the problem-solving entry;
- sets the values of the evidence nodes (i.e., *similarity* and *step*). The value of the similarity node is set via the same algorithm as used during simulation. Since the entry is correct, the value of the network step node that corresponds to the student's entry is set to '*True*' (see '*Step$_{n\text{-}force}$*' node in slice $t+1$, Figure 9);
- adds a 'View' node and links it to the step node corresponding to the student's entry (see '*View$_{n\text{-}force}$*' node in slice $t+1$, Figure 9). The view node encodes information on the student's example viewing related to this step, as we describe below.

A student's problem-solving entries help the model assess that student's knowledge for the corresponding rules (as mentioned above, all belief inference is realized via the cluster-update inference algorithm in the Smile Bayesian library (Smile, 2010)). In particular, if the probability of copying is low, then evidence from a student's correct entry results in belief propagation to the parent rule node, increasing the probability that the student knows the rule. If, on the other hand, the probability of copying is high, then the copy node 'explains away' much of the evidence so that it does not propagate to the parent rule node, since copied entries do not provide evidence that a student knows the related rules. To assess copying, the model relies on the same factors as during simulation (similarity, min-analogy tendency) as well as on information coming from a student's example-viewing actions in the masking interface.

Figure 9. Fragment of the EA-Coach dynamic Bayesian network used during assessment mode

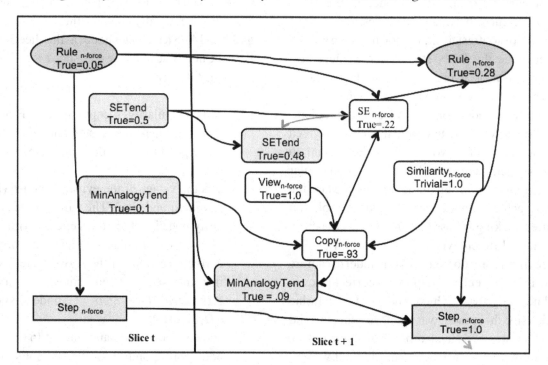

Specifically, the model takes into account whether prior to generating a problem-solving entry, the student actually viewed the corresponding step in the example solution. This information is encoded in the network by the view node that is linked to the copy node (see Figure 9). The view node's value is binary (*True/False*) and is set to:

- *True* if prior to generating her entry, the student viewed a corresponding step in the example solution. Only the last *three* steps viewed since the last problem-solving entry are considered, encoding the assumption that a student will not remember example steps viewed further back.
- *False* otherwise.

A student's example-viewing actions are also used to determine whether to add an SE node to the network. Specifically, an SE node is added if (i) the example affords the student the opportunity to learn the rule, i.e., a structurally identical step

exists in the example and (ii) the student viewed the corresponding step in the example. If the SE node is added, its value and influence on the corresponding rule node depends on the same factors as during simulation. If the SE node is not added, then the value of the parent rule node is simply transferred over to the child rule node.

During assessment, the model uses information on copying and self-explanation to infer how a student's meta-cognitive tendencies evolve during his interaction with the EA-Coach. To model the evolution for min-analogy tendency, the model uses its appraisal of the student's copying behaviors. For instance, belief in the student having copied (e.g., '$Copy_{n\text{-}force}$', *True* =.93 in Figure 9) decreases the model's belief in the student's tendency for min-analogy ('*MinAnalogyTend*', *True* =.1 in slice t decreases to *True* =.09 in slice $t + 1$). To model a student's evolution for self-explanation tendency, the model uses its appraisal of self-explanation episodes. For instance, if the probability of self-explanation is low, then belief in self-explanation tendency decreases ('*SETend*', *True* =.5 in slice *t* decreases to *True* =.48 in slice *t + 1*). Note that if an SE node is not added, then the SE tendency node has as its only parent the SE tendency node in the previous slice. In this case, the value of the parent tendency node is simply transferred over to the child tendency node via its temporal link.

As we described above, when the student closes the target problem, the current student model DBN for this problem is discarded. However, the posteriors for the rule and tendency nodes in the last slice of the DBN are stored in a data-structure that represents a long-term student model (not shown in Figure 1). The long-term model contains an assessment of student's tendencies and knowledge over all the EA-Coach's rules given all the problem solutions that the student has generated so far. When the student opens a new problem, a new DBN is built from this problem's solution graph. The priors for rule and tendency nodes in this DBN are set to the corresponding probabilities saved in the long-term model. This process allows the student model to have up-to-date information on the student each time he opens a new problem to work on.

EVALUATION OF THE EA-COACH DECISION-THEORETIC APPROACH

To verify how well the EA-Coach two-phase decision-theoretic process meets its selection objectives (learning, problem-solving success), we ran a study that compared the EA-Coach approach to the standard approach taken by ITS supporting APS, i.e., selecting the most similar example. Details may be found in (Muldner & Conati, in press); here we provide highlights of the methodology and results.

The study involved 16 university students. Each participant 1) completed a pencil and paper physics pre-test, 2) was introduced to the EA-Coach interface, 3) solved two Newton's Second Law problems using the EA-Coach (*experimental phase*) and 4) completed a pencil and paper physics post-test. The pre and post tests were specially designed to provide information on students' knowledge for solving the problems used during the experimental phase. During the experimental phase, for each problem, subjects had access to one example. For one of the problems, students were given an example selected by the EA-Coach (*adaptive-selection condition*; the example pool was populated with a total of six examples); for the other, students were given an example most similar to the target problem (*static-selection condition*). In contrast to the adaptive selection condition, the example in the static-selection condition was selected *a priori* so that all students saw the same problem/example pair. Subjects were given 45 minutes to complete each problem (this threshold was derived from pilot studies).

Note that we used a within-subjects design where each participant was exposed to both the adaptive selection and the static selection conditions. This design increases the experiment's power by accounting for the variability between subjects, arising from differences in, for instance, expertise or APS tendencies. To account for carry-over effects, the orders of the problems/ selection conditions were counterbalanced. The study data includes both logs of student interface actions, as well as students verbalizations of their thoughts, which we elicited by using a think-aloud protocol (Ericsson and Simon, 1980).

During the experimental phase, student characteristics influenced the EA-Coach's example selection, in that the same example was not always selected for a given student. Since this was the first evaluation of the EA-Coach, we focused on analyzing how in general the system influenced learning and problem solving; in the future, we will conduct further analysis and evaluations to better understand how the adaptive nature of the system interacted with individual differences between students.

As our primary data analysis technique, we used repeated-measures univariate ANOVA, performed separately for the dependent variables of interest (discussed below). The results from the ANOVA analysis are based on the data from the 14 subjects who used an example in both conditions (one subject only used the example in the adaptive condition, a second subject only used the example in the static condition).

Results

To assess how the EA-Coach adaptively-selected examples satisfied the learning goal, we analyzed students' behaviors that are known to impact learning, i.e., copying and self-explanation. While this approach makes the analysis challenging because it requires that students' reasoning is captured and analyzed, it provides in-depth insight on the impact of the EA-Coach selection mechanism. To identify copy events, we looked for instances when students: (1) accessed a step in the example solution (as identified by the verbal protocols and/or logged data on masking interface usage); (2) generated the corresponding step in their problem solution with no changes or only minor changes (e.g., changing the order of equation terms). The ANOVA revealed that students copied significantly less from the adaptively-selected examples, as compared to the statically-selected examples ($F(1,14) = 7.2$, $p = 0.023$; on average, 5.9 vs. 8.1 respectively). To identify self-explanation episodes, we analyzed the verbal protocol data to identify instances when students used self explanation to derive a new rule that they did not know before, following the approach in (VanLehn, 1999). Students derived significantly more new rules via self-explanation in the adaptive condition, as compared to the static condition ($F(1, 10)=12.8$, $p=0.005$; on average, 2.92 vs. 1.14 respectively).

In addition to analyzing behaviors that foster learning, we also measured pre/post test differences. In general, students improved significantly from pre to post test (on average, from 21.7 to 29.4;

2-tailed $t(15)=6.13$, $p<0.001$). However, because all students participated in both conditions and there was overlap in the domain rules involved in the solutions of the two problems, we needed to attribute learning to a particular selection condition. To do so, we first isolated rules that only appeared in one selection condition; next, we determined how many of these rules were learned from pre to post test. Although this left us with sparse data, we found more rules were learned in the adaptive condition than in the static condition (77% vs. 52%, respectively, $t(20)=1.72$, $p=0.056$).

To assess how well the EA-Coach adaptively-selected examples satisfied the problem-solving success goal, we identified how often students generated the problem solution in each condition. In the static condition, all 16 students generated a correct problem solution, while in the adaptive condition, 14 students did so (the other 2 students generated a partial solution; both used the example in both conditions). This difference between conditions, however, is not statistically significant (sign test, $p=0.5$), indicating that overall, both statically and adaptively selected examples helped students generate the problem solution.

Overall, the evaluation provided support for the pedagogical effectiveness of the EA-Coach's decision-theoretic example-selection mechanism. The adaptively-selected examples chosen by this mechanism encouraged students to engage in the target APS behaviors (min-analogy, self-explanation) better than statically-selected examples: students copied less and self-explained more when given adaptively-selected examples. It is important to note that as far as copying was concerned, students could copy as much or as little as they wished from both the statically and adaptively-selected examples. In particular, even the adaptively-selected examples were quite similar to the target problem and so how students would use them was an open question prior to the evaluation. As our evaluation showed, examples that are too similar do indeed facilitate copying, and that's why they are detrimental. Despite this, selecting the most similar examples is the approach used by all ITS that use examples to support problem solving.

Fostering the target APS behaviors did not come at the cost of problem-solving success, as the majority of students in both conditions were able to generate the problem solution. The fact that most students were able to achieve problem-solving success in the adaptive condition given the minimal scaffolding offered by the EA-Coach is a very positive result, because it shows that minor additions to the scaffolding may be sufficient to enable problem-solving success for all students.

DISCUSSION AND FUTURE WORK

Traditionally, a common application of decision theory corresponded to so-called decision-support systems, i.e., software tools that aim to help people make the optimal decision (for an overview, see (Shim et al., 2002)). While complex, such applications have an advantage over today's autonomous adaptive systems, since the latter need to make decisions without human intervention, often in the face of uncertain information and competing objectives. In this chapter, we focused on describing one such system, namely the EA-Coach. The design of this system in particular and autonomous decision-theoretic systems in general face a number of key challenges.

One challenge pertains to choosing the appropriate utility model to embed into the decision-theoretic application. Traditional decision support systems require a lengthy preference-elicitation process in order to identify a user's preferences, so that these preferences may be reflected in the decision-making process. Some of today's autonomous decision-theoretic systems choose to forego this elicitation step (Murray and VanLehn 2004, Mayo and Mitrovic 2001), instead relying on the system designers to hand select the utility function and corresponding weights. This is what we did for our work with the EA-Coach. We chose

a particular of type of multi-attribute function, namely a linearly additive one. Such a function greatly simplifies the expected utility calculation because it allows the utilities to be specified and calculated independently of each other. This is possible because additive independence among the agent's preferences is assumed. To illustrate additive independence, suppose we have two scenarios A and B, where a scenario corresponds to two possible outcomes, each with a 0.5 probability of occurring:

A (low Learning, low PS Success) with probability 0.5

(high Learning, high PS Success) with probability 0.5

B (low Learning, high PS Success) with probability 0.5

(high Learning, low PS Success) with probability 0.5

For instance, in scenario A, the two outcomes are (1) both learning and problem-solving success are low and (2) both learning and problem-solving success are high. If the decision maker is indifferent between the two scenarios then additive independence holds. However, if the decision-maker prefers scenario B over A because she prefers that at least one of *PS Success* or *Learning* is realized and does not want to risk neither happening, then additive independence does not hold. More formally, additive independence is defined as *"changes in lotteries in one attribute do not affect preferences for lotteries in the other attribute"* (Clement, 1996), where a lottery (i.e., scenario in our example above) is a probability distribution over outcomes. In the context of the EA-Coach, whether additive independence holds depends on the agent whose preferences the tutor is emulating (e.g., an instructor's, the researcher's). While assuming additive independence even when it does not hold has been shown to be acceptable in many practical applications (Clement, 1996), further investigation is needed to determine whether using this kind of function has any negative impact on the EA-Coach performance.

In addition to hand selecting the type of utility function used by the EA-Coach, currently we are also specifying the corresponding attribute weights (e.g., that learning and problem solving-success are equally important). An alternative approach is to elicit a preference function from an experienced tutor. While this approach has intuitive appeal, it is not without difficulty: research shows that there is a great deal of variance in terms of tutor behaviors, even across expert tutors (e.g., (VanLehn et al., 2003)). Thus, one tutor's utility function will likely not reflect another's, complicating the decision of which tutor to choose for the preference model. In general, it is an open question regarding whose preferences an adaptive system should be emulating, and whether these preferences should change to reflect those of the various users of an adaptive system.

Another approach for obtaining the attribute weights when using a linearly additive multi-attribute utility function is unique to adaptive systems. This approach involves setting the weights, observing system behavior, and then refining the weights until the desired system behavior is observed. Although this approach is clearly not feasible for human decision making, as trying out different alternatives is often not an option, researchers have started considering it for computational decision-making systems (e.g., (Murray, VanLehn et al., 2004)). However, judging desirability of a system's performance still relies on the evaluators' preferences, thus raising the same issue as stated above regarding whose preferences should be used to make the call.

Another challenge with respect to autonomous decision-theoretic applications relates to the specification of the other model parameters, e.g., priors for a DBN for a system relying on this type of probabilistic model. If the DBN priors are

initially inaccurate, then the system still functions, but its adaptation may not be adequately tailored to a users' characteristics. For instance, if the EA-Coach has inaccurate information on students' meta-cognitive tendencies, then it may choose examples that do not afford sufficient scaffolding for min-analogy and/or self-explanation. However, the EA-Coach also *assesses* a student as she interacts with the system, including that students' knowledge and meta-cognitive tendencies. Thus, with time, the initial assessment is refined with up to date information on the student. To illustrate, suppose the system assigns a generic prior to min-analogy tendency of 0.8, indicating that the student has a *high* min-analogy tendency, i.e., a low tendency for copying. Accordingly, the system chooses examples that do not aim to discourage copying (i.e., via non-trivial differences), because the system assumes that the student does not need such scaffolding. However, the student actually has a low min-analogy tendency, preferring to copy instead. The student's copying is captured by the system, and used to update the min-analogy tendency; each such update increases the probability that the student has a *low* min-analogy tendency, which in turn impacts subsequent example selection.

Yet another challenge relates to decision-theoretic application evaluation. These applications are a subset of a broader class of *adaptive systems*, i.e., ones that tailor their interaction to a given user to meet that user's needs. The evaluation of adaptive systems in general is known to be challenging, due to the presence of their many complex and inter-dependent components. Since decision-theoretic systems additionally include components related to the utility model and decision-making aspects, their evaluation may be especially difficult.

A common approach for evaluating an adaptive system involves measuring user attributes of interest before and after interacting with the system, e.g., student knowledge before and after interaction with an ITS (e.g., (Conati and VanLehn,

2000; Ringenberg and VanLehn, 2006). This approach, however, does not provide information on which aspects of the interaction triggered specific outcomes. For instance, if the outcome of interest is student learning and learning occurs, it is very difficult to attribute that result to a given component of the ITS, e.g., utility component, since the outcome could be the result of other factors (e.g., hints, feedback). One option to carefully evaluate individual system components is to run ablation studies, where users interact with different versions of the system, e.g., with and without meta-cognitive support, enabling an understanding of the impact of specific components on users' experience. An issue with this strategy is that system components are typically related, and so evaluating individual components may not accurately represent a fully-functioning system. Furthermore, ablation studies are very effort-intensive to run, and so this option is typically explored at the most basic level (i.e., an adaptive version of the system is compared against a non-adaptive counterpart). Another evaluation option is to rely on *process-oriented* methodologies, such as the one we employed in the evaluation of the EA-Coach, to obtain a richer picture of the system's impact on user behaviors (and not just outcomes). As was the case for ablation studies, this strategy is also very labor intensive, since it requires the copious amounts of data corresponding to users' *in situ* experience with the system are captured and analyzed.

Given the challenges associated with system evaluation, some researchers have proposed less-conventional evaluation methodologies, such as having expert judges rate the decisions made by the adaptive system (Murray and VanLehn, 2006). While such approaches do provide insight into the appropriateness of individual decisions taken by the system, they do not evaluate how the system decisions impact actual users. In general, the introduction of decision-theoretic components adds additional complexity that transfers to the evaluation of the system, and so more work is needed exploring the advantages and disadvantages of various evaluation methodologies. This is particularly salient as these systems are becoming more and more ubiquitous, and so ensuring their usability is crucial.

As far as our next steps with the EA-Coach are concerned, we are interested in analyzing if and how the EA-Coach utility model needs improvement, including investigating the suitability of using an additive utility function, as well as the weights assigned to this function. We currently assume that all weights are equal in the EA-Coach function, but this may be an overly simplistic conjecture. For instance, it may turn out that some rules are more important for students to master than others, in which case they should be assigned a higher weight to enable example-selection to reflect that preference. To address this issue, we plan to endow the EA-Coach with a preference-elicitation interface that will facilitate obtaining the preference functions of expert tutors. This functionality may be especially important to deploy the EA-Coach into actual classrooms, as various teachers may have different preferences that need to be reflected in the ITS's behavior. A challenge related to this endeavor, mentioned above, will be if and how to reconcile different tutor's preferences.

Another avenue of future research will involve analyzing the efficiency of the system in order to determine if and how it needs improvement. One possible refinement with this respect relates to which examples are included in the simulation phase. Currently, the simulation involves all of the examples in the system's example pool, but this approach will become infeasible with large pools. A remedy for this issue is to prune examples that are known a priori to be poor candidates, for instance because their solutions pertains to vastly different physics principles than that of the target problem. This pruning could be done by the system before any student interaction occurs, thereby increasing the simulation efficiency at run time. We are also planning on refining the dynamic Bayesian network student model parameters through machine learning from data with actual students interacting with the EA-Coach, which we've been collecting through various evaluations of the system.

REFERENCES

Anderson, J. R. (1993). *Rules of the mind*. Hillsdale, NJ: Lawrence Erlbaum Associates.

Arroyo, I., & Woolf, B. (2005). Inferring learning and attitudes from a Bayesian network of log file data. In *Proceeding of the Twelfth International Conference on Artificial Intelligence in Education (AIED'05)*, (pp. 33-40).

Bloom, B. S. (1984). The 2 sigma problem: The search for methods of group instruction as effective as one-to-one tutoring. *Educational Researcher, 13*, 4–16.

Bunt, A., Conati, C., & Muldner, K. (2004). Scaffolding self-explanation to improve learning in exploratory learning environments. In *Proceedings of the Seventh International Conference on Intelligent Tutoring Systems (ITS'04)*, (Maceo, Brazil), (pp. 656-667).

Chi, M. T. (2000). Self-explaining: The dual process of generating inferences and repairing mental models. In Glaser, R. (Ed.), *Advances in instructional psychology* (pp. 161–238). Lawrence Erlbaum Associates.

Chi, M. T., & VanLehn, K. (1991). The content of physics self-explanations. *Journal of the Learning Sciences, 1*, 69–105. doi:10.1207/s15327809jls0101_4

Clement, R. (1996). *Making hard decisions*. Pacific Grove, CA: Duxberry Press.

Conati, C., & Carenini, G. (2001). Generating tailored examples to support learning via self-explanation. In *Proceedings of IJCAI '01, the Seventeenth International Joint Conference on Artificial Intelligence*, (pp. 1301-1306).

Conati, C., Gertner, A., & VanLehn, K. (2002). Using Bayesian networks to manage uncertainty in student modeling. *User Modeling and User-Adapted Interaction, 12*(4), 371–417. doi:10.1023/A:1021258506583

Conati, C., and MacLaren, M. (2010). Empirically building and evaluating a probabilistic model of user affect. To appear in *User Modeling and User-Adapted Interaction.*

Conati, C., & Merten, C. (2007). Eye-tracking for user modeling in exploratory learning environments: An empirical evaluation. *Knowledge-Based Systems, 20*(6), 557–574. doi:10.1016/j.knosys.2007.04.010

Conati, C., Muldner, K., & Carenini, G. (2006). From example studying to problem solving via tailored computer-based meta-cognitive scaffolding: Hypotheses and design. *Technology, Instruction* [TICL]. *Cognition & Learning, 4*, 139–190.

Conati, C., & VanLehn, K. (2000). Toward computer-based support of meta-cognitive skills: A computational framework to coach self-explanation. *International Journal of Artificial Intelligence in Education, 11*, 389–415.

Cooper, D., Muldner, K., Arroyo, I., Woolf, B. P., Burleson, W., & Dolan, R. (2010). Ranking feature sets for emotion models used in classroom based intelligent tutoring systems. To appear in *the International Conference on User Modeling and Adaptive Presentation (UMAP'10)*, 12 pages.

Dean, T., & Kanazawa, K. (1989). A model for reasoning about persistence and causation. *Computational Intelligence, 5*(3), 142–150. doi:10.1111/j.1467-8640.1989.tb00324.x

Ericsson, K., & Simon, H. (1980). Verbal reports as data. *Psychological Review, 87*(3), 215–250. doi:10.1037/0033-295X.87.3.215

Gajos, K., Weld, D., & Wobbrock, J. (2008). Decision-theoretic user interface generation. *Proceedings of the 23rd National Conference on Artificial Intelligence (AIED'08)*, (pp. 1532-1536).

Heffernan, N., Koedinger, K., & Razzaq, L. (2008). Expanding the model-tracing architecture: A 3rd generation intelligent tutor for algebra symbolization. *International Journal of Artificial Intelligence in Education, 18*(2), 153–178.

Kabassi, K., & Virvou, M. (2006). Multi-attribute utility theory and adaptive techniques for intelligent web-based educational software. *Instructional Science, 34*, 131–158. doi:10.1007/s11251-005-6074-6

Keeney, R., & Raiffa, H. (1976). *Decisions with multiple objectives: Preferences and value trade-offs*. New York, NY: Wiley.

Mayo, M., & Mitrovic, A. (2001). Optimizing ITS behaviour with Bayesian networks and decision theory. *International Journal of Artificial Intelligence in Education, 12*, 124–153.

Mendicino, M., Razzaq, L., & Heffernan, N. T. (2009). Improving learning from homework using intelligent tutoring systems. [JRTE]. *Journal of Research on Technology in Education, 41*(3), 331–346.

Muldner, K. (2007a). *Tailored scaffolding for meta-cognitive skills during analogical problem solving*. Ph.D. Thesis, University of British Columbia, Canada.

Muldner, K., & Conati, C. (2007b). Evaluating a decision-theoretic approach to tailored example selection. In *Proceedings of the Twentieth International Joint Conference on Artificial Intelligence (IJCAI'07)*, (pp. 483-489).

Muldner, K., & Conati, C. (2010). Scaffolding meta-cognitive skills for effective analogical problem solving via tailored example selection. *Journal of Artificial Intelligence in Education, 20*(2).

Murray, C., & VanLehn, K. (2006). A comparison of decision-theoretic, fixed-policy and random tutorial action selection. In *Proceedings of the Eight International Conference on Intelligent Tutoring Systems (ITS'06)*, (pp. 114-123).

Murray, R. C., VanLehn, K., & Mostow, J. (2004). Looking ahead to select tutorial actions: A decision-theoretic approach. *Journal of Artificial Intelligence in Education, 14*(3), 235–278.

Novick, L. (1995). Some determinants of successful analogical transfer in the solution of algebra word problems. *Thinking & Reasoning, 1*(1), 1–30. doi:10.1080/13546789508256903

Novick, L. R. (1988). Analogical transfer, problem similarity and expertise. *Journal of Experimental Psychology. Learning, Memory, and Cognition, 14*, 510–520. doi:10.1037/0278-7393.14.3.510

Pack, T., & Horvitz, E. (2000). Conversation as action under uncertainty. In *Proceedings of the Sixteenth Conference on Uncertainty in Artificial Intelligence*, (pp. 455–464).

Pearl, J. (1988). *Probabilistic reasoning in intelligent systems: Networks of plausible inference*. San Mateo, CA: Morgan-Kaufmann.

Pek, P. K., & Poh, K. L. (2000). Using decision networks for adaptive tutoring. In *Proceedings of the International Conference on Computers in Education / International Conference on Computer-Assisted Instruction*, (pp. 1076-1084).

Pirolli, P. L., & Anderson, J. R. (1985). The role of learning from examples in the acquisition of recursive programming skills. *Canadian Journal of Psychology, 39*, 240–272. doi:10.1037/h0080061

Reed, S. K., & Bolstad, C. A. (1991). Use of examples and procedures in problem solving. *Journal of Experimental Psychology. Learning, Memory, and Cognition, 17*(4), 753–766. doi:10.1037/0278-7393.17.4.753

Reed, S. K., Dempster, A., & Ettinger, M. (1985). Usefulness of analogous solutions for solving algebra word problems. *Journal of Experimental Psychology. Learning, Memory, and Cognition, 11*, 106–125. doi:10.1037/0278-7393.11.1.106

Reed, S. K., Willis, D., & Guarino, J. (1994). Selecting examples for solving word problems. *Journal of Educational Psychology, 86*(3), 380–388. doi:10.1037/0022-0663.86.3.380

Ringenberg, M., & VanLehn, K. (2006). Scaffolding problem solving with annotated, worked-out examples to promote deep learning. In *Proceedings of the Eight International Conference on Intelligent Tutoring Systems (ITS'06)*, (pp. 625-634).

Roll, I., Aleven, V., McLaren, B. M., & Koedinger, K. R. (2011). Improving students' help seeking skills using meta-cognitive feedback in an intelligent tutoring system. *Learning and Instruction, 21.*

Shim, J., Warkentin, M., Courtney, J., Power, D., Sharda, R., & Carlsson, C. (2002). Past, present, and future of decision support. *Decision Support Systems, 33*(2), 111–126. doi:10.1016/S0167-9236(01)00139-7

SIS. (2010). *SMILE: Structural modeling, inference, & learning engine.* Retrieved May 2010 from http://genie.sis.pitt.edu

Ting, C.-Y., Beik, Z., Reza, M., & Chong, Y.-K. (2006). A decision-theoretic approach to scientific inquiry exploratory learning environment. In *Proceedings of the Eight International Conference on Intelligent Tutoring Systems (ITS'06)*, (pp. 85-94).

VanLehn, K. (1988). *Student modeling. Foundations of Intelligent Tutoring Systems* (pp. 55–78). Hillsdale, NJ: Lawrence Erlbaum Associates.

VanLehn, K. (1998). Analogy events: How examples are used during problem solving. *Cognitive Science, 22*(3), 347–388. doi:10.1207/s15516709cog2203_4

VanLehn, K. (1999). Rule-learning events in the acquisition of a complex skill: An evaluation of cascade. *Journal of the Learning Sciences, 8*(1), 71–125. doi:10.1207/s15327809jls0801_3

VanLehn, K., Jones, R. M., & Chi, M. (1992). A model of the self-explanation effect. *Journal of the Learning Sciences, 2*(1), 1–59. doi:10.1207/s15327809jls0201_1

VanLehn, K., Siler, S., Murray, R. C., Yamauchi, T., & Baggett, W. B. (2003). Why do only some events cause learning during human tutoring? *Cognition and Instruction, 21*(3), 209–249. doi:10.1207/S1532690XCI2103_01

Woolf, B. (2008). *Building intelligent interactive tutors: Student-centered strategies for revolutionizing e-learning.* San Francisco, CA: Elsevier Inc., Morgan Kauffman.

ADDITIONAL READING

Bohnenberger, T., & Jameson, A. (2001) When policies are better than plans: decision-theoretic planning of recommendation sequences. *In Proceedings of the 6th international conference on Intelligent user interfaces* (IUI'01), 21 – 24.

Conati C. (2002). Probabilistic Assessment of User's Emotions in Educational Games. *Journal of Applied Artificial Intelligence, special issue on Merging Cognition and Affect in HCI,* 16 (7-8), 555-575.

Fern, A., Natarajan, S., Judah, K., & Tadepalli, P. (2007). A Decision theoretic model of Assistance. *In Proceedings of the International Joint Conference in Artificial Intelligence (IJCAI'07),* 1879-1884.

Gajos, K. Z., & Weld, D. S. and Wobbrock, J. O. (2008). Decision-Theoretic User Interface Generation. In *Proceedings of AAAI'08,* 1532-1536.

Jameson, A., Grobmann-Hutter, B., March, L., & Rummer, R. (2000). Creating an Empirical Basis for Adaptation Decisions. *In Proceedings of the International Conference on Intelligent User Interfaces (IUI'00),* 149–156.

Jameson, A., Grobmann-Hutter, B., March, L., Rummer, R., Bohnenberger, T., & Wittig, F. (2001). When Actions Have Consequences: Empirically Based Decision Making for Intelligent User Interfaces. *Knowledge-Based Systems, 14*, 75–92. doi:10.1016/S0950-7051(00)00097-6

Liao, W., Zhang, W., Zhu, Z., Ji, Q., & Gray, W. (2006). Toward a decision-theoretic framework for affect recognition and user assistance. *International Journal of Human-Computer Interaction, 64*(9), 847–887.

Mott, B. W., & Lester, J. C. (2009). U-director: a decision-theoretic narrative planning architecture for storytelling environments. *In Proceedings of the fifth international joint conference on Autonomous agents and multiagent systems*, 977 – 984.

UserModeling and User-Adapted Interaction, Volume 17, Numbers 1-2, (2007), Special Issue on Statistical and Probabilistic Methods for User Modeling (Whole Issue).

KEY TERMS AND DEFINITIONS

Analogical Problem Solving (APS): Using examples to aid problem solving.

Intelligent Tutoring Systems (ITSs): Computer applications that employ artificial intelligence techniques to tailor their pedagogical support to suit individual students' needs.

Min-Analogy: Solving the problem on one's own as much as possible instead of by copying from examples.

Non-Trivial Similarity: A type of problem/example correspondence that does not allow the example solution to be copied directly over to the problem.

Self-Explanation: The process of explaining instructional material to oneself.

Trivial Similarity: A type of problem/example correspondence that allows the example solution to be copied directly over to the problem with minor or no changes.

User Model: A system component that (1) represents user states relevant for modifying system behaviour to suit individual users' needs and (2) generates inferences on those states based on information provided through the user's interaction with the system.

ENDNOTES

[1] Given a decision-theoretic stance, by definition an optimal action is one that maximizes an agent's expected utility.

[2] We will use a mix of feminine and masculine pronouns.

[3] The EA-Coach is implemented in Microsoft Visual Studio C++, with an Allegro Lisp back-end used for determining the correctness of student responses.

[4] The problem-solver is an off-the-shelf expert system.

[5] The simulation slice does not include the minAnalogyTend and SETend nodes because currently the simulation does not predict the impact of an example on a student's APS tendencies. This could be done following the approach used during assessment mode, discussed in Section 6 and shown in Figure 9, i.e., by having links from the copy / self explanation nodes to the respective tendency nodes. Doing so adds additional complexity to the simulation, and so we decided to leave this possibility for future work, after we have fully validated the approach on the simplified model.

[6] This occurs if the student generates a solution step(s) and then asks for an example. Accounting for this means that the model does not need to consider whether an example will help the student generate the step, since she already achieved problem-solving success on that step.

Chapter 11
Dynamic Decision Networks Applications in Active Learning Simulators

Julieta Noguez
Tecnológico de Monterrey, Mexico

Karla Muñoz
University of Ulster, Northern Ireland

Luis Neri
Tecnológico de Monterrey, Mexico

Víctor Robledo-Rella
Tecnológico de Monterrey, Mexico

Gerardo Aguilar
Tecnológico de Monterrey, Mexico

ABSTRACT

Active learning simulators (ALSs) allow students to practice and carry out experiments in a safe environment – anytime, anywhere. Well-designed simulations may enhance learning, and provide the bridge from concept to practical understanding. Nevertheless, learning with ALS depends largely on the student's ability to explore and interpret the performed experiments. By adding an Intelligent Tutoring System (ITS), it is possible to provide individualized personal guidance to students. The challenges are how an ITS properly assesses the cognitive state of the student based on the results of experiments and the student's interaction, and how it provides adaptive feedback to the student. In this chapter we describe how an ITS based on Dynamic Decision Networks (DDNs) is applied in an undergraduate Physics scenario where the aim is to adapt the learning experience to suit the learners' needs. We propose employing Probabilistic Relational Models (PRMs) to facilitate the construction of the model. These are frameworks that enable the definition of Probabilistic Graphical and Entity Relationship Models, starting from a domain, and in this case, environments of ALSs. With this representation, the tutor can be easily adapted to different experiments, domains, and student levels, thereby minimizing the development effort for building and integrating Intelligent Tutoring Systems (ITS) for ALSs. A discussion of the methodology is addressed, and preliminary results are presented.

DOI: 10.4018/978-1-60960-165-2.ch011

INTRODUCTION

Most Active Learning Simulators (ALSs) allow students (or users in general) to explore the effect that different variables have on the behavior of the system under a given scenario. These types of systems have also been called Open Learning Environments (OLEs). The main benefits of OLE systems are that they provide the student with the opportunity to learn through free exploration. The student has the freedom to modify different parameters and to observe their effects (Bunt, 2003). Nevertheless, students often repeat a given experiment several times without a clear understanding of the phenomenon behind the working scenario. For example, while interacting with OLEs some hyperactive students could try several options in the system, but the students' learning cannot be ensured. Another student could explore diverse variables and observe their behavior during simulation. However the student may not be able to connect the theory with the phenomenon that he is observing (McHaney, 2002). Another student could make a selection of parameters that may be enable him to create a link between the theoretical concepts and the behavior of the experiment. Several OLEs do not have specific goals for the student to attain. If there is not a defined experimental goal that the student is required to attain, it is not easy to infer the current knowledge state in an OLE. In addition, students' learning processes are not yet completely understood. It is expected that the student will be capable of constructing knowledge while interacting with the system. As a result, specific objectives are needed in order to attain and enable an effective assessment of the learning goals (Noguez J. & Sucar E., 2005). Even so, it is hard to detect and determine how much does the student actually knows at a given point in time, what they do not know and what skills have or have not been being acquired by the student, based only on the student's interaction with the OLE. Given the inherent uncertainty of these tasks, a decision model capable of reasoning under ambiguity is required.

To face the aforementioned learning problems, our aim is to include elements from Intelligent Tutoring Systems (ITSs) inside ALSs, which are capable of giving students (or users in general) the benefits of an adaptive learning environment. An ALS takes care of the balance between free exploration capabilities and the tutoring labor based on the best pedagogical action. For example, decisions such as when to interrupt a given experiment and to provide on time help for the user, and actions such as following-up the student's performance and planning the forthcoming task.

To handle uncertainty, student models, based on Bayesian Networks (BNs), have already been developed for ITSs (Pearl, 1988). These BNs are useful for diagnosing – or inferring – the student's current cognitive state, using observable data (Van-Lehn, 2001; Murray, 200; Mayo, 2001). However, the effort required to build the network structure, to obtain and define the related parameters, and to manage the computational complexity of the inference algorithms, makes the application of these types of models very difficult. This is particularly true in real time situations, such as simulators (Adams, 2007). Finding a general model for a variety of experiments, scenarios and domains is an additional challenge. In terms of development, efforts to create tutors for all simulators types are very laborious and time consuming. We have proposed using Probabilistic Relational Models (PRMs), which provide a new approach to student/user modeling, integrating the expressive power of BNs with the advantages of relational models (Noguez J. & Sucar E., 2005). PRMs enable starting with the domain problem, like object-oriented modeling, and continuing by defining the elements of probabilistic modeling. A general structure for each module of the ITS was designed. The first step was to identify the classes in the model. The next step was to define the dependency model at class level, allowing it to be used for any object in the class, thus facilitating the understanding of the model. The classes and their relationships provide a general schema. Based on this schema, a skeleton is derived that integrates the relevant variables and their dependencies into BNs or Dynamic Decision Networks (DDNs). Finally, a particular BN or DDN is obtained from the skeleton for each specific experiment in certain domains.

One important module necessary to adapt the feedback of the learning experience according to the learners' needs is the tutor model. Following each experiment, results are employed by the tutor module to decide the most appropriate response. If the experiment results are below specific and previously defined goals, the tutor uses specified pedagogical parameters, based on DDNs, to decide the best actions to be taken at a given time during a learning experience. A variety of instructive options and pedagogical feedback must be available to reinforce student learning. That is, the system is able to give ad hoc feedback using specific messages, according to the student's performance and interaction with the system.

Influence diagrams (Howard, 1984), also called relevance diagrams, are acyclic directed graphs representing decision problems. The goal of influence diagram modeling is to choose such an alternative decision that will lead to the highest expected gain (utility, see below). As with BNs, influence diagrams are very useful at showing the structure of the problem domain, i.e., the structure of the decision problem.

DDNs are an extension of BNs, incorporating decision and utility nodes as function of time (Tawfik, 2005). We focus here on the methodology to design an ALS capable of fostering the student's comprehension and learning. In addition, to providing the best pedagogical action according to the learner's particular needs the sufficient pedagogical reinforcement will be offered to the student during the learning process. An intelligent tutor, based on DDNs, provides the student with personalized and timely feedback whenever the learner makes a mistake. The DDN represents decision nodes containing the set of values cor-

responding to the best possible pedagogical actions, and employs utility nodes to select the best decision. The active learning environment will then provide feedback to the student so he will be able to understand the origin of his mistakes and take the necessary steps in order to find out the right answer.

We use PRMs to build the tutoring system based on DDNs. It holds some advantages over ad hoc methods because it can be easily extended to apply machine learning techniques in order to build adaptive tutors. In addition, a PRM is a general framework based on extensive research that can help to rationalize user behavior. The results of all the different instances during the student's interactions, which are retrieved from database and the probabilistic model, are kept by the PRM. With this information the PRM system generates a large database, which can be employed to search new patterns and behaviors of the variables. These patterns and behaviors are employed to validate or to find a new probabilistic structural model and its Conditional Probability Tables (CPTs).

As a case study, an undergraduate Physics learning scenario was chosen. It is a common fact that students enrolled in Physics bachelors usually have a tendency to learn Physics as a group of disjoint concepts. Very often, students do not understand the coherent structure underlying Physics, nor are they encouraged to do so. Based on our teaching experience, we believe that one of the most important factors that make Physics traditionally "difficult", it is precisely this lack of this understanding, which also has the effect of decreasing the student's confidence.

This chapter is focused on the application of a DDN to an ALS, which enables a given learning environment, with an academic or professional goal, to provide accurate and timely feedback to the user about the quality of his or her interaction with the system to achieve the desired goal. This chapter contributes by presenting a methodology for designing an ALS. The ALS accurately evaluates the learners' abilities, and provides the best suitable, personalized and immediate feedback to the learners' identified needs and common mistakes. The preliminary results, related to the usefulness of this tool while assisting students in their own learning, are presented. The discussion of the methodology is addressed and main conclusions are presented.

ACTIVE LEARNING SIMULATORS

ALSs bring together the concepts from active learning and computer simulations. Active learning is referenced as several models of instruction that focus the responsibility of learning on students. Bonwell and Eison popularized this approach to instruction of content (Bonwell & Eison 1991). A computer simulation is a reproduction of a scenario, an item or an event. Simulations can be developed in many fields including computer games, role-playing and building models, to name only a few. However, a useful simulation has a specific goal in mind, "a simulator is a real system so that we can explore it, perform experiments on it, and understand it before implementing it in the real world" (Novasim, 2009). These kinds of systems often involve simulation where learners can experiment with different aspects and parameters of a given phenomenon to observe the effects of decisions [Shute 1990]. The students are able to select different parameters in each system execution, trying to improve knowledge and understanding. Many advantages have been identified using ALSs (Lean, 2006): (i) reveal the connections between theory and physics phenomena throughout the visualization of experiments, (ii) engaging the student in a smart and graphical environment, (iii) students can practice in controlled and safe environments, (iv) the Information Technology (IT) resources are readily available, and (v) students can practice with experiments which are difficult to reproduce in the real world.

With the intelligent use of computer technology and media, e.g. animation and sound, the experi-

ence provided by an ALS can be personalized. The learner can be rewarded when making a correct decision, and can be brought back to a previous lesson when making a mistake that signaled a need to review previous material.

Additionally, ALSs allow students to practice and carry out experiments in a safe environment, anytime, anywhere. In addition, there are several important reasons to incorporate an ALS into a learning environment, such as:

a. Students are capable of constructing their own understanding about a given phenomenon (or law in the case of Physics).

b. The simulator separates and handles the effects of different parameters at a given time, allowing the student to explore the behavior of different variables, so improving the comprehension of fundamental concepts.

c. ALSs enable the use of several multimedia tools, such as images, animations, audio and graphs, which help to understand the main concepts, relations and processes involved within a given scenario.

d. ALSs also allow the investigation of different phenomena it would not otherwise be feasible to carry out in the classroom.

However, a substantial limitation of these systems is their effectiveness for learning, which strongly depends on the learner, the specific features that influence the student's ability to explore adequately, and the need for having a clear definition of what constitutes effective exploration behavior. There are several authors (Bunt 2003; Bull 2004; Mabbot 2004) that present OLE models. They argue that additional meta-cognitive skills such as self explanation should improve the effectiveness of a student's exploration. However, this hypothesis needs further study before drawing stronger conclusions.

On the other hand, many simulation training environments have added more intelligence to the simulation model than current intelligent tutoring systems (Mesbahi, 2007), (Liu, 2006). Some authors have included intelligent aspects to simulator environments, but it is no clear how generate the intelligent feedback or how the ITS was built. For example, a system that involves the development of an intelligent simulation based upon computer managed interactive media is presented in (Powell, 2008). It allows train a fire officer to deal intelligently with the command and control of a major fire event he will never have experienced. It includes firefighting demands where commanders impose their individual intelligence on each problem to solve it. However how the intelligent aspects work is no described, and additionally it is a standalone approach that doesn't allow the lecturer to monitor the knowledge gains of each student. In summary, the practice of including intelligence in modeling and simulation of next generation open, dynamic, and adaptive engineering applications is still in its infancy (Yilmaz, 2006).

DYNAMIC DECISION NETWORKS

As explained in chapter 2, utility theory extends probability theory to guide decision-making under uncertainty. Utilities are used to provide a quantitative measure of preferences among possible world states. To choose from alternative actions, the expected utility of each alternative is calculated by taking the sum of utilities corresponding to all the possible future world states, which follow from that alternative, weighted by the occurrence probabilities of those states (Tawfik, 2005).

A DDN is an extension of dynamic Bayesian networks (DBN) except that it has decision and utility nodes in addition to uncertainty or chance nodes. DDNs model decisions for situations in which decision, variables or preferences may change over time. These networks have been used in a variety of application like ITSs (Murray, 2000).

PROBABILISTIC RELATIONAL MODELS

Probabilistic relational models (PRMs) are an approach that integrates the expressive power of Bayesian networks and the facilities of relational models. PRMs make it possible to represent a given domain in terms of entities, their properties, and their relations (Koller, 2009). The basic entities in a PRM are objects or domain entities. Objects in the domain are partitioned into a set of disjoint classes X1,..., Xn, forming an schema. A set of attributes A(Xi) are associated with each class. The attributes can be information variables (provide general data, usually static) and random variables (correspond to the knowledge items related to the experiments, these are dynamic and uncertain). At the beginning, the dependency model is defined at the class level, allowing it to be used for any object in the class. For each class, its dependency relations with other classes are defined. Later, the specific dependencies between the attributes (random variables) of each object are defined based on attributes of related objects. A skeleton of a relational schema is defined as the partial specification of an instance of the schema, i.e. a skeleton represents a subset of variables and relations of the probabilistic model that are of interest at certain time.

A PRM allows the specification of the probability distribution of the skeletons using the same underlying principles used for Bayesian networks. The assumption is that each of the random variables in a PRM, in this case the attributes x.a of the individual object x, is directly influenced only by a few others. A PRM therefore defines for each attribute x.a, a set of parents, which have direct influence over it, and a local probabilistic model that specifies the probabilistic parameters. Once a specific network is generated from a skeleton, the inference mechanism is the same as for Bayesian networks.

Based on probabilistic relational models, we designed a general structure for modeling students in virtual laboratory environments (Noguez J. & Sucar E., 2005). The first step is to identify the classes in the model. The next step is to define the dependency model at class level, allowing it to be employed for any object in the class and facilitating the understanding of the model. The classes and their relations provide a general schema for the student model. Based on this schema, a skeleton is derived, which integrates in a BN the relevant variables and their dependencies. Finally, a particular BN is obtained from the skeleton for each specific experiment in certain domain. In the following sections we illustrate this methodology for the main elements in the student model of virtual laboratories.

ENHANCED LEARNING USING INTELLIGENT TUTORING SYSTEMS IN ACTIVE LEARNING SIMULATORS

As we mentioned before, ALSs using an ITS enhance learning by allowing students to explore several variables, to visualize displayed graphic results, and give suitable feedback. However, The incorporation of the ITS faces several challenges, such as how a student's level of comprehension can be determined based on student's interactions, what variables are involved in the inference learning process, how adapt it to diverse student profiles that include different levels of knowledge and skills, how the ITS can follow the student's progress while repeating a simulation to chose the most appropriate pedagogical action, how new experiments can be developed and be easily added to the ALS site without changing the student model, and how can reduce the time needed to develop new ALSs for other domains.

The student model is the main component of ITS. Because it adapts the learning experience to suit the learner's perceived needs (Self, 1999). However, the practical difficulty in building reliable student models is to define the appropriate role. The debate is really over what kind of

information the student model should provide. At one end, student models provide only information about the last student input to which the system has to react. At the other end, student models provide a detailed description of student's knowledge and psychological make-up. Neither extreme is feasible or desirable. In the student model the cognitive state of a learner is inferred from two parts: the previous data about the student and student's behavior during the interaction with the system (Collins, 1996). Due this fact, both involve uncertainty, a model that considers it is required. Additionally, the student's solution process does not always give enough information to obtain the student model, and it is hard to assess the student's effective exploration and define which learning objectives were reached using the same general model for different students (Richard, 1999). Thus, the main objective of this work is to provide a student model representation for an intelligent tutoring system of an ALS environment, using probabilistic relational models.

The developed ALS environment includes an ITS that keeps track of student's actions while conducting the experiment. It monitors student performance, updates the student model and gives appropriate feedback if required. When a student carries out an experiment in this learning environment, the student model propagates the evidence to specific Bayesian Nets. Based on this, and other accumulated information obtained from evidence of previous experiments, a behavior module updates the student model as needed. After each experiment is conducted, the results are then used by the tutor model that decides the most suitable feedback to respond to the student. The modular architecture is shown in Figure 1.

The ITS is based on PRMs, the ALS was designed by Physics, Mathematics, and Computer Science professors. Every simulation was adapted to enquire the student about reaching a specific goal or solving a problem. According to the benefits of an OLE, the system allows students free exploration in the learning environment in-

Figure 1. Modular architecture of an active learning simulator environment

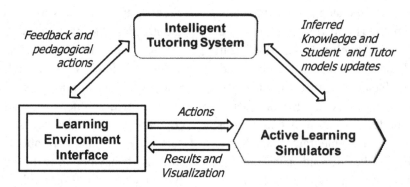

terface. However, the student needs to choose the best values for the exploration variables (in a range) to solve a problem or to reach a given goal. The ITS takes care of students' interactions and gives them the most suitable feedback. In the following sections, the methodology that we follow to define the main elements of an ITS is illustrated.

PROBABILISTIC RELATIONAL MODEL

The methodology used to implement the ITS is based on PRMs, which facilitate the development starting from the domain objects throughout the probabilistic models. The first step is to identify the classes in the model. We define the dependency model at class level, allowing it to be used for any knowledge-object in the class. This helped us to understand and build the probabilistic model. The classes and their relationships provided a general schema. Based on this schema, a skeleton is derived which integrates the relevant variables and their dependencies into a Bayesian network. Finally, a particular BN is obtained from the skeleton for each specific experiment in certain domains. Our ITS has four modules, which use PRMs as described below.

Figure 2. A PRM schema for the ALS's student model

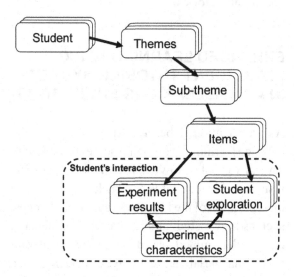

Student Model

In order to apply PRMs to student modeling (Sucar L.E. & Noguez J., 2008), the main knowledge-objects involved in the domain were identified. Then the dependency model at the class level was defined. The general schema for the student model and for the present case study is depicted in Figure 2.

For each class, a number of attributes (information variables and random variables) are defined, as shown in Figure 3.

Figure 3. A general probabilistic relational student model. The model specifies the main classes of objects, their attributes (information and random variables) and their dependencies.

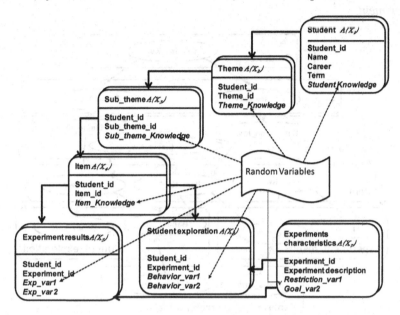

Once the model is specified at the class level (including the attributes and their dependencies), it is possible to extract a skeleton, which is a general Bayesian network model as a fragment of the main model. A skeleton obtained from the model in Figure 3 is depicted in Figure 4.

This network represents the dependencies among random or chance variables. Knowledge-objects are represented by different levels of granularity, and by the results of the experiments – in terms of performance and experiment results. Note that the general schema allows the creation of a skeleton representing a subset of random variables that may be of interest at a given time. It also supplies information variables used to build the database entities, in order to develop the PRM. From each skeleton, it is possible to define different instances according to the values of specific variables in the probabilistic model. The parameters of the PRM consist of a CPT for each variable (attribute) given its defined parents. These parameters are defined based on the skeleton of the relational schema.

The Knowledge-Base

The knowledge base refers to the database providing the means for the computerized collection, organization, and retrieval of knowledge of the specific domain. In this case the student's knowledge-base has different levels of granularity. It is organized in a hierarchical structure, from themes to sub-themes, and from sub-themes to knowledge items, and knowledge sub-items. When a student performs an experiment in the learning environment, the student model propagates the evidence from the experiment evaluation to the knowledge-objects in the knowledge-base. This knowledge base enables us to accumulate the knowledge evidence of the whole course for each student by combining information data with probabilistic values. These data could be useful to apply learning techniques to validate the structural probabilistic model and the conditional probabilistic tables.

Figure 4. A general skeleton obtained from the schema shown in Figure 3. This skeleton specifies a general probabilistic model for any experiment of the ALS environment, which is later instantiated for a particular experiment.

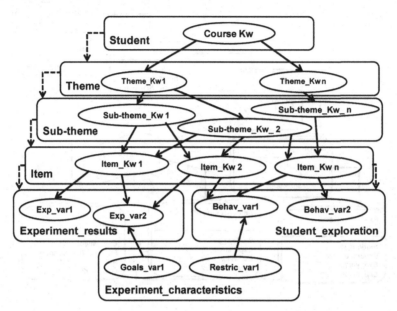

Interaction and Behavior Analysis

To evaluate student knowledge in each experiment, a set of exploration variables (student exploration), performance variables (experiment results), and knowledge items are defined. These form a general schema for interaction analysis. When the student finishes one experiment, the variable values are converted to probabilistic values in order to propagate the evidence and determine the student's inferred knowledge about each knowledge object.

The Tutor Model

After the student model is updated, the inferred results are used by the tutor module. Using PRMs, the main knowledge-objects involved in the tutor are identified. The dependency model at the class level is defined. The general schema for the tutor model is depicted in Figure 5.

To define the tutor skeleton we use the Decision Networks' features for addressing the provi-

sion of the best action as it is shown in Figure 6. The uncertainties associated with various variables of interest are represented by the probability distributions, which are encoded in the Decision Network. The powerful inference capability of decision networks enables the explanation of observations made about the student's interaction, as well as predictions based on the knowledge evidence. The use of Decision Networks provides a convenient way to control how the tutor makes decisions. Adjusting the conditional probabilities and the utility functions will influence how the decision is made. Another way to exert control is to adjust internal parameters, which are monitored at simulation time by the network in order to make inferences and assessments. The hierarchical structure helps to ensure a manageable number of variables in each individual network and reusability of the functionality of component networks.

A skeleton obtained from the model in Figure 6 is depicted in Figure 7. This network represents the dependencies among uncertainty or chance variables, but in this case we also include decision

Figure 5. A PRM schema for the ALS tutor model

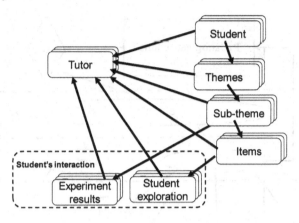

Figure 6. DN for ALSs

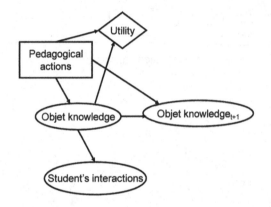

and utility nodes because the tutor should have the most suitable feedback according to the student's performance, i.e. we obtain an influence diagram. For example, for a good selection of variable values, the probability that a student knows a particular item, sub-theme, or theme increases. Then the tutor sends an appropriate congratulation message. The best pedagogical action in the DN of each ALS was initially defined by expert professors in the knowledge domain.

In the following sections, the proposed methodology for incorporating DDNs is described.

DDN APPLICATION IN ALS

The tutor model should also consider the dynamic properties of the student's learning when the student is interacting with simulators. Therefore we extend the model with a DDN in which some experiment results and the object knowledge at different levels of granularity are considered at different times to determine the best decision (pedagogical action). The pedagogical action is chosen by evaluating a utility function and influencing the same variable at the next time step.

This makes it possible to take into account the accumulated evidence from previous experiments and the results of the current experiment. The aim is to update the knowledge objects and choose the best pedagogical action. Figure 8 illustrates the dynamic model for an ALS environment.

The utility table entries are set based on the teacher experience about the best over all possible pedagogical actions according to the given knowledge state and experiment results inferred from the input factors (student's interaction). A generic example is shown in Table 1.

EXPERIMENT DESIGN

In order to design a learning simulator that fosters comprehension and learning, the instructor should

Figure 7. A skeleton for the tutor model

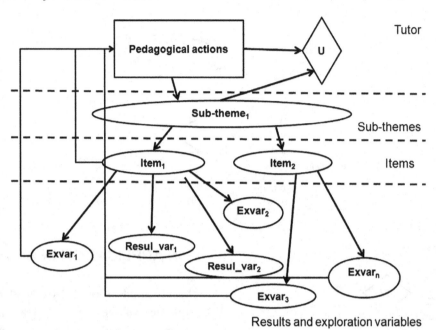

Figure 8. DDN for ALSs

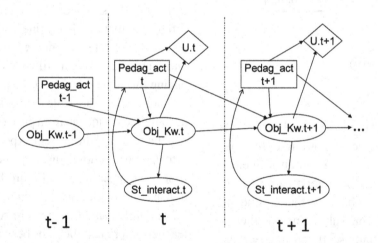

Table 1. Variables that affect the action selection decision

Var 1	Var 2	Var 3	Pedagogic Actions	Utility
Val 1.1	Val 2.1	Val 3.1	Act 1	U1
		Val 3.2	Act 2	U2
	Val 2.2	Val 3.1	Act 3	U3
		Val 3.2	Act 4	U4
Val 1.2	Val 2.3	--	Act 5	U5

consider an appropriate scenario with a challenging goal and with specific initial conditions. The goal should be motivating enough to enable student engagement through interaction with the simulator. The solution to the chosen problem involves the selection and manipulation of several physical quantities by the student. The physical quantities can take any value within specific ranges previously defined by the instructor. To attain the learning goal, students have to explore the consequences of choosing different values for each physical quantity. In each trial the student will learn more about the role of the chosen physical quantity. In each attempt the system will give appropriate feedback to the student, so that the student will learn more each time about the role of that chosen physical quantity. As a result, we expect that the student will make a better selection of parameters on successive attempts, until he or she finally attains the desired goal. It is necessary to be careful when designing a scenario. It must be non trivial, i.e., it should not be easily solved from the beginning. Also, to prevent simple memorization, the initial conditions must change randomly within specified ranges at each attempt. In addition, the initial conditions influence to some extent the level of challenge presented by the problem. Nevertheless, the values of physical quantities themselves are not so important: the main goal is the overall student understanding of the physical phenomena modeled by the simulator.

CASE STUDY

Conservation of Linear Momentum is one of the key topics of most first year Physics courses at undergraduate level. Therefore, a case study in Physics, a scenario where students can recognize and apply this law was chosen. The concept of linear momentum (or momentum) of an object is defined as the product of its mass and its velocity, the latter being expressed as a vector (Young, 2008). Also, the student must realize that

the total momentum of a given system is conserved only if the resultant external force on the system is zero. Hence, a scenario was envisaged describing the story of an astronaut in trouble (Muñoz, 2009). The astronaut is located in interplanetary space far from his spaceship with a limited oxygen supply in his tank. The astronaut attempts to save himself by returning to the spaceship before the oxygen supply is over. Initially, he is at rest relative to the spaceship and carries with him some hand tools. The hand tools should be thrown in such a way that the astronaut moves towards the spaceship. The problem statement is the following: *"The astronaut Neri Vela is on a mission on an asteroid near Europa, one of the four Galilean moons of Jupiter. He is outside of his spaceship repairing a sensor device set in the surface of the asteroid, when the security cable that connects him to the spaceship suddenly breaks up. He just has at this time a metal tank with a very limited supply of oxygen. If the astronaut carries with him a screwdriver, a pipe wrench and an adjustable wrench, how could he use these tools to arrive to his spaceship before his source of oxygen is completely exhausted? You should help the astronaut get back to his spaceship on time by selecting the astronaut's mass and the tools that must be thrown, along with their mass, velocity and direction"*. In this scenario, it is assumed that in interplanetary space, far away from massive bodies, the force of gravity on the system composed by the astronaut and his tools is small enough to be neglected in a first approximation. Hence, the total linear momentum of the system is conserved. In addition, it is implicitly assumed that the astronaut will be saved if he is able to arrive to the spaceship before his oxygen supply is exhausted. A range of values was set for some variables to offer a challenging problem to the student. The selected restriction variables were the distance between the astronaut and the spaceship, and the amount of oxygen available in the tank. We made several previous test calculations to determine the values of maximum distance to

Figure 9. The PRM schema for the case study

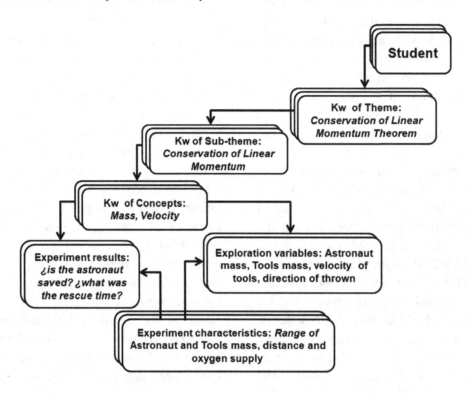

the spaceship and the minimum oxygen exhaustion time in order to provide a non trivial solution for this scenario. The instance of the general schema obtained is shown in Figure 9. Using this class diagram an experiment instance was defined for this scenario as shown in Figure 10.

The system then assigns, within previously defined ranges, random values to the initial distance from the astronaut to the spaceship, *D,* and the remaining time for the oxygen to be exhausted, T_{Oxygen}. The corresponding ranges are: 20 m $\leq$ $D \leq 25$ m and 40 s $\leq T_{\text{Oxygen}} \leq 60$ s. These values change every time the student initializes or resets the simulation. In this sense, the ALS is "dynamic", hindering the possibility that the student simply memorizes the values. The corresponding simulator interface is shown in Figure 11.

In order to save the astronaut, the student is asked to select: (i) the tools to be thrown, (ii) the mass of each tool, (iii) the velocity to throw the tools, (iv) the direction to throw the tools, and v)

suitable values for the astronaut's mass. These variables allow us to create a semi-open learning environment (Noguez J. & Sucar E., 2005), and they also are used to infer knowledge as explained above. The tools that can be selected are a pipe wrench, an adjustable wrench and a screwdriver. The possible mass ranges for the tools are: 0.80 kg $\leq M_{\text{Pipe Wrench}} \leq 1.2$ kg; 0.30 kg $\leq M_{\text{Adjustable Wrench}}$ ≤ 0.70 kg and 0.10 kg $\leq M_{\text{Screwdriver}} \leq 0.30$ kg. The velocity range to throw the tools is 0 m/s $\leq V_{\text{Tools}}$ ≤ 20m/s. The directions to throw the tools can be set *towards the spaceship,* "→", or *away from the spaceship,* "←". Finally, the astronaut's mass range is 60.0 kg $\leq M_{\text{Astronaut}} \leq 100$ kg.

If students fully understand the physical meaning of the law of conservation of linear momentum as well as the properties of linear momentum as a vector, they should recognize from the beginning that the tools must be thrown *away* from the spaceship to enable the astronaut to move *towards* the spaceship. Also they should realize

Figure 10. Experiment instance corresponding to the problem of conservation of linear momentum and obtained from the general skeleton

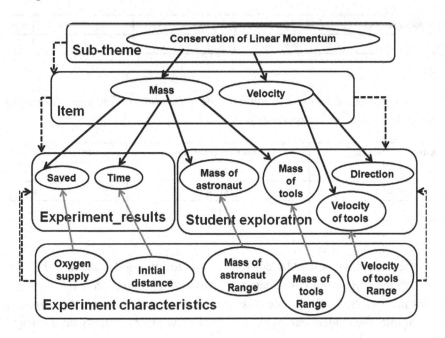

Figure 11. Active learning simulator interface

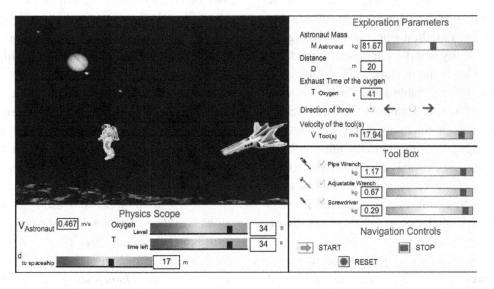

that the best choice is to simultaneously throw all the tools with their maximum velocities and to select the minimum astronaut's mass. The chosen set of values for the exploration parameters allow us to infer the student's level of comprehension about knowledge-items, sub-themes and themes.

To assess the cognitive state of the student, based on the results of the experiments as well as the student's interaction with the simulator, each

Table 2. Obtaining evidence from the student's selection for throwing the tools with a velocity (away from the spaceship) (marginal probabilities)

Selected Tools velocity (m/seg)	$15 \leq V_T < 20$	$10 \leq V_T < 15$	$5 \leq V_T < 10$	$V_T < 5$
Probabilities	**0.95**	0.6	0.3	0.1

Table 3. CPT used to propagate knowledge evidence based on the student's selection of the astronaut's mass: P(selected astronaut mass | mass concept)

Selected Astronaut Mass (kg)	P(Mass Concept=Known)	P(Mass Concept=Unknown)
$60 \leq M_A < 70$	**0.80**	0.1
$70 \leq M_A < 80$	**0.15**	0.2
$80 \leq M_A < 100$	**0.05**	0.7

selected value by the student is evaluated according to a carefully defined range of values selected by expert Physics professors, so the problem is not trivial. For example, the student can explore different values for the velocity to throw away the tools. As a result the astronaut will win linear momentum. The velocity range to avoid trivial problem solving is between 5 m/s and 20 m/s. The system defines the best selection as the highest possible velocity that the astronaut can obtain to attain more linear momentum while displacing in space. Accordingly, Table 2 is defined as follows.

As stated before, both the experiment results and the student interaction with the simulator are used to propagate evidence in the tutor probabilistic model. Each CPT corresponding to the experiment of conservation of linear momentum was defined by a group of expert professors teaching Physics. Table 3 shows the CPT used to assess the knowledge-item $M_{\text{Astronaut}}$.

After the evidence is propagated, the tutor model gives proper feedback using **DDNs**. A specific DN that addresses the best available feedback was defined and shown in Figure 12. The pedagogical actions include specific messages according to the student's performance. For example, if the direction to throw the tools is *towards* the spaceship "→", the ALS will give

the following feedback: "*YOU FAILED! The astronaut died.....You should repeat the experiment. In order to save the astronaut, in what direction must the tools be thrown?* Furthermore, even if students choose the correct direction to throw the tools (away from the spaceship), but they do not select suitable values for the remaining exploration parameters, the velocity acquired by the astronaut towards the spaceship will not be fast enough to arrive to the spaceship before the oxygen is exhausted. If they select unsuitable values for these variables and therefore the astronaut dies, the system gives the following feedback: "*YOU FAILED! the astronaut died....You should repeat the experiment. Please review the impact that the mass of the tools and the mass of the astronaut has on the Conservation of Momentum of the astronaut–tools–spaceship system. Are lighter tools or heavier tools better? Is a slim astronaut better than a fat one? Please review the impact that the tools throwing velocity has on the Conservation of Momentum of this system. Is high velocity or low velocity better?*"

In a similar way, Table 4 shows the CPT used to infer the knowledge-item, *Velocity*.

An example of relevant variables, feedback messages and utility values of the case study is shown in Table 5.

Figure 12. Decision network to determine the best pedagogic action

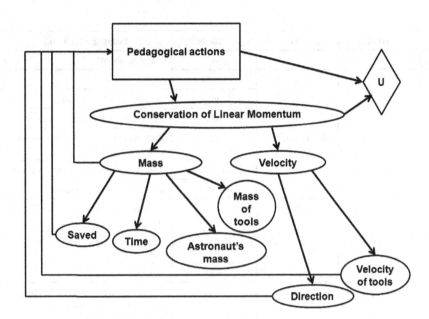

Table 4. CPT employed to propagate knowledge evidence based on the student's selection of the velocity of the tools: P(selected velocity of tools | velocity concept)

Velocity of tools (m/s)	P(Velocity Concept=Known)	P(Velocity Concept=Unknown)
$0 \leq V_T < 8$	0.1	0.75
$8 \leq V_T < 15$	0.2	0.15
$15 \leq V_T < 20$	0.7	0.10

As we mentioned before, it is important to note that the probability of success depends to some extent of the random initialization of the distance to the spaceship, D, and the remaining time to finish the oxygen supply, T_{Oxygen}, both set by the ALS. For the most restrictive case, that is, maximum D and minimum T_{Oxygen}, only the best selection of parameters will save the astronaut. In contrast, for the least restrictive case, minimum D and maximum T_{Oxygen}, there is a wider range of parameter combinations that will enable the astronaut to be saved. However, even in the latter case, the parameter ranges were selected in such a way that the astronaut will be saved by only 30% of the possible selection of values for the

defined parameters, making the problem non trivial.

To accumulate student's performance and knowledge inference results, the PRM model was enhanced in a dynamic way. The reason for this extension is to prevent a sudden drop in the DDN's belief regarding student knowledge between slices. This phenomenon happens when a student previously had been successful at performing an experiment and he involuntarily distracts, therefore, failing the experiment. This enhancement, described in Figure 13, was performed through propagating the previous object knowledge evidence obtained and pedagogical action delivered before the last student's interaction.

Table 5. Segment of the table used to determine the best pedagogical action of the tutor model using utility values

Direction	Saved	Mass	Velocity	Pedagogic Actions	Utility
Right	Yes	--	--	Congratulations!	10
	NO	Good choice	Good	NA	-20
			Regular	Check your velocity values	8
			Bad	Think, the tools need more velocity	4
		Regular choice	Good	The tools velocity is OK, but mass need to be improved	6
			Regular	Velocity and mass need to be improved	3
			Bad	The velocity is not enough	-3
		Bad choice	Good	Velocity is Ok, but how about chosen mass	5
			Regular	The astronaut mass affect the impulse gain	2
			Bad	Take care of astronaut and tools mass	-5
Wrong	NO	--	--	Wrong answer! Study the linear momentum conservation law in your textbook!	-10

Figure 13. Dynamic decision network corresponding to the case study

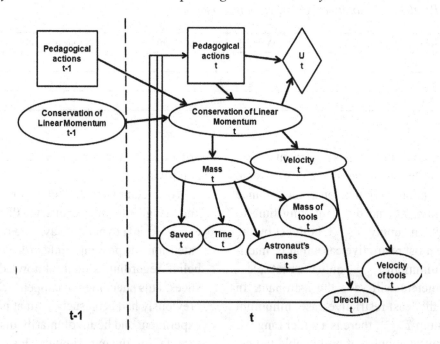

EVALUATION PROCESS

In our study we have analyzed the learners' exploration parameters while interacting with the ALS environment. We gained insight into the general effectiveness of the ALS, we conducted a study with a group of undergraduate students from different engineering majors coursing Physics I at Tecnológico de Monterrey, Mexico City campus in the January-May and August-December terms in the year 2009. The process of evaluation is described as follows:

January-May 2009 Term

The Pre-Phase

A written *Pre-test* including four questions related to the law of Conservation of Linear Momentum was applied to the student sample. To avoid the lecturer's influence over the results, the professors did not give the lectures of this theme while the students worked with our ALS.

Participants

A total of 45 students (N_{tot} = 45) participated in the study. They were divided randomly into two groups: one group interacted with the ALS (hereafter, the focus group, N_{focus} = 20) while the other group (hereafter, the control group, $N_{control}$ = 25) did not.

Experiment Design

The ALS was available to the focus group approximately during one week. This system also stored activity log files corresponding to the students' interaction sessions and results.

The Post-Phase

As with the pre-test, this was a written test comprised of four questions, or *Post-Test*, very similar to those applied in the *Pre-Test*. The post-tests were applied to the whole student sample once the focus group finished working with the ALS.

Analysis of Data and Results

Learning gains were calculated using the grades derived from the Pre-test and Post-test. In order to compare our results we computed a relative learning gain for each student in a similar way as defined by Hake (1998) and given in Equation (1):

$$G_{rel} = \frac{(PostTest - PreTest)}{(100 - PreTest)} \qquad (1)$$

Also, for comparison purposes, we have calculated a "simple" gain, as follows:

$$G = (PostTest - PreTest) \qquad (2)$$

Additionally, in order to assess how many attempts students made before saving the astronaut, we calculated an "efficiency", which was defined as the number of successful attempts relative to the total attempts made by the students.

We summarize our results in Tables 6 and 7, where we show the average values for the *pre-test*, the *post-test*, the *relative gain* and the *simple gain*, for the focus (N_{focus} = 20) and control ($N_{control}$ = 25) groups, respectively, with their corresponding standard deviations. As can be seen, students using the ALS had higher relative and simple learning gains when compared with those belonging to the students that did not interact with the ALS. Although N_{total} is still small, these results are encouraging and go in the right direction. It is interesting to note also that students in the average made a little more than 10 attempts and their average efficiency was one third, i.e. one successful attempt out of three. This shows that the proposed scenario was not trivial from the very beginning and presented some challenge to most students. This observation together with

Table 6. Summary of average learning gains and efficiency results for the focus group (N = 20)

Pre-Test	Post-Test	G_{rel}	G	Attempts	Efficiency
56 ± 21	76 ± 22	0.44 ± 0.32	20 ± 5	11	0.34

Table 7. Summary of average learning gains for the control group (N = 25)

Pre-Test	Post-Test	G_{rel}	G
60 ± 18	69 ± 13	0.13 ± 0.20	9 ± 5

Table 9. Summary of gains and efficiency results for the group using the ALS without tutor (ALS Group, N = 11)

Pre-Test	Post-Test	G_{rel}	G	Efficiency
59 ±23	73 ±26	0.27±0.33	14 ±13	0.28±0.15

Table 8. Summary of gains and efficiency results for the group not using any ALSs (Control Group, N = 34)

Pre-Test	Post-Test	G_{rel}	G	Efficiency
71 ±23	74 ±16	0.19±0.15	3 ±10	-

Table 10. Summary of gains and efficiency results for the group using the ALS with tutor (ALS with tutor Group, N = 12)

Pre-Test	Post-Test	G_{rel}	G	Efficiency
65 ±27	79 ±18	0.57±0.20	15 ±14	0.49±0.38

the higher gains obtained by the students in the focus group, when compared with those students in the control group, reinforces the assertion that the ALS promoted an enhanced comprehension of the Conservation of linear momentum law.

August-December 2009 Term

Another evaluation process was carried out with 57 engineering students from August to December in 2009. The students were enrolled in the course Physics I at Tecnológico de Monterrey, Mexico City. We had a control group (not using any ALSs) comprised of 34 students, a group comprised of 11 students using the ALS without tutor, and a group comprised of 12 students using the ALS with tutor. The pre-phase, experiment design, post-phase, data analysis was similar to that for the January-May 2009 term. The corresponding results are summarized in Table 8, 9 and 10.

From Tables 8 to 10 can be seen that the students using the ALS had higher relative and simple learning gains when compared with those

belonging to the students that did not interact with the ALS; and the students using ALS with ITS had higher relative and simple learning gains when compared with those belonging to the students that only interact with the ALS. Those results all go in the right direction in the sense that this ALS with ITS learning environment promoted an enhanced understanding of the linear momentum conservation law when is compared to ALS and control groups.

RESULTS AND DISCUSSION

We calculated the students' learning gains through the comparison of the students' marks achieved in the *post-tests* and *pre-tests*. The student sample was comprised of 45 students in the first semester in 2009 and 57 students in the second semester of this year. The first evaluation proved the enhancement of learning and understanding through employing ALSs and IT resources. In this case, the students' relative gains from using the ALS were almost twice the learning gains of the students that didn't interact with the ALS. In the second evaluation, we divided the students into groups as follows: (a) a control group, without any ALS environment, (b) a groups using an ALS without tutor, and (c) a group using an ALS with tutor. Also, the found learning gain for the ALS with ITS sample is longer than the ALS and control group. We also applied a qualitative survey enquiring students about the motivation experienced while interacting with the ALS. Some students said that the challenge involved in the situation encouraged them to think on the best way to solve the problem and act in the virtual environment. Therefore, we noted that the ALS stimulated the students' curiosity during the learning process.

CONCLUSION AND FUTURE WORK

Active Learning Simulators (ALSs) enable students to practice and conduct experiments in a safe environment - at anytime, and in anyplace. An ALS enhances learning and provides the bridge from concept to practical understanding. In order to design a learning simulator that fosters comprehension and learning, the instructor should consider an appropriate scenario with a challenging goal and with specific initial conditions. The goal should be motivating enough to enable student engagement through the interaction with the simulator. The solution to the problem that we designed involves the selection and manipulation of several physical quantities by the student. The physical quantities can take any value within specific ranges previously defined by the instructor. To attain the learning goal, students have to explore the consequences of choosing different values for each physical quantity. In each trial the student will learn more about the role of the chosen physical quantity. In each attempt the system will give appropriate feedback to the student, so that the student will learn more each time about the role of that chosen physical quantity. As a result, we

expect that the student will make a better selection of parameters on successive attempts, until he or she finally attains the desired goal. It is necessary to be careful when designing a scenario. First, it must be non trivial, i.e., it should not be easily solved from the beginning. Also, to prevent simple memorization, the initial conditions must change randomly within specific ranges at each attempt. In addition, the initial conditions influence to some extent the level of challenge presented by the problem. Nevertheless, the values of physical quantities themselves are not so important: the main goal is the overall student understanding of the physical phenomena modeled by the simulator

Through adding ITS into ALSs, guidance, assistance and support can be provided to the student as necessary. The intelligent tutor could assist the learner when the results of an experiment did not go well. The tutor must infer the level of student understanding, based on interactions when performing experiments. Thus, students are evaluated indirectly, based on the results of the experiments and their exploration behavior within the environment. Furthermore, based on learner interaction with the ALS, the tutor determines the student's level to decide the most suitable pedagogical action. Given the inherent uncertainty in these tasks, a student model that reasons under uncertainty is required. We have incorporated relational probabilistic models in BN in order to infer the most probable student's level of understanding of Physics concepts through the interaction with an ALS. The PRM was also used to define the tutor module. By adding an Intelligent Tutoring System, it is possible to provide personal *ad hoc* feedback to each student based upon Dynamic Decision Networks, the student interaction and student's behavior within the ALS.

The derived results for our case study in Physics go in the right direction in the sense that the learning gains for students using our ALS are higher than those obtained by students who did not use any ALS, and the gains are still higher when an ITS is added. Preliminary results give us confidence to elaborate other Physics scenarios within an appropriate ALS and ITS using DDNs. These intelligent environments enhance the students' learning about Physics concepts. We plan to increase the size of our student sample to give statistical significance to the derived learning gains. We also will carry out a study on how the feedback from the system correlates with learning outcomes, and how student interactions correlate with learning outcomes.

ACKNOWLEDGMENT

This work was supported by Tecnológico de Monterrey, Campus Ciudad de México, through the e-Learning research group. We want to recognize the contributions and support provided by Dr. Tom Lunney and Prof. Paul Mc Kevitt at the University of Ulster (UU), Magee campus. In addition we want to acknowledge the support provided by the European Union Scholarship "Alßan" to provide the funding during Karla Muñoz's M.Sc. studies at the UU. Finally, we want to acknowledge the support provided by the FONCICYT (European Union - National Research System of the Science and Technology Mexican Council) project number 95185.

REFERENCES

Adams, W. K., Reid, S., LeMaster, R., McKagan, S. B., Perkins, K. K., & Wieman, C. E. (2007). A study of educational simulations - Interface design. *Journal of Interactive Learning Research, 19*.

Bonwell, C., & Eison, J. (1991). *Active learning: Creating excitement in the classroom- AEHE-ERIC Higher Education Report No.1.* Washington, DC: Jossey-Bass.

Bull, S., & McKay, C. (2004). An open learner for children and teachers: Inspecting knowledge level of individuals level of individual and peers. *Proceedings of Intelligent Tutoring Systems 7th International Conference ITS2004,* Maceio, Alagoas, Brazil (pp. 646-655). Springer Verlag.

Bunt, A., & Conati, C. (2003). Probabilistic student modeling to improve exploratory behavior. *Journal of User Modeling and User-Adapted Interaction, 13*(3), 269–309. doi:10.1023/A:1024733008280

Collins, J., Greer, J., & Huang, S. (1996). Adaptive assessment using granularity hierarchies and Bayesian nets. *Proceedings of the Third International Conference ITS'96* (pp. 569-577). Springer-Verlag.

Hake, R. R. (1998). Interactive-engagement versus traditional methods: A six-thousand-student survey of mechanic test data for introductory physics courses. *American Journal of Physics, 66*(1), 64–74. doi:10.1119/1.18809

Howard, R. A., & Matheson, J. E. (1984). Influence diagrams. In *Readings on the principles and applications of decision analysis, II.* Menlo Park, CA: Strategic Decisions Group.

Jensen, F. V., & Nielsen, T. D. (2007). *Bayesian networks and decision diagrams. Information Science and Statistics* (p. 463). New York, NY: IEEE Computer Society.

Koller, D., & Friedman, N. (2009). *Probabilistic graphical models: Principles and techniques.* MIT Press.

Lean, J., Moizer, M., & Towler, C. A. (2006). Active learning in higher education. *Journal of Simulation and Games, 7*(3), 227–242.

Liu, X. M., Cao, Y. D., & Wang, E. Z. (2006). Numerical simulation of electric field with open boundary using intelligent optimum charge simulation method. *IEEE Transactions on Magnetics*, *42*(4), 1159–1162. doi:10.1109/TMAG.2006.872479

Mabbott, A., & Bull, S. (2004). Alternative views on knowledge: Presentation of open learner models. *Proceedings of Intelligent Tutoring Systems, 7th International Conference ITS2004*, Maceio, Alagoas, Brazil (pp. 689-698). Springer Verlag.

Mayo, M., & Mitrovic, A. (2001). Optimising ITS behaviour with Bayesian networks and decision theory. *International Journal of Artificial Intelligence in Education*, *12*(2), 124–153.

McHaney, R., White, D., & Heilman, G. E. (2002). Simulation project success and failure: Survey findings. *Simulation & Gaming*, *33*(1), 49–66. doi:10.1177/1046878102033001003

Mesbahi, E., Norman, R., & Peng, M. W. C. (2007). An intelligent simulation model for design and costing of high temperature ballast water treatment systems. *Marine Technology*, *44*(3), 194–202.

Muñoz, K., Noguez, J., Mc Kevitt, P., Neri, L., Robledo-Rella, V., & Lunney, T. (2009). Adding features of educational games for teaching physics. *Proceedings of the 39th IEEE International Conference on Frontiers in Education (FIE2009)*. San Antonio, Texas.

Murray, R. C., & VanLehn, K. (2000). DT Tutor: A decision-theoretic, dynamic approach for optimal selection of tutorial actions. In G. Gauthier, C. Frasson & K. VanLehn (Eds.), *Intelligent Tutoring Systems, Fifth International Conference, ITS 2000*, (pp. 153-162). Montreal, Canada. New York, NY: Springer.

Noguez, J., & Sucar, E. (2005). A semi-open learning environment for virtual laboratories. [Springer-Verlag.]. *Lectures Notes in Artificial Intelligence*, *3789*, 1185–1194.

Novasim. (2009). *What is Simulation?* Retrieved November 2009, from http://www.novasim.com

Pearl, J. (1988). *Probabilistic reasoning in intelligent systems: Networks of plausible inference*. San Mateo, CA: Morgan Kaufmann Publishers, Inc.

Powell, J., Wright, T., & Newland, P. (2008). Fire play: ICCARUS - Intelligent command and control, acquisition and review using simulation. *British Journal of Educational Technology*, *39*(2), 369–389. doi:10.1111/j.1467-8535.2008.00831.x

Richard, L., & Gourderes, G. (1999). An agent-operated simulation-base training system –Presentation of the CMOS project. In Lajoie, S. P., & Vivet, M. (Eds.), *Artificial intelligence in education* (pp. 343–351). IO Pres.

Self, J. (1999). The defining characteristics of intelligent tutoring systems research: ITSs care, precisely. *International Journal of Artificial Intelligence in Education*, *10*, 350–364.

Shute, V., & Glaser, R. (1990). A large scale evaluation of an intelligent discovery world. *Interactive Learning Environments*, *1*, 55–77. doi:10.1080/1049482900010104

Sucar, L. E., & Noguez, J. (2008). Student modeling. In Pourret, O., Naim, P., & Marcot, B. (Eds.), *Bayesian networks: A practical guide to applications* (pp. 173–185). Wiley & Sons.

Tawfik, A. Y., & Khan, S. (2005). Temporal relevance in dynamic decision networks with sparse evidence. *International Journal of Applied Intelligence, Special Issue on Uncertain Temporal Reasoning*, *23*(2).

VanLehn, K. (2001). Bayesian student modeling, user interfaces and feedback: A sensitive analysis. *International Journal of Artificial Intelligence in Education*, *12*(2), 154–184.

Yilmaz, L. (2006). Expanding our horizons in teaching the use of intelligent agents for simulation modeling of next generation engineering systems. *International Journal of Engineering Education, 22*(5), 1097–1104.

Young, H. D., & Freedman, R. A. (2008). *University physics* (12th ed.). Pearson, Addison Wesley.

ADDITIONAL READING

Available from. http://dx.doi.org/10.1007/s11257-009-9062-8. (Accessed 19th December 2010).

Available from. http://www.educause.edu/EDUCAUSE+Quarterly/EDUCAUSEQuarterlyMagazineVolum/ClickersintheClassroomAnActive/157458. (Accessed 19th December 2010).

Conati, C. & Maclaren, H. (2009) Empirically Building and Evaluating a Probabilistic Model of User Affect. User Modeling and User-Adapted Interaction [online].

For more information about active learning concepts we suggest (Martyn, 2007); an excellent introduction to influence diagrams is (Jensen, 2007); a detailed example of a technique employed to implement pedagogical actions using Dynamic Bayesian Networks (DBNs) in *PrimeClimb* is given in (Conati & Maclaren, 2009). Puterman (Puterman, 94) provides a comprehensive introduction to MDPs. Woolf (Woolf, 2009) provides a thorough and engaging introduction to the field of intelligent tutoring and related AI-based educational systems.

Information Science and Statistics, New York. IEEE Computer Society.

Jensen, F. V., Nielsen T. D., (2007). Bayesian Networks and Decision Diagrams.

Martyn, Margie (2007). "Clickers in the Classroom: An Active Learning Approach". EDUCAUSE. Quarterly (EQ) 30 (2).

Puterman, M. L. (1994). *Markov Decision Processes: Discrete Stochastic Dynamic Programming*. New York, NY: John Wiley and Sons.

Woolf, B. (2009). *Building Intelligent Interactive Tutors: Student-centered strategies for revolutionizing e-learning*. Morgan Kaufmann.

KEY TERMS AND DEFINITIONS

Active Learning Simulators (ALS): Simulators where learners can experiment with different aspects and parameters of a given phenomenon to observe the effects of their decisions. The students are able to select different parameters in each system execution, trying to improve knowledge and understanding.

Bayesian Networks (BN): Are probabilistic graphical models that represent a set of random variables and their conditional dependencies via a directed acyclic graph (DAG).

Dynamic Decision Networks (DDN): Represents decision nodes containing the set of values corresponding to the best possible actions, and employs utility nodes to select the best decision.

Influence diagrams: Acyclic directed graphs representing decision problems.

Intelligent Tutoring Systems (ITS): A system that tries to emulate a human tutor by adapting itself to the learner.

Probabilistic Relational Models (PRMs): Are a language based on relational logic for describing statistical models of structured data.

Student Model: Part of an ITS that is built for recognizing student plans or solution paths, or for evaluating student performance or problem solving skills.

Chapter 12

An Intelligent Assistant for Power Plant Operation and Training Based on Decision-Theoretic Planning

Alberto Reyes
Instituto de Investigaciones Eléctricas, México

Francisco Elizalde
Instituto de Investigaciones Eléctricas, México

ABSTRACT

In this chapter we present AsistO, a simulation-based intelligent assistant for power plant operators that provides on-line guidance in the form of ordered recommendations. These recommendations are generated using the formalism of Markov decision processes over an approximated factored representation of the plant. The decision model approximation is based on machine learning tools. We also described an explanation mechanism over these recommendations based on i) the selection of a relevant variable and ii) the automated construction of graphical explanations for operators. The explanation module analyzes the recommender system's decision model to support the reason why a recommendation should be followed.

INTRODUCTION

One of the essential requirements in the operation of complex processes, such as power plants, is to deal with a great amount of information for the decision making process. For instance, under unusual or abnormal situations, an operator must select the relevant information to rapidly identify the source of the problem, and effectively define the action plan to set the process into safe conditions. It is under these circumstances that the support of an intelligent assistant system (IAS), capable to interact with the operator and carry out

DOI: 10.4018/978-1-60960-165-2.ch012

some support functions required by the system, can become an important aid.

Intelligent assistants (IA) are knowledge-based systems for the decision support that provide users with accurate information at the right moment, and do suggestions and critiques during the decision making process. Optionally, an assistant could also adapt to users through simply observing their general behavior. In other words, the system could learn from users' experiences. Among the most representative work in the field of intelligent assistants applied to industry, ASTRAL (Caimi, Lanza, & Ruiz-Ruiz, 1999) is a simulator-based assistant for power operator's training. Its main functions are the recognition of the actions executed by an operator in a plant simulator, and the classification of detected errors with respect to an expected behavior. The main effort in this work is oriented to the development of explanation systems that support the operator's understanding about the plant state. SOCRATES (Vale et al., 1998) is a real time assistant for control center operators in alarm processing and energy restoration. The core of the system is SPARSE, an expert system initially developed to use it in power transmission and distribution control centers. SOCRATES also provides an intelligent tutor, SPARSE-IT, which fulfills two purposes: i) to show users how a trained operator solves problems and ii) to train the user to deal with specific situations and evaluate its performance. SART (Brézillion, Gentile, Saker, & Secron, 1997) is a traffic control support system for the French subway system, and implements an intelligent tutor with several functions such as: knowledge acquisition from operators, traffic simulation, model management of the network to test with alternative cases, enumeration of alternative solutions to incidents, and training of new operators.

In this chapter we present AsistO, a simulation-based intelligent assistant for power plant operators that provides on-line guidance in the form of ordered recommendations. It includes an explanation mechanism over these recommenda-tions to support the reason why a recommendation should be followed. The addition of this feature will allow the system to be an assistant not only for the decision support but also as an aid for operators training. As other authors, we consider the problem of generating recommedations as a sequential optimization problem that can be modeled as a Markov decision process (MDP). For instance, (Gui, David, & Ronen, 2002) de-scribe a particular MDP model, its initialization using a predictive model, the solution and update algorithm, and its actual performance on a com-mercial site. They also describe the particular predictive model they used which outperforms previous models. Their system is one of a small number of commercially deployed recommender systems. The work reported in (Reyes, Sucar, & Ibarguengoytia, 2005) was a pionneer in model-ling an industrial problem as a Markov decision process in which the action commands obtained help users to maintain a safe operation in the steam drum of a small power plant process. More recently, (Taghipour, Kardan, & Ghidary, 2007) proposed a reinforcement learning approach and a framework in which a web system interacts with the user and learns from its behavior.

The recent work on explanations for probabi-listic systems can be divided according to the type of models considered, basically Bayesian networks (BN's), decision networks and Markov decision processes. The main goal of explanations in BNs is to try to understand their inference process, and how it propagates through the network. One strategy is based on transforming the network to a qualitative representation, and using this more abstract model to explain the relations between variables and the inference process (Druzdzel, 1991), (Renooij & Gaag, 1998). The other strategy is based on the graphical representation of the model, using visual attributes (such as colors, line widths, etc.) to explain relations between nodes (variables) as well as the the inference process (Lacave, Atienza, & Díez, 2000). The explanation in decision networks has to do with understanding why a decision (or sequence of decisions) is optimal given the current evidence. Bielza et al. propose an explanation method for medical expert systems (Bielza, Pozo, & Lucas, 2003) which is based on reducing the table of optimal decisions obtained from an influence diagram, building a list that clusters sets of variable instances with the same decision. They propose to use this compact representation of the decision table as a form of explanation, showing the variables that are fixed as a rule for certain case. The explanation facilities for Bayesian networks proposed by Lacave et al. in (Lacave et al., 2000) were extended to influence diagrams in (Lacave, Luque, & Díez, 2007). Recently, an MDP model was integrated to a knowledge base for automated explanation generation (Elizalde, Sucar, Noguez, & Reyes, 2008). The use of templates and expert knowledge are a main issued for generating explanations automatically. In (Khan, Poupart, & Black, 2008) is also proposed an approach for the explanation of recommendations based on MDPs. They define a set of preferred scenarios that correspond to set of states with high expected utility, and generate explanations in terms of actions that will produce a preferred scenario based on predefined templates. In the present work, we consider that MDP models can also be explained exploiting the structure of a particular domain through the extraction of a relevant variable from a factored representation that can also be documented using a frame-based template.

FUNDAMENTALS

Learning Factored Models

A Markov decision process (MDP) (Puterman, 1994) models a sequential decision problem, in which a system evolves over time and is controlled by an agent. In a factored MDP, the set of states is described via a set of random variables $\mathbf{S} = \{X_1,..,X_n\}$, where each X_i takes on values in some finite domain $Dom(X_i)$. A factored MDP model might be learned from data based on a random exploration in a simulated environment. We assume that the agent can explore the state space, and that for each state–action cycle it can receive some immediate reward. Based on this random exploration, the reward and transition functions are induced.

Given a set of N non-ordered and rough (discrete and/or continuous) random variables $S^j = X_1,..,X_n$ defining a deterministic state, an action a^j executed by an agent from a finite set of actions $A = \{a_0,a_1\}$, and a reward (or cost) R^j associated to each state in an instant $j = 1,2,...,M$, we can learn a factored MDP model as follows:

1. Discretize the continuous attributes from the original sample $D = \{S,R,a\}$. This transformed data set is called the discrete data set $D_d = \{S_d,R_d,a_d\}$. For small state spaces, use conventional statistical discretization techniques. However, in complex state spaces, abstraction techniques are more efficient. For further details see (Munos & Moore, 1999; Reyes, Sucar, Morales, & Ibarguengoytia, 2006).

2. From the subset $\{S_d,R_d\}$ induce a decision tree, RDT, using the algorithm C4.5 (Quinlan, 1993). This predicts the reward function R_d in terms of the discrete state variables, $X_1,...,X_n$.

3. Format the discrete data set in such a way that the attributes follow a temporal causal ordering. For example variable $X_{0,t}$ before $X_{0,t+1}$, $X_{1,t}$ before $X_{1,t+1}$, and so on. The whole set of attributes should have the form X_t, X_{t+1}, a_t.

4. Prepare a data set for the induction of a set of 2-stage dynamic Bayesian nets. According to the action space dimension, split the discrete data set into $|A|$ subsets of samples for each action. Remove the attribute a_t from all of them.

5. Induce a transition model for each subset using the K2 algorithm (Cooper & Herskovits, 1992). The result is a 2-stage dynamic Bayesian net for each action $a \in A$.

This approximate model can be solved using value iteration to obtain the optimal policy. This approach has been successfully applied in a robot navigation domain (Reyes et al., 2005). For a more detailed description of MDPs and factored representations please refer to chapter 3 in this book.

Frame Systems

The frame based approach (Minsky, 1975) is a popular scheme for knowledge representation which has evolved over the years. This approach is particularly useful when not only a data structure is desirable, but when certain intelligence could be added to it. In general, a frame system can represent stereotyped situations through different levels of abstraction. Higher levels are fixed and are used to repre- sent things that usually are true. Lower levels have many terminals that can be instantiated with specific data. A frame has multiple slots used to define the various attributes of an object. The slots can have multiple facets for holding the value for the attributes, defaults, or procedures which are called to calculate a value. The various frames are linked together in a hierarchy with a-kind-of (ako) links that allow inheritance. There can also be defaults for attributes which might be overwritten for specific frames. Another feature of a frame based system is demons. These are procedures which are activated by various updating procedures.

Originally, frame-based systems were used to describe concepts and recognize specific instances of patterns. More recently, the frame based approach has been used to build spoken language applications by providing the meaning representation of a given sentence (Seneff, 1992). Frame systems also have a significant role in the

development of the semantic web (Lassila & McGuinness, 2001).

CASE STUDY

Modern power plants are following two clear trends. First, they are very complex processes working close to their limits. Second, they are highly automated and instrumented, leaving the operator with very few decisions. However, there still exist some maneuvers that require the experience and ability of the operator. In order to illustrate how important the decisions of a human operator are to overcome a transient, we have selected an electric load disturbance as a typical problem in the steam generation system of a combined cycle power plant.

In a combined cycle power plant, a gas turbine generates electricity and the waste heat is used to make steam to generate additional electricity via a steam turbine. The steam generation system of these type of plants starts in the heat recovery steam generator (*HRSG*), which is a process machinery capable of recovering residual energy from the exhaust gases of the gas turbine to heat up water. Eventually, the outlet of the HRSG is a mixture of steam and water (*Ffw*) flowing to the *steam drum* through the feedwater valve (*fwv*). The steam drum is a special vessel whose main function is the efficient separation of mixture that guarantees dry steam flow to the *steam turbine*. This steam flow is regulated by the main steam valve (*msv*). The *recirculation pump* is a device that extracts residual water from the steam drum to keep a water supply in the HRSG. The result of this process is a high-pressure steam flow (*Fms*) in the *steam turbine* that produce electric energy (*g*) in a *power generator*. The complete process control domain is shown in Figure 1.

An electric load disturbance (*d*) is an exogenous event that, as well as the control valves, could induce a state transition. The problem is to obtain a control strategy that considers stochastic com-

Figure 1. Simplified diagram of the steam generation system showing its main components, control devices and instrumentation. The gas turbine connection is not shown.

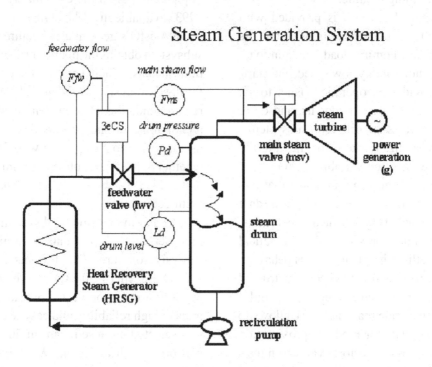

Steam Generation System

mands on the valves and, according to an experience-based preference function, maximizes the security in the drum, and/or the power generation. Since d is an event, it is not shown in the figure.

A practical solution is the use of a recommender system providing suggestions about how to make the best action on the process that corrects the problem. The recommendation system should be able to find an action policy according to the crisis dimension, taking into account that actuators are not perfect and can produce non-desired effects, and considering the performance, availability and reliability of the actual plant installations under these situations.

We consider that this problem is a sequential optimization problem that can be modeled as a Markov decision process (MDP) in which the state is observed directly through the process variables. We assume that the possible actions of opening and closing the main steam valve (*msv*) and the feedwater valve (*fwv*) can modify the system state

to eventually take the plant to a desired state. In this case, we are interested in minimizing the risk in the steam drum by rewarding safe states in this equipment.

In the following section, we describe the software modules required to build a recommender system in which the planning subsystem provides the optimal actions to maintain a secure operation when facing a load disturbance.

Recommender System for Operators Assistance

AsistO is an intelligent assistant that integrates a recommender system for on-line assistance and training in the power plant domain. The assistant is coupled to a power plant simulator capable of partially reproducing the operation of a combined cycle power plant, in particular, the steam generation process described in section. In this section we describe the on–line assistance module, and in section the training module.

The simulator (Figure 2) is provided with controls for setting power conditions in the gas and steam turbines (nominal load, medium load, minimum load, hot standby, low speed, and start-up). It also provides an operation panel to set load demands, unit trips, shutdowns, and other high-level operations in different subsystems. It includes a visualization tool for tracking the behavior of user-selected variables in time, and recording historical data. The simulator, that was implemented in MS Visual C++, can replicate data to MS SQL-Server and MySQL database formats. The core of the simulator is a set of mathematical equations modelling the plant process behavior. This process representation has been constructed through the years by domain experts. The simulator is used for two main reasons, first it allows to generate training data for model approximation and, second it allows to perform validation tests before the assistant can operate commercially.

The AsistO system is composed of a decision model base, a simulation data base, and the following subsystems:

1. Data management.
2. Model management.
3. Planning subsystem.
4. User interface.

The simulation data base comprises process signals generated in the simulator (outputs), and control signals (inputs) sent from the user interface to set a specific electric load or failure condition in the process.

The decision model base stores the transition and reward functions in a factored form. The transition model is implemented in Elvira (Consortium, 2002) (which was extended to handle Dynamic Bayesian Networks) and the reward function is implemented in Weka (Witten, 2005). The transition and reward functions are effectively learned using the K2 algorithm available in Elvira,

and the reward function is learned using a Java implementation of the C4.5 algorithm (Quinlan, 1993) available in Weka (J4.8).

In AsistO's general architecture the planning subsystem obtains the plant state from the simulation data base. Then it queries the policy function for the current state in the model base to obtain a recommendation. Both current state and recommendation, are shown graphically through the user interface to the operator who finally decides whether or not to execute the recommended command. Figure 3 shows the basic AsistO's general architecture.

The data management subsystem is composed of a set of tools for data administration and analysis software. The formats supported by AsistO are Microsoft SQL Server and MySQL. MySQL is open source and provides fast performance, high reliability and easy use. This format was selected because it can run in more than 20 platforms such as Linux, Windows, OS/X and HP-UX.

The model management subsystem manipulates the structures stored in the model base. It is also based on the academic tools Elvira and Weka.

The planning subsystem uses the decision models allocated in the model base and its inference algorithms to build an optimal policy plant state-recommendation. The resulting policy and utility functions are also stored in the model base. The planning subsystem in AsistO is based on SPUDD (Hoey, St-Aubin, Hu, & Boutilier, 1999), that includes a very efficient version of the value iteration algorithm for factored MDPs.

The user interface provides the communication with the environment. In this case, the power plant simulator is the environment, and the operator is the actor which provides the goals and executes the recommendations that modify the environment. The user interface is implemented in the Java language and it is provided with controls for command execution, load selection, failure simulation, and recommendation display. This module, that can also be used as a supervision

Figure 2. Steam Generation Simulator provided with controls, an operation panel, and data visualization tools. The top panel provides process setup features such as initial conditions or sampling frequency, and buttons for signal plotting and simulation control. The central panel allows to custumize the simulation by including or excluding HRSG's digital and analog signals. The bottom panel is splitted in two parts: one for custumizing the gas turbine signals and another for the steam turbine signals.

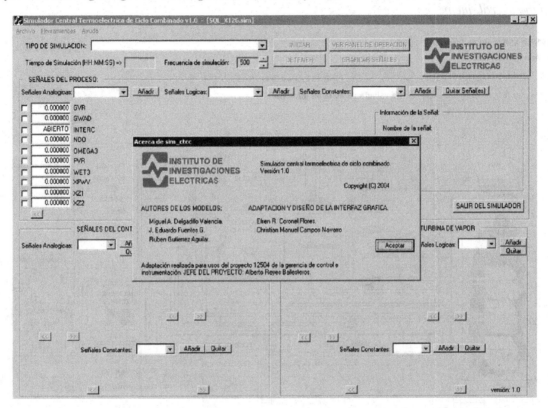

Figure 3. AsistO's general architecture. Given a current state, the planning subsystem queries a recommendation to the model base. This is presented to the user interface for the decision making.

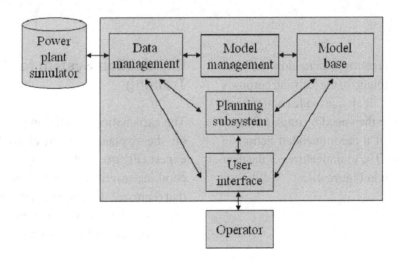

Figure 4. The user interface is the link between the recommender system and the operator. It includes supervision, problem specification and manual control capabilities. The top panel shows the messages area in which the recommendations are displayed. The central area contains a mimic panel either for process supervision and manual control. The bottom panel provides the operator a perspective of the optmization function, and controls to simulate disturbances. The model construction tools can be called from the overall menu.

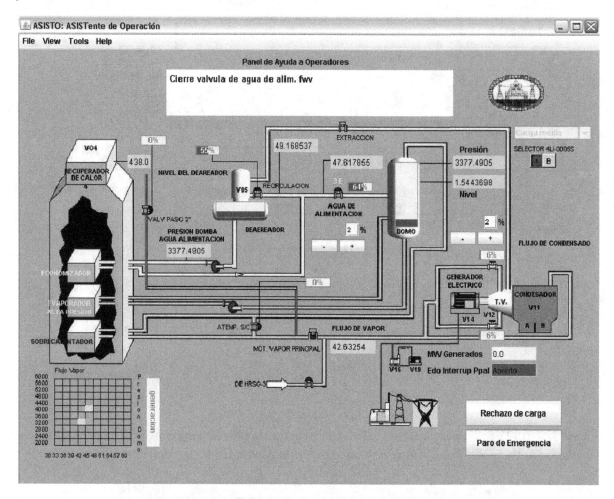

console, includes the controls for random exploration and system sampling for the learning purposes described in section. It also provides a graphical interface to observe the speed of impact from a correct execution of a recommended action in the plant operation. The main features of the user interface are shown in Figure 4.

Explanation System for Operators Training

The explanation generation mechanism is based on the explanations provided by the domain expert (Figure 5). To build the explanations we combine several knowledge sources: (i) the MDP that represents the process and defines the optimal actions; (ii) a domain knowledge base; (iii) a set of templates; and (iv) an operator model.

Figure 5. Explanation generation process. First, an optimal policy is obtained from an MDP. Using this policy and given the plant state, a recommendation is then obtained. Using the plant state and the recommendation, an explanation unit is selected and adjusted according to the user level. Explanation units are then gathered in order to make an explanation that will be displayed to the user.

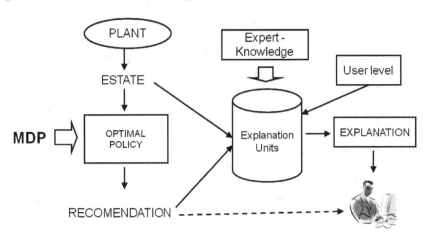

Although explanations generated manually are useful, they are difficult to obtain and to generalize for other plant subsystems or other domains. So that, we are interested in generating them automatically. When expert explanations were analyzed, we observe that they are focused on the most relevant variable, for example, the variable that in the current state of the system has the highest influence on the optimal action (Elizalde, Sucar, Reyes, & deBuen, 2007). Intuitively, we assume that the relevant variable X_R is the variable that has most impact in the expected utility (V), given the current state s and the optimal policy π^* (Elizalde, Sucar, Luque, Díez, & Reyes, 2008).

In this work, we consider at least 3 sources of knowledge: (i) a factored representation of the transition models in the MDP, (ii) an structured representation of the optimal policies and value functions, and (iii) domain knowledge stored in a knowledge base. Additionally, we have defined a set of general explanation templates based on the explanation units provides by the experts. Thus, our proposal for an automatic explanation mechanism, consists on extracting the relevant aspects from the knowledge sources to fill out an explanation template. This process is illustrated in Figure 6.

Relevant Variable Selection Algorithm

As mentioned before, our strategy for automatic explanation generation based on MDPs considers as a first step to find the most relevant variable X_R for certain state s and action a. All the explanations we obtained from the experts are based on a variable which they consider the most important under the current situation (state) and according to the optimal policy. Examples of some of these explanations in the power plant domain are given later on the paper. We expect that something similar may happen in other domains, so discovering the relevant variable is an important first step for policy explanation based on MDPs.

Intuitively, we can think that the relevant variable is the one with greater effect on the expected utility, given the current state and the optimal policy (Elizalde, Sucar, Luque, et al., 2008). So as an approximation to estimating the impact of each factor X_i in the utility, we estimate how much the utility, V, will change if we vary the value for each variable, compared to the utility of the cur-

Figure 6. Proposal for automatic explanations generation. In order to build an explanation, a selected template is filled out using values, trends, relations, and a relevant variable (X_R) extracted from a factored MDP model. Such as template is also complemented with the domain expert knowledge represented in a knowledge base (KB).

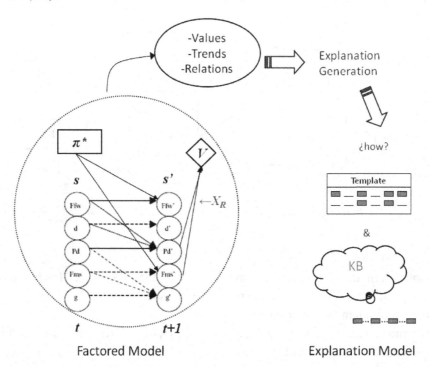

rent state. This is done by maintaining all the other variables, X_j, $j \neq i$, fixed. The process is repeated for all the variables, and the variable with the highest difference in value is selected as the relevant variable. An alternative criteria is to consider the action changes. That is, if the optimal action, a^*, in the current state, s, will change if a variable, X_i, has a different value. The variable that implies more changes will be in this case the relevant variable.

Thus, the algorithm to approximate the impact of each factor X_i in the expected utility is:

- estimate how much the utility, V, will change if we vary the value for each variable.
- this is compared versus the utility of the current state.

- maintain all the other variables, X_j, $j \neq i$, fixed.
- The process is repeated for all the variables.
- the variable with the highest difference in value is selected as the relevant variable (X_R).

Impact on Utility

The policy of an MDP is guided by the utility function, so the impact of a variable in the utility is an important aspect regarding its relevance for certain state. The idea is to evaluate how much will the utility function will change if we vary the value of one of the variables for the current state, keeping the other variables fixed. We analyze this potential change in utility for all the variables, and the one with the highest difference will be considered the most relevant variable.

Table 1. An example of the variable's impact. Analyzing each variable value maintaining the other variables fixed. In this example x5 has the biggest ΔV, therefore is selected as the relevant variable, X_R.

x1 (fms)	x2 (ffw)	x3 (d)	x1 (pd)	x5 (g)	V	ΔV	π^* vary?
0	**0**	**0**	**0**	**1**	**2601.29**		
1	0	0	0	1	2486.17		yes
2	0	0	0	1	3638.60		yes
3	0	0	0	1	3295.55		yes
4	0	0	0	1	2994.12		no
5	0	0	0	1	2761.32	1152.43	yes
0	**0**	**0**	**0**	**1**	**2601.29**		
0	0	0	0	1	2599.90	1.39	yes
0	**1**	**0**	**0**	**1**	**2601.29**		
0	0	0	0	1	2604.61	3.32	yes
0	**0**	**1**	**0**	**1**	**2601.29**		
0	0	0	1	1	2451.29		yes
0	0	0	2	1	2941.58		no
0	0	0	3	1	2791.82		no
0	0	0	4	1	2764.33		no
0	0	0	5	1	2624.39		no
0	0	0	6	1	2640.49		no
0	0	0	7	1	2601.29	490.29	yes
0	**0**	**0**	**0**	**1**	**2601.29**		
0	0	0	0	0	468.85	2132.44	yes

Let us assume that the process is in state s, then we measure the relevance of a variable X_i for the state s based on utility, denoted by

$rel_s^V(X_i)$, as:

$$rel_s^V(X_i) = \max_{s' \in neigh_{X_i}(s)} V(s') - \min_{s' \in neigh_{X_i}(s)} V(s')$$

where $neigh_{X_i}(s)$ is the set of states that take the same the values as s for all other variables $X_j, j \neq i$; and a different value for the variable of interest, X_i.

That is, the maximum change in utility when varying the value of X_i with respect to its value under the current state s. This expression is evaluated for all the variables, and the one with the highest value is considered the most relevant for state s, according to the value criteria:

$$X_R^V = argmax_i(rel_s^V(X_i)), \forall(i)$$

An example is depicted in Table 1. That is, the maximum change in utility when varying the value of X_i, maintaining all the other variables fixed.

Automatic Explanation Generation

The explanation generation mechanism is based on the explanations provided by the domain expert. To build the explanations we combine several knowledge sources: (i) the MDP that represents the process and defines the optimal actions; (ii) a

Figure 7. Block diagram of the explanation generation system. When the trainee makes an error (event), the current state, optimal action and relevant variable are obtained from the MDP. These are used as pointers to obtain the relevant elements from the KB to fill out an explanation template. The type of template is selected according to the user's model.

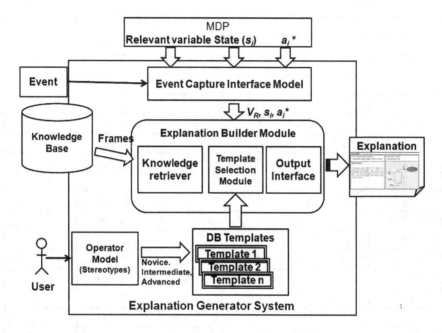

domain knowledge base; (iii) a set of templates; and (iv) an operator model.

The explanation system consists of three main stages (see Figure 7). As mentioned before, the relevant variable is a key factor for building an explanation. Therefore the first stage obtains the relevant variable and additional elements as the current state n_i and the optimal action a^*. In the second stage, according to the operator model (novice, intermediate or advanced), a template is selected. In the last stage, the template is filled out with information from a domain knowledge–base. Each of these stages are detailed in the following sections.

Explanation Template

The explanations are based on a predefined structure or *template*, inspired by the explanations obtained from the domain experts. Each template has a predefined structure and is configured to receive additional information from different sources. There are three types of templates according to the user: novice, intermediate and advanced. The main difference is in the amount and depth of the information provided, for novice users it is more detailed while for advanced operators a more concise explanation is given.

The explanation template has three main components:

1. The optimal action given the current state.
2. A verbal description of the main reasons for the previous action. The description depends on the user level.
3. A schematic diagram of the process, high-lighting the relevant variable.

The optimal action is directly obtained from an MDP given the current state of the plant, and the schematic diagram is previously defined for the process (or relevant process). Thus, the two

Figure 8. The KB represented as a frame hierarchy; it is divided in 3 parts: (i) actions, (ii) components, and (iii) variables

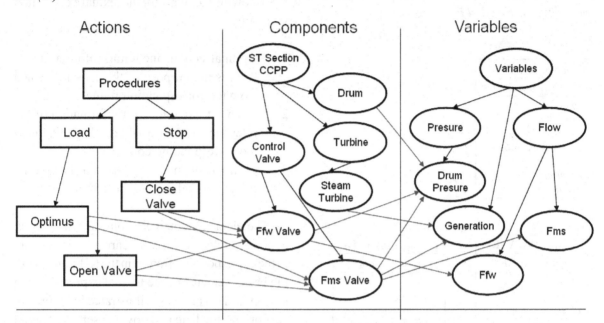

aspects that require a more complex procedure are the relevant variable (see previous sections) and the verbal component. The next section explains how to generate this verbal description by using a frame-based representation.

Knowledge Base

To complement the information obtained from the MDP model, additional domain knowledge is required about relevant concepts, components and actions in the process. A *frame* (Minsky, 1975) is a data structure with typical knowledge about a particular concept. Frames provide a natural way for representing the relevant elements and their relations, to fill out the explanations templates.

In the KB, the frames store the basic knowledge about the domain components, variables, actions, and their relationships (see Figure 8). This representation is an extension of the one proposed by (Vadillo-Zorita, Ilarraza, Fernández, Gutiérrez, & Elorriaga, 1994). The KB is conformed by three hierarchies: (i) procedures and actions, (ii)

components, and (iii) variables. It also includes relationships between the frames in different hierarchies: which actions affect a component and the variables associated to it. Part of the component hierarchy is depicted in Figure 9. It shows the frame for a *control valve*, and two subtypes, the feedwater valve (*Ffv*) and the main steam valve (*Msv*). A set of attributes is defined for each valve, with general aspects for the general valve and more specific ones for the others.

Each frame contains general knowledge for each procedure, component or variable; which is relatively easy to obtain from written documentation or expert explanations. The advantage of this representation is that the same KB can be used to generate explanations for any procedure related to the domain. To generate explanations in other domains a corresponding KB is required.

Next we describe how this KB is used to complete the explanation template.

Figure 9. A partial view of the component hierarchy. It shows the frame for a control valve and two subtypes: Ffw and Fms valves.

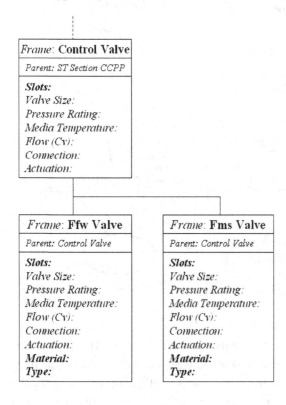

Filling the Template

As mentioned before, the template is adjusted according to the user level to fill it out. Next, the action is selected according to the optimal policy and the relevant variable is deduced with the described algorithm from the factored MDP model, and together, adding a schematic diagram of the process, are inserted in the corresponding template. The missing element is the textual explanation of *why* the action should be selected in the current situation. The explanation mechanism must then determine *what* should be included and *how much* detail to give to the user. *What* is determined by the template structure and *how much* by the operator level.

Inspired by the experts explanations, we define the following elements for the textual explanation structure:

1. Optimal action, including information on what is the purpose of the action obtained from the corresponding frame
2. Relevant variable, with information of the relevance of this variable and its relation to the corresponding component.
3. Component, including its main characteristics and its relation to the action.

The elements obtained from the MDP, state, action and relevant variables, are used as pointers to the corresponding frames in the KB from where the basic elements of the textual explanation are extracted. This process is illustrated in Figure 10.

For intermediate and novice users the textual explanation is extended by following the links in the KB hierarchies, adding information from frames in the upper part of the hierarchy. For instance, if the important component is the *feed water valve*, it includes additional information from the *control valve* frame for intermediate users, and more general knowledge on *valves* for the novice user. In this way, the amount of detail in the explanation is adapted to the user level.

The complete algorithm for explanation generation is depicted in Figure 11. In the following section we show specific examples of explanations generated in the domain of the power plants.

EXPERIMENTAL RESULTS

Recommender System

We used AsistO to run a series of experiments with different complexities. In the first set of experiments, we specified a 5-action hybrid problem with 5 variables (Fms, Ffw, Pd, g, d). We also defined a simple binary reward function based on the safety parameters of the drum (Pd and Fms). The

Figure 10. To fill the textual element in the explanation template, the information from the relevant variable, action and component frames are extracted and combined according to the user level. Through out an algorithm, the information is filled in using the corresponding frames. In this example, the template information is taken and selected from the Ffw valve-frame which is related to the variable Fms and also related to the Open Ffwv action-frame information.

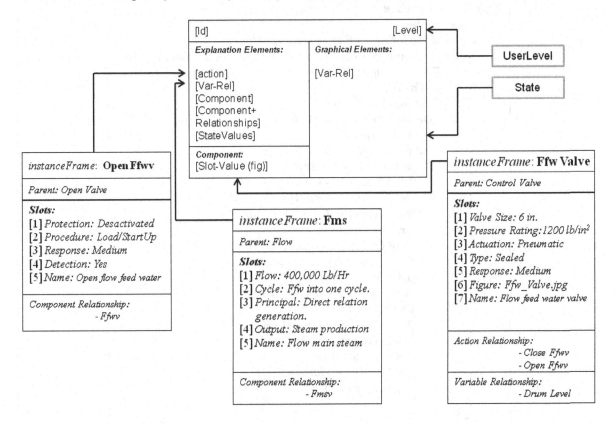

relationship between their values and the reward received can be seen in Figure 12 (left). Central black squares denote safe states (desired operation regions), and white zones represent non-rewarded zones (indifferent regions). To learn the model and the initial abstraction, samples of the system dynamics were gathered using simulation. Black dots in Figure 12 (right) represent sampled states with positive reward, red dots have no reward, and white zones were simply not explored. Figure 12 (left) shows the state partition and policy found (green arrows) by the learning system. For this simple example, although the resulting policy is not very detailed (discrete states are quite large), it follows the idea of going to the lower black

regions. When analyzed by an expert operator, this control strategy is near-optimal in most of the abstract states.

We solved the same problem but adding two extra variables, the position for valves *msv* and *fwv*, and using 9 actions (all the combinations of open-close valves *msv* and *fwv*). We also redefined the reward function to maximize power generation, *g*, under safe conditions in the drum. Although the problem increased significantly in complexity, the policy obtained is "smoother" than the 5-action simple version presented above. To give an idea about the computational effort, for a fine discretization (15,200 discrete states) this problem was solved in 859.2350 seconds, while using a

Figure 11. High–level algorithm for explanation generation. When an event occurs, the action and the relevant variable are instantiated. Via if–then rules, the information of the corresponding variables are adjusted to the user level to build an explanation, which is also correlated with the component information in the template.

```
ExplanationGeneration (a*, V_R, s, Comp, Exp, UsrLev)
    For each event e
    For each a*(s), V_R(x_i), s ∈ S, Comp, Exp, UsrLev;
    Where: a* = optimal action; V_R = relevant variable; s = current state;
        Comp = component; Exp = explanation; UsrLev = user level;
    IF e=true THEN {
            Get from MDP: a*(s)
            Get from ProbabilisticModel: V_R
            Get from Simulator: s
            Get from OperatorModel: UsrLev
            IF UsrLev = Novice THEN {
                Select Template = novice
                Get Frame(a*, Comp, V_R)
                Fill Template = Frame(a*, Comp, V_R) & s
                Exp = Template }
            ELSE IF UsrLev = Intermediate THEN {
                Select Template = Intermediate
                Get Frame(a*, V_R)
                Fill Template = Frame(a*, V_R) & s
                Exp = Template }
            ELSE IF UsrLev = Advanced THEN {
                Select Template = Advanced
                Get Frame(a*, V_R)
                Fill Template = Frame(a*, V_R) & s
                Exp = Template }
            }
    e = False;
    Return Exp;
```

more abstract representation (40 discrete states) it took only 14.2970 seconds. In both cases, the approximated models were found using the SPUDD system.

For a more detailed description about how to build the abstract factored representation used in these experiments please refer to (Reyes et al., 2006).

Explanation System

Relevant Variable Selection

In a first stage we evaluated the selection of the most relevant variable, and compared these to the ones given by the domain expert. In the power plant domain there are 5 state variables (three binary variables, one with 6 values and other with 8 values), with a total of 384 states. We analyzed a random sample of 30 states, nearly 10% of the total number of states. For the 30 cases we obtained the most relevant variable(s); and compared these

Figure 12. Process control problem. Left: reward function where black dots represent desired regions, discrete state partition (in this case 10 states) and policy found with value iteration. Right: exploration trace, where black dots represent sampled states with positive reward, red dots have no reward, and white regions represent unexplored zones.

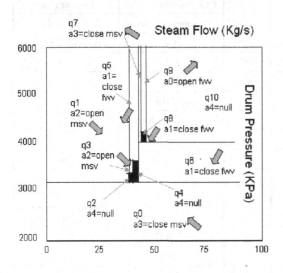
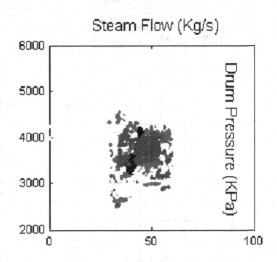

with the relevant variables given in the explanation units provided by the expert.

In order to perform a complexity analysis of the relevant variable selection algorithm, it is required to know how much the run–time increases given the size of the input (worst case analysis) (Aho, Hopcroft, & Ullman, 1998). The result is the term of the function that grows up faster, e.g. if the increment is equal to n^2 then the algorithm order has a complexity of O(n^2). In the 5 state–variable problem the computational effort to obtain the resulting inference from the factored MDP has a cost of 90.00 seconds.

Table 2 presents the results of the 30 cases. For each case we show: (i) the current state, (ii) the value, (iii) the optimal action, (iv) the variable selected according to the change in utility, including this change, and (v) the relevant variable(s) given by the expert. Note that for some cases the expert gives two relevant variables. The system selects in 100% of the 30 cases one of the most relevant variables according to the expert. In the future we plan to extend the relevant variable

selection mechanism so we can obtain more than one relevant variable.

Explanation Generation

To evaluate the explanations generated by the system, we generated explanations for different situations, and compared this to the explanations given for the same state by the domain expert (Figure 13). Figures 14 and 15 depict an example of an explanation template generated. It contains on the left side: (i) the optimal action, (ii) why is important to do this action, (iii) which component is related with optimal action, and (iv) a description of the current state. In the right side the relevant variable is highlighted in an schematic diagram of the process.

To evaluate the explanations generated by the system we adapted the methodology proposed by (Lester & Porter, 1997). The idea is to ask a panel of experts to compare the explanations given by the system to those given by a human, in terms of several evaluation criteria.

Table 2. Results for the relevant variable selection phase. It shows for each test case: the state (random variables), the expected value (V), the optimal action (π^*), the relevant variable with $|\Delta V|$, and the variable(s) selected by the expert.

| | selected S | | | | | | | Experimental results | Relevant Var |
| | Var | | | | | | | Changes in Utility | |
Test	fms	ffw	d	pd	g	V	π^*	$|\Delta V|$	Selected by Expert
1	0	0	0	0	1	2601.29	a1	g = 2132.44	g,fms
2	0	0	1	3	1	2514.00	a2	g = 2235.79	g,fms
3	1	1	0	4	0	796.95	a2	fms =2413.53	fms,g
4	2	0	0	7	1	3488.60	a4	pd = 2762.60	pd,fms
5	3	0	0	0	1	3295.55	a3	g = 2427.94	g,pd
6	3	1	0	2	1	3053.19	a2	g = 2109.73	g,pd
7	4	0	1	0	1	2986.18	a1	g = 2257.11	g,pd
8	4	1	1	7	0	843.27	a4	pd = 3271.43	pd,g
9	5	1	0	1	1	3632.66	a0	fms = 3720.05	fms
10	5	1	1	1	1	3287.13	a0	fms = 3642.53	fms
11	0	0	0	4	0	468.85	a2	g = 2295.48	g
12	0	0	0	5	1	2624.39	a0	g = 2155.54	g,fms
13	0	0	0	6	1	2640.49	a0	g = 2171.64	g,fms
14	0	0	0	7	1	2601.29	a1	g = 2132.44	g,fms
15	0	1	0	5	0	468.85	a2	g = 2150.45	g,pd
16	0	1	1	7	0	566.76	a4	g = 2036	g
17	1	0	0	5	1	2406.17	a2	fms = 2116.43	fms
18	1	0	1	4	0	794.72	a4	pd = 3762.20	pd,g
19	1	1	0	5	0	766.95	a2	g = 1719.22	g
20	1	1	1	7	0	819.82	a4	pd = 3666.26	pd,g
21	2	0	0	1	1	6251.20	a0	g = 5394.74	g
22	2	1	0	2	1	3484.47	a2	pd = 2685.48	pd,ffw
23	2	1	0	6	0	850.83	a2	g = 2783.64	g
24	2	1	1	1	1	6180.16	a0	g = 5004.11	g,pd
25	3	0	0	4	1	3295.55	a3	g = 2427.94	g,pd
26	3	0	1	0	0	679.67	a3	pd = 2615.88	pd,g
27	3	1	1	2	1	3045.10	a2	pd = 1521.18	pd
28	4	0	0	0	1	2994.12	a1	g = 2135.25	g,pd
29	4	0	1	4	0	729.07	a4	pd = 3304.97	pd,g
30	5	0	0	5	1	2761.32	a4	fms = 2116.43	fms

We consider 4 aspects: (i) coherence, (ii) contents, (iii) organization, and (iv) precision. We did not consider the fifth one, style, as we do not pretend to generate explanations in natural language. Each one is evaluated in a numerical scale: 1=bad, 2=regular, 3=good, 4=excellent. Each expert is presented with two explanations, side by side, for the same case; one given by a

Figure 13. An example of an explanation defined by a domain expert. In this example the relevant variable is generation, $X_R = G$, as the absence of generation is the main reason to close the feed–water valve.

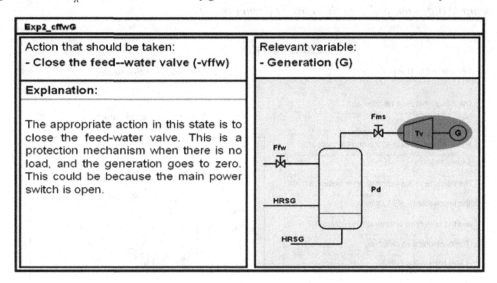

Figure 14. An example of an explanation template generated for a novice user. The template shows a detailed explanation for each section: the action (up-left), component (down-left) and relevant variable (up-right).

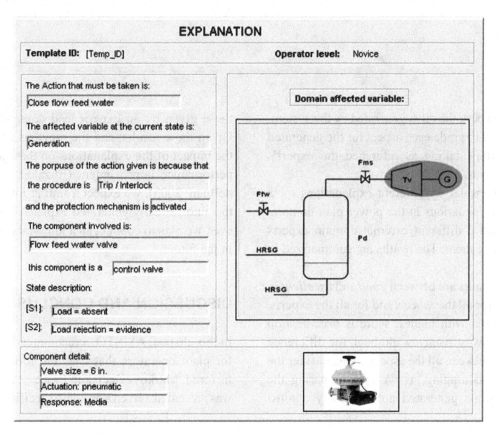

Figure 15. Another example of an explanation template generated for an intermediate user. The template shows an explanation about the action close flow feed water valve and it highlights the relevant variable in the schematic diagram, which in this case is drum pressure.

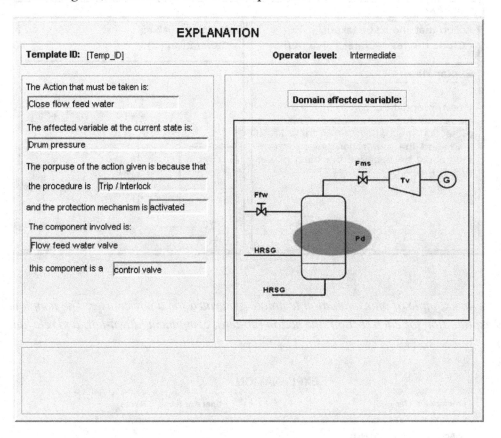

human expert, the other generated by the system. It is asked to grade each aspect for the generated explanations taking as reference the expert's explanations.

We consider 15 different explanations for a variety of situations in the power plan domain, and asked 6 different external domain experts to evaluate them. The results are summarized in table 3.

The results are between *good* and *excellent* in average for all the aspects and for all the experts. The criteria with highest score is *organization* and the lowest *contents*, although the difference is small between all the aspects. We consider the results encouraging, as we are comparing the explanations generated automatically against those given by an experienced domain expert. Given these results, and the previous results on the impact of the explanations on the operator's performance improvement (Elizalde, Sucar, & deBuen, 2005), we expect a similar impact with the automatically generated explanations; however, we plan to conduct an additional user study in the future.

DISCUSSION AND CONCLUSION

In this chapter, ASISTO, a recommender system for plant operators that uses the formalism of factored Markov Decision Processes (MDPs) was presented. Given a problem specification, the

Table 3. Results of the evaluation by a panel of experts. The table shows the average score per criteria–evaluator, and the totals for each dimension.

CRITERIA	CASES	EVALUATION PANEL							
		Eval 1	Eval 2	Eval 3	Eval 4	Eval 5	Eval 6	Average	Ranking
COHERENCE	C1 to C15	3.67	3.47	2.47	3.80	3.67	3.07	**3.36**	2⁰
CONTENT	C1 to C15	2.00	3.40	2.80	3.60	3.87	3.53	**3.20**	4⁰
ORGANIZATION	C1 to C15	2.87	2.93	2.93	4.00	3.93	3.67	**3.39**	1⁰
CORRECTNESS	C1 to C15	4.00	2.87	2.47	3.60	3.67	2.87	**3.24**	3⁰
Total		**3.13**	**3.17**	**2.67**	**3.75**	**3.78**	**3.28**	**3.30**	

objective of the MDP is to obtain useful recommendations (optimal policy) for getting a power plant to a state under optimal operation. AsistO uses a decision model base that represents the transition and reward functions in a factored form. The functions are represented through a two-stage Bayesian network and a decision tree, and they are effectively approximated from data using machine learning techniques. The recommender system aids operators not only during normal operation but under an unusual event.

The explanation system automatically explains the recommendations obtained from the recommender system to extend its usage for operator training. When analyzing the explanations provided by human experts, it was observed that they focused on the most relevant variable, i.e., the variable that in the current state of the system has the highest influence on the choice of the recommendation (optimal action). An algorithm based on the utility impact was used to select this relevant variable. The automatic generation explanation mechanism performs an analysis of the explanations given by the domain expert and a general template is displayed.

ASISTO will be extended to support partial observability, multiagent cooperation, and diagnosis capabilities. However, before this, a deeper review about how fast or how effective the system transients when applying an action has to be made and reported. A formal evaluation with real users and real plants should also be performed. Generally speaking, the assistant is still a laboratory system that has to be tested for commercial operation. We hope that in the near future, this prototype allows to model intelligent assistants for other domains with different scopes.

REFERENCES

Aho, A. V., Hopcroft, J. E., & Ullman, J. D. (1998). *The design and analysis of algorithms.* Addison-Wesley.

Bellman, R. (1957). *Dynamic programming.* Princeton, NJ: Princeton U. Press.

Bielza, C., del Pozo, J. F., & Lucas, P. (2003). Optimal decision explanation by extracting regularity patterns. In Coenen, F., Preece, A., & Macintosh, A. (Eds.), *Research and development in intelligent systems XX* (pp. 283–294). Springer-Verlag.

Boutilier, C., Dean, T., & Hanks, S. (1999). Decision-theoretic planning: Structural assumptions and computational leverage. *Journal of AI Research, 11,* 1–94.

Brézillion, P., Gentile, C., Saker, I., & Secron, M. (1997, February). SART: A system for supporting operators with contextual knowledge. In *Proceedings of the International and Interdisciplinary Conference on Modeling and Using Context (CONTEXT-97).* Rio de Janeiro, Brasil.

Caimi, M., Lanza, C., & Ruiz-Ruiz, B. (1999). *An assistant for simulator-based training of plant operator* (Tech. Rep.). Maria Curie Fellowships Annual Report.

Consortium, E. (2002). *Elvira: An environment for creating and using probabilistic graphical models (Tech. Rep.)*. Spain: U. de Granada.

Cooper, G. F., & Herskovits, E. (1992). A Bayesian method for the induction of probabilistic networks from data. *Machine Learning*.

Darwiche, A., & M., G. (1994). Action networks: A framework for reasoning about actions and change under understanding. In *Proceedings of the Tenth Conf. on Uncertainty in AI, UAI-94* (pp. 136–144). Seattle, WA.

Dean, T., & Givan, R. (1997). Model minimization in Markov decision processes. In *Proc. of the 14th National Conf. on AI* (pp. 106–111). AAAI.

Dean, T., & Kanazawa, K. (1989). A model for reasoning about persistence and causation. *Computational Intelligence, 5*, 142–150. doi:10.1111/j.1467-8640.1989.tb00324.x

Druzdzel, M. (1991). Explanation in probabilistic systems: Is it feasible? Will it work? In *Proc of the Workshop Intelligent Information Systems* (pp. 12-24). Poland.

Elizalde, F., Sucar, E., & deBuen, P. (2005). A prototype of an intelligent assistant for operator's training. In *International Colloquium for the Power Industry*. México: CIGRE-D2.

Elizalde, F., Sucar, E., Luque, M., Díez, J., & Reyes, A. (2008). Policy explanation in factored Markov decision processes. In M. Jaeger & Nielsen (Eds.), *Proceedings of 4rd European Workshop on Probabilistic Graphical Models PGM08* (p. 97-104). Hirtshals, Denmark.

Elizalde, F., Sucar, E., Noguez, J., & Reyes, A. (2008). Integrating probabilistic and knowledge-based systems for explanation generation. In *Proceedings of 3rd International Workshop on Explanation-Aware Computing ExaCt08* (vol. 391, p. 25-36). Patras, Greece: CEUR-WS.org.

Elizalde, F., Sucar, E., Reyes, A., & deBuen, P. (2007). An MDP approach for explanation generation. In *Proceedings of the 2nd Workshop on Explanation-Aware Computing, ExaCt07* (Vol. Technical Report WS-07-06, p. 28-33). Vancouver, Canada: AAAI Press.

Givan, R., Dean, T., & Greig, M. (2003). Equivalence notions and model minimization in Markov decision processes. *Artificial Intelligence, 147*(1-2), 163–223. doi:10.1016/S0004-3702(02)00376-4

Gui, S., David, H., & Ronen, B. I. (2002). An MDP-based recommender system. In *Proceedings of UAI-02*.

Hoey, J., St-Aubin, R., Hu, A., & Boutilier, C. (1999). Spudd: Stochastic planning using decision diagrams. In *Proc. of the 15th Conf. on Uncertainty in AI, UAI-99* (pp. 279–288).

Khan, O. Z., Poupart, P., & Black, J. (2008). Explaining recommendations generated by MDPs. In T. RB. et al. (Ed.), *Proceedings of the 3rd International Workshop on Explanation-Aware Computing ExaCt 2008*. Patras, Greece.

Khan, O. Z., Poupart, P., & Black, J. (2009). Minimal sufficient explanations for Factored Markov Decision Processes. In *Proceedings of the International Conference on Automated Planning and Scheduling (ICAPS)*. Thessaloniki, Greece.

Lacave, C., Atienza, R., & Díez, F. (2000). Graphical explanations in Bayesian networks. [ ]. Springer-Verlag.]. *Lecture Notes in Computer Science, 1933*, 122–129. doi:10.1007/3-540-39949-6_16

Lacave, C., Luque, M., & Dìez, F. J. (2007). Explanation of Bayesian networks and influence diagrams in Elvira. *IEEE Transactions on Systems, Man, and Cybernetics. Part B, Cybernetics, 37*, 952–965. doi:10.1109/TSMCB.2007.896018

Lassila, O., & McGuinness, D. L. (2001). The role of frame-based representation on the Semantic Web. *Electronic Transactions on Artificial Intelligence, 6*(5).

Lester, J. C., & Porter, B. W. (1997). Developing and empirically evaluating robust explanation generators: The knight experiments. *Computational Linguistics, 23*(1), 65–101.

Minsky, M. (1975). *A framework for representing knowledge* (Winston, P., Ed.). McGraw Hill.

Munos, R., & Moore, A. (1999, August). Variable resolution discretization for high-accuracy solutions of optimal control problems. In T. Dean (Ed.), *Proceedings of the 16th International Joint Conference on Artificial Intelligence (IJCAI-99)* (pp. 1348–1355). San Francisco, CA: Morgan Kaufmann Publishers.

Pearl, J. (1988). *Probabilistic reasoning in intelligent systems: Networks of plausible inference.* San Mateo, CA: Morgan Kaufmann.

Puterman, M. (1994). *Markov decision processes.* New York, NY: Wiley.

Quinlan, J. (1993). *C4.5: Programs for machine learning.* San Francisco, CA: Morgan Kaufmann.

Renooij, S., & van der Gaag, L. (1998). Decision making in qualitative influence diagrams. In *Proceedings of the Eleventh International FLAIRS Conference* (p. 410-414). Menlo Park, CA: AAAI Press.

Reyes, A., Sucar, L. E., & Ibarguengoytia, P. H. (2005, November). An operation auxiliary system for power plants based on decision-theoretic planning. In *Proceedings of the 13th IEEE International Conference on Intelligent Systems Applications to Power Systems ISAP05* (p. 286-290). Arlington, VA.

Reyes, A., Sucar, L. E., Morales, E., & Ibarguengoytia, P. H. (2006). Abstraction and refinement for solving Markov decision processes. In *Workshop on Probabilistic Graphical Models PGM06* (pp. 263-270). Czech Republic.

Seneff, S. (1992, March). TINA: A natural language system for spoken language applications. *Computational Linguistics, 18*, 61–86.

Taghipour, N., Kardan, A., & Ghidary, S. S. (2007, October). Usage-based web recommendations: A reinforcement learning approach. In *Proceedings of the 2007 ACM Conference on Recommender Systems.* Minneapolis, MN.

Vadillo-Zorita, J., de Ilarraza, A. D., Fernández, I., Gutiérrez, J., & Elorriaga, J. (1994). *Explicaciones en sistemas tutores de entrenamiento: Representacion del dominio y estrategias de explicacion.* Pais Vasco, España.

Vale, Z., Ramos, C., Silva, A., Faria, L., Santos, J., & Fernández, F. (1998). SOCRATES, an integrated intelligent system for power system control center operator assistance and training. In *Proceedings of the International Conference on Artificial Intelligence and Soft Computing (IASTED)* (pp. 27-30).

Wellman, M. (1990). Graphical inference in qualitative probabilistic networks. *Networks, 20*, 687–701. doi:10.1002/net.3230200511

Witten, I. (2005). *Data mining: Practical machine learning tools and techniques with Java implementations* (2nd ed.). USA: Morgan Kaufmann.

ADDITIONAL READING

The authors refer readers to (Wellman, 1990), (Khan, Poupart, & Black, 2009), (Pearl, 1988), (Dean & Kanazawa, 1989), (Darwiche & M., 1994), (Puterman, 1994), (Bellman, 1957), (Givan, Dean, & Greig, 2003), (Dean & Givan, 1997) and (Boutilier, Dean, & Hanks, 1999) for further information about the main topics on this chapter.

Chapter 13
POMDP Models for Assistive Technology

Jesse Hoey
University of Waterloo, Canada

Pascal Poupart
University of Waterloo, Canada

Craig Boutilier
University of Toronto, Canada

Alex Mihailidis
University of Toronto, Canada

ABSTRACT

This chapter presents a general decision theoretic model of interactions between users and cognitive assistive technologies for various tasks of importance to the elderly population. The model is a partially observable Markov decision process (POMDP) whose goal is to work in conjunction with a user towards the completion of a given activity or task. This requires the model to monitor and assist the user, to maintain indicators of overall user health, and to adapt to changes. The key strengths of the POMDP model are that it is able to deal with uncertainty, it is easy to specify, it can be applied to different tasks with little modification, and it is able to learn and adapt to changing tasks and situations. This chapter describes the model, gives a general learning method which enables the model to be learned from partially labeled data, and shows how the model can be applied within our research program on technologies for wellness. In particular, we show how the model is used in four tasks: assisted handwashing, stroke rehabilitation, health and safety monitoring, and wheelchair mobility. The first two have been fully implemented and tested, and results are summarized. The second two are meant to demonstrate how the POMDP can be applied across a wide variety of domains, but do not have specific implementations or results. The chapter gives an overview of ongoing work into each of these areas, and discusses future directions.

DOI: 10.4018/978-1-60960-165-2.ch013

INTRODUCTION

A growing area of activity in health technology is support systems for older adults, possibly with cognitive or physical disabilities, who want to continue to live independently in their own homes i.e. age-in-place. Such systems are typically engineered for a certain task to provide guidance, assistance, or emergency response (Mihailidis & Fernie, 2002, LoPresti, Mihailidis, & Kirsch, 2004). However, this approach is labour intensive, and the resulting systems tend to have no capacity to adapt over time or to different users or tasks. In this chapter, we discuss an approach to this problem: a ubiquitous modeling technique that can adapt to users over time. The idea is to have a single model and learning technique that can be easily applied to different tasks, without the need to re-engineer the model.

A typical task requiring assistance consists of four principal elements. We discuss these elements here in the context of the handwashing task for cognitively disabled people, who typically require assistance from a human caregiver to wash their hands. An example of this is shown in Figure 1, which shows key frames from about 15 seconds of a video of a user washing their hands, assisted by a human caregiver. First, the *task state* is a characterisation of the high-level state of the user, and is related to the goals in the task. For example, handwashing can be described by task states that describe whether the hands are wet or dry, dirty, soapy or clean. In Figure 1, the user's hands are dirty and wet at frame 1331, but become soapy and wet by frame 1745. Second, the *behavior* of the user is the course of action the user takes to change the task state. Common behaviors during handwashing may be things like *rinsing hands* or *using soap*, as in Figure 1. Third, the *caregiver's action* is what the caregiver does to help the user through the task. During handwashing, these actions are typically verbal prompts or reminders such as the *"I want you to use some soap now"* in Figure 1. However, as we will show, actions

can include more general dialogue iterations, calls to other response systems, or physical control of related systems. The fourth element, the users *ability*, is the cognitive state of the user, such as their level of responsiveness, attention, frustration with the system, and overall level of health. The user's expeditious reaction to the prompt in Figure 1, for example, might give us an indication that they are responsive, and are attending to the prompting system. Over a longer time period, the user's overall level of health may change. For example, their medical condition might take a turn for the worse, requiring attention from a professional. Such a change may be noticeable in their responses and behaviors.

Our goal is then to design a model of the interactions between these four elements, and to optimize an automated caregiving strategy by maximising (over the actions) some notion of utility over the possible outcomes. The model must be able to deal with uncertainty in the effects of actions and in sensor measurements, it must be able to tailor to specific individuals and circumstances, it must be able to trade off various objective criteria (e.g., task completion, caregiver burden, user frustration and independence), and it must be relatively easy to specify. A partially observable Markov decision process (POMDP), a decision theoretic model which has recently received much attention in the AI community, fulfills these constraints.

The general POMDP we present models the *task* and the *ability* as consequences of the *behavior* of the user, which is a reaction to the *actions* of the caregiver. We claim that the *task* will tend to be simple to specify, and can be defined by a non-specialised person, while the *ability* will require expert knowledge, but will tend to generalise across tasks. On the other hand, the *behaviors* will be much more difficult to specify. The standard approach to specifying models of behaviors occurs in two phases. In the first phase, expert knowledge is used to define the behaviors that will occur, and a supervised classifier is trained to recognise these

Figure 1. Example sequence in which a user is prompted to put soap on their hands

caregiver: "I want you to use some soap now"

1331 hands: wet,1395   1403   1422
        dirty

1445   1505   1546   1745hands: wet,
                                                    soapy

statically defined behaviors. In the second phase, a model of the relationship between the behaviors (as given by the learned classifier) and the task is learned (Peters, Wachsmuth, & Hoey, 2009). The problem with this approach is the need to specify behaviors *a priori*. This is a labor-intensive task requiring expert knowledge. Further, different individuals perform the same behaviors in different ways, exhibit different behaviors to perform the same task, and change their behaviors over time, usually as a result of their changing state of health. These considerations make it very difficult in many cases to define a single set of recognisable behaviors. This aspect is emphasised in the rehabilitation literature (LoPresti et al., 2004). Finally, users require assistance for very different aspects of a task, and so recognising all possible behaviors may be very wasteful. One approach is to *discover* the behaviors that are being exhibited, and to *learn* their relationship to the task simultaneously (Hoey & Little, 2004, Hoey, Poupart, Boutilier, & Mihailidis, 2005a). This learning method has the dual advantage of not requiring extensive *a priori* knowledge and training, and of being capable of adapting to users in different situations.

The chapter first describes related work, then describes a general POMDP model, including the observation function and the methods for specifying, learning, and solving the POMDP. We will then discuss the application of this general model in our own research program on technologies for wellness, where we focus on the development of systems that can assist older adults in a variety of contexts – specifically, completion of activities of daily living (ADL), health and safety monitoring, and improved mobility.

RELATED WORK

Cognitive Assistive technologies have been the subject of much research outside the artificial intelligence community, and are reviewed in (LoPresti et al., 2004, Pollack, 2005). Most relevant to our work, a system called COACH for monitoring handwashing using a ceiling-mounted camera was demonstrated in (Mihailidis, Barbenel, & Fernie, 2004, Mihailidis, Boger, Candido, & Hoey, 2008, Hoey et al., 2010). To date, several iterations of this technology have been developed and tested with this population for the specific activity of handwashing. COACH employs computer vision to track a user and objects of interest as s/he performs an activity of daily living and provides audio and/or visual assistance if, and only if, the user requires it (e.g., s/he performs a step in the handwashing activity out of sequence, gets sidetracked, or is not sure what to do next). A partially observable Markov decision process (POMDP) is employed to learn characteristics about each individual over time, such as what his/her level of independence is, what type of prompts are most effective with him/her, and the average amount of time it takes him/her to complete each step in handwashing. Not only does this approach enable COACH to customise guidance to each individual's needs, but also allows the system to adapt over time to changes in individuals' responsiveness and capabilities.

A POMDP model for a scheduling system for the care of the elderly was described in (Rudary, Singh, & Pollack, 2004). Their work is part of the *Autominder* project, which also includes design of a robotic nursing assistant that uses a POMDP for navigation purposes (Montemerlo, Pineau, Roy, Thrun, & Verma, 2002). POMDPs have recently been applied to dialogue management in care facilities (Roy, Gordon, & Thrun, 2003).

There has been significant progress in learning patterns of activity from a person's positional data. These include data mining techniques for discovering sequences of activities from discrete data (Guralnik & Haigh, 2002), and learning the parameters of a hierarchical hidden Markov model to explain GPS data of outdoor transportation patterns (Liao, Fox, & Kautz, 2004). This last work was done in the context of the Assisted Cognition project (Kautz et al., 2002).

The PROACT system infers tasks being completed based on sensor inputs. This system has three components: body worn RFID sensors, a probabilistic engine that infers activities given observations from these sensors, and a model creator that easily creates probabilistic models of activities (Philipose et al., 2004). PROACT uses a dynamic Bayesian network (DBN) to infer activi-

ties that represents daily activities such as making tea, washing, and brushing teeth. Each activity type that PROACT is intended to recognize is modeled as a linear series of steps, where specific objects that are involved in the completion of a step and the probability of seeing each such object are assigned. Recent work in the same direction has investigated how activites can be modeled with a combination of discriminative and generative approaches (Lester, Choudhury, Kern, Borriello, & Hannaford, 2005), how common sense models of everyday activities can be built automatically using data mining techniques (Pentney, Philipose, Bilmes, & Kautz, 2007, Pentney, Philipose, & Bilmes, 2008), and how human activities can be analyzed through the recognition of object use, rather than the recognition of human behavior (Wu, Osuntogun, Choudhury, Philipose, & Rehg, 2007). This last work uses DBNs as well to model various activities around the home, and a variety of radio frequency identification (RFID) tags to bootstrap the learning process. Other researchers use supervised techniques to build models of meeting dynamics (Rybski & Veloso, 2004), office activity (Nguyen, Bui, Venkatesh, & West, 2003), and other in-home activities (Hamid, Huang, & Essa, 2003).

Our previous work, (Hoey & Little, 2004, Hoey, Poupart, Boutilier, & Mihailidis, 2005b), showed how to learn the parameters of a fully observable Markov decision process, while *discovering* models of behaviors. We have also applied the systems presented here to handwashing (Boger et al., 2005, 2006, Hoey et al., 2010), art therapy (Blunsden et al., 2009, Mihailidis et al., 2010), stroke rehabilitation (Kan, Hoey, & Mihailidis, 2008, Lam et al., 2008, Patricia Kan & Mihailidis, 2010), emergency response (Mihailidis, Tam, McLean, & Lee, 2005) and fall detection (Lee & Mihailidis, 2005).

Figure 2. Two time slices of (a) a general POMDP and (b) a factored POMDP for modeling interactions with cognitive assistive technology. The state, S, is modified by action A, and produces observation O.

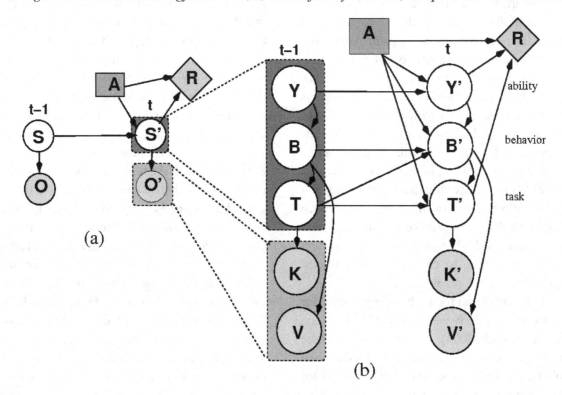

(a)

(b)

GENERAL MODEL

A discrete-time POMDP consists of: a finite set S of states; a finite set A of actions; a stochastic transition model Pr: $S \times A \rightarrow \Delta(S)$, with $\Pr(t|s,a)$ denoting the probability of moving from state s to t when action a is taken; a finite observation set O; a stochastic observation model with $\Pr(o|s)$ denoting the probability of making observation o while the system is in state s; and a reward function assigning reward $R(s,a,t)$ to state transition s to t induced by action a. Figure 2(a) shows the POMDP as a Bayesian network. Given a specific POMDP, our goal is to find a *policy* that maximizes the expected discounted sum of rewards attained by the system. Since the system state is not known with certainty, a policy maps either *belief states* (i.e., distributions over S) or action-observation *histories* into choices of actions. We will not delve into details of POMDP solution methods, but note

that current research has enabled the approximate solution of very large POMDPs (Pineau, Gordon, & Thrun, 2003, 2006, Poupart & Boutilier, 2004, Hoey & Poupart, 2005, Spaan & Vlassis, 2005). We refer to (Lovejoy, 1991) for an overview of POMDP concepts and algorithms.

Figure 2(b) shows the same model, except that the state, S, has been factored into three sets of variables: *task* (**T**), *ability* (**Y**) and *behavior* (**B**). Here we describe each of these sets, as well as the actions of the system, A, and the observations from which the state of the model is inferred.

Task, T: A characterisation of the domain in which the task is taking place in terms of a set of high-level variables. These will typically describe the physical state of items in the task, such as the cleanliness of hands during handwashing, or the location of a user in a mobility aid. These variables need to be specified for each task, but they characterise the world at a sufficiently high level to make this accessible to a wide variety of non-technical people.

Ability, Y: The cognitive or physical state of the user. This may include the level of dementia and the current responsiveness, the physical abilities, or perhaps the level of frustration the user is experiencing with the system itself. The *ability* variables essentially describe internal properties of the user that generalise across tasks, and would be specified by experts for the general system, and then carried over and possibly adapted for each task through learning.

Behavior, B: The task states and the user's ability are changed by the user's *behavior*, *B*. The user's *behavior* evolves depending on the previous states of the *ability* and the *task* as well as the system's action, *A*. The *behaviors* are probably the most difficult to manually specify, and so are learned by the system from data.

Action, A: The actions of the system modify the behavior, ability, and the task. These actions could be verbal prompts, calls to human caregivers or other response systems, or physical changes to the environment.

Observations, O: *Task* and *behavior* variables generate observations, **K** and **V**, respectively. We will assume here that these observations are generated from non-invasive sensors, such as cameras (in which case the observations are video streams), microphones (audio streams), or environmental switches such as thermostats.

Jointly, $S=\{T,B,Y\}$ is known as the state. The transition function can be factored as

$$Pr(S'|S,A)=Pr(T',B',Y'|T,B,Y,A)$$

$$=Pr(T'|B',Y',T,B,Y,A)Pr(B'|Y',T,B,Y,A)Pr(Y'|T,B,Y,A)$$

$$=Pr(T'|B',T,A)Pr(B'|Y'B,A)Pr(Y'|Y,B,A)$$

which is a product of three terms, as follows. $Pr(B'|Y',B,A)$ gives the expected behavior of the user given the previous state and the system action. $Pr(Y'|Y,B,A)$ gives the expected user state given the current behavior, the previous ability and task states and the system action. $Pr(T'|B',T,A)$ gives the expected task state given the current behavior, system action, and the previous task state.

Notice that the task state is independent of the ability, *Y*, given the behaviour, *B*. The idea is that changes in the *task* states are caused by the *behaviors* of the user (and possibly the system actions), independently of the user's ability given the behaviors.

The observations $O=\{K,V\}$ are generated by the *task* and *behavior* variables, *T* and *B*, respectively, through some observation functions $Pr(K|T)$ and $Pr(V|B)$. In general, the time scales at which observations occur will be of much shorter duration than those at which task or ability change. Observations of behaviors will typically be frames from some video camera (at 30Hz), or some segments of an audio stream (at 10kHz), whereas the task states will only change every few seconds. For example, during handwashing, a typical behavior may be "putting soap on hands", which may take a few seconds to perform, and result in 30 video frame observations (e.g. Figure 1), but only cause a single change of the *task* state: the hands become "soapy". Thus, the observation functions may introduce some hierarchical structure into the model. On the other hand, observations can be grouped together using some offline, heuristic method that produces a *virtual sensor*. An example is a computer vision algorithm that detects faces (Viola & Jones, 2004), variants of which can be found on most modern consumer digital cameras. This algorithm can be seen as a black box that maps video frames to a single bit (face/non-face) that can be treated as an observation by disregarding any noise or confidence information[1].

Specifying, Learning, and Solving POMDPs

There are three steps to obtaining a working POMDP-based system: specification, learning and solving. The POMDP is first *specified* by defining a set of *task* and *ability* variables, the observation space (what the sensors will be reporting to the system), a set of actions the system can take, a reward function, and the conditional dependencies in the associated Bayesian network (Figure 2). The transition function $Pr(S_{t+1}|S_t,A)$ and the observation function $Pr(O|S)$ can be further refined by *learning* them from data, in a supervised (Peters et al., 2009) or unsupervised (Hoey et al., 2005a) manner. The resulting POMDP is then *solved* to yield a policy, mapping observations to actions.

The size of our model puts it well beyond the reach of any exact solution techniques. Point-based algorithms (Pineau et al., 2006) use the approximate technique of only computing solutions at a finite set of belief points. Among the class of point-based algorithms, Perseus (Spaan & Vlassis, 2005) is very simple and yet quite effective, as it chooses belief points at random for value iteration backups, and only backs up enough belief points to improve the value function at all belief points, instead of backing up every belief point. Symbolic Perseus improves on Perseus by representing α-vectors *symbolically* with Algebraic Decision Diagrams (ADDs) (Bahar et al., 1993) instead of by enumerating the values for each state. The transition probabilities, rewards and α-vectors are represented with decision trees that aggregate identical values and allow branches to merge, potentially reducing memory and computation by an exponential factor. This idea was used successfully for MDPs (Hoey, St-Aubin, Hu, & Boutilier, 1999) and for POMDPs (Poupart, 2005). More details on the approximations used in symbolicPerseus can be found in (Poupart, 2005, Hoey et al., 2010). Software for SymbolicPerseus is available at http://www.cs.uwaterloo.ca/ppoupart/software.

Ideally, the learning and solving steps are combined in one, and the system learns both the model and the policy online as it interacts with users, known as reinforcement learning (RL). However, online learning requires a great deal of *exploration* for the system to discover how the domain works, so that it can exploit its knowledge (and reach goals, etc.). This exploration can be very costly, especially in a clinical setting with cognitively or physically disabled users. *Bayesian* reinforcement learning optimises the tradeoff between exploration and exploitation by including the model parameters as part of the state that is being estimated during online inference (Duff, 2002, P. Poupart, N. Vlassis, J. Hoey, K. Regan, 2006). The intuition is that the system should include its learning task as one of its goals (along with the goals defined by the domain itself). In a principled way, Bayesian RL also allows incorporation of prior knowledge to reduce the need for exploration.

ACTIVITY MODELS

We will demonstrate how to apply the POMDP model to four tasks: prompting assistance during handwashing for people with Alzheimer's, haptic stroke rehabilitation for upper arm recovery, emergency response for the elderly, and wheelchair control for the cognitively disabled. The first two have been fully implemented and tested and results are summarized. The second two are meant to demonstrate how the POMDP can be applied across a wide variety of domains, but do not have specific implementations or results. For each task, we introduce the domain, and then give an overview of the *task* and *ability* variables, and of the system actions. We then describe the observations and observation functions, the transition dynamics, and the reward function. Finally, we describe some of our current work.

Figure 3. Simplified view of the planstep transitions for the handwashing problem. The plansteps are shown along with the state of the hands (dirty,soapy,clean), the wetness of the hands (dry,wet) and the water flow (on/off). Transitions are for pairs of pre/post action behaviors for the null action. Transitions for prompting actions are slightly different (see text). The model is simplified for presentation in that some additional transitions and regressions are possible. An underscore (_) means any behavior and ~b means any behavior other than b. A question mark, ? indicates a probabilistic transition.

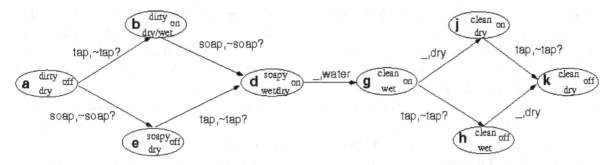

Handwashing

Older adults living with cognitive disabilities (such as Alzheimer's disease or other forms of dementia) have difficulty completing activities of daily living (ADLs), and are usually assisted by a human caregiver who prompts them when necessary. Assistive technology will allow this elderly population to age-in-place by non-invasively monitoring users in their homes during ADL, providing guidance or assistance when necessary (LoPresti et al., 2004). In the handwashing ADL, the user needs to get his hands clean by progressing through stages that include using soap, turning the water on and off, rinsing and drying his hands. A caregiver monitors the progress of the user, issuing reminders or prompts at appropriate times.

Task: The handwashing task can be described by three primary task variables: *hands_clean*, which can be *{dirty, soapy, clean}*, *hands_wet*, which can be *{wet, dry}*, and *water_flow*, which can be *{on, off}*. We assume the hands start *dirty* and *dry*, and the goal is to get them *clean* and *dry*, which can only happen if they become *soapy* and *wet* at some intermediate time. The water starts *off* and must be *off* for task completion. The water flow can have a corresponding observation (e.g. a

water flow switch), but this switch was not used in the experiments described below. The three variables above can be combined into a *planstep* variable, with 8 values corresponding to the possible states of the hands, as shown in Figure 3. Other task variables are involved with timing issues (such as how much time the system has waited for, how many prompts have been issued with no response, etc), and with issues related to the user's current performance (such as how many times they have regressed in the task).

Ability: The ability of the user can play a critical role in their ability to respond to prompts. We use two variables for handwashing: *awareness*, describing how likely they are do the task independently, and *responsiveness*, describing how likely they are to respond to a prompt.

Actions: The system actions are the possible reminders that can be given to the user in the form of audible cues, corresponding to the canonical steps of handwashing: *turn on water, wet hands, use soap, dry hands* and *turn off water*. The prompts can be issued at three levels of specificity. There is also one null action where the system waits (to give more independence to the user), and one action of calling for human assistance. This last action is important for such a system: it must know when its limitations have been reached. The goal is to reduce burden on caregivers, not to replace caregivers entirely. Audio cues have been found to be sufficient to decrease caregiver burden in previous studies (Mihailidis et al., 2004).

Observations: The user's behaviors are inferred from videos taken from an overhead camera. These behaviors have a temporal extent over multiple video frames and require a hierarchical observation function. The behaviors are either given by the (temporally averaged) location of the user's hands as reported by a handtracking system (Hoey et al., 2010), or are learned from data (Peters et al., 2009, Hoey et al., 2005b) as dynamic models of the usual activities in handwashing, such as using the soap, or reaching for the towel. The implementation we describe below uses a computer vision algorithm that tracks hands and towel (Hoey, 2006). This method uses a mixed-state data-driven Bayesian sequential estimation method using *flocks* of color features, which allow objects to be robustly tracked over long periods of time, through large changes in shape and through partial occlusions. The tracker locations are discretised into a fixed set of regions around each element of interest in the sink area (e.g. soap, taps), and a timeout function is applied.

Dynamics: The transition dynamics encode the progression of the handwashing task. For example, hands become clean if they are soapy and the user performs a behavior of rinsing. The probability of an appropriate user behavior as a response to prompts increases with prompt specificity and with user responsiveness.

Reward: The reward function gives a positive reward for task completion, small negative rewards for each prompt (encoding the preference of users to complete tasks on their own), and a large negative reward for calling a human caregiver. More specific prompts are more expensive, reflecting the increased impact these prompts have on feelings of independence. Thus, a policy for this model will typically start with the least specific prompt possible, until it learns that a person is not

responsive to that level of specificity, at which point it will be willing to pay the additional cost for a more specific prompt.

The handwashing POMDP has nine state variables, three observation variables, and 25 actions. There are 207360 states and 198 observations. Despite the size and complexity of this model, we are able to solve the POMDP, producing (approximately) sequentially optimal policies for ADL prompting. We solved the POMDP with SymbolicPerseus by using 150 alpha vectors and 65 iterations in 42 hours on a dual Intel® 2.40GHz XEON™ CPU with 4Gb of RAM, using about 2Gb of memory maximum.

The system was tested in an eight-week trial with our target users: six persons with moderate to severe dementia in a long-term care facility in Toronto, Canada (Figure 4). The subjects washed their hands once a day, with assistance given by our automated system, or by a human caregiver, in alternating two-week periods. The results showed that, when COACH was in use, those with moderate-level dementia completed on average 11% more handwashing steps and required 60% fewer interactions with a human caregiver. Four of the participants were nearly completely independent, and the majority of COACH's actions were considered clinically correct. Further, it was noted that individual idiosyncrasies seemed to play a larger role than participant's level of dementia. Our clinical findings (i.e. the effect of the system on users) are reported in (Mihailidis et al., 2008), whilst our technical findings, with more details on the POMDP and overall system are reported in (Hoey et al., 2010).

Figure 5 shows key frames and belief states from an example sequence of subject 4 (Avg. MMSE of 11.5) during trial 34 (the first day of the first system trial). In this case, the user independently uses the soap and lathers her hands (Figure 5-a), then turns the water on and rinses her hands (5-b), where the system correctly infers she is in planstep *g*. It gives her time to rinse, then her awareness shifts to *no*, and it prompts her to

Figure 4. COACH handwashing assistant in trial setting

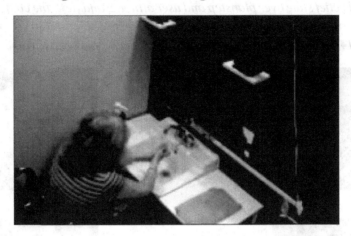

turn the water off, using a video prompt. Figure 5-c shows her responding, but then gets momentarily stuck with her hands at the taps during the act of turning them off (5-d). The system gives her a further prompt to turn the taps off, cuing her to continue to the towel. She follows this prompt, using the towel to finish the task (5-e).

We have also experimented with two simplified versions of this POMDP. The first version uses a simplified set of variables (ignoring ability and timing issues), and shows how models of behaviors could be learned from data, and how they could be subsequently used to monitor user progress in the task (Hoey et al., 2005b). The second version uses a simplified state space and investigates Bayesian reinforcement learning (P. Poupart, N. Vlassis, J. Hoey, K. Regan, 2006).

Stroke Rehabilitation

Stroke is the leading cause of physical disability and third leading cause of death in most countries around the world, including Canada (Canadian Stroke Network, 2010) and the United States (American Heart Association, 2010). The consequences of stroke are devastating with approximately 75% of stroke sufferers being left with a permanent disability (Heart & Stroke Canada, 2010). It is generally agreed that intensive, re-

petitive, and goal-directed rehabilitation improves motor function and cortical reorganization in stroke patients with both acute and long-term (chronic) impairment (Fasoli, Krebs, & Hogan, 2004). However, this recovery process is slow and labor-intensive, usually involving extensive interaction between one or more therapists and one patient. Rehabilitation robots can partially automate these interventions, provide intensive and reproducible movement training, and be used for assessment by therapists.

The system we describe in this section models the stroke rehabilitation task as an assistance task to autonomously facilitate upper-limb reaching rehabilitation for moderate level stroke patients, to tailor the exercise parameters for each individual, and to estimate user fatigue. The system consists of a haptic robotic device coupled to a POMDP model that tracks a user's progress over time, and adjusts the level of difficulty based on the user's current abilities. More details on this system can be found in (Kan et al., 2008, Lam et al., 2008, Patricia Kan & Mihailidis, 2010).

The robotic device, as detailed in (Lam et al., 2008), and shown in Figure 6, was built by Quanser Inc., a Toronto-based robotics company. It features a non-restraining platform for better usability and freedom of movement, and has two active and two passive degrees of freedom, which allow the

Figure 5. Key frames from subject 4, trial 34, showing (right) the overhead video and flock trackers (center) the marginal belief state over planstep and user attitude, and (left) the camcorder view (not used by the system). See text for description. 5-a (19 seconds) (frame 586). 5-b (30 seconds)(frame 929). 5-c (48 seconds)(frame 1454). 5-d (55 seconds)(frame 1657). 5-e (75 seconds)(frame 2251)

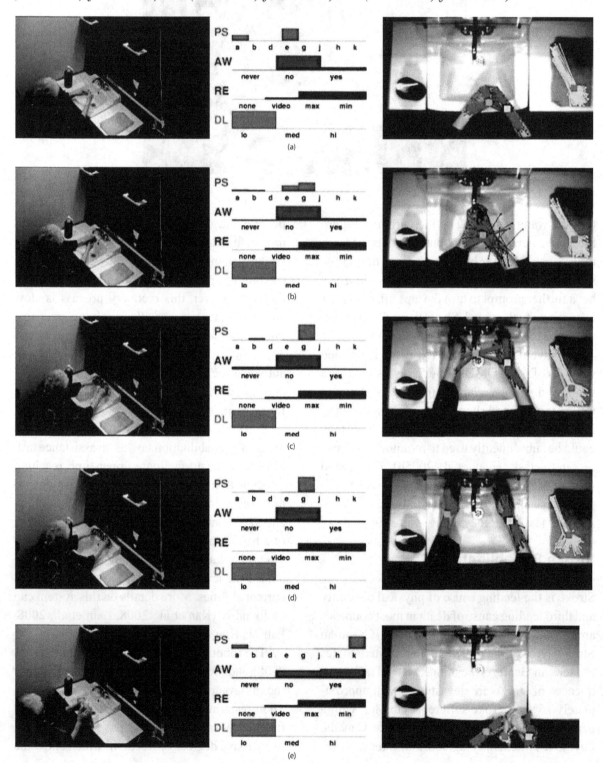

Figure 6. iSTRETCH haptic robotic device for stroke rehabilitation

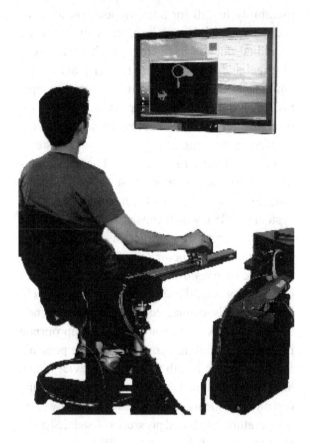

reaching exercise to be performed in 3D space. The robotic device also incorporates haptic technology, which provides feedback through sense of touch. Encoders in the end-effector of the robotic device provide data to indicate hand position and shoulder abduction/internal rotation (i.e. compensation) during the exercise. Unobtrusive trunk sensors provide data to indicate trunk rotation compensation. The trunk sensors are comprised of three photoresistors taped to the back of a chair, each in one of three locations: the lower back, lower left scapula, and lower right scapula. The detection of light during the exercise indicates trunk rotation, as it means a gap is present between the chair and user. Finally, the virtual environment provides the user with visual feedback on hand position and target location during the exercise.

The reaching exercise is represented in the form of a 2D bull's eye game. The goal of the game is for the user to move the robot's end-effector, which corresponds to the cross-tracker in the virtual environment, to the bull's eye target. The rectangular box is the virtual (haptic) boundary, which keeps the cross-tracker within those walls during the exercise.

Task The *task* state is only related to the virtual game, and encodes things such as whether the user has completed a level. At the present time, we do not include any of these elements, but these could be added in future.

Ability The user's *abilities* are modeled as a product of three factors: their range at each resistance level, their level of fatigue, and their learning rate (some users rehabilitate faster than others).

Actions: There are 10 possible actions the system can take. These are comprised of nine actions of which each is a different combination of setting a target distance $d \in \{d1, d2, d3\}$, and resistance level $r \in \{none, min, max\}$, and one action to stop the exercise when the user is fatigued.

Observation: The *behaviours* model the time it takes the user to reach the target, the amount of control they exhibit while reaching (the amount of 'wiggle' in the device as measured by the end-effector encoders), and whether they compensate or not (measured by the trunk photo-resistor sensors). The observations convert the time it takes the user to reach the target into three ranges: did not reach, slow or normal; and whether the user demonstrates sufficient control and does not compensate. These settings are done by the physical therapist to allow for the abilities of a particular user.

Dynamics: The dynamics of all variables were specified manually using simple parametric functions of the user's fatigue and the difference between the system's setting of resistance and distance and the user's range. For example, if the user is not fatigued and the system sets a target at the user's range, then the user might have a 90% chance of reaching the target. However, if the target is set further, or if the user is fatigued, then this chance might decrease to 50%. The functions have simple parameters that can be specified by therapists, giving them customisation of the POMDP model. More details can be found in (Kan et al., 2008).

Reward: The reward function was constructed to motivate the system to guide the user to exercise at maximum target distance and resistance level, while performing the task with maximum control and without compensation. Thus, the system was given a large reward for getting the user to reach the furthest target distance (d=d3) at maximum resistance (r=max). Smaller rewards were given when targets were set at or above the user's current range, and when the user was performing well. However, no reward was given when the user was fatigued, failed to reach the target, had no control, or showed signs of compensation during the exercise.

The system has been tested in a pilot study with a single patient and one therapist. In each session, the therapist reviewed each POMDP decision and either agreed or disagreed with it (in which case the therapist made the decision). Each session lasted for approximately one hour and was completed three times a week for two weeks. The therapist agreed with both the target distance and resistance level decisions made by the POMDP 94% and 90% of the time, respectively, but only 43% of the time for the stop decision. The POMDP wanted to stop the exercise to let the user take a break more often than the therapist wanted, but this could be changed by e.g. setting the cost for the stop action to be higher. More details can be found in (Patricia Kan & Mihailidis, 2010).

HEALTH MONITORING AND EMERGENCY RESPONSE

Aging-in-place is difficult for adults who live alone, possibly in rural areas where assistance may not be readily available (Mynatt, Essa, &

Rogers, 2000, Mihailidis & Fernie, 2002). For example, they may have a heart attack or stroke, fall, or become somehow incapacitated without the ability to call for help. In addition to these spontaneous adverse events, there may also be a gradual decline in overall health status, both physical and cognitive, that further places older adults at risk. There are currently several attempts to address these issues and support aging-in-place through the use of technological solutions, the most common being emergency response systems and health monitoring devices. The most common emergency response system (ERS) is the telephone-based personal emergency response system (PERS), which consists of the subscriber wearing a small help button as a necklace or wristband, and a home communicator that is connected to a residential phone line. In the event of an emergency, the subscriber presses the help button and is connected to a live emergency response centre, which arranges for appropriate help, such as calling paramedics or the person's family. Remote health monitoring devices have also been developed that measure and track various physiological parameters, such as pulse, skin temperature, and blood pressures (Asada, Shaltis, Reisner, Rhee, & Hutchinson, 2003).

However, these systems are invasive: they require the user to wear the device at all times and/or to manually take the required measurements. Many of the PERS and physiological-based monitoring systems are inappropriate, obtrusive and difficult for an older adult to operate for various reasons (e.g. require effort from the user, long training periods, etc.), and they become ineffective during more serious emergency situations (e.g. the person has a stroke). As a result, new systems are being developed that do not require manual interaction from the user, and that use non-physiological measures to determine health (Lee & Mihailidis, 2005). Here we show how the POMDP model we have discussed can be used to model the health monitoring and emergency response tasks.

The concept is to have cameras, microphones and speakers installed throughout a home, monitoring the user's activities during the day (for health monitoring) and providing assistance or emergency response when needed. In this case, there are two inputs: video and audio, which relate to visually observable behaviors of the user and their speech acts, respectively. This POMDP combines elements of human activity modeling (Wren, Azarbayejani, Darrell, & Pentland, 1997, Oliver, Horvitz, & Garg, 2002) and dialogue management (Roy et al., 2003, Williams, Poupart, & Young, 2005).

Task: Task variables include descriptors of the person's location, the time of day, the frequency of visits to different locations, and whether they have fallen or not.

Ability: Ability variables here can include overall level of health (such as fatigue, recurrence of disease symptoms, etc), responsiveness to prompts, current alertness level.

Actions: Possible actions are questions or speech acts (dialogue), or calls to neighbors, caregivers, or paramedics.

Observation: There are two *behavior* variables: the visually observable actions, such as motion (from room to room or within a room) and unusual events (falls), and the audible actions, such as speech acts or other noises. The visual and audio behaviors of a user are related to the observations of video (from cameras) and audio (from microphones) through separate observation functions. The information from the visual modality has also been used to help the speech recognition using a microphone array and a beam-forming algorithm. This allows sources of noise to be attenuated, so that the audio signal comes mainly from the area in which a person was observed to have fallen.

Dynamics: The model encodes two distinct, but related, functions. First, the monitoring of the overall level of health of the person is done by the dynamics of the *ability* and *task* variables. For example, if the frequency of visits to a particular location (e.g. the bathroom) suddenly increases, this may be an indication of the onset or recurrence of a health condition, and the transition function will assign a higher probability to this condition as a result of the observations of increased bathroom trips. Similarly, the presence of the person in an unusual location at some time of the day may also be an indication of a changing state of health. The responses to changes in these ability variables may be to schedule a visit to a doctor, or to call a family member. The second function of the system is emergency response in the case of a fall. In this case, it is not the *ability* variables that are important, but the *task* variables directly. The system's response will be to initiate a dialogue with the person to uncover more information, followed by possible calls to emergency response teams.

For both of these functions of the system, speech acts will be used to carry on dialogues in cases where the system attempts to uncover additional information from the user, such as whether they need help, etc. This requires some form of dialogue management encoded in the dynamics, which is an active area of research in POMDP modeling (Roy et al., 2003, Zhang, Cai, Mao, & Guo, 2001, Williams et al., 2005).

Reward: Rewards are given for calling for help if undesirable situations are encountered (e.g. unrecoverable falls, decline in health levels, etc.)

Wheelchair Mobility

Many older adults face various impairments and disabilities that result in their mobility being compromised. Furthermore, many of these people lack the strength to manually propel themselves, and require powered wheelchairs. However, powered wheelchairs are not appropriate for older adults with a cognitive impairment, such as dementia or Alzheimer's disease, as they do not have the cognitive capacity required to effectively and safely manoeuvre the wheelchair. In addition, their sometimes aggressive and unpredictable behavior makes wheelchair use unsafe for both themselves and others sharing the environment.

As a result, many care institutions (e.g. hospitals, long-term care facilities, etc.) have implemented policies that restrict driving for reasons of safety, especially for residents with cognitive impairment.

Reduced mobility results in reduced quality of life. The combination of social isolation, limited life space and choice, learned dependence (e.g. requiring someone to push a manual wheelchair), frustration, and limited autonomy likely contributes to symptoms of depression and exacerbation of cognitive impairment and undesirable behaviors. It should also be noted that this chain reaction of symptoms resulting from reduced mobility are also observed in other user groups beyond older adults (e.g. disabled children, adults with traumatic brain injury, etc.), thus broadening the scope of these problems and requirements from potential solutions.

In this case, our POMDP model implements a mixed initiative controller for the powered wheelchair (Mihailidis, Elinas, Boger, & Hoey, 2007). Such ideas have been explored before (Yanco, 1998, Nuttin, Demeester, Vanhooydonck, & Brussel, 2001), but not using a POMDP model. The idea is to let the user control their wheelchair independently until potentially dangerous situations arise, at which point the system will attempt to modify or stop the user's controls. The system can also act in a more passive way, issuing verbal prompts or reminders if unusual or detrimental activities are noticed.

Task: The wheelchair control problem can be characterised using a map of the environment in which the wheelchair operates, and maintaining the location and velocity of the wheelchair within the map. The map we use is an occupancy grid (Moravec & Elfes, 1985, Murray & Little, 1998), which estimates the presence of an obstacle at each 2D location $\{x,y\}$ in the reference frame of the (moving) wheelchair or in a global reference frame. Other task states may also include different aspects of the user's situation, such as their schedule, much like in the health monitoring POMDP described above.

Ability: The cognitive state of the user will have a significant impact on their ability to control a powered wheelchair, and so we include user alertness. User frustration (with the wheelchair control) could also be included here.

Actions: The actions of the system will be to modify the user actions (their behaviors), such as restricting movement in a certain direction, or modifying the user's control signal. Actions will also include audio prompts or alerts, since restricted movement on its own can cause confusion which can be mitigated by appropriate verbal cues.

Observation: The behaviors of the user are their driving actions on the wheelchair (use of the control joystick, for example). They are inferred from the joystick outputs (control to the wheelchair motors). The map and location variables are estimated simultaneously from stereo vision measurements (Murray & Little, 1998, Elinas, 2005).

Dynamics: The transition function characterises the effects of user and system controls on the map, location and velocity. The dynamics, when used to compute a policy, will give rise to implicit safety envelopes and times to collision in terms of the actions of the system and user. For example, if an obstacle suddenly appears in front of a moving wheelchair, the system can predict that the only action to avoid a collision is a hard braking one. The dynamics can also encode the larger scale patterns of a person's movement, such as their schedule, etc, as in the health monitoring case described above.

Reward: The reward function will assign a large penalty for the wheelchair coming into contact with any occupied cell in the map, but a positive reward for the wheelchair responding to the user's command (e.g. from a joystick). The control policy will therefore optimise satisfaction of user's needs for mobility (their control commands) with the requirements for safety in the wheelchair's location. Other rewards can be given for keeping the user on a schedule, for example.

We have implemented a preliminary version this system that uses local occupancy grid maps

Figure 7. Wheelchair collision avoidance (a) Nimble Rocket™ wheelchair and Bumblebee™ stereo vision camera (inset) (b) wheelchair camera view (c) occupancy grid map - the wheelchair is at the bottom center - white, black and gray cells are unoccupied, occupied and unknown (d) stereo image - brighter is closer

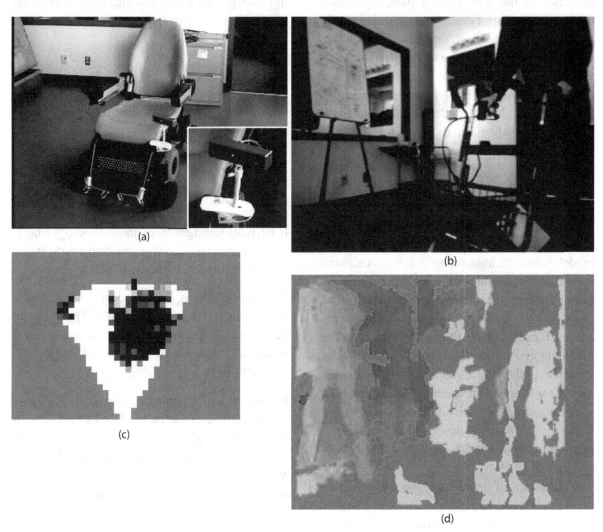

and a very simple collision detection/avoidance system. The wheelchair and sensor, and an example of a collision detection is shown in Figure 7. We have simply engineered a policy for this case, but our current work is focussed on implementing the system as POMDP and using it to derive policies of action. Methods for global mapping and Monte-Carlo localisation (Elinas, 2005) are also being investigated.

Using the proposed POMDP model, the intelligent wheelchair system will be able to assist in navigation by constructing maps of the user's environment using the global mapping and localisation techniques. The system will also learn locations of interest to the user by using his her daily schedule (provided to the system as input from a caregiver), observing his/her patterns of daily behaviour, and using any other available information, such as a schedule of special events held at the facility (e.g. a barbeque). Path planning will involve computing the optimal route based on the wheelchair's current and desired locations, obstacles in the wheelchair's path, and other contexts such as user preferences. Guidance will be provided to the user through visual and/or audio prompts. It is anticipated that this feedback will assist wheelchair users in getting to places of interest in a timely fashion, as well as encourage them to explore and interact with their environments in a safe manner.

CONCLUSION AND FUTURE WORK

We have described a general model for cognitive assistive technologies interacting with users. The model deals with uncertainty in action outcomes and in sensor measurements in a principled way, is able to learn and adapt over time to users and tasks, and avoids the need for extensive re-engineering for new tasks by defining a framework for modeling assistive technology. We showed four examples of the model's application to technologies for wellness. Our current work is involved with the implementation and testing of versions of the models we have described above, and the application to new tasks, such as toothbrushing and cooking.

A direction of interest is the combination of the models we have presented above in a single, hierarchical framework. Hierarchical POMDPs have already been described in the literature (Theocharous, Murphy, & Kaelbling, 2004), and we believe that similar concepts can be applied here. These types of models can have further application beyond that described for one type of tool, such as playing a significant role in achieving a fully integrated smart home. For example, while the health monitoring POMDP will take care of the gross movements of a user through their home, it can hand over control to the handwashing assistant POMDP when the user enters the washroom, or to the wheelchair controller when the user climbs

into their mobility device. An integrated system that can share infrastructure and resources across several different applications must be the final goal in order for these technologies to be successful and useful.

REFERENCES

American Heart Association. (n.d.). *Stroke statistics*. Retrieved November 10, 2010, from http://www.americanheart.org/presenter.jhtml?identifier=4725

Asada, H., Shaltis, P., Reisner, A., Rhee, S., & Hutchinson, R. (2003). *Wearable CV sensors*. IEEE Engineering in Medicine and Biology Magazine - Special Issue on Wearable Sensors/Systems and Their Impact on Biomedical Engineering.

Bahar, R. I., Frohm, E. A., Gaona, C. M., Hachtel, G. D., Macii, E., & Pardo, A. (1993). Algebraic decision diagrams and their applications. In *International Conference on Computer-Aided Design* (pp. 188–191).

Blunsden, S., Richards, B., Bartindale, T., Jackson, D., Olivier, P., & Boger, J. N. (2009). Design and prototype of a device to engage cognitively disabled older adults in visual artwork. In *Proceedings of the ACM 2nd International Conference on Pervasive Technologies Related to Assistive Environments*. Corfu, Greece.

Boger, J., Hoey, J., Poupart, P., Boutilier, C., Fernie, G., & Mihailidis, A. (2006, April). A planning system based on Markov decision processes to guide people with dementia through activities of daily living. *IEEE Transactions on Information Technology in Biomedicine*, *10*(2), 323–333. doi:10.1109/TITB.2006.864480

POMDP Models for Assistive Technology

Boger, J., Poupart, P., Hoey, J., Boutilier, C., Fernie, G., & Mihailidis, A. (2005, Jul). A decision-theoretic approach to task assistance for persons with dementia. In *Proc. IEEE International Joint Conference on Artificial Intelligence* (pp. 1293-1299). Edinburgh.

Canadian Stroke Network Website. (2010). *Stroke 101*. Retrieved November 10, 2010, from http://www.canadianstrokenetwork.ca/index.php/about/about-stroke/stroke-101/

Duff, M. O. (2002). *Optimal learning: Computational procedures for bayes-adaptive markov decision processes*. Unpublished doctoral dissertation, University of Massassachusetts Amherst.

Elinas, P. (2005, Jun). Monte-Carlo localization for mobile robots with stereo vision. In *Proc. Robotics: Science and Systems*. Cambridge, MA: Sigma-MCL.

Fasoli, S., Krebs, H., & Hogan, N. (2004). Robotic technology and stroke rehabilitation: Translating research into practice. *Topics in Stroke Rehabilitation, 11*(4), 11–19. doi:10.1310/G8XB-VM23-1TK7-PWQU

Guralnik, V., & Haigh, K. Z. (2002, Jul). Learning models of human behaviour with sequential patterns. In *AAAI-02 Workshop on Automation as Caregiver* (pp. 24-30).

Hamid, R., Huang, Y., & Essa, I. (2003, Jun). Argmode - Activity recognition using graphical models. In *Proc. CVPR Workshop on Detection and Recognition of Events in Video*. Madison, WI.

Heart & Stroke Foundation Canada. (2010). *Stroke statistics*. Retrieved November 10, 2010, from http://www.heartandstroke.com/site/c.ikIQLcMWJtE/b.3483991/k.34A8/Statistics.htm#stroke

Hoey, J. (2006, September). Tracking using flocks of features, with application to assisted handwashing. In M. J. Chantler, E. Trucco, & R. B. Fisher (Eds.), *Proc. of the British Machine Vision Conference* (vol. 1, pp. 367–376). Edinburgh.

Hoey, J., & Little, J. J. (2004). Value-directed learning of gestures and facial displays. In *Proc Intl. Conference on Computer Vision and Pattern Recognition*. Washington, DC.

Hoey, J., & Poupart, P. (2005, July). Solving POMDPs with continuous or large discrete observation spaces. In *Proc. International. Joint conference on Artificial Intelligence* (pp. 1332-1338).

Hoey, J., Poupart, P., Boutilier, C., & Mihailidis, A. (2005a). POMDP models for assistive technology. In *Proc. AAAI Fall Symposium on Caring Machines: AI in Eldercare*.

Hoey, J., Poupart, P., Boutilier, C., & Mihailidis, A. (2005b, July). Semi-supervised learning of a POMDP model of patient-caregiver interactions. In *Proc. IJCAI Workshop on Modeling Others from Observations* (pp. 101-110). Edinburgh.

Hoey, J., Poupart, P., von Bertoldi, A., Craig, T., Boutilier, C., & Mihailidis, A. (2010, May). Automated handwashing assistance for persons with dementia using video and a partially observable markov decision process. *Computer Vision and Image Understanding, 114*(5), 503–519. doi:10.1016/j.cviu.2009.06.008

Hoey, J., St-Aubin, R., Hu, A., & Boutilier, C. (1999). SPUDD: Stochastic planning using decision diagrams. In *Proceedings of Uncertainty in Artificial Intelligence* (pp. 279-288). Stockholm. Kan, P., Hoey, J., & Mihailidis, A. (2008). Stroke rehabilitation using haptics and a POMDP controller. In *AAAI Fall Symposium on Caring Machines: AI in Eldercare*.

311

Kan, P., Hoey, J., & Mihailidis, A. (2010). The development of an adaptive upper-limb stroke rehabilitation robotic system. *Journal of Neuroengineering and Rehabilitation*, 8.

Kautz, H., Arnstein, L., Borriello, G., Etzioni, O., & Fox, D. (2002). An overview of the assisted cognition project. In *Proc. AAAI-2002 Workshop on Automation as Caregiver: The Role of Intelligent Technology in Elder Care* (pp. 60-65).

Lam, P., Hébert, D., Boger, J., Lacheray, H., Gardner, D., & Apkarian, J. (2008). A haptic-robotic platform for upper-limb reaching stroke therapy: Preliminary design and evaluation results. *Journal of Neuroengineering and Rehabilitation*, 5(15), 1–13.

Lee, T., & Mihailidis, A. (2005). An intelligent emergency response system. *Journal of Telemedicine and Telecare*, 11(4).

Lester, J., Choudhury, T., Kern, N., Borriello, G., & Hannaford, B. (2005, July). A hybrid discriminative/generative approach for modeling human activities. In *Proc. IJCAI* (pp. 766-772). Edinburgh, Scotland.

Liao, L., Fox, D., & Kautz, H. (2004). Learning and inferring transportation routines. In *Proc Nineteenth National Conference on Artificial Intelligence (AAAI '04)* (pp. 348-353). San Jose, CA.

LoPresti, E. F., Mihailidis, A., & Kirsch, N. (2004). Assistive technology for cognitive rehabilitation: State of the art. *Neuropsychological Rehabilitation*, 14(1/2), 5–39. doi:10.1080/09602010343000101

Lovejoy, W. S. (1991). A survey of algorithmic methods for partially observed Markov decision processes. *Annals of Operations Research*, 28, 47–66. doi:10.1007/BF02055574

Mihailidis, A., Barbenel, J. C., & Fernie, G. (2004, March-May). The efficacy of an intelligent cognitive orthosis to facilitate handwashing by persons with moderate to severe dementia. *Neuropsychological Rehabilitation*, 14(1-2), 135–171. doi:10.1080/09602010343000156

Mihailidis, A., Blunsden, S., Boger, J., Richards, B., Zutis, K., & Young, L. (2010). Towards the development of a technology for art therapy and dementia: Definition of needs and design constraints. *The Arts in Psychotherapy*, 37(4). doi:10.1016/j.aip.2010.05.004

Mihailidis, A., Boger, J., Candido, M., & Hoey, J. (2008). The coach prompting system to assist older adults with dementia through handwashing: An efficacy study. *BMC Geriatrics*, 8(28).

Mihailidis, A., Elinas, P., Boger, J., & Hoey, J. (2007). An intelligent powered wheelchair to enable mobility of cognitively impaired older adults: an anticollision system. *IEEE Transactions on Neural Systems and Rehabilitation Engineering*, 15(1), 136–143. doi:10.1109/TNSRE.2007.891385

Mihailidis, A., & Fernie, G. R. (2002). Context-aware assistive devices for older adults with dementia. *Gerontechnology (Valkenswaard)*, 2, 173–189. doi:10.4017/gt.2002.02.02.002.00

Mihailidis, A., Tam, T., McLean, M., & Lee, T. (2005). *An intelligent health monitoring and emergency response system.* In ICOST.

Montemerlo, M., Pineau, J., Roy, N., Thrun, S., & Verma, V. (2002). Experiences with a mobile robotic guide for the elderly. In *Proceedings of the AAAI National Conference on Artificial Intelligence.* Edmonton, Canada: AAAI.

Moravec, H., & Elfes, A. (1985, Mar). High-resolution maps from wide-angle sonar. In *Proc. IEEE Int'l Conf. on Robotics and Automation.* St. Louis, Missouri.

Murray, D., & Little, J. (1998, June). Using real-time stereo vision for mobile robot navigation. In *Proceedings of the IEEE Workshop on Perception for Mobile Agents*. Santa Barbara, CA.

Mynatt, E., Essa, I., & Rogers, W. (2000). Increasing the opportunities for aging in place. In *ACM Conference on Universal Usability (CUU)*.

Nguyen, N. T., Bui, H. H., Venkatesh, S., & West, G. (2003, Jun). Recognising and monitoring high-level behaviours in complex spatial environments. In *Proc. CVPR*. Madison, WI.

Nuttin, M., Demeester, E., Vanhooydonck, D., & Brussel, H. V. (2001). Shared autonomy for wheel chair control: Attempts to assess the user's autonomy. In *Autonome Mobile Systeme 2001, 17 Fachgespräch* (pp. 127–133). London, UK: Springer-Verlag. doi:10.1007/978-3-642-56787-2_17

Oliver, N., Horvitz, E., & Garg, A. (2002, Oct). Layered representations for human activity recognition. In *Proceedings of International Conference on Multimodal Interfaces*. Pittsburgh, PA.

Pentney, W., Philipose, M., & Bilmes, J. (2008, July). Structure learning on large scale common sense statistical models of human state. In *Proc. AAAI*. Chicago.

Pentney, W., Philipose, M., Bilmes, J. A., & Kautz, H. A. (2007). Learning large scale common sense models of everyday life. In *Proceedings of AAAI* (p. 465-470).

Peters, C., Wachsmuth, S., & Hoey, J. (2009). Learning to recognise behaviours of persons with dementia using multiple cues in an hmm-based approach. In *Proceedings of the ACM 2nd International Conference on Pervasive Technologies Related to Assistive Environments*. Corfu, Greece.

Philipose, M., Fishkin, K., Patterson, D., Fox, D., Kautz, H., & Hahnel, D. (2004, October-December). Inferring activities from interactions with objects. *Pervasive Computing*, *3*(4), 10–17. doi:10.1109/MPRV.2004.7

Pineau, J., Gordon, G., & Thrun, S. (2003, Aug). Point-based value iteration: An anytime algorithm for POMDPs. In *Proc. of International Joint Conference on Artificial Intelligence* (pp. 1025-1032). Acapulco, Mexico.

Pineau, J., Gordon, G., & Thrun, S. (2006). Anytime point-based approximations for large POMDPs. *Journal of Artificial Intelligence Research*, *27*, 335–380.

Pollack, M. E. (2005, Summer). Intelligent technology for an aging population: The use of AI to assist elders with cognitive impairment. *AI Magazine*, *26*(2), 9–24.

Poupart, P. (2005). *Exploiting structure to efficiently solve large scale partially observable Markov decision processes*. Unpublished doctoral dissertation, University of Toronto, Toronto, Canada.

Poupart, P., & Boutilier, C. (2004). An approximate scalable algorithm for large scale POMDPs. In *Advances in Neural Information Processing Systems 17 (NIPS)* (pp. 1081–1088). Vancouver, BC: VDCBPI.

Roy, N., Gordon, G., & Thrun, S. (2003). Planning under uncertainty for reliable health care robotics. In *Proceedings of the International Conference on Field and Service Robotics*. Lake Yamanaka, Japan.

Rudary, M., Singh, S., & Pollack, M. E. (2004, Jul). Adaptive cognitive orthotics: Combining reinforcement learning and constraint-based temporal reasoning. In *Proc. 21st International Conference on Machine Learning (ICML 2004)*.

Rybski, P. E., & Veloso, M. M. (2004, Jul). Using sparse visual data to model human activities in meetings. In *Proc. IJCAI Workshop on Modeling Other Agents from Observations (MOO 2004)*. New York, NY.

Spaan, M. T. J., & Vlassis, N. (2005). Perseus: Randomized point-based value iteration for POMDPs. *Journal of Artificial Intelligence Research, 24*, 195–220.

Theocharous, G., Murphy, K., & Kaelbling, L. (2004). Representing hierarchical POMDPs as DBNs for multi-scale robot localization. In *Proc. International Conference on Robotics and Automation (ICRA 2004)*.

Viola, P. A., & Jones, M. J. (2004). Robust real-time face detection. *International Journal of Computer Vision, 57*(2), 137–154. doi:10.1023/B:VISI.0000013087.49260.fb

Williams, J., Poupart, P., & Young, S. (2005, Aug). Factored partially observable Markov decision processes for dialogue management. In *Proc. IJCAI Workshop on Knowledge and Reasoning in Practical Dialogue Systems* (pp. 76-82). Edinburgh, Scotland.

Wren, C. R., Azarbayejani, A., Darrell, T., & Pentland, A. (1997). Pfinder: Real-time tracking of the human body. *IEEE Transactions on Pattern Analysis and Machine Intelligence, 19*(7), 780–785. doi:10.1109/34.598236

Wu, J., Osuntogun, A., Choudhury, T., Philipose, M., & Rehg, J. M. (2007, October). A scalable approach to activity recognition based on object use. In *Proc. of International Conference on Computer Vision (ICCV)*. Rio de Janeiro, Brazil.

Yanco, H. A. (1998). Wheelesley, a robotic wheelchair system: Indoor navigation and user interface. In Mittal, V., Yanco, H., Aronis, J., & Simspon, R. (Eds.), *Lecture Notes in Artificial Intelligence: Assistive Technology and Artificial Intelligence* (pp. 256–268).

Zhang, B., Cai, Q., Mao, J., & Guo, B. (2001, August). Planning and acting under uncertainty: A new model for spoken dialogue system. In *Proceedings of Uncertainty in Artificial Intelligence* (pp. 572-579). Seattle, WA.

KEY TERMS AND DEFINITIONS

Algebraic Decision Diagram: A data structure consisting of a set of nodes and directed edges in which each node can have multiple parents and multiple children, and in which internal nodes (nodes with children) are labeled with symbols and leaves (nodes with no children) are labeled with real numbers.

Alzheimer's Disease: A incurable, degenerative and terminal disease of the nervous system which causes sufferers to lose short-term memory.

Cognitive Assistive Technology: A technology designed to assist a person cognitively in situations where their cognitive abilities are not properly matched to the task they are trying to perform, either due to a disability or due to task difficulty.

Cognitive Disability: an impairment of cognition, for example, due to an impairment of short-term memory as occurs in Alzheimer's disease.

Haptic: giving feedback via the sense of touch.

ENDNOTE

[1]   Confidence information can be included by added yet more observations corresponding to the confidences

Chapter 14
A Case Study of Applying Decision Theory in the Real World:
POMDPs and Spoken Dialog Systems

Jason D. Williams
AT&T Labs, USA

ABSTRACT

Spoken dialog systems present a classic example of planning under uncertainty. Speech recognition errors are ubiquitous and impossible to detect reliably, so the state of the conversation can never be known with certainty. Despite this, the system must choose actions to make progress to a long term goal. As such, decision theory, and in particular partially-observable Markov decision processes (POMDPs), present an attractive approach to building spoken dialog systems. Initial work on "toy" dialog systems validated the benefits of the POMDP approach; however, it also found that straightforward application of POMDPs could not scale to real-world problems. Subsequent work by a number of research teams has scaled up planning and belief monitoring, incorporated high-fidelity user simulations, and married commercial development practices with automatic optimization. Today, statistical dialog systems are being fielded by research labs for public use. This chapter traces the history of POMDP-based spoken dialog systems, and sketches avenues for future work.

INTRODUCTION

Spoken dialog systems (SDSs) are a widespread commercial technology with a broad range of applications. For example, currently deployed telephone-based SDSs enable callers to check their bank balance, get airline gate information, or find the status of a train. In a car, an SDS enables drivers to change the music, check traffic conditions or get driving directions. SDSs on mobile devices enable people to find a business, send a message, dial a contact, or set a social-networking status. Analysts estimate the total market for SDSs is in the billions of US dollars per year (Kowalke, 2008).

DOI: 10.4018/978-1-60960-165-2.ch014

Although widespread, spoken dialog systems remain challenging to build. First, to hear and understand users, spoken dialog systems use Automatic Speech Recognition (ASR) which is prone to errors. Despite years of research, ASR is still imperfect, and yields the wrong answer 20–30% of the time for non-trivial tasks. As a result, a dialog system can never know the user's true intentions – i.e., to the dialog system, the state of the world is *partially observable*. Moreover, dialog is a temporal process that requires careful *planning*: early decisions affect the long-term outcome, and there are important trade-offs between confirming current hypotheses ("Flying to Boston, is that right?"), gathering more information ("When would you like to travel?"), and committing to the current hypothesis ("Ok, issuing a ticket from New York to Boston for flight 103 on March 15.").

In industry, these two issues are addressed through hand-crafted heuristics. Directed questions ("Please say the time you would like to depart."), confirmations ("Eleven thirty, is that right?"), and local accept/reject decisions ("Sorry, I didn't understand. What time was that?") help reduce uncertainty; and dialog plans – carefully designed by experts – are highly constrained. Although these techniques are sufficient for certain commercial applications, their scope and robustness are inherently limited. Increasing automation by only a few percent would have real commercial impact. Moreover, increasing robustness is an important step toward moving new applications of spoken dialog systems out of the research lab into widespread use, in domains such as robotics (Roy, Pineau, & Thrun, 2000, Doshi & Roy, 2008b), eldercare (Mihailidis, Boger, Candido, & Hoey, 2008), handheld device interaction (Johnston et al., 2002), situated interaction (Bohus & Horvitz, 2009), and others.

With this in mind, researchers at several laboratories have turned to decision theory as a framework for building spoken dialog systems. With sequential decisions and a partially observ-

able state, dialog systems present a classic example of decision-making under uncertainty, for which *partially-observable Markov decision processes* (POMDPs) are an attractive method. Initial work at several research laboratories applying POMDPs to toy spoken dialog systems in 2000–2005 suggested that POMDPs were indeed capable of achieving significantly better performance than the traditional approach of hand-crafting dialog control. However, this early work also identified numerous barriers to commercial use.

Since that early pioneering work, the research community has made substantial progress. Current approaches are now capable of handling a virtually unbounded number of possible dialog states, system actions, and observations, yet perform on-line inference in real-time, and perform off-line planning quickly. Methods have been developed for incorporating business rules into the policy, encoding structured domain knowledge into the state, and automatically learning transition dynamics from unlabelled data. Together these techniques have enabled POMDPs to scale to real-world dialog systems, producing better robustness to speech recognition errors, better task completion rates, and shorter dialogs.

This chapter has three broad goals. First, the next two sections aim to present the spoken dialog task and explain why POMDPs are an attractive solution compared to current practice in industry and related approaches in research. Second, the following section details how POMDPs have been adapted to the requirements of this real-world task. Third, the final section identifies open problems for POMDP-based dialog systems, and suggests avenues for future research.

BACKGROUND: SPOKEN DIALOG SYSTEMS

In general spoken dialog systems have a common logical architecture, with three modules: input, output, and control (Figure 1). The input module

Figure 1. Components of a spoken dialog system

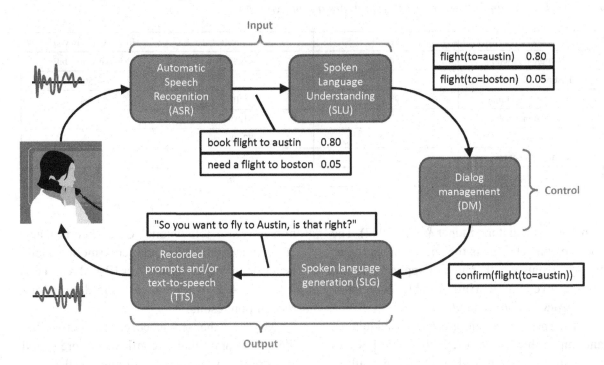

operates in two stages: automatic speech recognition (ASR) and spoken language understanding (SLU). First, ASR converts audio of the user's speech into an ordered *N-Best* list of the *N* best hypotheses for the words spoken, where the top (*n*=1) hypothesis is the recognizer's best guess. For example, hypothesis *n*=1 might be "Book a flight to Austin" and hypothesis *n*=2 might be "Need a flight to Boston". In the SLU step, each N-Best entry is converted to a dialog act, which expresses the user's intention. For example, hypothesis *n*=1 might be flight(to=austin) and hypothesis *n*=2 might be flight(to=boston).

The input module also produces a confidence score for each hypothesis, which is effectively a context-independent probability of correctness for each hypothesis on the N-Best list. For example, the confidence for *n*=1 might be 0.80 and the confidence for *n*=2 might be 0.05.

The control module receives the N-Best list of user dialog acts and performs two tasks. First, the control module tracks the current state of the

dialog, accumulating history as required. For example, the control module might track how many times each piece of information has been requested, and what has been recognized so far. Second, based on the current state, the control module chooses which dialog act to reply to the user, such as confirm(flight(to=austin)).

Finally the output module receives the system's dialog act and presents it to the user. The dialog act is converted to a string of words using natural language generation (NLG). For example, confirm(flight(to=austin)) might be converted to "So you want to fly to Austin, is that right?" Then the words are rendered as audio for the user, using pre-recorded prompts, text-to-speech (TTS), or a mixture of the two.

This architecture may be extended with additional modalities. For example, additional inputs might include the user's gesture, eye gaze, or keyboard entry; and additional outputs might include a graphical user interface (Johnston et al., 2002), an animated head (Bohus & Horvitz, 2009),

Table 1. Example accuracy of three grammars from commercially deployed spoken dialog systems running at AT&T. Even for simple tasks, ASR errors are unavoidable.

	Yes/no	City/state	How may I help you?
Example phrase(s)	yes; nope	Tucson Arizona	Help with um a bill
Distinct user intents	2	~30,000	~250
In-grammar accuracy	99.8%	85.1%	89.5%
In-grammar rate	92.3%	91.0%	86.8%
Overall accuracy	92.1%	77.6%	77.7%
Correct accept rate	89.6%	60.3%	73.3%
False accept rate	1.8%	4.9%	8.3%

or robotic articulators (Sidner & Lee, 2007). The focus of this chapter is the speech modality, as this underpins a wide range of applications and presents two important broad problems: *recognition errors* and *plan complexity*.

First, speech recognition errors are ubiquitous, and impossible to detect reliably. Table 1 shows accuracy for the top (n=1) recognition result in several commercially deployed dialog systems. Simple recognition tasks yield near-perfect accuracy when the user speaks "in-grammar" – within the catalog of words and phrases the recognizer is capable of recognizing. For example, a yes/no grammar might recognize "yes", "no", and synonyms like "nope", "yup", "yeah", etc. This grammar might be used following a question like "So you want to fly to Austin, is that right?". In-grammar accuracy for more complex recognition tasks is less than perfect but still rather high.

Unfortunately input to the ASR is often "out-of-grammar": words or other sounds which are outside the bounds of what the recognizer is capable of understanding. Table 1 shows only 86.8%-92.3% of utterances are in-grammar. Users sometimes provide additional information ("Yes and I'm leaving tomorrow"), change the topic ("Wait which airport do you have me leaving from?"), engage in dialog repair ("No I said tomorrow"), get distracted ([to a co-worker] "Just a minute, I'm on the phone."), hesitate ("Umm... well..."), or remain silent. In addition, background

noises (cars, televisions, other people) and communication channel problems (mobile phone network problems, Voice Over IP problems) can intrude. All of these can yield spurious recognition results.

Moreover, the confidence score cannot reliably identify errors. An ideal confidence score would assign 1.0 to accurate recognitions, and 0.0 to errors. In practice the probabilities are more evenly distributed. Figure 2 shows a receiver operating characteristic (ROC) curve for one question in a commercially spoken dialog system which illustrates that any choice of accept/reject threshold will result in admitting some errors and failing to admit some accurate recognitions.

The second challenge for spoken dialog systems is plan complexity. Dialog is a sequential process in which short-term actions affect the long-term outcome of the dialog, and it can be very difficult to anticipate what the consequences of different actions will be. For example:

• When is it better to ask an open question, such as "How may I help you?", and when is it better to ask more directed questions, such as "Which city are you leaving from?" Open questions can lead to faster dialogs when recognition is accurate, but engender more recognition errors since users' responses are more complex. Directed

Figure 2. Receiver operating characteristic (ROC) curve for ASR confidence score. A "False accept" is a recognition error which is admitted, and a "True accept" is a correct recognition which is admitted. Taken from a grammar running in a commercially deployed spoken dialog system at AT&T.

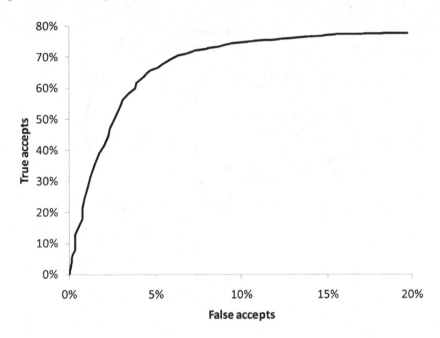

questions lead to more reliable recognitions but prolong the dialog.

- When is it better to confirm ("Was that Boston?") or commit ("Alright, I'm issuing a ticket from Boston to London.")? Confirming helps ensure information collected is reliable, but prolongs dialogs. In order to complete a task, the system must commit at some point.
- What is the best form for confirmations – explicit ("Are you leaving from Boston?") or implicit ("Ok, Boston. And where to?"). Explicit confirmations produce more regular speech and are thus more reliable, but they prolong the conversation and can be tedious.
- When is it better to provide more information ("I found five flights, here they are...") or less ("Here is a flight that matches your request...")? Listening to verbose system output is tedious, but users often want to know all of their options.

The conventional approach is for a dialog designer to create a flow chart that describes the dialog plan (example, Figure 3). Each node is labeled with a system action, and transitions are labeled with observations or other conditions. Unfortunately the size of the flowchart is bounded by the number of dialog situations that a designer can contemplate – in practice, on the order of 100 or 1000. Yet the space of possible dialog situations is astronomically larger: in practical systems, the space of possible system actions is often on the order of 10^{10} or more, and the space of possible observations – N-Best lists of dialog acts with their associated real-valued confidence scores – is unbounded. Thus the current practice of designing the dialog flow by hand ignores many possible dialog situations, resulting in sub-optimal plans.

Figure 3. Example of a dialog system design akin to those commonly used in industry. $asr[1] is the top recognition hypothesis and $conf[1] is its confidence score.

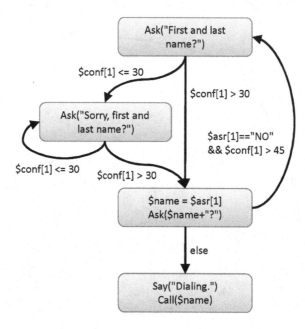

These two problems – ASR errors and plan complexity – conspire to produce spurious dialogs. Consider the dialog in Table 2. In turn 4, the user says their name, but this is mis-recognized as "Athens in Akron", which leads to a cascade of further errors. There is clear room for improvement in the dialog controller: for example, would it be better to have explicitly confirmed "Athens" in turn 5? Perhaps more confidence in "Athens" should have been required? Should off-topic recognitions for this question be disregarded altogether? These are all difficult design questions with consequences to the remainder of the dialog.

As this example illustrates, ASR errors render the true state of the dialog partially observable, and actions have long-term effects. In sum, dialog is an instance of planning under uncertainty, for which POMDPs provide a principled approach. The next section explains how dialog can be modeled as a POMDP and gives concrete examples

of its benefits compared to current practices in industry.

CASTING A SPOKEN DIALOG SYSTEM AS A POMDP

In this section, we first develop a model of spoken dialog as a POMDP, then illustrate how a POMDP-based dialog system can outperform traditional approaches. Finally, POMDP-based dialog systems are compared to related methods for learning dialog strategies.

Spoken Dialog as a POMDP

Recall from Chapter 3 that a POMDP consists of a tuple $\{\mathcal{A}, \mathcal{O}, \mathcal{S}, \mathcal{T}, \mathcal{Z}, R, \gamma\}$, where $\mathcal{A}$ is a set of actions $a \in \mathcal{A}$, $\mathcal{O}$ is a set of observations $o \in \mathcal{O}$, $\mathcal{S}$ is a set of states $s \in \mathcal{S}$, $\mathcal{T}$ is a transi-

Table 2. Sample conversation with a spoken dialog system affected by misunderstandings in the CMU Communicator spoken dialog system, taken from (Bohus & Rudnicky, 2002). U indicates a user turn and M indicates a machine turn. In turn 4 the user says their name (omitted for privacy reasons) but they are misrecognized as saying "Athens in Akron". This single error then leads to a complete misalignment between the user and system.

T	ID	System / user action
1	M	Are you a registered user ?
2	U	No I'm not. No [NO I'M NOT NO]
3	M	What is your full name ?
4	U	User Name [ATHENS IN AKRON]
5	M	There is an Athens in Georgia and in Greece. Which destination did you want ?
6	U	Neither [NEITHER]
7	M	I'm sorry, I didn't catch that. There is an Athens in Georgia and in Greece. Which destination did you want ?
8	U	Georgia [GEORGIA]
9	M	A flight from Athens... Where do you want to go ?
10	U	Start over [START OVER]
11	M	Do you really want to start over ?
12	U	Yes [YES]
13	M	What city are you leaving from ?
14	U	Hamilton, Ontario [HILTON ONTARIO]
15	M	......

tion function $P(s'|s,a)$, $\mathcal{Z}$ is an observation function $P(o'|s',a)$, R is a reward function $R(s,a) \in \mathbb{R}$, and γ is a discount factor $0 \le \gamma \le 1$.

To frame spoken dialog as a POMDP, the system's dialog act is cast as the POMDP action a and the ASR/SLU output is cast as the POMDP observation o. For example, POMDP action a might correspond to the system action ask(city) ("What city are you leaving from?"), confirm(city=boston) ("Was that Boston?"), or print-ticket(to=boston) ("Ok, issuing a ticket to Boston.") POMDP observation o might correspond to an N-Best list with 2 items (city=boston and city=austin), and their corresponding confidence scores.

The hidden state of the dialog – including all quantities which the system cannot directly observe – is cast as the hidden POMDP state s.

The exact elements of the hidden state can vary with the domain; here we describe one common factorization known as the SDS-POMDP model, which serves as a base framework for many information-seeking dialogs (Williams & Young, 2007a).

In the SDS-POMDP model, the hidden state contains three quantities, $s=(g,h,u)$. g is the *user's goal* – this is the user's long-term aim in the conversation, such as booking a flight from London to Boston on November 23 in economy class. u is the true, unobserved *user action*, such as yes,city=boston ("Yes, Boston"), remaining silent, or saying something out-of-grammar which the ASR/SLU cannot recognize. Finally, h is the *dialog history* – an accumulator variable which records aspects of hidden state which the dialog designer feels are important, such as whether the departure city has been asked, confirmed, or not yet discussed. Including this accumulator variable enables system and user behavior to be conditioned on distant history.

Depending on the domain, the SDS-POMDP model may be extended with other quantities, such as the user's level of expertise with the system or the user's emotional state or stress level (Bui, Poel, Nijholt, & Zwiers, 2009). Variables representing other world state may also be added – for example, in a dialog system for troubleshooting a network connection, the state of the network router (on/off, working/failed, status lights, etc.) might be included (Williams, 2007a).

Returning to the core SDS-POMDP model, we next substitute $s=(g,h,u)$ into the POMDP transition and observation functions. For the transition function we have:

$$P(s'|s,a)= P(g',h',u'|g,h,u,a)$$

$$= P(g'|g,h,u,a)P(u'|g',g,h,u,a)$$
$$P(h'|u',g',g,h,u,a). \qquad (1)$$

Conditional independence is then assumed as follows. The first term in Equation 1, called the *user goal model*, indicates how the user's goal changes (or does not change) at each time-step. It is assumed that the user's goal at each time-step depends only on the previous goal, the dialog history, and the machine's action:

$$P(g'|g,h,u,a)=P(g'|g,h,a). \qquad (2)$$

The second term, called the *user action model*, indicates what actions the user is likely to take at each time step. It is assumed the user's action depends on their (current) goal, the dialog history, and the machine action:

$$P(u'|g',g,h,u,a)=P(u'|g',h,a). \qquad (3)$$

The third term, called the *dialog history model*, captures relevant historical information about the dialog. This component has access to the most recent value of all variables:

$$P(h'|u',g',g,h,u,a)= P(h'|u',g',h,a). \qquad (4)$$

Thus the transition function becomes

$$P(s'|s,a)= P(g'|g,h,a)P(u'|g',h,a)P(h'|u',g',h,a). \qquad (5)$$

Similarly, substituting $s=(g,h,u)$ into the POMDP observation function yields $P(o'|g',h',u',a)$. It is assumed that the recognizer output depends only on the user's action:

$$P(o'|g',h',u',a)=P(o'|u'). \qquad (6)$$

The POMDP belief state update then becomes

$$b'(g',h',u')$$

$$= \eta \cdot p(o'|u') \sum_{g,h,u} P(g'|g,h,a)P(u'|g',h,a)P(h'|u',g',h,a)b(g,h,u) \qquad (7)$$

Figure 4 shows the SDS-POMDP model as an influence diagram.

The models themselves have to be estimated of course – in general this can be done by collecting dialogs, and fitting models to the data. In practice this requires relatively few dialogs – generally a few hundred or less.

Illustration of a POMDP-Based Dialog System

To illustrate, a simple dialog system is now reviewed. Full details are available in (Williams & Young, 2007a) and (Williams, 2006). In this system, the user is trying to book travel from one city to another in a world with 3 cities, resulting in 6 possible user goals. The system actions include asking for the origin or destination, confirmations, and printing a ticket. The dialog history indicates

Figure 4. The SDS-POMDP model shown as an influence diagram. The POMDP state s has been factored into 3 components: the user's goal g, the user's true goal u, and the dialog history h. The POMDP observation o is the output from the ASR/SLU.

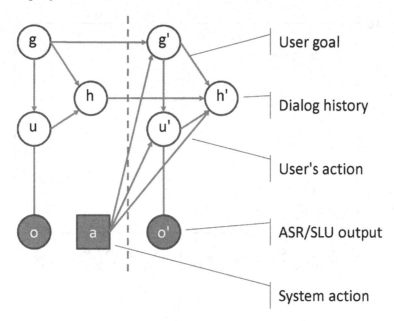

whether each slot is unasked, filled, or confirmed, yielding a set of 9 dialog histories. The user can say the name of a city, say "from" or "to" a city, say "from a to b", "yes", "no", and remain silent, yielding a set of 18 possible user actions. In addition there is a binary flag indicating whether the dialog is in its first turn or not. Taking the Cartesian product of these components yields 1944 POMDP states. The simulated ASR output includes one hypothesis and no confidence score, yielding 18 possible observations.

Simple transition function models are assumed – for example, it is assumed that the user's goal stays fixed and that the user sometimes provides additional information in their responses. The observation function is parameterized by p_{err}, the probability of making a uniformly distributed ASR confusion error. The reward function assigns +10 for printing the correct ticket, −10 for printing the wrong ticket, and −1 for each question asked.

With the transition function, observation function, and reward function in place, POMDP optimization can be applied to produce a dialog plan $\pi(b)$. Here the "Perseus" implementation (Spaan & Vlassis, 2005) of point-based value iteration is used (see Chapter 3). Running Perseus with 500 belief points finds good policies.

Two types of baseline policies were also developed on the same system: a (fully-observable) Markov decision process (MDP) akin to others used in the literature (Singh, Litman, Kearns, & Walker, 2002), and three hand-crafted controllers. The MDP (Chapter 3) is trained using the same reward function, but differs from the POMDP in that it does not model the partial observability of the user's goals. Rather, it tracks a single hypothesis for the user's goal, updating it whenever it sees a new recognition result. The three hand-crafted controllers implement three common dialog strategies found in commercial systems.

Figure 5. Expected or average return of POMDP policies and an MDP baseline. The horizontal axis p_{err} refers to the probability of making a simulated speech recognition error. As errors increase the POMDP outperforms the MDP by an increasing margin.

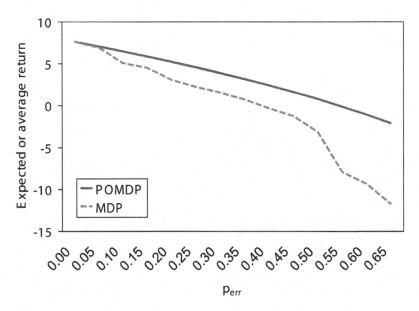

Average return for the POMDP and MDP are shown in Figure 5 for various ASR error rates on the horizontal axis. As errors increase performance of all systems decreases; however the POMDP outperforms the MDP by an increasing margin. The POMDP shows a similar performance gain over hand-crafted controllers (Williams, Poupart, & Young, 2005).

As this example illustrates, POMDPs are more robust to ASR errors, and in practice this leads to shorter dialogs with higher task completion rates. The POMDP achieves this by performing several types of reasoning which traditional systems cannot. First, POMDPs synthesize information across multiple dialog turns including multiple N-Best lists, whereas traditional systems make local accept/reject decisions considering only the top recognition result, and cannot accumulate noisy evidence over time. For example, consider Figure 6, in which the same hypothesis is recognized twice, with low confidence. Whereas a conventional system would discard each recogni-

tion, POMDP-based systems are able to use this information. Similarly, POMDP-based approaches are able to identify commonality across N-Best lists – for example, in Figure 7. Even though the $N=2$ item was never the single most likely item on a *local* N-Best list, it is the *globally* most likely user goal after the second turn. This behavior is not possible with traditional approaches.

In computing the belief state, POMDPs also incorporate prior expectations about users' behavior and goals. This additional information provides another source of robustness not available to traditional systems. For example, in Figure 8, the N-Best list contains two competing alternatives for the user's action. A traditional system would simply take the top hypothesis; a POMDP is able to view each of these in light of how likely they are given the current dialog context, and emerge with the correct answer. The same can be observed with competing user goals, as in Figure 9.

Figure 6. Example conversation with a spoken dialog system illustrating two successive low-confidence recognitions. In this example, both recognitions are correct. The POMDP accumulates weak evidence over time, whereas traditional methods would ignore both recognitions because they are below the rejection threshold (here set to 0.40). In effect, traditional methods are discarding possibly useful information.

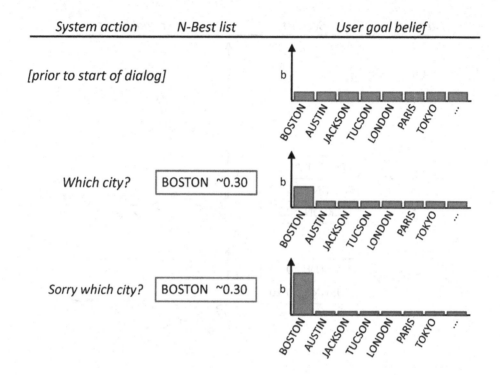

In sum, the belief state provides a *cumulative* confidence score for the user's goal over the entire dialog – including all N-Best lists and the confidence scores they contain – as well as prior expectations about user behavior and goal preferences. A distribution over multiple dialog state hypotheses adds inherent robustness, because even if an error is introduced into one dialog hypothesis, it can later be discarded in favor of other, uncontaminated dialog hypotheses.

POMDPs also choose actions differently than traditional approaches, and concretely the benefit is that POMDPs construct much more detailed dialog plans. A large-scale commercial dialog system design might contain 1000 pages of flowcharts (akin to Figure 3), comprising perhaps 1000 dialog situations. Increasing this by an order of magnitude is unimaginable, since no single human designer would be able to conceptualize the entire design in their mind. By contrast, POMDPs can consider many more dialog situations. Moreover, POMDP policies are performing explicit planning with respect to a global optimization criterion (the reward function), but with a hand-crafted dialog plan it is not known what the criteria are – indeed, dialog designers are often making educated guesses at the optimal choice of action (Williams, 2009).

Related Work

Many other approaches have been suggested for automatically choosing actions in a spoken dialog systems. One approach is to choose actions to maximize an immediate utility, rather than a long term reward (Horvitz & Paek, 1999, Paek & Horvitz, 2000, 200b, 2003, Bohus & Horvitz,

Figure 7. Example conversation with a spoken dialog system illustrating how tracking multiple dialog state hypotheses is able to identify commonality across ASR N-Best lists. In this example, the correct answer appears in the N=2 position on two successive recognitions. The POMDP is able to identify this commonality whereas traditional methods cannot.

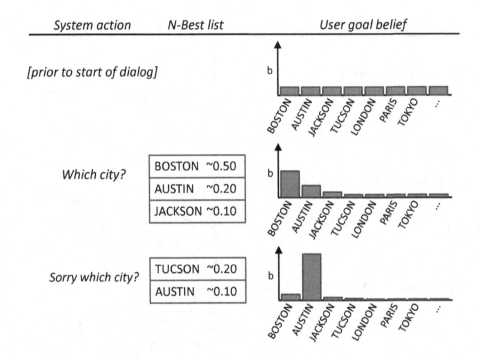

2009). This can be thought of as setting the POMDP discount factor to 0. This approach avoids the complexities of performing long-term planning, but requires that the immediate utilities ensure the agent makes progress toward a long-term goal. In this approach, designing a utility function can require more trial and error.

In a POMDP, the belief state is a strict probabilistic interpretations of a distribution over hidden states. Other techniques for tracking multiple dialog instead track *scores* which are monotonic but not necessarily probabilities (Higashinaka, Nakano, & Aikawa, 2003, Henderson, Lemon, & Georgila, 2008). These scores do not correspond to probabilities – in other words, they are an approximation to Eq 7. Scores can be easier to compute than probabilities; however, the effects of the approximations made have not been studied. Also, scores can be more difficult to interpret:

for example, a score of 0.5 may correspond to a probability of 0.9 or 0.1. At present, it is not known whether using scores degrades overall dialog performance compared to maintaining proper probabilities.

It is also possible to track multiple dialog states, but choose actions according to hand-crafted rules rather than by optimization (Higashinaka et al., 2003). In this approach, a person decides how to make use of the belief state. This is a difficult task to which dialog designers are generally not accustomed. Moreover, a dialog designer can only consider a small number of dialog situations, whereas an optimization process can create much more detailed dialog plans. Experiments with usability subjects have shown that optimization, done properly, yields more successful dialogs than hand-crafted design by better exploiting the information contained in the distribution

Figure 8. Illustration of how the POMDP is able to incorporate prior expectations about a user's behaviors. Here the N-Best list contains two competing hypotheses with similar ASR probabilities for the user's action; the effect of the user action model P(u'|g',h,a) is to prefer the more likely user action – TO=BOSTON – which more directly answers the system's question, even though it is recognized with a lower confidence score.

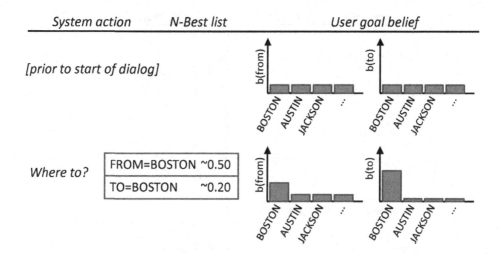

over multiple dialog states (Young et al., 2010, Thomson & Young, 2010).

Another method for dialog control is to mimic actions observed in a dialog corpus using supervised learning (Griol, Hurtado, Segarra, & Sanchis, 2008, Lee, Jung, Kim, & Lee, 2009b, Hori, Ohtake, Misu, Kashioka, & Nakamura, 2009). This approach may be attractive when there is a corpus of interactions with a dialog manager which is believed to be optimal – for example, a human "wizard" who sees the output of the speech recognition, and controls the dialog manager in real time. This approach allows for the creation of more detailed dialog plans than could be written by a human designer. However, it unclear whether a human wizard could make good use of distribution over dialog states, in real time, while interacting with real users.

Other approaches choose actions as POMDPs do, but track state differently. For example, there has been a large amount of work which tracks a single hypothesis for the current dialog state, casting optimization as an MDP rather than a POMDP (Walker, 2000, Levin, Pieraccini, & Eckert, 2000, Litman, Kearns, Singh, & Walker, 2000, Singh et al., 2002, Pietquin, 2004, Pietquin & Dutoit, 2006, Cuayáhuitl, Renals, Lemon, & Shimodaira, 2006, Lemon, Georgila, & Henderson, 2006, Tetreault & Litman, 2006, "Comparing User Simulation Models for Dialog Strategy Learning", 2007, Tetreault, Bohus, & Litman, 2007, Henderson et al., 2008, Rieser, 2008). In this approach it is difficult to aggregate information across recognitions, and also to make use of multiple entries on the N-Best list. Experiments have shown than POMDP-based dialog systems are more robust than MDP counterparts (Young et al., 2010, Thomson & Young, 2010).

In addition, numerous other aspects of the spoken dialog system can be "learned" for a specific task, such as application-specific grammars (Starkie et al., 2002, Suendermann, Liscombe, Dayanidhi, & Pieraccini, 2009), prompt wording (Chen, Bangalore, Rambow, & Walker, 2002, Paksima, Georgila, & Moore, 2009), choice of text-to-speech audio (Boidin, Rieser, Plas, Lemon,

Figure 9. Illustration of how the POMDP is able to integrate a prior over user goals. Here the same recognition result is received twice: TUCSON with low confidence. After the first update, the belief in TUCSON has increased, but the goal with the highest prior still has the most belief. After the second update, TUCSON now has the most belief. The POMDP is able to trade-off between prior beliefs and evidence – ultimately, sufficient evidence can overcome any non-zero prior.

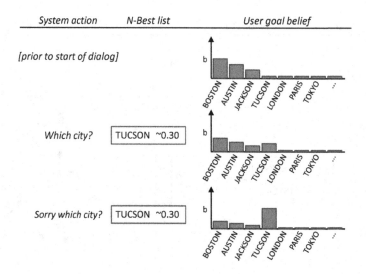

& Chevelu, 2009), and others. Learning in these areas can certainly improve performance of a spoken dialog system, but is separate from the dialog management task.

In sum, POMDPs provide a principled approach to building spoken dialog systems. However, building a real-world POMDP-based dialog system presents a host of obstacles. These challenges, and the techniques developed to overcome them, are covered in the next section.

REAL-WORLD POMDP-BASED DIALOG SYSTEMS

Early work applying POMDPs to SDSs made extensive use of toy problems like the one introduced in the previous section. Researchers at several labs initially followed in the POMDP tradition, creating abstract tasks akin to tiger (Cassandra, Kaelbling, & Littman, 1994), tiger-grid (Littman, Cassandra, & Kaelbling, 1995), chain-walk (Koller &

Parr, 2000), or rock-sample (Smith & Simmons, 2004). In this formula, first a designer specifies a flat POMDP state, observation, and action set, and then asserts a transition, observation, and reward function in tabular form. Optimization is performed to produce a policy, and that policy is evaluated by measuring its average return on the same system dynamics. The POMDPs developed in early work had on the order of 1000 states, 10 actions and 10 observations, and were optimized with techniques such as the augmented POMDP (Roy et al., 2000), grid-based approximations (Zhang, Cai, Mao, Chang, & Guo, 2001, Zhang, Cai, Mao, & Guo, 2001) point-based value iteration (Williams et al., 2005, Williams & Young, 2007a, Pineau, Gordon, & Thrun, 2003, Spaan & Vlassis, 2005), and heuristic search value iteration (Smith & Simmons, 2005), among others.

These preliminary studies confirmed that as speech recognition errors increase, POMDPs outperform both the traditional commercial practice of hand-crafting a policy, and other emerging research techniques such as MDP optimization. Analysis showed that POMDPs were realizing many of the behaviors predicted in the previous section. Spurred on by these preliminary results, the research community set out to scale POMDPs to real dialog systems.

Applying the SDS-POMDP model to real systems presented a series of substantial obstacles. After about 5 years of steady progress, researchers achieved the aim of scaling the POMDP approach to real systems: today, statistical dialog systems are capable of handling a virtually unbounded number of possible dialog states, system actions, and observations, yet perform on-line inference in real-time, and perform off-line planning quickly. Methods have been developed for incorporating business rules into the policy, encoding structured domain knowledge into the state, and learning from a high-fidelity simulated user. These systems have been demonstrated to the research community (Young, Schatzmann, Thomson, Weilhammer, & Ye, 2007, K. Kim & Lee, 2007, Williams, 2008b, Varges, Quarteroni, Riccardi, Ivanov, & Roberti, 2009) and are available for public use (Young et al., n.d., Williams, n.d.). Recently, toolkits have been released to assist non-experts build statistical dialog systems (Bui, Hofs, & Schooten, n.d., Williams, 2010).

This section reviews five crucial advances which enabled the SDS-POMDP model to be scaled to real systems. First, two of these advances address the problem of *tracking* a distribution over dialog states quickly and accurately. The remaining three of these advances tackle the problem of *choosing actions* optimally, in very large state spaces.

Incorporating the N-Best List into the Observation Function

Early work cast the POMDP observation function as a single ASR hypothesis without a confidence score. However, as mentioned above, real ASR outputs is an "N-Best" of N hypotheses $\tilde{\mathbf{u}} = (\tilde{u}_1, \ldots, \tilde{u}_N)$, each with a *local*, context-in-

dependent probability of correctness $P(u = \tilde{u}_n \mid o)$. For example, an N-Best list of length 2 with $\tilde{\mathbf{u}} = (\text{austin}, \text{boston})$ might assign $P(u = \text{austin} \mid o) = 0.7$ and $P(u = \text{boston}|o) = 0.1$. The residual mass can be used to determine the probability of correctness for items not on the N-Best list – for example, if there were 100 items in this grammar, then $P(u = \text{cleveland}|o) = (1.0-0.7-0.1)/(100-2) = 0.2/98 \approx 0.002$.

In practice, when the correct answer is not in the N=1 position, about half the time it is further down the N-Best list – so making full use of the information on the N-Best list will produce more accurate belief state updates. Computing $P(u|o)$ can be done quite accurately by creating a regression model that takes features from the ASR and SLU process and yields a vector of probabilities (Thomson, Yu, et al., 2008, Williams & Balakrishnan, 2009). However incorporating $P(u|o)$ into the belief state update requires some care. The POMDP observation function calls for $P(o|u)$, where o is the *entire* N-Best list and all of the associated probabilities. In other words, the POMDP calls for a model of how the N-Best lists and their probabilities are *generated* $P(o|u)$, but the ASR is providing a model of how likely its entries are to be correct $P(u|o)$.

One solution is to apply Bayes' rule:

$$P(o \mid u) = \frac{P(u \mid o)P(o)}{P(u)} \qquad (8)$$

$$= k_1 \cdot \frac{P(u \mid o)}{P(u)} \qquad (9)$$

$$\approx k_2 \cdot P(u \mid o). \qquad (10)$$

During the update, $P(o)$ is constant; this is absorbed into the normalization constant k_1. The key assumption is that $P(u)$ is uniform over all actions, and can also be absorbed into the normalizing constant k_2 in Eq 10. Of course this is not strictly true, but in practice the error introduced is small since the full belief state update (Eq. 7) includes the term $P(u'|g',a,h)$, which is more informative than $P(u)$.

Overall this approach enables all of the information in the observed N-Best list to be used, which yields a more accurate belief state (Williams & Balakrishnan, 2009).

Scaling Up Belief Tracking

Computing the belief state update itself (Eq 7) in real time is problematic for real-world dialog systems. To illustrate this, consider a small dialog task with four slots (e.g., origin city, destination city, time of travel, etc.), where each slot takes on 1000 values. This implies $O(1000^4) = O(10^{12})$ possible values for g, and similarly $O(10^{12})$ possible values for u. In a flat representation, the update iterates over each value of the 4 elements g, g', u, and u'; thus the whole update is $O((10^{12})^4) = O(10^{48})$ which is inconceivable in real time. The picture is even worse for more sophisticated dialog tasks.

One way of speeding up the belief state update is to *factor* the influence diagram further, assume conditional independences as appropriate, and apply *approximate* inference. For example, the user's goal g and user's action u could be decomposed into slots (such as origin city, destination city, time, etc.) (Williams & Young, 2005, 2006, 2007b, Bui, Poel, Nijholt, & Zwiers, 2007, Thomson & Young, 2010). It might then be assumed that the origin city is conditionally independent of the date of departure, or that a user's preference for characteristics of a restaurant or bar are independent of the location. With conditional independences in place, a speed-up over exhaustive enumeration can be realized by using *approximate* inference techniques to compute *marginal* distributions over each variable. For example, researchers in two different labs have applied particle filters (Williams, 2007b), and loopy belief propagation (Thomson, Schatzmann, & Young, 2008). Factoring approaches enable the number of hidden

variables to be scaled, but their computation still grows with the number of values in each variable.

An alternative is to track only a handful of hidden states, and to track all the remaining states *en masse* without distinguishing between them. One implementation of this idea is to track hidden states in *partitions*, where each partition contains one or more user goals (Young, Williams, Schatzmann, Stuttle, & Weilhammer, 2006, Young, Schatzmann, Weilhammer, & Ye, 2007, Young et al., 2010, Williams, 2010). At first there is one root partition that contains all user goals. Then partitions are sub-divided as necessary based on N-Best lists and system actions. For example, if a voice dialer system recognized "Jason", then the root partition would divide into two partitions: all listings with the first name equal to jason, and all listings with the first name *not* jason (denoted ¬jason). Then if "Williams" were recognized, each of these partitions would split, yielding four partitions: ¬jason∧¬williams, ¬jason∧williams, jason∧¬ williams, and jason∧williams. If the number of partitions grows larger than a threshold, then low-probability partitions can be *recombined*, summing their beliefs and ignoring the distinctions between them. This recombination ensures that the belief update can run in real-time regardless of the length of the dialog. An example of the partitioning process is shown in Figure 10.

One key benefit of partitioning is that it allows a proper joint distribution to be tracked over all of the elements of the user's goal. This is important because there are often meaningful dependencies between slots. For example, business names and locations, people's first and last names, and flight departure and arrival cities are all highly coupled.

Another benefit of partitioning is that its update time is not dependent on the number of underlying user goals – in other words, it enables both the number of variables and the number of variable values to be scaled. However, partitioning makes several important assumptions – chiefly, that the

Figure 10. Illustration of belief monitoring with partitions. Initially there are two partitions (two upper right boxes in blue outline): jason and ¬jason. The number in the lower right of each partition indicates its prior probability; the number in the lower left is the belief (posterior). In this example, the N-Best list (shown in red outline) contains two entries: wilson and williams. In the split phase, partitions are sub-divided for each N-Best entry – first on wilson which increases the number of partitions from 2 to 4, then on williams which increases the number of partitions from 4 to 6. In the figure, new partitions are shown with blue shading. In the update and recombine phase, the belief in each partition is updated, and low probability partitions are re-combined. In this example the maximum number of partitions is limited to 3.

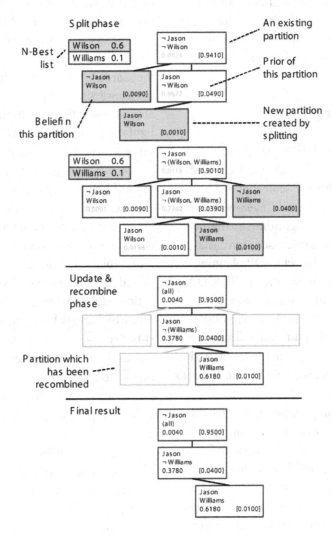

user's goal is generally fixed, and can change in only highly regulated ways.

On the one hand, factoring has the benefit of allowing arbitrary changes in hidden variables, whereas partitioning does not. On the other hand, partitioning is capable of modeling a proper joint distribution and scales to arbitrary numbers of values per variable whereas factoring does not. Recognizing their complementary strengths, recent work has started to unify the two, for example by factoring with variables that may be partitioned (Thomson & Young, 2010). However, at present no technique is able to scale to an arbitrary number of hidden values, handle user goal changes, and track a joint distribution over all goals.

In sum, factoring and partitioning enable POMDP-based dialog systems to track a distribution over a very large number of dialog states in real time, where complete enumeration is hopeless (Williams, 2007b, Young et al., 2010, Thomson & Young, 2010, Williams, 2010). However, both factoring and partitioning have implications for planning, discussed next.

Scaling Up Planning

Optimal planning in POMDPs is notoriously intractable. Indeed, early work verified that POMDP planners could not scale beyond toy tasks with a handful of user goals, even with the most sophisticated planning algorithms available. Moreover, the two advances discussed above present challenges for traditional POMDP planning. The main problem is that traditional POMDP optimization enumerates all possible hidden states, yet as discussed above, the scale of the dialog task renders this impossible for even the simpler problem of belief tracking. Performing traditional POMDP planning over all possible hidden states is completely hopeless.

The key to scaling up planning is the insight that planning can be done in a small *feature space* by exploiting properties of the dialog domain. The basic idea is to map the belief state and action into smaller feature spaces, perform planning and choose actions in feature space, and then map that action back to the full space (Williams & Young, 2005, 2006, 2007b).

As an illustration, consider a slot-filling dialog, in which the system's goal is to obtain the value of the user's goal for a set of *slots*. For simplicity first consider a dialog problem with a single slot – for example, a weather information service with N cities. The system can ask for the slot value ("What city do you want the weather for?"), confirm the slot's value ("The weather in Seattle, is that right?"), or submit the slot's value ("The weather in Seattle today will be overcast and rainy."). There is a single ask action, and N confirm and submit actions, for a total of $1+2N$ actions. The key insight is that the confirm and submit actions can be limited *a priori* to act on only *the most likely slot value*, reducing the set of useful actions to 3. In other words, even though there are a very large set of *possible* actions available to the dialog system, only a small number of these are *useful* in a given dialog context. Further, to choose among these actions, it can be reasonably assumed that only the belief held by the most likely value (or the top M values) is relevant. In other words, the planner can act on a small set of *features* of the belief state, rather than considering the full belief simplex.

Recall that in real-world dialog systems, the belief state cannot be maintained explicitly, but is rather represented in a factored or partitioned representation. Fortunately, factored and partitioned belief states marry well with feature-based action selection. First, the designer creates a function which maps from the partitioned or factored belief state to feature vector $\hat{b}$. This feature vector might contain, for example, the amount of belief held by the most likely user goals. The designer also specifies a small set of *summary* actions $\{\hat{a}_1, \ldots, \hat{a}_N\}$, and a method for mapping these to fully-instantiated dialog actions. For example, the confirm summary action could be mapped to confirm the most likely slot value, such as "Boston, is that right?"

The aim of optimization is then to estimate $\hat{\pi}$ which maps from the feature vector $\hat{b}$ to a summary action $\hat{a}$, $\hat{\pi}(\hat{b}) = \hat{a}$. Unlike in traditional POMDP optimization, the learner does not have direct access to the transition function or reward function $\hat{R}(\hat{b}, \hat{a})$, because in general these cannot be computed analytically from the underlying dynamics. Instead, the learner is presented with a simulator, or trajectories of the form $(\hat{b}_0, \hat{a}_1, r_1, \hat{b}_1, \hat{a}_2, r_2, \hat{b}_2, \ldots)$. Thus learning is now a general reinforcement learning problem, and can be accomplished in a variety of ways. Chapter 4 describes reinforcement learning in detail; in this domain, early work sampled trajectories through summary space $(\hat{b}_0, \hat{a}_1, r_1, \hat{b}_1, \hat{a}_2, r_2, \hat{b}_2, \ldots)$, used these to estimate a reward function $\hat{R}(\hat{b}, \hat{a})$ and grid-based transition function $\hat{P}(\hat{b}' \mid \hat{b}, \hat{a})$, and applied simple value iteration (Williams & Young, 2006, 2007b, Williams, 2008c). Subsequently, many other approaches have been explored, including eligibility traces (Scheffler & Young, 2002), SARSA (Henderson, Lemon, & Georgila, 2005, Henderson & Lemon, 2008), Monte Carlo methods (Young et al., 2010), novel variants of Least-Squares Policy Iteration (Li, Williams, & Balakrishnan, 2009), and Natural Actor-Critic (Thomson & Young, 2010).

An alternative for planning using summary actions which *does* admit traditional POMDP planning is the *Permutable POMDP* (Doshi & Roy, 2008a). Here states are dynamically re-ordered by their belief, allowing planning in master space using summary-style actions. While elegant, this approach requires that the state variables are enumerated – as discussed above, this is impossible with the large state spaces required in real-world dialog problems.

Adding More Sophisticated Simulated Users

In traditional POMDPs it is usually assumed that the model of the environment $P(s'|s,a)$ is correct. In spoken dialog systems, the "environment" is the users of the system and the ASR/SLU input channel. The behavior of real people is highly complex, and modeling this behavior is an unsolved problem and active area of research in its own right. Studies have found that modeling user behavior well requires non-trivial data structures – for example, modeling persistent goals over

long dialog segments requires a dynamic stack of intentions (Schatzmann, Georgila, & Young, 2005, Schatzmann, Weilhammer, Stuttle, & Young, 2007, Thomson, Schatzmann, Welhammer, Ye, & Young, 2007, Schatzmann, Thomson, Weilhammer, Ye, & Young, 2007, Schatzmann, Thomson, & Young, 2007b). Implementations of these models generally contain complex series of deterministic and random decisions, and this complexity makes it extremely difficult to incorporate them into an influence diagram. In addition, research has shown that optimizing a dialog system with an overly simplistic simulated user may yield promising results when tested on the same simplistic simulated user, but very poor results on more realistic simulated users (or real users!) (Schatzmann, Stuttle, Weilhammer, & Young, 2005, D. Kim et al., 2008). Similarly, other studies have found that the most reliable ASR/SLU simulations rely on sequences of operations which would be problematic to encode in an influence diagram (Schatzmann, Thomson, & Young, 2007a).

In sum, it would be beneficial to make use of a high-fidelity simulator during the optimization process, but that simulator can't be encoded into the transition function. As a result, state-of-the-art POMDP-based dialog systems make use of *two* distinct user models: a *simplified, internal* simulated user which can readily be incorporated into an influence diagram, and a *complex, external* simulated user which runs in a purely generative mode. The internal model is used to perform inference to compute the belief state; the external model is used to simulate dialogs for policy learning (Young et al., 2010, Thomson & Young, 2010).

Adding Business Rules and Domain Knowledge to Planning

In many dialog tasks, dialog designers know a great deal about the structure of the optimal policy. For example, it is easy to articulate rules such as "don't attempt to confirm a value before it has been requested." In addition, in commercial settings, dialog systems must be guaranteed to follow certain business rules, such as always verifying a password before allowing a caller to transfer funds. Thus there are constraints available on when actions can be taken.

One solution is to apply a *partial program* (Andre & Russell, 2002) to dialog systems (Williams, 2008a, Gasic et al., 2009). A hand-crafted dialog manager *with its own internal state* runs in parallel with the belief state. At each time-step, the hand-crafted dialog manager outputs a vector of features, and nominates a set of one or more *allowed* actions; the planner chooses which action is *optimal* from this limited set based on the feature vector.

Experiments have shown that this approach not only enables expert knowledge and business rules to be encoded in the policy, but also that optimization runs faster and more reliably as compared to standard exhaustive exploration (Williams, 2008a, Gasic et al., 2009). The intuition is that the expert knowledge avoids taking spurious actions and focuses planning effort on the set of plausible plans.

From an engineering standpoint, this formulation provides an important bridge from current commercial practices to statistical approaches. Dialog designers currently write computer programs that output a single action at each time-step, possibly with the help of a dialog design tool – for example, (*VoiceObjects application design tool*, 2010, *SpeechDraw application design tool*, 2010, *Audium Studio application design tool*, 2010, *Nuance OpenSpeech dialog design tool*, 2010). It is relatively straightforward to extend this model to output a small set of actions at each time-step. In effect, this approach captures the strengths of both human expertise in providing high-level structure and cohesion and the robustness and fine-grained control afforded by statistical techniques.

Crucially, the feature vector can contain elements drawn from either the belief state or the hand-crafted dialog manager state, and the features themselves can take any form, including categorical, binary, integral, or real-valued elements. For example, consider a voice dialer in which a caller says the name of a listing they want to call (Williams, 2008b, 2008c). In this problem, the hidden state enumerates all the user's possible goals (the listings), and the belief state maintains a distribution over these. There are two probability features: one for the belief in the top listing, and another in the belief in the top type of phone (office or cell). In addition, the planner needs information about whether the most likely listing has an office phone and/or cellphone available, whether there are multiple listings with the same name in the directory, and how many times the caller has been asked each question. Unlike the user's goal (the listings), there is no uncertainty in these items. Thus the feature vector includes categorical features for how many phone types are available for the most likely listing ("none","one","two"), and binary features ("true" or "false") for whether the most likely listing is ambiguous and whether confirmation has been requested by the system. As this example illustrates, a heterogeneous feature vector is useful because there are often fully observable features useful for planning, and tracking a distribution over these adds additional computation with no benefit.

Section Summary

This section has described five key advances for decision-theoretic approaches to dialog control: incorporating the N-Best list into the observation function, speeding up the belief state update, scaling up planning, employing more sophisticated user simulations, and injecting business rules and domain knowledge into planning. Each of these has played an important role in moving the POMDP approach closer to commercial readiness. Although state-of-the-art dialog systems are implemented rather differently to a traditional POMDP, it is important to realize that all of their machinery is in service of the two fundamental ideas of POMDPs: tracking a distribution over multiple states, and choosing actions to maximize a sum of rewards. It is these two fundamental ideas which are responsible for the gains in performance achieved by POMDP-based dialog systems over competing approaches.

Research into statistical approaches to dialog remains an active area, and a number of international research teams are currently working on this topic. Although researchers at different labs have made good progress in the past five years, important open questions remain, and there is still interesting work ahead. The next section concludes by discussing suggesting some opportunities.

CONCLUSION AND OPEN PROBLEMS

Spoken dialog systems are a classic example of planning under uncertainty: dialog is a control problem where speech recognition errors render the true state of the world only partially observable, yet the agent must choose actions to make progress toward a long-term goal. Difficult trade-offs exist between actions which gather information but prolong the dialog, and actions which can conclude the dialog but have high cost if taken in error.

The dialog management problem is well modeled as a POMDP. In a POMDP, the state of the world isn't observed directly, so a *distribution* over many dialog states is maintained. Actions are then chosen to maximize the expected *sum* of rewards until the end of the interaction.

In early work, toy dialog problems were solved using traditional POMDP optimization techniques. To apply POMDP-based dialog systems to real-world dialog problems, numerous extensions have been made to tailor the POMDP approach to the dialog domain. Several POMDP-based dialog systems have been trialed with paid usability subjects (Young et al., 2010, Thomson & Young,

2010), and currently dialog systems incorporating elements of the POMDP approach are being fielded with real users in the 2010 Spoken Dialog Challenge (Black, Burger, Langner, Parent, & Eskenazi, 2010).

Despite this progress, several important open questions remain:

- The analysis in this chapter suggests that first-order "lifted" POMDPs would be a natural fit with SDSs. As discussed above, lifted inference (in the form of partitions) is required to perform the belief update in real time. To scale, planning ought to operate on the same representation of state. Although first-order POMDPs are in their infancy today (Sanner, 2009), perhaps spoken dialog systems will provide a fertile testbed for emerging first-order POMDP work.

- There is a clear opportunity for a POMDP-based dialog system to refine its models as it interacts with users. While there has been some work exploring learning models of user behavior from logs of dialog data (Syed & Williams, 2008, Thomson et al., 2007), there are many issues remaining to explore: for example, there is an interdependence between the user's actual behavior, the system's model of the user's behavior, and the system's current policy. More work is needed to understand how to jointly optimize the models of user behavior and the system's policy.

- Currently, it is not well understood how to set the reward function used to guide action selection. In practice, practitioners try different values until optimization yields a reasonable dialog policy. There is a clear need for specific guidance on how to set the reward function. One possibility is to examine existing (hand-designed) dialog systems to infer what reward function would make their policy optimal. This process is known as *inverse reinforcement learning*, and algorithms have been suggested for inferring reward functions from expert trajectories (Ng & Russell, 2000), including in the partially observable case (Choi & Kim, 2009).

- Substantial work is needed to make POMDP-based SDSs accessible to commercial practitioners. Tools are needed in general-purpose programming language such as Python or Java which encapsulate common functions, such as policy optimization, model representation and estimation, simulated dialog execution, etc.

Although interesting research questions such as these remain, POMDP-based dialog systems are rapidly maturing, and it seems promising that they will be applied in industry in the near future.

REFERENCES

Ai, H., Tetreault, J. R., & Litman, D. J. (2007). Comparing user simulation models for dialog strategy learning. In *Proc Human Language Technologies: The Annual Conference of the North American Chapter of the Association for Computational Linguistics (NAACL-HLT)*, Rochester, New York, USA.

Andre, D., & Russell, S. J. (2002). State abstraction for programmable reinforcement learning agents. In *Proc National Conference on Artificial Intelligence*, Edmonton, Alberta, Canada (pp. 119–125).

Audium. (2010). *Studio application design tool.* Retrieved from http://www.audiumcorp.com/Products/

Black, A. W., Burger, S., Langner, B., Parent, G., & Eskenazi, M. (2010). Spoken dialog challenge 2010. In *Proc Workshop on Spoken Language Technologies (SLT), Spoken Dialog Challenge 2010 Special Session*, Berkeley, CA.

Bohus, D., & Horvitz, E. (2009). Models for multiparty engagement in open-world dialog. In *Proc SIGDIAL Workshop on Discourse and Dialogue*, London, UK.

Bohus, D., & Rudnicky, A. I. (2002). *Integrating multiple knowledge sources for utterance-level confidence annotation in the CMU Communicator spoken dialog system* (Technical Report No. CMU-CS-02-190). Carnegie Mellon University.

Boidin, C., Rieser, V., van der Plas, L., Lemon, O., & Chevelu, J. (2009). Predicting how it sounds: Re-ranking dialogue prompts based on TTS quality for adaptive spoken dialogue systems. In *Proc Interspeech*. Brighton, UK: Special Session on Machine Learning for Adaptivity in Spoken Dialogue.

Bui, T. H., Hofs, D., & van Schooten, B. (n.d.). *POMDP toolkit for spoken dialog systems.* Retrieved from http://wwwhome.ewi.utwente.nl/~hofs/pomdp/index.html

Bui, T. H., Poel, M., Nijholt, A., & Zwiers, J. (2007). A tractable DDN-POMDP approach to affective dialogue modeling for general probabilistic frame-based dialogue systems. In *Proc Workshop on Knowledge and Reasoning in Practical Dialogue Systems, Intl Joint Conf on Artificial Intelligence (IJCAI)*, Hyderabad, India (pp. 34–37).

Bui, T. H., Poel, M., Nijholt, A., & Zwiers, J. (2009). A tractable hybrid DDN-POMDP approach to affective dialogue modeling for probabilistic frame-based dialogue systems. *Natural Language Engineering, 15*(2), 273–307. doi:10.1017/S1351324908005032

Cassandra, A. R., Kaelbling, L. P., & Littman, M. L. (1994). Acting optimally in partially observable stochastic domains. In *Proc Conf on Artificial Intelligence, (AAAI)*, Seattle.

Chen, J., Bangalore, S., Rambow, O., & Walker, M. A. (2002). Towards automatic generation of natural language generation systems. In *Proc Intl Conf on Computational Linguistics (COLING)*, Taipei.

Choi, J., & Kim, K. E. (2009). *Inverse reinforcement learning in partially observable environments* (pp. 1028–1033). IJCAI.

Cuayáhuitl, H., Renals, S., Lemon, O., & Shimodaira, H. (2006). Reinforcement learning of dialogue strategies with hierarchical abstract machines. In *Proc Workshop on Spoken Language Technologies (SLT)*, Aruba (pp. 182–185).

Doshi, F., & Roy, N. (2008a). The permutable POMDP: Fast solutions to POMDPs for preference elicitation. In *Proc International Joint Conference on Autonomous Agents and Multiagent Systems*, Estoril, Portugal (pp. 493–-500).

Doshi, F., & Roy, N. (2008b). Spoken language interaction with model uncertainty: An adaptive human–robot interaction system. *Connection Science*, *20*(4), 299–318. doi:10.1080/09540090802413145

Gasic, M., Lefevre, F., Jurcicek, F., Keizer, S., Mairesse, F., & Thomson, B. (2009). Back-off action selection in summary space-based POMDP dialogue systems. In *Proc IEEE Workshop on Automatic Speech Recognition and Understanding (ASRU)*, Merano, Italy.

Griol, D., Hurtado, L. F., Segarra, E., & Sanchis, E. (2008). A statistical approach to spoken dialog systems design and evaluation. *Speech Communication*, *50*(8-9), 666–682. doi:10.1016/j.specom.2008.04.001

Henderson, J., & Lemon, O. (2008). Mixture model POMDPs for efficient handling of uncertainty in dialogue management. In *Proc Association for Computational Linguistics Human Language Technologies*. Columbus, Ohio: ACL-HLT.

Henderson, J., Lemon, O., & Georgila, K. (2005). Hybrid reinforcement/supervised learning for dialogue policies from communicator data. In *Proc Workshop on Knowledge and Reasoning in Practical Dialogue Systems, Intl Joint Conf on Artificial Intelligence (IJCAI)*, Edinburgh (pp. 68–75).

Henderson, J., Lemon, O., & Georgila, K. (2008). Hybrid reinforcement/supervised learning of dialogue policies from fixed data sets. *Computational Linguistics*, *34*(4), 487–511. doi:10.1162/coli.2008.07-028-R2-05-82

Higashinaka, R., Nakano, M., & Aikawa, K. (2003). Corpus-based discourse understanding in spoken dialogue systems. In *Proc Association for Computational Linguistics*. Sapporo, Japan: ACL.

Hori, C., Ohtake, K., Misu, T., Kashioka, H., & Nakamura, S. (2009). Statistical dialog management applied to WFST-based dialog systems. In *Proc Intl Conf on Acoustics, Speech, and Signal Processing (ICASSP), Taipei, Taiwan* (pp. 4793–4796).

Horvitz, E., & Paek, T. (1999). A computational architecture for conversation. In *Proc 7th International Conference on User Modeling (UM)*, Banff, Canada (pp. 201–210).

Johnston, M., Bangalore, S., Vasireddy, G., Stent, A., Ehlen, P., & Walker, M. (2002). An architecture for multimodal dialogue systems. In *Proc Association for Computational Linguistics (ACL)*. Philadelphia, USA: MATCH.

Kim, D., Sim, H. S., Kim, K.-E., Kim, J. H., Kim, H., & Sung, J. W. (2008). Effects of user modeling on POMDP-based dialogue systems. In *Proc Interspeech*, Brisbane, Australia.

Kim, K., & Lee, G. G. (2007). Multimodal dialog system using hidden information state dialog manager. In *Proceedings of the Ninth International Conference on Multimodal Interfaces (ICMI 2007) Demonstration Session*, Nagoya.

Koller, D., & Parr, R. (2000). Policy iteration for factored MDPs. In *Proceedings of the Sixteenth Conference on Uncertainty in Artificial Intelligence,* Stanford, California (pp. 326--334).

Kowalke, M. (2008, October 28). *DMG: Recession won't hamper IVR market growth.* Retrieved from http://www.tmcnet.com/channels/ivr/articles/44089-dmg-recession-wont-hamper-ivr-market-growth.htm

Lee, C., Jung, S., Kim, K., & Lee, G. G. (2009b). Hybrid approach to robust dialog management using agenda and dialog examples. *Computer Speech & Language, 24*(4).

Lee, C., Jung, S., Kim, S., & Lee, G. G. (2009a, May). Example-based dialog modeling for practical multi-domain dialog system. *Speech Communication, 51*(5), 466–484. doi:10.1016/j.specom.2009.01.008

Lemon, O., Georgila, K., & Henderson, J. (2006). Evaluating effectiveness and portability of reinforcement learned dialogue strategies with real users: The TALK TownInfo evaluation. In *Proc Workshop on Spoken Language Technologies (SLT),* Aruba (pp. 178–181).

Levin, E., Pieraccini, R., & Eckert, W. (2000). A stochastic model of human-machine interaction for learning dialogue strategies. *IEEE Transactions on Speech and Audio Processing, 8*(1), 11–23. doi:10.1109/89.817450

Li, L., Williams, J. D., & Balakrishnan, S. (2009). Reinforcement learning for dialog management using least-squares policy iteration and fast feature selection. In *Proc Interspeech,* Brighton, UK.

Litman, D. J., Kearns, M. S., Singh, S. B., & Walker, M. A. (2000). Automatic optimization of dialogue management. In *Proc Association for Computational Linguistics.* Hong Kong: ACL.

Littman, M., Cassandra, A., & Kaelbling, L. (1995). Learning policies for partially observable environments: Scaling up. In *Proceedings of the Twelfth International Conference on Machine Learning,* San Francisco, CA (pp. 362–370). Morgan Kaufmann.

Mihailidis, A., Boger, J. N., Candido, M., & Hoey, J. (2008). The COACH prompting system to assist older adults with dementia through handwashing: An efficacy study. *BMC Geriatrics, 28*(8).

Ng, A. Y., & Russell, S. (2000). Algorithms for inverse reinforcement learning. In *Proc Intl Conf on Machine Learning (ICML),* Stanford, California.

Nuance. (2010). *Openspeech dialog design tool.* Retrieved from http://www.nuance.com/dialog/

Paek, T., & Horvitz, E. (2000). *Grounding criterion: Toward a formal theory of grounding* (Technical Report No. MSR-TR-2000-40). Microsoft Research.

Paek, T., & Horvitz, E. (2000b). Conversation as action under uncertainty. In *Proc Conf on Uncertainty in Artificial Intelligence (UAI),* Stanford, California (pp. 455–464).

Paek, T., & Horvitz, E. (2003). On the utility of decision-theoretic hidden subdialog. In *Proc ISCA Workshop on Error Handling in Spoken Dialogue Systems,* Chateau-D'oex-Vaud, Switzerland (pp. 95–100).

Paksima, T., Georgila, K., & Moore, J. (2009). Evaluating the effectiveness of information presentation in a full end-to-end dialogue system. In *Proc Sigdial Workshop on Discourse and Dialogue,* London, UK.

Pietquin, O. (2004). *A framework for unsupervised learning of dialogue strategies.* Unpublished doctoral dissertation, Faculty of Engineering, Mons (TCTS Lab), Belgium.

Pietquin, O., & Dutoit, T. (2006). A probabilistic framework for dialog simulation and optimal strategy learning. *IEEE Transactions on Audio, Speech and Language Processing, 14*(2), 589–599. doi:10.1109/TSA.2005.855836

Pineau, J., Gordon, G., & Thrun, S. (2003). Point-based value iteration: An anytime algorithm for POMDPs. In *Proc Intl Joint Conf on Artificial Intelligence (IJCAI),* Acapulco, Mexico (pp. 1025–1032).

Rieser, V. (2008). *Bootstrapping reinforcement learning-based dialogue strategies from Wizard-of-Oz data.* Unpublished doctoral dissertation, Saarland University.

Roy, N., Pineau, J., & Thrun, S. (2000). Spoken dialog management for robots. In *Proc Association for Computational Linguistics* (pp. 93–100). Hong Kong: ACL.

Sanner, S. (2009, July). *First-order models for sequential decision-making.* Retrieved from http://videolectures.net/ilpmlgsrl09_sanner_fomsdm/

Schatzmann, J., Georgila, K., & Young, S. (2005). Quantitative evaluation of user simulation techniques for spoken dialogue systems. In *Proc Sigdial Workshop on Discourse and Dialogue,* Lisbon, Portugal (pp. 178–181).

Schatzmann, J., Stuttle, M. N., Weilhammer, K., & Young, S. (2005). Effects of the user model on simulation-based learning of dialogue strategies. In *Proc IEEE Workshop on Automatic Speech Recognition and Understanding (ASRU),* San Juan, Puerto Rico, USA.

Schatzmann, J., Thomson, B., Weilhammer, K., Ye, H., & Young, S. (2007). Agenda-based user simulation for bootstrapping a POMDP dialogue system. In *Proceedings of Human Language Technologies / North American Chapter of the Association for Computational Linguistics (HLT/NAACL).*

Schatzmann, J., Thomson, B., & Young, S. (2007a). Error simulation for training statistical dialogue systems. In *Proc IEEE Workshop on Automatic Speech Recognition and Understanding (ASRU),* Kyoto, Japan (pp. 526–531).

Schatzmann, J., Thomson, B., & Young, S. (2007b). Statistical user simulation with a hidden agenda. In *Proc Sigdial Workshop on Discourse and Dialogue,* Antwerp, Belgium (pp. 273–282).

Schatzmann, J., Weilhammer, K., Stuttle, M. N., & Young, S. (2007, June). A survey of statistical user simulation techniques for reinforcement-learning of dialogue management strategies. *The Knowledge Engineering Review, 21*(2), 97–126. doi:10.1017/S0269888906000944

Scheffler, K., & Young, S. (2002). Automatic learning of dialogue strategy using dialogue simulation and reinforcement learning. In *Proc Human Language Technologies* (pp. 12–18). San Diego, USA: HLT.

Sidner, C. L., & Lee, C. (2007). Conversational informatics: An engineering approach. In *Attentional gestures in dialogues between people and robots.* Wiley and Sons.

Singh, S., Litman, D., Kearns, M., & Walker, M. (2002). Optimizing dialogue management with reinforcement leaning: Experiments with the NJFun system. *Journal of Artificial Intelligence, 16,* 105–133.

Smith, T., & Simmons, R. (2004, July). Heuristic search value iteration for POMDPs. In *Proceedings of the 20th Conference on Uncertainty in Artificial Intelligence.*

Smith, T., & Simmons, R. (2005). Point-based POMDP algorithms: Improved analysis and implementation. In *Proc Conference on Uncertainty in Artificial Intelligence* (pp. 542–549).

Spaan, M. T. J., & Vlassis, N. (2005). Perseus: Randomized point-based value iteration for POM-DPs. *Journal of Artificial Intelligence Research, 24*, 195–220.

Speechdraw. (2010). *Application design tool.* Retreived from http://www.speechvillage.com/home/

Starkie, B., Findlow, G., Ho, K., Hui, A., Law, L., & Lightwood, L. (2002). Lyrebird™: Developing spoken dialog systems using examples. In *Grammatical inference: Algorithms and applications; 6th International Colloquium, ICGI,* Amsterdam (p. 354-358). Springer-Verlag Lecture Notes in Computer Science.

Suendermann, D., Liscombe, J., Dayanidhi, K., & Pieraccini, R. (2009, September). A handsome set of metrics to measure utterance classification performance in spoken dialog systems. In *Proceedings of the Sigdial 2009 Conference* (pp. 349–356). London, UK: Association for Computational Linguistics.

Syed, U., & Williams, J. D. (2008). Using automatically transcribed dialogs to learn user models in a spoken dialog system. In *Proc Association for Computational Linguistics Human Language Technologies.* Columbus, Ohio: Acl-Hlt.

Tetreault, J. R., Bohus, D., & Litman, D. J. (2007). Estimating the reliability of MDP policies: A confidence interval approach. In *Proc Human Language Technologies: The Annual Conference of the North American Chapter of the Association for Computational Linguistics (NAACL-HLT),* Rochester, New York, USA.

Tetreault, J. R., & Litman, D. J. (2006). Using reinforcement learning to build a better model of dialogue state. In *Proc European Association for Computational Linguistics.* Trento, Italy: EACL.

Thomson, B., Schatzmann, J., Welhammer, K., Ye, H., & Young, S. (2007). Training a real-world POMDP-based dialog system. In *Proc Human Language Technologies: The Annual Conference of the North American Chapter of the Association for Computational Linguistics (NAACL-HLT) Workshop on Bridging the Gap: Academic and Industrial Research in Dialog Technologies,* Rochester, New York, *USA* (pp. 9–17).

Thomson, B., Schatzmann, J., & Young, S. (2008). Bayesian update of dialogue state for robust dialogue systems. In *Proc Intl Conf on Acoustics, Speech, and Signal Processing (ICASSP),* Las Vegas, USA.

Thomson, B., & Young, S. (2010). Bayesian update of dialogue state: A POMDP framework for spoken dialogue systems. *Computer Speech & Language, 24*, 562–588. doi:10.1016/j.csl.2009.07.003

Thomson, B., Yu, K., Gasic, M., Keizer, S., Mairesse, F., & Schatzmann, J. (2008). Evaluating semantic-level confidence scores with multiple hypotheses. In *Proc Interspeech,* Brisbane, Australia.

Varges, S., Quarteroni, S., Riccardi, G., Ivanov, A. V., & Roberti, P. (2009). *Combining POMDPs trained with user simulations and rule-based dialogue management in a spoken dialogue system.* In ACL-IJCNLP Demonstrations.

Voiceobjects. (2010). *application design tool.* Retrieved from http://www.voiceobjects.com

Walker, M. A. (2000). An application of reinforcement learning to dialogue strategy selection in a spoken dialogue system for email. *Journal of Artificial Intelligence Research, 12*, 387–416.

Williams, J. D. (2006). *Partially observable Markov decison processes for spoken dialogue management.* Unpublished doctoral dissertation, Cambridge University.

Williams, J. D. (2007a). Applying POMDPs to dialog systems in the troubleshooting domain. In *NAACL-HLT Workshop on Bridging the Gap: Academic and Industrial Research in Dialog Technologies*, Rochester, New York, USA (pp. 1–8).

Williams, J. D. (2007b). Using particle filters to track dialogue state. In *Proc IEEE Workshop on Automatic Speech Recognition and Understanding (ASRU)*, Kyoto, Japan.

Williams, J. D. (2008a). The best of both worlds: Unifying conventional dialog systems and POMDPs. In *Proc Interspeech*, Brisbane, Australia.

Williams, J. D. (2008b). Demonstration of a POMDP voice dialer. In *Proc Demonstration Session of Association for Computational Linguistics Human Language Technologies*. Columbus, Ohio: ACL-HLT.

Williams, J. D. (2008c). Integrating expert knowledge into POMDP optimization for spoken dialog systems. In *Proc AAAI Workshop on Advancements in POMDP Solvers*, Chicago.

Williams, J. D. (2009). Spoken dialogue systems: Challenges, and opportunities for research. In *Proc IEEE Workshop on Automatic Speech Recognition and Understanding (ASRU)*, Merano, Italy.

Williams, J. D. (2010). Incremental partition recombination for efficient tracking of multiple dialog states. In *Proc Intl Conf on Acoustics, Speech, and Signal Processing (ICASSP)*, Dallas, USA.

Williams, J. D. (n.d.). *AT&T voice dialer demonstration*. Retrieved from http://www.research.att.com/people/Williams_Jason_D

Williams, J. D., & Balakrishnan, S. (2009). Estimating probability of correctness for ASR N-best lists. In *Proc Sigdial Workshop on Discourse and Dialogue*, London, UK.

Williams, J. D., Poupart, P., & Young, S. (2005). Factored partially observable Markov decision processes for dialogue management. In *Proc Workshop on Knowledge and Reasoning in Practical Dialogue Systems, Intl Joint Conf on Artificial Intelligence (IJCAI)*, Edinburgh.

Williams, J. D., & Young, S. (2005). Scaling up POMDPs for dialog management: The "summary POMDP" method. In *Proc IEEE Workshop on Automatic Speech Recognition and Understanding (ASRU)*, San Juan, Puerto Rico, USA (pp. 177–182).

Williams, J. D., & Young, S. (2007a). Partially observable Markov decision processes for spoken dialog systems. *Computer Speech & Language, 21*(2), 393–422. doi:10.1016/j.csl.2006.06.008

Williams, J. D., & Young, S. (2007b). Scaling POMDPs for spoken dialog management. *IEEE Trans. on Audio, Speech, and Language Processing, 15*(7), 2116–2129. doi:10.1109/TASL.2007.902050

Williams, J. D., & Young, S. J. (2006). Scaling POMDPs for dialog management with composite summary point-based value iteration (CSPBVI). In *Proc American Association for Artificial Intelligence (AAAI) Workshop on Statistical and Empirical Approaches for Spoken Dialogue Systems*, Boston.

Young, S., Gašić, M., Keizer, S., Mairesse, F., Schatzmann, J., & Thomson, B. (2010, April). The hidden information state model: A practical framework for POMDP-based spoken dialogue management. *Computer Speech & Language, 24*(2), 150–174. doi:10.1016/j.csl.2009.04.001

Young, S., Keizer, S., Yu, K., Mairesse, F., Jurcícek, F., & Thomson, B. (n.d.). *Tourist information system for Cambridge*. Retrieved from http://mi.eng.cam.ac.uk/research/dialogue/demo.html

Young, S., Schatzmann, J., Thomson, B., Weilhammer, K., & Ye, H. (2007). The hidden information state dialogue manager: A real-world POMDP-based system. In *Proc Demonstration Session of Human Language Technologies: The Annual Conference of the North American Chapter of the Association for Computational Linguistics (NAACL-HLT),* Rochester, New York, USA.

Young, S., Schatzmann, J., Weilhammer, K., & Ye, H. (2007). The hidden information state approach to dialog management. In *Proc Intl Conf on Acoustics, Speech, and Signal Processing (ICASSP),* Honolulu, Hawaii, USA (pp. IV149–IV152).

Young, S., Williams, J. D., Schatzmann, J., Stuttle, M. N., & Weilhammer, K. (2006). *The hidden information state approach to dialogue management* (Technical Report No. CUED/F-INFENG/TR.544). Cambridge University Engineering Department.

Zhang, B., Cai, Q., Mao, J., Chang, E., & Guo, B. (2001). Spoken dialogue management as planning and acting under uncertainty. In *Proc Interspeech, Aalborg, Denmark* (pp. 2169–2172).

Zhang, B., Cai, Q., Mao, J., & Guo, B. (2001). Planning and acting under uncertainty: A new model for spoken dialogue systems. In *Proc Conf on Uncertainty in Artificial Intelligence (UAI),* Seattle, Washington (pp. 572–579).

ADDITIONAL READING

Balentine, B. 2001. *How to Build a Speech Recognition Application: Second Edition: A Style Guide for Telephony Dialogues.* Enterprise Integration Group; second edition.

Cohen, M. H., Giangola, J. P., & Balogh, J. (2004). *Voice User Interface Design.* Addison-Wesley Professional.

Jelinek, F. (1998). *Statistical Methods for Speech Recognition (Language, Speech, and Communication).* The MIT Press.

Kristiina Jokinen and Michael McTear. 2010. *Spoken Dialogue Systems.* Morgan and Claypool Publishers. Daniel Jurafsky and James H. Martin. 2008. *Speech and Language Processing.* Prentice Hall; second edition. Christopher D. Manning and Hinrich Schütze. 1999. *Foundations of Statistical Natural Language Processing.* The MIT Press.

KEY TERMS AND DEFINTIONS

Automatic Speech Recognition (ASR): A computer algorithm that takes speech audio as input and outputs a hypothesis for the text of the words in the audio.

Dialog Manager (DM): Within a spoken dialog system, a dialog manager is the module that tracks the state of the conversations and decides what to say or do to respond to the user. The dialog manager takes a meaning representation of the user's speech as input, and outputs a meaning representation to be relayed back to the user.

N-Best List: In the output of an ASR, an N-Best list is an ordered list of alternate hypotheses for the speech contained within the audio. The list is in order of likelihood, with the most likely hypothesis first.

Spoken Dialog System (SDS): A computer program that interacts with a person using spoken language.

Spoken Language Generation (SLG): A computer algorithm that takes a meaning representation as input and outputs a string of words which represents that meaning in a human language (eg English).

Spoken Language Understanding (SLU): A computer algorithm that takes text of words as input and outputs a representation of the meaning of those words in some taxonomy.

Text-to-Speech (TTS): A computer algorithm that takes text as input, and outputs speech audio of that text being read.

Chapter 15
Task Coordination for Service Robots Based on Multiple Markov Decision Processes

Elva Corona
National Institute of Astrophysics, Optics and Electronics, Mexico

L. Enrique Sucar
National Institute of Astrophysics, Optics and Electronics, Mexico

ABSTRACT

Markov Decision Processes (MDPs) provide a principled framework for planing under uncertainty. However, in general they assume a single action per decision epoch. In service robot applications, multiple tasks are required simultaneously, such as navigation, localization and interaction. We have developed a novel framework based on functional decomposition that divides a complex problem into several sub-problems. Each sub-problem is defined as an MDP and solved independently, and their individual policies are combined to obtain a global policy. In contrast to most previous approaches for hierarchical MDPs, in our approach all the MDPs work in parallel, so we obtain a reactive system based on a decision theoretic framework. We initially solved each MDP independently and combined their policies assuming no conflicts. Then we defined two kinds of conflicts, resource and behavior conflicts, and proposed solutions for both. The first kind of conflict is solved off-line using a two phase process which guarantees a near-optimal global policy. Behavior conflicts are solved on-line based on a set of restrictions specified by the user, and a constraint satisfaction module that selects the action set with higher expected utility. We have used these methods for task coordination in service robots, and present experimental results for a messenger robot.

DOI: 10.4018/978-1-60960-165-2.ch015

INTRODUCTION

Our work is motivated by planning under uncertainty in robotics. Consider a mobile robot that has to perform a complex task in an uncertain environment. To accomplish its goal, the robot has to do several subtasks simultaneously, such as finding the shortest route to certain location, and, at the same time, avoiding obstacles and maintaining its location in the map. It might also need to recognize objects in the environment and interact with people. A popular approach to solve this problem in robotics is based on Brooks' *subsumption architecture* (Brooks, 1986), in which several processes can sense and act in *parallel*. The conflicts that could arise between the different *behaviors* are usually solved by a fixed priority structure. However, this type of task coordination has several drawbacks: (i) as the number of subtasks increases, defining the priority structure becomes very difficult, (ii) the priority is fixed, and can not change depending on the current situation. We consider an alternative approach based on decision–theoretic planning, in which the priority of the subtasks can be decided dynamically such that the *best* actions can be taken at each decision point.

Markov Decision Processes (MDPs) (Bellman, 1957, Puterman, 1994) have developed as a standard method for representing uncertainty in decision-theoretic planning. They are simple for domain experts to specify, or can be learned from data. However, if we represent the robot task coordination problem as a single MDP, we have to consider all possible combinations of all the possible simultaneous actions. This implies an explosion in the action—state space and thus an important increase in complexity for solving the MDP. It also becomes much more difficult to specify or learn the model. Given that each subtask is usually implemented as a separate software module, it is natural to try to view each subtask as a different MDP and then in some way combine their policies to obtain the optimal global policy.

Although there has been some work on MDPs with concurrent or parallel actions (Meuleau et al., 1998, Rohanimanesh & Mahadevan, 2008, Younes & Simmons, 2004, Marthi, Russell, Latham & Guestrin, 2005, Little & Thiebaux, 2006, Sucar, 2007, Muausam & Weld, 2008), in general they assume that the subtasks are independent and they do not consider explicitly the conflicts between the policies of each subtask.

We have developed a novel framework for task coordination for service robots based on multiple MDPs, that considers and solves conflicts between the individual policies. Based on functional decomposition, a complex task is partitioned into several subtasks which are solved independently, so that the combined policy can execute concurrent actions. Each subtask is represented as an MDP and solved independently, obtaining an optimal policy. These policies are executed in parallel assuming no conflicts. All the subtasks have a common goal and can share part of the state space, that is represented in a factored form.

We consider that conflicts may arise between the subtasks. We define and solve two types of conflicts: (i) *resource conflicts*, and (ii) *behavior conflicts*. Resource conflicts occur when two actions require the same physical resource (i.e., to control the wheels of a robot) and cannot be executed concurrently. This type of conflict is solved off–line by a two-phase process. In the first phase we obtained an optimal policy for each subtask (MDP). An initial global policy is obtained by combining the local policies, such that if there is a conflict between the actions selected by each MDP for certain state, the one with maximum value is considered, and the state is marked as a *conflict* state. This initial solution is improved in a second phase using policy iteration. Taking the previous policy as its initial policy and considering only the states marked as conflicts, with this consideration the time complexity is drastically reduced and a near-optimal global policy is obtained.

Behavior conflicts arise in situations in which it is possible to execute two (or more) actions at the same time but it is not desirable given the application. For example, it is not desirable for a mobile robot to be navigating and handing out an object to a person at the same time (this situation is also difficult for a person). Behavior conflicts are solved on–line based on a set of restrictions specified by the user. If there are no restrictions, all the actions are executed concurrently; otherwise, a constraint satisfaction module selects the set of actions with the higher expected utility.

We have applied our proposed solutions to a *messenger* robot. We consider initially no conflicts between the MDPs and demonstrate that a complex robot task can be solved efficiently using our approach. Then we consider a more difficult scenario with conflicts, and show that our method can solve these conflicts and still solve the problem effectively. We also compared it with a solution without restrictions and confirmed that by incorporating restrictions the robot can accomplish the task more efficiently, with a significant reduction in the number of time steps required to complete the task.

MARKOV DECISION PROCESSES

A Markov Decision Process (Puterman, 1994) models a sequential decision problem, in which a system evolves in time and is controlled by an agent. A policy for an MDP is a mapping $\pi : S \rightarrow A$ that selects an action for each state. A solution to an MDP is a policy that maximizes its expected value. Two popular methods for finding an optimal policy for an MDP are: (a) value iteration and (2) policy iteration (Puterman, 1994) (see Chapter 3).

The main drawback of the MDP approach is that the solution complexity is polynomial on size of the state–action space, and this can be *very large* for most applications. To deal with the complexity problem for MDPs there are three main approaches:

- **Factorization,** in which the state space is represented in a factored form (Boutilier, Dearden & Goldszmidt, 1995, Hoey, St-Aubin, Hu & Boutilier, 1999).
- **Abstraction,** that creates an abstract model where states with similar features are grouped together (Parr & Russell, 1997, T. G. Dietterich, 1998, Jong & Stone, 2005, Li, Walsh & Littman, 2006, Dean & Givan, 1997).
- **Decomposition,** that divides the global problem into smaller problems that are solved independently and their solutions are combined (Meuleau et al., 1998, Laroche, Boniface & Schott, 2001).

We briefly review these 3 approaches, with emphasis on decomposition, which is the approach we follow.

Factorization

Traditional MDP solution techniques have the drawback that they require an explicit state space representation, limiting their applicability to real-world problems. Factored representations address this drawback by compactly specifying the state-space in factored form. In a factored MDP, the set of states is described via a set of random variables, $X = \{X_1, ..., X_n\}$, where each X_1 takes on values in some finite domain, $Dom(X_1)$. The framework of dynamic Bayesian networks (DBNs) gives us the tools to describe the transition function concisely (see Chapter 2). For each action, a two-stage DBN specifies the transition function. An even more compact representation can be obtained by representing the transition tables and value functions as decision trees (Boutilier, Dean & Hanks, 1999) or algebraic decision diagrams (Hoey et al., 1999).

Abstraction

A further reduction in complexity can be obtained by state abstraction and aggregation techniques (Boutilier et al., 1999). Dean and Givan (Dean & Givan, 1997) describe an algorithm that partitions the state space into a set of blocks such that the each block is *stable*; that is, it preserves the same transition probabilities as the original model. Although this algorithm produces an exact partition, this could still be too complex. In many applications an approximate model could be sufficient to construct near–optimal policies. Pineau (Pineau, Gordon & Thrun, 2003) uses the notions of abstraction and aggregation to group states that are similar with respect to certain problem characteristics to further reduce the complexity of the representation or the solution.

Feng (Feng, Dearden, Meuleau & Washington, 2004) proposes a state aggregation approach for exploiting the structure of MDPs with continuous variables. The state space is dynamically partitioned into regions where the value function is the same throughout each region. Li et al. (Li & Littman, 2005) address hybrid state spaces using a discretization-free approach called *lazy approximation* and present a comparison with Feng's work finding that their method produced reasonable and consistent results.

Reyes et al. (Reyes, Sucar, Morales & Ibarguen-goytia, 2006) proposed a representation based on *qualitative models*, which are particularly useful for domains with continuous state variables. They used training data to learn a decision tree for the reward function, from which they obtained an abstraction called *qualitative states*. The initial abstraction is refined and improved via a local iterative process. States with high variance in their value with respect to neighboring states are partitioned, and the MDP is solved locally to improve the policy.

Decomposition

Other approaches consider problem decomposition, in which an MDP is partitioned in several problems that are solved independently and then pieced together (Boutilier et al., 1999), called hierarchical MDPs.

Hierarchical MDPs accelerate the solution of complex problems by defining different subtasks that correspond to intermediate goals, solving for each subgoal, and then combining these subprocesses to solve the overall problem. Hierarchical MDP approaches include MAXQ (T. Dietterich, 2000) and HAM (Parr & Russell, 1997), among others. Most of these approaches assume that the domain hierarchy is given; a notable exception that learns the decomposition is HEXQ (Hengst, 2002). More recently, Hengst (Hengst, 2007) proposes a hierarchical reinforcement learning method that extends previous techniques to discounted value functions and infinite horizon learning problems.

Although our approach also considers a decomposition of the problem, it is a different one. Hierarchical MDPs provide a *sequential* decomposition, in which different subgoals are solved in sequence to reach the final goal. That is, at the execution phase, only one task is *active* at a given time. In concurrent or parallel MDPs, the subtasks are executed in parallel to solve the global task.

There are few previous works on *parallel decomposition* (e.g. (Meuleau et al., 1998, Rohani-manesh & Mahadevan, 2008, Elinas, Sucar, Reyes & Hoey, 2004b, Marthi et al., 2005, Muausam & Weld, 2008)), where the subtasks are executed concurrently, so in principle they can execute several actions simultaneously. Next we briefly summarize the main approaches.

Concurrent MDPs.

Loosely coupled MDPs (Meuleau et al., 1998) consider several independent subprocesses whose reward and transition functions are independent of each other, but these are coupled due to common resource constraints. Their solution is divided in two phases. In the first, off–line phase, value functions are calculated for the individual subtasks. In the second, on–line phase, the value functions are used to calculate the next action for each process. To choose the actions, they use an iterative procedure based on a heuristic allocation of resources to each task. There are important differences in the types of problems we are solving and also in the solutions. We are interested in problems in which the subtasks have a common goal, but each consider a different aspect of the problem.

Rohanimanesh and Mahadevan (Rohanimanesh & Mahadevan, 2008) extend the *options* framework for concurrent, temporally extended, actions. An option is a kind of *macro–action* that considers a temporally extended series of actions or policy. Rohanimanesh and Mahadevan (Rohanimanesh & Mahadevan, 2008) consider a set of concurrent actions that do not compete for shared resources so they can run in parallel. For this they assume that the set of options is partitioned in disjoint classes, such that the actions in each class do not affect the state of the other classes; options from different classes can run in parallel.

Concurrent Markov Decision Processes (Muausam & Weld, 2008) extend MDPs by allowing multiple actions with variable durations. Their approach allows executing multiple actions at a time; they define a set of actions that can safely be executed concurrently such that they do not interact (based on probabilistic STRIPS). They solve an MDP with multiple actions by using *sampled real-time dynamic programming*, a version of dynamic programming that does not visit all the states. Thus, in sake of efficiency, this solution does not visit all the states in each sample backup and does not consider all possible actions' combinations.

Marthi et al. (Marthi et al., 2005) introduce a Lisp-based language for concurrent hierarchical reinforcement learning that allows multi-threaded partial programs, where each thread corresponds to a task. They use linear function approximation to represent the Q-functions and implement a feature template that considers only the active features in a joint state, in conjunction with potential-based shaping. They show how several concurrent actions can be achieved in a computer game domain, however they need to define an adequate set of features, assume that the Q-function can be represented as a linear combination of such features and need to define an adequate shaping function.

Younes and Simmons (Younes & Simmons, 2004) transform the original problem into a planning problem that can be solved with conventional systems, and then use the solution to find a solution to the original problem. They first ignore the uncertainty of the original problem, splitting effects with probabilistic effects into multiple events with deterministic effects. Then they solve the resulting deterministic planning problem using an existing temporal planner, which can have concurrent actions. Finally, to generate a policy, they create examples from the plan and use a regular decision tree algorithm to create a policy.

A fairly similar approach is followed in (Little & Thiebaux, 2006), who extend *Graphplan* to concurrent probabilistic planning. Again additional nodes are created for probabilistic actions and they use an efficient method for finding optimal contingency plans using goal regression. Whereas most of the research on probabilistic planning has been based on MDPs, in this paper they extend the more traditional classical planning into a probabilistic setting.

In general, previous approaches that consider conflicts in concurrent actions limit the problem *a priori* so that conflicts cannot arise. We take a different approach by considering initially each sub-task independently and finding its local optimal policy; solving conflicts later as we combine the local policies.

MDPS WITH MULTIPLE ACTIONS: NO CONFLICTS

Architecture

We consider an architecture designed as a modular software system composed of a number of modules or *behaviors* (Arkin, 1998). A behavior is an independent software module that solves a particular problem, such as navigation or face detection. We consider that each module is represented as an MDP; so the solution to the MDP provides the actions the will be executed by the corresponding module according to the current state.

We use a factored, structured, MDP solver, SPUDD (Hoey et al., 1999), that uses the value iteration algorithm to compute an optimal infinite-horizon policy of action for each state, with *expected total discounted reward* as the optimality criterion. SPUDD uses a representation of MDPs as decision diagrams, and is able to take advantage of structure in the underlying process to make computation more efficient and scalable towards larger environments. The modularity of our architecture makes representation as a factored MDP simple and typically results in a sparsely connected Markov network. Such sparseness leads to very efficient calculations when using a structured solution approach as in SPUDD. However, if we require simultaneous actions using a single MDP, we need to consider all the possible action combinations, which will imply an additional increase in the size of the state-action space. So we propose a framework for task coordination based on multiple MDPs, that we call *Parallel Markov Decision Processes (P-MDPs)* (Sucar, 2007).

Parallel MDPs

A parallel MDP or P-MDP is a set of N MDPs, all of which share the same goal and state space, but have different action sets. We assume, initially, that the actions of each MDP do not *conflict* with the other processes, so that each action set can be executed concurrently with the others. We do not find optimal solutions for the global MDP, but simply simultaneously execute the optimal solutions from each sub-MDP. Intuitively, we can think that each MDP is solving one aspect of the global task, coordinated by a common state vector, and in this way accomplishes the common goal.

Given that we have a factored representation of the state space, each MDP only needs to consider the state variables that directly influence its actions and reward. This implies that each MDP, P_i, will in general have a subset of the state variables spanning its local state space, S_i. Further, we do not consider the effects of combined actions. Each MDP executes an action from each action set, A_i, so that the combinations of actions do no need to be considered, as it will be the case for a single MDP. These two aspects can make a considerable reduction in the action-state space of the problem.

At the design phase, we specify each MDP to solve one aspect of the global task. For instance, for a service robot, one MDP can focus on the navigation part, another on the speech dialog, another on gesture interaction, etc. Each MDP can be specified relatively independently of the others, although the goal (utility function) is the same and the designer should be aware of the other subtasks. Then, each MDP can be solved independently to obtain the optimal policies for each subtask. At the execution stage, all the MDPs are executed concurrently, and the best actions for each MDP are selected according to each policy and the current state.

A final consideration is conflicts between the actions of the different MDPs. Conflict in this case is simply a constraint that would preclude two actions from being executed. For example, a robot might not be able navigate and recognize people simultaneously because the robotic head must be facing in different directions for each. Next we define the possible conflicts that might arise and propose solutions for these conflicts.

MDPS WITH MULTIPLE ACTIONS: SOLVING POLICY CONFLICTS

Once the *MDP*, P_i, for each subtask is solved, in principle their policies can be executed simultaneously to solve the global problem. That is, at each time state (s_i), each P_i selects an action to execute according to its local optimal policy: $\{\pi_1^*(s_i) = a_1,$ $\pi_2^*(s_i) = a_2, ..., \pi_k^*(s_i) = a_k\}$. This set of actions is denoted by $A_{s_i} = \{a_1, a_2, ., a_k\}$. When these policies are combined conflicts between them can arise. We have identified two types of conflicts: *Resource conflicts* and *Behavior conflicts*. In the following sections we describe the solutions for both types of conflicts.

Resource Conflicts

This type of conflict arises when two or more actions require the same resource, so it is impossible to execute them at the same time. For example, suppose that a robot is delivering an urgent message, but the battery is running low. In this state, the *navigation* function may want to turn left to reach the target point, while the *energy* function may want to turn right to recharge the battery. That is, two (or more) actions are trying to control the same physical resource (the wheel motors in the example) so they cannot be executed concurrently. In the case of resource conflicts there are no concurrent actions, the initial individual policies are combined into a global policy so a single action is selected at each time step, avoiding potential conflicts.

This type of conflict is solved off–line via a two-phase process. An initial global policy is obtained by combining the local policies, such that if there is a conflict between the actions selected by each *MDP* for certain state, the one with maximum value is considered, and the state is marked as a conflict state. Thus, the initial policy ($\pi_{initial}$) is obtained by: (i) obtaining a global state vector, S, which is the union of the local state variables, S_i, of each

MDP; (ii) for each s_i: if the optimal action is the same for all *MDPs*, assign this action; otherwise, assign the action with greatest expected value and mark the states with conflicts in their actions.

This initial solution is improved in a second phase using a modified policy iteration (PI) (Puterman, 1994) algorithm. The policy obtained in the first phase is the initial policy for the policy iteration algorithm. PI is executed considering only the marked (conflict) states at each iteration to improve the initial policy. With these considerations the time complexity of policy iteration is drastically reduced.

The algorithm for solving resource conflicts is in Algorithm 1. First, it initializes two arrays, $\pi_{initial}$ and *states*$_{inconflict}$, to save the global policy and the states in conflict, respectively. An initial global policy is obtained by combining the local policies (lines 4 to 8), such that if there is a conflict between the actions selected by each *MDP* for certain state, the one with maximum value is considered (line 8), and the state is marked as a *conflict* state (lines 9 and 10). Finally, it calls the policy improvement algorithm (line 14).

The initial solution is improved in a second phase (see Algorithm 2) using policy iteration (Puterman, 1994). The previous policy is the initial policy (lines 1 and 2), and considers only the states marked as conflicts (line 3) to improve the initial policy (lines 4 to 12). The main differences with policy iteration are: (i) it starts from the initial policy ($\pi_{initial}$) instead of a random policy, (ii) it only visits the states marked as conflict. Algorithm 2 returns the final policy (line 13) that solves resource conflicts; in this case no simultaneous actions are allowed.

Behavior Conflicts

Behavior conflicts arise when the execution of concurrent actions, although in principle it is possible, produces an undesirable behavior. For instance, imagine a service robot interacting with a user. The *manipulation* module is delivering

Algorithm 1. Resource-Conflicts-p1 ($sMDP_1$, $sMDP_2$, ..., $sMDP_k$)

```
1: MDP = {MDP_1 ∪ bMDP_2 ∪ MDP_k}
2: do π_initial(s)= a for all states s ∈ S
3: states_inconflict = NULL
4: for each state s_i ∈ S do
5: if all π*_k(s_i) = a_j then
6: π_initial(s_i) = a_j
7: else
8: π_initial(s_i) = action a with the largest accumulated V^a_k(S_i).
9: if V_k(s_i) ≠ 0 then
10: add the s_i state in states_inconflict
11: end if
12: end if
13: end for
14: π* = PItoRC(S, A, Φ, R, γ, π_initial).
```

Algorithm 2. Resource-Conflicts-p2 (S, A, Φ, R, γ, $\pi_{initial}$, $states_{inconflict}$)

```
1: Let Π = π_initial be the initial policy
2: Compute V_Π(S)
3: for each s ∈ states_inconflict and each a ∈ A do
4: if V_a(s) > V_Π(s) then
5: Π'(s) = a
6: else
7: Π'(s) = Π(s)
8: end if
9: end for
10: if Π'(s) ≠ Π(s) for any s then
11: go to 2
12: end if
13: Return Π
```

an object to the user while at the same time the *navigation* module is trying to evade an obstacle (in this case the same person); these two behaviors should not be executed concurrently. To solve this type of conflicts we also consider two phases: (i) *define restrictions* (off–line); and (ii) *execute concurrent actions* (on–line).

The user establishes a restriction set (**RS**) in terms of the actions from the different *MDPs* that should not be executed at the same time. We consider that given a functional decomposition of the problem and domain knowledge, it is relatively easy for a person to specify these restrictions (we have established a simple syntax for the RS). We have defined four restriction operators:

1. a_i **not_start** a_j. The actions a_i and a_j must not start at the same state.
2. a_i **not_before** a_j. The action a_i must not start before a_j.
3. a_i **not_after** a_j. The action a_i must not start after a_j.
4. a_i **not_during** a_j. If the action a_j is running a_i must not start.

Conjunction (AND) and disjunction (OR) of *actions* within the restrictions are allowed (e.g., interact_with_user AND recognize_user **not_during** robot_turning).

Once the **RS** is defined, and the optimal policies are obtained for all *MDPs*, the system executes the optimal individual policies for the *kMDPs* simultaneously. At each time step, the agent consults the optimal action a_i^* for all the *MDPs*. If there are no restrictions between the actions for all *MDPs*, all actions are performed concurrently. Otherwise, we use a constraint satisfaction module (CSM) to choose the best subset of actions.

The CSM modules receives as inputs:

- The best action for each *MDP* at the current time step, $a_i^*(t)$.
- The action executed for each *MDP* at the previous time step, $a_i^*(t-1)$.
- The expected value for each *MDP* given its current state and action, that is its Q value: $Q_i(s, a)$.

The CSM selects the action subset that satisfies all the constraints and maximizes the expected additive value, maximizing $\sum_i Q_i(s, a)$. All the actions in this subset are executed concurrently. The CSM is based on the constraint satisfaction module of SWI-Prolog (Schrijvers & Demoen, 2004).

In principle, it is possible that the user specifies a set of restrictions such that in certain situation these become unsatisfiable. This could happen if for certain combination of actions for the k MDPs, the subset of actions that satisfies all the restrictions is empty. However, these cases can be detected off-line in a validation stage, in which all actions combinations are tested and unsatisfiable combinations are detected. This result could be given to the user so that the restrictions are modified. In the domain of service robots there are usually a low number of subtasks and actions per subtask, so the number of action combinations is not too large and testing all combinations is feasible (in the order of 1000 action combinations in our experiments). In our experiments we have not encountered a case of unsatisfiable restrictions.

ANALYSIS

Next we make a preliminary theoretical analysis of our approach in terms of optimality and complexity.

Optimality

When we decompose a task in N subtasks and represent and solve each subtask as an MDP, in general we cannot guarantee optimality for the global task. The policy for each subtask is optimal, but the interactions between these policies might render their combination sub-optimal from the point of view of the complete task. If all the subtasks are independent, and we assume that the global reward (R) is the sum of the individual rewards (r_i), $R = \sum_i r_i$, then the combination of the individual policies will give an optimal global policy (Sucar, 2007). However, in general, there are interactions between the subtasks, so by combining their policy we expect a sub-optimal global policy. In this case we are trading-off optimality for simplicity by specifying and solving the task as N independent MDPs.

In the case of resource conflicts, we propose a two phase process in which the initial optimal policies of the N subtasks are combined in a second phase using policy iteration. In Algorithm 2 only states marked as *conflict* are considered in this modified policy iteration. This in general does not guarantee optimality, as these conflicts can *expand* to other states which are not visited in the algorithm, and their actions are not modified. To guarantee optimality we will require to consider all the states in Algorithm 2; but we lose in terms of efficiency of the algorithm. In this case there is still some gain given by the initial policy, as in general we expect that the algorithm converges faster than starting from a random policy.

Finally, with regards to behavior conflicts, the analysis is similar as for the decomposition approach. We cannot guarantee global optimality, only that each subtask is optimal, and that the combined policy does not violate any of the restrictions. However, in practice, the resulting policies considering the restrictions tend to achieve the goal faster than without restrictions, see . Give that the optimality criteria is based on expected total discounted reward, the policy that gets faster to the goal will have a greater value. An interesting open question is if we can demonstrate that by incorporating restrictions to a parallel MDP we can get closer to global optimality.

Complexity

When we decompose a factored MDP with K state variable in N MDPs, in general we consider that some of the state variable will be in two or more MDPs, and not all the K variables are in all the MDPs. There are two extreme cases: (i) worst case, all the K variables appear in the all the MDPs, (ii) best case, there are not common variables, so that each MDP has in average K/N state variables. Assuming for now a single action at each time epoch, in the worst case solving the N MDPs will result in an increase in time complexity by N compared to solving the global MDP; this is a linear increase in time complexity. In the best case, given that both value and policy iteration are quadratic in terms of the number of states, there is an exponential decrease in time (and space) complexity with respect to solving the task as a single MDP. In general, each MDP will have $K - i$ state variables, and even if $i = 1$, there is a significant reduction in time and space complexity.

If we consider multiple actions per time epoch the gain is much more significant, as solving the problem as a single MDP will imply considering all possible action combinations, implying an exponential growth of the state-action space. When we decompose the problem we consider a single action per MDP, so this explosion is avoided.

In the case of resource conflicts the complexity reduction is not as important, given that in the second phase all the MDPs are combined and solved together using modified policy iteration. In this case there is some gain only in terms of time complexity depending on how close the initial policy is to the optimal one (number of iterations), and how many states are marked in conflict with respect to the total state space.

For behavior conflicts we have a similar reduction as for the general task decomposition analyzed above, in terms of solving the MDPs and obtaining the optimal policy. There is an extra cost during the policy execution phase due to the constraint satisfaction process.

EXPERIMENTAL RESULTS

We describe two sets of experiments with messenger robots. The first set was performed by the robot *HOMER* and does not consider conflicts. The second set includes conflict resolution and it was done with the robot *Markovito*.

Messenger Robot Without Conflicts

We have tested the parallel MDPs approach with a real robot in a message delivery task. In this case we consider simultaneous actions and no conflicts,

so each MDP selects its action independently and all are executed concurrently, coordinated implicitly with common state variables. By assuming no conflicts, there is, in principle, no need for an arbiter. In practice, we give priority to one of the tasks. A detailed description of the application of multiple MDPs for task coordination for the messenger robot *HOMER* is given in (Elinas, Sucar, Reyes & Hoey, 2004a). Next we just present a brief summary of the main results.

HOMER (Elinas, Hoey & Little, 2003), the Human Oriented MEssenger Robot, is a mobile robot that communicates messages between humans in a workspace. The message delivery task is a challenging domain for an interactive robot. It presents all the difficulties associated with uncertain navigation in a changing environment, as well as those associated with exchanging information and taking commands from humans using a natural interface. For this task we use 3 MDPs: the navigator, the dialog manager and the gesture generator. Together they coordinate 10 behaviors (Elinas & Little, 2002) for accomplishing the message delivery task.

The robot, HOMER, shown in Figure 1, is a Real World Interface B-14 robot, and has a single sensor: a Point Grey Research Bumblebee™ stereo vision camera (Murray & Little, 2000).

HOMER's message delivery task consists of accepting messages, finding recipients and delivering messages. In his quiescent state, HOMER explores the environment looking for a message sender. A potential sender can initiate an interaction with HOMER by calling his name, or by presenting herself to the robot. HOMER asks the person for her name (sender), the recipient's name, and the message. During the interactions, HOMER uses speech recognition, speech generation and gesture generation to communicate with people. Once HOMER has a message to deliver, he must find the recipient. This requires some model of the typical behavioral patterns of people within HOMER's workspace. We use a static map of person locations, which is updated when new

Figure 1. (a) HOMER the messenger robot interacting with a person and (b) closeup of HOMER's head

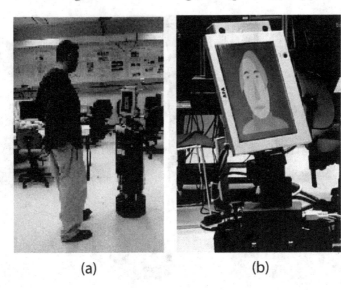

(a)   (b)

information is obtained about the presence or absence of persons. This map allows HOMER to assess the most likely location to find a person at any time. Navigation to that location is then attempted. If the location is not reachable, HOMER finds another location and re-plans. If the location is reached, then HOMER attempts to find a potential receiver using face and voice detection. Upon verifying the receivers name, HOMER delivers the message. During the entire process, HOMER will localize in the map if necessary, or it will go *home* to recharge if its battery is low.

The message delivery task can be divided in 3 subtasks, each one controlled by an MDP. The **N**avigator controls the navigation and localization of the robot, the **D**ialogue Manager controls the interaction with people using speech, and the **G**esture Generator controls the interaction with people using gestures performed by an animated face. Each MDP includes the relevant variables as its state space, and controls several behaviors through its actions. The actions for each MDP are the following:

- **Navigator:** *explore, navigate, localize, get-new-goal, go-home, wait.*

- **Dialogue Manager:** *ask, confirm, give-message.*
- **Gesture Generator:** *neutral, happy, sad, angry.*

The complete state is represented by 13 state variables (Elinas et al., 2004a): *has-message, receiver-name, sender-name, at-location, has-location, location-unreachable, receiver-unreachable, battery-low, uncertain-location, voice-heard, person-close, called-Homer, yes-no.* The goal of the message delivery task is encoded in the reward function: a *small* reward for receipt of a message, a *big* reward for message delivery, and a negative reward for a low battery. The Dialog and Gesture planners only include rewards for message receipt and delivery, while the navigator includes all three.

We solved the 3 MDPs using SPUDD (Hoey et al., 1999) and generated the optimal policies for each one. During concurrent execution of the policies, potential conflicts are avoided by simply giving priority to the Navigator. Thus, if HOMER is navigating to a location, such as *home*, it does not stop for an interaction.

Figure 2. (a) Markovito, (b) entering the arena at RoboCup 2009.

(a)   (b)

We ran several experiments with HOMER. Each experiment involves the robot receiving and delivering a message by visiting locations as necessary. Initially, we performed a guided exploration task in order to build all the necessary maps for navigation and localization. We also manually specified a list of possible users and the most likely areas they inhabit. HOMER then ran autonomously for the message delivery task. Based on our task decomposition and concurrent execution approach, HOMER was able to successfully execute the message delivery task under different conditions, showing experimentally that the method works well for a complex task.

Messenger Robot with Conflicts

The second set of experiments were done with *Markovito*, a service robot, which also performed a delivery task; but in this case conflicts were considered.

Markovito is based on an ActivMedia People-Bot robot platform. It has two rings of sonars, a Laser SICK LMS200, one video camera Canon VCC5, two infrared sensors, a directional mi-

crophone SHURE SM81, a gripper, the robot's internal computer, a Laptop, bumpers and a frame grabber WinTV USB 2 (see Figure 2).

In the task we consider for Markovito, the goal is for the robot to receive and deliver a message, an object or both, under a user's request. The interaction again is through natural language. The user gives an order to send a message/object and the robot asks for the name of the sender and the receiver. The robot either records a message or uses its gripper to hold an object, and navigates to the receiver's position and delivers. We decompose the task into five subtasks, each represented as an MDP:

1. *navigation*, the robot navigates safely on different scenarios;
2. *vision*, for looking and recognizing people and objects;
3. *interaction*, for listening and talking with a user;
4. *manipulation*, to get and deliver an object safely; and
5. *expression*, to show *emotions* using an animated face.

Each subtask is represented as a factored MDP, next we briefly describe each model:

- **Navigation:** States: 256 decomposed into 6 state variables (*located, has-place, has-path, direction, see-user, listen-user*). Actions: 4 (*goto, stop, turn, move*).

- **Vision:** States: 24 decomposed into 3 state variables (*user-position, user-known, user-in-db*). Actions: 3 (*look-for people, recognize-user, register-user*).

- **Interaction:** States: 9216 decomposed into 10 state variables (*user-position, user-known, listen, offer-service, has-petition, has-message, has-object, has-user-id, has-reciever-id, greeting*). Actions: 8 (*hear, offer-service, get-message, deliver-message, ask-reciever-name, ask-user-name, hello, bye*).

- **Manipulation:** States: 32 decomposed into 3 state variables (*has-petition, see-user, has-object*). Actions: 3 (*get-object, deliver-object, move-gripper*).

- **Expression:** States: 192 decomposed into 5 state variables (*located, has-petition, see-user, see-reciever, greeting*). Actions: 4 (*normal, happy, sad, angry*).

Note that several state variables are common to two or more MDPs. If we represent this task as a single, flat MDP, there are 1,179,648 states (considering all the non-duplicated state variables) and 1,536 action combinations, given a total of nearly two billion state-actions. So to solve this task as a single MDP will be difficult even for state of the art MDP solvers.

The MDP model for each subtask was defined user SPUDD's structured representation (Hoey et al., 1999). The transition and reward functions were specified by the user based on task knowledge and intuition. Given that the MDP for each subtask is relatively simple, its manual specification is not too difficult. In contrast, if we wanted

to specify a single MDP for the complete task it will be practically impossible.

In this task, conflicts might arise between the different subtasks, so we need to include our conflict resolution strategies. For comparison, we solve this problem under two conditions: (1) without restrictions and (2) with restrictions.

Solution Without Restrictions

For this case the 5 MDPs were solved independently using SPUDD and their individual optimal policies were executed concurrently, without any restriction. Figure 3 summarizes the results of a typical run without restrictions, depicting the actions executed for each *MDP*, P_i, per time step. This figure has in the X axis the different actions of the five MDPs, for navigation at the bottom, followed by vision, interaction, manipulation and expression, at the top. In principle, all actions can be executed concurrently, but as shown in Figure 3 the robot performs some undesirable behaviors. For example, the system is not able to identify a person until s_{33} after which it is able to complete the task. This is because the *visionMDP* cannot get a good image to analyze and recognize the user because the *navigationMDP* is moving trying to avoid the user. Also, because of this, the user has to follow the robot to provide an adequate input to the microphone.

Solution With Restrictions

In this case we consider behavior conflicts and introduce a set of restrictions that are summarized in Table 1. As for the previous experiment, the five MDPs were solved with SPUDD to obtain the optimal policies. During execution, at each decision epoch, the actions selected by each MDP are sent to the conflict resolution module, which executes the actions that satisfy all the restrictions.

The results, presented in the same way as the previous case, are shown in Figure 4. The restrictions introduced allowed a more fluid and efficient

Figure 3. Messenger robot without restrictions. The graphs shows the actions executed for each time step, for each of the 5 MDPs. From top to bottom: expression, manipulation, interaction, vision, navigation. Without restrictions several conflicts arise between the MDPs and it takes 59 time steps to complete the task (see text for details).

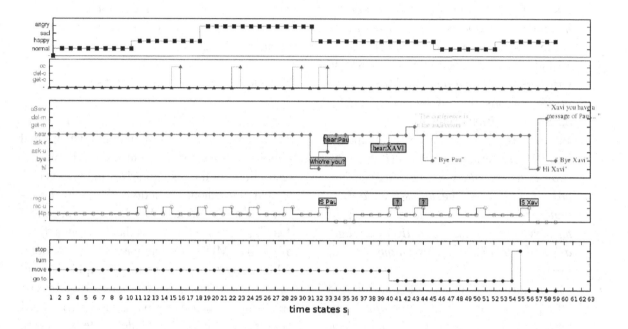

Table 1. Restriction set for the messenger robot.

action(s)	restriction	action(s)
get message	not_during	turn OR advance
ask_user_name	not_before	recognize_user
recognize_user	not_start	avoid_obstacle
get_object OR deliver_object	not_during	directed towards OR turn OR moving

solution. For example, Figure 4 shows that the *visionMDP* with the restriction set is now able to detect and recognize the user much earlier. When the *interactionMDP* is activated, the *navigation-MDP* actions are not executed (shown with larger black squares), allowing an effective inter-action and recognition.

In summary, not only does the robot performs the expected behavior, but also it has a more robust performance, avoids conflicts, and there is a significant reduction in the time required to complete the task.

CONCLUSION AND FUTURE WORK

Our work has been motivated by planning under uncertainty in robotics, in particular for task coordination for service robots. We developed a framework for executing multiple actions concurrently based on MDPs and applied it to task coordination in service robots. The global task is divided into several subtasks, each one represented as an MDP. We initially solved each MDP independently and combined their policies assuming no conflicts. Then we defined two kinds of conflicts, resource

Figure 4. Messenger robot with restrictions. The graphs shows the actions executed for each time step, for each of the 5 MDPs (same order as figure 3). In this case it takes only 34 time steps to complete the task (see text for details).

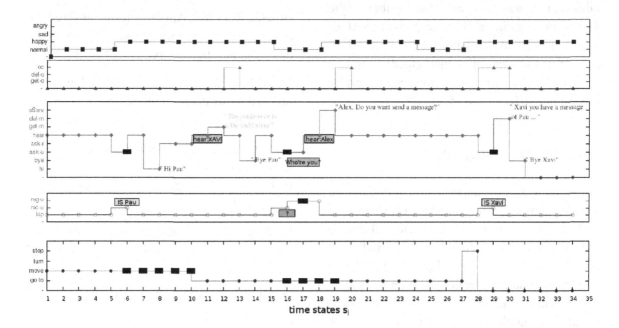

and behavior conflicts, and proposed solutions for both. The first kind of conflict is solved offline using a two phase process which guarantees a near-optimal global policy. Behavior conflicts are solved on-line based on a set of restrictions, and a constraint satisfaction module that selects the action set with higher expected utility.

The proposed framework has been applied to messenger robots with good results. We showed experimentally that we can solve complex tasks successfully with a significant reduction in complexity for specifying and solving the MDP representation of the problem. We also showed that by considering and solving conflicts between the individual policies, the robot can accomplish its goals more efficiently.

An initial theoretical analysis of the proposed approach shows in general a significant reduction in complexity by sacrificing optimality for the global task. We can only guarantee global optimality in the case that all the subtasks are independent.

An interesting question for future research is if we can give certain bounds on optimality based on the dependence or interactions between the subtasks. Another open question is the relationship between restrictions and optimality.

In this work we have assumed that the MDPs are specified by a person, and we do not have considered learning. Given the nature of the service robot tasks it is difficult to apply reinforcement learning, as each trail with a real robot takes a lot of time and effort. An alternative could be to try a model–based learning approach, in which we start form a subjective estimate of the transition probabilities and these are refined based on experience. An additional line for future research is performing sensitivity analysis, to evaluate the impact of changes in transition functions and rewards in the optimal policy.

ACKNOWLEDGMENT

We will like to acknowledge the contributions of Eduardo F. Morales and rest of the members of the *Markovito* team in the Robotics Lab at INAOE. We also thank that anonymous reviewers for their comments and suggestions that helped to improve this chapter. This work was supported in part by Project FONCICYT 95185 and INAOE.

ADDITIONAL READINGS

For a general introduction to computational aspects of mobile robots we suggest (Dudek & Jenkin, 2000); an excellent overview of probabilistic robotics, including the use of MDPs and POMDPs is (Thrun, Burgard & Fox, 2005), and a more concise introduction is given in (Thrun, 2000). A collection of articles on the application of artificial intelligence techniques for mobile robots is given in (Kortenkam, Bonasso & Murphy, 1998). Brooks (Brooks, 1986) introduces the reactive approach to robotics, and Arkin (Arkin, 1998) behavior–based robotics.

Puterman (Puterman, 1994) provides a comprehensive introduction to MDPs. A technical analysis of the use of decision–theoretic models in planning is included in (Boutilier et al., 1999).

REFERENCES

Arkin, R. C. (1998). *Behavior-based robotics*. MIT Press.

Bellman, R. (1957). *Dynamic programming*. Princeton, N.J.: Princeton U. Press.

Boutilier, C., Dean, T., & Hanks, S. (1999). Decision-theoretic planning: structural assumptions and computational leverage. *Journal of Artificial Intelligence Research, 11*, 1–94.

Boutilier, C., Dearden, R., & Goldszmidt, M. (1995). *Exploiting structure in policy construction* (pp. 1104–1113). Ijcai.

Brooks, R. (1986, April). A robust layered control system for a mobile robot. *IEEE Journal on Robotics and Automation, 2*(1), 14–23.

Dean, T., & Givan, R. (1997). Model minimization in markov decision processes. In *Proc. of the 14th national conf. on ai* (pp. 106–111). AAAI.

Dietterich, T. (2000). Hierarchical reinforcement learning with the maxq value function decomposition. *Journal of Artificial Intelligence Research, 13*, 227–303.

Dietterich, T. G. (1998). *The maxq method for hierarchical reinforcement learning* (pp. 118–126). Icml.

Dudek, G., & Jenkin, M. (2000). *Computational principles of mobile robotics*. Cambridge University Press.

Elinas, P., Hoey, J., & Little, J. J. (2003, March). Human oriented messenger robot. In *Proc. of aaai spring symposium on human interaction with autonomous systems*. Stanford, CA.

Elinas, P., & Little, J. J. (2002, March). A robot control architecture for guiding a vision-based mobile robot. In *Proc. of aaai spring symposium in intelligent distributed and embedded systems*. Stanford, CA.

Elinas, P., Sucar, E., Reyes, A., & Hoey, J. (2004b, September 20 - 22). A decision theoretic approach for task coordination in social robots. In *13th ieee international workshop on robot and human interactive communication*.

Elinas, P., Sucar, L., Reyes, A., & Hoey, J. (2004a). A decision theoretic approach for task coordination in social robots. In *Proc. of the ieee international workshop on robot and human interactive communication (ro-man)* (pp. 679–684). Japan.

Feng, Z., Dearden, R., Meuleau, N., & Washington, R. (2004). Dynamic programming for structured continuous markov decision problems. In *Proc. of the 20th conf. on uncertainty in AI (UAI-2004)*. Banff, Canada.

Hengst, B. (2002). *Discovering hierarchy in reinforcement learning with hexq* (pp. 243–250). Icml.

Hengst, B. (2007). Safe state abstraction and reusable continuing subtasks in hierarchical reinforcement learning. In M. A. Orgun & J. Thornton (Eds.), *Artificial intelligence* (Vol. 4830, pp. 58–67). Springer.

Hoey, J., St-Aubin, R., Hu, A., & Boutilier, C. (1999). Stochastic planning using decision diagrams. In *Proceedings of international conference on uncertainty in artificial intelligence (uai '99)*. Stockholm: SPUDD.

Jong, N. K., & Stone, P. (2005, August). State abstraction discovery from irrelevant state variables. In *Proceedings of the nineteenth international joint conference on artificial intelligence* (pp. 752–757).

Kortenkam, D., Bonasso, P., & Murphy, R. (1998). *Artificial intelligence for mobile robots*. MIT Press.

Laroche, P., Boniface, Y., & Schott, R. (2001). A new decomposition technique for solving markov decision processes. In *Sac* (p. 12-16).

Li, L., & Littman, M. L. (2005). Lazy approximation for solving continuous finite-horizon mdps. In *AAAI-05* (p. 1175-1180). Pittsburgh, PA.

Li, L., Walsh, T. J., & Littman, M. L. (2006, January). Towards a unified theory of state abstraction for mdps. In *Ninth international symposium on artificial intelligence and mathematics* (p. 21-30).

Little, I., & Thiebaux, S. (2006). Concurrent probabilistic planning in the graphplan framework. In *proceedings ICAPS-2006*.

Marthi, B., Russell, S., Latham, D., & Guestrin, C. (2005). Concurrent hierarchical reinforcement learning. In *proceedings IJCAI-2005* (pp. 779–785).

Meuleau, N., Hauskrecht, M., Kim, K. E., Peshkin, L., Kaelbling, L. P., & Dean, T. (1998). Solving very large weakly coupled markov decision processes. In *AAAI/IAAI* (p. 165-172).

Muausam, & Weld, D. (2008). Planning with durative actions in stochastic domains. *J. Artif. Intell. Res. (JAIR), 31*, 33–82.

Murray, D., & Little, J. (2000). Using real-time stereo vision for mobile robot navigation. *Autonomous Robots, 8*, 161–171.

Parr, R., & Russell, S. J. (1997). *Reinforcement learning with hierarchies of machines*. NIPS.

Pineau, J., Gordon, G., & Thrun, S. (2003). Policy-contingent abstraction for robust control. In *Proc. of the 19th conf. on uncertainty in ai, UAI-03* (pp. 477–484).

Puterman, M. L. (1994). *Markov decision processes: Discrete stochastic dynamic programming*. New York, NY: Wiley.

Reyes, A., Sucar, L. E., Morales, E., & Ibarguengoytia, P. H. (2006). Abstraction and refinement for solving Markov Decision Processes. In *Workshop on probabilistic graphical models PGM-2006* (p. 263-270). Czech Republic.

Rohanimanesh, K., & Mahadevan, S. (2008). Decision-Theoretic planning with concurrent temporally extended actions. In *Proceedings of the seventeenth conference on uncertainty in artificial intelligence (UAI)* (pp. 472–479).

Schrijvers, T., & Demoen, B. (2004). *The K. U. Leuven CHR system: Implementation and application*. First Workshop on Constraint Handling Rules: Selected Contributions.

Sucar, L. E. (2007, June). Parallel markov decision processes. *Studies in Fuzziness and Soft Computing. Advances in Probabilistic Graphical Models, 214/2007*, 295–309.

Thrun, S. (2000). Probabilistic algorithms in robotics. *AI Magazine, 21*(4), 93–109.

Thrun, S., Burgard, W., & Fox, D. (2005). *Probabilistic robotics*. MIT.

Younes, H. L. S., & Simmons, R. (2004). Policy generation for continuous-time stochastic domains with concurrency. In *proceedings ICAPS-2004*.

KEY TERMS AND DEFINITIONS

Behavior: An independent software module that solves a particular problem.

Behavior Conflict: Behavior conflicts arise in situations in which it is possible to execute two (or more) actions at the same time but it is not desirable given the application.

Concurrent Markov Decision Processes: It refers to the concurrent execution of the policies from two or more MDPs, such that several actions can be performed at the same time.

Conflict: A constraint that would preclude two or more actions from being executed concurrently.

Constraint Satisfaction: Is the process of finding a solution to a set of constraints that impose conditions that the variables must satisfy.

Resource Conflict: Resource conflicts occur when two actions require the same physical resource and cannot be executed concurrently.

Service Robot: Service robot is a robot which operates semi- or fully autonomously to perform services useful to the well-being of humans and equipment.

Chapter 16
Applications of DEC–MDPs in Multi–Robot Systems

Aurélie Beynier
University Pierre and Marie Curie, France

Abdel-Illah Mouaddib
University of Caen, France

ABSTRACT

Optimizing the operation of cooperative multi-robot systems that can cooperatively act in large and complex environments has become an important focal area of research. This issue is motivated by many applications involving a set of cooperative robots that have to decide in a decentralized way how to execute a large set of tasks in partially observable and uncertain environments. Such decision problems are encountered while developing exploration rovers, teams of patrolling robots, rescue-robot colonies, mine-clearance robots, et cetera.

In this chapter, we introduce problematics related to the decentralized control of multi-robot systems. We first describe some applicative domains and review the main characteristics of the decision problems the robots must deal with. Then, we review some existing approaches to solve problems of multiagent decentralized control in stochastic environments. We present the Decentralized Markov Decision Processes and discuss their applicability to real-world multi-robot applications. Then, we introduce OC-DEC-MDPs and 2V-DEC-MDPs which have been developed to increase the applicability of DEC-MDPs.

INTRODUCTION

Recent robotic researches have demonstrated the feasibility of projects such as space exploration by mobile robots, mine clearance of risky area, search and rescue of civilians in urban disaster environments, etc. In order to increase the performance and abilities of these robots, researchers aim at developing multi-robot systems where the robots could interact. As explained by Estlin et al. (Estlin et al., 1999) about multi-rover exploration of Mars, such teams of robots will be able to collect more data by dividing tasks among the robots. More complex tasks that require several robots

DOI: 10.4018/978-1-60960-165-2.ch016

to cooperate, could also be executed. Moreover, abilities of the team could be improved by enabling each rover to have special skills. Finally, if one robot fails (robot breakdown or failure of task execution), another robot will be able to repair the damage to the first robot or will complete the unexecuted tasks. Teams of robots can also be used to increase the efficiency of rescue robots, patrolling robots or to develop constellations of satellites (Damiani et al., 2005). All these applications share common characteristics: they are composed of a set of robots that must autonomously and cooperatively act in uncertain and partially observable environments. Thus, each robot must be able to decide on its own, how to act so as to maximize the global performance of the system. In order these robots to be able to optimize their behaviors, decision making approaches that take into account characteristics of real-world applications (large systems, constraints on task execution, uncertainty and partial observability) have then to be developed.

Markov Decision Processes (MDPs) and Partially Observable Markov Decision Processes (POMDPs) have proved to be efficient tools for solving problems of single-agent control in stochastic environments (Puterman, 2005, Kaelbling et al., 1998, Zilberstein et al., 2002). The application of MDPs has therefore been extended to multiagent settings. Thus, Decentralized Markov Decision Processes (DEC-MDPs) have been proposed (Bernstein et al., 2002). They allow for modeling cooperative and distributed decision problems under uncertainty and partial observability. This chapter will describe how DEC-MDP approaches can contribute to solve multi-robot decision problems.

The chapter will be divided into three main parts. The first part will describe multi-robot real-world applications and we will introduce problematics related to the decentralized control of robot teams. The second part will introduce the DEC-MDP framework and the last part of the chapter will present existing DEC-MDP approaches that are concerned with solving multi-robot decision problems.

DECENTRALIZED CONTROL IN MULTI-ROBOT SYSTEMS

This section introduces problematics related to the decentralized control of multi-robot systems. Optimizing the operation of cooperative multi-robot systems that can cooperatively act in large and complex environments has become an important focal area of research. This issue is motivated by many applications involving a set of cooperative robots that have to decide in a decentralized way how to execute a large set of tasks in partially observable and uncertain environments.

Mars Exploration Scenario

The first problem we consider consists in controlling task execution of a cooperative team of Mars exploration rovers. Once a day, the team receives, from a ground center, a set of tasks to execute (observations, measurements, moves) which is intended to increase science knowledge. As the amount of useful scientific data returned to the ground measures the success of the mission, rovers aim at maximizing science return. This performance measure can be represented by an expected value function. In order to optimize this function, several kinds of constraints must be respected while executing the tasks (Cardon et al., 2001, Bresina et al., 2002, Zilberstein et al., 2002):

- **Temporal Constraints:** start times and end times of tasks have to respect temporal constraints. Since robots are solar-powered, most operations must be executed during the day. Moreover, because of illumination constraints, pictures must be taken at sunset or sunrise. On the other hand, some operations must be performed at night (atmospheric measurements).

- **Preconditions:** Some tasks have setup conditions that must hold before they can be performed. For instance, instruments must be turned on and calibrated in order an agent to perform measurements. If these preconditions do not hold, the agent will fail to perform its task. Preconditions lead to precedence constraints between the tasks and to dependencies between the agents. Let us consider that a robot must take a sample of the ground in order for another robot to analyse it: the second robot cannot start analysis before the first robot has finished to take the sample. The success of the second robot relies therefore on the first robot.

- **Resource Constraints:** Executing a task requires power, storage (storing pictures or measurements) or bandwidth (data communication). These resources must be available to complete a task.

Moreover, robots must handle uncertainty on task execution and partial observability of the environment. Since accuracy and capacity of sensors are limited, each rover partially senses its environment. Because the environment is unknown and the issue of a task may depend on environment parameters (temperature, slope and roughness of the terrain, etc.), durations and resource consumptions of tasks are uncertain. Thus, each task takes differing amounts of time and consumes differing amounts of resources.

Furthermore, robots must deal with limited communications. Mars rovers communicate with operators via a satellite which is often unavailable due to its orbital rotation. Moreover, communications take time and consume resources. Consequently, communications with operators are limited to once a day. During this communication window, the robots send the data they have collected and they receive a new set of tasks to execute. During the rest of the day, the robots cannot communicate with the operators and they

must act in an autonomous way. If there is no obstacle between the robots and they are close enough to each other, direct communication is possible. Nonetheless, as rovers cover large area with many obstacles, such direct communication is often impossible. They must therefore be able to perform their tasks without direct information exchange. Then, each rover must be able to autonomously decide how it will act and decision processes have to be decentralized. Finally, space robots have limited computation resources and data storage. Thus, in order to maximize collected data, each rover must be able to efficiently decide (with little computing power and data storage) which task to execute.

RESCUE MISSIONS

There has been a growing interest in the recent years in disaster management crisis (Morimoto, 2000, RoboCup, 2000). The RoboCup Rescue Competition has been organized since 2001 to promote research and development in this domain. The scenarios that are considered involve a team of rescue robots that must rescue civilians and prevent buildings from burning, after an earthquake occurs. A team is composed of three kinds of robots: fire brigade robots that must extinguish fires, ambulance robots that must rescue injured people and drive them to hospital, and police robots that can unblock roads. Such skills lead to dependencies between the robots. For instance, ambulance robots and fire robots cannot pass a blockade. Thus, police robots must unblock roads before the other robots can pass.

Rescue robots share many characteristics with planetary rovers. Rescue robots must face uncertainty and partial observability of the environment. Task durations and resource consumptions are uncertain. For instance, extinguishing a fire can take different amounts of time and consumes different amounts of water. Since communication installations often breakdown in such scenarios, it is assumed that communications between the agents are impossible. Moreover, resources are limited: an ambulance can load only one civilian at a time, a fire brigade robot has a limited amount of water, etc. Finally, temporal constraints must be considered. First, a crisis deadline is set. Next, temporal constraints can be deduced from scenarios' characteristics. For instance, a fire robots must have extinguished a fire before the building is entirely destroyed.

Multi-robot exploration and rescue rover missions are closely related to the problem of Decentralized Simultaneous Localization and Mapping (DSLAM) (Kleiner and Sun, 2007, Nettleton et al., 2003). Decentralized SLAM addresses the problem of cooperatively building a map of an envrionment: a set of agents navigate in an unknown environment and jointly build a map of this environment while simultaneously localising themselves relatively to the map. DSLAM approaches have been applied to the problem of fire searching in an unknown environment (Marjovi et al., 2009).

Multi-Robot Flocking and Platooning

The purpose of robot platooning (Michaud et al., 2006) is to build and to maintain a formation for a group of mobile robots from a starting point to a goal. Because the environments are unknown and the robots have imperfect sensing of the environment, environments are assumed to have unpredictable properties so actions have nondeterministic effects (for example, an agent can skid on a wet ground). Those kind of problems have been studied with flocking approach, where the agents have to maintain a global shape thanks to few simple local basic rules. Flocking rules (Reynolds, 1987) are a set of three very simple rules describing the behaviour of the agents. Those rules are:

1. **Cohesion:** Steer to move toward the average position of local flockmates,

Figure 1. Flocking rules: (1) cohesion, (2) separation, (3) alignment

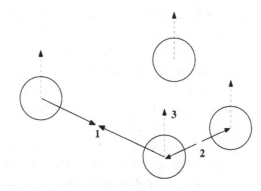

2. **Separation:** Steer to avoid crowding local flockmates,
3. **Alignment:** Steer towards the average heading of local flockmates.

Despite the simplicity of those rules, agents manage to maintain the shape of the group. The main advantage of this approach is that it is fully decentralized, with no communication at all.

The platooning can be seen as a particular form of flocking, where agents try to maintain a line shape and to move toward the platoon's objective (in this line, each agent has the same orientation as the previous agent if it is possible, and the leader heads to the objective. The global shape will then be a straight line or, if agents do not have enough space, a broken straight line). This can be done by giving particular flocking rules to each agent:

1. **Cohesion:** Steer to wait for agents behind it,
2. **Separation:** Steer to avoid agents in front of it,
3. **Alignment:** Steer to move toward the near agent in front of it, or toward the objective if no one is in front of it.

The multi-robot teams presented in this section can be easily considered as cooperative multiagent systems. These consist of a set of agents that have to autonomously execute a set of tasks in the same environment so as to maximize a common performance measure[1]. The problems that are considered involve large sets of tasks and agents. For instance, regarding Mars exploration, the set of tasks to execute is sent once a day and may involve about ten robots that have to complete hundreds of tasks. Different kinds of constraints must be considered in order to achieve good performance. These include temporal constraints, precedence constraints, resource constraints, limited or impossible communication, limited computation capacities.

DECENTRALIZED MARKOV DECISION PROCESSES

The above mentioned multi-robot applications require a decentralized control approach that enables each robot to decide how to act in a partially observable environments and in a coordinated way with the other robots. Classical multiagent planning approaches are not suitable to handle such decision problems since they are not able to consider uncertainty and partial observability (Shoham and Tennenholtz, 1992, Weld, 1994a, Decker and Lesser, 1993a, Decker and Lesser, 1992, Clement and Barrett, 2003). Some classical planning approaches, such as STRIPS, GRAPH-PLAN or PGRAPHPLAN, have been adapted for planning under uncertainty (Blythe, 1999a, Blum and Furst, 1997, Blum and Langford, 1999). Most of these approaches search for a plan that meets a threshold probability of success or that exceeds a minimum expected utility. During task execution, if the agent deviates from the computed plan, a new plan has to be re-computed. To limit re-planning, some approaches compute a contingent plan that encodes a tree of possible courses of actions. Nonetheless, a contingent plan may not consider all possible courses of actions so, re-planning remains and optimality is not guaranteed.

Markov Decision Processes (MDP) provide a stochastic planning approach that allows for computing optimal policies (see Chapter 3). As a policy maps each possible state of the agent to an action, there is no need for on-line re-planning. The agent's objectives are expressed as a utility function and efficient algorithms have been developed to efficiently compute a policy that maximizes the utility (Puterman, 2005, Howard, 1960). MDPs have been successfully applied to many domains such as mobile robots (Bernstein et al., 2001), spoken dialog managers (Roy et al., 2000) or inventory management (Puterman, 2005). Then, MDPs have been extended to deal with multiagent settings and Decentralized Markov Decision Processes (DEC-MDPs) (Bernstein et al., 2002) have been defined.

Model Description

DEC-MDPs provide a mathematical framework to model and solve problems of decentralized control in stochastic environments. So as to modelize partial observability and uncertainty, the DEC-MDP model is composed of a set of observations, a probabilistic observation function and a probabilistic transition function. A reward function to maximize formalizes the objectives of the system.

Definition 1. *A Decentralized Markov Decision Process (DEC-MDP) for n agents is defined by a tuple* $< \mathcal{S}, \mathcal{A}, \mathcal{P}, \Omega, \mathcal{O}, \mathcal{R} >$ *where:*

- $\mathcal{S}$ is a finite set of system states. The state of the system is assumed to be jointly observable [2].
- $\mathcal{A} = \langle \mathcal{A}_1, \cdots, \mathcal{A}_n \rangle$ is a set of joint actions, $\mathcal{A}_i$ is the set of actions a_i that can be executed by the agent $\mathcal{A}g_i$.
- $\mathcal{P} = \mathcal{S} \times \mathcal{A} \times \mathcal{S} \to [0,1]$ is a transition function. $\mathcal{P}(s, a, s')$ is the probability of the outcome state s' when the agents execute the joint action a in s.

- $\Omega = \Omega_1 \times \Omega_2 \times \cdots \times \Omega_n$ is a finite state of observations where Ω_i is agent $\mathcal{A}g_i$'s set of observations.
- $\mathcal{O} = \mathcal{S} \times \mathcal{A} \times \mathcal{S} \times \Omega \rightarrow [0,1]$ is the observation function. $\mathcal{O}(s,a,s',o = \langle o_1, \cdots, o_n \rangle)$ is the probability that each agent $\mathcal{A}g_i$ observes o_i when the agents execute the joint action a from state s and the system moves to state s'.
- $\mathcal{R}$ is a reward function. $\mathcal{R}(s,a,s')$ is the reward the system obtains when the agents execute joint action a from state s and the system moves to state s'..

Problem Solving

Optimally solving a DEC-MDP consists in finding a joint policy which maximizes the expected reward of the system.

Definition 2. *A joint policy π in an n-agent DEC-MDP is a set of individual policies* $\langle \pi_1, \ldots, \pi_n \rangle$ where π_i is the individual policy of the agent $\mathcal{A}g_i$. The individual policy π_i of an agent $\mathcal{A}g_i$ is a mapping from each possible state of the agent's information (its state, its observations or its belief state) to an action $a_i \in \mathcal{A}_i$.

Note that an individual policy π_i takes into account every possible information state of the agent while methods based on classical planners find a sequence of actions based on a set of possible initial states (Blythe, 1999b).

Recent works have focused on developing off-line planning algorithms to solve problems formalized by DEC-MDPs. They consist in computing a set of individual policies, one per agent, describing the agents' behaviors. Each individual policy maps the agent's information (its state, its observations or its belief state) to an action. Since solving optimally a DEC-MDP is a very hard problem (NEXP-hard) (Bernstein et al., 2002), most approaches search for methods that reduce the complexity of the problem.

Two kinds of approaches can be identified to overcome the high complexity of DEC-MDPs. The first set of approaches aims at identifying properties of DEC-MDPs that reduce their complexity. Thus, Goldman and Zilberstein (Goldman and Zilberstein, 2004) have introduced transition independence and observation independence. These properties enable identifying classes of problems that are easier to solve (Goldman and Zilberstein, 2004). For instance, it has been proved that a DEC-MDP with independent transitions and observations is NP-complete. Based on this study, an optimal algorithm, the Coverage Set Algorithm (CSA), has been developed to solve DEC-MDPs with independent observations and transitions (Becker et al., 2003).

Other attempts to solve DEC-MDPs have focused on finding approximate solutions instead of computing the optimum. (Nair et al., 2003) describe an approach, the Joint Equilibrium Based Search for Policies (JESP), to solve transition and observation independent DEC-MDPs. JESP relies on co-alternative improvement of policies: the policies of a set of agents are fixed and the policies of the remaining agents are improved. Policy improvement is executed in a centralized way and only a part of the agents' policies is improved at each step. Finally, the algorithm converges to a Nash equilibrium. Chadès et al. describe a similar approach based on the definition of subjective MDPs and the use of empathy (Chadès et al., 2002). Improvements of JESP have also been proposed: DP-JESP (Nair et al., 2003) speeds up JESP algorithm using dynamic programming and LID-JESP (Nair et al., 2005) combines JESP and distributed constraints optimization algorithms. Thus, LID-JESP exploits the locality of interactions to improve the efficiency of JESP. SPIDER (Varakantham et al., 2007) also exploits the locality of interactions to compute an approximate solution. Moreover, SPIDER uses branch and bound search and abstraction to speed up policy computation. (Peshkin et al., 2000) propose a distributed learning approach based on gradient descent method that also allows finding a Nash equilibrium. (Emery-Montemerlo et al., 2004) approximate DEC-MDP solutions using one-step Bayesian games that are solved by a heuristic method. Alternatives to Hansen's exact dynamic programming algorithm (Hansen et al., 2004) have also been proposed by Bernstein et al.(Bernstein et al., 2005) and Amato et al. (Amato et al., 2007). They use memory bounded controllers to limit the required amount of space to solve the problem. Recently, Wu et al. (Wu et al., 2010) have improved the scalability of Amato et al.'s approach (Amato et al., 2007) by avoiding the full backup performed at each step of the policy computation.

Finally, some approaches introduce direct communication so as to increase each agent observability (Goldman and Zilberstein, 2003, Xuan et al., 2001, Pynadath and Tambe, 2002). The agents communicate to inform the other agents of their local state or observation. If communication is free and instantaneous and the system state is jointly observable, the problem is reduced to a Multiagent Markov Decision Process (MMDP) (Boutilier et al., 1999) that is easier to solve. Otherwise, the problem complexity remains unchanged and heuristic methods are described to find near optimal policies.

DEC-MDP Approaches for Multi-Robot Systems

Even if DEC-MDP approaches describe a powerful framework to formalize and solve multiagent decision problems, several issues arise while considering problems of decentralized control in real-world multi-robot systems. Bresina et al. (Bresina et al., 2002) point out some difficulties in formalizing robotic planning problems using markovian models. Indeed, this framework considers a simple model of time and actions. All actions are assumed to have the same duration (one time unit) so the agents are assumed to be fully synchronized. Moreover, DEC-MDPs do

not take into account temporal and precedence constraints on action execution. The high complexity of optimally solving DEC-MDPs also reduced their applicability since it is difficult to solve problems involving more than two agents.

In this section we introduce two approaches based on DEC-MDPs that have been proposed to reduce the gap between the kinds of problems DEC-MDPs can solve and real world multi-robot applications. These models improve time and action representations and propose efficient approximate algorithms that can solve large problems considering constraints on task execution.

OC-DEC-MDP

The Opportunity Cost Decentralized Markov Decision Process (OC-DEC-MDP) framework (Beynier and Mouaddib, 2005, Beynier and Mouaddib, 2006) has been proposed to modelize and solve problems of decentralized control in multi-robot systems such as the ones presented at the beginning of the chapter. Because of communication limitations and unreliability of information exchange, communication between the agents (i.e. the robots) is assumed to be impossible during task execution. In order for a task to be successfully executed, temporal, precedence and resource constraints must be respected. Temporal constraints define, for each task t_i, a temporal window during which the task should be executed. Precedence constraints partially order the tasks by representing preconditions on task execution such as "task t_j must be finished before t_i can start". Finally, resource constraints guarantee that an agent has enough resources to execute a task.

Mission Definition

Problems of decentralized control in multi-agent systems that are considered in the OC-DEC-MDP framework, are defined as a mission $\mathcal{X}$ which stands for a couple $\langle \mathcal{Ag}, \mathcal{T} \rangle$ where:

Figure 2. Mission graph

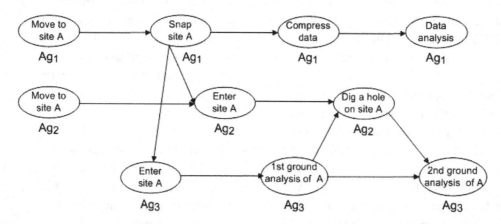

- $Ag = \{Ag_1, \cdots, Ag_n\}$ is a set of n agents $Ag_i \in Ag$.
- $T = \{t_1, \cdots, t_p\}$ is the set of tasks to execute.

The problem is for the agents $Ag_i \in Ag$ to execute the set of tasks T. The problem of task allocation is out of the scope of this chapter and tasks are supposed to be divided among the agents. Note that task allocation must take into account each agent's skills and must result in a feasible mission. Thus, there must be at least one interval of execution per task which respects temporal and precedence constraints. Hanna and Mouaddib (Hanna and Mouaddib, 2002), and more recently Abdallah and Lesser (Abdallah and Lesser, 2005), have developed MDP based algorithms that can perform such an allocation. Allocation of tasks among physical robots have also been studied by Gerkey et al. (Gerkey and Matarić, 2002) and Esben et al. (Esben et al., 2002) using auction principles.

As shown on Figure 2, a mission can be represented by an acyclic graph. This example describes a mission involving three planetary rovers. Edges stand for precedence constraints and nodes represent the tasks.

Each task $t_i \in T$ is characterized by:

- an agent Ag_i that has to execute the task.
- different possible durations δ^i. $P_t(\delta^i)$ is the probability the execution of t_i takes δ^i time units.
- different possible resource consumptions Δ_r^i. $P_r(\Delta_r^i)$ is the probability the execution of t_i consumes Δ_r^i resources.
- **temporal constraints:** each task t_i is assigned a temporal window $TC_i = [EST_i, LET_i]$ during which it should be executed. EST_i is the Earliest Start Time of the task and LET_i is its Latest End Time.
- **precedence constraints:** each task t_i has a set of predecessors $Pred_i$ which defines the tasks to be executed before t_i can start.

$$\forall t_i \in T, t_i \notin root \Leftrightarrow \exists t_j \in T : t_j \in Pred(t_i)$$

where *root* refers to the first tasks to be executed, i.e. the tasks without predecessors. Coordination constraints similar to our precedence constraints are described in frameworks such as TAEMS (Task Analysis, Environment Modeling and Simulation) (Decker and Lesser, 1993b) which is used to describe task structures of multiagent systems.

- a reward R_{ti} which is the reward the agents obtain when t_i is successfully executed (respecting temporal, precedence and resource constraints).

Given a mission $\mathcal{X}$, the agents' aim consists in maximizing the sum of the cumulative reward they obtain during task execution. Because of the decentralized nature of the decision process and communication limitations, each agent must be able to decide, in a cooperative way, which task to execute and when, without communicating (during task execution) and with respect to constraints.

OC-DEC-MDP Model

In order to model large problems, the OC-DEC-MDP model represents the multiagent decision problem as a set of MDPs where each MDP stands for a single agent decision problem. The policy of an agent $\mathcal{A}g_i$ will therefore be deduced from $\mathcal{A}g_i$'s MDP. Since each agent observe all the information it needs to make a local decision, MDPs are defined (not POMDPs) and the framework is referred as OC-DEC-MDPs.

Definition 3. *An n-agent OC-DEC-MDP is a set of n MDPs, one for each agent. The MDP of an agent $\mathcal{A}g_i$ is defined as a tuple $<\mathcal{S}_i, \mathcal{T}_i, \mathcal{P}_i, \mathcal{R}_i>$ where:*

- $\mathcal{S}_i$ is the finite set of states of the agent $\mathcal{A}g_i$,

- $\mathcal{T}_i$ is the finite set of tasks of the agent $\mathcal{A}g_i$,

- $\mathcal{P}_i$ is the transition function of the agent $\mathcal{A}g_i$,

- $\mathcal{R}_i : \mathcal{T}_i \to \mathbb{R}$ is the reward function of the agent $\mathcal{A}g_i$.

Because of interactions between the agents, local MDPs are not independent of each others. Moreover, the components of the MDPs must be defined so as to represent constraints on task

execution. The remaining of this section details each component of a local MDP.

States

The state space of an agent (i.e. of its MDP) is composed of three kinds of states: success states, partial failure states and failure states.

- **Success states:** Let us consider an agent $\mathcal{A}g_i$ which has just successfully executed a task t_i during an interval I and let r be the agent's remaining resources. At the end of t_i's execution, the agent $\mathcal{A}g_i$ moves to a success state and must decide its next action. This action depends on the last successfully executed task t_i, its interval I and the remaining resources r. Thus, a success state of $\mathcal{A}g_i$ is defined as a triplet $[t_i, I, r]$.

- **Partial failure states:** When an agent $\mathcal{A}g_i$ starts to execute a task t_{i+1} at st but fails because the predecessors of t_{i+1} are not finished, it moves to a partial failure state $[t_i, [st, st+1], et(I'), r]$ where t_i stands for $\mathcal{A}g_i$ last successfully executed task, $et(I')$ is the end time of t_i and r is $\mathcal{A}g_i$'s remaining resources after it partially fails.

When an agent starts to execute a task t_{i+1} before the predecessors of t_{i+1} have finished their execution, the agent immediately realizes that the execution of the task partially fails. This means that the agent $\mathcal{A}g_i$, at $st + 1$, realizes that it fails. As the agent could retry to execute the task later, this state is called a partial failure state. Thus, if precedence constraints are respected when the agent retries to execute t_{i+1}, the task could be successfully executed.

- **Failure states:** When an agent $\mathcal{A}g_i$ starts to execute a task t_{i+1} and it lacks resources or it violates temporal constraints, it moves to the failure state $[failure_{t_{i+1}}, *, *]$ associated to t_{i+1}.

Tasks-Actions

At each decision step, the agent must decide when to start its next task. The actions to perform thus consist of *"Executing the next task t_{i+1} at time st: $E(t_{i+1}, st)$"*, that is the action to start executing task t_{i+1} at time st where st respects temporal constraints. Actions are probabilistic since the processing time and the resource consumption of the task are uncertain. Precedence and temporal constraints restrict the possible start times of each task. Consequently, there is a finite set of start times for each task and a finite action set.

Transition Function

The transition function of an agent Ag_i gives the probability that Ag_i moves from a state s_i to a state s_j when it starts to execute a task t_{i+1} at st. Since the execution of t_{i+1} can lead to three different kinds of states, three kinds of transitions have to be considered: successful transitions, partial failure transitions and failure transitions. Transition probability computation differs for each kind of transition. Let us assume that an agent Ag_i tries to execute a task t_{i+1} at st.

- **Successful transitions:** The probability that Ag_i successfully executes t_{i+1} relies on: the probability the predecessors of t_{i+1} have finished at st (given by the probabilities on resource consumptions of t_{i+1}, and the probability Ag_i finishes the execution of the task before its deadline (given by probabilities on the durations of t_{i+1}).
- **Partial failure transitions:** The probability that Ag_i moves to a partial failure state is the probability that the predecessors of t_{i+1} have not finished at st and Ag_i has enough resources to be aware of its partial

failure. The probability that the predecessors have not finished at st is the probability that they will finish later or they will never finish.

- **Failure transitions:** An agent fails to execute its task if it lacks resources or temporal constraints are violated. The probability that Ag_i lacks of resources is given by the probability the execution of t_{i+1} consumes more resources than available or the agent partially fails and the necessary resources to be aware of it are not sufficient.

If $st > LET_{i+1} - min(\delta^{i+1})$, the agent starts the execution of t_{i+1} before the latest end time of t_{i+1} ($LET_{i+1} - min(\delta^{i+1})$). Temporal constraints are therefore violated and the agent fails.

When $st \le LET_{i+1} - min(\delta^{i+1})$, the agent may also violate temporal constraints. Indeed, if the duration δ^{i+1} is so long that the deadline is met ($st + \delta^{i+1} > LET_{i+1}$), the agent fails. The probability of violating the deadline therefore relies on duration probabilities.

In order to define transition functions, probabilities on start times and end times of the tasks must be known. The probability an agent starts to execute a task t_{i+1} at st relies on the agent's policy, on its available resources and on the ends times of the predecessors of t_{i+1}. Moreover, the predecessors' end times depend on the policies of their agents. Thus, the agents' policies have to be known to compute probabilities on start times and end times. Assuming an initial set of policies for the agents (one policy per agent), a propagation algorithms has been developed (Beynier and Mouaddib, 2005) to compute such probabilities. This algorithm propagates constraints through the mission graph from the roots to the leaves. Each time a node (i.e. a task) t_i is considered, its temporal probabilities (probabilities on start times and end times) and resource probabilities are computed using temporal and resource probabilities of the predecessors of t_i and using the policy of t_i. Once all the nodes have been considered, transition probabilities can be deduced from temporal probabilities and probabilities on resource consumptions.

Reward Function

When it successfully executes a task t_{i+1}, the agent $\mathcal{A}g_i$ moves to a success state and obtains the reward associated with t_{i+1}. If the agent partially fails, no reward is obtained. Finally, if the agent permanently fails the execution of t_{i+1}, it is penalized for all the tasks it will not be able to execute due to the failure of t_{i+1}.

Complexity Analysis

A joint policy for the agents in an OC-DEC-MDP is a set of individual policies $\langle \pi_1 \cdots \pi_n \rangle$ where π_i is a local policy for an agent $\mathcal{A}g_i$ in the OC-DEC-MDP.

Theorem 1. *Optimally solving an OC-DEC-MDP requires an exponential amount of computation time.*

Proof: Optimally solving an OC-DEC-MDP consists in finding a joint policy that maximizes the global performance (Bernstein et al., 2002). From the definition of a joint policy for an n-agent OC-DEC-MDP, we can deduce that the number of possible joint policies is exponential in the number of joint states. Evaluating a joint policy can be done in polynomial time through the use of dynamic programming (Goldman and Zilberstein, 2004). In fact, we use standard policy evaluation algorithms for MDPs since the policy to evaluate is a mapping from joint states to joint actions: the states of the MDPs are the joint states $s = \langle s_1 \cdots s_n \rangle$ where s_i is a local state of $\mathcal{A}g_i$ in the OC-DEC-MDP and the actions of the MDP are the joint actions $a = \langle a_1, \cdots a_n \rangle$ where a_i is an action of $\mathcal{A}g_i$ in the OC-DEC-MDP. Finding an optimal policy for an n-agent OC-DEC-MDP consists in evaluating all the possible local policies and therefore requires an exponential amount of computation time.

Constraints affect the policy space but have no effect on the worst case complexity. They reduce the state space and the action space. Thus, the policy space can be reduced. Nonetheless, the number of policies remains exponential. Consequently, dealing with constraints does not result in lower complexity.

Due to the high complexity of OC-DEC-MDPs, it is untractable to optimally solve large size of problems. It is thus better to turn towards an approximate planning approach that can solve large size of problems and computes a solution that is closed to the optimum. Indeed, developing an optimal algorithm would limit the size of problems that can be solved in practice and real-world multi-rover applications could not be considered.

Decision Problem

During task execution, each agent has a local view of the system and does not know the other agents' states nor actions. If the execution of a task t_i starts before its predecessors finish, it partially fails. Partial failures consume restricted resources and can lead to insufficient resources. If an agent lacks resources it will be unable to execute its remaining tasks. Consequently, the agents tend to avoid partial failures. One way to restrict partial failures consists in delaying the execution of the tasks. As a result, the likelihood that the predecessors have finished when an agent starts to execute a task increases and less resources are "wasted" by partial failures. Nonetheless, the more the execution of a task is delayed, the more the successors are delayed and the higher the probability of violating temporal constraints. In fact, the probability the deadline is met and the agent fails permanently executing the task increases.

The problem is to find a local policy for each agent that maximizes the sum of the rewards of all the agents. Thus, the agents must trade off the probability of partially failing and consuming resources to no avail against the consequences of delaying the execution of a task. Indeed, to maximize the sum of the expected rewards, each agent must consider the consequences of a delay on itself and on its successors.

Opportunity Cost and Expected Value

For purposes of coordinating the agents, the notion of Opportunity Cost has been introduced by Beynier and Mouaddib (Beynier and Mouaddib, 2005, Beynier and Mouaddib, 2006). It is borrowed from economics and refers to hidden indirect costs associated with a decision. In the OC-DEC-MDP framework, Opportunity Cost measures the indirect effect of an agent's decision on the other agents. More specifically, the Opportunity Cost is the loss of expected value resulting from delaying the execution of the other agents' tasks. Taking this cost into account leads to better coordination among the agents: it allows each agent to consider how its decisions influence the other agents.

Consequently, the policy of an agent Ag_i in a state s_i is computed using two equations. The first one is a standard Bellman equation that computes the expected utility of an agent Ag_i and considers the tasks Ag_i still has to execute:

$$V(s_i) = \overbrace{R(s_i)}^{Immediate\,Gain} + \overbrace{\max_{E(t_{i+1}, st_{i+1}), st_{i+1} \geq t}(V(E(t_{i+1}, st_{i+1}), s_i))}^{Expected\,Utility}$$

$$(1)$$

where $s_i = <t_i, [st_i, et_i], r_{t_i}>$ (and $et_i = t$) or $s_i = <t_i, [t-1, t], et_i, r_{t_i}>$. If s_i is a success state ($s_i = <t_i, [st_i, et_i], r_{t_i}>$), the agent obtains a reward for successfully executing task t_i and $R(s_i) = \mathcal{R}(t_i)$. Otherwise, $R(s_i) = 0$.

$V(E(t_{i+1}, st_{i+1}), s_i))$ denotes the expected utility of the agent while executing $E(t_{i+1}, st_{i+1})$ from state s_i. Since the execution of the action can lead to different types of transitions, $V(E(t_{i+1}, st_{i+1}), s_i))$ is defined as:

$$V(E(t_{i+1}, st_{i+1}), s_i) = V_{suc}(E(t_{i+1}, st_{i+1}), s_i)$$
$$+V_{PCV}(E(t_{i+1}, st_{i+1}), s_i) + V_{fail}(E(t_{i+1}, st_{i+1}), s_i)$$

where $V_{suc}(E(t_{i+1}, st_{i+1}), s_i)$ is the expected value of the agent when t_{i+1} is successfully executed at st_{i+1}, V_{PCV} is the expected value of the agent when the execution of t_{i+1} starts at st_{i+1} and partially fails, and V_{fail} is the expected value if the agent start executing t_{i+1} at st_{i+1} and it lacks resources or temporal constraints are violated.

The second equation computes the best foregone action using a modified Bellman equation in which an Expected Opportunity Cost (EOC) is introduced. It allows the agent to select the best action to execute in a state s_i, considering its expected utility and the EOC induced on the other agents:

$$\pi_i(s_i) = \arg\max_{E(t_{i+1}, st_{i+1}), st_{i+1} \geq et_i}\left(\overbrace{V(E(t_{i+1}, st_{i+1}), s_i)}^{Expected\,Utility}\right.$$
$$\left. - \overbrace{EOC(t_{i+1}, st_{i+1})}^{Expected\,Opportunity\,Cost}\right)$$

$$(2)$$

where:

- *argmax* denotes the operator which returns the action $E(t_{i+1}, st_{i+1})$ which maximizes the trade-off between the expected utility V of the agent and the expected opportunity cost provoked on the other agents.
- $EOC(t_{i+1}, st_{i+1})$ is the expected opportunity cost the execution of t_{i+1} will induce if it starts at st_{i+1}.

Thus, the most valuable foregone action is selected by considering:

- The expected value, computed using a standard Bellman equation (Equation 1). It takes into account the expected value of executing the agent's remaining task.
- The expected opportunity cost provoked on the other agents.

The EOC induced on the other agents when t_{i+1} starts at st is defined as follows:

$$EOC(t_{i+1}, st) = P_{suc} \cdot \sum_{Ag_j \in Ag, j \neq i} EOC_{Ag_j, t_{i+1}}(et_{i+1})$$

(3)

$$+P_{fail} \sum_{Ag_j \in Ag, j \neq i} EOC_{Ag_j, t_{i+1}}(fail) + P_{PCV} \cdot EOC(t_{i+1}, st')$$

where et_{i+1} is a possible end time of t_{i+1}, $EOC_{Ag_j, t_{i+1}}(et_{i+1})$ is the EOC induced on the agent Ag_j when t_{i+1} ends at et_{i+1}. It is computed using Equation 4. $EOC(t_{i+1}, st')$ is the OC when the execution of t_{i+1} partially fails and the agents retries to execute the task at st' (the next start time of the task). P_{suc} stands for the probability to successfully execute the task, P_{PCV} is the probability to fail partially because the predecessors have not finished. P_{fail} is the probability to fail permanently.

EOC values can be deduced by considering the delay provoked on the successors. The Expected Opportunity Cost described in Equation 3 is given by:

$$EOC_{Ag_j, t_{i+1}}(et_{t_{i+1}}) = \sum_{r_{t_j}} P_{ra}^{t_j}(r_{t_j}) \cdot OC_{t_j}(\Delta t, r_{t_j})$$

(4)

where t_j is the nearest task that will be executed by Ag_j (the distance between two tasks t_i and t_j is given by the number of nodes that belongs to the shortest path between t_i and t_j in the mission graph). $P_{ra}^{t_j}(r_{t_j})$ is the probability that Ag_j has r_{t_j} resources when it starts to execute t_j. Δt is the delay induced on t_j when t_{i+1} ends at $et_{t_{i+1}}$. This delay is computed by propagating temporal constraints between t_{i+1} and t_j. $OC_{t_j}(\Delta t, r_{t_j})$ is the Opportunity Cost provoked on t_j when it is delayed by Δt. It stands for a difference in expected value computed as follows:

$$OC_{t_j}(\Delta t, r_{t_j}) = V_{t_j}^{0, r_{t_j}} - V_{t_j}^{\Delta t, r_{t_j}}$$

(5)

where $V_{t_j}^{0, r_{t_j}}$ is the expected value of Ag_j if the execution of t_j is not delayed and the agent has r_{t_j} resources when it starts to execute t_j. $V_{t_j}^{\Delta t, r_{t_j}}$ is the expected value of the agent Ag_j when the execution of t_j is delayed by Δt and the agent has r_{t_j} resources when it starts to execute t_j.

If the execution of t_{i+1} fails, t_j could not be executed because of violation of precedence constraints. Then, $EOC_{Ag_j, t_{i+1}}(fail)$ is given by:

$$EOC_{Ag_j, t_{i+1}}(fail) = OC_{t_j}(fail)$$

$$= \sum_{r_{t_j}} P_{ra}^{t_j}(r_{t_j})\left(V_{t_j, r_{t_j}}^0 - V([failure_{t_j}, *, *])\right)$$

Policy Computation

Given a state s_i of an agent Ag_i, Equation 2 allows for the agent to decide its policy from s_i. Beynier and Mouaddib (Beynier and Mouaddib, 2006) have proposed an iterative revision algorithm which applies this decision method to each state of each agent and computes an approximate solution to the multiagent decision problem. The algorithm consists in iteratively improving an initial policy set. At each iteration step, the agents improve their initial local policy at the same time. Given the initial policies that have been used to compute temporal and resource probabilities, each agent tries to improve its own policy. At each iteration step, each agent Ag_i traverses the task graph in the reverse topological order and, revises the execution policy of each task (node), using Equation 2. While revising the policy of t_i, Ag_i considers all the states s_i from which t_i can be executed (states associated to the previous task t_{i-1} of Ag_i). The expected value of s_i is then computed and its policy is deduced. This process is repeated until no changes are made. An equilibrium is then reached.

Experiments

Experiments have been developed to prove the scalability, the efficency and the applicability of OC-DEC-MDPs. Experiments show that large problems can be solved using the OC-DEC-MDP framework. Indeed, missions of hundreds of tasks and more than twenty agents can be considered. The performances obtained at each iteration step have also been studied by running mission executions. Experiments illustrate that the performance of the agents increases with the number of iterations. By iterating the process, the likelihood the agents fail because of partial failure resource consumption and because of lack of resources, decreases. The resulting policy is safer than policies of previous iterations and the gain of the agents is steady over executions. A near optimal policy is obtained at the end of the first iteration. Second iteration leads to small improvements but it diminishes the number of partial failures.

Finally, the OC-DEC-MDP framework has been applied to real-world scenarios using Koala robots. Scenarios derived from Mars rover missions were considered. Figure 3 represents a scenario involving two robots that have to explore a set of 8 interesting places. The first robot (robot Ag_1) can take pictures and the second one (robot Ag_2) can take and analyse ground samples. Robot Ag_1 must take picture of sites A, B, D, E, F,

H and J, and robot Ag_2 must analyse sites C, D, F, H and I. Sites are ordered so as to minimize travelling resource consumptions. Furthermore, precedence constraints have to be taken into account. As taking samples of the ground may change the topology of the site, pictures of a site must be taken before the other robot starts to analyse it. Moreover, robot Ag_1 must have left a site before robot Ag_2 can start to analyse it. Thus, robot Ag_1 must have taken a picture of site D before robot Ag_1 enters this site. Temporal constraints have also to be considered: visiting earliest start times and latest end times are associated with each site.

The mission was represented using a mission graph (Figure 4). Then, the corresponding OC-DEC-MDP was automatically built and solved by the iterative algorithm. Finally, resulting policies were implemented on Koala robots. During task execution, robots only have to execute their policies which map each state to an action. Thus, initial ambitions about the limitation of computational resources needed to make a decision have been fulfilled. Coordination performs well even if robots cannot communicate. Temporal and precedence constraints are respected. As shown on Figure 5 for the crossing point D, while deciding when to start its action, the first robot takes into account the fact that the other robot waits for him (thanks to the OC). The decision of the second robot is based on the probability that robot Ag_1 has left the site, the cost of a partial failure, and the robot's own expected value. Thus, robot Ag_1 enters site D, completes its task (Picture 2) and leaves the site (Picture 3). Then, robot Ag_2 tries to enter the site (Picture 4). As robot Ag_1 does not know the other robot actions, it may try to enter the site and fails because the other robot has not finished to take the picture. The second robot realizes that it fails when it tries to enter the site. If precedence constraints are not respected the robot returns to its last position. If temporal constraints are respected, the robot enters the site (Picture 4). These experiments show that the

Figure 3. Two-robot exploration scenario

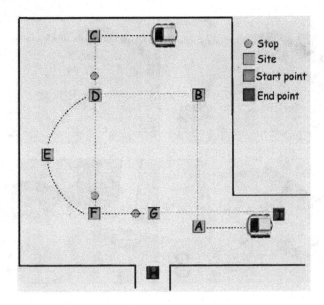

Figure 4. Mission graph of the two-robot exploration scenario

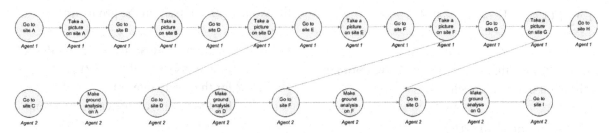

OC-DEC-MDP approach can be used by physical robots which are thus able to successfully and cooperatively complete their mission.

2V-DEC-MDP FOR FLOCKING AND PLATOONING

In (Mouaddib et al., 2007), the Vector-Valued Decentralized Markov Decision Process (2V-DEC-MDP) framework has been proposed to coordinate locally the actions of a group of agents. It is based on MDP with an online coordination part. Assuming without loss of generality that all agents are identical, a 2V-DEC-MDP is a set of 2V-MDP, one per agent. A 2V-MDP is composed

by an off-line part, an MDP, and an on-line part to adapt its actions with the other agents.

The MDP is a tuple $\langle S, A, P, R \rangle$, with:

- S a set of states,
- A a set of actions,
- $P : S \times A \times S \rightarrow [0;1]$, the transition function,
- $R : S \times A \times S \rightarrow \mathbb{R}$, the reward function which expresses both positive reward for goal states and negative reward for hazardous states.

For the optimality criteria, an expected reward is defined on a finite horizon T. The optimal value function V^* of a state is defined by:

Figure 5. Execution of the mission (crossing point of site D)

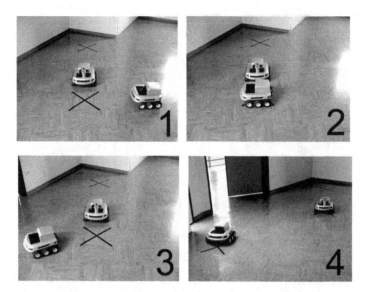

$$V^*(s) = \max_{a \in A}(R(s,a)$$
$$+\sum_{s' \in S} P(s,a,s') \cdot V^*(s')), \forall s \in S$$

A policy is a function $\pi : S \rightarrow A$, the optimal policy is a policy π^*, such that:

$$\pi^*(s) = argmax_a(R(s,a)$$
$$+\sum_{s' \in S} P(s,a,s') \cdot V^*(s')), \forall s \in S$$

The neighborhood for an agent i is defined as the set of states of (detected) agents who can interact with i. Until now, it is assumed that all the agents near enough (according to a fixed maximum distance d) could be detected and their states could be known. Taking into account partial observability will be the subject of some future works. If the neighborhood is too big, it can be restricted to a subset (more the neighborhood will be big and more the policy will be good but more the computation of this policy will take time).

The on-line part of a 2V-MDP is built with the computation of local social impact, according to local observations. The functions for computing the value of the impact on the group are:

- *ER* for the individual award (the value of the optimal policy of the MDP),
- *JER* for the group interest,
- *JEP* for the negative impact on the group.

Using those functions, the agents will use a *LexDiff* operator to choose the best policy (i.e. the best action) to apply.

LexDiff builds a vector $v = (ER(\pi_i), JER(\pi_i), JEP(\pi_i))$ for every π_i and normalize each values vector $v_i = (v_i^1, v_i^2, v_i^3)$ to a utilities vector $v_u = (v_u^1, v_u^2, v_u^3)$. *LexDiff* then permutes those utilities vectors so that each vector (v^1, v^2, v^3) be such that $v^1 \geq v^2 \geq v^3$. The best vector is then founded by a lexicographic order: for two vectors $v_a = (v_a^1, v_a^2, v_a^3)$ and $v_b = (v_b^1, v_b^2, v_b^3)$, we choose v_a if $v_a^1 > v_b^1$ and v_b if $v_a^1 < v_b^1$. If $v_a^1 = v_b^1$, we compare v_a^2 and v_b^2, and so on.

Thanks to this design, the DEC-MDP is expressed as a set of 2V-MDP, allowing the coordination problem to be tractable. In (Boussard et al., 2008), *ER*, *JER* and *JEP* have been defined for platoon emergence, but this work does not try to keep the shape of the platoon. s_i^j is the state *j* of agent *i* (the environment being reduced to a discrete set of possible positions, a state is one position of this set and one orientation),

- $\vec{s} = (s_1, \ldots, s_N)$ is the joint state vector,
- *face*(s) gives all the agents the are closer to the objective than *s*,
- *distance*(s^1,s^2) gives the number of actions needed to go from s^1 to s^2,

  angle(s^1,s^2) gives the angle between the orientation of s^1 and the one of s^2:

$$angle(s^1, s^2) = \frac{\left\| orientation_{s^1} - orientation_{s^2} \right\|}{angle_{max}}$$

- *back*(s) gives the next place available behind *s* (if s^1, the location just behind *s* according to the orientation of *s*, is available, s^1 is returned. If it is not available, *back*(s^1)) is returned.

So now, using those definitions, the formulae for *ER*, *JER* and *JEP* can be written in the platooning context.

Alignment

$$ER(s, a) = \sum_{s' \in S} p(s, a, s') ER_i, \quad i = 1, 2, 3$$

Depending on the situation, ER_i are defined by:

$$ER_1 = V^*(s')$$

$$ER_2 = -\min_{s_j \in face(s')} (distance(s', s_{b1}) + \frac{angle(s', s_{b1})}{angle_{max}})$$

$$ER_3 = -(distance(s', s_{b2}) + \frac{angle(s', s_{b2})}{angle_{max}})$$

where $s_{b1} = back(s_j)$, $s_{b2} = back(leader)$ and $V^*(s)$ a function of the expected distance between *s* and the objective of the platoon. *Distance*(s^1,s^2) gives the cost of going from a state s^1 to a state s^2 and *angle*(s^1, s^2) gives the cost of rotating from the orientation of s^1 to the one of s^2. Thus, it has been added to those equations two costs: the cost of going from a state s^1 to a state s^2, wich means the cost of reaching the position of s^2 AND rotating to the good orientation. The angle is divided by the maximum angle to be sure that the cost of the distance will always be bigger than the cost of the angle, so the agent will not choose to stay on a distant place for saving the cost of a rotation. In ER_2 and ER_3, *back*(target) is used instead of *targett*, because the agent wants to go behind its target.

An agent does not have the same objectives whether it is on a leader position or inside a platoon. Indeed, a leader will move in the direction of its objective, while a non-leader agent follow the one in front of it. Hence, an agent have to choose which equation to follow before resolve its 2V-MDP.

So, if the agent is a leader, or if it is out of range of any platoon, it chooses ER_1. If it is inside a platoon but it knows that the leader is behind it, it chooses ER_3. Finally, if it is inside a platoon and have no leader behind it, it chooses ER_2.

Separation

$$JEP(s, a) = \sum_{s' \in S} [p(s, a, s') \cdot \sum_{s_j \in D} (\sum_{a_j^k, k=1}^{|A_j|} p(s_j, a_j^k, s') \cdot C)]$$

Where *D* is the set of states of detected agents in neighborhood and C a constant equal to the cost of a collision between two agents.

Cohesion

$$JER(s, a) = \sum_{s' \in S} (p(s, a, s') \cdot K(s'))$$

Figure 6. Scenario of multi-robot platooning

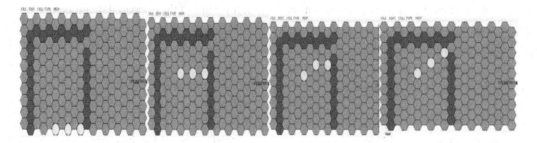

Where $K(s)$ is the function which estimate the gain of a given situation for the group. $K(s)$ gives a reward if at least one agent is behind s.

After choosing an equation for the ER criteria, the agent has to fix the weight of *ER*, *JER* and *JEP*. For a leader, it is set w_{JEP} to 0 since the criterion is with no sense for it and, typically, w_{ER} to 0.49 and w_{JER} to 0.51. For a non-leader, $w_{JEP} = 0.35$, $w_{ER} = 0.32$ and $w_{JER} = 0.33$ (except if a leader is detected behind the agent, in which case $w_{JER} = w_{JEP} = 0$, and $w_{ER} = 1$). Finally, for any agent, $w_{JER} = 0$ as soon as it is near to the objective of the platoon. Experimentations proved that values of those weights do not change anything on the behavior of the agents. The only important thing is the order of those weights: the most important criteria has to have the biggest weight, the second criteria has to have the second weight, etc., so values for those weights could be chosen arbitrary.

Experiments with Real Robots

After testing the approach on a simulator, tests on real robots (Koalas) have been developed. Those robots know the "map" of the environment they are evolving in and have local visibility, so they know the position and orientation of the agents around them. A 2V-DEC-MDP, parameterized as described before, is running on them. An example with 3 robots is shown on Figure 6. Robots are placed on a same line, and an objective in front of them is given (the door on the right side). Figure 7, Figure 8 and Figure 9 are captions of those tests.

When the test starts, the closest robot to the objective chooses the *ER*1 function and goes toward its objective. Because of the *JER* function, it waits for the other agents. In the same time, the two other agents follow the first one: according to the *ER*2 function, one of them chooses to follow the first agent, while the other one chooses to take the third place.

The platoon then emerges from those interactions: we can see the robots in their initial position in Figure 7, and their position after a few moves in Figure 8. Then, in Figure 9, we can see the fully shaped platoon.

Many other initial configurations were considered and we can see that, for each configuration, robots fully form a platoon after some moves.

CONCLUSION

Decentralized decision making is an appropriate approach for multi-robot applications since they are able to support uncertainty, partial observability and decentralized control. Even if Decentralized Markov Decision Processes suffer from a high complexity, the structure of multi-robot decision problems such as constraints on task execution (exploration mission) or locality of interactions (platooning) can be exploited to reduce the complexity. This chapter presented two approaches based on DEC-MDPs that have been proved to solve efficiently multi-robot cooperative problems. These approaches allow us to derive

Figure 7. Initial situation

Figure 8. After few moves

Figure 9. Platoon is formed

individual cooperative policies for the robots such that a global utility is maximized. The coordination in those approaches is considered during the computation of the policies by evaluating the effect of a local decision on the other robots. In the opposite to that, classical multiagent planning techniques address the problem of coordination in two steps: computing plans and then coordinating them. The second step requires in general a costly communication between the robots that limits their applicability in real-world applications (communication not always available, costly and time consuming). Another drawback of classical approaches is when the execution deviates from the expected behavior and thus re-planification and re-coordination are required that can reduce the performance of the system during the execution. Another contribution of decentralized decision models is to better formalize the flocking techniques by improving their robustness, supporting the uncertainty and assessing the quality of the global behavior.

Markov Decision Processes have also been successfully used to solve decentralized decision problems in non Artificial Intelligence domains. For instance, decision problems of search and storage in peer-to-peer server networks have been solved using a set of Interactive Markov Decision Processes (Beynier and Mouaddib, 2009).

Future works in multi-robot domain should concern the extension of the DEC-MDPs to deal with problems involving human and robot interactions such as mixed initiative techniques (Weld, 1994b, Sidner and Lee, 2005, Freedy et al., 2008). These systems can operate mostly autonomously, but may need supervision or help in particular situations. Examples include mobile robots or intelligent vehicles navigating in a narrow corridor or heavy traffic, or avoiding risky areas that could cause costly failures. Similarly, robots performing complex surgical operations may require supervision and intervention of the specialist. In these applications, a supervision unit, often a human operator, can take over control when the situation is too complex for the autonomous system (Crandall and Goddrich, 2005). While the supervision unit (e.g., a driver, a surgeon, or a control center operator) may be able to perform each task by manually controlling the system, this would normally result in a time-consuming, costly operation. The problem is therefore to develop a general framework for supervision unit - autonomous unit teaming, to optimize performance and reduce the supervision unit work-load, costs, fatigue-driven errors and risks (Green et al., 2008).

REFERENCES

Abdallah, S., & Lesser, V. (2005). Modeling task allocation using a decision theoretic model. In *Proceedings of Fourth International Joint Conference on Autonomous Agents and Multiagent Systems*, (pp. 719–726). Utrecht, Netherlands. ACM Press.

Amato, C., & Zilberstein, S. (2007). Optimizing memory-bounded controllers for decentralized POMDPs. In *Proceedings of the Twenty Third Conference on Uncertainty in Artificial Intelligence*.

Becker, R., Zilberstein, S., Lesser, V., & Goldman, C. (2003). Transition-independent decentralized markov decision processes. In *Proceedings of the Second International Joint Conference on Autonomous Agents and Multi Agent Systems*, (pp. 41–48). Melbourne, Australia.

Bernstein, D., Hansen, E. A., & Zilberstein, S. (2005). Bounded policy iteration for decentralized POMDPs. In *Proceedings of the Nineteenth International Joint Conference on Artificial Intelligence*, Edinburgh, Scotland.

Bernstein, D., Zilberstein, S., & Immerman, N. (2002). The complexity of decentralized control of MDPs. *Mathematics of Operations Research, 27*(4), 819–840. doi:10.1287/moor.27.4.819.297

Bernstein, D., Zilberstein, S., Washington, R., & Bresina, J. (2001). Planetary rover control as a Markov decision process. In *The 6th International Symposium on Artificial Intelligence, Robotics and Automation in Space*, Montreal, Canada.

Beynier, A., & Mouaddib, A. (2009). Decentralized decision making process for document server networks. In *Proceeding of the International Conference on Game Theory and Networks*.

Beynier, A., & Mouaddib, A. I. (2005). A polynomial algorithm for decentralized Markov decision processes with temporal constraints. *Proceedings of the Fourth Interantional Joint Conference on Autonomous Agents and MultiAgent Systems*, (pp. 963–969).

Beynier, A., & Mouaddib, A. I. (2006). An iterative algorithm for solving constrained decentralized Markov decision processes. In *The Twenty-First National Conference on Artificial Intelligence (AAAI-06)*.

Blum, A., & Furst, M. (1997). Fast planning through planning graph analysis. *Artificial Intelligence, 90*, 281–300. doi:10.1016/S0004-3702(96)00047-1

Blum, A., & Langford, J. (1999). Probabilistic planning in the graphplan framework. In *Proceedings of ECP'99*.

Blythe, J. (1999a). Decision-theoretic planning. *AI Magazine*.

Blythe, J. (1999b). *Planning under uncertainty in Dynamic domains*. PhD thesis, Carnegie Mellon University.

Boussard, M., Bouzid, M., & Mouaddib, A. (2008). Vector valued Markov decision process for robot platooning. In *Proceedings of the European Conference on Artificial Intelligence (ECAI 2008)*.

Boutilier, C., Dean, T., & Hanks, S. (1999). Decision-theoretic planning: Structural asumptions and computational leverage. *Journal of Artificial Intelligence Research, 1,* 1–93.

Bresina, J., Dearden, R., Meuleau, N., Ramakrishnan, S., Smith, D., & Washington, R. (2002). *Planning under continuous time and resource uncertainty: A challenge for AI.* In UAI.

Cardon, S., Mouaddib, A., Zilberstein, S., & Washington, R. (2001). Adaptive control of acyclic progressive processing task structures. In *Proceedings of the 17th International Joint Conference on Artificial Intelligence, IJCAI-2001,* (pp. 701–706).

Chadès, I., Scherrer, B., & Charpillet, F. (2002). A heuristic approach for solving decentralized-POMDP: Assessment on the pursuit problem. In *Proceedings of the Sixteenth ACM Symposium on Applied Computing.*

Clement, B., & Barrett, A. (2003). *Continual coordination through shared activities.* In International Joint Conference on Autonomous Agents and MulAgent Systems, AAMAS.

Crandall, P., & Goddrich, M. (2005). Validating human-robot interaction schemes in multitasking environments. *IEEE Transaction Systems, Man, and Cybernetics. Part A: Systems and Humans, 35*(4), 438–449. doi:10.1109/TSMCA.2005.850587

Damiani, S., Verfaillie, G., & Charmeau, M. (2005). An earth watching satellite constellation: How to manage a team of watching agents with limited communications. In *Proceedings of the Fourth International Joint Conference on Autonomous Agents and MultiAgent Systems (AAMAS 2005),* (pp. 455–462).

Decker, K., & Lesser, V. (1992). Generalizing the partial global planning algorithm. *Journal on Intelligent Cooperative Information Systems, 1*(2), 319–346. doi:10.1142/S0218215792000222

Decker, K., & Lesser, V. (1993a). Quantitative modeling of complex computational task environnement. In *Proceedings of the Eleventh National Conference on Artificial Intelligence,* (pp. 217–224).

Decker, K., & Lesser, V. (1993b). Quantitative modeling of complex environments. *International Journal of Intelligent Systems in Accounting Finance & Management, 2*(4), 215–234.

Emery-Montemerlo, R., Gordon, G., Schneider, J., & Thrun, S. (2004). Approximate solutions for partially observable stochastic games with common payoffs. In *Proceedings of the Third Joint Conference on Autonomous Agents and Multi Agent Systems.*

Esben, H. O., Maja, J. M., & Gaurav, S. S. (2002). Multi-robot task allocation in the light of uncertainty. In *Proceedings of IEEE International Conference on Robotics and Automation,* (pp. 3002–3007).

Estlin, T., Tobias, A., Rabideau, G., Castana, R., Chien, S., & Mjolsness, E. (1999). *An integrated system for multi-rover scientific exploration.* In The Sixteenth National Conference on Artificial Intelligence.

Freedy, A., Sert, O., Freedy, E., Weltman, G., Mcdonough, J., Tambe, M., & Gupta, T. (2008). Multiagent adjustable autonomy framework (MAAF) for multirobot, multihuman teams. In *International Symposium on Collaborative Technologies (CTS) 2008.*

Gerkey, B. P., & Matarić, M. J. (2002). Sold! Auction methods for multi-robot coordination. *IEEE Transactions on Robotics and Automation, 18*(5), 758–768. doi:10.1109/TRA.2002.803462

Goldman, C., & Zilberstein, S. (2003). Optimizing information exchange in cooperative multiagent systems. In *International Joint Conference on Autonomous Agents and Multi Agent Systems,* (pp. 137–144).

Goldman, C., & Zilberstein, S. (2004). Decentralized control of cooperative systems: Categorization and complexity analysis. *Journal of Artificial Intelligence Research, 22*, 143–174.

Green, A. S., Billinghurst, M., Chen, W., & Chase, J. (2008). Human-robot collaboration: A literature review and augmented reality approach in design. *International Journal of Advanced Robotic Systems, 5*(1), 1–16.

Hanna, H., & Mouaddib, A. (2002). Task selection as decision making in multiagent system. In *International Joint Conference on Autonomous Agents and Multi Agent Systems*, (pp. 616–623).

Hansen, E. A., Bernstein, D., & Zilberstein, S. (2004). Dynamic programming for partially observable stochastic games. In *Proceedings of the Nineteenth National Conference on Artificial Intelligence.*

Howard, R. A. (1960). *Dynamic programming and Markov processes.* MIT Press.

Kaelbling, L. P., Littman, M. L., & Cassandra, A. R. (1998). Planning and acting in partially observable stochastic domains. *Artificial Intelligence, 101*, 99–134. doi:10.1016/S0004-3702(98)00023-X

Kleiner, A., & Sun, D. (2007). Decentralized slam for pedestrians without direct communication. In. *Proceedings of IROS, 2007*, 1461–1466.

Marjovi, A., Nunes, J., Marques, L., & de Almeida, A. (2009). Multi-robot fire searching in unknown environment. In *Intelligent Robots and Systems (IROS 2009)*, (pp. 1929–1934).

Michaud, F., Lepage, P., Frenette, P., Letourneau, D., & Gaubert, N. (2006). Coordinated maneuvering of automated vehicles in platoons. *ITS, 7*(4), 437–447.

Morimoto, T. (2000). *How to develop a RoboCupRescue agent.* RoboCupRescue Technical Committee.

Mouaddib, A., Boussard, M., & Bouzid, M. (2007). Towards multiobjective multiagent planning. In *Proceedings of the International Joint Conference on Autonomous Agents and Multiagent Systems (AAMAS 2007).*

Nair, R., Pradeep, V., Milind, T., & Makoto, Y. (2005). Networked distributed POMDPs: A synthesis of distributed constraint optimization and POMDPs. In *Proceedings of the Twentieth National Conference on Artificial Intelligence (AAAI-05).*

Nair, R., Tambe, M., Yokoo, M., Marsella, S., & Pynadath, D. V. (2003). Taming decentralized pomdps: Towards efficient policy computation for multiagent settings. In *Proceedings of the International Joint Conference on Artificial Intelligence*, (pp. 705–711).

Nettleton, E., Thru, S., Durrant-Whyte, H., & Sukkarieh, S. (2003). Decentralized slam with low-bandwith communication for teams of vehicles. In *Proceedings of the International Conference on Field and Service Robotics.*

Peshkin, L., Kim, K., Meuleu, N., & Kaelbling, L. (2000). Learning to cooperate via policy search. In *Sixteenth Conference on Uncertainty in Artificial Intelligence*, (pp. 307–314).

Puterman, M. L. (2005). *Markov Decision processes: Discrete stochastic dynamic programming.* New York, NY: Wiley-Interscience.

Pynadath, D., & Tambe, M. (2002). The communicative multiagent team decision problem: Analyzing teamwork theories and models. *Journal of Artificial Intelligence Research*, 389–423.

Reynolds, C. W. (1987). Flocks, herds, and schools: A distributed behavioral model. *Computer Graphics, 21*(4), 25–34. doi:10.1145/37402.37406

RoboCup. (2000). *RoboCup-Rescue simulator manual.*

Roy, N., Pineau, J., & Thrun, S. (2000). Spoken dialogue management using probabilistic reasoning. In *Proceedings of the 38th Annual Meeting of the Association for Computational Linguistics (ACL-2000)*, Hong Kong.

Shoham, Y., & Tennenholtz, M. (1992). On social laws for artificial agent societies: Off-line design. *Artificial Intelligence, 73*(1-2), 231–252. doi:10.1016/0004-3702(94)00007-N

Sidner, C., & Lee, C. (2005). Robots as laboratory hosts. *Interaction, 12*(2), 24–26. doi:10.1145/1052438.1052457

Varakantham, P., & Marecki, J. Yabu, y., Milind, T., & Makoto, Y. (2007). Letting loose a SPIDER on a network of POMDPs: Generating quality guaranteed policies. In *Proceedings of the International Joint Conference on Agents and Multiagent Systems (AAMAS-07)*.

Weld, D. (1994a). An introduction to least-commitment planning. *Artificial Intelligence Magazine, 15*(4), 27–61.

Weld, D. (1994b). Robots that work in collaboration with people. *AAAI Fall Symposium on the intersection of Robotics and Cognitive Sciences*.

Wu, F., Zilberstein, S., & Chen, X. (2010). Point-based policy generation for decentralized pomdps. In *Proceedings of the Ninth International Joint Conference on Autonomous Agents and Multi-Agent Systems*.

Xuan, P., Lesser, V., & Zilberstein, S. (2001). Communication decisions in multiagent cooperation: Model and experiments. In *Proceedings of the Fifth International Conference on Autonomous Agents*, (pp. 616–623). Montreal. ACM Press.

Zilberstein, S., Washington, R., Bernstein, D., & Mouaddib, A. I. (2002). Decision-theoretic control of planteray rovers. In Beetz, M. (Eds.), *Plan-based control of robotic agents, LNCS 2466* (pp. 270–289). doi:10.1007/3-540-37724-7_16

ADDITIONAL READING

An extention of MDP/POMDPs to multiagent settings is given in (Sigaud & Buffet, 2010) where an introduction to DEC-POMDPs/DEC-MDPs and appropriate algorithms is given. Stochastic games are also an important concept described in an interesting chapter in (Shoham & Leyton-Brown, 2009) and in (Sigaud & Buffet, 2010).

Shoham, Y., & Leyton-Brown, K. (2009). *Multiagent Systems: Algorithmic, Game Theoretic and Logical Foundations*. Cambridge, UK: Cambridge University Press.

Sigaud, O., & Buffet, O. (2010). *Markov Decision Processes in Artificial Intelligence*. New York, NY: Wiley.

ENDNOTES

[1] The Robocup rescue competition defines a score based on the number of rescued civilians, the rate of burned buildings, etc.

[2] Decentralized Partially Observable Markov Decision Processes (DEC-POMDPs) generalize DEC-MDPs to formalize problems where the state of the system is partially observable (Bernstein et al., 2002).

Compilation of References

Aamodt, A., & Plaza, E. (1994). Case-based reasoning: Foundational issues, methodological variations, and system approaches. *AI Communications, 7*(1), 39–59.

Abbeel, P., Coates, A., & Ng, A. Y. (2010). Autonomous helicopter aerobatics through apprenticeship learning. *The International Journal of Robotics Research, 29*(13), 1608–1639. doi:10.1177/0278364910371999

Abbeel, P., & Ng, A. (2004). Apprenticeship learning via inverse reinforcement learning, *International Conference on Machine Learning (ICML)*, Banff, Alberta, (pp. 1-8).

Abdallah, S., & Lesser, V. (2005). Modeling task allocation using a decision theoretic model. In *Proceedings of Fourth International Joint Conference on Autonomous Agents and Multiagent Systems*, (pp. 719–726). Utrecht, Netherlands. ACM Press.

Adams, W. K., Reid, S., LeMaster, R., McKagan, S. B., Perkins, K. K., & Wieman, C. E. (2007). A study of educational simulations - Interface design. *Journal of Interactive Learning Research, 19*.

Aho, A. V., Hopcroft, J. E., & Ullman, J. D. (1998). *The design and analysis of algorithms*. Addison-Wesley.

Ai, H., Tetreault, J. R., & Litman, D. J. (2007). Comparing user simulation models for dialog strategy learning. In *Proc Human Language Technologies: The Annual Conference of the North American Chapter of the Association for Computational Linguistics (NAACL-HLT)*, Rochester, New York, USA.

Altman, E. (1999). *Constrained Markov Decision Processes*. Boca Raton, FL: Chapman & Hall/CRC.

Amato, C., Bernstein, D. S., & Zilberstein, S. (2007). *Solving POMDPs using quadratically constrained linear programs*. International Joint Conferences on Artificial Intelligence (pp. 2418–2424). IJCAI.

Amato, C., Bernstein, D. S., & Zilberstein, S. (2010). Optimizing fixed-size stochastic controllers for POMDPs and decentralized POMDPs. *Autonomous Agents and Multi-Agent Systems, 21*(3), 293–320. doi:10.1007/s10458-009-9103-z

Amato, C., & Zilberstein, S. (2007). Optimizing memory-bounded controllers for decentralized POMDPs. In *Proceedings of the Twenty Third Conference on Uncertainty in Artificial Intelligence*.

American Heart Association. (n.d.). *Stroke statistics*. Retrieved November 10, 2010, from http://www.americanheart.org/presenter.jhtml? identifier=4725

Anderson, J. R. (1993). *Rules of the mind*. Hillsdale, NJ: Lawrence Erlbaum Associates.

Andre, D., & Russell, S. J. (2002). State abstraction for programmable reinforcement learning agents. In *Proc National Conference on Artificial Intelligence*, Edmonton, Alberta, Canada (pp. 119–125).

Antos, A., Munos, R., & Szepesvári, C. (2008). Fitted Q-iteration in continuous action-space MDPs. In *Advances in Neural Information Processing Systems 20 (NIPS-2007)* (pp. 9–16). Cambridge, MA: MIT Press.

Applegate, D. L., Bixby, R. E., Chvátal, V., & Cook, W. J. (2007). *The traveling salesman problem: A computational study*. Princeton, NJ: Princeton University Press.

Argall, B., Browning, B., & Veloso, M. (2007). Learning by demonstration with critique from a human teacher. In *2nd Conf. on Human-Robot Interaction* (pp. 57–64).

Arkin, R. C. (1998). *Behavior-based robotics*. MIT Press.

Arroyo, I., & Woolf, B. (2005). Inferring learning and attitudes from a Bayesian network of log file data. In *Proceeding of the Twelfth International Conference on Artificial Intelligence in Education (AIED'05)*, (pp. 33-40).

Arroyo-Figueroa, G., & Sucar, L. (1999, July). A temporal Bayesian network for diagnosis and prediction. In K. Laskey & H. Prade (Eds.), *Proc. of the Fifteenth Conference on Uncertainty in Artificial Intelligence* (pp. 13–20). Stockholm, Sweden: Morgan Kaufmann Publishers, San Francisco, CA.

Artzner, P., Delbaen, F., Eber, J.-M., Heath, D., & Ku, H. (2007). Coherent multiperiod risk adjusted values and Bellman's principle. *Annals of Operations Research, 152*(1), 5–22. doi:10.1007/s10479-006-0132-6

Asada, H., Shaltis, P., Reisner, A., Rhee, S., & Hutchinson, R. (2003). *Wearable CV sensors*. IEEE Engineering in Medicine and Biology Magazine - Special Issue on Wearable Sensors/Systems and Their Impact on Biomedical Engineering.

Åström, K. J. (1965). Optimal control of Markov decision processes with incomplete state estimation. *Journal of Mathematical Analysis and Applications, 10*, 174–205. doi:10.1016/0022-247X(65)90154-X

Attias, H. (2003). Planning by probabilistic inference. In *Proceedings of the International Conference on Artificial Intelligence and Statistics.*

Audium. (2010). *Studio application design tool*. Retrieved from http://www.audiumcorp.com/Products/

Bagnell, D., Kakade, S., Ng, A. Y., & Schneider, J. (2004). Policy search by dynamic programming. In *Advances in Neural Information Processing Systems 16 (NIPS-2003)* (pp. 831–838). Cambridge, MA: MIT Press.

Bahar, R. I., Frohm, E. A., Gaona, C. M., Hachtel, G. D., Macii, E., & Pardo, A. (1993). Algebraic decision diagrams and their applications. In *International Conference on Computer-Aided Design* (pp. 188–191).

Baird, L. (1995). Residual algorithms: Reinforcement learning with function approximation. In *Proceedings of the Twelfth International Conference on Machine Learning* (pp. 30–37). Morgan Kaufmann.

Balasubramanian, J., & Grossmann, I. E. (2003). Approximation to multistage stochastic optimization in multiperiod batch plant scheduling under demand uncertainty. *Industrial & Engineering Chemistry Research, 43*, 3695–3713. doi:10.1021/ie030308+

Baxter, J., & Bartlett, P. (2001). Infinite-horizon policy-gradient estimation. *Journal of Artificial Intelligence Research, 15*(4).

Becker, R., Zilberstein, S., Lesser, V., & Goldman, C. (2003). Transition-independent decentralized markov decision processes. In *Proceedings of the Second International Joint Conference on Autonomous Agents and Multi Agent Systems*, (pp. 41–48). Melbourne, Australia.

Bellman, R. (1957). A Markov decision process. *Indiana University Mathematics Journal, 6*(4), 679–684. doi:10.1512/iumj.1957.6.06038

Bellman, R. (1957). *Dynamic programming*. Princeton, NJ: Princeton University Press.

Bellman, R. (1962). Dynamic programming treatment of the travelling salesman problem. *Journal of the ACM, 9*, 61–63. doi:10.1145/321105.321111

Bellman, R. (1957). *Dynamic programming*. Princeton, NJ: Princeton U. Press.

Bengio, Y., & Frasconi, P. (1996). Input/output HMMs for sequence processing. *IEEE Transactions on Neural Networks, 7*(5), 1231–1249. doi:10.1109/72.536317

Ben-Tal, A., El Ghaoui, L., & Nemirovski, A. (2009). *Robust optimization*. Princeton, NJ: Princeton University Press.

Bernstein, D. S., Amato, C., Hanse, E. A., & Zilberstein, S. (2009). Policy iteration for decentralized control of Markov decision processes. [JAIR]. *Journal of Artificial Intelligence Research, 34*, 89–132.

Bernstein, D., Zilberstein, S., & Immerman, N. (2002). The complexity of decentralized control of MDPs. *Mathematics of Operations Research, 27*(4), 819–840. doi:10.1287/moor.27.4.819.297

Bernstein, D., Hansen, E. A., & Zilberstein, S. (2005). Bounded policy iteration for decentralized POMDPs. In *Proceedings of the Nineteenth International Joint Conference on Artificial Intelligence*, Edinburgh, Scotland.

Bernstein, D., Zilberstein, S., Washington, R., & Bresina, J. (2001). Planetary rover control as a Markov decision process. In *The 6th International Symposium on Artificial Intelligence, Robotics and Automation in Space*, Montreal, Canada.

Bertsekas, D. P., & Tsitsiklis, J. (1996). *Neuro-dynamic programming*. Belmont, MA: Athena Scientific.

Bertsekas, D. P. (2005). *Dynamic programming and optimal control* (3rd ed.). Belmont, MA: Athena Scientific.

Beynier, A., & Mouaddib, A. (2009). Decentralized decision making process for document server networks. In *Proceeding of the International Conference on Game Theory and Networks*.

Beynier, A., & Mouaddib, A. I. (2005). A polynomial algorithm for decentralized Markov decision processes with temporal constraints. *Proceedings of the Fourth Interantional Joint Conference on Autonomous Agents and MultiAgent Systems*, (pp. 963–969).

Beynier, A., & Mouaddib, A. I. (2006). An iterative algorithm for solving constrained decentralized Markov decision processes. In *The Twenty-First National Conference on Artificial Intelligence (AAAI-06)*.

Bielza, C., del Pozo, J. F., & Lucas, P. (2003). Optimal decision explanation by extracting regularity patterns. In Coenen, F., Preece, A., & Macintosh, A. (Eds.), *Research and development in intelligent systems XX* (pp. 283–294). Springer-Verlag.

Billard, A., Calinon, S., Dillmann, R., & Schaal, S. (2008). *Robot programming program by demonstration*. MIT Press.

Billingsley, P. (1995). *Probability and measure* (3rd ed.). New York, NY: Wiley-Interscience.

Birge, J. R. (1992). The value of the stochastic solution in stochastic linear programs with fixed recourse. *Mathematical Programming*, *24*, 314–325. doi:10.1007/BF01585113

Birge, J. R., & Louveaux, F. (1997). *Introduction to stochastic programming*. New York, NY: Springer.

Bishop, C. (2006). *Pattern recognition and machine learning*. Springer-Verlag.

Black, A. W., Burger, S., Langner, B., Parent, G., & Eskenazi, M. (2010). Spoken dialog challenge 2010. In *Proc Workshop on Spoken Language Technologies (SLT), Spoken Dialog Challenge 2010 Special Session*, Berkeley, CA.

Blockeel, H., & Raedt, L. D. (1998, June). Top-down induction of logical decision trees. *Artificial Intelligence*, *101*, 285–297. doi:10.1016/S0004-3702(98)00034-4

Bloom, B. S. (1984). The 2 sigma problem: The search for methods of group instruction as effective as one-to-one tutoring. *Educational Researcher*, *13*, 4–16.

Blum, A., & Furst, M. (1997). Fast planning through planning graph analysis. *Artificial Intelligence*, *90*, 281–300. doi:10.1016/S0004-3702(96)00047-1

Blum, A., & Langford, J. (1999). Probabilistic planning in the graphplan framework. In *Proceedings of ECP'99*.

Blunsden, S., Richards, B., Bartindale, T., Jackson, D., Olivier, P., & Boger, J. N. (2009). Design and prototype of a device to engage cognitively disabled older adults in visual artwork. In *Proceedings of the ACM 2nd International Conference on Pervasive Technologies Related to Assistive Environments*. Corfu, Greece.

Blythe, J. (1999a). Decision-theoretic planning. *AI Magazine*.

Blythe, J. (1999b). *Planning under uncertainty in Dynamic domains*. PhD thesis, Carnegie Mellon University.

Boda, K., & Filar, J. A. (2006). Time consistent dynamic risk measures. *Mathematical Methods of Operations Research*, *63*, 169–186. doi:10.1007/s00186-005-0045-1

Boger, J., Hoey, J., Poupart, P., Boutilier, C., Fernie, G., & Mihailidis, A. (2006, April). A planning system based on Markov decision processes to guide people with dementia through activities of daily living. *IEEE Transactions on Information Technology in Biomedicine*, *10*(2), 323–333. doi:10.1109/TITB.2006.864480

Boger, J., Poupart, P., Hoey, J., Boutilier, C., Fernie, G., & Mihailidis, A. (2005, Jul). A decision-theoretic approach to task assistance for persons with dementia. In *Proc. IEEE International Joint Conference on Artificial Intelligence* (pp. 1293-1299). Edinburgh.

Bohus, D., & Horvitz, E. (2009). Models for multiparty engagement in open-world dialog. In *Proc SIGDIAL Workshop on Discourse and Dialogue,* London, UK.

Bohus, D., & Rudnicky, A. I. (2002). *Integrating multiple knowledge sources for utterance-level confidence annotation in the CMU Communicator spoken dialog system* (Technical Report No. CMU-CS-02-190). Carnegie Mellon University.

Boidin, C., Rieser, V., van der Plas, L., Lemon, O., & Chevelu, J. (2009). Predicting how it sounds: Re-ranking dialogue prompts based on TTS quality for adaptive spoken dialogue systems. In *Proc Interspeech.* Brighton, UK: Special Session on Machine Learning for Adaptivity in Spoken Dialogue.

Bonwell, C., & Eison, J. (1991). *Active learning: Creating excitement in the classroom- AEHE-ERIC Higher Education Report No.1.* Washington, DC: Jossey-Bass.

Borrás, R. (2001). *Análisis de incertidumbre y riesgo para la toma de decisiones.* Orizaba, Mexico: Comunidad Morelos. (in Spanish)

Boussard, M., Bouzid, M., & Mouaddib, A. (2008). Vector valued Markov decision process for robot platooning. In *Proceedings of the European Conference on Artificial Intelligence (ECAI 2008).*

Boutilier, C., Patrascu, R., Poupart, P., & Schuurmans, D. (2006). Constraint-based optimization and utility elicitation using the minimax decision criterion. *Artificial Intelligence, 170*(8), 686–713. doi:10.1016/j.artint.2006.02.003

Boutilier, C., Dearden, R., & Goldszmidt, M. (2000). Stochastic dynamic programming with factored representations. *Artificial Intelligence, 121*(1-2), 49–107. doi:10.1016/S0004-3702(00)00033-3

Boutilier, C., Dean, T., & Hanks, S. (1999). Decision-theoretic planning: Structural assumptions and computational leverage. *Journal of AI Research, 11,* 1–94.

Boutilier, C., Dean, T., & Hanks, S. (1996). Planning under uncertainty: Structural assumptions and computational leverage. In Ghallab, M., & Milani, A. (Eds.), *New directions in AI planning* (pp. 157–171). Amsterdam, The Netherlands: IOS Press.

Boutilier, C. (2003, August 9—15). On the foundations of expected expected utility. *Eighteenth International Joint Conference on Artificial Intelligence* (pp. 285-290). Acapulco, Mexico.

Boutilier, C., & Poole, D. (1996). Computing optimal policies for partially observable decision processes using compact representations. In W. J. Clancey & D. Weld (Eds.), *Proceedings of the Thirteenth National Conference on Artificial Intelligence (AAAI-96)* (pp. 1168–1175). Portland, OR: AAAI Press.

Boutilier, C., Dearden, R., & Goldszmidt, M. (1995). Exploiting structure in policy construction. In *Proceedings of the 14th International Joint Conference on Artificial Intelligence (IJCAI–95)* (p. 1104-1111). Montreal, Canada.

Boyd, S., & Vandenberghe, L. (2004). *Convex optimization.* Cambridge, UK: Cambridge University Press.

Brafman, R. I., & Tennenholtz, M. (2002). R-max - A general polynomial time algorithm for near-optimal reinforcement learning. *Journal of Machine Learning Research, 3,* 213–231.

Bratko, I., Urbančič, T., & Sammut, C. (1998). Behavioural cloning: phenomena, results and problems. Automated systems based on human skill. In *Proc. of the International Federation of Automatic Control Symposium.* Berlin.

Braziunas, D., & Boutilier, C. (2004). Stochastic local search for POMDP controllers. *National Conference on Artificial Intelligence (AAAI)*, San Jose, California, (pp. 690-696).

Breiman, L., Friedman, J., Stone, C. J., & Olshen, R. A. (1984). *Classification and regression trees.* Boca Raton, FL: Chapman and Hall/CRC.

Bresina, J., Dearden, R., Meuleau, N., Ramakrishnan, S., Smith, D., & Washington, R. (2002). *Planning under continuous time and resource uncertainty: A challenge for AI.* In UAI.

Brézillion, P., Gentile, C., Saker, I., & Secron, M. (1997, February). SART: A system for supporting operators with contextual knowledge. In *Proceedings of the International and Interdisciplinary Conference on Modeling and Using Context (CONTEXT-97).* Rio de Janeiro, Brasil.

Brooks, R. (1986, April). A robust layered control system for a mobile robot. *IEEE Journal on Robotics and Automation, 2*(1), 14–23. doi:10.1109/JRA.1986.1087032

Bui, T. H., Poel, M., Nijholt, A., & Zwiers, J. (2009). A tractable hybrid DDN-POMDP approach to affective dialogue modeling for probabilistic frame-based dialogue systems. *Natural Language Engineering, 15*(2), 273–307. doi:10.1017/S1351324908005032

Bui, T. H., Hofs, D., & van Schooten, B. (n.d.). *POMDP toolkit for spoken dialog systems.* Retrieved from http://wwwhome.ewi.utwente.nl/~hofs/pomdp/index.html

Bui, T. H., Poel, M., Nijholt, A., & Zwiers, J. (2007). A tractable DDN-POMDP approach to affective dialogue modeling for general probabilistic frame-based dialogue systems. In *Proc Workshop on Knowledge and Reasoning in Practical Dialogue Systems, Intl Joint Conf on Artificial Intelligence (IJCAI),* Hyderabad, India (pp. 34–37).

Bull, S., & McKay, C. (2004). An open learner for children and teachers: Inspecting knowledge level of individuals level of individual and peers. *Proceedings of Intelligent Tutoring Systems 7th International Conference ITS2004,* Maceio, Alagoas, Brazil (pp. 646-655). Springer Verlag.

Bunt, A., & Conati, C. (2003). Probabilistic student modeling to improve exploratory behavior. *Journal of User Modeling and User-Adapted Interaction, 13*(3), 269–309. doi:10.1023/A:1024733008280

Bunt, A., Conati, C., & Muldner, K. (2004). Scaffolding self-explanation to improve learning in exploratory learning environments. In *Proceedings of the Seventh International Conference on Intelligent Tutoring Systems (ITS'04),* (Maceo, Brazil), (pp. 656-667).

Caimi, M., Lanza, C., & Ruiz-Ruiz, B. (1999). *An assistant for simulator-based training of plant operator* (Tech. Rep.). Maria Curie Fellowships Annual Report.

Canadian Stroke Network Website. (2010). *Stroke 101.* Retrieved November 10, 2010, from http://www.canadianstrokenetwork.ca/index.php/about/about-stroke/stroke-101/

Capella, C., Heitz, P. U., Hofler, H., Solcia, E., & Kloppel, G. (1995). Revised classification of neuroendocrine tumours of the lung, pancreas and gut. *Virchows Archiv, 425*(6), 547–560. doi:10.1007/BF00199342

Cardon, S., Mouaddib, A., Zilberstein, S., & Washington, R. (2001). Adaptive control of acyclic progressive processing task structures. In *Proceedings of the 17th International Joint Conference on Artificial Intelligence, IJCAI-2001,* (pp. 701–706).

Carpentier, P., Cohen, G., & Culioli, J. C. (1996). Stochastic optimization of unit commitment: A new decomposition framework. *IEEE Transactions on Power Systems, 11,* 1067–1073. doi:10.1109/59.496196

Cassandra, A. R., Kaelbling, L. P., & Littman, M. L. (1994). Acting optimally in partially observable stochastic domains. In *Proc Conf on Artificial Intelligence, (AAAI),* Seattle.

Chadès, I., Scherrer, B., & Charpillet, F. (2002). A heuristic approach for solving decentralized-POMDP: Assessment on the pursuit problem. In *Proceedings of the Sixteenth ACM Symposium on Applied Computing.*

Chajewska, U., Koller, D., & Ormoneit, D. (2001, June 28-July 1). Learning an agent's utility function by observing behavior. *Eighteenth International Conference on Machine Learning* (pp. 35–42). Williamstown, MA: Morgan Kaufmann.

Chandrasekaran, B., Tanner, M. C., & Josephson, J. R. (1989). Explaining control strategies in problem solving. *IEEE Expert: Intelligent Systems and Their Applications, 4*(1), 9–15, 19-24.

Chapman, D., & Kaelbling, L. (1991). Input generalization in delayed reinforcement learning: An algorithm and performance comparison. In *Proc. of the International Joint Conference on Artificial Intelligence* (p. 726-731). San Francisco, CA: Morgan Kaufmann.

Charness, N. (1977). Human chess skill. In Frey, P. (Ed.), *Chess skill in man and machine* (pp. 35–53). Springer-Verlag.

Chen, J., Bangalore, S., Rambow, O., & Walker, M. A. (2002). Towards automatic generation of natural language generation systems. In *Proc Intl Conf on Computational Linguistics (COLING),* Taipei.

Chi, M. T., & VanLehn, K. (1991). The content of physics self-explanations. *Journal of the Learning Sciences, 1,* 69–105. doi:10.1207/s15327809jls0101_4

Chi, M. T. (2000). Self-explaining: The dual process of generating inferences and repairing mental models. In Glaser, R. (Ed.), *Advances in instructional psychology* (pp. 161–238). Lawrence Erlbaum Associates.

Chiralaksanakul, A. (2003). *Monte Carlo methods for multi-stage stochastic programs*. Unpublished doctoral dissertation, University of Texas at Austin, Austin, TX.

Choi, J., & Kim, K.-E. (2011). Inverse reinforcement learning in partially observable domains. [JMLR]. *Journal of Machine Learning Research*, *12*, 691–730.

Chow, C., & Liu, C. (1968). Approximating discrete probability distributions with dependence trees. *IEEE Transactions on Information Theory*, *14*, 462–467. doi:10.1109/TIT.1968.1054142

Chung, K.-J., & Sobel, M. (1987). Discounted MDP's: Distribution functions and exponential utility maximization. *SIAM Journal on Control and Optimization*, *25*(1), 49–62. doi:10.1137/0325004

Clancey, W. J. (1983). The epistemology of a rule-based expert system – A framework for explanation. *Artificial Intelligence*, *20*, 215–251. doi:10.1016/0004-3702(83)90008-5

Clemen, R., & Reilly, T. (2001). *Making hard decisions*. Pacific Grove, CA: Duxbury.

Clement, B., & Barrett, A. (2003). *Continual coordination through shared activities*. In International Joint Conference on Autonomous Agents and MulAgent Systems, AAMAS.

Cocora, A., Kersting, K., Plagemanny, C., Burgardy, W., & Raedt, L. D. (2006). Octuber). Learning relational navigation policies. *Journal of Intelligent & Robotic Systems*, 2792–2797.

Cole, S., & Rowley, J. (1995). Revisiting decision trees. *Management Decision*, *33*(8), 46–50. doi:10.1108/00251749510093932

Collins, J., Greer, J., & Huang, S. (1996). Adaptive assessment using granularity hierarchies and Bayesian nets. *Proceedings of the Third International Conference ITS'96* (pp. 569-577). Springer-Verlag.

Conati, C., Gertner, A., & VanLehn, K. (2002). Using Bayesian networks to manage uncertainty in student modeling. *User Modeling and User-Adapted Interaction*, *12*(4), 371–417. doi:10.1023/A:1021258506583

Conati, C., & Merten, C. (2007). Eye-tracking for user modeling in exploratory learning environments: An empirical evaluation. *Knowledge-Based Systems*, *20*(6), 557–574. doi:10.1016/j.knosys.2007.04.010

Conati, C., Muldner, K., & Carenini, G. (2006). From example studying to problem solving via tailored computer-based meta-cognitive scaffolding: Hypotheses and design. *Technology, Instruction* [TICL]. *Cognition & Learning*, *4*, 139–190.

Conati, C., & VanLehn, K. (2000). Toward computer-based support of meta-cognitive skills: A computational framework to coach self-explanation. *International Journal of Artificial Intelligence in Education*, *11*, 389–415.

Conati, C., & Carenini, G. (2001). Generating tailored examples to support learning via self-explanation. In *Proceedings of IJCAI '01, the Seventeenth International Joint Conference on Artificial Intelligence*, (pp. 1301-1306).

Conati, C., and MacLaren, M. (2010). Empirically building and evaluating a probabilistic model of user affect. To appear in *User Modeling and User-Adapted Interaction*.

Consortium, E. (2002). *Elvira: An environment for creating and using probabilistic graphical models (Tech. Rep.)*. Spain: U. de Granada.

Cooper, G. (1990). The computational complexity of probabilistic inference using Bayesian networks. *Artificial Intelligence*, *42*, 393–405. doi:10.1016/0004-3702(90)90060-D

Cooper, G., & Herskovitz, E. (1992). A Bayesian method for the induction of probabilistic networks from data. *Machine Learning*, *9*(4), 309–348. doi:10.1007/BF00994110

Cooper, D., Muldner, K., Arroyo, I., Woolf, B. P., Burleson, W., & Dolan, R. (2010). Ranking feature sets for emotion models used in classroom based intelligent tutoring systems. To appear in *the International Conference on User Modeling and Adaptive Presentation (UMAP'10)*, 12 pages.

Cooper, G. (1988). A method for using belief networks as influence diagrams. In *Proceedings of the Twelfth Conference on Uncertainty in Artificial Intelligence*, (pp. 55 63).

Coquelin, P.-A., Deguest, R., & Munos, R. (2009). Particle filter-based policy gradient in POMDPs. In *Advances in Neural Information Processing Systems 21 (NIPS-2008)* (pp. 337–344). Cambridge, MA: MIT Press.

Crandall, P., & Goddrich, M. (2005). Validating human-robot interaction schemes in multitasking environments. *IEEE Transaction Systems, Man, and Cybernetics. Part A: Systems and Humans*, *35*(4), 438–449. doi:10.1109/TSMCA.2005.850587

Crites, R. H., & Barto, A. G. (1995). *Improving elevator performance using reinforcement learning* (pp. 1017–1023). Proc. of the Neural Information Processing Systems.

Croonenborghs, T., Driessens, K., & Bruynooghe, M. (2007, June). Learning relational options for inductive transfer in relational reinforcement learning. In *Proceedings of the 17th Conference on Inductive Logic Programming* (pp. 88–97). Springer.

Crowley, M. (2004). *Evaluating influence diagrams.* Retrieved from http://www.cs.ubc.ca/~crowley/papers/aiproj.pdf

Csáji, B., & Monostori, L. (2008). Value function based reinforcement learning in changing Markovian environments. *Journal of Machine Learning Research*, *9*, 1679–1709.

Cuaya, G., & Muñoz-Meléndez, A. (2007, September). *Control de un robot hexapodo basado en procesos de decision de markov.* Primer Encuentro de Estudiantes en Ciencias de la Computación (CIC-IPN).

Cuayáhuitl, H., Renals, S., Lemon, O., & Shimodaira, H. (2006). Reinforcement learning of dialogue strategies with hierarchical abstract machines. In *Proc Workshop on Spoken Language Technologies (SLT)*, Aruba (pp. 182–185).

Damiani, S., Verfaillie, G., & Charmeau, M. (2005). An earth watching satellite constellation: How to manage a team of watching agents with limited communications. In *Proceedings of the Fourth International Joint Conference on Autonomous Agents and MultiAgent Systems (AAMAS 2005)*, (pp. 455–462).

Dantzig, G. B. (1955). Linear programming under uncertainty. *Management Science*, *1*, 197–206. doi:10.1287/mnsc.1.3-4.197

Darwiche, A. (2009). *Modeling and reasoning with Bayesian networks.* Cambridge University Press. doi:10.1017/CBO9780511811357

Darwiche, A., & M., G. (1994). Action networks: A framework for reasoning about actions and change under understanding. In *Proceedings of the Tenth Conf. on Uncertainty in AI, UAI-94* (pp. 136–144). Seattle, WA.

Das, T., Gosavi, A., Mahadevan, S., & Marchalleck, N. (1999). Solving semi-Markov decision problems using average reward reinforcement learning. *Management Science*, *45*(4). doi:10.1287/mnsc.45.4.560

Dayan, P., & Hinton, G. (1997). Using expectation-maximization for reinforcement learning. *Neural Computation*, *9*(2). doi:10.1162/neco.1997.9.2.271

de Freitas, N., Dearden, R., Hutter, F., Morales-Menendez, R., Mutch, J., & Poole, D. (2004). Diagnosis by a waiter and a Mars explorer. *Proceedings of the IEEE, Special Issue on Sequential State Estimation*, *92*(3).

de Groot, A. (1965). *Thought and choice in chess.* The Hague, The Netherlands: Mouton.

Dean, T., & Kanazawa, K. (1989). A model for reasoning about persistence and causation. *Computational Intelligence*, *5*(3), 142–150. doi:10.1111/j.1467-8640.1989.tb00324.x

Dean, T., & Givan, R. (1997). Model minimization in Markov decision processes. In *Proc. of the 14th National Conf. on AI* (pp. 106–111). AAAI.

Dearden, R., Friedman, N., & Russell, S. (1998). Bayesian q-learning. In *Proc. of the AAAI Conference on Artificial Intelligence* (pp. 761–768). AAAI Press.

Decker, K., & Lesser, V. (1992). Generalizing the partial global planning algorithm. *Journal on Intelligent Cooperative Information Systems*, *1*(2), 319–346. doi:10.1142/S0218215792000222

Decker, K., & Lesser, V. (1993b). Quantitative modeling of complex environments. *International Journal of Intelligent Systems in Accounting Finance & Management*, *2*(4), 215–234.

Defourny, B., Ernst, D., & Wehenkel, L. (2008, December). *Risk-aware decision making and dynamic programming*. Paper presented at the NIPS-08 Workshop on Model Uncertainty and Risk in Reinforcement Learning, Whistler, BC.

Defourny, B., Ernst, D., & Wehenkel, L. (2009). Bounds for multistage stochastic programs using supervised learning strategies. In *Stochastic Algorithms: Foundations and Applications. Fifth International Symposium, SAGA 2009* (pp. 61-73). Berlin, Germany: Springer-Verlag.

Delage, E., & Ye, Y. (2010). Distributionally robust optimization under moment uncertainty with application to data-driven problems. *Operations Research, 58*(3), 596–612. doi:10.1287/opre.1090.0741

Delgado, K. V., Sanner, S., & Nunes de Barros, L. (2011). Efficient solutions to factored MDPs with imprecise transition probabilities. [AIJ]. *Artificial Intelligence, 175*(9-10), 1498–1527. doi:10.1016/j.artint.2011.01.001

Dempster, A., Laird, L., & Rubin, D. (1977). Maximum likelihood from incomplete data via the EM algorithm. *Journal of the Royal Statistical Society. Series B. Methodological, 39*(1), 1–38.

Dempster, M. A. H., Pflug, G., & Mitra, G. (Eds.). (2008). *Quantitative fund management*. Boca Raton, FL: Chapman & Hall/CRC.

Demuth, H., & Beale, M. (1993). *Neural network toolbox for use with Matlab*.

Dentcheva, D., & Römisch, W. (2004). Duality gaps in nonconvex stochastic optimization. *Mathematical Programming, 101*(3), 515–535. doi:10.1007/s10107-003-0496-1

Dietterich, T. G. (2000). Hierarchical reinforcement learning with the maxq value function decomposition. *Journal of Artificial Intelligence Research, 13*, 227–303.

Dietterich, T. G., & Wang, X. (2002). Batch value function approximation via support vectors. In *Advances in Neural Information Processing Systems* (pp. 1491–1498). Cambridge, MA: MIT Press.

Dietterich, T. G. (1998). *The MAXQ method for hierarchical reinforcement learning* (pp. 118–126). Proc. Internation Confence on Machine Learning.

Dietterich, T. G. (2000). Ensemble methods in machine learning. In *Proceedings of the First International Workshop on Multiple Classifier Systems* (pp. 1-15). Berlin, Germany: Springer-Verlag.

Doshi, F., & Roy, N. (2008b). Spoken language interaction with model uncertainty: An adaptive human–robot interaction system. *Connection Science, 20*(4), 299–318. doi:10.1080/09540090802413145

Doshi, F., & Roy, N. (2008a). The permutable POMDP: Fast solutions to POMDPs for preference elicitation. In *Proc International Joint Conference on Autonomous Agents and Multiagent Systems,* Estoril, Portugal (pp. 493–-500).

Doyle, D., Cunningham, P., Bridge, D., & Rahman, Y. (2004). *Advances in case-based reasoning* (pp. 157–168). Berlin, Germany: Springer. doi:10.1007/978-3-540-28631-8_13

Driessens, K., & Dzeroski, S. (2002). Integrating experimentation and guidance in relational reinforcement learning. In *Proc. of the Nineteenth International Conference on Machine Learning* (p. 115-122). Morgan Kaufmann.

Driessens, K., & Ramon, J. (2003). Relational instance based regression for relational reinforcement learning. In *Proc. of the International Conference on Machine Learning (icml '03)*.

Driessens, K., Ramon, J., & Blockeel, H. (2001). Speeding up relational reinforcement learning through the use of an incremental first order decision tree learner. In *Proc. of the 13th. European Conference on Machine Learning (ecml-01)* (p. 97-108). Springer.

Drummond, M. F., Sculpher, M. J., Torrance, G. W., O'Brien, B. J., & Stoddart, G. L. (2005). *Methods for the economic evaluation of health care programmes* (3rd ed.). Oxford, UK: Oxford University Press.

Druzdzel, M. (1991). Explanation in probabilistic systems: Is it feasible? Will it work? In *Proc of the Workshop Intelligent Information Systems* (pp. 12-24). Poland.

Dudek, G., & Jenkin, M. (2000). *Computational principles of mobile robotics*. Cambridge University Press.

Duff, M. O. (2002). *Optimal learning: Computational procedures for bayes-adaptive markov decision processes.* Unpublished doctoral dissertation, University of Massachusetts Amherst.

Dupacova, J. (1987). The minimax approach to stochastic programming and an illustrative application. *Stochastics, 20,* 73–88. doi:10.1080/17442508708833436

Dzeroski, S., Raedt, L. D., & Driessens, K. (2001). Relational reinforcement learning. *Machine Learning, 43*(2), 5–52. doi:10.1023/A:1007694015589

Eglese, R. W. (1990). Simulated annealing: A tool for operational research. *European Journal of Operational Research, 46,* 271–281. doi:10.1016/0377-2217(90)90001-R

Elinas, P. (2005, Jun). Monte-Carlo localization for mobile robots with stereo vision. In *Proc. Robotics: Science and Systems.* Cambridge, MA: Sigma-MCL.

Elinas, P., & Little, J. J. (2002, March). A robot control architecture for guiding a vision-based mobile robot. In *Proc. of AAAI Spring Symposium in Intelligent Distributed and Embedded Systems.* Stanford, CA.

Elinas, P., Hoey, J., & Little, J. J. (2003, March). Human oriented messenger robot. In *Proc. of AAAI Spring Symposium on Human Interaction with Autonomous Systems.* Stanford, CA.

Elinas, P., Sucar, E., Reyes, A., & Hoey, J. (2004, September). A decision theoretic approach for task coordination in social robots. In *Proc. 13th IEEE International Workshop on Robot and Human Interactive Communication.* (pp. 679–684). Japan.

Elizalde, F., Sucar, L. E., Luque, M., Diez, F. J., & Reyes, A. (2008). Policy explanation in factored Markov decision processes. *European Workshop on Probabilistic Graphical Models,* (pp. 97-104).

Elizalde, F., Sucar, E., Reyes, A., & deBuen, P. (2007). *An MDP approach for explanation generation.* Workshop on Explanation-Aware Computing with American Association of Artificial Intelligence.

Elizalde, F., Sucar, L. E., Noguez, J., & Reyes, A. (2008b). *Integrating probabilistic and knowledge-based systems for explanation generation.* European Conference on Artificial Intelligence 2008 Workshop on Explanation Aware Computing.

Elizalde, F., Sucar, E., & deBuen, P. (2005). A prototype of an intelligent assistant for operator's training. In *International Colloquium for the Power Industry.* México: CIGRE-D2.

Elizalde, F., Sucar, E., Noguez, J., & Reyes, A. (2008). Integrating probabilistic and knowledge-based systems for explanation generation. In *Proceedings of 3rd International Workshop on Explanation-Aware Computing ExaCt08* (vol. 391, p. 25-36). Patras, Greece: CEUR-WS.org.

Elizalde, F., Sucar, E., Reyes, A., & deBuen, P. (2007). An MDP approach for explanation generation. In *Proceedings of the 2nd Workshop on Explanation-Aware Computing, ExaCt07* (Vol. Technical Report WS-07-06, p. 28-33). Vancouver, Canada: AAAI Press.

Emery-Montemerlo, R., Gordon, G., Schneider, J., & Thrun, S. (2004). Approximate solutions for partially observable stochastic games with common payoffs. In *Proceedings of the Third Joint Conference on Autonomous Agents and Multi Agent Systems.*

Epstein, L., & Schneider, M. (2003). Recursive multiple-priors. *Journal of Economic Theory, 113,* 1–13. doi:10.1016/S0022-0531(03)00097-8

Ericsson, K., & Simon, H. (1980). Verbal reports as data. *Psychological Review, 87*(3), 215–250. doi:10.1037/0033-295X.87.3.215

Ernst, D., Geurts, P., & Wehenkel, L. (2005). Tree-based batch mode reinforcement learning. *Journal of Machine Learning Research, 6,* 503–556.

Ernst, D., Glavic, M., Capitanescu, F., & Wehenkel, L. (2009). Reinforcement learning versus model predictive control: A comparison on a power system problem. *IEEE Transactions on Systems, Man, and Cybernetics. Part B, Cybernetics, 39*(2), 517–529. doi:10.1109/TSMCB.2008.2007630

Esben, H. O., Maja, J. M., & Gaurav, S. S. (2002). Multirobot task allocation in the light of uncertainty. In *Proceedings of IEEE International Conference on Robotics and Automation,* (pp. 3002–3007).

Escudero, L. F. (2009). On a mixture of the fix-and-relax coordination and Lagrangian substitution schemes for multistage stochastic mixed integer programming. *Top (Madrid), 17,* 5–29. doi:10.1007/s11750-009-0090-7

Estlin, T., Tobias, A., Rabideau, G., Castana, R., Chien, S., & Mjolsness, E. (1999). *An integrated system for multi-rover scientific exploration*. In The Sixteenth National Conference on Artificial Intelligence.

Fard, M. M., & Pineau, J. (2011). Non-deterministic policies in Markovian decision processes. [JAIR]. *Journal of Artificial Intelligence Research, 40*, 1–24.

Fasoli, S., Krebs, H., & Hogan, N. (2004). Robotic technology and stroke rehabilitation: Translating research into practice. *Topics in Stroke Rehabilitation, 11*(4), 11–19. doi:10.1310/G8XB-VM23-1TK7-PWQU

Feng, Z., Dearden, R., Meuleau, N., & Washington, R. (2004). Dynamic programming for structured continuous Markov decision problems. *International Conference on Uncertainty in Artificial Intelligence (UAI)*, (pp. 154-161).

Ferguson, K., & Mahadevan, S. (2006). Proto-transfer learning in markov decision processes using spectral methods. In *Proc. of the ICML Workshop on Transfer Learning*.

Fern, A., Yoon, S., & Givan, R. (2003). Approximate policy iteration with a policy language bias. In *Proc. of the Neural and Information Processing Conference (NIPS'03)*.

Fernandez, F., & Veloso, M. (2006). Probabilistic policy reuse in a reinforcement learning agent. In *Proceedings of the Fifth International Joint Conference on Autonomous Agents and Multiagent Systems* (pp. 720–727). ACM Press.

Freedy, A., Sert, O., Freedy, E., Weltman, G., Mcdonough, J., Tambe, M., & Gupta, T. (2008). Multiagent adjustable autonomy framework (MAAF) for multirobot, multihuman teams. In *International Symposium on Collaborative Technologies (CTS) 2008*.

Friedman, J. H. (2001). Greedy function approximation: A gradient boosting machine. *Annals of Statistics, 29*(5), 1189–1232. doi:10.1214/aos/1013203451

Gajos, K., Weld, D., & Wobbrock, J. (2008). Decision-theoretic user interface generation. *Proceedings of the 23rd National Conference on Artificial Intelligence (AIED '08)*, (pp. 1532-1536).

Galán, S. F., Arroyo-Figueroa, G., Díez, F. J., & Sucar, L. E. (2007). Comparison of two types of event Bayesian networks: A case study. *Applied Artificial Intelligence, 21*(3), 185–209. doi:10.1080/08839510601170754

Gasic, M., Lefevre, F., Jurcicek, F., Keizer, S., Mairesse, F., & Thomson, B. (2009). Back-off action selection in summary space-based POMDP dialogue systems. In *Proc IEEE Workshop on Automatic Speech Recognition and Understanding (ASRU)*, Merano, Italy.

Gerkey, B. P., & Matarić, M. J. (2002). Sold! Auction methods for multi-robot coordination. *IEEE Transactions on Robotics and Automation, 18*(5), 758–768. doi:10.1109/TRA.2002.803462

Getoor, L., & Taskar, B. (2007). *Introduction to statistical relational learning: Adaptive computation and machine learning*. Boston, MA: MIT Press.

Getoor, L., Koller, D., Taskar, B., & Friedman, N. (2000). Learning probabilistic relational models with structural uncertainty. In *Proceedings of the ICML-2000 Workshop on Attribute-Value and Relational Learning: Crossing the Boundaries* (pp. 13–20).

Geurts, P., Ernst, D., & Wehenkel, L. (2006). Extremely randomized trees. *Machine Learning, 63*, 3–42. doi:10.1007/s10994-006-6226-1

Ghahramani, Z. (1998). Learning dynamic Bayesian networks. *Lecture Notes in Computer Science, 1387*, 168–197. doi:10.1007/BFb0053999

Ghavamzadeh, M., & Mahadevan, S. (2007). Hierarchical average reward reinforcement learning. *Journal of Machine Learning Research, 8*.

Ghavamzadeh, M., & Engel, Y. (2007). Bayesian policy gradient algorithms. In *Advances in Neural Information Processing Systems 19 (NIPS-2006)* (pp. 457–464). Cambridge, MA: MIT Press.

Gillies, D. (2000). *Philosophical theories of probability*. London, UK: Routledge.

Givan, R., Dean, T., & Greig, M. (2003). Equivalence notions and model minimization in Markov decision processes. *Artificial Intelligence, 147*(1-2), 163–223. doi:10.1016/S0004-3702(02)00376-4

Gmytrasiewicz, P., & Doshi, P. (2005). A framework for sequential planning in multiagent settings [JAIR]. *Journal of Artificial Intelligence Research, 24*, 49–79.

Goel, V., & Grossmann, I. E. (2006). A class of stochastic programs with decision dependent uncertainty. *Mathematical Programming, 108*, 355–394. doi:10.1007/s10107-006-0715-7

Goldman, C., & Zilberstein, S. (2004). Decentralized control of cooperative systems: Categorization and complexity analysis. *Journal of Artificial Intelligence Research, 22*, 143–174.

Goldman, C., & Zilberstein, S. (2003). Optimizing information exchange in cooperative multiagent systems. In *International Joint Conference on Autonomous Agents and Multi Agent Systems*, (pp. 137–144).

Goodman, N., Mansinghka, V., Roy, D., Bonawitz, K., & Tenenbaum, J. (2008). Church: A language for generative models. In *Proceedings of the Conference on Uncertainty in Artificial Intelligence.*

Gosavi, A. (2008). Reinforcement learning: A tutorial survey and recent advances. *INFORMS Journal on Computing*, 1–45.

Govea, B. V., & Morales, E. (2006). *Learning navigation teleo-operators with behavioural cloning.*

Grant, M., & Boyd, S. (2008). Graph implementations for nonsmooth convex programs. In Blondel, V., Boyd, S., & Kimura, H. (Eds.), *Recent advances in learning and control. Lecture Notes in Control and Information Sciences* (*Vol. 371*, pp. 95–110). London, UK: Springer-Verlag.

Grant, M., & Boyd, S. (2009, February). *CVX: Matlab software for disciplined convex programming (web page and software).* Retrieved from http://stanford.edu/~boyd/cvx

Green, A. S., Billinghurst, M., Chen, W., & Chase, J. (2008). Human-robot collaboration: A literature review and augmented reality approach in design. *International Journal of Advanced Robotic Systems, 5*(1), 1–16.

Gregor, S., & Benbasat, I. (1999). Explanations from intelligent systems: Theoretical foundations and implications for practice. *Management Information Systems Quarterly, 23*(4), 497–530. doi:10.2307/249487

Griol, D., Hurtado, L. F., Segarra, E., & Sanchis, E. (2008). A statistical approach to spoken dialog systems design and evaluation. *Speech Communication, 50*(8-9), 666–682. doi:10.1016/j.specom.2008.04.001

Grzes, M., & Kudenko, D. (2009). Theoretical and empirical analysis of reward shaping in reinforcement learning. In *Proc. of the International Conference on Machine Learning and Applications* (p. 337-344).

Guestrin, C., Koller, D., Parr, R., & Venkataraman, S. (2003). Efficient solution algorithms for factored MDPs. [JAIR]. *Journal of Artificial Intelligence Research, 19*, 399–468.

Gui, S., David, H., & Ronen, B. I. (2002). An MDP-based recommender system. In *Proceedings of UAI-02.*

Guo, X., & Hernandez-Lerma, O. (2009). Continuous time Markov decision processes. *Applications of Mathematics, 62*, 9–18.

Guralnik, V., & Haigh, K. Z. (2002, Jul). Learning models of human behaviour with sequential patterns. In *AAAI-02 Workshop on Automation as Caregiver* (pp. 24-30).

Haddix, A., Teutsch, S., Shaffer, P., & Dunet, D. (1996). *Prevention effectiveness: A guide to decision analysis and economic evaluation.* Oxford, UK: Oxford University Press.

Hake, R. R. (1998). Interactive-engagement versus traditional methods: A six-thousand-student survey of mechanic test data for introductory physics courses. *American Journal of Physics, 66*(1), 64–74. doi:10.1119/1.18809

Hamid, R., Huang, Y., & Essa, I. (2003, Jun). Argmode - Activity recognition using graphical models. In *Proc. CVPR Workshop on Detection and Recognition of Events in Video.* Madison, WI.

Hammond, P. J. (1976). Changing tastes and coherent dynamic choice. *The Review of Economic Studies, 43*, 159–173. doi:10.2307/2296609

Hanna, H., & Mouaddib, A. (2002). Task selection as decision making in multiagent system. In *International Joint Conference on Autonomous Agents and Multi Agent Systems*, (pp. 616–623).

Hansen, E. A. (1997). *An improved policy iteration algorithm for partially observable MDPs. Advances in Neural Information Processing systems* (pp. 1015–1021). Denver, Colorado: NIPS.

Hansen, E. A. (1998). Solving POMDPs by searching in the policy space. *International Conference on Uncertainty in Artificial Intelligence (UAI)*, Madison, Wisconsin, (pp. 211-219).

Hansen, E. A., & Zhou, R. (2003). Synthesis of hierarchical finite-state controllers for POMDPs. *International Conference on Automated Planning and Scheduling (ICAPS)*, (pp. 113-122).

Hansen, E. A., Bernstein, D., & Zilberstein, S. (2004). Dynamic programming for partially observable stochastic games. In *Proceedings of the Nineteenth National Conference on Artificial Intelligence*.

Hastie, T., Tibshirani, R., & Friedman, J. (2009). *The elements of statistical learning: Data mining, inference, and prediction* (2nd ed.). New York, NY: Springer.

Heart & Stroke Foundation Canada. (2010). *Stroke statistics.* Retrieved November 10, 2010, from http://www.heartandstroke.com/site/c.ikIQLcMWJtE/b.3483991/k.34A8/Statistics.htm#stroke

Heckerman, D. (2008). A tutorial on learning with Bayesian networks. *Innovations in Bayesian Networks*, 33–82.

Heffernan, N., Koedinger, K., & Razzaq, L. (2008). Expanding the model-tracing architecture: A 3rd generation intelligent tutor for algebra symbolization. *International Journal of Artificial Intelligence in Education, 18*(2), 153–178.

Heitsch, H., & Römisch, W. (2003). Scenario reduction algorithms in stochastic programming. *Computational Optimization and Applications, 24*, 187–206. doi:10.1023/A:1021805924152

Heitsch, H., & Römisch, W. (2009). Scenario tree modeling for multistage stochastic programs. *Mathematical Programming, 118*(2), 371–406. doi:10.1007/s10107-007-0197-2

Hempel, C. G., & Oppenheim, P. (1948). Studies in the logic of explanation. *Philosophy of Science, 15*, 135–175. doi:10.1086/286983

Henderson, J., & Lemon, O. (2008). Mixture model POMDPs for efficient handling of uncertainty in dialogue management. In *Proc Association for Computational Linguistics Human Language Technologies*. Columbus, Ohio: ACL-HLT.

Henderson, J., Lemon, O., & Georgila, K. (2005). Hybrid reinforcement/supervised learning for dialogue policies from communicator data. In *Proc Workshop on Knowledge and Reasoning in Practical Dialogue Systems, Intl Joint Conf on Artificial Intelligence (IJCAI)*, Edinburgh (pp. 68–75).

Hengst, B. (2002). Discovering hierarchy in reinforcement learning with hexq. In *Proceedings of the Nineteenth International Conference on Machine Learning* (pp. 243–250). Morgan Kaufmann.

Hengst, B. (2007). Safe state abstraction and reusable continuing subtasks in hierarchical reinforcement learning. In M. A. Orgun & J. Thornton (Eds.), *Artificial intelligence* (vol. 4830, pp. 58–67). Springer.

Herlocker, J. (1999). *Explanations in recommender systems.* Computer Human Interaction 1999 Workshop on Interacting with Recommender Systems.

Hernández, S. F., & Morales, E. F. (2006, Septemer). Global localization of mobile robots for indoor environments using natural landmarks. *Proc. of the IEEE 2006 ICRAM*, (pp. 29-30).

Herrera-Vega, J. (2009). *Mobile robot localization in topological maps using visual information.* Master's thesis (to be published).

Higashinaka, R., Nakano, M., & Aikawa, K. (2003). Corpus-based discourse understanding in spoken dialogue systems. In *Proc Association for Computational Linguistics*. Sapporo, Japan: ACL.

Hilli, P., & Pennanen, T. (2008). Numerical study of discretizations of multistage stochastic programs. *Kybernetika, 44*, 185–204.

Hinton, G. E., Osindero, S., & Teh, Y.-W. (2006). A fast learning algorithm for deep belief nets. *Neural Computation, 18*, 1527–1554. doi:10.1162/neco.2006.18.7.1527

Hinton, G. (1984). *Distributed representations* (Tech. Rep. No. CMU-CS-84-157). Pittsburgh, PA: Carnegie-Mellon University, Department of Computer Science.

Hochreiter, R., & Pflug, G. C. (2007). Financial scenario generation for stochastic multi-stage decision processes as facility location problems. *Annals of Operations Research, 152*, 257–272. doi:10.1007/s10479-006-0140-6

Hoey, J., & Poupart, P. (2005). *Solving POMDPs with continuous or large discrete observation spaces. International Joint Conferences on Artificial Intelligence* (pp. 1332–1338). IJCAI.

Hoey, J., Poupart, P., von Bertoldi, A., Craig, T., Boutilier, C., & Mihailidis, A. (2010, May). Automated handwashing assistance for persons with dementia using video and a partially observable markov decision process. *Computer Vision and Image Understanding, 114*(5), 503–519. doi:10.1016/j.cviu.2009.06.008

Hoey, J. (2006, September). Tracking using flocks of features, with application to assisted handwashing. In M. J. Chantler, E. Trucco, & R. B. Fisher (Eds.), *Proc. of the British Machine Vision Conference* (vol. 1, pp. 367–376). Edinburgh.

Hoey, J., & Little, J. J. (2004). Value-directed learning of gestures and facial displays. In *Proc Intl. Conference on Computer Vision and Pattern Recognition.* Washington, DC.

Hoey, J., Poupart, P., Boutilier, C., & Mihailidis, A. (2005a). POMDP models for assistive technology. In *Proc. AAAI Fall Symposium on Caring Machines: AI in Eldercare.*

Hoey, J., Poupart, P., Boutilier, C., & Mihailidis, A. (2005b, July). Semi-supervised learning of a POMDP model of patient-caregiver interactions. In *Proc. IJCAI Workshop on Modeling Others from Observations* (pp. 101-110). Edinburgh.

Hoey, J., St-Aubin, R., Hu, J. A., & Boutilier, C. (1999). SPUDD: stochastic planning using decision diagrams. *International Conference on Uncertainty in Artificial Intelligence (UAI),* (pp. 279-288).

Hoey, J., St-Aubin, R., Hu, A., & Boutilier, C. (1999). SPUDD: Stochastic planning using decision diagrams. In *Proceedings of Uncertainty in Artificial Intelligence* (pp. 279-288). Stockholm. Kan, P., Hoey, J., & Mihailidis, A. (2008). Stroke rehabilitation using haptics and a POMDP controller. In *AAAI Fall Symposium on Caring Machines: AI in Eldercare.*

Hoey, J., von Bertoldi, A., Poupart, P., & Mihailidis, A. (2007). *Assisting persons with dementia during handwashing using a partially observable Markov decision process.* International Conference on Computer Vision Systems.

Hoffman, M., de Freitas, N., Doucet, A., & Peters, J. (2009). An expectation maximization algorithm for continuous Markov decision processes with arbitrary reward. In *Proceedings of the International Conference on Artificial Intelligence and Statistics.*

Hoffman, M., Doucet, A., de Freitas, N., & Jasra, A. (2007). Bayesian policy learning with trans-dimensional MCMC. In *Advances in Neural Information Processing Systems.*

Hoffman, M., Kück, H., de Freitas, N., & Doucet, A. (2009). New inference strategies for solving Markov decision processes using reversible jump MCMC. In *Proceedings of the Conference on Uncertainty in Artificial Intelligence.*

Hori, C., Ohtake, K., Misu, T., Kashioka, H., & Nakamura, S. (2009). Statistical dialog management applied to WFST-based dialog systems. In *Proc Intl Conf on Acoustics, Speech, and Signal Processing (ICASSP), Taipei, Taiwan* (pp. 4793–4796).

Horvitz, E., & Paek, T. (1999). A computational architecture for conversation. In *Proc 7th International Conference on User Modeling (UM),* Banff, Canada (pp. 201–210).

Howard, R. A. (1971). *Dynamic Probabilistic Systems (Vol. II).* New York, NY: John Wiley & Sons.

Howard, R. A., & Matheson, J. (1972). Risk-sensitive Markov decision processes. *Management Science, 18*(7), 356–369. doi:10.1287/mnsc.18.7.356

Howard, R. A., & Matheson, J. E. (1984). Influence diagrams. In *Readings on the principles and applications of decision analysis, II.* Menlo Park, CA: Strategic Decisions Group.

Howard, R. A. (1960). *Dynamic programming and Markov processes.* MIT Press.

Howard, R., & Matheson, J. (1984). Influence diagrams. In Howard, R., & Matheson, J. (Eds.), *Readings on the principles and applications of decision analysis.* Menlo Park, CA: Strategic Decisions Group.

Høyland, K., Kaut, M., & Wallace, S. W. (2003). A heuristic for moment matching scenario generation. *Computational Optimization and Applications, 24*, 169–185. doi:10.1023/A:1021853807313

Huang, K., & Ahmed, S. (2009). The value of multistage stochastic programming in capacity planning under uncertainty. *Operations Research, 57*, 893–904. doi:10.1287/opre.1080.0623

Infanger, G. (1992). Monte Carlo (importance) sampling within a Benders decomposition algorithm for stochastic linear programs. *Annals of Operations Research, 39*, 69–95. doi:10.1007/BF02060936

Jaynes, E. T. (2003). *Probability theory: The logic of science*. Cambridge, UK: Cambridge U Press. doi:10.1017/CBO9780511790423

Jensen, F. (2001). *Bayesian networks and decision graphs*. New York, NY: Springer-Verlag.

Jensen, F. V., & Nielsen, T. D. (2007). *Bayesian networks and decision diagrams. Information Science and Statistics* (p. 463). New York, NY: IEEE Computer Society.

Johnston, M., Bangalore, S., Vasireddy, G., Stent, A., Ehlen, P., & Walker, M. (2002). An architecture for multimodal dialogue systems. In *Proc Association for Computational Linguistics (ACL)*. Philadelphia, USA: MATCH.

Jong, N. K., & Stone, P. (2005, August). State abstraction discovery from irrelevant state variables. In *Proceedings of the Nineteenth International Joint Conference on Artificial Intelligence* (pp. 752–757).

Judah, K., Roy, S., Fern, A., & Dietterich, T. G. (2010). Reinforcement learning via practice and critique advice. In *Proceedings of the Twenty-Fourth AAAI Conference on Artificial Intelligence* (pp. 481–486). AAAI Press.

Kabassi, K., & Virvou, M. (2006). Multi-attribute utility theory and adaptive techniques for intelligent web-based educational software. *Instructional Science, 34*, 131–158. doi:10.1007/s11251-005-6074-6

Kaelbling, L. P., Littman, M., & Cassandra, A. R. (1998). Planning and acting in partially observable stochastic domains. *Artificial Intelligence, 101*, 99–134. doi:10.1016/S0004-3702(98)00023-X

Kaelbling, L. P., Littman, M. L., & Moore, A. W. (1996). Reinforcement learning: A survey. *Journal of Artificial Intelligence Research, 4*, 237–285.

Kallrath, J., Pardalos, P. M., Rebennack, S., & Scheidt, M. (Eds.). (2009). *Optimization in the energy industry*. Berlin, Germany: Springer-Verlag. doi:10.1007/978-3-540-88965-6

Kalman, R. (1960). A new approach to linear filtering and prediction problems. *Journal of Basic Engineering, 82*(1).

Kan, P., Hoey, J., & Mihailidis, A. (2010). The development of an adaptive upper-limb stroke rehabilitation robotic system. *Journal of Neuroengineering and Rehabilitation, 8*.

Kanerva, P. (1993). Sparse distributed memory and related models. In Hassoun, M. (Ed.), *Associate neural memories: Theory and implementation* (pp. 50–76). New York, NY: Oxford University Press.

Kaplan, R. M., & Anderson, J. P. (1988). A general health policy model: Update and applications. *Health Services Management Research, 23*(2), 203–235.

Kautz, H., Arnstein, L., Borriello, G., Etzioni, O., & Fox, D. (2002). An overview of the assisted cognition project. In *Proc. AAAI-2002 Workshop on Automation as Caregiver: The Role of Intelligent Technology in Elder Care* (pp. 60–65).

Kearns, M., Mansour, Y., & Ng, A. Y. (1999). *A sparse sampling algorithm for near-optimal planning in large Markov decision processes. International Joint Conferences on Artificial Intelligence* (pp. 1324–1331). Stockholm, Sweden: IJCAI.

Kearns, M. (1998). Near-optimal reinforcement learning in polynomial time. In *Machine learning* (pp. 260–268). Morgan Kaufmann.

Keeney, R., & Raiffa, H. (1976). *Decisions with multiple objectives: Preferences and value tradeoffs*. New York, NY: Wiley.

Kersting, K., & Driessens, K. (2008, July). Non-parametric policy gradients: A unified treatment of propositional and relational domains. In *Proceedings of the 25th International Conference on Machine Learning* (vol. 307, pp. 456–463). ACM.

Kersting, K., & Raedt, L. D. (2003). Logical Markov decision programs. In *Proc. of the IJCAI-03 Workshop on Learning Statistical Models of Relational Data*.

Kersting, K., Raedt, L. D., & Kramer, S. (2000). Interpreting Bayesian logic programs. In *Proceedings of the Work-In-Progress Track at the 10th International Conference on Inductive Logic Programming* (pp. 138–155).

Khan, O. Z., Poupart, P., & Black, J. (2008). Explaining recommendations generated by MDPs. In T. RB. et al. (Ed.), *Proceedings of the 3rd International Workshop on Explanation-Aware Computing ExaCt 2008*. Patras, Greece.

Khan, O. Z., Poupart, P., & Black, J. (2009). Minimal sufficient explanations for Factored Markov Decision Processes. In *Proceedings of the International Conference on Automated Planning and Scheduling (ICAPS)*. Thessaloniki, Greece.

Kim, D., Lee, J., Kim, K.-E., & Poupart, P. (2011). *Point-Based Value Iteration for Constrained POMDPs. International Joint conferences on Artificial Intelligence* (pp. 1968–1974). IJCAI.

Kim, D., Sim, H. S., Kim, K.-E., Kim, J. H., Kim, H., & Sung, J. W. (2008). Effects of user modeling on POMDP-based dialogue systems. In *Proc Interspeech*, Brisbane, Australia.

Kim, K., & Lee, G. G. (2007). Multimodal dialog system using hidden information state dialog manager. In *Proceedings of the Ninth International Conference on Multimodal Interfaces (ICMI 2007) Demonstration Session*, Nagoya.

Kirkpatrick, S., Gelatt, C. D. Jr, & Vecchi, M. P. (1983). Optimization by simulated annealing. *Science, 220*, 671–680. doi:10.1126/science.220.4598.671

Kleiner, A., & Sun, D. (2007). Decentralized slam for pedestrians without direct communication. In. *Proceedings of IROS, 2007*, 1461–1466.

Knox, W. B., & Stone, P. (2010). Combining manual feedback with subsequent MDP reward signals for reinforcement learning. In *Proc. of 9th int. Conf. on Autonomous Agents and Multiagent Systems* (pp. 5–12).

Kober, J., & Peters, J. (2008). Policy search for motor primitives in robotics. In *Advances in Neural Information Processing Systems*.

Koivu, M., & Pennanen, T. (2010). Galerkin methods in dynamic stochastic programming. *Optimization, 59*, 339–354. doi:10.1080/02331931003696368

Koller, D., & Friedman, N. (2009). *Probabilistic graphical models: Principles and techniques*. MIT Press.

Koller, D., & Parr, R. (2000). Policy iteration for factored MDPs. In *Proceedings of the Sixteenth Conference on Uncertainty in Artificial Intelligence*, Stanford, California (pp. 326–334).

Kortenkam, D., Bonasso, P., & Murphy, R. (1998). *Artificial intelligence for mobile robots*. MIT Press.

Kouwenberg, R. (2001). Scenario generation and stochastic programming models for asset liability management. *European Journal of Operational Research, 134*, 279–292. doi:10.1016/S0377-2217(00)00261-7

Kowalke, M. (2008, October 28). *DMG: Recession won't hamper IVR market growth*. Retrieved from http://www.tmcnet.com/channels/ivr/articles/44089-dmg-recession-wont-hamper-ivr-market-growth.htm

Küchler, C., & Vigerske, S. (2010). Numerical evaluation of approximation methods in stochastic programming. *Optimization, 59*, 401–415. doi:10.1080/02331931003700756

Kuhn, D. (2005). *Generalized bounds for convex multistage stochastic programs. Lecture Notes in Economics and Mathematical Systems* (*Vol. 548*). Berlin, Germany: Springer-Verlag.

Kurniawati, H., Hsu, D., & Lee, W. (2008). SARSOP: Efficient point-based POMDP planning by approximating optimally reachable belief spaces. *International Conference on Robotics: Science and Systems (RSS)*.

Kveton, B., Hauskrecht, M., & Guestrin, C. (2006). Solving factored MDPs with hybrid state and action variables. [JAIR]. *Journal of Artificial Intelligence Research, 27*, 153–201.

Kydland, F. E., & Prescott, E. C. (1977). Rules rather than discretion: The inconsistency of optimal plans. *The Journal of Political Economy, 85*, 473–492. doi:10.1086/260580

Lacave, C., & Díez, F. J. (2002). A review of explanation methods for Bayesian networks. *The Knowledge Engineering Review, 17*, 107–127. doi:10.1017/S026988890200019X

Lacave, C., Luque, M., & Díez, F. (2007). Explanation of Bayesian networks and influence diagrams in Elvira. *IEEE Transactions on Systems, Man, and Cybernetics, 37*(4), 952–965. doi:10.1109/TSMCB.2007.896018

Lacave, C., Atienza, R., & Díez, F. (2000). Graphical explanations in Bayesian networks. []. Springer-Verlag.]. *Lecture Notes in Computer Science, 1933*, 122–129. doi:10.1007/3-540-39949-6_16

Lacave, C., Luque, M., & Diez, F. J. (2007). Explanation of Bayesian networks and influence diagrams in Elvira. *IEEE Transactions on Systems, Man, and Cybernetics. Part B, Cybernetics, 37*, 952–965. doi:10.1109/TSMCB.2007.896018

Lagoudakis, M. G., & Parr, R. (2003). Reinforcement learning as classification: Leveraging modern classifiers. In *Proceedings of the Twentieth International Conference on Machine Learning (ICML-2003)* (pp. 424-431). Menlo Park, CA: AAAI Press.

Lam, W., & Bacchus, F. (1994). Learning Bayesian belief netwoks: An aproach based on the MDL principle. *Computational Intelligence, 10*, 269–293. doi:10.1111/j.1467-8640.1994.tb00166.x

Lam, P., Hébert, D., Boger, J., Lacheray, H., Gardner, D., & Apkarian, J. (2008). A haptic-robotic platform for upper-limb reaching stroke therapy: Preliminary design and evaluation results. *Journal of Neuroengineering and Rehabilitation, 5*(15), 1–13.

Langford, J., & Zadrozny, B. (2005). Relating reinforcement learning performance to classification performance. In *Proceedings of the Twenty-Second International Conference on Machine Learning (ICML-2005)* (pp. 473-480). New York, NY: ACM.

Laroche, P., Boniface, Y., & Schott, R. (2001). A new decomposition technique for solving Markov decision processes. In *Proc. ACM Symposium on Applied Computing* (pp. 12-16). ACM.

Lassila, O., & McGuinness, D. L. (2001). The role of frame-based representation on the Semantic Web. *Electronic Transactions on Artificial Intelligence, 6*(5).

Lauritzen, S., & Nilsson, D. (2001). Representing and solving decision problems with limited information. *Management Science, 47*, 1235–1251. doi:10.1287/mnsc.47.9.1235.9779

lbling, L. P. K., Littman, M. L., & Cassandra, A. R. (1998). Planning and acting in partially observable stochastic domains. *Artificial Intelligence, 101*, 99–134.

Lean, J., Moizer, M., & Towler, C. A. (2006). Active learning in higher education. *Journal of Simulation and Games, 7*(3), 227–242.

Lee, T., & Mihailidis, A. (2005). An intelligent emergency response system. *Journal of Telemedicine and Telecare, 11*(4).

Lee, C., Jung, S., Kim, K., & Lee, G. G. (2009b). Hybrid approach to robust dialog management using agenda and dialog examples. *Computer Speech & Language, 24*(4).

Lee, C., Jung, S., Kim, S., & Lee, G. G. (2009a, May). Example-based dialog modeling for practical multidomain dialog system. *Speech Communication, 51*(5), 466–484. doi:10.1016/j.specom.2009.01.008

Lemon, O., Georgila, K., & Henderson, J. (2006). Evaluating effectiveness and portability of reinforcement learned dialogue strategies with real users: The TALK TownInfo evaluation. In *Proc Workshop on Spoken Language Technologies (SLT),* Aruba (pp. 178–181).

Lester, J. C., & Porter, B. W. (1997). Developing and empirically evaluating robust explanation generators: The knight experiments. *Computational Linguistics, 23*(1), 65–101.

Lester, J., Choudhury, T., Kern, N., Borriello, G., & Hannaford, B. (2005, July). A hybrid discriminative/generative approach for modeling human activities. In *Proc. IJCAI* (pp. 766-772). Edinburgh, Scotland.

Levin, E., Pieraccini, R., & Eckert, W. (2000). A stochastic model of human-machine interaction for learning dialogue strategies. *IEEE Transactions on Speech and Audio Processing, 8*(1), 11–23. doi:10.1109/89.817450

Li, L., & Littman, M. L. (2005). Lazy approximation for solving continuous finite-horizon mdps. In *Proceedings National Conference on Artificial Intelligence* (p. 1175-1180). Pittsburgh, PA. AAAI.

Li, L., Walsh, T. J., & Littman, M. L. (2006, January). Towards a unified theory of state abstraction for mdps. In *Proc. Ninth International Symposium on Artificial Intelligence and Mathematics* (pp. 21-30).

Li, L., Williams, J. D., & Balakrishnan, S. (2009). Reinforcement learning for dialog management using least-squares policy iteration and fast feature selection. In *Proc Interspeech*, Brighton, UK.

Liao, L., Fox, D., & Kautz, H. (2004). Learning and inferring transportation routines. In *Proc Nineteenth National Conference on Artificial Intelligence (AAAI '04)* (pp. 348-353). San Jose, CA.

Lim, C., & Kim, H. (1991). Cmac-based adaptive critic self-lerning control. *IEEE Transactions on Neural Networks, 2*, 530–533. doi:10.1109/72.134290

Litman, D. J., Kearns, M. S., Singh, S. B., & Walker, M. A. (2000). Automatic optimization of dialogue management. In *Proc Association for Computational Linguistics*. Hong Kong: ACL.

Little, I., & Thiebaux, S. (2006). Concurrent probabilistic planning in the Graphplan framework. In *Proceedings International Conference on Planning and Scheduling*.

Littman, M. L. (1994). Markov games as a framework for multi-agent reinforcement learning. In *Proceedings of the Eleventh International Conference on Machine Learning* (pp. 157–163). Morgan Kaufmann.

Littman, M. L., Dean, T. L., & Kaelbling, L. P. (1995). On the complexity of solving Markov decision problems. In *Proceedings of the Eleventh Conference on Uncertainty in Artificial Intelligence (UAI-1995)* (pp. 394-402). San Francisco, CA: Morgan Kaufmann.

Littman, M., Cassandra, A., & Kaelbling, L. (1995). Learning policies for partially observable environments: Scaling up. In *Proceedings of the Twelfth International Conference on Machine Learning*, San Francisco, CA (pp. 362–370). Morgan Kaufmann.

Liu, X. M., Cao, Y. D., & Wang, E. Z. (2006). Numerical simulation of electric field with open boundary using intelligent optimum charge simulation method. *IEEE Transactions on Magnetics, 42*(4), 1159–1162. doi:10.1109/TMAG.2006.872479

Lloyd, J. (1987). *Foundations of logic programming* (2nd ed.). Berlin, Germany: Springer-Verlag.

LoPresti, E. F., Mihailidis, A., & Kirsch, N. (2004). Assistive technology for cognitive rehabilitation: State of the art. *Neuropsychological Rehabilitation, 14*(1/2), 5–39. doi:10.1080/09602010343000101

Lovejoy, W. S. (1991). A survey of algorithmic methods for partially observed Markov decision processes. *Annals of Operations Research, 28*, 47–66. doi:10.1007/BF02055574

Lusena, C., Goldsmith, J., & Mundhenk, M. (2001). Nonapproximability results for partially observable Markov decision processes. [JAIR]. *Journal of Artificial Intelligence Research, 14*, 83–103.

Mabbott, A., & Bull, S. (2004). Alternative views on knowledge: Presentation of open learner models. *Proceedings of Intelligent Tutoring Systems, 7th International Conference ITS2004*, Maceio, Alagoas, Brazil (pp. 689-698). Springer Verlag.

MacKay, D. J. C. (2003). *Information theory, inference and learning algorithms*. Cambridge, UK: Cambridge University Press.

Mak, W.-K., Morton, D. P., & Wood, R. K. (1999). Monte Carlo bounding techniques for determining solution quality in stochastic programs. *Operations Research Letters, 24*(1-2), 47–56. doi:10.1016/S0167-6377(98)00054-6

Marjovi, A., Nunes, J., Marques, L., & de Almeida, A. (2009). Multi-robot fire searching in unknown environment. In *Intelligent Robots and Systems (IROS 2009)*, (pp. 1929–1934).

Marthi, B. (2007). Automatic shaping and decomposition of reward functions. In *Proceedings of the International Conference on Machine Learning*. ICML.

Marthi, B., Russell, S., Latham, D., & Guestrin, C. (2005). Concurrent hierarchical reinforcement learning. In *Proceedings International Joint Conference on Artificial Intelligence* (pp. 779–785).

Mayo, M., & Mitrovic, A. (2001). Optimizing ITS behaviour with Bayesian networks and decision theory. *International Journal of Artificial Intelligence in Education, 12*, 124–153.

McDermott, D. V. (1998). *The planning domain definition language manual.* Technical Report 98-003, Department of Computer Science, Yale University.

McGuinness, D., Glass, A., Wolverton, M., & da Silva, P. (2007). *Explaining task processing in cognitive assistants that learn.* National Conference on Artificial Intelligence Spring Symposium on Interaction Challenges for Intelligent Assistants.

McHaney, R., White, D., & Heilman, G. E. (2002). Simulation project success and failure: Survey findings. *Simulation & Gaming, 33*(1), 49–66. doi:10.1177/1046878102033001003

McLachlan, G., & Krishnan, T. (1997). *The EM algorithm and extensions.* New York, NY: Wiley.

Mendicino, M., Razzaq, L., & Heffernan, N. T. (2009). Improving learning from homework using intelligent tutoring systems. [JRTE]. *Journal of Research on Technology in Education, 41*(3), 331–346.

Mercier, L., & Van Hentenryck, P. (2007). Performance analysis of online anticipatory algorithms for large multistage stochastic integer programs. In *Proceedings of the Twentieth International Joint Conference on Artificial Intelligence (IJCAI-07)* (pp. 1979-1984). San Francisco, CA: Morgan Kaufmann.

Mesbahi, E., Norman, R., & Peng, M. W. C. (2007). An intelligent simulation model for design and costing of high temperature ballast water treatment systems. *Marine Technology, 44*(3), 194–202.

Meuleau, N., Benazera, E., Brafman, R.I., & Hansen, E.A. & Mausam. (2009). A Heuristic Search Approach to Planning with Continuous Resources in Stochastic Domains. [JAIR]. *Journal of Artificial Intelligence Research, 34*, 27–59.

Meuleau, N., Hauskrecht, M., Kim, K. E., Peshkin, L., Kaelbling, L. P., & Dean, T. (1998). Solving very large weakly coupled Markov decision processes. In *Proceedings National Conference on Artificial Intelligence* (pp. 165-172). AAAI.

Meuleau, N., Kim, K. E., Kaelbling, L. P., & Cassandra, A. R. (1999). Solving POMDPs by searching the space of finite policies. In *Proceedings of the 15th Conference on Uncertainty in Artificial Intelligence (UAI'99)* (pp. 417–426). Stockholm, Sweden: Morgan Kaufmann, San Francisco, CA.

Michaud, F., Lepage, P., Frenette, P., Letourneau, D., & Gaubert, N. (2006). Coordinated maneuvering of automated vehicles in platoons. *ITS, 7*(4), 437–447.

Michie, D., Bain, M., & Hayes-Michie, J. (1990). Cognitive models from subcognitive skills. In Grimble, M., McGhee, J., & Mowforth, P. (Eds.), *Knowledge-based systems in industrial control* (pp. 71–90). Peter Peregrinus. doi:10.1049/PBCE044E_ch5

Mihailidis, A., Barbenel, J. C., & Fernie, G. (2004, March-May). The efficacy of an intelligent cognitive orthosis to facilitate handwashing by persons with moderate to severe dementia. *Neuropsychological Rehabilitation, 14*(1-2), 135–171. doi:10.1080/09602010343000156

Mihailidis, A., Blunsden, S., Boger, J., Richards, B., Zutis, K., & Young, L. (2010). Towards the development of a technology for art therapy and dementia: Definition of needs and design constraints. *The Arts in Psychotherapy, 37*(4). doi:10.1016/j.aip.2010.05.004

Mihailidis, A., Boger, J., Candido, M., & Hoey, J. (2008). The coach prompting system to assist older adults with dementia through handwashing: An efficacy study. *BMC Geriatrics, 8*(28).

Mihailidis, A., Elinas, P., Boger, J., & Hoey, J. (2007). An intelligent powered wheelchair to enable mobility of cognitively impaired older adults: an anticollision system. *IEEE Transactions on Neural Systems and Rehabilitation Engineering, 15*(1), 136–143. doi:10.1109/TNSRE.2007.891385

Mihailidis, A., & Fernie, G. R. (2002). Context-aware assistive devices for older adults with dementia. *Gerontechnology (Valkenswaard), 2*, 173–189. doi:10.4017/gt.2002.02.02.002.00

Mihailidis, A., Tam, T., McLean, M., & Lee, T. (2005). *An intelligent health monitoring and emergency response system.* In ICOST.

Mihailidis, A., Boger, J. N., Candido, M., & Hoey, J. (2008). The COACH prompting system to assist older adults with dementia through handwashing: An efficacy study. *BMC Geriatrics, 28*(8).

Minsky, M. (1975). *A framework for representing knowledge* (Winston, P., Ed.). McGraw Hill.

Modlin, I. M., Kidd, M., Latich, I., Zikusoka, M. N., & Shapiro, M. D. (2005). Current status of gastrointestinal carcinoids. *Gastroenterology, 128*, 1717–1751. doi:10.1053/j.gastro.2005.03.038

Moertel, C. G., Kvols, L. K., O'Connell, M. J., & Rubin, J. (1991). Treatment of neuroendocrine carcinomas with combined etoposide and cisplatin. Evidence of major therapeutic activity in the anaplastic variants of these neoplasms. *Cancer, 68*(2), 227–232. doi:10.1002/1097-0142(19910715)68:2<227::AID-CNCR2820680202>3.0.CO;2-I

Montemerlo, M., Pineau, J., Roy, N., Thrun, S., & Verma, V. (2002, July 28-August 1). Experiences with a mobile robotic guide for the elderly. *Eighteenth National Conference on Artificial Intelligence* (pp. 587–592). Edmonton, AB, Canada.

Morales, E. (1997). On learning how to play. In van den Herik, H., & Uiterwijk, J. (Eds.), *Advances in computer chess 8* (pp. 235–250). The Netherlands: Universiteit Maastricht.

Morales, E. (2003). Scaling up reinforcement learning with a relational representation. In *Proc. of the Workshop on Adaptability in Multi-Agent Systems* (p. 15-26).

Morales, E., & Sammut, C. (2004). Learning to fly by combining reinforcement learning with behavioural cloning. In *Proc. of the Twenty-First International Conference on Machine Learning* (p. 598-605).

Moravec, H., & Elfes, A. (1985, Mar). High-resolution maps from wide-angle sonar. In *Proc. IEEE Int'l Conf. on Robotics and Automation.* St. Louis, Missouri.

Morimoto, T. (2000). *How to develop a RoboCupRescue agent.* RoboCupRescue Technical Committee.

Mouaddib, A., Boussard, M., & Bouzid, M. (2007). Towards multiobjective multiagent planning. In *Proceedings of the International Joint Conference on Autonomous Agents and Multiagent Systems (AAMAS 2007).*

Muausam, & Weld, D. (2008). Planning with durative actions in stochastic domains. *J. Artif. Intell. Res. (JAIR), 31*, 33–82.

Muldner, K., & Conati, C. (2010). Scaffolding metacognitive skills for effective analogical problem solving via tailored example selection. *Journal of Artificial Intelligence in Education, 20*(2).

Muldner, K. (2007a). *Tailored scaffolding for metacognitive skills during analogical problem solving.* Ph.D. Thesis, University of British Columbia, Canada.

Muldner, K., & Conati, C. (2007b). Evaluating a decision-theoretic approach to tailored example selection. In *Proceedings of the Twentieth International Joint Conference on Artificial Intelligence (IJCAI'07)*, (pp. 483-489).

Munos, R., & Szepesvári, C. (2008). Finite-time bound for fitted value iteration. *Journal of Machine Learning Research, 9*, 815–857.

Munos, R., & Moore, A. (1999, August). Variable resolution discretization for high-accuracy solutions of optimal control problems. In T. Dean (Ed.), *Proceedings of the 16th International Joint Conference on Artificial Intelligence (IJCAI-99)* (pp. 1348–1355). San Francisco, CA: Morgan Kaufmann Publishers.

Muñoz, K., Noguez, J., Mc Kevitt, P., Neri, L., Robledo-Rella, V., & Lunney, T. (2009). Adding features of educational games for teaching physics. *Proceedings of the 39th IEEE International Conference on Frontiers in Education (FIE2009)*. San Antonio, Texas.

Murphy, K. (2001). The Bayes Net Toolbox for Matlab. *Computing Science and Statistics, 33*, 1–20.

Murphy, K. (2002). *Dynamic Bayesian networks: Representation, inference and learning.* Unpublished doctoral dissertation, Computer Science Division, University of California, Berkeley.

Murray, R. C., VanLehn, K., & Mostow, J. (2004). Looking ahead to select tutorial actions: A decision-theoretic approach. *Journal of Artificial Intelligence in Education, 14*(3), 235–278.

Murray, D., & Little, J. (2000). Using real-time stereo vision for mobile robot navigation. *Autonomous Robots, 8*, 161–171. doi:10.1023/A:1008987612352

Murray, C., & VanLehn, K. (2006). A comparison of decision-theoretic, fixed-policy and random tutorial action selection. In *Proceedings of the Eight International Conference on Intelligent Tutoring Systems (ITS'06)*, (pp. 114-123).

Murray, R. C., & VanLehn, K. (2000). DT Tutor: A decision-theoretic, dynamic approach for optimal selection of tutorial actions. In G. Gauthier, C. Frasson & K. VanLehn (Eds.), *Intelligent Tutoring Systems, Fifth International Conference, ITS 2000*, (pp. 153-162). Montreal, Canada. New York, NY: Springer.

Mynatt, E., Essa, I., & Rogers, W. (2000). Increasing the opportunities for aging in place. In *ACM Conference on Universal Usability (CUU)*.

Nair, R., Pradeep, V., Milind, T., & Makoto, Y. (2005). Networked distributed POMDPs: A synthesis of distributed constraint optimization and POMDPs. In *Proceedings of the Twentieth National Conference on Artificial Intelligence (AAAI-05)*.

Nair, R., Tambe, M., Yokoo, M., Marsella, S., & Pynadath, D. V. (2003). Taming decentralized pomdps: Towards efficient policy computation for multiagent settings. In *Proceedings of the International Joint Conference on Artificial Intelligence*, (pp. 705–711).

Natarajan, S., Tadepalli, P., Altendorf, E., Dietterich, T. G., Fern, A., & Restificar, A. (2005). Learning first-order probabilistic models with combining rules. In *ICML '05: Proceedings of the 22nd International Conference on Machine Learning* (pp. 609–616). New York, NY: ACM.

Neapolitan, R. (2004). *Learning Bayesian networks*. New Jersey: Prentice Hall.

Neapolitan, R. E. (1990). *Probabilistic reasoning in expert systems*. New York, NY: John Wiley & Sons.

Nemirovski, A., Juditsky, A., Lan, G., & Shapiro, A. (2009). Stochastic approximation approach to stochastic programming. *SIAM Journal on Optimization, 19*, 1574–1609. doi:10.1137/070704277

Nesterov, Y. (2003). *Introductory lectures on convex optimization*. Dordrecht, The Netherlands: Kluwer Academic Publishers.

Nettleton, E., Thru, S., Durrant-Whyte, H., & Sukkarieh, S. (2003). Decentralized slam with low-bandwith communication for teams of vehicles. In *Proceedings of the International Conference on Field and Service Robotics*.

Neu, G., & Szepesvari, C. (2007) Apprenticeship learning using inverse reinforcement learning and gradient methods. *International Conference on Uncertainty in Artificial Intelligence (UAI)*, Vancouver, Canada, (pp. 295-302).

Neumann, J. V., & Morgenstern, O. (1944). *Theory of games and economic behavior*. Princeton University Press.

Neumann, G., Maass, W., & Peters, J. (2009). Learning complex motions by sequencing simpler motion templates. In *Proceedings of the International Conference on Machine Learning*.

Ng, A. Y., & Jordan, M. (1999). PEGASUS: A policy search method for large MDPs and POMDPs. In *Proceedings of the Sixteenth Conference on Uncertainty in Artificial Intelligence (UAI-2000)* (pp. 406-415). San Francisco, CA: Morgan Kaufmann.

Ng, A. Y., & Russell, S. J. (2000, June 29 to July 2). Algorithms for inverse reinforcement learning. *Seventeenth International Conference on Machine Learning* (pp. 663–670). Stanford, CA: Morgan Kaufmann Publishers Inc.

Ng, A. Y., & Russell, S. (2000). Algorithms for inverse reinforcement learning. In *Proc Intl Conf on Machine Learning (ICML)*, Stanford, California.

Ng, A. Y., Harada, D., & Russell, S. (1999). Policy invariance under reward transformations: Theory and application to reward shaping. In *Proceedings of the Sixteenth International Conference on Machine Learning* (pp. 278–287). Morgan Kaufmann.

Nguyen, N. T., Bui, H. H., Venkatesh, S., & West, G. (2003, Jun). Recognising and monitoring high-level behaviours in complex spatial environments. In *Proc. CVPR*. Madison, WI.

Nielsen, T. D., & Jensen, F. V. (2004). Learning a decision maker's utility function from (possibly) inconsistent behavior. *Artificial Intelligence, 160*(1), 53–78. doi:10.1016/j.artint.2004.08.003

Noguez, J., & Sucar, E. (2005). A semi-open learning environment for virtual laboratories. [Springer-Verlag.]. *Lectures Notes in Artificial Intelligence, 3789*, 1185–1194.

Norkin, V. I., Ermoliev, Y. M., & Ruszczyński, A. (1998). On optimal allocation of indivisibles under uncertainty. *Operations Research*, *46*, 381–395. doi:10.1287/opre.46.3.381

Novasim. (2009). *What is Simulation?* Retrieved November 2009, from http://www.novasim.com

Novick, L. (1995). Some determinants of successful analogical transfer in the solution of algebra word problems. *Thinking & Reasoning*, *1*(1), 1–30. doi:10.1080/13546789508256903

Novick, L. R. (1988). Analogical transfer, problem similarity and expertise. *Journal of Experimental Psychology. Learning, Memory, and Cognition*, *14*, 510–520. doi:10.1037/0278-7393.14.3.510

Nuance. (2010). *Openspeech dialog design tool.* Retrieved from http://www.nuance.com/dialog/

Nugent, C., & Cunningham, P. (2005). A case-based explanation system for black-box systems. *Artificial Intelligence Review*, *24*(2), 163–178. doi:10.1007/s10462-005-4609-5

Nuttin, M., Demeester, E., Vanhooydonck, D., & Brussel, H. V. (2001). Shared autonomy for wheel chair control: Attempts to assess the user's autonomy. In *Autonome Mobile Systeme 2001, 17 Fachgespräch* (pp. 127–133). London, UK: Springer-Verlag. doi:10.1007/978-3-642-56787-2_17

Oh, E., & Kim, K.-E. (2011). A geometric traversal algorithm for reward-uncertain MDPs. *International Conference on Uncertainty in Artificial Intelligence (UAI)*, Barcelona, Spain.

Oken, M. M., Creech, R. H., Tormey, D. C., Horton, J., Davis, T. E., & McFadden, E. T. (1982). Toxicity and response criteria of the eastern cooperative oncology group. *American Journal of Clinical Oncology*, *5*, 649–655. doi:10.1097/00000421-198212000-00014

Oliver, N., Horvitz, E., & Garg, A. (2002, Oct). Layered representations for human activity recognition. In *Proceedings of International Conference on Multimodal Interfaces.* Pittsburgh, PA.

Olmsted, S. M. (1983). *On representing and solving decision problems.* Unpublished doctoral dissertation, Engineering-Economic Systems Dept., Stanford University, CA, U.S.A.

Ormoneit, D., & Sen, S. (2002, November-December). Kernel-based reinforcement learning. *Machine Learning*, *49*(2-3), 161–178. doi:10.1023/A:1017928328829

Pack, T., & Horvitz, E. (2000). Conversation as action under uncertainty. In *Proceedings of the Sixteenth Conference on Uncertainty in Artificial Intelligence*, (pp. 455–464).

Paek, T., & Horvitz, E. (2000). *Grounding criterion: Toward a formal theory of grounding* (Technical Report No. MSR-TR-2000-40). Microsoft Research.

Paek, T., & Horvitz, E. (2000b). Conversation as action under uncertainty. In *Proc Conf on Uncertainty in Artificial Intelligence (UAI)*, Stanford, California (pp. 455–464).

Paek, T., & Horvitz, E. (2003). On the utility of decision-theoretic hidden subdialog. In *Proc ISCA Workshop on Error Handling in Spoken Dialogue Systems*, Chateau-D'oex-Vaud, Switzerland (pp. 95–100).

Pages, G., & Printems, J. (2003). Optimal quadratic quantization for numerics: The Gaussian case. *Monte Carlo Methods and Applications*, *9*, 135–166. doi:10.1515/156939603322663321

Paksima, T., Georgila, K., & Moore, J. (2009). Evaluating the effectiveness of information presentation in a full end-to-end dialogue system. In *Proc Sigdial Workshop on Discourse and Dialogue*, London, UK.

Papadimitriou, C. H., & Tsitsilis, J. N. (1987). The complexity of Markov decision processes. *Mathematics of Operations Research*, *12*(3), 441–450. doi:10.1287/moor.12.3.441

Parr, R., & Russell, S. J. (1997). *Reinforcement learning with hierarchies of machines. Advances in Neural Information Processing Systems.* NIPS.

Pearl, J. (1988). *Probabilistic reasoning in intelligent systems: networks of plausible inference.* San Francisco, CA: Morgan Kaufmann.

Pedersen, L., Bualat, M. G., Lees, D., Smith, D. E., & Washington, R. (2003, May). *Integrated demonstration of instrument placement, robust execution and contingent planning.* International Symposium on Artificial Intelligence, Robotics and Automation for Space. Tokyo, Japan.

Pek, P. K., & Poh, K. L. (2000). Using decision networks for adaptive tutoring. In *Proceedings of the International Conference on Computers in Education / International Conference on Computer-Assisted Instruction,* (pp. 1076-1084).

Pennanen, T. (2009). Epi-convergent discretizations of multistage stochastic programs via integration quadratures. *Mathematical Programming, 116,* 461–479. doi:10.1007/s10107-007-0113-9

Pentney, W., Philipose, M., & Bilmes, J. (2008, July). Structure learning on large scale common sense statistical models of human state. In *Proc. AAAI.* Chicago.

Pentney, W., Philipose, M., Bilmes, J. A., & Kautz, H. A. (2007). Learning large scale common sense models of everyday life. In *Proceedings of AAAI* (p. 465-470).

Peshkin, L., Kim, K., Meuleu, N., & Kaelbling, L. (2000). Learning to cooperate via policy search. In *Sixteenth Conference on Uncertainty in Artificial Intelligence,* (pp. 307–314).

Peters, C., Wachsmuth, S., & Hoey, J. (2009). Learning to recognise behaviours of persons with dementia using multiple cues in an hmm-based approach. In *Proceedings of the ACM 2nd International Conference on Pervasive Technologies Related to Assistive Environments.* Corfu, Greece.

Peters, J., & Schaal, S. (2007). Reinforcement learning for operational space control. In *Proceedings of the IEEE International Conference on Robotics and Automation.*

Peters, J., Vijayakumar, S., & Schaal, S. (2003a). Reinforcement learning for humanoid robotics. In *Proceedings of the Third IEEE-RAS International Conference on Humanoid Robots* (pp. 1–20).

Pflug, G. C., & Römisch, W. (2007). *Modeling, measuring and managing risk.* Hackensack, NJ: World Scientific Publishing Company. doi:10.1142/9789812708724

Philipose, M., Fishkin, K., Patterson, D., Fox, D., Kautz, H., & Hahnel, D. (2004, October-December). Inferring activities from interactions with objects. *Pervasive Computing, 3*(4), 10–17. doi:10.1109/MPRV.2004.7

Pietquin, O., & Dutoit, T. (2006). A probabilistic framework for dialog simulation and optimal strategy learning. *IEEE Transactions on Audio. Speech and Language Processing, 14*(2), 589–599. doi:10.1109/TSA.2005.855836

Pietquin, O. (2004). *A framework for unsupervised learning of dialogue strategies.* Unpublished doctoral dissertation, Faculty of Engineering, Mons (TCTS Lab), Belgium.

Pineau, J., Gordon, G., & Thrun, S. (2006). Anytime point-based approximations for large POMDPs. [JAIR]. *Journal of Artificial Intelligence Research, 27,* 335–380.

Pineau, J., Gordon, G. J., & Thrun, S. (2003) Policy-contingent abstraction for robust robot control. *International Conference on Uncertainty in Artificial Intelligence (UAI),* (pp. 477-484).

Pineau, J., Gordon, G., & Thrun, S. (2003, Aug). Point-based value iteration: An anytime algorithm for POMDPs. In *Proc. of International Joint Conference on Artificial Intelligence* (pp. 1025-1032). Acapulco, Mexico.

Pirolli, P. L., & Anderson, J. R. (1985). The role of learning from examples in the acquisition of recursive programming skills. *Canadian Journal of Psychology, 39,* 240–272. doi:10.1037/h0080061

Piunovskiy, A. B., & Mao, X. (2000). Constrained Markovian decision processes: the dynamic programming approach. *Operations Research Letters, 27*(3), 119–126. doi:10.1016/S0167-6377(00)00039-0

Poggio, T., & Girosi, F. (1990). Regularizationn algorithms for learning that are equivalent to multilayer networks. *Science, 247,* 978–982. doi:10.1126/science.247.4945.978

Poggio, T., & Girosi, F. (1989). A theory of networks for approximation and learning. Laboratory, Massachusetts Institute of Technology, 1140.

Pollack, M. E. (2005, Summer). Intelligent technology for an aging population: The use of AI to assist elders with cognitive impairment. *AI Magazine, 26*(2), 9–24.

Porta, J. M., Vlassis, N. A., Spaan, M. T. J., & Poupart, P. (2006). Point-Based Value Iteration for Continuous POMDPs. [JMLR]. *Journal of Machine Learning Research, 7,* 2329–2367.

Poupart, P., & Boutilier, C. (2003). *Bounded finite state controllers, Advances in Neural Information Processing Systems*. Vancouver, Canada: NIPS.

Poupart, P., & Boutilier, C. (2004). An approximate scalable algorithm for large scale POMDPs. In *Advances in Neural Information Processing Systems 17 (NIPS)* (pp. 1081–1088). Vancouver, BC: VDCBPI.

Poupart, P. (2005). *Exploiting structure to efficiently solve large scale partially observable markov decision processes*. Unpublished doctoral dissertation, University of Toronto.

Poupart, P., Kim, K. E., & Kim, D. (2011). Closing the Gap: Improved Bounds on Optimal POMDP Solutions, *International Conference on Automated Planning and Scheduling (ICAPS)*, Freiburg, Germany.

Poupart, P., Lang, T., & Toussaint, M. (2011). Analyzing and Escaping Local Optima in Planning as Inference for Partially Observable Domains. *European Conference on Machine Learning (ECML)*, Athens, Greece.

Powell, W. B. (2007). *Approximate dynamic programming: Solving the curses of dimensionality*. Hoboken, NJ: Wiley-Interscience. doi:10.1002/9780470182963

Powell, J., Wright, T., & Newland, P. (2008). Fire play: ICCARUS - Intelligent command and control, acquisition and review using simulation. *British Journal of Educational Technology*, *39*(2), 369–389. doi:10.1111/j.1467-8535.2008.00831.x

Powell, W. B., & Topaloglu, H. (2003). Stochastic programming in transportation and logistics. In Ruszczyński, A., & Shapiro, A. (Eds.), *Stochastic programming. Handbooks in operations research and management science* (*Vol. 10*, pp. 555–635). Amsterdam, The Netherlands: Elsevier.

Prékopa, A. (1995). *Stochastic programming*. Dordrecht, The Netherlands: Kluwer Academic Publishers.

Puterman, M. (2005). *Markov Decision Processes: Discrete Stochastic Dynamic Programming* (2nd ed.). New York, NY: John Wiley & Sons.

Pynadath, D., & Tambe, M. (2002). The communicative multiagent team decision problem: Analyzing teamwork theories and models. *Journal of Artificial Intelligence Research*, 389–423.

Quinlan, J. (1993). *C4.5: Programs for machine learning*. San Francisco, CA: Morgan Kaufmann.

Rabiner, L., & Juang, B. (1993). *Fundamentals of speech recognition. Signal Processing Series*. New Jersey, USA: Prentice Hall.

Rachev, S. T., & Römisch, W. (2002). Quantitative stability in stochastic programming: The method of probability metrics. *Mathematical Programming*, *27*(4), 792–818.

Raedt, L. D., Kimmig, A., & Toivonen, H. (2007, January). Problog: A probabilistic prolog and its application in link discovery. In *Proceedings of 20th International Joint Conference on Artificial Intelligence* (pp. 2468–2473). AAAI Press.

Raiffa, H., & Schlaifer, R. (1961). *Applied statistical decision theory*. Cambridge, MA: Harvard University Press.

Raiffa, H. (1968). *Decision analysis. Introductory lectures on choices under uncertainty*. Reading, MA: Addison-Wesley.

Ramachandran, D. (2007). Bayesian inverse reinforcement learning. In *Proceedings of the 20th International Joint Conference on Artificial Intelligence* (pp. 2586–2591).

Rasmussen, C. E., & Williams, C. K. I. (2006). *Gaussian processes for machine learning*. Cambridge, MA: MIT Press.

Rebane, G., & Pearl, J. (1987). The recovery of causal poly-trees from statistical data. In L. N. Kanal, T. S. Levitt, & J. F. Lemmer (Eds.), *Uncertainty in artificial intelligence* (pp. 175–182). Elsevier. Retrieved from http://www2.sis.pitt.edu/~dsl/UAI/UAI87/Rebane.UAI87.html

Reed, S. K., & Bolstad, C. A. (1991). Use of examples and procedures in problem solving. *Journal of Experimental Psychology. Learning, Memory, and Cognition*, *17*(4), 753–766. doi:10.1037/0278-7393.17.4.753

Reed, S. K., Dempster, A., & Ettinger, M. (1985). Usefulness of analogous solutions for solving algebra word problems. *Journal of Experimental Psychology. Learning, Memory, and Cognition*, *11*, 106–125. doi:10.1037/0278-7393.11.1.106

Reed, S. K., Willis, D., & Guarino, J. (1994). Selecting examples for solving word problems. *Journal of Educational Psychology*, 86(3), 380–388. doi:10.1037/0022-0663.86.3.380

Regan, K., & Boutilier, C. (2011a). *Eliciting additive reward functions for Markov decision processes. International Joint Conferences on Artificial Intelligence* (pp. 2159–2164). Barcelona, Spain: IJCAI.

Regan, K., & Boutilier, C. (2011b). *Robust Online Optimization of Reward-Uncertain MDPs. International Joint Conferences on Artificial Intelligence* (pp. 2165–2171). Barcelona, Spain: IJCAI.

Regan, K., & Boutilier, C. (2010). Robust policy computation in reward-uncertain MDPs using nondominated policies. *National Conference on Artificial Intelligence (AAAI)*.

Renooij, S., & van der Gaag, L. (1998). Decision making in qualitative influence diagrams. In *Proceedings of the Eleventh International FLAIRS Conference* (p. 410-414). Menlo Park, CA: AAAI Press.

Reyes, A., Sucar, L. E., & Ibarguengoytia, P. H. (2005, November). An operation auxiliary system for power plants based on decision-theoretic planning. In *Proceedings of the 13th IEEE International Conference on Intelligent Systems Applications to Power Systems ISAP05* (p. 286-290). Arlington, VA.

Reyes, A., Sucar, L. E., Morales, E., & Ibarguengoytia, P. H. (2006). Abstraction and refinement for solving Markov decision processes. In *Workshop on Probabilistic Graphical Models PGM06* (pp. 263-270). Czech Republic.

Reynolds, C. W. (1987). Flocks, herds, and schools: A distributed behavioral model. *Computer Graphics*, 21(4), 25–34. doi:10.1145/37402.37406

Richard, L., & Gourderes, G. (1999). An agent-operated simulation-base training system –Presentation of the CMOS project. In Lajoie, S. P., & Vivet, M. (Eds.), *Artificial intelligence in education* (pp. 343–351). IO Pres.

Richardson, M., & Domingos, P. (2006). Markov logic networks. *Machine Learning*, 62(1-2), 107–136. doi:10.1007/s10994-006-5833-1

Rieser, V. (2008). *Bootstrapping reinforcement learning-based dialogue strategies from Wizard-of-Oz data.* Unpublished doctoral dissertation, Saarland University.

Ringenberg, M., & VanLehn, K. (2006). Scaffolding problem solving with annotated, worked-out examples to promote deep learning. In *Proceedings of the Eight International Conference on Intelligent Tutoring Systems (ITS'06)*, (pp. 625-634).

RoboCup. (2000). *RoboCup-Rescue simulator manual.*

Rockafellar, R. T. (1970). *Convex analysis.* Princeton, NJ: Princeton University Press.

Rockafellar, R. T., & Uryasev, S. (2000). Optimization of conditional value-at-risk. *Journal of Risk*, 2(3), 21–41.

Rockafellar, R. T., & Wets, R. J.-B. (1991). Scenarios and policy aggregation in optimization under uncertainty. *Mathematics of Operations Research*, 16, 119–147. doi:10.1287/moor.16.1.119

Rohanimanesh, K., & Mahadevan, S. (2008). Decision-theoretic planning with concurrent temporally extended actions. In *Proceedings of the Seventeenth Conference on Uncertainty in Artificial Intelligence, UAI-08* (pp. 472–479).

Roll, I., Aleven, V., McLaren, B. M., & Koedinger, K. R. (2011). Improving students' help seeking skills using meta-cognitive feedback in an intelligent tutoring system. *Learning and Instruction*, 21.

Romero, L., Morales, E., & Sucar, L. E. (2001). An exploration and navigation approach for indoor mobile robots considering sensor's perceptual limitations. *Proc. of the IEEE ICRA*, (pp. 3092-3097).

Ross, S., Pineau, J., Paquet, S., & Chaib-Draa, B. (2008). Online planning algorithms for POMDPs. [JAIR]. *Journal of Artificial Intelligence Research*, 32, 663–704.

Roy, N., Gordon, G., & Thrun, S. (2003). Planning under uncertainty for reliable health care robotics. In *Proceedings of the International Conference on Field and Service Robotics.* Lake Yamanaka, Japan.

Roy, N., Pineau, J., & Thrun, S. (2000). Spoken dialogue management using probabilistic reasoning. In *Proceedings of the 38th Annual Meeting of the Association for Computational Linguistics (ACL-2000)*, Hong Kong.

Royalty, J., Holland, R., Dekhtyar, A., & Goldsmith, J. (2002). *POET, the online preference elicitation tool.* In National Conference on Artificial Intelligence Workshop on Preferences in Artificial Intelligence and Constraint Programming: Symbolic Approaches.

Rudary, M., Singh, S., & Pollack, M. E. (2004, Jul). Adaptive cognitive orthotics: Combining reinforcement learning and constraint-based temporal reasoning. In *Proc. 21ˢᵗ International Conference on Machine Learning (ICML 2004).*

Ryan, M. (1998). Rl-tops: An architecture for modularity and re-use in reinforcement learning. In *Proc. of the Fifteenth International Conference on Machine Learning* (p. 481-487). San Francisco, CA: Morgan Kaufmann.

Rybski, P. E., & Veloso, M. M. (2004, Jul). Using sparse visual data to model human activities in meetings. In *Proc. IJCAI Workshop on Modeling Other Agents from Observations (MOO 2004).* New York, NY.

Sammut, C., Hurst, S., Kedzier, D., & Michie, D. (1992). Learning to fly. In *Proc. of the Ninth International Conference on Machine Learning* (p. 385-393). Morgan Kaufmann.

Samuelson, P. A. (1937). A note on measurement of utility. *The Review of Economic Studies, 4*(2), 155–161. doi:10.2307/2967612

Sanner, S. (2009, July). *First-order models for sequential decision-making.* Retrieved from http://videolectures.net/ilpmlgsrl09_sanner_fomsdm/

Sanner, S., & McAllester, D. (2005). Affine algebraic decision diagrams (AADDs) and their application to structured probabilistic inference. *International Joint Conference on Artificial Intelligence (IJCAI).*

Sanner, S., Delgado, K. V., & de Barros, L. N. (2011). Symbolic dynamic programming for discrete and continuous state MDPs. *International Conference on Uncertainty in Artificial Intelligence (UAI),* Barcelona, Spain.

Satia, J. K., & Lave, R. E. Jr. (1970). Markovian decision processes with uncertain transition probabilities. *Operations Research, 21,* 728–740. doi:10.1287/opre.21.3.728

Schaal, S. (1997). Learning from demonstration. In *Advances in Neural Information Processing Systems, 9.* MIT Press.

Schatzmann, J., Weilhammer, K., Stuttle, M. N., & Young, S. (2007, June). A survey of statistical user simulation techniques for reinforcement learning of dialogue management strategies. *The Knowledge Engineering Review, 21*(2), 97–126. doi:10.1017/S0269888906000944

Schatzmann, J., Georgila, K., & Young, S. (2005). Quantitative evaluation of user simulation techniques for spoken dialogue systems. In *Proc Sigdial Workshop on Discourse and Dialogue,* Lisbon, Portugal (pp. 178–181).

Schatzmann, J., Stuttle, M. N., Weilhammer, K., & Young, S. (2005). Effects of the user model on simulation-based learning of dialogue strategies. In *Proc IEEE Workshop on Automatic Speech Recognition and Understanding (ASRU),* San Juan, Puerto Rico, USA.

Schatzmann, J., Thomson, B., Weilhammer, K., Ye, H., & Young, S. (2007). Agenda-based user simulation for bootstrapping a POMDP dialogue system. In *Proceedings of Human Language Technologies / North American Chapter of the Association for Computational Linguistics (HLT/NAACL).*

Schatzmann, J., Thomson, B., & Young, S. (2007a). Error simulation for training statistical dialogue systems. In *Proc IEEE Workshop on Automatic Speech Recognition and Understanding (ASRU),* Kyoto, Japan (pp. 526–531).

Schatzmann, J., Thomson, B., & Young, S. (2007b). Statistical user simulation with a hidden agenda. In *Proc Sigdial Workshop on Discourse and Dialogue,* Antwerp, Belgium (pp. 273–282).

Scheffler, K., & Young, S. (2002). Automatic learning of dialogue strategy using dialogue simulation and reinforcement learning. In *Proc Human Language Technologies* (pp. 12–18). San Diego, USA: HLT.

Schrijvers, T., & Demoen, B. (2004). *The K.U. Leuven CHR system: Implementation and application.* Belgium: Leuven University.

Schultz, R., Stougie, L., & Van der Vlerk, M. H. (1998). Solving stochastic programs with integer recourse by enumeration: A framework using Gröbner basis reduction. *Mathematical Programming, 83,* 229–252. doi:10.1007/BF02680560

Schuurmans, D., & Patrascu, R. (2001). *Direct value-approximation for factored MDPs. Advances in Neural Information Processing Systems* (pp. 1579–1586). Vancouver, BC: NIPS.

Self, J. (1999). The defining characteristics of intelligent tutoring systems research: ITSs care, precisely. *International Journal of Artificial Intelligence in Education*, *10*, 350–364.

Sen, S., Doverspike, R. D., & Cosares, S. (1994). Network planning with random demand. *Telecommunication Systems*, *3*, 11–30. doi:10.1007/BF02110042

Sen, S., & Sherali, H. (2006). Decomposition with branch-and-cut approaches for two-stage stochastic mixed-integer programming. *Mathematical Programming*, *106*, 203–223. doi:10.1007/s10107-005-0592-5

Sen, S., Yu, L., & Genc, T. (2006). A stochastic programming approach to power portfolio optimization. *Operations Research*, *54*, 55–72. doi:10.1287/opre.1050.0264

Seneff, S. (1992, March). TINA: A natural language system for spoken language applications. *Computational Linguistics*, *18*, 61–86.

Shachter, R. D. (1986). Evaluating influence diagrams. *Operations Research*, *34*(6), 871–882. doi:10.1287/opre.34.6.871

Shachter, R. (1988). Probabilistic inference and influence diagrams. *Operations Research*, *36*(4). doi:10.1287/opre.36.4.589

Shachter, R. D., & Peot, M. (1992). Decision making using probabilistic inference methods. In *Proc. of the Eight Conference on Uncertainty Artificial Intelligence* (pp. 276–283).

Shani, G., Brafman, R. I., & Shimony, S. E. (2007). *Forward search value iteration for POMDPs. International Joint Conferences on Artificial Intelligence* (pp. 2619–2624). IJCAI.

Shani, G., Poupart, P., Brafman, R. I., & Shimony, S. E. (2008). Efficient ADD Operations for Point-Based Algorithms. *International Conference on Automated Planning and Scheduling (ICAPS)*, pp. 330-337.

Shapiro, A. (2003a). Inference of statistical bounds for multistage stochastic programming problems. *Mathematical Methods of Operations Research*, *58*(1), 57–68. doi:10.1007/s001860300280

Shapiro, A. (2006). On complexity of multistage stochastic programs. *Operations Research Letters*, *34*(1), 1–8. doi:10.1016/j.orl.2005.02.003

Shapiro, A. (2009). On a time-consistency concept in risk averse multistage stochastic programming. *Operations Research Letters*, *37*, 143–147. doi:10.1016/j.orl.2009.02.005

Shapiro, A., Dentcheva, D., & Ruszczyński, A. (2009). *Lectures on stochastic programming: Modeling and theory*. Philadelphia, PA: SIAM. doi:10.1137/1.9780898718751

Shapiro, A. (2003b). Monte Carlo sampling methods. In Ruszczyński, A., & Shapiro, A. (Eds.), *Stochastic programming. Handbooks in operations research and management science* (*Vol. 10*, pp. 353–425). Amsterdam, The Netherlands: Elsevier.

Shim, J., Warkentin, M., Courtney, J., Power, D., Sharda, R., & Carlsson, C. (2002). Past, present, and future of decision support. *Decision Support Systems*, *33*(2), 111–126. doi:10.1016/S0167-9236(01)00139-7

Shoham, Y., & Tennenholtz, M. (1992). On social laws for artificial agent societies: Off-line design. *Artificial Intelligence*, *73*(1-2), 231–252. doi:10.1016/0004-3702(94)00007-N

Shute, V., & Glaser, R. (1990). A large scale evaluation of an intelligent discovery world. *Interactive Learning Environments*, *1*, 55–77. doi:10.1080/1049482900010104

Sidner, C. L., & Lee, C. (2007). Conversational informatics: An engineering approach. In *Attentional gestures in dialogues between people and robots*. Wiley and Sons.

Sidner, C., & Lee, C. (2005). Robots as laboratory hosts. *Interaction*, *12*(2), 24–26. doi:10.1145/1052438.1052457

Silver, D., & Veness, J. (2010). *Monte Carlo planning in large POMDPs, Advances in Neural Information Processing Systems*. Vancouver, BC: NIPS.

Sim, H. S., Kim, K.-E., Kim, J. H., Chang, D.-S., & Koo, M.-Y. (2008). Symbolic heuristic search value iteration for factored POMDPs. *National Conference on Artificial Intelligence (AAAI)*, pp. 1088-1093.

Simon, H. A. (1956). Rational choice and the structure of the environment. *Psychological Review, 63*, 129–138. doi:10.1037/h0042769

Singh, S., Jaakkola, T., & Jordan, M. (1996). Reinforcement learning with soft state aggregation. In *Neural Information Processing Systems 7*. Cambridge, MA: MIT Press.

Singh, S., Tadic, V., & Doucet, A. (2007). A policy gradient method for semi-Markov decision processes with application to call admission control. *European Journal of Operational Research, 178*(3), 808–818. doi:10.1016/j.ejor.2006.02.023

Singh, S. S., Kantas, N., Vo, B.-N., Doucet, A., & Evans, R. J. (2007). Simulation-based optimal sensor scheduling with application to observer trajectory planning. *Automatica, 43*, 817–830. doi:10.1016/j.automatica.2006.11.019

Singh, S., Jaakkola, T., & Jordan, M. (1996). Reinforcement learning with soft state aggregation. In *Neural information processing systems 7*. Cambridge, MA: MIT Press.

Singh, S., Litman, D., Kearns, M., & Walker, M. (2002). Optimizing dialogue management with reinforcement leaning: Experiments with the NJFun system. *Journal of Artificial Intelligence, 16*, 105–133.

Singh, S., Sutton, R. S., & Kaelbling, P. (1996). Reinforcement learning with replacing eligibility traces. In *Machine learning* (pp. 123–158).

SIS. (2010). *SMILE: Structural modeling, inference, & learning engine.* Retrieved May 2010 from http://genie.sis.pitt.edu

Smallwood, R. D., & Sondik, E. J. (1973). The optimal control of partially observable Markov processes over a finite horizon. *Operations Research, 21*, 1071–1088. doi:10.1287/opre.21.5.1071

Smith, T., & Simmons, R. G. (2005). Point-based POMDP algorithms: improved analysis and implementation, *International Conference on Uncertainty in Artificial Intelligence (UAI)*, pp. 542-547.

Smith, T., & Simmons, R. (2004, July). Heuristic search value iteration for POMDPs. In *Proceedings of the 20th Conference on Uncertainty in Artificial Intelligence*.

Sørmo, F., Cassens, J., & Aamodt, A. (2005). Explanation in case-based reasoning—Perspectives and goals. *Artificial Intelligence Review, 24*(2), 109–143. doi:10.1007/s10462-005-4607-7

Spaan, M. T. J., & Vlassis, N. A. (2005). Perseus: randomized point-based value iteration for POMDPs. [JAIR]. *Journal of Artificial Intelligence Research, 24*, 195–220.

Speechdraw. (2010). *Application design tool.* Retrieved from http://www.speechvillage.com/home/

Spirtes, P., Glymour, C., & Scheines, R. (1993). *Causation, prediction, and search.* Berlin, Germany: Springer-Verlag.

Starkie, B., Findlow, G., Ho, K., Hui, A., Law, L., & Lightwood, L. (2002). Lyrebird™: Developing spoken dialog systems using examples. In *Grammatical inference: Algorithms and applications; 6th International Colloquium, ICGI*, Amsterdam (p. 354-358). Springer-Verlag Lecture Notes in Computer Science.

Steinwart, I., & Christman, A. (2008). *Support vector machines.* New York, NY: Springer.

Strens, M. (2000). A Bayesian framework for reinforcement learning. In *Proceedings of the Seventeenth International Conference on Machine Learning* (pp. 943–950). ICML.

Strotz, R. H. (1955). Myopia and inconsistency in dynamic utility maximization. *The Review of Economic Studies, 23*, 165–180. doi:10.2307/2295722

Sucar, L. E. (2007, June). Parallel Markov decision processes. *Studies in Fuzziness and Soft Computing. Advances in Probabilistic Graphical Models, 214*, 295–309. doi:10.1007/978-3-540-68996-6_14

Sucar, L. E., & Noguez, J. (2008). Student modeling. In Pourret, O., Naim, P., & Marcot, B. (Eds.), *Bayesian networks: A practical guide to applications* (pp. 173–185). Wiley & Sons.

Suendermann, D., Liscombe, J., Dayanidhi, K., & Pieraccini, R. (2009, September). A handsome set of metrics to measure utterance classification performance in spoken dialog systems. In *Proceedings of the Sigdial 2009 Conference* (pp. 349–356). London, UK: Association for Computational Linguistics.

Sunmola, F. T., & Laboratory, W. C. (2006). Model transfer for Markov decision tasks via parameter matching. In *Workshop of the UK Planning and Scheduling Special Interest Group.*

Sutton, R., Precup, D., & Singh, S. P. (1999). Between MDPs and semi-MDPs: a framework for temporal abstraction in reinforcement learning. [AIJ]. *Artificial Intelligence, 112*(1-2), 181–211. doi:10.1016/S0004-3702(99)00052-1

Sutton, R., & Barto, A. (1989). *Reinforcement learning an introduction.* Cambridge, MA: MIT Press.

Sutton, R., Precup, D., & Singh, S. (1998). Between MDPs and semi-MDPs: A framework for temporal abstraction in reinforcement learning. *Artificial Intelligence, 112*(1).

Sutton, R. S., & Barto, A. G. (1998). *Reinforcement learning, an introduction.* Cambridge, MA: MIT Press.

Swartout, W. R. (1983). Xplain: A system for creating and explaining expert consulting programs. *Artificial Intelligence, 21,* 285–325. doi:10.1016/S0004-3702(83)80014-9

Swartout, W. R. (1977, August). A digitalis therapy advisor with explanations. Fifth International Joint Conference on Artificial Intelligence. Cambridge, MA, USA.

Syed, U., & Williams, J. D. (2008). Using automatically transcribed dialogs to learn user models in a spoken dialog system. In *Proc Association for Computational Linguistics Human Language Technologies.* Columbus, Ohio: Acl-Hlt.

Tadepalli, P., & Ok, D. (1998). Model-based average reward reinforcement learning. In *Artificial intelligence* (pp. 881–887). AAAI Press/MIT Press.

Taghipour, N., Kardan, A., & Ghidary, S. S. (2007, October). Usage-based web recommendations: A reinforcement learning approach. In *Proceedings of the 2007 ACM Conference on Recommender Systems.* Minneapolis, MN.

Tang, J., Singh, A., Goehausen, N., & Abbeel, P. (2010). Parameterized maneuver learning for autonomous helicopter flight. In *Proc. of the International Conference on Robotics and Automation* (pp. 1142–1148).

Tawfik, A. Y., & Khan, S. (2005). Temporal relevance in dynamic decision networks with sparse evidence. *International Journal of Applied Intelligence, Special Issue on Uncertain Temporal Reasoning, 23*(2).

Taylor, M. E., & Stone, P. (2009). Transfer learning for reinforcement learning domains: A survey. *Journal of Machine Learning Research, 10*(1), 1633–1685.

Tenorio-Gonzalez, A. C., Morales, E. F., & Pineda, L. V. (2010). Dynamic reward shaping: Training a robot by voice. In *Proc. of the Ibero-American Conference on Artificial Intelligence* (pp. 483–492).

Tesauro, G. (1992, May). Practical issues in temporal difference learning. *Machine Learning, 8,* 257–277. doi:10.1007/BF00992697

Tetreault, J. R., & Litman, D. J. (2006). Using reinforcement learning to build a better model of dialogue state. In *Proc European Association for Computational Linguistics.* Trento, Italy: EACL.

Tetreault, J. R., Bohus, D., & Litman, D. J. (2007). Estimating the reliability of MDP policies: A confidence interval approach. In *Proc Human Language Technologies: The Annual Conference of the North American Chapter of the Association for Computational Linguistics (NAACL-HLT),* Rochester, New York, USA.

The MathWorks, Inc. (2004). *Matlab.* Retrieved from http://www.mathworks.com

Theocharous, G., Murphy, K., & Kaelbling, L. (2004). Representing hierarchical POMDPs as DBNs for multi-scale robot localization. In *Proc. International Conference on Robotics and Automation (ICRA 2004).*

Theodorou, E., Buchli, J., & Schaal, S. (2010). A generalized path integral control approach to reinforcement learning. *Journal of Machine Learning Research, 11,* 3137–3181.

Thomson, B., & Young, S. (2010). Bayesian update of dialogue state: A POMDP framework for spoken dialogue systems. *Computer Speech & Language, 24,* 562–588. doi:10.1016/j.csl.2009.07.003

Thomson, B., Schatzmann, J., Welhammer, K., Ye, H., & Young, S. (2007). Training a real-world POMDP-based dialog system. In *Proc Human Language Technologies: The Annual Conference of the North American Chapter of the Association for Computational Linguistics (NAACL-HLT) Workshop on Bridging the Gap: Academic and Industrial Research in Dialog Technologies*, Rochester, New York, *USA* (pp. 9–17).

Thomson, B., Schatzmann, J., & Young, S. (2008). Bayesian update of dialogue state for robust dialogue systems. In *Proc Intl Conf on Acoustics, Speech, and Signal Processing (ICASSP)*, Las Vegas, USA.

Thomson, B., Yu, K., Gasic, M., Keizer, S., Mairesse, F., & Schatzmann, J. (2008). Evaluating semantic-level confidence scores with multiple hypotheses. In *Proc Interspeech*, Brisbane, Australia.

Thrun, S. (1999). Monte Carlo POMDPs. [NIPS]. *Advances in Neural Information Processing Systems*, 1064–1070.

Thrun, S. (2000). Probabilistic algorithms in robotics. *Artificial Intelligence Magazine*, *21*(4), 93–109.

Thrun, S., Burgard, W., & Fox, D. (2005). *Probabilistic robotics*. MIT Press.

Ting, C.-Y., Beik, Z., Reza, M., & Chong, Y.-K. (2006). A decision-theoretic approach to scientific inquiry exploratory learning environment. In *Proceedings of the Eight International Conference on Intelligent Tutoring Systems (ITS'06)*, (pp. 85-94).

Tintarev, N., & Masthoff, J. (2007). A survey of explanations in recommender systems. *International Conference on Data Engineering Workshop on Recommender Systems & Intelligent User Interfaces*.

Todorov, E., & Li, W. (2005). A generalized iterative LQG method for locally-optimal feedback control of constrained nonlinear stochastic systems. In *Proceedings of the 2005 American Control Conference*.

Torrey, L., Shavlik, J., Walker, T., & Maclin, R. (2008). Relational macros for transfer in reinforcement learning. *ILP*, 254-268.

Toussaint, M. (2009). Robot trajectory optimization using approximate inference. In *Proceedings of the International Conference on Machine Learning*.

Toussaint, M., & Storkey, A. (2006). Probabilistic inference for solving discrete and continuous state Markov decision processes. In *Proceedings of the International Conference on Machine Learning*.

Toussaint, M., Harmeling, S., & Storkey, A. (2006). Probabilistic inference for solving (PO)MDPs, *Technical Report EDI-INF-RR-0934*, School of Informatics, University of Edinburgh.

Vadillo-Zorita, J., de Ilarraza, A. D., Fernández, I., Gutiérrez, J., & Elorriaga, J. (1994). *Explicaciones en sistemas tutores de entrenamiento: Representacion del dominio y estrategias de explicacion*. Pais Vasco, España.

Vale, Z., Ramos, C., Silva, A., Faria, L., Santos, J., & Fernández, F. (1998). SOCRATES, an integrated intelligent system for power system control center operator assistance and training. In *Proceedings of the International Conference on Artificial Intelligence and Soft Computing (IASTED)* (pp. 27-30).

Van der Vlerk, M. H. (2010). Convex approximations for a class of mixed-integer recourse models. *Annals of Operations Research*, *177*, 139–151. doi:10.1007/s10479-009-0591-7

van Gerven, M. A. J., Díez, F. J., Taal, B. G., & Lucas, P. J. F. (2007). Selecting treatment strategies with dynamic limited-memory influence diagrams. *Artificial Intelligence in Medicine*, *40*, 171–186. doi:10.1016/j.artmed.2007.04.004

van Gerven, M. A. J., & Díez, F. J. (2006). Selecting strategies for infinite-horizon dynamic LIMIDs. In M. Studený & J. Vomlel (Eds.), *Proceedings of the Third European Workshop on Probabilistic Graphical Models (PGM'06)* (pp. 131-138). Prague, Czech Republic.

Van Hentenryck, P., & Bent, R. (2006). *Online stochastic combinatorial optimization*. Cambridge, MA: MIT Press.

van Otterlo, M. (2009). *The logic of adaptive behavior: Knowledge representation and algorithms for adaptive sequential decision making under uncertainty in first-order and relational domains*. The Netherlands: IOS Press.

van Otterlo, M. (2003). Efficient reinforcement learning using relational aggregation. In *Proc. of the Sixth European Workshop on Reinfocement Learning*. Nancy, France.

413

van Otterlo, M. (2004). Reinforcement learning for relational mdps. In A. Nowé, T. Lenaerts, & K. Steenhaut (Eds.), *Proc. of the Machine Learning Conference of Belgium and The Netherlands* (pp. 138-145).

VanLehn, K. (1988). *Student modeling. Foundations of Intelligent Tutoring Systems* (pp. 55–78). Hillsdale, NJ: Lawrence Erlbaum Associates.

VanLehn, K. (1998). Analogy events: How examples are used during problem solving. *Cognitive Science*, *22*(3), 347–388. doi:10.1207/s15516709cog2203_4

VanLehn, K. (1999). Rule-learning events in the acquisition of a complex skill: An evaluation of cascade. *Journal of the Learning Sciences*, *8*(1), 71–125. doi:10.1207/s15327809jls0801_3

VanLehn, K., Jones, R. M., & Chi, M. (1992). A model of the self-explanation effect. *Journal of the Learning Sciences*, *2*(1), 1–59. doi:10.1207/s15327809jls0201_1

VanLehn, K., Siler, S., Murray, R. C., Yamauchi, T., & Baggett, W. B. (2003). Why do only some events cause learning during human tutoring? *Cognition and Instruction*, *21*(3), 209–249. doi:10.1207/S1532690XCI2103_01

VanLehn, K. (2001). Bayesian student modeling, user interfaces and feedback: A sensitive analysis. *International Journal of Artificial Intelligence in Education*, *12*(2), 154–184.

Vapnik, V. N. (1998). *Statistical learning theory*. New York, NY: John Wiley & Sons.

Varakantham, P., & Marecki, J. Yabu, y., Milind, T., & Makoto, Y. (2007). Letting loose a SPIDER on a network of POMDPs: Generating quality guaranteed policies. In *Proceedings of the International Joint Conference on Agents and Multiagent Systems (AAMAS-07)*.

Varges, S., Quarteroni, S., Riccardi, G., Ivanov, A. V., & Roberti, P. (2009). *Combining POMDPs trained with user simulations and rule-based dialogue management in a spoken dialogue system*. In ACL-IJCNLP Demonstrations.

Vaughan, R., Gerkey, B., & Howard, A. (2003). On device abstractions for portable, reusable robot code. *Proc. of the 2003 IEEE/RSJ IROS*, (pp. 11-15).

Verma, D., & Rao, R. (2006). Planning and acting in uncertain environments using probabilistic inference. In *Intelligent robots and systems*.

Verweij, B., Ahmed, S., Kleywegt, A., Nemhauser, G., & Shapiro, A. (2003). The sample average approximation method applied to stochastic routing problems: A computational study. *Computational Optimization and Applications*, *24*(2-3), 289–333. doi:10.1023/A:1021814225969

Vijayakumar, S., Toussaint, M., Petkos, G., & Howard, M. (2009). Planning and moving in dynamic environments: A statistical machine learning approach. In *Creating brain like intelligence: From principles to complex intelligent systems*. Springer-Verlag.

Viola, P. A., & Jones, M. J. (2004). Robust real-time face detection. *International Journal of Computer Vision*, *57*(2), 137–154. doi:10.1023/B:VISI.0000013087.49260.fb

Vlassis, N., & Toussaint, M. (2009). Model-free reinforcement learning as mixture learning. In *Proceedings of the 26th International Conference on Machine Learning*.

Voiceobjects. (2010). *application design tool*. Retrieved from http://www.voiceobjects.com

Walker, M. A. (2000). An application of reinforcement learning to dialogue strategy selection in a spoken dialogue system for email. *Journal of Artificial Intelligence Research*, *12*, 387–416.

Wallace, S. W., & Ziemba, W. T. (Eds.). (2005). *Applications of stochastic programming*. Philadelphia, PA: SIAM. doi:10.1137/1.9780898718799

Watkins, C. (1989). *Learning from delayed rewards*. Unpublished doctoral dissertation. Cambridge, MA: Cambridge University.

Weinstein, M., & Stason, W. (1977). Foundations of cost-effectiveness analysis for health and medical practices. *The New England Journal of Medicine*, *296*(13), 716–721. doi:10.1056/NEJM197703312961304

Weld, D. (1994a). An introduction to least-commitment planning. *Artificial Intelligence Magazine*, *15*(4), 27–61.

Weld, D. (1994b). Robots that work in collaboration with people. *AAAI Fall Symposium on the intersection of Robotics and Cognitive Sciences*.

Wellman, M. (1990). Graphical inference in qualitative probabilistic networks. *Networks*, *20*, 687–701. doi:10.1002/net.3230200511

Wets, R. J.-B. (1974). Stochastic programs with fixed recourse: The equivalent deterministic program. *SIAM Review, 16*, 309–339. doi:10.1137/1016053

White, C. C. III, & El-Deib, H. K. (1994). Markov decision processes with imprecise transition probabilities. *Operations Research, 42*(4), 739–749. doi:10.1287/opre.42.4.739

Whitehead, S. D., & Ballard, D. H. (1991). Learning to perceive and act by trial and error. *Machine Learning, 7*, 45–83. doi:10.1007/BF00058926

Wick, M. R., & Thompson, W. B. (1992). Reconstructive expert system explanation. *Artificial Intelligence, 54*(1-2), 33–70. doi:10.1016/0004-3702(92)90087-E

Williams, J. D. (2008b). Demonstration of a POMDP voice dialer. In *Proc Demonstration Session of Association for Computational Linguistics Human Language Technologies*. Columbus, Ohio: ACL-HLT.

Williams, J. D., & Young, S. (2007a). Partially observable Markov decision processes for spoken dialog systems. *Computer Speech & Language, 21*(2), 393–422. doi:10.1016/j.csl.2006.06.008

Williams, J. D., & Young, S. (2007b). Scaling POMDPs for spoken dialog management. *IEEE Trans. on Audio, Speech, and Language Processing, 15*(7), 2116–2129. doi:10.1109/TASL.2007.902050

Williams, J. D. (2007a). Applying POMDPs to dialog systems in the troubleshooting domain. In *NAACL-HLT Workshop on Bridging the Gap: Academic and Industrial Research in Dialog Technologies*, Rochester, New York, USA (pp. 1–8).

Williams, J. D. (2007b). Using particle filters to track dialogue state. In *Proc IEEE Workshop on Automatic Speech Recognition and Understanding (ASRU)*, Kyoto, Japan.

Williams, J. D. (2008a). The best of both worlds: Unifying conventional dialog systems and POMDPs. In *Proc Interspeech*, Brisbane, Australia.

Williams, J. D. (2008c). Integrating expert knowledge into POMDP optimization for spoken dialog systems. In *Proc AAAI Workshop on Advancements in POMDP Solvers*, Chicago.

Williams, J. D. (2009). Spoken dialogue systems: Challenges, and opportunities for research. In *Proc IEEE Workshop on Automatic Speech Recognition and Understanding (ASRU)*, Merano, Italy.

Williams, J. D. (2010). Incremental partition recombination for efficient tracking of multiple dialog states. In *Proc Intl Conf on Acoustics, Speech, and Signal Processing (ICASSP)*, Dallas, USA.

Williams, J. D. (n.d.). *AT&T voice dialer demonstration.* Retrieved from http://www.research.att.com/people/Williams_Jason_D

Williams, J. D., & Balakrishnan, S. (2009). Estimating probability of correctness for ASR N-best lists. In *Proc Sigdial Workshop on Discourse and Dialogue*, London, UK.

Williams, J. D., & Young, S. (2005). Scaling up POMDPs for dialog management: The "summary POMDP" method. In *Proc IEEE Workshop on Automatic Speech Recognition and Understanding (ASRU)*, San Juan, Puerto Rico, USA (pp. 177–182).

Williams, J. D., & Young, S. J. (2006). Scaling POMDPs for dialog management with composite summary point-based value iteration (CSPBVI). In *Proc American Association for Artificial Intelligence (AAAI) Workshop on Statistical and Empirical Approaches for Spoken Dialogue Systems*, Boston.

Williams, J. D., Poupart, P., & Young, S. (2005). Factored partially observable Markov decision processes for dialogue management. In *Proc Workshop on Knowledge and Reasoning in Practical Dialogue Systems, Intl Joint Conf on Artificial Intelligence (IJCAI)*, Edinburgh.

Wilson, A., Fern, A., Ray, S., & Tadepalli, P. (2007). Multi-task reinforcement learning: A hierarchical bayesian approach. In *Proceedings of the 24th International Conference on Machine Learning* (p. 1015). ACM Press.

Witten, I. (2005). *Data mining: Practical machine learning tools and techniques with Java implementations* (2nd ed.). USA: Morgan Kaufmann.

Woolf, B. (2008). *Building intelligent interactive tutors: Student-centered strategies for revolutionizing e-learning.* San Francisco, CA: Elsevier Inc., Morgan Kauffman.

Wren, C. R., Azarbayejani, A., Darrell, T., & Pentland, A. (1997). Pfinder: Real-time tracking of the human body. *IEEE Transactions on Pattern Analysis and Machine Intelligence, 19*(7), 780–785. doi:10.1109/34.598236

Wu, F., Zilberstein, S., & Chen, X. (2010). Point-based policy generation for decentralized pomdps. In *Proceedings of the Ninth International Joint Conference on Autonomous Agents and Multi-Agent Systems.*

Wu, J., Osuntogun, A., Choudhury, T., Philipose, M., & Rehg, J. M. (2007, October). A scalable approach to activity recognition based on object use. In *Proc. of International Conference on Computer Vision (ICCV)*. Rio de Janeiro, Brazil.

Xuan, P., Lesser, V., & Zilberstein, S. (2001). Communication decisions in multiagent cooperation: Model and experiments. In *Proceedings of the Fifth International Conference on Autonomous Agents*, (pp. 616–623). Montreal. ACM Press.

Yanco, H. A. (1998). Wheelesley, a robotic wheelchair system: Indoor navigation and user interface. In Mittal, V., Yanco, H., Aronis, J., & Simspon, R. (Eds.), *Lecture Notes in Artificial Intelligence: Assistive Technology and Artificial Intelligence* (pp. 256–268).

Yilmaz, L. (2006). Expanding our horizons in teaching the use of intelligent agents for simulation modeling of next generation engineering systems. *International Journal of Engineering Education, 22*(5), 1097–1104.

Younes, H. L. S., & Simmons, R. (2004). Policy generation for continuous-time stochastic domains with concurrency. In *Proceedings International Conference on Automated Planning and Scheduling.*

Younes, H., & Littman, M. (2004). *Ppddl1.0: An extension to pddl for expressing planning domains with probabilistic effects*. Technical Report CMU-CS-04-167, Department of Computer Science, Carnegie-Mellon University.

Young, H. D., & Freedman, R. A. (2008). *University physics* (12th ed.). Pearson, Addison Wesley.

Young, S., Gašić, M., Keizer, S., Mairesse, F., Schatzmann, J., & Thomson, B. (2010, April). The hidden information state model: A practical framework for POMDP-based spoken dialogue management. *Computer Speech & Language, 24*(2), 150–174. doi:10.1016/j.csl.2009.04.001

Young, S., Keizer, S., Yu, K., Mairesse, F., Jurcícek, F., & Thomson, B. (n.d.). *Tourist information system for Cambridge*. Retrieved from http://mi.eng.cam.ac.uk/research/dialogue/demo.html

Young, S., Schatzmann, J., Thomson, B., Weilhammer, K., & Ye, H. (2007). The hidden information state dialogue manager: A real-world POMDP-based system. In *Proc Demonstration Session of Human Language Technologies: The Annual Conference of the North American Chapter of the Association for Computational Linguistics (NAACL-HLT)*, Rochester, New York, USA.

Young, S., Williams, J. D., Schatzmann, J., Stuttle, M. N., & Weilhammer, K. (2006). *The hidden information state approach to dialogue management* (Technical Report No. CUED/F-INFENG/TR.544). Cambridge University Engineering Department.

Zaragoza, J. H. (2010). Relational reinforcement learning with continuous actions by combining behavioral cloning and locally weighted regression. *Journal of Intelligent Learning Systems and Applications, 2*, 69–79. doi:10.4236/jilsa.2010.22010

Zhang, B., Cai, Q., Mao, J., & Guo, B. (2001, August). Planning and acting under uncertainty: A new model for spoken dialogue system. In *Proceedings of Uncertainty in Artificial Intelligence* (pp. 572-579). Seattle, WA.

Zhang, B., Cai, Q., Mao, J., Chang, E., & Guo, B. (2001). Spoken dialogue management as planning and acting under uncertainty. In *Proc Interspeech, Aalborg, Denmark* (pp. 2169–2172).

Zhang, N. L., & Liu, W. (1996). Planning in stochastic domains: problem characteristics and approximation. *Technical Report HKUST-CS96-31*, Hong Kong University of Science and Technology.

Zhang, W., & Dieterich, T. G. (1995). Value function approximations and job-shop scheduling. In *Proceedings of the Workshop on Value Function Approximation*, Carnegie-Mellon University, School of Computer Science (pp. 95–206).

Zilberstein, S., Washington, R., Bernstein, D., & Mouaddib, A. I. (2002). Decision-theoretic control of planteray rovers. In Beetz, M. (Eds.), *Plan-based control of robotic agents, LNCS 2466* (pp. 270–289). doi:10.1007/3-540-37724-7_16

About the Contributors

Luis Enrique Sucar has a Ph.D in computing from Imperial College, London; a M.Sc. in electrical engineering from Stanford University; and a B.Sc. in electronics and communications engineering from ITESM, Monterrey, Mexico. He has been a Researcher at the Electrical Research Institute and Professor at ITESM Cuernavaca, and is currently a Senior Researcher at INAOE, Puebla, Mexico. He has more than 100 publications in journals and conference proceedings, and has directed 16 Ph.D. thesis. Dr. Sucar is Member of the National Research System, the Mexican Science Academy, and Senior Member of the IEEE. He has served as president of the Mexican AI Society, has been member of the Advisory Board of IJCAI, and is Associate Editor of the journals Computación y Sistemas and Revista Iberoamericana de Inteligencia Artificial. His main research interest are in graphical models and probabilistic reasoning, and their applications in computer vision, robotics and biomedicine.

Eduardo F. Morales is a research scientist since 2006 of the National Institute for Astrophysics, Optics and Electronics (INAOE) in Mexico where he conducts research in Machine Learning and Robotics. He has a B.Sc. degree (1974) in Physics Engineering from Universidad Autonoma Metropolitana (Mexico), an M.Sc. degree (1985) in Information Technology: Knowledge-based Systems from the University of Edinburgh (U.K.), and a PhD degree (1992) in Computer Science from the Turing Institute - University of Strathclyde (U.K.). He has been responsible for 20 research projects sponsored by different funding agencies and private companies and has more than 100 articles in journals and conference proceedings.

Jesse Hoey is an assistant professor in the David R. Cheriton School of Computer Science at the University of Waterloo. Hoey is also an adjunct scientist at the Toronto Rehabilitation Institute in Toronto, Canada. His research focuses on planning and acting in large scale real-world uncertain domains. He has worked extensively on systems to assist persons with cognitive and physical disabilities. He won the Best Paper award at the International Conference on Vision Systems (ICVS) in 2007 for his paper describing an assistive system for persons with dementia during hand washing. Hoey won a Microsoft/AAAI Distinguished Contribution Award at the 2009 IJCAI Workshop on Intelligent Systems for Assisted Cognition, for his paper on technology to facilitate creative expression in persons with dementia. He also works on devices for ambient assistance in the kitchen, on stroke rehabilitation devices, and on spoken dialogue assistance systems. Hoey was co-Chair of the 2008 Medical Image Understanding and Analysis (MIUA) conference and he is Program Chair for the British Machine Vision Conference (BMVC) in 2011.

* * *

Jay Black is an Adjunct Associate Professor in the David R. Cheriton School of Computer Science at the University of Waterloo (Canada). He received his Ph.D. in Computer Science from the University of Waterloo in 1982, having previously studied at the University of Calgary and the Institut National Polytechnique de Grenoble, France. His research interests include pervasive, mobile, and wireless computing, distributed systems, wireless networks; the behaviour of distributed applications and systems; and computer system performance analysis, modelling and simulation.

Aurélie Beynier was born in 1980 and received a PhD in computer science from the University of Caen Basse-Normandie (France) in 2006, entitled « An approach to solve Decentralized Markov Decision Processes with temporal constraints ». During her PhD, she proposed the OC-DEC-MDP model that improves time and action representation of Decentralized Markov Decision Processes. She also did some work on approximate approaches to efficiently solves OC-DEC-MDPs and I applied my work to multirobot exploration scenarios. She currently holds a position of assistant professor at the University Pierre and Marie Curie (University of Paris 6, France). She is a member of the multiagent group (SMA) of the LIP6 (Laboratoire d'Informatique de Paris 6). Her research interests are in coordination and decentralized control of multiagent systems. She is interested in decentralized decision making in uncertain and partially observable environments.

Craig Boutilier is a Professor of Computer Science at the University of Toronto. He received his Ph.D from of Toronto in 1992. Boutilier's research has spanned topics ranging from knowledge representation, revision, default reasoning, and philosophical logic, to probabilistic reasoning, decision making under uncertainty, multiagent systems, and machine learning. His current research efforts focus on various aspects of decision making under uncertainty: preference elicitation, mechanism design, game theory and multiagent decision processes, economic models, social choice, computational advertising, Markov decision processes and reinforcement learning. Boutilier served as Program Chair for both the 16th Conference on Uncertainty in Artificial Intelligence (UAI-2000) and the 21st International Joint Conference on Artificial Intelligence (IJCAI-09). He will serve as Associate Editor-in-Chief/Editor-in-Chief of the Journal of Artificial Intelligence Research (JAIR) from 2011-2015 Boutilier is a Fellow of the Association for the Advancement of Artificial Intelligence (AAAI). He has been awarded the Isaac Walton Killam Fellowship and an IBM Faculty Award. He also received the Killam Teaching Award from the University of British Columbia.

Cristina Conati is an associate Professor in Department of Computer Science at the University of British Columbia. Her research interests include Artificial Intelligence, Cognitive Science and Human Computer interaction, with a focus on user-adaptive interaction. She is especially interested in comprehensive user-modeling: extending the range of user features used for adaptation from purely cognitive features (knowledge, goals, preferences), to meta-cognitive skills (e.g., the capability of effectively exploring a large information space), personality traits and emotional reactions.

Elva Corona-Xelhuantzi is pursuing a Ph.D. in Computer Science at the National Institute for Astrophysics, Optics and Electronics (INAOE) in Puebla, Mexico. Her research interests are in decision-theoretic planning and service robots.

Boris Defourny received his Electrical Engineering degree from the University of Liège in 2005, and will receive his PhD degree in 2010. He is with the Systems and Modeling Research Unit of the University of Liège, where he has carried out research on applications of machine learning techniques and multistage stochastic programming for sequential decision making under uncertainty. His research interests include optimization, operations research, and artificial intelligence in general.

Francisco Javier Díez was born in Burgos, Spain, in 1965. He received a M.S. in Theoretical Physics from the Universidad Autónoma de Madrid and a Ph.D. from the Universidad Nacional de Eduación a Distancia (UNED) in 1994. In 1992 he was a visiting scholar at the University of California Los Angeles (UCLA), invited by Prof. Judea Pearl. He is currently associate professor at the Department of Artificial Intelligence of the UNED, in Madrid, and Director of the Research Center on Intelligent Decision-Support Systems (CISIAD), at the same university. His current research interests include probabilistic graphical models (Bayesian networks, influence diagrams, factored MDPs and POMDPs, etc.) and medical decision making, especially cost-effectiveness analysis.

Francisco Elizalde is a researcher at the Electrical Research Institute in México (IIE) since 1992. His research interests include decision-theoretic planning and intelligent assistant systems and their applications in control and industrial processes. He received a PhD degree in computer science from Tec de Monterrey (ITESM) campus Cuernavaca in 2008, and is currently involved in research applications projects to Mexico energy facilities.

Damien Ernst received the MSc and PhD degrees from the University of Liège in 1998 and 2003, respectively. He is currently a Research Associate of the Belgian FRS-FNRS and he is affiliated with the Systems and Modeling Research Unit of the University of Liège. Damien Ernst spent the period 2003-2006 with the University of Liège as a Postdoctoral Researcher of the FRS-FNRS and held during this period positions as visiting researcher at CMU, MIT and ETH. He spent the academic year 2006-2007 working at SUPELEC (France) as professor. His main research interests are in the field of power system dynamics, optimal control, reinforcement learning and design of dynamic treatment regimes.

Nando de Freitas is an Associate Professor in computer science at the University of British Columbia (UBC). He is also an associate member of the statistics department and one of the faculty members of the cognitive systems program. His areas of specialization are machine learning, computational statistics and computational neuroscience. From 1999 to 2001, he was a visiting post-doctoral scholar with Stuart Russell at the University of California, Berkeley, where he worked on structured probabilistic modeling and Monte Carlo methods. He obtained his Ph.D. on Bayesian methods for neural networks in 1999 from Trinity College, Cambridge University, following B.Sc. and M.Sc. degrees (with distinction) from the University of the Witwatersrand, Johannesburg. He was the first recipient of the MITACS Young Investigator Award (2010) and is a Fellow of the Neural Computation and Adaptive Perception CIFAR program. His research is also supported by NSERC.

Marcel van Gerven received a BSc in Cognitive Science and an MSc in knowledge engineering from the Radboud University Nijmegen, The Netherlands. He obtained a Ph.D. degree from the same university in 2007. His Ph.D. work deals with the construction of large-scale probabilistic and decision-theoretic models for monitoring disease progession and treatment planning in clinical oncology. He is currently senior postdoctoral researcher at the Institute for Computing and Information Sciences at Radboud University Nijmegen. He is engaged in the development of sparse Bayesian methods for Brain-Computer Interfacing (BCI) applications. His experimental work at the Donders Institute for Brain, Cognition and Behaviour has led to the development of a novel covert attention BCI paradigm. His latest work deals with the use of generative models for the decoding of mental state from functional magnetic resonance imaging data.

Matthew Hoffman is a Ph.D. student in the department of computer science at the University of British Columbia. He specializes in machine learning, with a focus on planning and reinforcement learning problems, under the supervision of Nando de Freitas and Arnaud Doucet. In 2005 he received a B.Sc. in computer science and a B.Sc. in mathematics from the University of Washington, where he worked with Rajesh Rao on robotic imitation learning.

Omar Zia Khan is a Ph.D. candidate in the David R. Cheriton School of Computer Science at the University of Waterloo, Waterloo (Canada). He received B.S. in Computer Science at National University of Computer and Emerging Sciences (Islamabad, Pakistan) in 2003, and M.Math in Computer Science at University of Waterloo (Canada). His research focuses on making decision-theoretic systems, such as Markov Decision Processes (MDPs) and Partially Observable MDPs, more usable by generating automated explanations for their policies and developing techniques for automatically refining their models.

Alex Mihailidis, Ph.D., P.Eng., is the Barbara G. Stymiest Research Chair in Rehabilitation Technology at the University of Toronto and Toronto Rehab Institute. He is an Associate Professor in the Department of Occupational Science and Occupational Therapy (U of T) and in the Institute of Biomaterials and Biomedical Engineering (U of T), with a cross appointment in the Department of Computer Science (U of T). He has been conducting research in the field of pervasive computing and intelligent systems in health for the past 13 years, having published over 100 journal papers, conference papers, and abstracts in this field. He has specifically focused on the development of intelligent home systems for elder care and wellness, technology for children with autism, and adaptive tools for nurses and clinical applications. Dr. Mihailidis is also very active in the rehabilitation engineering profession, currently as the President-Elect for RESNA (Rehabilitation Engineering and Assistive Technology Society of North America).

Julieta Noguez Monroy is associated professor researcher at the Computer Science Department of the *Tecnológico de Monterrey, Campus Ciudad de México*. Julieta Noguez has a M.Sc. and a Ph.D. in Computer Science from *Tecnológico de Monterrey*. She has more than 50 publications in journals and international conference proceedings, and has supervised six M.Sc., and two PhD theses. She is member of the Mexican AI Society. She has been a reviewer for the FIE Conferences from 2005 to 2010. She received the Best Professor Award in 2000 and Best Professor of Graduate Level Award in 2009 at the Tecnológico de Monterrey, Campus Ciudad de México. She belongs to National Research System (SNI level 1) of Science and Technology Mexican Council. She is the leader of e-Learning research group at ITESM-CCM since April, 2005, and her main research interests include Intelligent Tutoring Systems, Virtual Laboratories, Collaborative Learning, Probabilistic Reasoning, Project Oriented Learning, Active Learning, and e-Learning.

Abdel-Illah Mouaddib is Professor of Computer and Director of the Model, Agent and Decision Group of "Groupe de Recherche en Informatique, Image, Instrumentation et Automatique (GREYC)" Lab at the University of Caen Basse-Normandie, since 2001. He received a Master and a Ph.D. in Computer Science from the University of Nancy in 1993. Professor Mouaddib's research focuses on the foundations and applications of resource-bounded reasoning and deicion-making techniques, which allow complex systems to make decisions while coping with uncertainty, missing information, and limited computational resources. His research interests include decision theory, reasoning under uncertainty, Markov decision processes, design of autonomous systems, multi-agent systems and automated coordination and communication. He has published over 100 refereed papers on these topics. Professor Mouaddib is a recipient of Best Paper Awards from ECAI (1998) and nominated for the best paper awards from IJCAI (1999). He was involved in many national and international projects (collaborator in Mars Rover project from 1999-2003, Multi-robot systems Agence National de Recherche projects 2007-2012. He serves on the program committees of many AI-related conferences and workshops.

Kasia Muldner is a Post-doctoral researcher in the Department of Psychology at Arizona State University, working with Dr. Michelene Chi in the *Learning and Cognition* Lab. Her work focuses on (1) understanding how to foster constructive and engaged student learning through a variety of activities, including by self-explaining, from tutoring, and from observing others learn; (2) designing computational, adaptive support to foster such constructive learning, including innovative ways to unobtrusively obtain information on students' states of interest, such as cognitive effort, reasoning style, and affect.

Karla Cristina Muñoz Esquivel is full time Ph.D. student at the *University of Ulster, Magee campus*. She has a M.Sc. in Computing and Intelligent Systems from the *University of Ulster* and a B.Sc. in Electronic Systems Engineering from *Tecnológico de Monterrey, Mexico City*. In 2008 she was granted a Vice Chancellor's Research Scholarship (VCRS) by the University of Ulster to sponsor her Ph.D. studies. In 2008, she was awarded with 8over8 prize, which is allocated to the top performing student on the M.Sc. Computing with Specialism course at the University of Ulster. In 2007 she was granted a high level scholarship for Latin America (ALBAN) by the European Union Program for pursuing her M.Sc. studies at the University of Ulster. She has presented papers in workshops and international conferences. Karla's research interests include e-learning, Affective Computing, Problem-Based Learning, User-modeling, Virtual and Game Learning Environments, Intelligent Tutoring Systems and Artificial Intelligence techniques for reasoning and making decisions under uncertainty.

Pascal Poupart is an Associate Professor in the David R. Cheriton School of Computer Science at the University of Waterloo, Waterloo (Canada). He received the B.Sc. in Mathematics and Computer Science at McGill University, Montreal (Canada) in 1998, the M.Sc. in Computer Science at the University of British Columbia, Vancouver (Canada) in 2000 and the Ph.D. in Computer Science at the University of Toronto, Toronto (Canada) in 2005. His research focuses on the development of algorithms for reasoning under uncertainty and machine learning with application to Assistive Technologies, Natural Language Processing and Information Retrieval.

Víctor Robledo Rella is full-time professor at the Physics and Mathematics Department of the Engineering and Architecture School of the *Tecnológico de Monterrey, Mexico City Campus*. He is the Head of the Honours-Courses Program for the EIA and the Coordinator of Introductory Physics courses at the Campus. He holds a MS in Astronomy from *Universidad Nacional Autónoma de México* (UNAM) and has more that 10 years of experience teaching science at the graduate level. He has developed a couple of courses for Blackboard approved by Tecnológico de Monterrey and has made important contributions to the Educative Model of Tecnológico de Monterrey, and his main research interests include Collaborative Learning, Active Learning in Physics, Problem Based Learning, M-Learning, and e-Learning.

Alberto Reyes is a researcher at the Electrical Research Institute in México (IIE) and part-time professor at Instituto Tecnológico y de Estudios Superiores de Monterrey (ITESM). His research interests include decision-theoretic planning and machine learning, and their applications in robotics and industrial processes. He received a PhD degree in computer science from ITESM-campus Cuernavaca, and was recently involved in a postdoctoral program at the Instituto Superior Técnico (IST) in Lisbon. He is a member of the National Research System (SNI) in Mexico.

Gerardo P. Aguilar Sánchez is a Mathematician and Master in Science (Mathematics) by the Facultad de Ciencias UNAM. He was a scholarship holder in the Institute of Mathematics of *Universidad Nacional Autónoma de México* (UNAM). He has a PhD in Business Administration from *Tecnológico de Monterrey, Campus Ciudad de México*. He worked as a full time professor at the Universidad Autonoma Metropolitana (Iztapalapa) from 1983 to 1992 where he was coordinator of the general trunk of subject and divisional director of CBI from 1987 to 1988. It is co-author of 3 research articles and 3 textbooks of undergraduate level. Is full time professor in the Department of Physics and Mathematics, School of Engineering and Architecture of the Tecnológico de Monterrey Campus Ciudad de México since January 1993, where he has been Coordinator of the subjects of Math for the Social Sciences I, Mathematics for Social Sciences II, Mathematics for Engineering II, and Remedial Math and he was the Director of the Mathematics Department in May 2005 to May 2009. His investigation areas are e-Learning, Ring Theory, Collaborative Learning and Mobile Learning.

Luis Neri Vitela is full-time professor at the Physics and Mathematics Department (DFM) of the Engineering and Architecture School (EIA) at *Tecnológico de Monterrey* (ITESM), Mexico City Campus (CCM). He holds a PhD. in Physics from *Universidad Nacional Autónoma de México* (UNAM) and has 29 years of experience as a Physics and Mathematics professor. He is author and co-author of several Physics textbooks and Handbooks, and also of Blackboard courses approved by ITESM. He is a reviewer for the Frontiers in Education Conferences (FIE) sponsored by IEEE, since 2008. He is certified in Problem Based Learning and Collaborative Learning techniques by ITESM, and he gives seminars to qualify teachers about Active Learning methods at CCM, and his main research interests include Collaborative Learning, Active Learning in Physics, Problem Based Learning, M-Learning, and e-Learning.

Louis Wehenkel graduated in Electrical Engineering (Electronics) in 1986 and received the Ph.D. degree in 1990, both from the University of Liège, where he is full Professor of Electrical Engineering and Computer Science. His research interests lie in the design of computational methods for modeling, analyzing and designing complex and/or stochastic systems, based on principles from machine learning and optimization. He works on applications in the context of large scale electric power systems planning and operation, industrial process control, bioinformatics and biomedical image analysis.

Jason Williams is Principal Member of Technical Staff at AT&T Labs - Research. His research interests include applying statistical approaches and machine learning to spoken dialog systems to improve robustness. He is on the Scientific Committee of the Special Interest Group on Dialog and Discourse, and is an elected member of the IEEE Speech and Language Technical Committee (SLTC). Jason holds a PhD and Masters in Speech and Language Processing from Cambridge University (UK), and a BSE in Electrical Engineering from Princeton University (USA). Before joining AT&T he held positions at Tellme Networks, Edify (now Convergys), and the management consultancy McKinsey & Company.

Julio Zaragoza is a research assistant of the National Institute for Astrophysics, Optics and Electronics (INAOE) in Mexico where he conducts research in Bayesian Networks and Reinforcement Learning. He has a B.Sc. degree (2005) in Computer Systems from Instituto Tecnologico de Morelia (Mexico) and an M.Sc. degree (2009) in Computer Sciences from the National Institute for Astrophysics, Optics and Electronics.

Index

T

Temporal Differences 68, 70, 80
text-to-speech (TTS) 317, 327, 336, 342
tile coding 72
time-consistency 135-136, 142
transition functions 29-30, 35-37, 41-44, 56, 64-65, 72, 145, 150, 193, 197, 273, 299-300, 307-308, 320, 322-323, 332-333, 345, 347, 357, 365, 369-370, 375
trivial similarity 247
tutor module 250, 256, 267
two-stage stochastic program 103, 117-118

U

Utility Principle 4-5

V

value functions 37-39, 41-42, 47-51, 55-57, 65-73, 75, 77, 80, 94, 136-138, 152, 193-194, 215, 279, 300, 345-347, 358, 362, 375
value of multistage programming (VMS) 113-114, 116
value of the stochastic solution (VSS) 113-117, 138
variable elimination 17, 28, 30, 43, 154-155

W

wheelchair mobility 8, 294, 307